James Kay

SEEING BEYOND THE WORD

Seeing beyond the Word

Visual Arts and the Calvinist Tradition

Edited by

Paul Corby Finney

William B. Eerdmans Publishing Company
Grand Rapids, Michigan / Cambridge, U.K.

Published 1999 by Wm. B. Eerdmans Publishing Co.
255 Jefferson Ave. S.E., Grand Rapids, Michigan 49503 /
P.O. Box 163, Cambridge CB3 9PU U.K.

Published with the cooperation of
Huguenot Heritage, New York

Printed in Canada

04 03 02 01 00 99   7 6 5 4 3 2 1

Library of Congress Cataloging-in-Publication Data

Seeing beyond the word: visual arts and the Calvinist tradition /
edited by Paul Corby Finney.
p.   cm.
Includes bibliographical references and index.
ISBN 0-8028-3860-X (cloth: alk. paper)
1. Christianity and art — Reformed Church.
I. Finney, Paul Corby.
BX9423.A77S44   1999
261.5′7′088242 — dc21   98-6060
                                                   CIP

Dedicated to the memory of James I. McCord,
theologian of the Reformed tradition,
ecumenist,
founder and chancellor (1978-1989)
of the Center of Theological Inquiry

Contents

FRANCE/SWITZERLAND

GERMANY

HUNGARY

NETHERLANDS

THE NEW WORLD

NEW WORLD COMMENTARY

CONTENTS

Foreword

JANE DEMPSEY DOUGLASS

A fresh perspective on the long-debated question of Calvinism's relation to the visual arts is long overdue. This rich collection of articles, approaching the question from detailed study in varying contexts of Europe and North America, points to the complexity necessary for any appropriate response.

This complexity is already rooted in the views of John Calvin himself. It may be helpful to call attention here to four elements of Calvin's thought which are especially relevant to the role of the visual arts in Calvinism. At various times and places in the history of Calvinism, some of these elements of Calvin's thought have been emphasized at the expense of others. Yet in the collection of articles within this volume, all of the elements can be seen to be at work.

First is Calvin's fundamental conviction that God alone is Lord, that God alone is to be worshipped and adored, and that the knowledge of God necessary for proper worship is to be found in Scripture. Without a biblical knowledge of God, the human mind superstitiously creates idols. This conviction supported the Reformed program, which predated Calvin's arrival in Geneva, of removing all visual presentations of God and of the saints from places of worship, both to avoid any danger that they might be superstitiously worshipped and to allow the Scriptures and preaching, not art, to be the teacher of the people. So important is this conviction that Calvin and the Reformed tradition renumbered the Ten Commandments. The traditional Catholic and Lutheran first commandment was divided into two, so that "You shall not make for yourself an idol . . ." became a separate and very visible second commandment; the last two commandments in the traditional numbering were then combined to keep the total number at ten.

Second is the deep concern for simplicity of lifestyle, so that available resources can meet human needs. If the rich live extravagantly, the poor will go hungry, Calvin thought, especially in a city like Geneva, crowded with refugees and vulnerable to food shortages. Calvin believed that God had created such a bountiful world that all could enjoy the means of life if resources were fairly shared. The church and its leaders were expected to model simplicity of life in an effort to reform the broader society and its values and to be good stewards of financial resources so that the poor could be cared for. Ostentatious decoration or luxury in the church's own lifestyle would undermine the church's mission, so places of worship should be simple.

Third is the doctrine of vocation. Calvin taught that God calls Christians to work faithfully in their vocation in the world. A religious vocation is not limited to pastors. Rulers, farmers, artisans, and craftspeople can live out a Christian vocation in their daily work. Parents should urge their children to choose vocations which would be useful to their neighbors and in which they could earn honestly the means to support their families and to share their means with those in need. Whatever they have has been given by God in trust for the needy.

Fourth is Calvin's love of creation and its beauty. This element may be the least known and appreciated of the four. Calvin marveled at the new scientific insights into the nature of the heavens and the earth and of the human body; he urged people to admire creation as God's handiwork and give praise to God. God did not order creation just to be useful; God also intended it to be a source of delight to human beings. Calvin says in the *Institutes:*

> Has the Lord given to the flowers so great beauty that meets our eyes, so great sweetness of fragrance that flows upon our nose, and yet will it be unlawful for our eyes to be affected by that beauty, or our sense of smell by the pleasantness of that odor? What? Did he not so distinguish colors as to make some more lovely than others? What? Did he not endow gold and silver, ivory and marble with a loveliness by which they are rendered more precious than other metals or stones? Did he not, in short, render many things praiseworthy to us, apart from their necessary use? (*Inst.* 3.10.2)

One senses the tension and yet also the harmony of these elements of Calvin's thought as one reflects on the Calvinist silversmith with a sense of vocation for his work, creating with delight simple but elegant silver flagons, chalices, and patens for use at the Lord's Supper. There is no idolatry here, and the beautiful vessels created are useful in the community's worship. Yet are they not costly and even luxurious vessels? Will they be purchased with church funds? What of the poor? How are the earnings of the craftsman's family used? The complexity of the relation of these elements in Calvin's thought underlies the complexity in the Calvinist tradition of its relation to the visual arts.

The studies which follow point to another sort of complexity, the variety of styles of Calvinist art, the "vernacular" quality of much Calvinist art. Though this art reflects in some ways the common elements of Calvin's thought which we have highlighted, yet it also profoundly reflects the particular social and cultural contexts in which it lives. Perhaps one can see in this inculturation an echo of the broadly Protestant insistence on using the language of the common people to teach and preach and sing the Psalms, but more must be said. It is instructive that it has been customary since the sixteenth century for the Reformed church in each region to articulate its faith in its own confession, speaking out of its particular circumstances. Unlike the Lutherans who have held to a single confession, the Augsburg Confession, Reformed people have many confessions, yet they believe that they represent different ways of articulating a common faith. Is there evidence that Calvinist art speaks any more directly out of its many contexts than that of other traditions?

The historical studies before us will interest those in the World Alliance of Reformed Churches and ecumenical bodies who are currently exploring the relation of gospel and culture. Still these studies reflect only the Calvinism of Europe and North America. A next very fascinating project might be a comparative study of Calvinist visual art in the countries of the South: Asia, Africa, and Latin America, where about three-fourths of Reformed churches are located today.

I am deeply appreciative of the imagination and persistence of Professor Corby Finney in seeking out and assembling this group of scholars who out of their wide experience have indeed brought fresh perspective to our thinking about Calvinism and the visual arts.

Editor's Preface

PAUL CORBY FINNEY

At Princeton in May of 1995 the Center of Theological Inquiry (CTI) hosted a four-day symposium to explore the relationship between Calvinist (Reformed Christian) traditions and the visual arts, including architecture, painting, sculpture, and the decorative arts. Most of the papers that follow were first delivered in a lecture format at the symposium. A few (notably those by Finney, Koch, Rosasco, and Winkler) came later. It is sometimes assumed either that Reformed Christianity has had no bearing on the development of European and New World visual traditions or that the Reformed influence on the visual arts has been purely negative, amounting to an iconoclastic undoing of medieval religious art, especially figural iconography depicting biblical subjects. Neither of these characterizations is entirely unjustified, but at the same time neither does justice to a subject that is complex and complicated due to vagaries of time and place and circumstance. A more nuanced approach is clearly needed.

The essays that follow fall under the revisionist rubric. They seek to redefine a subject that has long lain dormant, and they seek to lay out the critical terms and perspectives that might serve for future research and scholarly discussion of this complex subject. This collection of essays does not presume to constitute an exhaustive or definitive treatment of any given subject, but it does set a new standard of discourse in the definition of a subject that constitutes an important crossroad in early modern history, a place where religion and culture, society, economy, and politics intersect.

There is not a great deal to be said on Calvin's view of the visual arts — it appears this is a subject that did not interest him in any great degree. Insofar as his opinions and convictions on art or art-related subjects had any lasting direct influence on the history of art, they can be subsumed under two headings: opposition to what he styled "external idolatry" (*Inst.* 2.8.17) and opposition to pictures (especially figural iconography) in places of Christian worship (*Inst.* 1.11.1-16). After his conversion (1534) to an evangelical form of Christianity, Calvin devoted a sizable part of his literary output (consisting in exegesis, homilies, letters, and constructive theology) to an attack on the material and visual signs of idolatry which he believed were especially conspicuous in medieval Catholic churches. His position on the suppression of pictures within churches was a direct implication of his obsession with the evils of external idolatry.

Calvin was not a visual person; he knew very little in detail about the visual arts. His true métier was literature. From his earliest student years to his full maturity, Calvin's heroes, his friends, his colleagues were all literary personalities, grammarians, lexicographers, rhetoricians, Latinists, Hellenists, prose and verse writers — in a word, literati. Calvin was clearly committed to a negative view of medieval Catholicism as a visually defined (and hence false) religious culture, and he also quite clearly managed to convince himself that pictures never can be an effective didactic/cognitive or communicative medium, a means of teaching, a mode of communicating. As one commentator has observed, Calvin's opinion of visual art was that in content it was "too ambiguous and too subject to personal interpretation."[1] At the same time, Calvin was unwilling to endorse iconoclasm — he consistently opposed the use of violence in reforming Christian houses of worship: "Car iamais Dieu n'a commendé d'abatre les idoles. . . ."[2] His views on the reforming of churches are best described as temperate, and his concept of reform as it applied to the real-life, material condition of church buildings was gradualistic. In short, Calvin held clear and unmistakable views on the subject of idolatry, and he expressed these views in strong language, but his real-life implementation of these views within the practical arena tended to fall on the moderate side. It was really his associates and followers who put into iconoclastic practice Calvin's literary invective against idolatry, and hence in terms of pragmatic precedents it is these later Reformed Christians, Calvin's followers more than Calvin himself, who had a direct effect on the development of Western religious art.

In the fifth of his six Stone Lectures delivered (1898) at Princeton Theological Seminary, Abraham Kuyper[3] (1837-1920) observed that historical Calvinism has never developed "an art-style of its own." The point is well taken and goes to the heart of the present volume. One of the persistent themes that emerges from the pages of this volume is the chameleon-like quality of art that can be classified under the Reformed rubric. Within the architectural idiom, for example, many early modern Reformed places of worship represent exercises in the appropriation of already exist-

1. John H. Leith, *Introduction to the Reformed Tradition* (Atlanta, 1981), p. 201.

2. Writing 13 August 1561 to the Consistory at Sauve against their iconoclasm; *Ioannis Calvini opera quae supersunt omnia* 18, ed. W. Baum, E. Cunitz, and E. Reuss (*Corpus Reformatorum* 46; Braunschweig, 1878), col. 581.

3. *Lectures on Calvinism* (Grand Rapids, 1931; reprinted 1994), pp. 142-70.

ing buildings, the assimilation of Reformed intents and purposes to already existing styles and architectonic forms, the adaptation and reconfiguration of interior spaces and furnishings to suit the needs of an immigrant religious community. Appropriation, assimilation, adaptation, reconfiguration: these are the operative analytical paradigms which describe a great deal of what we call the Reformed phenomenon in architecture. The same is true in greater or lesser degree for painting, the graphic arts, Reformed sculpture (insofar as it has any historical existence), and the decorative arts. Wherever in the early modern period we encounter material evidence that can be denominated under the Reformed rubric, we are likely to encounter these selfsame attributes.

Historically, in both Old World and New World settings, Reformed Christians have created a separate and distinct denominational identity. They have constructed their own boundaries which invariably have included a clearly defined set of confessional conditions wrapped within a distinctive polity as criteria for membership within the church. Reformed identity is not an accident, and it is not ambiguous. But these same communities have tended not to develop their own specific visual identity. Instead they have appropriated already existing stylistic traditions which they have reshaped to meet their own special needs. To repeat, this a striking feature of the Reformed tradition, past and present. This is also what makes the subject of this book so exciting and so challenging; namely, the liminal character of Reformed art; the layering of Reformed intentions on top of Catholic, secular, and other matrices; the ambiguity of an art that can and cannot be called Reformed; the appropriation of widely diverse styles and their reworking for the benefit of Reformed patrons with their distinctive Calvinist ideology.

*   *   *

A word about the Center of Theological Inquiry is in order. In 1978, after his retirement as president of Princeton Theological Seminary, Dr. James I. McCord founded the Center. Dr. McCord's vision for CTI was that it should become the premier North American research institution of its kind, an ecumenical institute devoted to interdisciplinary research in the field of religion. In dedicating this volume to the memory of Dr. McCord, I am mindful of the lofty aspirations and high purposes he had for CTI. I think this is a book of which he would have been proud. This is the first major publication in which CTI has been officially involved as affiliate and sponsor.

In organizing the CTI symposium and in editing this volume of essays, I have accumulated numerous debts which it is my pleasure to acknowledge here. I want to thank the CTI Selection Committee and Board of Trustees for approving this project. I am most grateful to CTI Director

Emeritus Daniel W. Hardy. And I am especially indebted to Henry Luce III, Chairman and CEO of the Henry Luce Foundation, and to John Wesley Cook, President of the Henry Luce Foundation. Without the combined generosity of CTI and of Mr. Luce and Dr. Cook, this book would not have seen the light of day.

I also want to thank the CTI staff members (past and present) for their assistance. This includes two former staffers, Mrs. Kate Le Van and Calvin Ratcliffe, along with current staff members Maureen Montgomery and Mary Beth Lewis, Hal Erdmans, Cecilio Otrantes, and Linda Sheldon. I also want to acknowledge the assistance of Princeton Theological Seminary audiovisual engineer Bobby Marshall. And to Dr. Mark Brombaugh, who regaled us midway through the symposium with a splendid harpsichord recital *(Keyboard Music of Early Seventeenth Century Netherlands and Its Elizabethan English Progenitors)*, my warmest thanks.

Among colleagues and friends, my primary debt is to Professor Jane Dempsey Douglass, who served as an adviser to this project in both of its phases, symposium and book. To Professors Jamie Deming, Egbert Haverkamp-Begemann, and John Wilson, for their expert participation in the symposium, my thanks. And in addition, for support and advice in various kinds, I am indebted to Professors Susan Caroselli, Natalie Davis, Taube Greenspan, Steve Hause, Thomas DaCosta Kaufman, Raymond A. Mentzer Jr., Howard Miller, Victor Nuovo, Leigh Eric Schmidt, Anita Schorsch, and Jean-Loup Seban.

To my friend Steve Rosenthal, who graciously agreed to interrupt his busy schedule to photograph the Rocky Hill Meetinghouse in Amesbury, I extend my sincere thanks. And last but not least, I want to thank William B. Eerdmans Jr., a good friend whose support throughout this project has been extraordinary. In these times of declining standards and shrinking budgets within the world of academic publishing, Bill Eerdmans has honored my request that this become a book of which humanists like Calvin and bibliophiles like de Bèze would have been proud to claim a part.

Calvinism and the Visual Arts: A Theological Introduction

DANIEL W. HARDY

Introduction

While it was done with the best motives, the Reformers' action of disallowing a direct contribution to religion from the visual arts was a very serious step, with deep and long-lasting consequences for both, separately and in their relation to each other. It leaves a lingering question: Was it based on a failure to understand the arts, or Christianity, or both? To understand the full significance of this action, we must consider the special character of the visual arts, the position which they might have — and had previously — occupied in Christian faith, why and how they were rejected by the Reformers, and the implications of this rejection for the future relationship of Christianity and these arts. Throughout, our concern will be with theological issues. Other parts of this book explore these matters from cultural, religious, and artistic perspectives.

The Special Character of the Visual Arts

A major issue is what the arts *are*. It is often overlooked that the world as we know it is a reality that is, so to speak, spread out or distributed. It is not an undifferentiated mass which is "all at once," but various and time laden. In it things are different, related, and differently phased in time. In this distributed, time-laden world, things are not evenly spread: nature is "clumped" in certain ways, as things of different kinds related to each other in complex ways, and through events in complex dynamic patterns we call "history." These "clumps" and "movements" are what we are, and what surrounds us.

1

Of course, these movements may be instantaneous, but even such events are usually complex, and originate from, and give rise to, complex spatial and time-laden sequences from which they are not easily separable. To act in such a world is to invoke complex and time-laden prior conditions and consequences. Before and after, actions imply the shaping of the distributed reality of the world and the phasing of its time.

Broadly speaking, the arts are the means by which human beings *capture* ("*hold*") and *portray* the richness of this reality in its time-laden and instantaneous complexity. The fact that they can do so is one of the unique features of human beings. And they appear always to have done so. The world and history have always been *summarized* or *concentrated* by human beings, as one finds them doing in prehistoric cave paintings, ritual behavior, dance forms, their imaginations, or literature, for example.

They do so in many ways. One key difference between these is in their use of *extension*. The visual arts compress one spatio-temporal extension into another, much smaller one, reducing the one to the other. These "compressed extensions" vary in kind. Some are "flat," on one plane. Some are multidimensional, like sculptures. Some are "spatial configurations" in which people live and move, as with buildings, gardens, and cities. All of these "extensions" involve time somehow, but some are more explicitly time laden, whether because of the medium which they employ or because they represent or shape movement. By contrast, performed music is nonspatial; it employs phased movement, as when sounds are patterned as temporal configurations in music

The literary arts, however, transpose spatio-temporal extension into words, a very different kind of extension. Again, this medium varies enormously. Literature may begin from a "flood of talk"[1] which captures certain situations and range to the other extreme, to the subjection of words to cognitive control through which they are made to "serve the purposes of intellect."[2] On the one hand, the rich portrayal of a situation may be primary, and metaphor and narrative predominate. On the other hand, words may be used analytically and made to correspond closely — usually as propositions — to the reality which they are used to express. Grammar and logic can further intellectualize language as specialized symbols and formulas which capture timeless operations like the laws of nature. Inevitably, the use of language in these ways carries implications for the reality expressed.

Other factors enter the process by which the arts and language are pro-

---

1. "Actually, if the linguistic theorist can obtain access to a nursery, he . . . will hear the mother not enunciating single words to her child, but pouring out a flood of talk mostly devoted not to the naming of certain things but to the expression of her pleasure in its society . . . sooner or later the child is heard imitating in garbled phrases which it has heard on certain kinds of occasion. . . ." R. G. Collingwood, *Principles of Art* (Oxford, 1938), p. 227.

2. Collingwood, p. 252.

duced — material, social, cultural, commercial, and personal. What is the significance of the play of ideas — whereby minds "are both active and receptive in . . . imagination" — by which the mind "illuminates our images so that they can affect our receptive mind, just as light activates colours to affect our sight"?[3] Whether independent of, or immediately conjoined with, artistic or literary expression, the imagination is an extraordinarily rich medium for ideas, memories, and hopes, and their active illumination. In that sense, it is vital to knowledge. But at the same time, it has the power to free itself — in flights of imagination — of the constraints of reality, and thus to be a danger where the presentation of reality is the issue.

When the real and the imaginative are combined in the visual and literary arts, there is a "projection" in different mediums. The visual and literary arts provide an addition to the "reality" from which they begin, utilizing a new "surface" — a two-dimensional plane, a three-dimensional extension, or a counterpart in words. In so doing, they are expressed and embodied for others: some measure of the fullness of reality is expressed within the compass of the artistic forms available.

Conceptions of the Visual Arts in Christian Faith

The capacity of the visual arts for concentration of reality in different forms of extension (as "flat," multidimensional, architectural, musical, and dance), or that of language for analytical or narrative representation of reality, conceivably permits them to be used as "fields" in which the "extension" of God's history with humankind can be presented. Church buildings and liturgical worship, for example, can serve as architectural and performative "extensions" in which God's long-term presence with humankind can be presented, through which the former can become the "language" for the other. Conceivably, any of these forms of art, as the elemental ways by which human beings concentrate reality in front of, around, and in them, might be religiously transposed in such fashion. Are we to conclude that such religious presentations are only the product of human endeavor, and therefore *prima facie* idolatrous? Or are they "concentrated extensions" of the self-concentration of God in historical reality, and apprehended through artistic expression?

To respond to this question, one must ask about the forms of representation used in religious art. To take the most obvious case, the use of inverted perspective in the Orthodox art of the East provides pictures whose representation of objects is such that they are seen to "belong to another, spiritual world, rather than the three-dimensional material world of

---

3. St. Thomas Aquinas, *Summa Theologiae*, ed. T. McDermott (Westminster, 1989), 54.4, p. 97.

time and space," thus avoiding the dangers of idolatry.[4] But for those incapable of grasping such forms of representation, there is the possibility that anomalous forms of artistic representation will not be grasped, and such pictures will be viewed as representing objects belonging to *thisworldly time and space.* Hence, those who read them in straightforward realistic ways, simple presentations of the *other,* spiritual world in terms of the reality of *this* world, will consider them idolatrous — a misconception based on the supposition that artistic presentations are of the same nature (consubstantial) with what is represented.[5]

The fact that such anomalous forms of artistic representation are not grasped fuels the long-standing debate between iconophiles and iconoclasts. How could that which is held to be anti-idolatrous (e.g., Orthodox art) come to be seen in the modern West as intrinsically idolatrous — the self-projection of God as human projection? One answer may lie in a long-standing Western conviction about reality itself, that there is such an unbridgeable gap between the spiritual and the material that the material is incapable of representing the spiritual — *finitum non capax infiniti* — except where this is made possible by God. By contrast, the Eastern notion is anti-dualist: "the very existence of the icon is based on the Incarnation of the second person of the Holy Trinity, this Incarnation, in turn . . . confirmed and proven by the image."[6]

Western Conceptions

In the Western view, the question is *how* the material may represent the spiritual, and how narrowly this possibility is construed. This is the major issue between the Reformers and "the rest" — including both Roman Catholics and Orthodox — *and* between the Reformers themselves.

Generally speaking, those who insist on a narrow construal maintain that the possibility of representing the spiritual (God) arises only within the *act of God* in Jesus Christ where this is received *in faith* by those transformed by it (through justification). No neutral, quasi-objective form of representation would be suitable to such a powerfully "actualist" notion, but only witness in which the Word of God identifies, judges, and corrects human evil. Amongst the Reformers, as we will see, there is some difference about the implications which are to be drawn. But there is still general agreement that it is safe to concentrate only on the "self-accommodation" of God (in Calvin's term) in his Word to human language, and therefore to human understanding; this was what was to be sought in the language of Scripture, as

---

4. John Willats, *Art and Representation* (Princeton, 1997), p. 27.

5. Leonid Ouspensky, *Theology of the Icon* (Crestwood, 1992), vol. I, p. 122.

6. Ouspensky, p. 121.

read (and heard) in faith. This has the advantage of "double invisibility," as we might call it. Language — unless defined otherwise, as in logical positivism — has the advantage of allowing the invisibility of that to which it refers, hiding any visibility its referent might have. And its reception is also invisible, the quality being dependent on the power of its referent — in the reading or hearing — to convince the recipient.

The alternative, of course, is not to suppose a lesser gap between the spiritual and the material, or to suppose that the material as such represents the spiritual, but to believe that God makes the material capable of representing God. "Since the sacred realities signified by the sacraments are spiritual things that only mind can grasp, the sacraments must signify them with things our senses can perceive, just as the scriptures express them with analogies drawn from the perceptible world."[7] By extension, the same can be applied to the visual arts: images of perceptible things can provide analogies to the spiritual insofar as they are used within the faith of believers in the church.

The larger question here is *what in the world* can and should be used to represent the work of God in the world. How, for example, might language and visual arts be used in ways which are appropriate to, but do not pretend adequacy to, God's work in the world? The answer turns on several issues about representation. (a) *Relative to what* is their capacity to represent to be judged — to the nature and activity of God or/and to the comprehension of human beings? (b) What is suitable for representational use? And (c) what forms of representational system are suitable — an optical denotational system that provides effective representation of their shape, or something else? The answers to such questions are not, furthermore, a matter of arbitrary choice by individuals; they are interwoven with the purpose of representations within the life of the Church. They are the issues that came to concern the Reformers.

As we turn to the Reformers themselves, we must not assume that *all* kinds of artistic view of God's work were rejected by those who objected to the religious use of the visual arts in general. Second-generation Calvinists like Theodore Beza and William Perkins employed what can be called "topological" charts of salvation, making use of what we can now recognize as topological geometrical representational systems. Schematic diagrams of such a kind are used, for example, in the London Underground; "based on the most elementary and general types of spatial properties, which include relations like touching, separation, spatial order, and enclosure,"[8] they represent not true scales and shapes, but only the connections between stations and their order along the route. The "Golden Chain" used by Beza

7. Aquinas, *Summa Theologiae*, 60.4, p. 547.
8. Aquinas, p. 13.

5

and Perkins represents no spatial order, and no exact historical order, but only the order of connections within the inner communication of the God-head and between them and the acts of God wherein are the "causes of Salvation and Damnation, according to God's word," eventually leading to God's justice and mercy, and the fullness of God's glory. There is the topographically ordered connection between God's foreknowledge and predestination, God's double decree (of election and reprobation), creation and fall, and the "double line" which connects the destiny of those elected to salvation and of those to reprobation to the salvation by which all creation is returned to the glory of God. For those elected to salvation, after creation and fall Christ and his benefits are connected, and the calling, justification, and sanctification to which they give rise are also connected. Like any topological map, this portrays relations, separation, and enclosure within the saving work of God — a capturing of this work in a concentrated topological form which is nonetheless not seen as pictorially representative at all.

The History of the Debate

If we go back two thousand years, the use of the visual arts in Christianity is already widespread; they were employed for the nonverbal mediation of religious belief. To some extent, therefore, they clarified the content of faith; presentation and content interacted.

The arts appear to have been used by Christians from earliest times, in all the forms we have seen — including the verbal, two- and three-dimensional — and with the clear intention of concentrating those fundamental aspects of Christian belief and life which involve God's activity in the world. At first, under the very restrictive conditions in which Christianity began, abstractive and nonnaturalistic line-drawings prevailed, as in ideograms like the fish, anchor, or lamb. With the establishment of Christianity by Constantine, however, the position of the Church changed drastically. It now needed to express and embody the Christian religious basis for all existing institutions. Hence Christianity needed to weld together a variety of loosely linked churches and to engage with the existing Roman polity, buildings, and art. Architecture and art, making use of existing forms, became important means of "summarizing" the interaction of God with worldly reality. As it has been claimed,[9] there was an "essential shift . . . of meanings related to perhaps the most remarkable change in society that the Western world has seen." Through Christianity, the arts of Rome were given "new energy, focus and fervour."

At the same time, there was a concerted effort to preserve Christian

9. Elsner, *Art and the Roman Viewer* (Cambridge, 1995), p. 245.

6

faith from degradation. "Christian art worked — perhaps harder than any other aspect of Christianization — towards what has been described as draining the secular from society, toward eliminating non-exegetic ways of viewing."[10] The chief means for doing so was the development of a deeply symbolic and typological tradition in Christian imagery through which the world was made transparent to the activity of God, as distinct from the naturalism characteristic of Roman art.

In the late Middle Ages, it appears that this tradition in the use of the visual arts in Christianity underwent a further transformation. To a large extent, the arts were "renaturalized," which implicated the faith they represented in this naturalism. While the typological/symbolic use of visual arts had served to focus the eye on what lay *beyond* the natural as such, particularly in presenting God as normative for history, the arts now tended to reduce the infinite to the finite, and the normative to what was familiar and undemanding. The use of images, the product of the "unlimited desire to bestow form on everything that is sacred . . . so that it exists in the mind like a crisply printed picture . . . overloaded belief itself."[11] So widely were images used, turning everything holy into pictorial images, that direct aesthetic perception overcame religious meanings, and the mystery and demand of the holy were lost. Worse still, perhaps, was the readiness with which people acquiesced in this state of affairs; even their attempts to stir themselves to apprehend the sacred showed trumped-up enthusiasm.

The situation was still more complex. To take one example, the demise of the classical world and its replacement by an early medieval one severely damaged traditional suppositions about the nature of truth and how knowledge was to be found. With such uncertainties, and with the emphasis then placed on the hiddenness of divine truth and the inadequacy of language to it, signs came to be seen as material manifestations of the spiritual world through which knowledge of God was revealed. The argument centered on whether or not images were to be "an important element in a sign-system through which knowledge, no longer accessible in the old way, could still be reliably assessed."[12] Fundamentally, this was an "argument about the correct representation of God" which involved basic issues about how God is to be known. If, as the Byzantine iconoclasts claimed, "only certain signs were to be allowed, principally the Eucharist, the 'one true image' of God, all other figural images should be destroyed."[13] The argument was not about returning to an imageless religion, but about what signs are allowed, and how they are important.

10. Elsner, p. 251.

11. Johan Huizinga, *The Autumn of the Middle Ages* (Chicago, 1996), p. 173.

12. Averil Cameron, "The Language of Images," in *The Church and the Arts* (Studies in Church History xxviii; Oxford, 1992), p. 4.

13. Cameron, p. 37.

The situation was exacerbated by the tendencies of the Renaissance, with the revival of subjects and styles antedating Christian influence. Renaissance influences came through both artists and humanists. On the one hand, "the achievements of Renaissance painters and sculptors . . . were instrumental in establishing a canon of taste in which ancient art came to occupy the supreme place."[14] And, on the other hand, the humanists created a climate in which the preferred subject-matter was ever more "natural," that is, "portraiture, secular history, classical mythology and allegory."[15] Interestingly, the Renaissance both heightened the situation — in art and literature — to which the Reformers found it necessary to react, and provided the vehicle through which they reacted, *textuality as the medium of truth*.

Why Reformation? Reaction and Relation

In the complex situation just indicated, it is quite understandable that there should have been a reaction. But with the Reformers, a suspicion for the arts began which is remarkable for its clarity and severity. In itself, this justifies the attention given in this book to "The Visual Arts and the Calvinist Tradition." The fact is that the Reformed tradition has been unusual in the sharpness and severity of its suspicion for the arts, a suspicion expressed in an unusual variety of strategies to limit their use in Christianity. And this is good reason for considering the significance of the Reformed tradition and the arts for each other. It is a "hard case" which illuminates major features of the interaction of religion and the arts in general, not least because the views are clearly expressed, often in extreme forms, and artistic reactions to them are — at least to some extent — definite.

But the Reformed "tradition" is not monolithic and historically unvarying. The Reformers vary in their views, and these undergo further modifications during their transmission to later generations and different places. Wider influences, philosophical, cultural, and artistic, play a role in these transitions. The influence is not only one-way, therefore, as if the influence of the Reformed tradition was determinative for the arts, while the arts had no effect on it. While Reformed religion did attempt to control the place of the arts in religion, there were reciprocal effects of the arts on both religious practice and the place of religion in public life, and not necessarily ones of which the Reformed tradition would disapprove. It is therefore necessary to examine the importance of the Reformed tradition and the arts *for each other* during the historical transitions of each.

14. Charles Hope and Elizabeth McGrath, "Artists and Humanists," in *The Cambridge Companion to Renaissance Humanism*, ed. Jill Kraye (Cambridge, 1996), p. 165.
15. Hope and McGrath, p. 170.

A notable illustration of the interaction between the arts and religion is architectural. When the meetinghouse replaced the church building, this configuration of space reinforced perceptions of what was primary in religion, focusing attention on the preaching of the Word of God. The issues involved were profoundly theological. Churches had been intended to concentrate — through their form and embellishment — the presence of the triune God *in and with the secular.*[16] These, however, were gradually replaced by meetinghouses intended only to house Word-governed witness to God's act in Jesus Christ. The effect of this replacement — somewhat like replacing a lamp with a searchlight — was to displace the visibly sacred from wider spheres of public activity and to transfer attention to prophetic witness directed at discernible evil. Furthermore, where *churches* had enacted communal society by extended liturgical performances, *meetinghouses* housed the inner transformation of individuals by the preached Word of God. In due course, it would become difficult to maintain the requirements of Christian communal life where they conflicted with emerging social norms. Despite his previous success in the revivals in New England, when Jonathan Edwards attempted to ensure that church membership was necessary for acceptance in the community, his people rejected him and he was forced to leave.[17]

Better understanding of the Reformed tradition and the visual arts requires that we examine their importance *for each other* with careful attention to the differences made by new historical situations. Religious suppositions, artistic expressions, and their interrelation will vary. In the case just mentioned, it is plainly not the case that meetinghouses were always of one kind, but they reflected new combinations of religious supposition, architectural form, and local social practices. The interaction of religion and the arts varied, even in the dissociation (attempted by the Reformers) of the two from each other. In an important sense, they were formative for each other, whether by mutual resistance or by collaboration, and in different ways, during the centuries to follow. That is the fascination of the material presented in this book.

Sources of Reformation

The need for the Reformers' suspension of the arts did not arise only from "outside." An artistic situation highly problematic for religion met a *passionately purified form of religion,* and a collision between the two was inevitable. In a fashion reminiscent of Augustine, the Reformers' demand was for radical purification.

16. See J. G. Davies, *The Secular Use of Church Buildings* (London, 1968).
17. Patricia J. Tracy, *Jonathan Edwards, Pastor* (New York, 1979), p. 175.

It has been said, rather mildly, that the impulse of the Reformation was one of clearing up, and in that sense it was but a further example of the religious attempts to reform, to purify the Christian faith and practice which have featured in the history of Christianity from the beginning. That is considerably to underestimate it.

This was a movement of purification that began not from the practical wish to control excesses, but from a deep transformation in the mode of Christian existence as such. It is significant that the reforming movements originated from definite and powerful "turnings" to the purifying touch of God, which changed the life-direction of those involved. To those thus transformed, anything less was seen as inadequate or false.

Martin Luther's reforming movement began from his own struggle with the inadequacy of the accepted formalist interpretation of Romans 1 ("the righteousness [*justitia*] of God is revealed in [the gospel]"), and such satisfaction as he could offer to meet his "most unquiet conscience" as a sinner in the presence of God. Only when "God showed mercy and [he] turned [his] attention to the connection of the words, namely — 'The righteousness of God is revealed, as it is written: the righteous shall live by faith,'" was he "straightway born afresh."[18] The God-given change from unrighteousness to righteous life, which occurred through faith alone, was pivotal for Luther.

John Calvin's reforming also began from an "unexpected conversion," although different from Luther's. "When I was too firmly addicted to the papal superstitions to be drawn easily out of such a deep mire, by a sudden conversion He brought my mind (already more rigid than suited my age) to submission."[19] Calvin was acutely aware of the active glory of God which "stripped men of all their glory . . . to clothe them with something better," whose only Mediator is Christ, "through whom the fullness of all heavenly gifts flows down to us and through whom we on our part may ascend to God."[20] To be transformed was a total reorientation of human capacities, in which the change to righteousness implicated everything human.

Whether these accounts refer to sudden conversions at the outset of their major contributions, or are to be treated as summary statements of their lifetime transformation, it is clear that both Luther and Calvin identified a *distinctive modality for Christian faith*. It occurred entirely by the activity of God as this took place in the justifying of human beings by Christ through faith. This was the springboard for the fundamental reform they advocated.

At this level, Huldreich Zwingli's "turning" was similar. It was to utter trust in God as God speaks in the Bible; without such trust all created

18. E. G. Rupp and Benjamin Drewery, ed., *Martin Luther* (London, 1970), pp. 5-6.
19. *Calvin's Commentaries*, ed. Joseph Haroutunian (London, 1958), p. 52.
20. Haroutunian, p. 147.

reality, including human beings, is incapable of goodness, and inclined to idolatry.[21] Zwingli's turning was a spiritual one, to trust, grace, and freedom received from God through Jesus Christ by the activity of the Holy Spirit. A spiritual reformation was necessary — matched by a "concomitant institutional and liturgical reformation as well."[22]

The distinctive modality of being Christian uncovered by these Reformers had certain common *religious* features. But each Reformer elucidated these in distinct *theological* ways. It is these theological differences which are especially important for their views of the visual arts.

Theological Differences and the Visual Arts

As he saw it, Luther's conversion was rooted in the active righteousness of God imparting righteousness to the faithful even in their sin, making them genuinely righteous even in their sin *(simul iustus et peccator)*. God's revelation in Scripture was therefore not so much informative as transforming, and what was pivotal was that this should be *confessed* by those who were transformed. If the issue is the conferring of righteousness on sinful human beings, and if — despite their sin — their Christ-given faith makes them capable of receiving it, the existing liturgies and devotions as well as the use of visual arts were no problem except insofar as they obstructed this justification. Furthermore, God's justification in Christ and the dynamic of human transformation were deeply historical, that is, temporally extended. It was for this reason, apparently, that Luther was open to the arts: his attention to liturgy and churches was no accident: "I would like to see all the arts, especially music, used in the service of Him who gave and made them."[23]

Luther was convinced that the transformative power of the Word would show how ineffective images as such were ("then they would have fallen by themselves"[24]), but there were others — like Andreas Carlstadt — who advocated immediate abolition of images. Luther, however, counseled reliance on the Word: "it should be left to God, and his Word should be allowed to work alone, without our work or interference . . . for faith must come freely without compulsion."[25] As in his view of justification by faith,

21. "For the flesh is always against God and everything which is against him, knows of no rest or comfort. . . . Where the Spirit of God is not, there is no freedom." Huldreich Zwingli, *The Defense of the Reformed Faith*, trans. E. J. Furcha (Allison Park, 1984), p. 68.

22. John Phillips, *The Reformation of Images: Destruction of Art in England, 1535-1660* (Berkeley, 1973), p. 108.

23. Martin Luther, *Luther's Works*, vol. 53 (Philadelphia, 1959), p. 316.

24. Luther, Third Sermon at Wittenberg, in *Luther's Works*, vol. 51 (Philadelphia, 1959), p. 83.

25. Luther, Second Sermon at Wittenberg, in *Luther's Works*, vol. 51, pp. 76-77.

Luther concentrated on the action of God in changing human beings to righteousness, while the consequences of sin remained. In the case of the arts, Luther was more concerned with change from wrong use than with the arts as such. In a world where anything could be used idolatrously, "abuses must be met as abuses, not as occasions for removing that which gives offense."[26] Faith transforms life while leaving its essentials intact.

Calvin's "conversion" yielded different theological implications, focused as it was on the glory of the one true God, and how this God might rightly be known, worshipped, and served by those without the capacity to do so (non capax infiniti). The glory of God was such that he could be accessible only insofar as he freely and graciously "unveils" himself by accommodating himself to the human condition, coming in Christ to dwell in the finite and sinful and thereby making it possible for human beings to know, honor, and serve him. Calvin therefore saw God's self-revelation as both informative (through unveiling and self-accommodation) and transformative (through redeeming the sinful), and human beings were entirely dependent for truth on his initiative in his Word. This was not entirely to disqualify human knowledge, for the self and the world could be known within certain limits, but such knowledge would become idolatrous when used beyond its limits. Calvin's notorious disinterest in the arts is not therefore based on a trait of character, but on twin theological premises — that the arts are not interesting to those concerned for the truth as God known in God's Word, and that in themselves they are legitimate only within strictly defined limits.

The consequences of Calvin's view for the arts are to be seen in his *Institutes of the Christian Religion* and in the efforts of his followers to agree on church reform — at the Colloquy of St. Germain-en-Laye in 1562, for example. There it is clear that human beings must rely wholly on God's freely given justification by grace, thereby to be freed from the attempt to achieve righteousness by their works. They must learn to rely only on the one mediator Jesus Christ, in whom alone God accommodates himself to human capacities through the Word (and by the Spirit) in preaching and sacraments. This self-accommodation in the Word is so full that any addition or substitution is unnecessary; images can only be a substitute for the Word, and they are no genuine aid to devotion.

For Calvin, images undermine God's self-witness, the fact that "God himself is the sole and proper witness of himself."[27] As the Second Commandment shows, all visible representations of God are "unfitting and absurd fictions" that sully God's immeasurable majesty, displease God, and conflict with his universality. In effect, they draw human attention down-

26. John Dillenberger, *A Theology of Artistic Sensibilities* (New York, 1986), p. 62.
27. John Calvin, *Institutes of the Christian Religion*, trans. Ford Lewis Battles (Philadelphia, 1959), 1.11.100.

ward, rather than lifting human minds above themselves in admiration. Calvin traces the repudiation of images through Scripture and the fathers and doctors of the church, concluding that such things — far from being necessary concessions to the uneducated — are "examples of the most abandoned lust and obscenity."[28]

Hence it has been suggested[29] that the Second Commandment, by indicating that images must not be used to refer to God, provides a *via negativa*: human beings may know God's glory by setting aside what is incompatible with it. If, however, they use images to refer directly to God, this constitutes a *via positiva* which is in fact blasphemous, confining God's glory to that of images. The art involved is also false, a deception deludes viewers into thinking God visible, and self-destructive, since it promotes the improper construction of images. There is a "true" art, but it consists only of the portrayal of sensible — not imagined — things or events, whether present or remembered. Calvin thereby provides a very restricted place for the arts, and a very limited view of what they may attempt.

Zwingli's position was of another kind, uncompromisingly spiritual and scriptural. He was concerned above all to promote prayer to God "which recognizes Him truly and calls on God with heart free from doubt, not with hypocrisy, but with right, true acknowledgment and recognition . . . Christ [Matt. 6:7] prohibited much babbling and has taught that we should pray in spirit and in truth [John 4:24] where He frees us from particular localities."[30] Accordingly, Zwingli sought a form of worship conducive to such prayer, free of visual arts and music, which were powerless to aid the worshipper and tended always to distract: "taking from God his honour and giving it to anything else is for Zwingli the true idolatry."[31]

So spiritual was this conception of worship that all relationships between Christianity and the arts were to be severed. The result of Zwingli's views was the methodical removal of images from the churches of Zurich, until he could declare: "in Zurich we have churches which are positively luminous; the walls are beautifully white."[32]

As this suggests, Zwingli closely aligned the act of God with human spiritual response, when the living Word of God occurred for people when the Bible was preached, or when the congregation "spiritually ate" the Lord's Supper. All else was at best an external sign, for fleshly human beings. Short of a view which prohibits the arts altogether, Zwingli's is the most extreme in disallowing the visual and musical arts from Christian worship and life, allowing them no legitimacy in this sphere. This did not,

28. *Inst.* 1.11.106.
29. David Willis Watkins, *The Second Commandment and Church Reform: The Colloquy of St. Germain-en-Laye* (Studies in Reformed Theology and History; Princeton, 1994), p. 41.
30. Watkins, p. 40.
31. Watkins, p. 70.
32. Charles Garside Jr., *Zwingli and the Arts* (New Haven, 1966), p. 160.

however, disallow the arts altogether, but limited them to a non-reverential use in the home and public places, "so long as they were merely *geschichteswyss,* historical representations" and not devotional aids.[33]

As we saw, despite these *theological* differences the distinctive modality of being Christian uncovered by these Reformers had certain features common to them all. All three directed human beings to concentrate on the *act* of God by which they came to their "truth." Through the reconciliation with God effected by Christ, and by the agency of the Holy Spirit, God activated their faith and saved them from their sin.

We see, then, that the distinctive modality common to Reformed Christianity was religious, but that it was accompanied in each of the Reformers by a different *theological* explication. Luther's theology unfolded justification as such (the transformation to righteousness in sin); Calvin's theology explicated the implications of the unveiling of the glory of God for human thought and life (a noetic as well as a justifying transformation); and Zwingli's reiterated complete reliance on truth learned from God as the Spirit of God inspired understanding of God's own word in Scripture. The implication of the Reformed modality as such was only the *suspension* of the position that the arts had formerly occupied, but the implications of the distinctive theological positions that resulted provided distinctive notions of the place to be accorded to the arts in Christian life.

Another way to state this is to distinguish between what can be called "natural suspicion" and its particular consequences. Simply by virtue of the Reformers' concentration on God and the activity of God in Christ, on things invisible and unlocatable except in the transformed self, all three are naturally suspicious of what is visible and externally locatable. And in the course of time, that suspicion might have consequences for the arts, through attempts to redirect attention to the character of the activity of God. But what, except for the different theological expositions of this modality, would account for the differences in the ways the arts were treated? One kind of theological explication might lead to a relatively passive *allowing* of continued use of the arts in a religious context, another to an active *disengagement* from the arts so far as used religiously, and a third to direct action *against* the arts used even for human edification. All three, of course, are markedly different from the redirected engagement with the arts which was favored in Roman Catholicism after the Council of Trent (1545-63).

Identifying Theological Strategies

In a time when the importance of the arts has grown greatly and informed understanding of Christianity has declined, it is too easy to underestimate

33. Garside, p. 181.

14

the importance of the views of the Reformers and to avoid their significance for the relation of Christian faith and the visual arts. Nonetheless, the Reformers' views of the visual arts are of pivotal importance for establishing the relation of Christian faith to the arts.

It is important to appreciate fully the issues at stake. The use of the arts in Christianity goes to the core of what Christian faith is, to the nature of God and God's activity in Christ, how these appear in the world, and how they involve the spatio-temporal character of human life in the world. One major aspect of the importance of the visual arts is that they press these issues home.

How are the spatio-temporal implications of God's activity in Christ to be sustained in Christianity and in the arts without compromising either to the other? It is one thing to provide general answers, of course, and quite another to find out how — in the practice of Christian faith and that of the arts — they are mutually involved without loss to either. How can the arts and Christian faith be "drawn through" each other? That is a question which has never been fully answered, whether for the arts or for other mediations of life in the world.

The response of the Reformers was far-reaching in its significance, both historically and theologically, not least because it was concentrated on the *intensive act* of God. God had acted toward the world in accordance with God's will, in a way which was suitable to God and appropriate to the condition of humanity, that is, in the intensity of his judgment and love in Jesus Christ, God's Word of justification to reconcile human beings to God. The intensity of this act was to be received by human beings in comparable fashion, through a justifying faith that transformed them, as this was made possible for them by Christ through the Holy Spirit.

The implication of this concentration upon God's act of justification was that all existing human capacities — perception, imagination, and cognition — needed to be capacitated by the action of God if they were to be humanly adequate to the apprehension of God's act. For this was a theology whose core was the intensity of the act of God by which human beings were morally and cognitively transformed in such a way as to be fit to respond to and know God. Since nothing untouched by this act could contribute to the relationship between human beings and God, the effect was to confine anything "outside" to the secular sphere — where it could not even prepare human beings for the act of God.

Concentrated as they were on the intensity of God's act, there were still discernible differences in the strategy of the Reformers as regards the arts. Both Calvin and Zwingli located God's act in its intensity for the individual, in knowledge and spiritual awareness respectively. The consequence was disengagement from the religious use of the visual, whether representing the real or expressing the imagination, as simply inadequate to God. This did not eliminate their value in private or public life, so long

15

as such uses were nonreverential. In effect, therefore, Calvin and Zwingli opposed all *religious use* of the visual arts. Recalling the categories mentioned earlier, we may conclude that for them the *intensity* of God's act for human awareness cancelled the possibility of *extensive* artistic representation of God's involvement in the spatio-temporality of the world.

While Luther was just as much concerned for the intensity of God's act, his view was somewhat different. He located this act more directly in the *dynamics of life* as *temporally extended human history*. Human activity was as much contingent upon the activity of God as it was for Calvin and Zwingli, but — not content with tracing God's act in faith as such — Luther seemed to regard human history as such as the theater for God's action. This opened a possibility for the arts not present in the others, as the *extended representation* of God's action in the spatio-temporality of human existence. This may explain Luther's greater attention to buildings, liturgy, and music as allies in Christian faith, which sharply distinguishes his views from the others'.

The developments in culture, architecture, and art traced elsewhere in this book suggest, however, that the vitality of the visual arts eventually outstripped the clear principles laid down by the Reformers, allowing the arts to escape the limitations the Reformers placed on them. It would be a mistake to suppose that this points to the inadequacy of the Reformers' views of the visual arts, for they are powerfully self-consistent in their conception of the manner in which God acts in the world, and in drawing its implications for the arts.

What the development of the visual arts throughout the centuries does suggest, however, is that the question of the right relation of Christian faith and the arts must be reopened. By doing so, and inquiring deeply into the implications of this development for both Christian faith and the arts, we may yet find how they can be mutually involved without loss to either. Perhaps that is the conversation to which this book will give rise. If so, these ventures into a new field of exploration will have proved their value.

EUROPE
(GENERAL)

Calvinism as a Culture?
Preliminary Remarks on Calvinism
and the Visual Arts

PHILIP BENEDICT

Those who seek in scholarship nothing more than an honored
occupation with which to beguile the tedium of idleness I would
compare to those who pass their lives looking at paintings.[1]

John Calvin made this remark in a letter that he wrote in 1540 to an unknown young man whose progress in his studies he praised but whom he
sought at the same time to inspire to greater devotion to the cause of true
religion. Although little more than an offhand comment, the sentence still
reveals basic aspects of the Genevan reformer's attitude toward the visual
arts. Implying, characteristically, that all activities should be performed for
the greater glory of God, it situates the act of looking at paintings at the
very antipode of such behavior. Not only is there no suggestion that this
activity might be morally or devotionally edifying; there is also no hint of
the fetishization or sacralization of the work of art on aesthetic grounds
that a few theorists of art were just beginning to promote in Calvin's own
lifetime and that would become so central to Western discussions of art
from the eighteenth century onward. But if looking at pictures is in no way

---

This paper owes a great deal to conversations with Jeffrey Muller and to comments and critical questions posed by my fellow symposiasts at the CTI symposium. I wish to express my
thanks to all of them.

1. *Ioannis Calvini opera quae supersunt omnia*, ed. W. Baum, E. Cunitz, and E. Reuss
(Brunswick and Berlin, 1863-1900), vol. XI, p. 56.

ennobling or improving, it is a pastime in which Calvin can imagine acquaintances engaging. Although idle, it may amuse.

This quotation from Calvin has not been chosen as the starting point for this essay in order to emphasize the importance of Calvin himself for the subject of this volume or to imply that his passing comments represent normative pronouncements for the religious tradition that we often label for convenience "Calvinism." Calvin in fact only expressed a broader consensus among Reformed theologians on matters pertaining to the visual arts, and while his prestige was great within the different churches and religious movements that constitute this tradition, recent scholarship has underscored the variety and changeableness of the theological influences shaping the different branches of this tradition. "Reformed," not "Calvinist," is now the generic classification of choice among specialists, even if "Calvinist" retains the advantage of greater accessibility for nonspecialists.

What the quotation does offer, however — beyond a certain puckish appropriateness to the subject at hand — is an immediate dip into the words of the sixteenth century. That in turn is perhaps the best antidote to anachronism and special pleading. And this is valuable because these two qualities long abounded in discussions of the subject of Calvinism and the visual arts, and still threaten to cast their shadow over the way in which the subject is approached.

The history of scholarship about the topic of Calvinism and the visual arts can be roughly divided into two eras. In the nineteenth century, and for the better part of the twentieth, the question was cast in a manner heavily tinged by confessional polemics and the prevailing conceptions of the nature of art and of culture. As the elements of apologetics and anachronism became more and more apparent in the work produced within the parameters of this discussion, interest in the question declined. But then, in the past fifteen years or so, a new generation of scholars has begun to approach the topic with very different assumptions, generating a revival of interest that is just beginning to gather steam. Today, the issues at stake look quite different, and far more complex, than they once did.[2]

For an introduction to the way in which the question of Calvinism and the visual arts was traditionally framed, we can do no better than to turn to two lectures delivered within four years of one another nearly a century ago by a pair of leading theologians and Calvin scholars of that era, Abraham Kuyper and Émile Doumergue. Kuyper, a prominent Dutch political leader as well as a theologian, chose the subject of "Calvinism and Art" for one of the six L. P. Stone Lectures that he delivered at Prince-

---

2. For an excellent bibliography of the relevant literature, focused primarily on the sixteenth century, see Linda B. Parshall and Peter W. Parshall, *Art and the Reformation: An Annotated Bibliography* (Boston, 1986). The preface, pp. xv-xlvi, surveys the trends that have promoted the recent revival of interest in this topic.

ton Theological Seminary in 1898 and subsequently published under the title *Lectures on Calvinism*. The work was reprinted as recently as 1994.[3] Doumergue, the scarcely less distinguished French Calvin scholar, took up the same question in a series of lectures given in the Salle de la Réformation in Geneva that he entitled *L'art et le sentiment dans l'oeuvre de Calvin*.[4]

The context in which both men worked was that of the still-bitter confessional and clericalist-against-anticlericalist rivalries of the late nineteenth and early twentieth century. Already in the eighteenth century Voltaire had mocked dour Geneva's hostility to the pleasures of the theater and the arts. This tradition was still alive among French critics of art and literature at the end of the subsequent century. Ferdinand Brunetière, a leading literary scholar of the Third Republic, asserted that "Horror of art was and would remain one of the essential, characteristic traits of the Reformation in general and the Calvinist Reformation in particular." The prominent art critic Eugène Müntz asked about "the proud and cruel Calvin": "Where and when can one find that the author of the *Institutes* ever demonstrated the slightest interest in any branch of art?"[5] Doumergue felt himself compelled to rebut such views. To do so, he deployed "the protestant method, which consists of putting listeners in the situation where they can decide for themselves against error and in favor of the truth." He cited passages from the *Institutes* where Calvin indicates that the arts are gifts of God to man, and that inventions such as musical instruments should not be condemned, even though they serve pleasure and delectation more than utility. The Genevan reformer was thus no joyless enemy of all beauty and amusement, Doumergue asserted. He then, quickly and typically, moved on to a discussion of Dutch art of the Golden Age, and in particular of Rembrandt, whose painting represented "the most brilliant and logical expression of the artistic temperament of his country and his people." Further equating Holland's spirit with Calvinism, he found in Rembrandt's art the emancipation, the laicization, and the interiorization of the visual arts. These, he concluded, had been the genuine consequence of the Calvinist Reformation for art.[6] Kuyper similarly responded to the charge that Calvinism had not produced a great architectural style in the manner of other great world religions by emphasizing that Calvinism refused to embody its religious spirit in monuments. As the alliance of religion and art represented a lower stage of human development, the emancipation of art from the guardianship of the church and its separation in a distinctive

3. Abraham Kuyper, *Lectures on Calvinism* (Grand Rapids, 1931; 2nd ed. Grand Rapids, 1994).

4. Doumergue, *L'art et le sentiment dans l'oeuvre de Calvin* (Geneva, 1902).

5. Both quoted in Doumergue, pp. 9, 33.

6. Doumergue, pp. 8, 13-14, 36-41.

aesthetic sphere, the true achievements of Calvinism, in fact demonstrated its superiority.[7]

Today, the element of confessional apologetics in these interpretations is immediately evident. It is equally apparent in the Catholic tradition of scholarship of the same era that chronicles the Calvinist destruction of Catholic churches and works of art, within the tradition of what Louis Réau called in 1959 the "history of vandalism."[8] Suspended between history and apologetics, these works cast the central question about the subject of Calvinism and the visual arts as an essentially evaluative one: Did Reformed theology comprise purely negative prohibitions that encouraged the destruction of existing works of art and were antithetical to the creation of new ones, or did it also act as a creative force that helped to shape an alternative aesthetic within post-Reformation Europe and North America? This manner of posing the question dominated thinking about this issue until at least 1960, when no less a figure than Erwin Panofsky delivered a series of remarks that still stand clearly within this tradition.[9]

But it is not simply the heavy overtones of confessional apologetics in these works that now make their conceptualization of the basic issues appear to be potentially misleading. In their efforts to attribute praise or blame to the Reformed tradition according to the standard of the degree to which it contributed to the progress of the arts, they also replicate the modern sacralization of art. The process of extending our knowledge of the social world often involves both historicization and disenchantment, as deeply valorized and sentimentalized features of social organization or culture are revealed to be not natural features of all human life, but temporally and culturally specific. Art history has undergone such a process of disenchantment in the past generation, coming to recognize that works of art do not simply express timeless aesthetic impulses but have served very different functions in different societies — indeed, that the modern Western category of "art" is a historically specific category of the past several centuries that may have very little to do with the way in which other cultures or more distant eras of the Western past categorized and thought about those objects that we today classify as works of art. The very title of a recent book on the history of icons and holy images, *Likeness and Presence:*

7. Kuyper, pp. 142-52.

8. See, e.g., Victor Carrière, *Introduction aux études d'histoire ecclésiastique locale* (Paris, 1936), III, part 6: "Les épreuves de l'église de France au XVIe siècle"; Louis Réau, *Les monuments detruits de l'art français. Histoire du vandalisme* (Paris, 1959).

9. Erwin Panofsky, "Comments on Art and Reformation," in *Symbols in Transformation: Iconographic Themes at the Time of the Reformation* (exhibition catalogue, Princeton, 1969), pp. 9-14. Panofsky's comments were originally delivered in 1960, largely in response to Alexander Rüstow, "Lutherana Tragoedia Artis," *Schweizer Monatshefte* 39 (December 1959): 891-906. Perhaps the most important twentieth-century work in the apologetic tradition is G. G. Coulton, *Art and the Reformation* (New York, 1928; 2nd ed. Cambridge, 1953).

A History of the Image before the Era of Art, testifies clearly to the new awareness of the historicity of the idea of art that developed in Europe between
the Renaissance and the age of romanticism, with its claim to constitute an
autonomous realm in which artists gave expression to their particular vision of the world and, by virtue of their genius, revealed the aesthetic values and worldview of their times.[10] With the recognition that the functions of the visual arts and of art objects within the culture of the sixteenth
and seventeenth centuries may have been very different from what they
subsequently became has come an awareness of the anachronism involved
in judging the people or doctrines of that era according to their relationship to "art."

Still another feature that is visible in the work of both Kuyper and
Doumergue is a tendency to interpret works of art in Hegelian or romantic
idealist ways as manifestations of a larger guiding spirit. Doumergue, we
have seen, postulated a Dutch national spirit that expressed itself in the art
of Rembrandt and could be equated with Calvinism. Kuyper explicitly
spoke of Calvinism as a "life system," a *Weltanschauung.* The faith's deepest
life principle sprang from its particular religious consciousness, he asserted. From there it worked its way out into the various realms of theology, church life, politics, science, and art.[11] This aspect of their work raises
theoretical questions that deserve particularly close attention, for if the imperative to avoid anachronistic understandings of the character of art and
its function in society is now broadly accepted by historians of art, the issue of how to conceptualize the relationship of individual works of art to
the larger collectivities in which these are produced remains a field where
competing assumptions still contend for dominance.

For much of the twentieth century, and particularly in the half-
century since World War II, the tendency seemed clearly to be that the
Hegelianism and romantic idealism so palpable in these works, and whose
influence could also be detected in the writings of such exemplary cultural
historians as Jakob Burckhardt and Panofsky, were in decline within the
different branches of cultural history. In the past decade or two, however,
this trend has been partially reversed. Views of culture that postulate considerable internal coherence and unity within the various forms of thought
and expression of a given group are making a comeback in important corners of cultural history and cultural studies, thanks most obviously to the
influence of Michel Foucault, of contemporary American versions of romantic nationalism, and of the ways in which these mesh with identity
politics. The highbrow vernacular speaks about America today as if every
group has its own culture, expressed most clearly in its literature and art,

10. Hans Belting, *Likeness and Presence: A History of the Image before the Era of Art* (Chicago, 1994).
11. Kuyper, p. 17 and passim.

23

which reveals that group's experience and perhaps even essence. Comparable issues of group formation and mobilization, it might be noted, were part of Kuyper's political project in a very different historical context.

Nearly thirty years ago, Ernst Gombrich subjected the often unconscious Hegelianism that still informed so much cultural history in his lifetime to a penetrating critique in his *In Search of Cultural History*.[12] The particular object of his critique was the view that periods formed coherent wholes, held together by the spirit of the age. On the contrary, he observed, the art of any given moment was typically characterized by rival schools and movements. Individuals and movements, not periods, formed the proper subject of study of cultural history. It was at once unjustifiable and misleading to assume that the different aspects of the culture of a period — its art, its literature, its customs, its political life — were all expressions of a single spirit. Each one of these areas had its own internal traditions, what literary scholars now call intertextuality. While changes in one area might be influenced by contemporaneous developments in another, no necessary connections could properly be assumed in advance.

In discussing the subject of Calvinism and the visual arts, the question that must be confronted is whether or not Calvinism formed a distinctive culture of such strength and coherence that works of art produced by Calvinist artists or for a Calvinist audience can properly be interpreted as expressing a Calvinist sensibility. A critique similar to that which Gombrich develops of the idea of a spirit of the age can easily be extended to the view that religious or ethnic groups within a larger population constitute distinctive cultures. In complex, pluralistic societies, many cultural practices are shared across different groups. Groups have their own internal cultural differences that may be far more salient than the common features that hold them together. To speak of French as opposed to Dutch culture may seem to be doing nothing more than expressing the truism that in some ways the Dutch are or were different from the French. For ethnic minorities to assert the existence and dignity of their own culture is unquestionably a useful political strategy for increasing their cultural capital. But insofar as a culture is understood to be, in the widely influential definition of Clifford Geertz, a "system of meanings embodied in symbols," the a priori postulation of a proliferating variety of such systems is only likely to cloud our understanding of the actual dynamics of culture and cultural history, by suggesting systematic differences and boundaries where there is in fact much overlap, and by promoting the narcissism of petty differences. As one anthropologist has observed, "This use of culture as a blanket term for intuited or assumed similarities within a group of people is usually misleading. Not only do cultural groupings tend not to correspond neatly with geographical, national, religious and other sorts of groupings, but

12. Gombrich, *In Search of Cultural History* (Oxford, 1969).

24

those things which constitute culture tend not to occur together in neat bundles which contrast sharply with other such bundles."[13]

The thrust of recent historical studies of individual regions of Calvinist strength, as well as the historiography of the Reformation more generally, provides empirical substantiation of these rather abstract theoretical considerations. Many historical discussions of Calvinism have treated the faith as if it were so all-pervasive an ideology, so hostile to all forms of cultural expression arising from folkloric or nonreligious sources, that it constituted a highly distinctive culture. As important a work of historical scholarship as Emmanuel LeRoy Ladurie's *The Peasants of Languedoc*, for instance, reiterates the view that the Huguenots of the Cévennes, that mountainous region of southern France where Protestantism took deeper root than anywhere else in France, became so imbued with Calvinist biblical culture that this obliterated all preexisting elements of profane culture. Nineteenth-century folklorists who visited the region, it is said, found no trace of any indigenous lullabies. Babies were rocked to sleep with psalms.[14]

While such cultural patterns would have conformed to the aspirations of certain godly Calvinist ministers — Pierre Jurieu wrote in 1675, for instance, "it would be necessary, if it were possible, to train our heart so that it conceives its thoughts and forms its meditations only in the terms of the Holy Spirit as expressed in the Psalms"[15] — abundant historical evidence shows that such aspirations were indeed unrealizable and that the Bible always had to make its peace with beliefs, motifs, and genres derived from nonbiblical sources, even in the greatest strongholds of Calvinist fidelity. When the folkloric belief that May was an unlucky time for couples to be married spread across southern France in the early seventeenth century, it took hold among the Huguenots of the Cévennes just as it did among the Catholics of neighboring areas, despite what we might postulate to be Calvinism's greater hostility to superstitious practices and its insistence upon calendrical regularity.[16] Folklorists studying the region may not have found local lullabies, but they have reported a vigorous undergrowth of beliefs in the efficacy of magical healing and the evil eye, despite the church's long hostility to such practices.[17] Many elements of the folkloric culture of this region, in short, were shared between Calvinists and Catholics alike.

---

13. Kenneth A. Rice, *Geertz and Culture* (Ann Arbor, 1980), p. 241.

14. LeRoy Ladurie, *Les paysans de Languedoc* (Paris, 1966), vol. I, p. 613.

15. Jurieu, *Traité de la devotion* (Rouen, 1675), p. 184.

16. Philip Benedict, *The Huguenot Population of France, 1600-1685: The Demographic Fate and Customs of a Religious Minority*, Transactions of the American Philosophical Society 81, part 5 (Philadelphia, 1991), pp. 86-90.

17. Philippe Joutard, "Protestantisme populaire et univers magique: le cas cévenol," *Le Monde Alpin et Rhodanien*, vol. V (1977), pp. 145-71.

In similar fashion, studies of elite culture in seventeenth-century France have revealed that the circles of those given to literary, artistic, scientific, or antiquarian interests were among the locales where the confessional differences of the era were most easily overcome. Catholics and Huguenots gathered together in such places to cultivate their common interests, and it is far from certain that the way in which individual members did so was significantly inflected by their religious views. The thrust of much recent work in the history of the Reformation more generally has likewise been to point out the very substantial areas of agreement between the different post-Reformation confessional families on matters such as political theory. There were even substantial areas of borrowing and overlap in their devotional literature.[18] If practices and precepts were often shared between the different confessions even in this realm where we might think that the differences between them would be the most marked, we clearly need to be cautious about postulating from the outset a distinctive Calvinist culture or life system that found expression in the art that Calvinists produced or commissioned.

Rather than beginning from such postulates, the most fruitful way of approaching the problem of Calvinism and the visual arts would appear to be to start with some simpler observations and questions. Whether or not Calvinism was a culture, it was undeniably a certain set of theological pronouncements, some of which had direct implications for what might be depicted in works of art, the ways in which paintings and sculptures might be used, and how churches ought to be decorated. Just what did various generations of Reformed theologians say about these theological matters with relevance for the visual arts? How much room for disagreement was there about these principles? How vigorously were they enforced by authoritative church bodies? These are the most basic questions from which to

18. The exploration of the shared features and parallel consequences of the Lutheran, Calvinist, and Catholic Reformations was pioneered with particular influence by E. W. Zeeden in Germany, Jean Delumeau in France, and John Bossy in England. See especially Zeeden, *Die Entstehung der Konfessionen: Grundlagen und Formen der Konfessionsbildung im Zeitalter der Glaubenskämpfe* (Munich, 1965); Delumeau, *Naissance et affirmation de la Réforme* (Paris, 1965); Delumeau, *Le Catholicisme entre Luther et Voltaire* (Paris, 1971); Bossy, *Christianity in the West, 1400-1700* (Oxford, 1985). For more detailed research demonstrating the shared features within political thought and devotional culture, see Quentin Skinner, "The Origins of the Calvinist Theory of Revolution," in *After the Reformation: Essays in Honor of J. H. Hexter*, ed. Barbara C. Malament (Philadelphia, 1980), pp. 309-30; Heinz Schilling, "Between the Territorial State and Urban Liberty: Lutheranism and Calvinism in the County of Lippe," in R. Po-chia Hsia, *The German People and the Reformation* (Ithaca, N.Y., 1988), pp. 263-83; Schilling, *Civic Calvinism in Northwestern Germany and the Netherlands: Sixteenth to Nineteenth Centuries* (Kirksville, Mo., 1991), esp. pp. 5-6, 100; Charles E. Hambrick-Stowe, *The Practice of Piety: Puritan Devotional Disciplines in Seventeenth-Century New England* (Chapel Hill, 1982), pp. 25-39; Udo Sträter, *Sonthom, Bayly, Dyke und Hall: Studien zur Rezeption der englischen Erbauungsliteratur in Deutschland im 17. Jahrhundert* (Tübingen, 1987).

26

start. Once these questions have been explored, it then becomes possible to move on to a series of further questions. What were the consequences for artistic production of the establishment of Calvinist churches in different parts of Europe? As Calvinist artists and architects explored their crafts within the confines of the permissible and the impermissible as defined by Calvinist theology, did they develop distinctive styles or interpretations of their subject matter? If so, were these directly influenced by the religious beliefs of either the artists who produced them or the individuals who commissioned them, or did such innovations as appeared spring simply from the process of working within a new set of parameters? Since many of these questions involve trying to locate aspects of the art produced by Calvinist artists or in Calvinist areas that can be demonstrated to have been distinctively influenced by Calvinist precepts, it deserves some stress that these questions cannot be answered by looking at Calvinist artists or countries alone. Instead, they may often be best answered by looking comparatively at work produced in Calvinist and non-Calvinist countries, or by Calvinist and non-Calvinist artists within the same country.

A considerable body of recent literature has explored the theology of images and the phenomenon of iconoclasm during the era of the Reformation. It is abundantly clear from this work that an adequate treatment of Reformed theological pronouncements on this issue must recognize two fundamental points. The first is that central to the Reformed tradition from its very inception was a particularly strict and insistent interpretation of the biblical commandments against idolatry, and a sensibility that saw any excessive investment in the adornment of churches as a misuse of funds that could better be spent on the poor.

The first Reformation expression of such views came in Wittenberg in late 1521 and early 1522, where Carlstadt parted company with Luther over precisely the image question. He took the position that the Old Testament prohibition of graven images was clear, binding on Christians, and required them to purge their churches of statues and altarpieces. Devotional actions involving physical representations of God were antithetical to the proper worship of a spiritual being, for Christ is not known through the flesh.[19] Luther also opposed the idolatrous veneration of images, but he was willing to retain statues or altarpieces that were not objects of such veneration. When the issue of images was debated in Zurich in October 1523, Zwingli followed Carlstadt in advocating the removal of all paintings

19. James S. Preus, *Carlstadt's "Ordinaciones" and Luther's Liberty: A Study of the Wittenberg Movement, 1521-22* (Cambridge, Mass., 1974); M. Stirm, *Die Bilderfrage in der Reformation* (Gütersloh, 1977), pp. 38-44; Giuseppe Scavizzi, *Arte e architettura sacra. Cronache e documenti sulla controversia tra riformati et cattolici (1500-1550)* (Rome, 1981), pp. 42-83; Carlos Eire, *War against the Idols: The Reformation of Worship from Erasmus to Calvin* (Cambridge, 1986), pp. 55-73; Sergiusz Michalski, *The Reformation and the Visual Arts: The Protestant Image Question in Western and Eastern Europe* (London, 1993), pp. 43-50.

and sculptures from the city's churches. To the considerations highlighted by Carlstadt he added a third argument: that it was wasteful and unchristian to spend money on church decoration that could better go to the poor.[20] In Strasbourg, Martin Bucer reached similar conclusions by 1524.[21] Calvin consequently expressed little that was novel when he devoted a long chapter of the first book of the *Institutes* to the propositions "It Is Unlawful to Attribute a Visible Form to God, and Generally Whoever Sets Up Idols Revolts against the True God." The chapter stresses that any figurative representation of a purely spiritual God is a betrayal of both the character and the commandments of the divinity. Far from being the books of the unlettered, images in church are a standing invitation to idolatry, not to mention often "examples of the most abandoned lust and obscenity" because of the manner in which they were painted.[22] If Calvin stood out in any way from his Reformed predecessors, it was in the depth of the abhorrence he displayed for the polluting consequences of idolatry. At one point in his *Excuse à MM les Nicodémites*, he likens idolaters with latrine cleaners, who cannot understand why people find them so foul-smelling. "Hardened by habit, they sit in their own excrement, and yet believe they are surrounded by roses."[23]

Undergirding Reformed belief in the inappropriateness of representing the divine in physical form was the Platonic dualism between matter and spirit, communicated to the leading Reformed theologians via Erasmus and Lefèvre d'Étaples.[24] Here Lutheran orthodoxy would always part company with Reformed, as subsequent Lutheran theologians not only retained Luther's acceptance of paintings and sculptures in church so long as they did not become cult objects, but also developed the eucharistic doctrine of ubiquity to explain how Christ could be physically present in the bread and wine of communion. The Lutherans also preserved the dominant medieval system of numbering the Ten Commandments, which subsumed the prohibition against graven images within the first commandment ("Thou shalt have no other gods before me") and typically did not even cite the words warning against idolatry in basic expositions of the commandments. The Reformed, by contrast, elevated the prohibition of

20. Charles Garside Jr., *Zwingli and the Arts* (New Haven, 1966), pp. 76-178; Stirm, pp. 138-53; Scavizzi, pp. 83-102; Eire, pp. 73-86; Michalski, pp. 51-59.

21. Frank Muller, "Bucer et les images," in *Martin Bucer and Sixteenth Century Europe*, ed. Christian Krieger and Marc Lienhard (Leiden, 1993), pp. 227-37.

22. Calvin, *Institutes of the Christian Religion* 1.11. In quoting from the *Institutes*, I have generally relied upon the translation of John T. McNeill and Ford Lewis Battles (Philadelphia, 1960), but I have occasionally ventured my own translation. The most extended secondary discussion of Calvin's views on art, although heavily apologetic in character, may be found in Léon Wencelius, *L'esthétique de Calvin* (Paris, 1937). See also Eire, pp. 195-233; Stirm, pp. 161-228; Michalski, pp. 59-73.

23. Quoted in Eire, p. 220.

24. Highlighted well in Eire, passim, esp. pp. 31-36, 168-77.

graven images to the rank of a separate commandment, a reorganization of the Decalogue that they could make without spoiling the round number of ten commandments by at the same time bundling into a single rule the prohibition against coveting one's neighbor's house, wife, children, servants, or goods. These prohibitions were split between two commandments in the Catholic and Lutheran versions.[25]

The particularly intense Reformed concern with the danger of idolatry and the consequent emphasis on the need to banish images from churches was codified in many Reformed confessions and church ordinances. The Tetrapolitan Confession of the South German cities of 1530 asserted that "when all have begun to adore [images] they should be universally removed from the churches, on account of the offence which they occasion."[26] The Heidelberg Catechism included the following questions and answers:

> Should we, then, not make any images at all?

> God cannot and should not be pictured in any way. As for creatures, although they may indeed be portrayed, God forbids making or having any likeness of them in order to worship them, or to use them to serve him.

> But may not pictures be tolerated in churches in place of books for unlearned people?

> No, for we must not try to be wiser than God, who does not want his people to be taught by means of lifeless idols, but through the living preaching of his word.[27]

The Second Helvetic Confession likewise forbade depicting the person of Christ or employing pictures instead of the Bible to teach the laity.[28] Elizabethan legislation of 1559 required the destruction of all "monuments of feigned miracles, pilgrimages, idolatry and suspicion" and criticized "abused images, tables, pictures, and paintings," although the Thirty-nine Articles of the faith were silent on the matter.[29] The church order established in Scotland in 1560 that subsequently became known as the first

---

25. See especially Stirm, pp. 17-22, 134-40, 154-61, 235-39.

26. Arthur C. Cochrane, ed., *Reformed Confessions of the Sixteenth Century* (Philadelphia, 1966), p. 80.

27. Cochrane, p. 324.

28. Cochrane, pp. 229-30.

29. John Phillips, *The Reformation of Images: Destruction of Art in England, 1535-1660* (Berkeley, 1973), p. 114; Margaret Aston, *England's Iconoclasts*, vol. 1, *Laws against Images* (Oxford, 1988), pp. 298-302. These two works offer an excellent guide through the full, complicated history of English legislation concerning images, set in the larger context of the debates inspired by Lollardy and the Reformation.

Book of Discipline ordered the abolition of idolatry, including the "adoration of images and the keeping and retaining of the same."[30]

It is hard to overemphasize the force and significance of the anti-idolatrous impulse in shaping Reformed attitudes toward the visual arts. Certain sacred images had become the objects of passionate veneration in the later Middle Ages. Many other works of art were used in devotion to help believers visualize beloved religious figures or events such as the episodes of the Passion for use in contemplative prayer. Representations of sacred scenes or figures were justified as the Bible of the poor, and the rich decoration of churches was taken to be a worthy expression of human love for the divine. When Reformed theologians attacked these practices, they cut to the heart of late medieval religious culture and achieved one of their most powerful transvaluations of values. No other rallying cry appears to have mobilized crowds as galvanically across the length and breadth of Europe as the cry to purge the churches of their idols.[31] Théodore de Bèze declared at the colloquy of Saint-Germain in 1562 that the abuse of images was a key reason why he and many others left the Catholic Church.[32] Students of the various iconoclastic episodes that dotted the history of the Reformation have observed that the church purifiers often displayed a clear hierarchy of concerns. Sculptures were attacked first and destroyed most consistently since they particularly lent themselves to personification and veneration; paintings occupied something of a middle position; and stained glass was most often spared, in some cases because it was deemed least likely to become the object of behavior deemed idolatrous, in others simply because it was difficult to reach and costly and time-consuming to replace.[33]

The Reformed castigation of idolatry, furthermore, was quickly reinforced by an interpretation of Christian history that saw the reintroduction

30. James K. Cameron, ed., *The First Book of Discipline* (Edinburgh, 1972), p. 95.

31. Martin Haas, "Der Weg der Täufer in de Absonderung. Zur Interdependenz von Theologie und sozialen Verhalten," in *Umstrittenes Täufertum 1525-1975. Neue Forschungen*, ed. Hans-Jürgen Goertz (Göttingen, 1975), p. 69; Claire Cross, *Church and People, 1450-1660* (London, 1976), pp. 76-77; Eire, p. 159. Many excellent studies have recently been devoted to the place of images in pre-Reformation devotional life and the dynamics, motivation, and significance of Reformation iconoclasm. In addition to the works already cited, see especially Solange Deyon and Alain Lottin, *Les 'Casseurs' de l'été 1566: L'iconoclasme dans le nord de la France* (Paris, 1981); David Freedberg, *Iconoclasm and Painting in the Revolt of the Netherlands, 1566-1609* (New York, 1987); R. W. Scribner and M. Warnke, eds., *Bilder und Bildersturm im Spätmittelalter und der frühen Neuzeit* (Wiesbaden, 1990); Olivier Christin, *Une révolution symbolique: L'iconoclasme huguenot et la reconstruction catholique* (Paris, 1991); Belting; Eamon Duffy, *The Stripping of the Altars: Traditional Religion in England, 1400-1580* (New Haven, 1992); Lee Palmer Wandel, *Voracious Idols and Violent Hands: Iconoclasm in Reformation Zurich, Strasbourg, and Basel* (Cambridge, 1995).

32. Donald Nugent, *Ecumenism in the Age of the Reformation: The Colloquy of Poissy* (Cambridge, Mass., 1974), p. 193.

33. Muller, p. 231; Christin, pp. 152-54.

of false forms of worship into the church as an ever-present danger against which constant vigilance was necessary. In this view, to whose elaboration Zwingli, Bullinger, and Calvin all contributed important elements, the idolatrous practices of the church of Rome had gradually corrupted the pristine worship of the early church as a consequence of the innate human tendency to depict God in human form and to wish to demonstrate reverence in new manners. Since such impulses were basic elements of human nature, constant vigilance was necessary lest worship, once properly reformed, be corrupted anew. The call to such vigilance provoked continuing, anxious scrutiny of the legitimacy of different artistic practices and could generate some extremely strict definitions of what might constitute idolatry, as in William Prynne's later warning against stained glass — "Popery may creep in at a glasse-window" — or in the reticence of a number of churchmen in Zurich in 1550 to allow the painting or export of portraits of the city's leading theologians, lest "a window to idolatry might therefore be opened to posterity."[34] Patrick Collinson has even argued that English Protestantism passed through a two-stage process of development that took it from iconoclasm to outright iconophobia. At first, the cause of the Reformation was willing to embrace existing cultural forms and to use them for its own purposes, as was done for instance by employing certain forms of visual propaganda for the Protestant cause. After about 1580, however, suspicion of possibly illegitimate uses of images became so intense that what Collinson characterizes as "visual anorexia" set in. He illustrates his thesis with several telling episodes. When a Flemish ship ran aground off Sussex during the Civil War, the parliamentary authorities who impounded it sputtered with indignation at the paintings in its cargo, including a "monstrous" image of the Trinity. The 1610 devotional work entitled *Contemplative Pictures with Wholesome Precepts* was in fact a blind emblem book with no pictures.[35]

While recent scholarship has made abundantly clear the depth of Reformed concern at the misuse of images and the powerful iconoclastic impulses that this encouraged, this scholarship has also underscored a second point of equal importance: If Reformed warnings against idolatry should not be underestimated, neither should they be taken to constitute a blanket condemnation of all use or enjoyment of the visual arts. On the contrary, Zwingli wrote in 1525 that "No one is a greater admirer than I of paintings and statuary." He was willing to allow stained glass in churches, and felt that images of a historical nature, including historical episodes

---

34. Michalski, p. 56; Mary G. Winkler, "A Divided Heart: Idolatry and the Portraiture of Hans Asper," *Sixteenth Century Journal* 18 (1987): 222-23.

35. Patrick Collinson, *From Iconoclasm to Iconophobia: The Cultural Impact of the Second English Reformation* (Reading, 1986), esp. pp. 22-25. Collinson restates much of his argument in *The Birthpangs of Protestant England: Religious and Cultural Change in the Sixteenth and Seventeenth Centuries* (New York, 1988), pp. 45-51.

from the Bible, were appropriate for private homes, where the same rules did not apply as in the decoration of churches.[36] Calvin and after him the great English theologian William Perkins likewise stressed the distinction between private homes and churches, allowing biblical scenes in private households.[37] In his extensive treatment of the dangers of idolatry in the *Institutes,* Calvin also paused for a moment to state, "I am not so scrupulous as to think no images are to be tolerated." "Only those things are to be sculpted or painted which the eyes are capable of seeing," he quickly added; "let not God's majesty, which is far above the perception of the eyes, be debased through unseemly representations." Histories, trees, landscapes, and persons were all fit subjects for paintings. "The histories are instructive; the others are only to give pleasure."[38] The tradition of defending the appropriateness of most sorts of pictures in private homes continued to define the majority position within Reformed ranks into the seventeenth century. In the first part of the century, for instance, the Dutch Reformed theologian Jacobus Trigland defended the private possession of paintings, except for those that contained naked figures, against Quaker criticisms that the possession of all pictures whatsoever was sinful.[39] A suspicious, begrudging quality marks certain of these statements about the permissible uses of the visual arts, and they do not add up to a very detailed positive program or set of guidelines about how the skills of painters or sculptors are to be used, but they demonstrate an interest in and appreciation of the visual arts within defined boundaries.

Additional aspects of the attitude of leading Reformed theologians toward the appropriate uses of the visual arts may be inferred from the nature of certain works of art produced in the cities and regions over which they exercised so much influence. Thus, the growing volume of works of devotion and propaganda produced in Geneva during Calvin's lifetime for export throughout western Europe included works of graphic satire or propaganda, among them no fewer than nine editions of a reworked version of Lucas Cranach's famous antipapal visual satire, the *Passional Christi und Antichristi.*[40] As the powerful Company of Pastors is not known to have made any protest about this work, it can be assumed that Calvin accepted

36. Huldreich Zwingli, *Commentary on True and False Religion,* ed. Samuel Macauley Jackson and Clarence Nevin Heller (Philadelphia, 1929), pp. 330-37, esp. p. 337; Garside, p. 76; Michalski, p. 56.

37. Wencelius, p. 166; Aston, p. 451.

38. *Inst.* 1.11.12.

39. R. B. Evenhuis, *Ook dat was Amsterdam,* vol. 2, *De Kerk der Hervoming in de Gouden Eeuw* (Amsterdam, 1967), p. 131.

40. Paul Chaix, "Un pamphlet genevois du XVIe siècle: l'*Antithèse* de S. DuRosier: Recherche iconographique," in *Mélanges offerts à M. Paul-E. Martin* (Geneva, 1961), pp. 467-82; Philip Benedict, "Of Marmites and Martyrs: Images and Polemics in the Wars of Religion," in *The French Renaissance in Prints* (exhibition catalogue, Los Angeles, 1994), pp. 117-20.

recruiting the talents of woodcutters or engravers to aid in the spread of Reformation ideas (see Betsey Rosasco's article, pp. 231-42 in this volume). Illustrated Bibles produced in both Strasbourg and Zurich in the early Reformation were characterized by far greater richness and originality of illustration than those printed in Wittenberg at the same time. Bucer and Zwingli's insistence that all instruction in God's word pass through the medium of Scripture thus did not preclude illustrated Scriptures, although the production of illustrated Bibles would be discouraged in Geneva after 1566 because the illustrators were introducing improper novelties into their plates.[41] Vernacular emblem books with illustrations also began to appear in England from 1580 onward, the date when Collinson diagnoses the onset of visual anorexia. These were used even in advanced Protestant circles to drive home moral and spiritual lessons. Within limits, then, images continued to be used within Reformed circles for meditative and didactic purposes of a religious character.[42]

As Tessa Watt has persuasively shown, Collinson's larger thesis that Reformed suspicion of images bred nothing less than visual anorexia in English culture after 1580 cannot be accepted. In permitting only certain forms of visual material within devotional literature, Reformed theology may have had significant consequences for the character of religious practice and the religious imagination. Barbara Lewalski has suggested that where Catholic devotional practice encouraged believers to meditate upon or to summon up in their minds religious scenes, with which they were then to develop a vicarious personal identification, English Protestant works of devotion encouraged believers to apply the salvific or moral implications of biblical scenes to their own lives, to focus, in other words, not on the scene itself but upon its implications for belief and behavior.[43] The manuals of practical devotion that began to multiply within the Reformed tradition from the late sixteenth century onward did not seek to evoke mental images as consistently as their Catholic counterparts, or so at least some selective reading in the genre seems to indicate. Yet in assessing Collinson's thesis, it must be remembered that sixteenth-century England was a technological backwater with few graphic artists or highly skilled painters, where most of such painting as was done took the form of wall paintings that have subsequently been largely obliterated rather than framed canvases of a character and quality likely to have survived down to the present day. Within this artistically underdeveloped society, Watt's careful inventory of all visual works in circulation reveals their continued

41. Muller, p. 234; W. Deonna, *Les arts à Genève des origines à la fin du XVIIIe siècle* (Geneva, 1942), p. 300.

42. Tessa Watt, *Cheap Print and Popular Piety, 1550-1640* (Cambridge, 1991), pp. 138, 238-53; Hambrick-Stowe, pp. 29ff.; Rosemary Freeman, *English Emblem Books* (London, 1967).

43. Barbara Kiefer Lewalski, *Protestant Poetics and the Seventeenth-Century Religious Lyric* (Princeton, 1979), chap. 4.

and even expanded production in the later sixteenth and early seventeenth century. The subject matter of most of this work fell within the admittedly restrictive parameters set by the dominant Reformed consensus within the English church at the time, but the trend was toward the expansion of the volume and variety of images in circulation in English society, not toward its desiccation.[44] A larger methodological point is illustrated here. Scholars have recurrently attributed the absence or only modest production of certain kinds of images in Calvinist regions to Reformed concern about the dangers of idolatry, yet the cause may often have been the simple absence of the relevant traditions or technology. Questions of this sort cannot be discussed outside the context of the highly regionally differentiated economic geography of European artistic production at the time.[45]

Issues of church architecture other than the appropriateness of images in churches generated much less discussion than questions of painting and sculpture among the early Reformed theologians, for the simple reason that the initial thrust of the Reformation involved taking over already constructed Catholic churches and adapting them for properly reformed worship, rather than establishing new churches whose physical form required extended attention. Calvin nonetheless warned in the *Institutes* against confusing the physical structures of church buildings with God's proper dwelling place and asserted that "What is bestowed upon the adornment of churches . . . is wrongly applied if that moderation is not used which both the nature of sacred things prescribes and the apostles and other holy fathers have prescribed." Such was hardly the case in the Roman church, where money was squandered on church buildings that ought to go to God's living temples, the poor.[46] The Second Helvetic Confession also specified a modest architectural program. "The places where the faithful meet are to be decent, and in all respects fit for God's Church. Therefore, spacious buildings or temples are to be chosen, but they are to be purged of everything that is not fitting for a church. And everything is to be arranged for decorum, necessity, and godly decency. . . . All luxurious attire, all pride, and everything unbecoming to Christian humility, discipline and modesty are to be banished from the sanctuaries and places of

44. Watt, pp. 41-42, 131-253, 324-25.

45. Another example to illustrate this point: the leading expert on early French evangelical propaganda, Francis M. Higman, attributes the smaller quantities of illustrated propaganda produced in Geneva than in Germany in the early years of the Reformation to the distinctive Reformed theology of images. Higman, "Le domaine français 1520-1562," in Jean-François Gilmont et al., *La Réforme et le livre, L'Europe de l'imprimé (1517–v. 1570)* (Paris, 1990), pp. 121-23. But French propaganda in defense of the Catholic Church was also very sparing in its use of visual materials until the last decades of the century. The paucity of illustrated Reformation propaganda produced in Geneva or France probably should be attributed primarily to the rarity of French-speaking woodcutters and engravers and the still far more limited uses to which their technologies were put in Francophone than in Germanophone Europe.

46. *Inst.* 3.20.30, 4.5.18.

prayer of Christians. . . . Let all things be done decently and in order in the church, and finally, let all things be done for edification."[47]

If these were the theological principles of the various Reformed theologians and confessional statements with regard to the practice of the visual arts, how energetically did the churches actually seek to ensure that the artists within their ranks followed these precepts? Several early synods of the French Reformed churches legislated about such matters, the 1562 synod of Orléans decreeing that printers, painters, and other members of the faith should not make anything that would abet Roman superstitions, and the 1567 synod of Verteuil warning painters, sculptors, and masons against making anything that was in any way idolatrous.[48] In 1613 the presbytery of Glasgow censured a painter who had recently painted the crucifix in many houses, "quhilk [which] is liklie . . . to turne the hearts of the ignorant to idolatrie."[49] Also in 1613, the elders of the church of Amsterdam spoke to the sculptor Hendrik de Keyser and got him to cease working on a statue of Saint John the Evangelist for a church in Den Bosch (see Ilja Veldman's article, pp. 397-420 in this volume) that they feared would be "misused for idolatry by all who come to the church."[50] A generation earlier, the consistories of both Le Mans and Nîmes took similar action on several occasions against goldsmiths or other artisans working on Catholic liturgical objects or churches, with the Le Mans consistory even offering in 1561 to compensate one goldsmith for his financial loss if he would renounce a commission to produce a silver crucifix.[51] Thus, measures were passed that entered into the disciplinary system of the Reformed churches, and disciplinary agencies occasionally acted to uphold these measures.

But it does not appear that these agencies were especially energetic in the quest to dissuade craftsmen from accepting idolatrous commissions. At any rate, they did not stop Reformed artists from producing monuments of idolatry. Biographies of Calvinist artists living in majority Catholic countries in the seventeenth century have meanwhile shown that many were quite willing to accept commissions from the Catholic Church that entailed the violation of the rules articulated by the French national synods, including commissions of such importance and public notoriety that the

47. Cochrane, p. 289.

48. Jean Aymon, *Tous les Synodes Nationales des Eglises Reformées de France* (The Hague, 1710), pp. 27, 73, 75.

49. Walter Roland Foster, *The Church before the Covenants: The Church of Scotland, 1596-1638* (Edinburgh, 1975), p. 98.

50. Volker Manuth, "Denomination and Iconography: The Choice of Subject Matter in the Biblical Paintings of the Rembrandt Circle," *Simiolus* 22 (1993-94): 242.

51. "Papier et registre du consistoire de l'Eglise du Mans réformée selon l'Evangile 1560-1561," in P.-A. Anjubault and H. Chardon, eds., *Recueil de pièces inédites pour servir à l'histoire de la Réforme et de la Ligue dans le Maine* (Le Mans, 1867), p. 7; Philippe Chareyre, "Le Consistoire de Nîmes 1561-1685" (thèse de doctorat d'etat, Université Paul Valéry, 1987), pp. 571-72.

local consistory could hardly have been unaware of them. The Huguenot Sébastien Bourdon, for instance, found himself in a violent quarrel with a rival artist after painting *The Fall of Simon Magus* for the high altar of Montpellier's cathedral — a building, ironically enough, whose refurbishing was largely necessitated by the wave of iconoclasm that accompanied the Protestant domination of Montpellier in 1621-22 — but there is no evidence that he fell afoul of the consistory for taking this commission. The equally Huguenot Salomon de Brosse collaborated in the design of an engraving in honor of Pope Gregory IV. Perhaps the most remarkable case of a Calvinist artist active in a Catholic artistic center was Jacob Jordaens, who was a member of the clandestine Reformed congregation that met in Antwerp from 1650 onward even as he continued to receive commissions for Catholic altarpieces that he painted in his lavish baroque.[52]

These last cases are extremely significant. One of the distinctive features of the sociology of the early Calvinist movement in places like France and the Low Countries was the disproportionately large number of converts who came from the ranks of the skilled artisans, including many painters, sculptors, and goldsmiths.[53] As the Reformed became a permanent minority in France and the southern Netherlands, it would appear that the consistories stepped lightly when it came to denying church members work that may have been necessary to their livelihood and professional success. It would remain a feature of the French art world in the seventeenth century that an important fraction of leading painters and graphic artists were Calvinists, including at least a fifth of the original members of the Academy of Painting and Sculpture.[54]

52. Charles Ponsonailhe, *Sébastien Bourdon* (Paris, 1886), pp. 175-79; Rosalyn Coope, *Salomon de Brosse and the Development of the Classical Style in French Architecture from 1565 to 1630* (University Park, Pa., 1972), p. 6; Menna Prestwich, "Patronage and the Protestants in France, 1598-1661: Architects and Painters," in *L'age d'or du Mécénat (1598-1661)*, ed. Roland Mousnier and Jean Mesnard (Paris, 1985), pp. 82-84; Christian Tümpel, "Jordaens, a Protestant Artist in a Catholic Stronghold: Notes on Protestant Artists in Catholic Centres," in *Jordaens (1593-1678)* (exhibition catalogue, Antwerp, 1993), vol. I, pp. 31-37.

53. Natalie Zemon Davis, "Strikes and Salvation at Lyon," in *Society and Culture in Early Modern France* (Stanford, 1975), p. 7; Joan Davies, "Persecution and Protestantism: Toulouse 1562-1575," *Historical Journal* 22 (1979): 40; Philip Benedict, *Rouen during the Wars of Religion* (Cambridge, 1981), pp. 73-85, esp. p. 80; James R. Farr, "Popular Religious Solidarity in Sixteenth-Century Dijon," *French Historical Studies* 14 (1985): 202-4; Guido Marnef, *Antwerp in the Age of Reformation: Underground Protestantism in a Commercial Metropolis, 1550-1577* (Baltimore, 1996), pp. 176, 182.

54. Prestwich, p. 82. It must be said that reliable statistics on the full extent of Protestant representation within the ranks of seventeenth-century French artists remain difficult to establish. Prestwich asserts that seven of the first twenty-three members of the Academy were Protestant, but her count appears mistakenly to include Jean Michelin among the ranks of the original members. From the evidence provided in her article and in standard biographical dictionaries of the period, it is nonetheless certain that six of the first twenty-four members of the body were Huguenots. Such a figure reveals the continuing overrepresentation of

Calvinist artists are known who did not simply accept whatever commissions came their way, but sought scrupulously to avoid indecent subjects or improper representations of the divinity. In this context, scholars have recently highlighted the Amsterdam painter Jan Victors. A conscientious member of the Reformed church, Victors avoided in his oeuvre all depictions of Christ, shunned Old Testament scenes involving angels, and developed unusual interpretations of scenes such as the Finding of Moses in order to avoid the inclusion of nude figures.[55] It may also be significant in this context that while several of the leading French sculptors of the mid–sixteenth century, including Jean Goujon and Ligier Richier, joined the Reformed churches as they took shape in the kingdom after 1555, relatively few Huguenots appear to have gained prominence working in this medium in the seventeenth century.[56] If this impression is correct, the lower representation of Huguenots in this branch of the visual arts may have stemmed from a shared conviction that three-dimensional images were particularly likely to evoke the kinds of responses that the Reformed deemed idolatrous. The willingness of many Calvinist artists to paint altarpieces that expressed elements of Catholic theology or violated Reformed rules of what was appropriate in artistic representation nonetheless underscores how substantially the content of works of art at this time was controlled by those who commissioned them. The postromantic assumption that paintings express the particular viewpoint or sensibility of the artist who produced them simply does not apply to this period without significant quali-

---

Protestants in this sector of the economy, for in this period Protestants made up only 5 to 6 percent of the total French population. But Nathalie Heinich, *Du peintre à l'artiste. Artisans et académiciens à l'age classique* (Paris, 1993), p. 149, reports considerably lower Protestant representation among the 140 individuals admitted to the Academy from 1648 to 1681: just 9 Huguenots. Unfortunately, her work fails to indicate the sources used in reaching this conclusion, which is more controversial than the author appears to be aware. In verifying the undeniably important representation of Protestants among the initial members of the Academy, I have relied upon the list of original academicians in Heinich, p. 240; Prestwich; François Bluche, ed., *Dictionnaire du Grand Siècle* (Paris, 1990); Emmanuel Bénézit, *Dictionnaire critique et documentaire des peintres, sculpteurs, dessinateurs et graveurs*, 2nd ed. (Paris, 1966); and E. and E. Haag, *La France protestante* (Paris, 1877-88).

55. Christian Tümpel, "Die Reformation und die Kunst der Niederlande," in *Luther und die Folgen für die Kunst*, ed. Werner Hoffman (Munich, 1983), p. 317; Manuth, p. 240.

56. Stanislas Lami, *Dictionnaire des sculpteurs de l'école française du moyen age au règne de Louis XIV* (Paris, 1898), and *Dictionnaire des sculpteurs de l'école française sous le règne de Louis XIV* (Paris, 1906), reveal just three sculptors identified as Protestant among fifty sculptors active between 1600 and 1680 for whom the most extensive biographical information is supplied (Jean Richier, d. 1625; Barthélemy Prieur, d. 1611; and Mathieu Lespagnandelle, 1617-89). The actual percentage of Protestants may, however, have been somewhat higher, with gaps in the available information accounting for some underrepresentation of Protestants in this sample. For only thirty of the fifty sculptors in question is burial in the Catholic Church noted, and in some of these instances the individual in question died after 1685, when this was the only legally tolerated church in the country.

fication. These cases also provoke further questions. Did Calvinist artists working for Catholic patrons seek to introduce details or inflections into their depictions of the subjects they were commissioned to produce that might have made their finished works slightly less offensive to Reformed sensibilities than they otherwise might have been? Just how, if at all, did artists of different religious affiliation working in the same places and the same sectors of the marketplace differ from one another in their choices of subject matter or style? Only through such detailed investigation of the oeuvre of artists of different religious affiliations working alongside one another in religiously plural localities will it become possible to determine just how the personal religious affiliation of individual artists may have affected the shape and content of their work. It is clear that too direct a link cannot simply be assumed.

If no simple relation can be assumed between the theological implications of a given canvas and the religious beliefs of the artist who produced it, there can be no doubt that wherever a Reformed Reformation triumphed, it immediately and substantially altered the conditions of artistic patronage and production. As early as 1525-26, painters and sculptors in both Strasbourg and Basel, two cities caught up in the ferment of the early evangelical movement, addressed pleas for help to the civic authorities. Since the pure word of God had come to be announced in their cities, they claimed, their business had fallen off. No more altarpieces or other works of art destined for churches were being commissioned, and several painters had already been obliged to abandon their craft. As Carl Christensen has demonstrated, the ranks of artists subsequently thinned significantly in four such South German and Swiss cities where the early evangelical movement bore a heavy Reformed imprint.[57] (See table 1 on page 39.) Sculptors particularly suffered. In another corner of Europe where Reformed churches became the state-supported ecclesiastical establishment, the Netherlands, the painter and art theorist Samuel van Hoogstraten still lamented the Reformation's negative consequences for his trade a century after the fact. "Art in Holland has not been entirely destroyed since the Iconoclasm of the previous century," he wrote in 1678, "but the best avenue has been closed to it, namely the painting of altars and histories for churches, as a result of which most painters have been obliged to paint modest things, even banalities."[58] Hoogstraten's assertion must be evaluated in light of the hierarchy of genres at the time that accorded history painting the greatest prestige, and it fails to mention that the numerous Catholic congregations that met throughout Holland behind the plain fa-

57. Carl C. Christensen, "The Reformation and the Decline of German Art," *Central European History* 6 (1973): 207-32.

58. Quoted in Tümpel, "Die Reformation und die Kunst der Niederlande," p. 314; Manuth, p. 239.

cades of ordinary houses in the seventeenth century commissioned their share of altarpieces and paintings.[59] Still, the most obvious consequence of a Reformed Reformation for the livelihoods of painters and sculptors was the virtual disappearance of ecclesiastical patronage. Since this was the source of many of the most valuable commissions for artists on the eve of the Reformation, the economic impact of this is hard to overstate. If today Holland appears to us as the Calvinist-dominated region where the painter's art weathered the crisis of the Reformation most successfully, this must be attributed to the extraordinary number of artists working in the broader region even before the Reformation, as well as to the high level of general prosperity in the newly independent Dutch Republic that gave rise to strong demand for individual ownership of paintings.

TABLE 1

Painters and Sculptors Appearing in the Public Records
of Four Swiss and South German Cities, 1500-1575

City	Painters			Sculptors		
	1501-25	1526-50	1551-75	1501-25	1526-50	1551-75
Basel	33	14	13	13	4	2
Constance	15	10	10	11	0	5
Strasbourg	20	17	29	13	4	3
Ulm	21	14	14	13	8	2
Total	89	55	66	50	16	12

Note: Catholicism was restored in Constance after 1548, while Lutheran orthodoxy increasingly came to define the church life of Strasbourg and Ulm after 1555.

Source: Carl C. Christensen, "The Reformation and the Decline of German Art," *Central European History* 6 (1973), Appendix A.

In addition to eliminating most forms of ecclesiastical patronage, the triumph of a Reformed Reformation also generated dramatic shifts in the sorts of themes favored by those who purchased paintings for display in their homes. Several examinations of probate inventories from religiously divided communities have shown well the influence of religious affiliation both on the degree of interest in owning works of art and on preferences for different painted subjects owned by individuals. In seventeenth-century Metz, an outpost of French control in Lorraine with a significant Huguenot minority, Calvinism only modestly diminished the desire of its adherents

59. Xander van Eck, "From Doubt to Conviction: Clandestine Catholic Churches as Patrons of Dutch Caravaggesque Painting," *Simiolus* 22 (1993-94): 217-34.

to possess and display paintings in their homes. Canvases appear in virtually the same percentage of Calvinist and Catholic households, with the Catholic painting owners possessing a mean of 8.9 works, as opposed to 6.5 for the Huguenots. But the sorts of works favored by each group were quite different. While 61 percent of the paintings in Catholic hands were religious in character, just 27 percent of those owned by Calvinists were. In their choice of subject matter within the religious category, Metz's Huguenots shunned almost completely the canvases of the Virgin, the saints, the crucifixion, and the Magdalene that were the favored subjects of paintings in the Catholic homes of the city. Instead the largest single category of religious paintings that they owned was Old Testament histories; the second largest, New Testament stories; with depictions of the nativity coming third. The Calvinists were meanwhile more likely to own genre scenes, paintings of the twelve months of the year or the five senses, and mythological scenes, although these kinds of works, like landscapes and portraits as well — which appear evenly distributed between the two confessions — also appeared often in Catholic households.[60]

The contrast between Catholic and Calvinist preferences was less sharp in seventeenth-century Amsterdam, where secular genres that were less confessionally marked accounted for a far higher percentage of the total output of local artists. The pattern was nonetheless similar. Thirty-eight percent of the canvases owned by a sample of Amsterdam Catholic picture owners between 1620 and 1679 were religious in character, while just 16 percent of the canvases owned by Calvinists were. The most common works of a religious character owned by Amsterdam's Calvinists were once again Old Testament histories first, New Testament histories second, and nativities third, while Catholics demonstrated a preference for scenes of the crucifixion, the Virgin, and the saints.[61]

Clearly, these differences reflect important differences in the religious sensibilities of the two groups. The ordinary Calvinist inhabitants of these towns had largely accepted and internalized the Reformed insistence that biblical histories were the sorts of religious images most appropriate for private homes, while avoiding fairly scrupulously those images that were the classic accompaniments to private prayer and devotion or that represented elements of sacred history that the Reformed rejected as fabulous. These statistical investigations also demonstrate that the consequence of the triumph of a Reformed Reformation would have been to shift demand

60. Philip Benedict, "Towards the Comparative Study of the Popular Market for Art: The Ownership of Paintings in Seventeenth-Century Metz," *Past and Present* 109 (1985): 108-12.

61. John Michael Montias, "Works of Art in Seventeenth-Century Amsterdam: An Analysis of Subjects and Attributions," in *Art in History/History in Art: Studies in Seventeenth-Century Dutch Culture*, ed. David Freedberg and Jan de Vries (Santa Monica, 1991), table 5 (figures combined and recalculated).

for works of art toward the production of intimate biblical histories and nonreligious genres such as landscapes and genre paintings, while diminishing interest in such previous staples of religious art as scenes of the crucifixion or the holy family. Christian Tümpel has declared that the Dutch tradition of intimate biblical histories epitomized by artists such as Rembrandt represents "a fundamental Protestant contribution to art," even though he also notes the important role played in the development of this genre by Rembrandt's Catholic teacher Pieter Lastman; the key, in his view, was that the genre developed within an artistic milieu whose contours and possibilities were shaped by Calvinism.[62]

More broadly, it might be hypothesized that Calvinism exercised its most powerful influence on the visual arts through the ways in which it restructured the contours of artistic patronage and altered dominant understandings of the nature and appropriate uses of works of painting and sculpture. From such a hypothesis flows a series of further questions that clearly merit additional study. Where similar sorts of works were purchased by Catholics and Protestants alike, were they understood and appreciated in a similar fashion? Did the Calvinist sensitivity to the dangers of iconoclasm create a different psychological relationship to visual images of all sorts than was characteristic of Catholics, or were the differences confined to the way in which certain sorts of works of art were thought of and used as aids to devotion? (There may yet remain some merit in Doumergue's argument that Calvinism promoted the emancipation and laicization of the work of art.) Were the differences in subject preferences between Catholics and Calvinists matched by differences in stylistic preferences? Insofar as shifting market preferences directed artists in Protestant lands toward exploring subjects such as landscape or genre scenes, did Protestant artists do so in a different manner from their Catholic counterparts specializing in similar themes?

In the realm of architecture, the chief consequences of the establishment of Reformed churches in any given area stemmed at least as much from the process by which these churches came into being and the degree of political power they obtained, as they did from the faith's relevant theological precepts. In those areas where Reformed churches became established as state churches, the Reformed simply took over existing church buildings and modified them for their own purposes. The volume of new church construction was very small over the subsequent centuries, as new churches were required only in new towns, in rapidly growing cities, or in the wake of disasters such as the Great Fire of London that gave Christopher Wren such an opportunity to leave his architectural mark on London. It was first and foremost in areas such as France, where the Reformed church became a legally tolerated minority faith expected to finance its

---

62. Tümpel, "Die Reformation und die Kunst der Niederlande," pp. 314-15.

41

own houses of worship, or in overseas territories newly colonized by Calvinist settlers, that substantial numbers of new Calvinist churches had to be constructed.

The challenge for those who designed these churches was to create buildings suited for the public activities of Calvinist worship, which centered primarily around the preaching of the word and secondarily around the eucharistic ritual. (The manner in which the Lord's Supper was celebrated differed among the Reformed, with the Eucharist generally being celebrated by parishioners being seated at a long table in Scotland and the Netherlands; with the congregation coming forward in a line to receive the elements and then standing at a table in Geneva, France, and the German Reformed churches; and with congregants served at their places in Zwinglian Switzerland and among the English Independents and New England Congregationalists.)[63] The challenge was also to respect the injunctions against wasting money unnecessarily on the ornamentation of the building itself while respecting the requirements of decorum, decency, and edification.[64]

To conclude, we have seen that among the members of Antwerp's clandestine Reformed church was the baroque painter Jacob Jordaens, whose commissioned altarpieces for that city's Catholic churches run as sharply counter as it is possible to imagine to what preconceived notions might suggest that "Calvinist art" ought to look like. Among the works of art listed in the postmortem inventories of seventeenth-century Metz were certain kinds of paintings that appear in Catholic and Huguenot households alike. Evidence such as this underscores that Calvinism did not constitute a distinctive cultural system of such force that all works of art produced by or for Calvinists expressed something distinctively Calvinist. Calvinist artists often worked for Catholic patrons. Even when they

63. James Hasting Nichols, *Corporate Worship in the Reformed Tradition* (Philadelphia, 1968), p. 49; Horton Davies, *The Worship of the English Puritans* (Westminster, 1948), p. 214; Davies, *The Worship of the American Puritans, 1629-1730* (New York, 1990), pp. 163-66.

64. Good architectural histories explore how builders met these challenges in three parts of Europe where the Reformed largely took over existing pre-Reformation church structures but constructed a modest but growing number of new churches over the subsequent centuries: M. D. Ozinga, *De Protestantsche Kerkenbouw in Nederland van Hervorming tot Franschen Tijd* (Amsterdam, 1929); George Hay, *The Architecture of Scottish Reformation* (Oxford, 1957); and Georg Germann, *Der protestantische Kirchenbau in der Schweiz von der Reformation bis zur Romantik* (Zurich, 1963). (This last work is also excellent on Huguenot church architecture in France and its international influence.) Brief historical surveys may be found in Andrew Landale Drummond, *The Church Architecture of Protestantism: An Historical and Constructive Study* (Edinburgh, 1934), pp. 19-140; James F. White, *Protestant Worship and Church Architecture: Theological and Historical Considerations* (New York, 1964), pp. 78-117. And see further G. W. O. Addleshaw and Frederick Etchells, *The Architectural Setting of Anglican Worship* (London, 1950); George Yule, "James VI and I: Furnishing the Churches in His Two Kingdoms," in *Religion, Culture, and Society in Early Modern Britain: Essays in Honour of Patrick Collinson*, ed. Anthony Fletcher and Peter Roberts (Cambridge, 1994), pp. 182-208.

worked for Calvinist patrons or an anonymous market composed largely or exclusively of Reformed believers, they did so in genres and iconographic traditions that had developed gradually over time and were the common property of artists of all post-Reformation confessional families. The appeal of many works cut across confessional boundaries.

Evidence such as this now makes unconvincing the quick steps that interpreters once made from works of art to the ambient "national genius" or "religious life-systems" of the societies or the artists who produced them. It makes it difficult to sustain an interpretation of a pre-eighteenth-century artist's oeuvre in light of his or her personal confessional affiliation without a careful investigation of the artistic vocabulary more broadly characteristic of the artist's time and milieu and a clear demonstration that the artist employed that vocabulary in ways that different from peers of another religious outlook. But if the guiding assumptions and relevant parameters of the topic of Calvinism and the visual arts have thus changed since the generation of Kuyper and Doumergue, the questions that this topic opens up are no less interesting for scholars today, at a moment when art history is increasingly seeking to integrate itself with contemporary developments in cultural studies and sociocultural history, while historians of the early modern and modern worlds are increasingly recognizing the value of material objects and visual images as sources.

The Reformed tradition embraced a set of theological positions regarding the legitimacy of visual images within churches and the degree of ornamentation appropriate for church buildings that set it distinctively apart from Lutheranism as well as Catholicism. For the history of humanity's psychological relationship to images that David Freedberg and Hans Belting have begun to explore, that theology's stigmatization as profoundly offensive to God of certain manners of interacting with visual images that were so prevalent in pre-Reformation Europe is a central part of the story.[65] The issue of how those raised within this tradition subsequently used images of all sorts, and whether or not Calvinist theology served to promote a consistently different kind of relationship with visual materials, also stands as a potentially fruitful avenue of investigation within the sort of cultural history that Roger Chartier has recently pioneered, focused on practices of appropriation and the ways in which different groups use cultural materials common to a given culture as a whole.[66]

Wherever a Reformed Reformation triumphed, the principles of Reformed theology brought about the desiccation of ecclesiastical patronage

65. Belting; Freedberg, *The Power of Images: Studies in the History and Theory of Response* (Chicago, 1989).

66. See especially Chartier, "Culture as Appropriation: Popular Cultural Uses in Early Modern France," in *Understanding Popular Culture: Europe from the Middle Ages to the Nineteenth Century,* ed. Steven L. Kaplan (Berlin, 1984), pp. 229-53; and Chartier's two edited collections, *Pratiques de la lecture* (Marseille, 1985) and *Les usages de l'imprimé* (Paris, 1987).

for painters and sculptors and important shifts in the character of private demand for works of art, although only modest apparent decline in the level of such private demand. Where the course of the Reformation brought into existence a minority Reformed church that had to construct a new set of church buildings on its own, or where the processes of demographic and geographic expansion led to the need for new churches, it also confronted architects with a novel set of guidelines and constraints within which to carry out their church designs. The churches, for the most part, do not appear to have been consistently watchful about trying to ensure that those of their members who were artists themselves cleaved strictly to the principles that they deemed appropriate for the fabrication of art objects, leaving it largely up to the individual artists to make whatever compromises between the demands of the market and the demands of their faith that their consciences allowed. Nor were the guidelines shaping Reformed church architecture particularly detailed. The changing ways in which different architects or anonymous craftsmen interpreted the architectural commandments of this church tradition can thus illuminate how, in this domain of culture as in so many others, theological precept came to be blended with nonecclesiastical cultural elements and traditions, both vernacular and learned, and how this blend changed over time in ways that reveal broader processes of religious or cultural change within Calvinist communities. The ways in which individual artists reconciled the competing demands of theological precept and the wishes of the market or of individual patrons can illuminate the extent and limits of artistic autonomy in this era, as well as the force of theological prescription in the lives of individual believers. The transformations of the market that occurred wherever a Reformed Reformation triumphed and the ways in which this might have spurred artists to explore in new ways those genres that continued to be deemed acceptable represent important elements in the emerging economic history of artistic production that J. M. Montias has done so much to inspire.[67]

In short, the topic of Calvinism and the visual arts takes one today into a rich set of questions about processes of cultural appropriation, cultural change, and individual creativity within the constraints of inherited traditions, market forces, and institutional oversight. The topic raises important questions about the force of theological systems and their interaction with other elements of a culture. It asks its student to consider the changing uses and appreciations of images and material objects over time.

67. John Michael Montias, *Artists and Artisans in Delft: A Socio-Economic Study of the Seventeenth Century* (Princeton, 1982); Montias, "Cost and Value in Seventeenth-Century Dutch Art," *Art History* 10 (1987): 455-66; Freedberg and de Vries, eds., especially the articles by de Vries, van der Woude, and Montias; Richard A. Goldthwaite, *Wealth and the Demand for Art in Italy, 1300-1600* (Baltimore, 1993).

Whether or not the investigation of such questions would amount in Calvin's eyes to more than just a way of beguiling the tedium of idleness is, of course, an open question. In light of the ways in which this corresponds to the aspirations and preoccupations of more than one contemporary scholarly discipline, it is nonetheless no wonder that the topic should suddenly appear an exciting one for scholars approaching the subject from a variety of methodological perspectives, even if the confessional impulses that once motivated so much discussion of this topic have now lost most of their force.

Bibliography

Chartier, Roger. "Culture as Appropriation: Popular Cultural Uses in Early Modern France." In *Understanding Popular Culture: Europe from the Middle Ages to the Nineteenth Century,* edited by Steven L. Kaplan. Berlin, 1984.

Collinson, Patrick. *From Iconoclasm to Iconophobia: The Cultural Impact of the Second English Reformation.* Reading, 1986.

Coulton, G. G. *Art and the Reformation.* 2nd ed. Cambridge, 1953.

Doumergue, Émile. *L'art et le sentiment dans l'oeuvre de Calvin.* Geneva, 1902.

Michalski, Sergiusz. *The Reformation and the Visual Arts: The Protestant Image Question in Western and Eastern Europe.* London, 1993.

Parshall, Linda B., and Peter W. Parshall. *Art and the Reformation: An Annotated Bibliography.* Reference Publication in Art History, edited by Craig Harbison. Boston, 1986.

Tümpel, Christian. "Die Reformation und die Kunst der Niederlande." In *Luther und die Folgen für die Kunst,* edited by Werner Hoffman. Munich, 1983.

Watt, Tessa. *Cheap Print and Popular Piety, 1550-1640.* Cambridge, 1991.

ENGLAND

Puritan and Nonconformist Meetinghouses in England

CHRISTOPHER STELL

Sixteenth-century England saw many changes in religious thought and practice. The old certainties which hitherto had served to keep enthusiasm in check were increasingly being brought into question. The harder the state and the established church sought to impose a uniformity in religious matters, the harder did the forces of change react against the shackles forged to control them. Reformation once commenced was not so readily halted. While the good intentions of all parties need not be questioned, the result was a diversity of belief and practice — the releasing of a genie which twentieth-century proponents of church reunion will have found difficult putting back into its bottle.

Puritan reaction against the Elizabethan church settlement, directed initially toward further reformation within, took the form of religious polemics rather than built structures to house separatist congregations. Some town "lecturers" sailed very close to the wind in their desire for reform and paid scant heed to the restraining hands of episcopal authority, but with the backing of town corporations, such as that in Northampton, they remained within the structure of the established church.

I am greatly indebted to the Royal Commission on the Historical Monuments of England (subsequently abbreviated RCHME) for permission to reproduce photographs and other illustrations from the three published volumes and one forthcoming on nonconformist chapels and meetinghouses in England. These works are cited in the bibliography.

Separatist Congregations

Separatists, unable to accept the existing church organization, formed "gathered churches" more in accord with their own ideas of church polity but were still too insecure to meet regularly in any specially constructed meetinghouse. The literature[1] of nonconformity is scattered with references to meetings in woods and obscure places where the long arm of the law might, God willing, pass them by. But how much of this is now capable of corroboration or distinguishable from pious fiction may well be questioned.

One case where a building has long been claimed for a separatist congregation is the thatched meetinghouse at Horningsham in Wiltshire (see plate 1).[2] It would be most interesting to know just how long the story has been current that the congregation which still worships there was formed by Presbyterian masons working on the erection of nearby Longleat House and that the meetinghouse, proudly displaying the date 1566 in its end wall, was built for their use. It is a pretty story to go with a very charming chapel of stone and thatch which deserves a place in any discussion of English meetinghouses, but it is a story quite incapable of proof. On the contrary, the building appears to be one described in 1700 as "newly erected" when it was registered as a place of worship, extended at one end in 1754 and at the other in 1816. The last date is interesting because it is in this end, behind the pulpit, that the clearly early nineteenth-century stone dated 1566 is to be found, placed there just 250 years after the supposed event. Wiltshire is a county where separatists could well have met at an early period,[3] and it is only the date of the meetinghouse that need be questioned.

The eastern counties[4] of England were also places where separatists gathered, encouraged by trade connections with the Continent, to which many migrated when their liberty was threatened. There we come across another early congregation at Walpole,[5] a village less than ten miles from the coast. This is better documented: the church book of a large congregation of

---

1. See, for example, K. W. H. Howard, ed., *The Axminster Ecclesiastica, 1660-1698* (Sheffield: Gospel Tidings, 1976). This is a theme running through much of the folklore of early dissent in England and repeated in numerous published histories of the earliest congregations.

2. H. M. Gunn, *History of Nonconformity in Warminster* (1853); *The Congregational Year Book* (London, 1855), pp. 258-59; E. G. Atkinson, "The Horningsham Tradition," *Journal of the Presbyterian Historical Society of England* 1 (1914-19): 79-87; R. B. Pugh and E. Crittall, eds., *Victoria History of Wiltshire*, III (London, 1956), p. 99.

3. Pugh and Crittall, p. 99.

4. See *Religious Dissent in East Anglia* (Cambridge, 1991; Norwich, 1993), the proceedings of two symposia on the history of religious dissent in East Anglia.

5. J. Browne, *History of Congregationalism and Memorials of the Churches in Norfolk and Suffolk* (London, 1877), pp. 437-40; J. W. Newby, *A History of Independency . . . in Halesworth and District* (Halesworth, 1936), pp. 40-63; C. F. Stell, *Interiors* (London, 1982), pp. 164-73.

Independents at Great Yarmouth records that in June 1649 "on the 21st of this instant month the saints in and about Couckley did intend to set down in gospel order."[6] Cookley is little more than a mile northwest of Walpole, and it was there, so it seems, that the church first met, assisted by several of the neighboring parish clergy. The Walpole meetinghouse (see plate 2), to which the church may have moved at a very early date, began its existence as a timber-framed cottage, or pair of cottages, built perhaps in the early sixteenth century. It could well have served as a meeting place even before being fitted up as a more regular place of worship; that event may have had to await the easing of restrictions on dissenters in 1689 with the passing of the Toleration Act.[7] It serves as an example of the simple accommodation occupied by the earlier separatists and the manner in which, as they achieved some degree of freedom, they provided more suitable surroundings. On the outside it might still be mistaken for cottages were it not for the gravestones which raise their heads above the long grass of the burial ground in front. Inside (see plate 3) is a full panoply of galleries on three sides, a row of posts to hold up the double roof, put on when the back wall was extended to enlarge the space; against the back wall stands a big canopied pulpit between a pair of large, round-arched windows.

Much the same story might be told of the Old Baptist meetinghouse in Tewkesbury,[8] Gloucestershire, which began its existence about 1500 as a timber-framed hall house hidden away down an alley not far from the famous Abbey Church. In the mid–seventeenth century Baptists had a burial ground in the garden, and soon afterward converted the body of the house into a meetinghouse, much after the fashion of Walpole. Both of these places still stand and are being cared for, though neither is in regular use. Walpole has passed to the care of a newly formed organization, the Historic Chapels Trust,[9] which has been set up to preserve some of the best of the surviving nonconformist chapels in England.

6. Newby, p. 41; J. E. Clowes, *Chronicles of the Old Congregational Church at Great Yarmouth, 1642-1858* (Great Yarmouth, 1912), p. 86. Cookley is the modern spelling of the parish name.

7. The "Toleration Act" (1 William & Mary, cap. 18, 1689), entitled *An Act for exempting their Majesties' Protestant Subjects, dissenting from the Church of England, from the Penalties of certain Laws*, allowed the registration of meetinghouses by orthodox Protestant dissenters. For text, see D. Neal, *The History of the Puritans or Protestant Non-Conformists . . .* , IV (London, 1738), pp. 627-33.

8. B. R. White, ed., *Association Records of the Particular Baptists of England, Wales, and Ireland to 1660*, pt. 1 (London: Baptist Historical Society, 1971), pp. 18-50 passim. Also H. G. Arnold, "Early Meeting Houses," *Transactions of the Ancient Monuments Society*, n.s., 8 (1960): 103-4, 110.

9. The Historic Chapels Trust (29 Thurloe Street, London SW7 2LQ, England) was established in 1993 to take into care redundant places of worship in England other than those of the established church, for which the Churches Conservation Trust is responsible. It is grant-aided by public funds and private donations.

The three places thus far named preserve something of the memory of those separatist congregations which continued a rather nebulous existence in the late sixteenth and early seventeenth century. Elsewhere historical connections are rather tenuously maintained, as in Gainsborough, Lincolnshire, where the name of John Robinson is attached to a late nineteenth-century chapel,[10] or in London where the "Church of the Pilgrim Fathers" in Southwark laid claim to a singularly early ancestry.[11] What time has destroyed, the eye of faith has always diligently striven to restore, and we should not be too hard on those who, like the church at Horningsham, seem to require a tangible witness to their origins.

The Puritan Evidence

Puritans who sought to remain within the church establishment have left a few reminders of their presence, though fashionable uniformity[12] such as prevailed during the period of the Gothic revival, and subsequently with even more drastic "reorderings," has swept away much that might now be more highly valued. Their emphasis on preaching and particularly on the corporate nature of the Lord's Supper left its mark on the arrangement of the chancels of some remote churches where change was less welcome, and these survivals are precious memorials of practices now almost forgotten.

Langley Chapel,[13] standing in lonely majesty in a field in Shropshire, has long been known for its Puritan fittings. It was built, or rather rebuilt, in the late sixteenth century and perhaps repaired in 1601, the date on one of the roof timbers. Its precise status is unclear, though it seems to be related to the nearby Langley Hall and may have been regarded as a chapel of ease, losing its *raison d'être* by the early nineteenth century when the hall and any local community had effectively ceased to exist. The chapel is a simple, rect-

10. The "John Robinson Memorial Church," erected in memory of Robinson, "pastor and exile" who ministered to the church in Leyden, has a foundation stone laid 29 June 1896 by the American ambassador. *Congregational Year Book* (London, 1895), p. 186.

11. The church claimed a rather tenuous descent from several early congregations. The chapel built in 1864 as a memorial to the Pilgrim fathers no longer exists. E. E. Cleal, *The Story of Congregationalism in Surrey* (London, 1908), pp. 1-16.

12. "The improvement in public taste which has been seen in our national edifices and private habitations, during the last twenty-five years, has at length reached the meeting-houses of Nonconformists, and in those quarters least likely to be moved from the pattern adopted by their forefathers, we now witness a conformity to ecclesiastical models which is to us as unexpected as it is agreeable." "Remarks on Ecclesiastical Architecture as applied to Nonconformist chapels," *Congregational Year Book* (London, 1847), pp. 150-63.

13. M. H. Bloxham, *Companion to the principles of Gothic Ecclesiastical Architecture* (London, 1882), p. 174; *Victoria History of Shropshire*, VIII (London, 1968), pp. 145-46. The chapel, long disused, is in the care of the Historic Buildings and Monuments Commission for England ("English Heritage"). The present communion table is a modern replica.

1. Communion table
in Langley Chapel,
Shropshire

angular, stone building without any structural chancel. It is oriented in the traditional medieval manner, with a priest's door on the south side of the chancel and a three-light mullioned window at the east end.

On the inside its significance is at once apparent in the arrangement of the fittings. Centrally in the easternmost bay, raised up by just one step from the floor of the nave, is the communion table (see fig. 1). Around it, on north, south, and east sides, are the seats for the communicants. In some churches the seating even extended around all four sides. Next to the priest's door is a small pulpit, and on the opposite side, to the north, is a much larger canopied pew, described as the "reading pew." This arrangement is, in some respects, a compromise with what might be thought to be Puritan preferences. The table is very small and could not adequately serve those who might have preferred to sit around it, as was later to be the practice in many Presbyterian churches.[14] The Puritans were not in favor of kneeling for communion,[15] whereas these pews have a kneeling board attached, though it may not be original.

14. For this usage in Scottish Presbyterian churches, see G. Hay, *The Architecture of Scottish Post-Reformation Churches, 1560-1843* (Oxford, 1957), pp. 178-83. The longest communion table known to the writer in an English nonconformist chapel is in the Bunyan Meeting, Bedford, now in two sections, originally measuring twelve feet in length.

15. Kneeling at communion was regarded by Puritans as condoning a belief in the real presence and as such contrary to one of the basic tenets of Protestantism. In the examination of Daniel Buck, a separatist, in 1593, he describes the manner of administration of the Lord's Supper: ". . . the pastor did breake the bread and then delivered yt unto some of them, and the deacons delivered the rest, some of the said congregacion sittinge and some standinge aboute the table and that the pastor delivered the cupp unto one and he to an other, and so from one to another till they had all dronken. . . ." L. H. Carlson, ed., *The Writings of John Greenwood and Henry Barrow, 1591-1593*, Elizabethan Nonconformist texts, VI (London, 1970), p. 307.

A chapel a little later in date than Langley and architecturally distinct, but with particular Puritan and transatlantic associations, is "The Ancient Chapel of Toxteth."[16] Ever since the days of King John in the early thirteenth century, "Toxteth Park," a few miles south of the once small port of Liverpool but now quite engulfed by this great conurbation, had been an enclosed deer park. This use ceased in 1604 and the land was brought into cultivation. The new inhabitants soon felt the need for a school, and in 1611 they appointed as schoolmaster the young Richard Mather,[17] then only fifteen years of age. Mather went up to Oxford University in 1618 but very soon afterward was invited to return to Toxteth as minister of a newly built chapel, for which office he was reluctantly obliged to accept episcopal ordination.

Mather's ministry at Toxteth lasted for seventeen years, during which his relationship with the established church remained strained, although the remoteness of Toxteth at that time allowed him for most of that period to continue in office without much interference. In 1633 conditions changed. Mather was accused of unorthodox practices, omitting the sign of the cross in baptism, and failing to administer the sacrament to communicants kneeling. In 1635 he followed in the footsteps of many of his fellow Puritans and set sail for the New World. As to the great achievements and benefits he and his successors brought to their new country, that is another story which cannot be more than hinted at in this paper.

Richard Mather's chapel in Toxteth (see figs. 2 and 3) still stands, although not quite in the form in which he last cast eyes upon it. It is a sandstone building given an eighteenth-century appearance as the result of much rebuilding and heightening in 1774. The building stands on a small site on the southeast side of Park Road, an ancient track leading to Liverpool; at the southwest end is the original entrance and on the roof a bell cote housing a single bell dated 1751. At the opposite end is now a much grander entrance, built in 1841, which stands on the site of a two-storied school building of about 1795. Of greatest importance here, in view of the Puritan worship conducted in the chapel from its inception, is to consider what stood on this part of the site before 1795. The only visible evidence is the surviving northeast end wall of the main body of the chapel (see fig. 4).

16. This style was adopted in the nineteenth century to distinguish it from the many other places of worship then being built in the district. It was earlier known as Toxteth Chapel or Toxteth Park Chapel. See V. D. Davis, *Some Account of the Ancient Chapel of Toxteth Park, Liverpool* (Liverpool, 1884); L. Hall, "Toxteth Park Chapel in the Seventeenth Century," *Transactions of the Unitarian Historical Society*, V (London, 1931-34), pp. 351-83; L. Hall, "The Ancient Chapel of Toxteth Park and Toxteth School," *Transactions of the Historic Society of Lancashire and Cheshire* 87 (Liverpool, 1936): 23-57; B. Nightingale, *Lancashire Nonconformity*, VI (Manchester, 1893), pp. 66-110.

17. Richard Mather (1596-1669) entered Brasenose College, Oxford, in May 1618 but preached his first sermon at Toxteth in November of that year. *Dictionary of National Biography* (London, 1894 and later); R. Middlekauff, *The Mathers: Three Generations of Puritan Intellectuals, 1596-1728* (New York, 1971).

2. Toxteth Chapel,
Liverpool

In this wall immediately opposite the original entrance is a large pointed
arch which is clearly part of the original structure; above it, in the now
heightened roof space, is an area of original wall plaster marking the previous height of the wall, and a similar patch of wall plaster, slightly lower,
marking the roof line of the pre-1795 building beyond. The arch is, without a doubt, a chancel arch, and the structure beyond was a chancel. One
further item of evidence which remains in the chapel archives is a roughly
drawn plan dated 1773, just before the major reconstruction which raised
the walls to their present height. This shows a school building occupying
the site of the chancel and a gallery cutting across the line of the arch.

After the Restoration in 1660 the chapel continued in the hands of
Presbyterians who had used it during the Commonwealth; it was never reclaimed by the Church of England and remained thereafter a dissenters'
meetinghouse. At first it had a single gallery above the southwest entrance;
then by 1773, perhaps well before, a second gallery was built across the
chancel arch and the pulpit placed between them on the side wall, as was
usual in contemporary meetinghouses. These two galleries are shown on
the 1773 plan, and a third cross gallery was added later. The chancel had
long before this date come to be used for a school, but burial rights remained within it, occasioning a welcome half-holiday for scholars when an
interment was to take place.

It takes some imagination to visualize Toxteth Chapel as it was when
its first minister, while initially avoiding too great a conflict with the authorities, came to conduct worship in accordance with his Puritan persua-

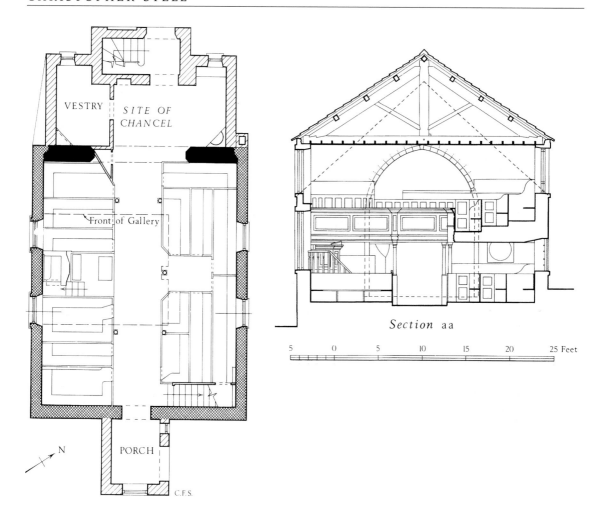

3. Toxteth Chapel,
plan and section

sion. When viewed from the old entrance, with the large arch beyond, it may seem more orthodox than might be expected. Probably the chapel was built or completed while Mather was at Oxford and was what the local people or their builder thought appropriate without reference to the proclivities of their new minister. What does seem clear is that a chancel, possibly fitted out as was Langley Chapel, was not unacceptable.

Toxteth Chapel is a very instructive example of the way in which Puritanism could tolerate architectural orthodoxy even though ecclesiastical orthodoxy found Puritanism intolerable. In its later history and its unusual survival within the nonconformist fold, it also illustrates the typical eighteenth-century meetinghouse layout, with the pulpit against a longer side wall, but retains some of the earlier fittings such as a pew dated 1650 near the entrance, or the grave of Edward Aspinwall, who was responsible for Mather's conversion to Puritanism, appropriately sited immediately in front of the chancel arch.

56

Nonconformist Squires

4. Interior of Toxteth
Chapel

Chancels, symbolic of Gothic churches and the unreformed religion, have
not been thought of as belonging much to the early years of English nonconformity, but the Calvinism which was preached in barns could be, and was
during the Commonwealth, preached in cathedrals, while the piper who
called the tune or the landed proprietor who built the chapel often had ideas
in architecture beyond those of small impoverished congregations for whom
mere protection from the weather was as far as their aspirations extended.

A second Lancashire chapel, now gone, the general proportions of
which must have been close to those of Toxteth before its heightening
(though nearly a century later in date), was Risley Chapel (see fig. 5),[18] built
about 1707 by Thomas Risley — as reluctant a nonconformist as Mather was
an Anglican. Risley was a fellow of Pembroke College, Oxford, who surren-
dered his fellowship when the Act of Uniformity[19] came into force on 24 Au-

18. B. Nightingale, *Lancashire Nonconformity*, IV (Manchester, 1892), pp. 252-61; C. F.
Stell, in *Transactions of the Ancient Monuments Society*, n.s., 30 (London, 1986), pp. 131-38.

19. The Act of Uniformity (14 Charles II, cap. IV, 1662), requiring entire consent by

57

5. Risley Chapel,
Lancashire

West Elevation   East Elevation   Section, looking East

South Elevation

C.F.S.

Plan

gust 1662 (Saint Bartholomew's Day), but so far relented as to accept episcopal ordination. Then his latent nonconformity led him to retire to his
family estate in southern Lancashire, to preach, to teach, and eventually to
build a simple Presbyterian chapel, of brick, covered in stone slates, and oriented in the orthodox manner, with nave, chancel, and bell cote.

Of external decoration there was none, except for a brick band carried

clergy to a revised *Book of Common Prayer* and submission to the established Church of England, was objected to by many serving ministers who either withdrew from public life or
conducted meetings illegally and at considerable risk to themselves and their hearers.

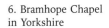
6. Bramhope Chapel
in Yorkshire

across the heads of the formerly segmentally arched windows. The chancel at the east end, which by the early nineteenth century had become a vestry, had its own doorway for the minister and an east window centrally located on the main axis of the chapel. The history of this congregation is typical of many early Presbyterian societies in England in that it gradually exchanged Calvinistic orthodoxy for Unitarianism, but at Risley Chapel legal action in the early nineteenth century forced its transfer to orthodox Presbyterian trustees who were responsible for the various structural changes which subsequently took place. One of these may have been the closing off of the chancel by a boarded partition.

Risley Chapel, like Toxteth, had its chancel arch, though in its latest manifestation this was a semicircular arch of very recent date. Fortunately old photographs record its predecessor, which was a very depressed, almost flat, segmental arch with a keystone in the plaster, of clearly early eighteenth-century date.

What the reason may have been for providing chancels in these small chapels, whether it was due to Lancastrian conservatism or other causes, is hard to say.[20] It does not, however, represent the usual design for a meetinghouse. If we return to the mid–seventeenth century, the period of the Commonwealth, a few chapels are found which more nearly follow the pattern of Langley Chapel, with its simple rectangular plan and perhaps a bell cote at one end. Of these the most significant is Bramhope Chapel in York-

---

20. Another Lancashire chapel, Tunley Chapel, Wrightington, built 1691, appears to have been built with a chancel, but since rebuilt. One reason for these chancels may have been a desire of some nonconforming landowners to worship in a building with some of the visible attributes of the established church.

59

7. Bullhouse Chapel,
Yorkshire

shire (see fig. 6),[21] built in 1649 by Robert Dyneley of Bramhope Hall. Although he owned the property, he left the appointment of what he describes as a "godly and able minister" in the hands of trustees. In the south wall are two identical doorways, while at the east end is a window of four lights marking the location of the communion table.

This is a very long and narrow building, only seventeen and a half feet across but sixty feet long, twice the length of the body of Toxteth Chapel; these proportions are most frequent in the north of England, not only in nonconformist chapels but also in many chapels of ease, which they sometimes closely resemble. The original chancel fittings do not survive, but much else does, in the pews and particularly in the fine pulpit which was filled by many a godly and able minister in the twenty-two years or so before the chapel passed into the hands of the established church. One who filled the pulpit in a very literal sense was the great Yorkshire itinerant preacher Oliver Heywood, a seventeenth-century John Wesley, who records having preached here in 1665 on the occasion of a public fast, to "a great congregation . . . with abundance of inlargement from 11 o'clock til half an hour past 3," adding that "blessed, blessed be our gracious God for that precious and unexpected opportunity."

A comparable chapel, again the product of a sympathetic local squire, though a generation later, is Bullhouse Chapel (see fig. 7),[22] built in 1692 by Elkanah Rich, who occupied the adjacent Bullhouse Hall. The hall had

21. *The Bradford Antiquary*, III (Bradford, 1900), pp. 325-34; *Thoresby Society Publications*, IX (Leeds, 1899), pp. 228-45.

22. Bullhouse Chapel, near Penistone. See C. F. Stell, *Archaeological Journal* 138 (1980): 99.

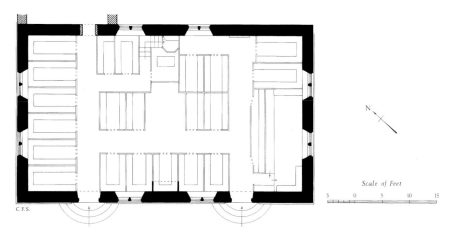

8. Rivington
Chapel, Lancashire
plan

Scale of Feet

been built in 1655 by his father, Sylvanus Rich, who provided shelter for several nonconforming ministers during the difficult years following the Restoration. The chapel is in the usual Pennine vernacular style with stone walls and roof and mullioned and transomed windows. The front faces east and is symmetrical, with a central porch and ball finials on the gables.

The much refitted interior has a directional emphasis along the longer north-south axis to face a contemporary canopied pulpit set between a pair of windows in the north wall. At the opposite end is a single window of three lights; it is tempting to speculate whether the communion table might have been placed at that end rather than in front of the pulpit, but the refitting, which resulted from a very checkered history over the past century, has left no visible evidence. This was at least nominally Presbyterian in its early days, as were many of the older meetinghouses, but that cause failed by the early nineteenth century and the present church is Independent.

Another of these "squires' meetinghouses," as they might be called, whose erection and possible resemblance to chapels of ease may be attributed to the patronage of some local landowner or other dignitary well disposed toward dissenters, is found in Lancashire. The Presbyterians at Rivington[23] continued to occupy the old chapel of ease, now the parish church, for many years after the attempted ejection of the minister in 1662; in fact, they remained in possession until 1702 due to the influence of Hugh, Lord Willoughby of Parham, who was a local magistrate. With the accession of Queen Anne, Lord Willoughby's influence waned, and the dissenters were belatedly ejected from the parochial chapel and forced to fend for themselves. The result was the erection of Rivington Presbyterian Chapel (see plate 4 and fig. 8), a rectangular stone chapel of much the same proportions as Bullhouse Chapel but a few

23. P. J. W. Higson, "Some Leading Promoters of Nonconformity," *Transactions of the Lancashire and Cheshire Antiquarian Society* LXXV-VI (Manchester, 1965-66): 135-38; B. Nightingale, *Lancashire Nonconformity*, III (Manchester, 1892), pp. 81-98.

feet wider, and with a bell cote over the northwest gable, but for which the front with its two doorways is entirely symmetrical.

Most significant here is the change of axis in the inside. It reflects what occurred at Toxteth Chapel when the chancel fell out of use, requiring that the pulpit be placed in the most logical position halfway along one of the longer walls, with the pews and galleries ranged around it. But at Rivington the meetinghouse style was adopted from the first. The windows in the front wall are repeated at the back, with the pulpit set high up between them. Two similar cross-framed windows occupy the end walls, while the space between the front windows directly facing the pulpit is taken up by Lord Willoughby's family pew. The pew is little different from the other pews and is distinguished only by a modest canopy. Between pew and pulpit is the space allocated to the communion table, which is safely set within the confines of the table pew. Of additional embellishment there is none — for the good wine of scriptural exposition needed no bush while the simple proportions and straightforward country craftsmanship of the period were sufficient to endow the chapel with an aurora of peace and purpose which could brook no meretricious or supererogatory distractions.

Urban Meetinghouses

Those buildings so far named have been, at least in origin, country meetinghouses where the builders have on the whole needed to accommodate relatively modest congregations without undue pressure upon space. In towns the situation was somewhat different; larger buildings were needed. Stepney Meetinghouse in London, for example, long since replaced by a big Gothic chapel which has also passed away, was said to date from 1674, well before the Toleration Act of 1689. Few meetinghouses are to be found from the years between the Restoration and the "Glorious Revolution" (1660-88), but there seems no good reason to doubt that this was one. It had about it a generally domestic air, as has the earliest Quaker meetinghouse to survive, that of 1670 in Hertford.

Stepney Meetinghouse,[24] London, built for a Congregational church under the ejected minister Matthew Meade and long since demolished, may have been altered in the eighteenth century, but the broad proportions of its plan resembled those of Rivington Chapel: six windows wide in the front but only four in the depth, while two lower windows in front sat between a pair of doorways, here with pedimented heads, in a very similar manner. With all large meetinghouses the support of the roof structure was a primary consideration; at Stepney it was upheld by "four huge wooden pillars."

24. J. J. Green, "Matthew Meade, A.M., and His Sermons," *Transactions of the Congregational Historical Society*, II (London, 1911-12), pp. 116-21; A. T. Jones, *Notes on the Early Days of Stepney Meeting, 1644-89* (London, 1887).

9. Saint Nicholas Street Meetinghouse, Ipswich

Several large town meetinghouses surviving from the years immediately following Toleration indicate the quality which some of the more generously endowed meetings were able to achieve. One of the better known is the Old Meetinghouse, Norwich (see plate 5),[25] built in 1693 by a Congregational church formed fifty years before. During the Commonwealth they had the use of one of the many parish churches in the town, and following that they occupied a converted granary and a brewhouse. The Old Meetinghouse does not stand on a prominent site; it is set well back from the street and makes no pretense to be other than a house, that is, a house for meetings. It is built in the domestic style of the day, of brick with giant Corinthian pilasters dividing the broad front wall into five bays. At each end is a doorway with a canopy supported by carved brackets, and below the eaves is an elaborate wooden cornice. The windows, formerly cross-framed, were altered in the eighteenth century, and it seems likely that the roof, now in a single span of low pitch, has also been replaced. Galleries continue around three sides and are supported by columns which rise up to the level of the ceiling.

The meetinghouse next in date, though first in quality, is at Ipswich (see fig. 9),[26] still on the eastern side of England where Continental influences were greatest. Superficially it may not seem to resemble the Norwich Old Meetinghouse — its rendered timber-framed construction is very different — but the broad front is again in five bays with three windows between

25. Browne, pp. 152-74; *A Miscellany*, Norfolk Record Society, XXII (London, 1951), pp. 1-9.

26. W. H. Godfrey, "The Unitarian Chapels of Ipswich and Bury St Edmunds," *Archaeological Journal* 108 (London, 1951): 121-26; A. P. Hewett, *A Short History of St Nicholas Old Meeting House Now Called the Unitarian Meeting House, Ipswich* (Ipswich, 1960); S. A. Notcutt et al., *Reflections on an Old Meeting House* (Ipswich, 1976).

10. Interior view of
Saint Nicholas Street
Meetinghouse, Ipswich

the principal entrances. Decoration is confined to the door cases with their
carved brackets and to the eaves cornice, while the oval windows at each end
serve in a practical way to strengthen the design of the end bays.

This was originally known as the Saint Nicholas Street Meetinghouse, after the street from which it was then approached, through a
narrow archway and almost hidden from sight. Since then the main approach has changed, and its Presbyterian congregation, in common with
many others, has left whatever Calvinism it once had for a Unitarian
theology. Nevertheless, it remains of crucial importance in demonstrating the degree of sophistication to which English dissenters could rise,
given the opportunity.

The Ipswich meetinghouse was completed in 1700, and we are fortu-
nate in having the building contract[27] dated 5 August 1699 "between Joseph Clarke of Ipswich in the county of Suffolk, housecarpinter," and six
persons, of whom two are described as gentlemen and the others as wool-
en draper, weaver, clothier, and beer brewer. This shows that the meetinghouse was to be built on the site of some outhouses at the rear of a "capital
messuage" lately bought by Bantoft, the woolen draper. "The good new

27. The contract is transcribed in Godfrey.

64

11. Rook Lane Chapel, Frome

strong and substantiall house for a meeting place" was to be sixty feet long and fifty feet broad with a double roof "boorne up in the middle with four good and substanciall Cullums," and was to measure twenty-one feet from floor to ceiling.

The internal arrangements (see fig. 10) are now predictable, with galleries on three sides and the pulpit on the fourth; the four substantial columns are still in place, two freestanding and two aligned with the gallery fronts. Behind the pulpit is a row of round-arched windows, set rather low to allow for the framing of the walls, and four circular windows above. In front of the pulpit is a clear space where it is likely the communion table was placed within a distinct enclosure. Elaboration is confined principally to some very ornamental carving on the pulpit and a brass chandelier at the center, a necessary feature in all meetinghouses, though few as fine as this now remain. On the gallery front facing the pulpit is the chapel clock, while unseen and now seldom exhibited is a set of very fine communion cups. This is a building which greatly attracted Daniel Defoe on his journey throughout Great Britain. Of Ipswich he wrote:

> There is one meeting-house for the Presbyterians, one for the Independents, and one for the Quakers; the first is as large and as fine a building of that kind as most on this side of England, and on the inside the best finished of any I have seen, London not excepted; that for the Independents is a handsome new-built building, but not so gay or so large as the other.[28]

28. Daniel Defoe, *A Tour through the Whole Island of Great Britain*, Folio Society edition, I (London, 1983), p. 59.

65

12. Churchgate Street
Chapel, Bury St.
Edmunds, Suffolk

The Meetinghouse Style

A still loosely domestic design, or at least one of a civic rather than recognizably religious form, appears in one notable chapel in the small manufacturing town of Frome in the west of England. The West Country abounds in good building stone, which was used here to excellent effect by the dissenters at Rook Lane Chapel (see fig. 11).[29] This chapel, dated 1707, must surely owe its excellence to the support of some of the wealthier members of the congregation. There have been some slight changes to the exterior, notably to the staircase wings at either side which were added in the early nineteenth century and the cast-iron window frames which date from a major refurbishment in 1862.

Little remains to be seen of the original internal features apart from two very substantial stone columns of the Roman Doric order surmounted by entablature blocks which support the main timbers of the roof. It was a more complex roof structure than most: we might expect a simple double roof with a central valley such as became common practice in the eighteenth century. Instead of this the middle bay of the ceiling rose up into the roof space as a four-sided plaster dome, of which the formwork remained above the Victorian ceiling. Apart from this variation, the meetinghouse proportions and the double-columned interior continue to be the standard design for the majority of the larger meetinghouses of this period.

29. Rook Lane Chapel is poorly documented, a fact which may be accounted for by a lengthy period of benevolent oversight by one or more private individuals. *Congregational Year Book* (London, 1847), p. 156; (1863), p. 335.

13. Mary Street
Chapel, Taunton

The quality of architecture expressed in Frome is repeated, or even surpassed, in another medium, at Churchgate Street, Bury St. Edmunds, Suffolk (see fig. 12).[30] This has long attracted attention for the quality of its brickwork. Bury St. Edmunds is a town where good building stone was nonexistent and timber-framed construction more the order of the day. English Presbyterian societies which generally attracted the wealthier of the dissenters were more inclined to put their comfort before their Calvinism and better able to appreciate and to afford the pleasures of good architectural design. This was built in 1711; it is smaller than Ipswich, but the oval window above the single entrance is reminiscent of the same combination of features in the end bays at the latter. The central bay has lost a small pediment, the base of which alone remains above the sundial, but otherwise this is remarkably complete even to the window glazing with its small, clear-glass, leaded panes set in substantial timber frames.

The plan is square rather than the usual rectangle, perhaps due to the nature of a restricted town site, though it is always tempting to see the

30. J. Duncan, "The Presbyterians in Bury St Edmunds," *Journal of the Presbyterian Historical Society* 12 (1960-63): 100-109; Godfrey; N. Lloyd, *A History of English Brickwork* (London, 1925), pp. 77, 211: "a fine building, probably the most distinguished architectural feature in the town."

67

14. Congregational
Chapel at Lyme Regis
in Dorset

square plan as symbolic of something. Undoubtedly the shape is very satisfying, and the proximity of the congregation in the gallery to the minister
in his tall canopied pulpit might seem to imply a religious as well as a
physical superiority over those in the pit below — all of which is quite unjustified! On more practical matters, some square chapels have pyramid
roofs devoid of internal supports, but at Bury St. Edmunds the gallery columns rise up to add their assistance, and instead of the more usual two
columns there is a single, slender, central post.

Presbyterians may have represented the elite in Protestant dissent, at
least in worldly terms, but the Baptists of Taunton were an exception. At Mary
Street Chapel (see fig. 13)[31] they were able to fit out a meetinghouse worthy
to be compared with any other of its time. It was built in 1721, though just
how much of their early Calvinism they had retained at that date may well be
open to question. Be that as it may, "Jachin and Boaz," the two pillars of the
temple as nonconformists were wont to regard them, were tricked out in full
Corinthian finery, and the embellishment of their meeting place was completed in 1728 by the gift of a magnificent twenty-four-branch chandelier.

The double-roofed, double-columned meetinghouse continued well into
the eighteenth century as the customary design for use by dissenting congregations, so much so that one might suppose that it was only necessary to give
the required dimensions and the local builder would do the rest. The building
contract for Saint Nicholas Street Meetinghouse, Ipswich (see fig. 9), simply
called on the contractor to "perform and finish all Carpenters work and Ma-

31. J. Murch, *A History of the Presbyterian and General Baptist Churches in the West of England* (London, 1835), pp. 192-210.

68

15. Interior of Congregational chapel in Lyme Regis

sons' work as is usual and necessary to be done in the building of such a house as well not mentioned as mentioned," and the result was one of the best buildings of its kind. Details of course varied, and at Lyme Regis in Dorset (see fig. 14),[32] in a chapel of the mid–eighteenth century, the tradition continued within the same general provisions. Materials depended on the locality, and at Lyme Regis rather poor local stone needed external rendering; oval windows light the gallery, but the double roof is basic to the design; sometimes the ends of the valley are concealed, but more often, as here, they are exposed between the hipped ends of the individual roofs.

A late nineteenth-century photograph (see fig. 15) of the interior of the Congregational chapel in Lyme Regis before a series of alterations destroyed some of its character illustrates the two fluted columns which conceal the structural posts holding up the roof valley. The pulpit was set high between two tall arched windows in the back wall, reglazed in the early nineteenth century but still unaltered in size, while we are told that the minister of the day, the Reverend Mr. Whitty, "made the pulpit and front of the galleries, and adorned them with all their mouldings, with his own hands." Undoubtedly the work was lovingly done, and it seems likely, if this tradition is correct, that he also had a hand in ordering the design of the meetinghouse itself.

32. *The Builder* (London, 21 April 1922), measured drawing by A. Durst; W. Densham and J. Ogle, *The Story of the Congregational Churches of Dorset* (Bournemouth, 1899), pp. 143-56.

16. Meetinghouse
at Stevington in
Bedfordshire

Not all meetinghouses were built in the grand style; not all congregations could afford the luxury of fine fittings or appointments. Another aspect of the story is found at Stevington in Bedfordshire (see fig. 16),[33] where the Particular Baptists met for a long time in a converted barn. When a new meetinghouse was needed in 1720, constructing it was a communal effort in which one member gave the land and others helped with labor and in other ways; nor was the effort confined to the local church, for it seems that responsibility for carting the stone was undertaken by a Roman Catholic living nearby. But what brings this close to all the other more polite versions of the meetinghouse so far mentioned is the basic design: a broad front, a double roof with a central valley, and two plain oak posts of octagonal section to support it.

Some variations in the layout of these broad-fronted chapels are found, of which the most noticeable is to place the pulpit at the front between the entrances. This allows the two big pulpit windows to form an architectural feature and, to that extent, detracts from the domestic two-storied appearance when gallery windows cross the main facade. It is very much a characteristic of northern England and is seen at its best at

33. H. G. Tibbutt, *Stevington Baptist Meeting, 1655-1955* (Stevington, 1955); H. G. Tibbutt, ed., *Some Early Nonconformist Church Books*, LI (Bedford: Bedford Record Society, 1972).

17. Underbank Chapel, Stannington, Yorkshire

Underbank Chapel, Stannington (see fig. 17),[34] just outside Sheffield, which dates from 1742. This building is also notable in having a clear span roof without intermediate supports.

Plans, Precedents, and the New Dissent

There are some chapels in which more ambitious planning was attempted. Most were built by Presbyterian congregations whose innovations in design led to innovations in theology or were possibly already symptomatic of a tendency toward so-called liberal thinking. The most interesting of these is the chapel in St. Saviourgate, York (see fig. 18),[35] built in 1692-93 for what was doubtless regarded as a very "respectable" congregation. Several ladies of title were supporters of the cause, notably Lady Hewley, whose benefactions gave rise to much litigation in the nineteenth century. With such support it is hardly surprising that a building was erected with due regard to the status or aspirations of its occupants. So in this cathedral city we have a meetinghouse of cruciform plan with a central tower. The plain brickwork, altered windows, and changes to the pitch of the main roofs have given it a spartan appearance, but when it had two small win-

34. *Transactions of the Unitarian Historical Society*, III (London, 1923-26), pp. 160-65; F. T. Wood, *A History of Underbank Chapel, Stannington* (Sheffield, 1944).

35. B. Dale, *Historical Sketch of Early Nonconformity in the City of York* (York, 1904); J. Kenrick, *Memorials of the Presbyterian Chapel, St Saviourgate, York* (York, 1869).

18. Chapel in St.
Saviourgate, York

dows in each face of the tower, steeper tiled roofs, and appropriate glazing, the picture would have been very different.

A refitting in 1860 swept away much of the internal interest, but above the flat plaster ceilings are remains of earlier plaster barrel-vaults terminating at the crossing in great pointed arches with the ceiling in the tower raised up to roof level to make a lantern lit by the upper windows. In this highly ortho-dox arrangement, the chancel formed the northwestern arm and the pulpit stood, at least in the years prior to the refurbishment, adjacent to one of the piers of the crossing, while Lady Hewley occupied "a spacious pew directly fronting the pulpit."

How then does this fit in with the generality of nonconformist build-ings? I would suggest that it illustrates the close ties which once existed in the north of England with Presbyterians north of the border, where much more ambitious church planning produced quite a variety of designs, all suitable for reformed worship. One building closely akin to St. Saviourgate is the parish church at Lauder in Berwickshire built in 1673. The plan is very similar, and the central tower, though rising to an octagon, is sufficiently like to bear com-parison.

Of greater relevancy to the planning of English chapels is the octagon, a style which several denominations used for a time until its limitations became apparent. The earliest and most elaborate of these stands is in

Norwich, not many yards from the Old Meetinghouse. "The Octagon Chapel" (see plate 6)[36] was designed by Thomas Ivory, a carpenter turned architect, and built in 1754-56 for a Presbyterian, latterly Unitarian, congregation whose standards of doctrinal orthodoxy were already open to question. Shortly after opening, it was visited by John Wesley, who confided his opinions to his journal in the following words:

> *Wednesday 23 November 1757.* I was shown Dr Taylor's new meetinghouse, perhaps the most elegant one in Europe. It is eight-square, built of the finest brick, with sixteen sash windows below, as many above, and eight skylights in the dome, which indeed are purely ornamental. . . .
>
> . . . The inside is finished in the highest taste, and is as clean as any nobleman's saloon. The communion table is fine mahogany; the very latches of the pew doors are polished brass. . . .[37]

Bearing in mind the changed attitudes of the congregation, Wesley's final comment will be readily understood:

> . . . How can it be thought that the old, coarse gospel should find admission here?

Wesley was no Calvinist, but he clearly felt the danger of architectural elaboration exceeding acceptable bounds, and all the octagonal chapels which he encouraged to be built for Methodist use were relatively simple and unadorned.[38]

The mid–eighteenth century was a period of change. Denominational differences were becoming more marked, new denominations were springing up, and chapel design was undergoing a radical overhaul. The old broad-fronted meetinghouse style was looking old-fashioned; experimentation with architectural geometry was expensive; and popular leaning was toward the longer, narrow-fronted chapels best suited to restricted town sites. In Exeter one old-established congregation built a new meetinghouse close to the cathedral in 1760 which was given the name of "George's Meeting" (see fig. 19)[39] in honor of the accession of King George III in that year. Such a mark of loyalty was not uncommon in an age which was still suspicious of dissenters and fearful of any revival of the Stuart cause.

The pulpit, a remarkably elaborate affair with a carved wooden canopy, stands against the wall opposite the entrance at the far end of the lon-

36. J. Taylor and E. Taylor, *History of the Octagon Chapel, Norwich* (London, 1848).

37. N. Curnock, ed., *The Journal of the Rev. John Wesley, A.M.* (London, 1938), IV, p. 244.

38. G. W. Dolbey, *The Architectural Expression of Methodism: The First Hundred Years* (London, 1964), pp. 99-115.

39. Murch, pp. 372-452; *Transactions of the Unitarian Historical Society*, V (London, 1931-34), pp. 384-92; VI (1935-38), pp. 253-56.

19. George's Meeting-
house, Exeter, Devon

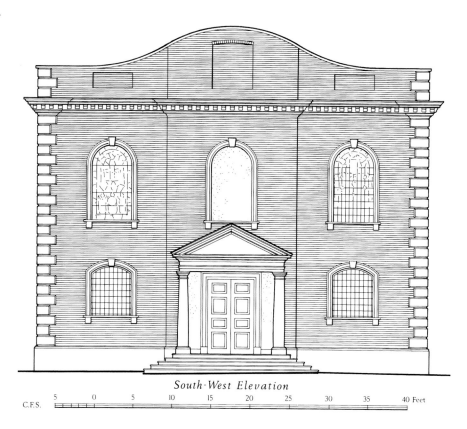

South-West Elevation

C.F.S.

ger axis. There was no central aisle between the pews, but it is not difficult
to see the resemblance to a traditional eighteenth-century parish church.
The outward trappings of orthodoxy have ever proved a temptation to dissenters — all the more so as their religious orthodoxy or distinctive traditions have become clouded. In its later years a cross was added over the
pulpit, after the congregation had turned Unitarian. Some responsibility
for the axial change in chapel planning may also be ascribed to the Wesleyan Methodists, whose founder claimed a continuing personal link for
himself and his followers with the established church.

John Wesley was by no means the only reluctant dissenter. The
countess of Huntingdon was another who sought to evangelize her peers
and to spread the Calvinist gospel, which Wesley feared even more than
Unitarianism, by means of her own private chaplains. The countess's chapel in Bath[40] is of particular interest for the description of it left by Horace
Walpole in a letter dated 1766. He writes:

40. [B. G. Medd], *A Bicentenary Record, 1765-1965, Trinity Presbyterian Church Formerly
Countess of Huntingdon's Chapel, Vineyards, Bath* [Bath, 1965]; [A. C. H. Seymour], *The Life and
Times of Selina, Countess of Huntingdon* (London, 1839), I, pp. 466-88.

The chapel is very neat, with true Gothic windows (yet I am not converted); but I was glad to see that luxury is creeping in upon them before persecution: they have very neat mahogany stands for branches, and brackets of the same in taste. At the upper end is a broad *hautpas* of four steps, advancing in the middle: at each end of the broadest part are two of *my* eagles, with red cushions for the parson and clerk. Behind them rise three more steps, in the midst of which is a third eagle for pulpit. Scarlet armed chairs to all three. On either hand, a balcony for elect ladies. The rest of the congregation sit on forms. Behind the pit, in a dark niche, is a plain table within rails. . . .[41]

In spite of much later alteration the three eagles remain and are also found in other chapels of this connection. But most interesting here is the "dark niche" in which the communion table evidently stood at the opposite end to the pulpit.

If luxury had begun to creep into the chapel in Bath — not surprising in a fashionable watering place — it was hardly a feature of the chapels of the countess's spiritual mentor, George Whitefield. It was Whitefield's espousal of the Calvinistic cause that occasioned the rift between himself and John Wesley and the formation of the rather loosely organized body of Calvinistic Methodists, now best known for its success in Wales. Whitefield seems to have preferred the name "tabernacle" for his preaching houses and to have favored the square, tentlike design which was used in his tabernacle in Moorfields, London, in 1753. Something very similar was used for the Tottenham Court Road Chapel, which was built three years later in the same vicinity. In these instances the square plan does seem to be used to express particular theological sentiments.

How far we would be justified in reading such deep meanings into other buildings may be a matter for conjecture, but undoubtedly the square had its supporters where site conditions allowed. Square Chapel, Halifax (see fig. 20),[42] built in 1772 for Congregationalists, is one of the most notable of these, with a clear internal span of seventy feet. Nor was it free from criticism over the cost or the elaborate decoration with which it was finished.

One instance which I note in passing where a square meetinghouse has been interpreted as having some hidden meaning was the Temple of the New Church, or Church of the New Jerusalem, in Birmingham,[43] commonly called Swedenborgian. It was built in 1790 and was nearly square,

41. Letter to John Chute, 10 October 1766, in J. Aitken, ed., *English Letters of the Eighteenth Century* (Harmondsworth: Pelican Books, 1946), pp. 109-10.

42. Although square in plan, the chapel is so named from its proximity to a projected town square. *Hhadash Hamishcan: or, the New Chapel, at Halifax, in Yorkshire: A Poem* (Halifax, 1772).

43. E. J. E. Schreck, *Early History of the New Church in Birmingham* (London, 1916).

20. Square Chapel,
Halifax, Yorkshire

though with a curved back wall. The historian of the New Church in Birmingham comments on the fascination of the early Swedenborgians with what he calls "the new science of correspondences revealed in Swedenborg's writings." He goes on to claim that the equality of length and breadth symbolizes that of goodness and truth, that the many windows symbolize the light of divine truth, and that their number, three on each of the four sides at the upper level, is reminiscent "of the three gates on each of the four quarters of the holy city that was seen by John to descend from God out of heaven," while the double tier of windows signified the twofold character of a true Christian, both spiritual and natural."[44] This is something which makes even the wildest theories of art historians pale into insignificance!

Three Huntingtonian Chapels

What then might we make of the multifaceted front to the former Calvinistic Independent "Providence Chapel" at Cranbrook in Kent (see fig. 21)?[45] Its seven faces float serenely between heaven and earth, supported, one might almost say, more by the prayers of the faithful than by the foundations laid by man. The truth, unfortunately, is more mundane.

44. Schreck, pp. 23-24.
45. [R. J. Honeysett], *Providence Chapel, Cranbrook, 1803-1953* [Cranbrook, 1953]; S. F. Paul, *Further History of the Gospel Standard Baptists*, V (Brighton, 1966), pp. 243-67.

76

21. Former Calvinistic Independent "Providence Chapel" at Cranbrook in Kent

The Calvinism of the Old Dissent in England suffered changes and even complete transformation as a result of the eighteenth-century Age of Reason; the New Dissent had a different agenda. On the other hand, some groups of Particular Baptists and unattached Independents remained faithful to the old ways, with leaders such as William Gadsby and William Huntington coming readily to mind. Many were small churches, seemingly "the chosen few" rather than the many that were called. They built according to their means, and the Calvinistic Independents of Cranbrook began their worship in a storeroom at the back of the present site. Soon an upper floor was added to the room, and that formed the nucleus of the chapel. This was extended on several occasions, always at the upper level, leaving the strange structure which remains to this day.

Internally it is galleried and has the pulpit against the blind center window of the front. The pulpit is small, as are most in this denomination, and the minister remains within it throughout the service. In front is a small music stand for the singers; after all, not all of these chapels were equipped with organs, instruments derided by the more extreme Scottish Presbyterians as mere "kists of whistles."

Cranbrook was the native place of William Huntington,[46] a man in no way to be confused with the countess of Huntingdon; he rose from very humble beginnings to become an immensely popular if controversial London preacher. Several portraits of him exist, including a naive painting (see plate 7) which hangs in Providence Chapel. Huntington sometimes de-

46. William Hunt, alias Huntington (1745-1813); T. Wright, *The Life of William Huntington S.S.* (London, 1909).

77

22. Interior view of Providence Chapel at Chichester

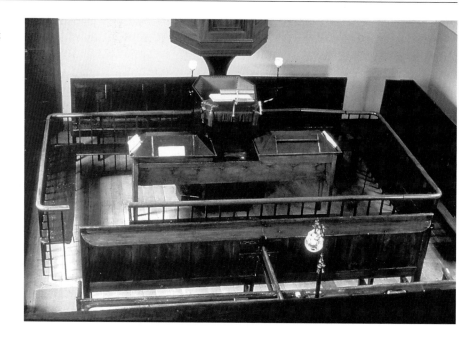

scribed himself as "the coalheaver," a name derived from one of his earlier occupations, and also went by the pseudonym "the archbishop of Titchfield Street," which was the location of his first London chapel. He was undoubtedly an eccentric preacher, and perhaps some of his popularity stemmed from that source. It may not even be too wide of the mark to liken him to Ireland's Dr. Paisley.

Huntington was personally responsible for the cost of the first Cranbrook chapel, and he was involved in others too, such as a small chapel in Chichester,[47] also named Providence, which he opened in 1809. This is of a much more standard design with a gabled front of three bays. It is partly hidden behind a high wall and has a small cottage at the back originally intended for the minister.

Here it is the fittings (see fig. 22) that deserve attention, most of which are original to the building. Thus, it may be taken as representative of a chapel of its period in the high-Calvinist tradition. No one who has worshiped there can easily forget the hard, open-backed benches, which are no wider than necessary. Rising from them when the chapel clerk, seated in front of the pulpit, gives out a hymn, is in itself a blessed deliverance. The pulpit is accessible only from the minister's vestry, which is at first-floor level, an arrangement which was quite common at the time and one adopted by many different denominations.

Below the preacher lies a second focus of attention, the table pew. It

47. J. S. Reynolds, *Providence Chapel, Chichester,* The Chichester Papers, no. 19 (Chichester, 1961).

23. Jireh Chapel in Lewes, Sussex

is also the singers' pew, with a table at the center which ingeniously does duty both as a communion table and a desk for the singers. When required for communion, one of the two desktops is lifted away, leaving a flat surface sufficient for the necessary vessels to stand on. This may not quite resemble the chancel fittings at Langley Chapel, though it is impossible not to feel that those early Puritans might recognize something which they held in common.

Finally we come to the greatest of these Calvinistic Independent chapels, all of which lie in the southeast corner of England: Jireh Chapel in Lewes (see fig. 23).[48] From the outside it looks like a brick building, but it is entirely timber framed, clad in part in what are called "mathematical tiles," so shaped that they resemble brickwork. This congregation originated with a minister from the Countess of Huntingdon's Connection, Jenkin Jenkins, whose brand of Calvinism was not appreciated by the more sedate trustees of the Cliffe Chapel at which he officiated. Jireh Chapel was built for him in 1805 and was opened by the indefatigable William Huntington. In the gable is a tablet inscribed:

> Jireh Chapel erected by J. Jenkins W.A. with the
> voluntary Contributions of the Citizens of Zion;
> Anno Domini MDCCCV

48. C. F. Stell, *The World of Interiors* (London, 1988), pp. 124-27. See also Wright.

79

The initials W.A. were a foible of Huntington, who called Jenkins "the Welsh Ambassador," while he took to himself the letters S.S. after his name, standing for "Sinner Saved," saying he adopted them not having the learning to acquire an M.A. nor the money to purchase a D.D.

Behind the chapel is a plain tomb in which William Huntington is buried. The inscription on the monument, written by himself, reads:

> Here lies the coalheaver who departed this life July 1 1813 in the 69th year of his age. Beloved of his God but abhorred of men, the omniscient Judge at the grand assize shall ratify and confirm this to the confusion of many thousands, for England and its metropolis shall know that there hath been a prophet among them.

Jireh is quite the largest of the Calvinistic Independent chapels. It was enlarged in 1826 by extension to the front, and much of its present appearance is of that date. It has a gallery (see plate 8) around all four sides with columns rising to support a barrel vault above the central space. Most of the woodwork is of unvarnished pine, and substantial box pews line the galleries. Time was when the chapel was filled with worshipers. Sadly that has not been so for many years, and its only user, other than those gathering in the vestry for services, has been one of the Protestant bonfire societies, a notable feature of Lewes, who met for their annual service to commemorate the failure of the "gunpowder plot" and the apprehension of Guy Fawkes and his associates in words once annexed to the Anglican *Book of Common Prayer*.

As in Chichester the minister's vestry is at first-floor level, is equipped with a small library, and is adorned, as is many another nonconformist vestry, with portraits of past ministers, as well as a large portrait of William Huntington. From the vestry the preacher proceeds down a flight of steps between the pews of the end gallery and across a short bridge into the pulpit, in front of which is the clerk's desk and the railed table pew.

The architecture of Calvinism, real no-nonsense Calvinism, which admits no blurring of the edges of belief, which sees and does not hesitate to distinguish between the saved and the damned, is to be found at its best in Jireh Chapel, Lewes. An appreciation of the genius which pervades the architecture of the traditional English meetinghouse requires not only an empathy between the viewer and the builders for whom architectural expression was subservient to pastoral needs, but a realization of the infinite gradation which exists between the beliefs and practices of the multitude of the many and disparate religious societies — Calvinistic or otherwise — which from the seventeenth century came to constitute the body of English dissent. When these denominational requirements are reduced to their basic essentials, we find that the simple gospel message, unadorned by the niceties of a liturgical service, called for a corresponding simplicity in buildings. The meetinghouse is not a shrine for a god to inhabit requiring palatial embellishments; it is a house suitable for corporate worship. The central pulpit dominates an interior where the eye is not diverted by an excess of decoration, nor the mind allowed to stray from the work in hand. A domestic atmosphere, with the people gathered around the preacher, was all that the faithful desired, a building of good proportions and seemly construction, which is itself the basis of all good architecture.

Bibliography

Most of the buildings referred to are discussed in the following four volumes, prepared by the writer on behalf of the Royal Commission on the Historical Monuments of England.

[Stell, C. F.]. *An Inventory of Nonconformist Chapels and Meeting-houses in Central England*. London: Her Majesty's Stationery Office [HMSO], 1986.

Stell, C. *An Inventory of Nonconformist Chapels and Meeting-houses in South-West England*. London: HMSO, 1991.

———. *An Inventory of Nonconformist Chapels and Meeting-houses in the North of England*. London: HMSO, 1994.

———. *An Inventory of Nonconformist Chapels and Meeting-houses in Eastern England*. London: HMSO, in progress.

Other principal publications relevant to individual buildings are cited in the respective footnotes. The following more general works should also be noted.

Addleshaw, G. W. O., and F. Etchells. *The Architectural Setting of Anglican Worship*. London, 1948.

Briggs, M. S. *Puritan Architecture and Its Future*. London, 1946.

[Creasey, J., ed.]. *Nonconformist Congregations in Great Britain: A List of Histories and Other Material in Dr Williams's Library*. London, 1973.

Drummond, A. L. *The Church Architecture of Protestantism*. Edinburgh, 1934.

Watts, M. R. *The Dissenters: From the Reformation to the French Revolution*. Oxford, 1975.

Huguenot Goldsmiths in England

JAMES LOMAX

Summary

The main subject of this paper is the effect of the Revocation of the Edict of Nantes (1685) on the development of the goldsmiths' art and trade in England. This event has often been seen as a turning point in the history of British decorative arts, historians since Samuel Smiles[1] having long since recognized that the luxury trades in particular[2] were major beneficiaries of its consequences. The newly arrived Huguenot goldsmiths brought with them a tradition of exceptional technical virtuosity along with a fresh repertory of Continental style and ornament unknown in England. Their high standards were swiftly taken up by their English colleagues with long-term beneficial results for the future. France at this time was the center of most avant-garde developments within this craft.

We will begin, however, by looking briefly at the first wave of immigration and the context within which the Continental refugees came to England from the early part of the Reformation until the Civil War. Lack of hard evidence makes it impossible to quantify the significance of specifically Calvinist goldsmiths at this time. The conservative nature of native craftsmanship and design makes it likely that most of the outstanding pieces made for the crown and nobility were indeed the work of foreigners, who were also the agents for any changes in style and ornament. The effect of the new liturgy of Protestantism on the design of church plates, both for Anglican and Continental Reformed churches, will also be discussed.

We will then consider the effect that approximately 150 goldsmiths of French origin had in transforming and elevating a moribund English craft into one that became proverbial for its standards of excellence that

---

1. Samuel Smiles, *The Huguenots* (London, 1867), p. 320.
2. The term "goldsmiths" is used throughout and includes silversmiths.

prevailed for generations to come. The development of a distinctive French baroque style as part of the great policy of centralization by Colbert and Louis XIV will be examined, and also the way in which the latter was able to use the guild system in his persecution of his highly skilled Huguenot subjects. Their arrival in England was officially welcomed by the government but deeply resented by the native goldsmiths, to whom they posed a considerable threat. We will see how they were able to overcome these difficulties and how they were able to find clients among the greatest in the land. Within a single generation their influence was profound: they remained a close-knit group and in the second generation were the natural leaders in the development of the rococo style — in any case an essentially French phenomenon.

It is misleading in my view to find any specifically religious significance in the work of the immigrant Huguenot craftsmen. And the role that religion played in their success story is also difficult to evaluate. To be sure, many of them were devout in adhering to the Calvinist ethics of hard work, frugality, and mutual support — but all of these would have been crucial for any refugee minority attempting to establish itself in a new environment. It will be seen here that although the primary motive for the Huguenots' departure from France was to seek religious toleration, the goldsmiths in particular were anxious to find a new market for their products at a time of considerable economic recession at home. In England they received much sympathy from official sources, not only on account of their Protestantism (although mainstream Anglicanism and Calvinism were not easily reconciled), but also because their skills were seen to be highly desirable in the development of native crafts and industry. In addition, in the popular mind they were seen as victims of the despotic government of Britain's archenemy, Louis XIV. In due course they were able to overcome the conservative elements among the native craftsmen, and within a generation their influence was to permeate all aspects of the trade.

The evidence from their work will be seen to support this view. Their most prestigious output would have consisted in the grand ceremonial pieces destined for the sideboards of their wealthiest clients — scarcely objects which reflected the austere lifestyle enjoined by the strictest tenets of Reformed faith and practice. Even the so-called Queen Anne plain style — simple but elegant tea and toilet wares based on classicizing geometric shapes — can be seen as an interpretation of fashionable Oriental porcelain prototypes. Likewise the apparently unostentatious character of much everyday silver at this time more often reflects the client's taste and ability to pay the goldsmith's surcharge for "fashion." Indeed, the role of the client was all-important: even their grandest English patrons appear to have had a commonsense outlook on the relative appropriateness of ornament or elaboration, often ordering the most showy objects for the "public" rooms of a house, while simpler but beautifully finished pieces were considered more suitable for private apartments.

Thus the Huguenot goldsmiths' great success in England was to develop and supply a market for fashionable silverware, both useful and ornamental, at precisely the moment when conditions were most propitious. In the contemporary debate on the ethics of luxury (in its widest sense), the work of the Huguenot craftsmen, for all the reticence of their personal lives, represented some of the most advanced features of artistic and economic sophistication.

The First Phase

During the Middle Ages foreign goldsmiths played a highly significant role in the commercial and financial life of the City of London. By the end of the medieval period, between 1479 and 1514, there were some four hundred "strangers" licensed by the Goldsmiths' Company, which was the sole guild charged to regulate the trade, receive masters, and "assay" and mark all wrought plate.[3] Most of these alien craftspeople were probably Germans, Flemings, and French who provided luxury finishes to the trade: gilding, engraving and chasing, jewel setting and die cutting. No doubt they were lured to England by tales of her great wealth and by the market for prestigious foreign-made luxury goods. Their very success and their presence in the capital in considerable numbers prompted the authorities to control their activities.[4]

Beginning in 1483 it became necessary for foreigners to seek (and pay for) "denization" status in order to set up a business, keep a shop, lease property, or take on apprentices. Undoubtedly a considerable number sought to evade this requirement, but as Europe became increasingly divided, it also became important to comply with legal and other formalities.

---

3. T. W. Reddaway and L. E. Walker, *The Early History of the Goldsmiths' Company, 1327-1509* (London, 1975), p. 171. Lists of foreigners working in London in Tudor and Stuart periods (and some analyses of their occupations) have been published in a number of sources, notably R. E. G. Kirk and E. F. Kirk, "Returns of Aliens Dwelling in the City and Suburbs of London from the Reign of Henry VIII to that of James I," *Publications of the Huguenot Society of London*, X (1900-1908), 4 parts; Joan Evans, "Huguenot Goldsmiths in England and Ireland," *Proceedings of the Huguenot Society of London* (hereafter *Proc Hug*), XIV (1930-33), pp. 496ff. Recent analyses include those of Irene Scouloudi, "Alien Immigration into and Alien Communities in London, 1558-1640," *Proc Hug*, XVI (1937-41); and "The Stranger Community in the Metropolis, 1558-1640," in *Huguenots in Britain and Their French Background, 1550-1800*, ed. Irene Scouloudi (London, 1985), pp. 42-55; also Hugh Tait, "London Huguenot Silver," in *Huguenots in Britain and Their French Background, 1550-1800*, ed. Irene Scouloudi (London, 1985), pp. 89-112; and Philippa Glanville, *Silver in Tudor and Early Stuart England* (London, 1990), esp. pp. 92ff.

4. The most recent published account of this subject is by Glanville, pp. 85-99.

In 1544, just prior to Henry VIII's proposed invasion of France, some three thousand new denizens were enrolled — many of these being craftsmen who had lived in London for a considerable number of years.

One effect of the Henrician Reformation was to change the character of the emerging English Renaissance, which in its early stages had been largely inspired by court patronage of Italian craftsmen. Increasingly their place was taken (both at court and at large) by French and "Dutch" (Flemings and Germans), many with undoubted Protestant sympathies. These newcomers also fulfilled the government's policy of employing skilled foreign workers specifically to improve the royal ordnance foundries and workshops, but also to work as goldsmiths, jewelers, silk weavers, printers, and felt hat makers. It was obviously hoped that their physical presence in London and elsewhere would help spread the knowledge of new techniques and design as well as reduce dependence on imported goods.

With the temporary triumph of the Reformed church during Edward VI's short reign (1547-53) came the official establishment of the independent Dutch and French churches at Austin Friars and Threadneedle Street in 1550. It has been suggested by Andrew Pettegree that the government's close interest in these advanced religious organizations served as a model for the development of a new and established Reformed church in England.[5] Their congregations, included numbers of skilled craftsmen who were crucial to the economic development of the nation. At least thirty metalworkers (including twelve goldsmiths) were present in the Dutch congregations, which had a membership of approximately 350.[6]

After the brief restoration (1553-58) of Catholicism under Mary I, Queen Elizabeth (who took a violent personal exception to Calvin's misogyny) declared for a milder version of the Reformed church. In her foreign policy she came out (1562) in support of the Huguenots. The following year there were some 4,534 foreigners recorded as domiciled in London, out of a total City population of about 95,000. By 1573 their numbers had risen to 7,143, of which about 30 percent (2,541) declared unequivocally that they had come for reasons of employment rather than religion.

Of these, however, only a relatively small number appear to have been goldsmiths: their figures for the whole period between 1558 and 1625 were just 150 Dutch, Germans, and Flemings. Thus it seems somewhat of an exaggeration to learn from a German observer in 1613 that "It is not a long time hence since the majority of artificers and mechanics were aliens and foreigners and all the goldsmiths were Germans."[7]

Obviously the perceived presence of so many foreigners was the

5. Andrew Pettegree, *Foreign Protestant Communities in Sixteenth Century London* (Oxford, 1986), p. 45.

6. Pettegree, p. 82.

7. Daniel von Wensin, *Oratio contra Brittaniam* (Tübingen, 1613), quoted by W. B. Rye, *England as Seen by Foreigners in the Days of Elizabeth and James I* (London, 1865), p. cviii.

cause of great resentment among the indigenous craftsmen, and as a consequence there were several serious riots, the worst probably in 1593 with more than two thousand participants. The government suppressed activities like these, but only with the greatest difficulty. The story of this battle between foreigners and natives, a conflict which was institutionalized and hence exacerbated in the form of closed shop policies in the various guilds, was to be repeated well into the eighteenth century.

Since it lacked supporting statistics, what would account for this impression of huge numbers of foreign goldsmiths in London? Strictly speaking, foreign-run premises should have been forbidden under the exclusive guild regulations, and even where such premises existed they were obliged to be extremely inconspicuous and situated well away from Cheapside, the street in the heart of the City where most goldsmiths had their shops. But it was more likely the presence of large numbers of young foreign journeymen on their *Wanderjahr* which conveyed the impression that London was swarming with German goldsmiths. A year (or more) of travel abroad was a well-established practice on the Continent, but was almost unknown in England. This was one of many Continental practices that promoted the flow of new ideas across borders and kept many of the leading northern European goldsmiths in direct contact with each other.

It is impossible to identify any surviving work by really first-rate or well-established foreign masters (Calvinists included) working in London in the early sixteenth century. The most celebrated of these was Hans of Antwerp,[8] who was first recorded in London in 1511, long before the beginnings of the English Reformation. Despite all the legal restrictions Hans had a large London workshop staffed by Flemish journeymen. He became a close friend of Hans Holbein and executed a number of the latter's Italianate designs intended for Henry VIII and the court — indeed, some of the most memorable objects of the English High Renaissance.

Like many others, and despite his superior skills, Hans of Antwerp was unable to gain the "freedom" of the Goldsmiths' Company, which would have entitled him to ownership of his own workshop, to a maker's mark, and to the free assay of his products. Technically speaking (unless he was working within certain exempted areas of the City which continued to claim immunity from the law because of their previous monastic privileges), Hans would even have been debarred from having a retail establishment within the City (or two miles beyond its perimeter), and he was also required to cover the windows of any workshop he operated to prevent passersby from seeing inside. But in this particular case, under the express

8. For an account of his career, see J. F. Hayward, *Virtuoso Goldsmiths and the Triumph of Mannerism, 1540-1620* (London, 1976), pp. 112-15. Recently the covers of a silver girdle prayer book, circa 1540, in the British Museum, with inscriptions from the English Bibles of 1539 and 1540, have been attributed to him. See Hugh Tait, "The Girdle Prayer Book or 'Tablett,'" *Jewellery Studies* 2 (1985): 29-58.

command of Thomas Cromwell, the King's Lord Privy Seal, the Court of the Goldsmiths' Company was finally (1537) ordered to admit Hans, albeit some twenty-six years after he first set foot on English soil.

Despite the statutory and social constraints, however, it is clear that many highly skilled foreign goldsmiths worked in sixteenth- and early seventeenth-century London. The records of the Goldsmiths' Company[9] provide the names of those who were officially licensed, while some others can be established from a wide variety of archival sources. Matching these names to surviving work is, however, extremely difficult since some of the most sophisticated objects of the mid to late sixteenth century apparently bear unidentifiable English marks. Objects of such sophistication as the Wyndham Ewer and Basin of 1554 (see plate 9)[10] or the Rutland Ewer and Basin (Belvoir Castle, Leicestershire) (1579 and 1581) are so unlike anything being produced by the native goldsmiths that we must infer that they were made by foreigners who managed to persuade (no doubt with compensation) a freeman of the Goldsmiths' Company to submit them for assay. Whether these "aliens" were Protestant or Catholic, working in England for opportunistic economic gain or on account of religious persecution (or both), is not known.

But Nicaise Roussel,[11] a native of Bruges who arrived in London circa 1573, is one foreign craftsman whose work and influence can be identified. He was a member of the Dutch church, and in 1617 was described as "amongst the Goldsmiths, Diamond Cutter and Jewelers within ye City."[12] He was almost certainly dead by 1623, the year in which a set of twelve grotesque designs by him was published.[13] These consist of fantastical leafy tendrils sprouting strange monsters and demi-figures and represent a sophisticated development of a well-established and popular decorative style.

Roussel was clearly a significant entrepreneur: he was involved, for example, after the death of Queen Elizabeth, in the dispersion and exchange for new plate of the queen's jewels; he also had business dealings with Prince Henry and his circle. If he was also a working goldsmith, as reported by the contemporary description, then none of his work can be

---

9. The official history of the Goldsmiths' Company for the period under discussion is in preparation and should provide further details.

10. Hugh Tait, "The Wyndham Ewer and Basin and Subsequent Additions to Tudor and Stuart Silver Plate at the British Museum," *Silver Society Journal* 5 (spring 1994): 195-205.

11. Charles Oman, "Nicaise Roussel and the Mostyn Flagons," *Leeds Arts Calendar*, 83 (1978), pp. 4-8; for another view see James Lomax, *British Silver at Temple Newsam and Lotherton Hall* (Leeds, 1992), pp. 45-49.

12. "Register of the Dutch Church," *Proc Hug*, X, pt. 3 (1907), pp. 46, 160, 177.

13. *De grotesco perutilis atq. omnibus quibus pertinebit valde necessari Liber. Per Nicasius Rousseel, ornatissimo atq. varium artium peritissimo viro. Domino G. Heriot. Johan Barra sculp. Londinii, 1623.*

identified for certain because of the lack of a signature or maker's mark. There is, however, a group of extremely finely engraved objects,[14] some of which have ornament very similar to Roussel's published grotesque designs but are marked by a number of different goldsmiths (see plate 10). Whether these were made by independent goldsmiths in Roussel's workshops and engraved there by the master himself or merely sent to Roussel for engraving will never be known. Nor indeed will it be known whether they are the work of clever plagiarists anxious to adopt a new interpretation of the ever-popular grotesque decoration. At all events, there is nothing specifically Protestant about any of this: they are best described as examples of imported design brought about, once again, by a combination of religious persecution and economic opportunism.

Early Sacramental Plate of the English Reformed Church

The one area where there is evidence of a Reformed influence on the goldsmiths' art is in the commissioning of new and suitable plate for the advanced Reformed church which assumed establishment status after Edward VI's accession in 1547. We can witness the changeover from chalices intended for the Catholic Eucharist to the new and more commodious Reformed communion cups intended for the whole congregation. The change can also be seen in the large flagons designed to hold the additional wine required for the Protestant order of worship, in the alms dishes designed for a service of worship in which almsgiving acquired greater prominence, and (after 1552) in the larger patens to accommodate household breads instead of the tradition of eucharistic wafers. Other liturgical changes which may have affected the appearance of vessels included the increasing requirement for the clergy to face the people during the service and the laity's own handling of the vessels during the administration of communion. Interestingly, in Lutheran areas of Germany and Scandinavia there seemed to be no opposition to using old Catholic mass chalices. In England, however, the impetus to trade these in seems to have come from the Calvinist injunction to use the simplest forms of domestic drinking vessels.

Almost immediately on Edward's accession a number of churches, particularly in the City of London, began to order new plate suitable for communion in both kinds in compliance with the Order in Council of March 1548 and confirmed in the 1549 *Book of Common Prayer*. According to the late Charles Oman,[15] by 1552 over half the City's churches had new communion cups, and at least eight of them were well on their way to provisioning themselves with plate for the new requirements of worship. Three different

14. See Glanville, pp. 95, 163; Oman, "Nicaise Roussel," pp. 5-6.
15. Charles Oman, *English Church Plate* (Oxford, 1957), pp. 129-31, 191-93, 310-11.

groups can be identified from this period. The first (or common) type, as found at Beddington, Surrey (1551), has a tall, bucket-shaped bowl, a spool-shaped stem, and a stepped foot.[16] Secondly, there is the alternative large and heavy design, as in the example (see plate 11) from St. Mary Aldermary (1549), with a wider and lower bowl, a pear-shaped stem with a flanged knop joined to a low-spreading foot. This example also has a fitting and footed paten (or cover) with a handsome enameled royal coat of arms, indicating that it may have come from a royal chapel. Thirdly, there are a number of eccentric designs which subsume a range of interesting vessel shapes. These are perhaps experimental types that attempt to adopt and adapt secular forms for sacred purposes — the cup and paten from St. Michael's, Southampton (1551),[17] are among the most elegant exemplars in this third category, while the cup from Great Houghton, Northamptonshire (1553),[18] is arguably one of the least successful examples in this group. They all have one feature in common — that their stems all have flanges at the point where the priest's fingers meet when elevating the cup at the consecration. This replaced the use of a knop in this position on Catholic chalices, and it may reflect the communicants' need to handle the vessel during the administration of the sacrament.

It was from these experiments (as directed by the Reformers) with the simplest contemporary wine cups that the classic Anglican communion cup emerged during the reign of Queen Elizabeth. Her archbishops conducted systematic campaigns in the 1560s and 1570s to replace the remaining Catholic chalices in the parishes with "decent communion cups."[19] It is difficult to evaluate to what degree the decoration of these new cups was dictated by theological or canonical considerations. This was a decoration confined to engraved annular bands of arabesque ornament. The goldsmiths, whose primary concern was to sell their products, may have judged that the abstract nature of this type of decoration (which was otherwise entirely associated with secular objects) could not possibly cause offense.

Church Plate of the Immigrant Communities

It might be interesting at this point to consider the sacramental plate the early foreign adherents of the Reformed churches in England, and later the Huguenots, made for their own use, as well as the liturgical vessels they

16. Oman, *English Church Plate,* pl. 49.

17. Oman, *English Church Plate,* pl. 52A.

18. Oman, *English Church Plate,* pl. 53B.

19. This phrase is often found in contemporary sources. See W. H. Frere, "Visitation Articles and Injunctions of the Period of the Reformation," III (1910), *Alcuin Club Collections,* XIV, pp. xxxii, xlv.

24. From Bernard
Picart, *Ceremonies and
Religious Customs of the
Various Nations. . . .*
(vol. v, 1733;
engraving)

made for others.[20] The best pictorial evidence showing a Reformed liturgy
in the early eighteenth century comes in an engraving (see fig. 24) published by Bernard Picart.[21] Uncut loaves of communion bread and flagons
of wine are on the altar-table with the ministers seated facing the congregation. Below them the women are seated on benches at a long table receiving the cup from each other as it is passed down from the minister,
who sits in the center. Likewise the bread has been cut and put onto plates
which are also being passed down the table. To the left other women stand
in line until a place becomes available for them. Obviously a considerable
number of vessels was required for such an arrangement, and frequently
these expensive objects were the gifts of prosperous members of the congregation. As one might expect, they were often made by goldsmiths in the
community. Generally speaking, and in accordance with Calvinist principles, they take the form of contemporary or, later, archaic secular drinking
vessels: either late-Elizabethan/Jacobean wine cups, or occasionally Elizabethan-style communion cups.

20. For the earliest discussion of the plate of the foreign Reformed churches, see E. A.
Jones, *The Old Silver Sacramental Vessels of the Foreign Protestant Churches in England* (London,
1908). A number of the pieces were shown in the exhibition *The Quiet Conquest: The Huguenots,
1685 to 1985* (Museum of London, 1985) and discussed in the catalogue by Tessa Murdoch.

21. B. Picart, *Ceremonies and Religious Customs of the Various Nations* (various editions
translated from the French) (London, 1733), vol. 5, opposite p. 468. The text gives a full explanation of the liturgy.

25. (left) Beaker (from a set of four) formerly at the Dutch church, Norwich, silver, circa 1575, maker's mark: William Cobbold

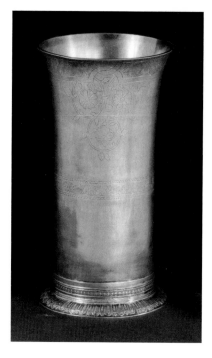

26. (right) Beaker (from a set of four) formerly at the Dutch church, Austin Friars, London, silver, London, 1669, maker's mark: Jacob Bodendick

No examples seem to have survived from the early French or Dutch churches established in London during Edward VI's reign. Instead the earliest surviving foreign Protestant plate are the four beakers (one is illustrated in fig. 25), circa 1575, from the Dutch church at Norwich with the maker's mark of William Cobbold (formerly attributed to Peter Peterson).[22] Beakers are not a very common drinking form in England and are rarely found for liturgical use, although they are seen in churches in Scotland north of the river Tay, and at least one, by David Jesse, circa 1672, was noted at the First Church in Dorchester, Massachusetts.[23]

There is also a set of four fine, but very foreign-looking, covered beakers (see fig. 26) from the Dutch church at Austin Friars, London, by the Restoration goldsmith IB, probably Jacob Bodendick, a goldsmith from Limburg who was responsible for some of the most glamorous secular plate to be found in England in the 1660s and 1670s. These beakers are exceptions in that they have a band of formal, leafy, cut-card work around the foot and on the cover — a decorative technique rarely used by English goldsmiths at this date (although it was becoming commonplace on the

22. Jones, *Sacramental Vessels,* pp. 20-21; for Cobbold, see G. N. Barrett, *Norwich Silver and Its Marks, 1565-1702: The Goldsmiths of Norwich, 1141-1750* (Norwich, 1981), pp. 82-83 (it also contains biographical information about immigrant goldsmiths); and Robin Emmerson, *Norwich Silver in the Collection of the Norwich Castle Museum* (Norwich, 1981), pp. 37-38.

23. Jones, *Sacramental Vessels,* p. xii.

27. (Left) Covered cup from All Hallows, Thames Street, London, silver gilt. Cup 1608, mark: "T.F." Cover 1544

28. (Right) Communion cup (from a set of eight) from the Walloon church, Canterbury Cathedral, silver, London, 1631, maker's mark: "IT."

Continent) and which the Huguenots of the 1680s are usually credited with having introduced. Obviously these vessels would have been used only by foreign communicants, and at this point in time would not have been known to English craftsmen.

The earliest surviving examples from the French-speaking communities are the thistle-shaped cup (see fig. 27) and flagon dating from 1608 from the Church of All Hallows, Thames Street — the former shape is clearly derived from the basic beaker form. It is a handsome but fairly workaday example of a secular type, but it is of special interest because its cover (year-marked 1544) obviously comes from a much older vessel. Both components fit well, not only by virtue of size but also in style — the lobes on the lid are repeated again on the lower part of the bowl and also on the foot. One must infer that the cup was made specifically to accommodate the earlier cover.

A set of eight cups (see fig. 28) dating from 1631 and with the unidentified maker's mark "IT" was made for the Walloon church (established 1548) situated in the crypt of Canterbury Cathedral. They take their form from the absolutely standard wine cups which had emerged at the end of Queen Elizabeth's reign and which remained popular up to the Civil War. Eight cups would most certainly have been needed for this large congregation who did not conform to Anglicanism until 1789.

What is particularly interesting is that no less than six almost identical copies were made nearly 170 years later in 1717 by two well-known Huguenot goldsmiths of the new Emigration. Two of these by

29. Communion cup from the French church, Hoxton, London, silver, London, 1717, maker's mark: "HI" (possibly Robert Hill)

Louis Cuny[24] were for the conformist French Church of the Savoy, and four by Jacob Margas[25] for the church at Threadneedle Street. Another pair of cups (see fig. 29) and patens were made in the same year for the French church at Hoxton, with the maker's mark "HI," probably for Robert Hill.[26] This latter goldsmith was obviously no stranger to religious minorities: he is usually associated with the annual presenation dish given to the Lord Mayor of London by the Jewish community at this time.[27] This last-named group of cups, made for Hoxton, is quite different from the others and really represents a pastiche Elizabethan communion cup type; one of the patens and two of the cups are inscribed with their donors' names.[28]

This small group of objects, all dating from 1717, raises a number of interesting questions, the answers to which are simply not known at this stage: Was there a directive by the London Consistory that year requiring numbers of new cups to be made, as Tessa Murdoch has suggested?[29] Why did they choose these archaic forms? Certainly it seems likely that the Canterbury cups must have been known by these goldsmiths, who may have deliberately chosen them as prototypes as an act of sentimental piety. Or was the shape of these cups the choice of the donors? Could it be that the six based on the wine cup form were actually the work of only one of these goldsmiths, either Cuny or Margas, who marked two with his own maker's mark and then sold the rest to the other goldsmith, as a wholesaler might have done, who then gave them his own maker's mark? There would have

24. Jones, *Sacramental Vessels*, pp. 10-11; see also Arthur G. Grimwade, *London Goldsmiths, 1697-1837: Their Lives and Marks*, 3rd ed. (London, 1990), p. 482.

25. Jones, *Sacramental Vessels*, pp. 5-6; Grimwade, *London Goldsmiths*, pp. 590-91.

26. Jones, *Sacramental Vessels*, pp. 12-14.

27. Grimwade, *London Goldsmiths*, p. 546.

28. Jones, *Sacramental Vessels*, pp. 12-14: "The Gift of Mr Stephen Romilly/To the French Congregation at Hoxton/The 25: March 1717"; "The Gift of Mrs Rachel Ribeaut/To the French Congregation at Hoxton/The 25: March 1717"; "The Gift of Lewis De Tudert Esqr to ye French/Congregation at Hoxton ye 25: March 1717."

29. Verbally to the author. See also her article "The Double Ethic: Huguenot Forms of Worship, Belief and Practice," in *Handmaids to Religion: Festivals, Images, and Sacred Objects 1500-1800*.

been nothing unusual about doing this — it would have been very much in accordance with trade practice of the time.

Another interesting pair of communion cups, virtually identical to the Elizabethan-style examples at Hoxton, were made a few years earlier for the French church at Southampton in the year in which the congregation decided to conform to a French translation of the Anglican liturgy in 1711.[30] Was this perhaps a deliberate attempt to identify even more strongly with the established church of their adopted country? At the same time it should be remembered that by this date there was no such thing as a contemporary secular prototype for a wine cup in silver: from the late seventeenth century onward wine was drunk almost exclusively from glasses.

But undoubtedly the finest sacramental plate made by the Huguenots for their own use was the communion plate (see fig. 30) made in 1714 and given to the French church at Portarlington, Ireland, by Princess Caroline of Wales, consort of the future George II. It was made by one of the most successful émigré goldsmiths, David Willaume, son of Adam Willaume of Metz, first recorded in London as an alien resident in 1687. It is most beautifully engraved with the royal arms and inscribed, but apart from the extra-large communion cups there is nothing to distinguish them from standard Anglican church plate of this time.[31]

Silver for the Established Church, 1660-1770

What then of the church plate made by the Huguenots for non-Calvinist congregations? In many ways this is the area where their complete detachment from their clients' agenda is most obvious. We find Huguenot craftsmen working with great skill and application not only for Anglican but also for Roman Catholic patrons. However, it is almost impossible to identify any objects of this type made before the 1680s, unless one were to count the spectacular chased auricular plate worked by Wolfgang Howzer of Zurich (fl. 1652-88) for Bishop Cosin of Durham and for the Chapels Royal at Saint George's, Windsor and Whitehall.[32]

With the appearance of the chapel plate for Sir Christopher Wren's Royal Hospital at Chelsea (1688),[33] however, certain distinctive features

---

30. Jones, *Sacramental Vessels,* p. 7, pl. iv.

31. In Scotland the Huguenot community commissioned two communion cups in the form of old-fashioned wine cups in 1685 for James Penman; Hubert Fenwick, "Silver for Huguenot and Catholic," *Country Life,* 25 April 1968, pp. 1058-59.

32. Oman, *English Church Plate,* passim. More biographical information in Charles Oman, *Caroline Silver* (London, 1970), pp. 33-34.

33. Oman, *English Church Plate,* pls. 93 and 143; Oman, *Caroline Silver,* p. 30. The Jewel Office was later to become an important patron of Huguenot goldsmiths. See Christopher

30. Communion plate (cup, tankard, three patens) of the French church, Portarlington, Ireland, silver, London, 1714, maker's mark for David Willaume

appear which were shortly to become popularized by the new wave of Huguenot immigrants. The order was an official one from the King's Jewel Office and included the somewhat austere communion cup and paten, but also the magnificent pair of altar candlesticks. Each of these items incorporated unmistakably French characteristics. For example, the base of the communion cup has a calyx of leafy cut-card work, while the stem is cast in the form of a classical baluster. The stems of the candlesticks continue to use the baluster motif and the feet rest on scrolling volutes. Two other features are particularly noteworthy: despite the fact that this set is intended for Anglican liturgy, it is engraved, ironically, with the arms of the staunch Catholic monarch James II (r. 1685-88), who was nevertheless obliged by public opinion to continue to support the established church. Secondly, the plate bears the maker's mark of the prolific English banker-goldsmith Ralph Leeke,[34] who has almost certainly used a newly arrived Huguenot journeyman-goldsmith in his workshop for this job. This becomes even more apparent when one compares the advanced French features of this

Hartop, *The Huguenot Legacy: English Silver 1680-1760 from the Alan and Simone Hartman Collection* (1996), passim.

34. Grimwade, *London Goldsmiths*, p. 579; Oman, *Caroline Silver*, pp. 29-30.

31. Communion cup and cover from Christchurch, Oxford, silver gilt, London, 1699, maker's mark for Jean Chartier

piece with the plate supplied by him only five years earlier for Saint James's, Piccadilly, in an embossed and highly florid Anglo-Dutch late-Restoration style.[35]

If the Chelsea plate is somewhat hesitant, the same cannot be said of the elegantly proportioned communion cup and cover of 1699 at Christchurch, Oxford (see fig. 31), made by the highly gifted goldsmith Jean Chartier, a Huguenot formerly of Blois. His name is first recorded in London in 1688, and he was closely related to two other goldsmiths' families, the Garniers and the Pilleaus.[36] The smaller bowl of the cup is more akin to a Catholic chalice and employs cut-card work, a vase-shaped baluster stem, and a consistent use of lobes and gadroons.

It would be good to think that this might have ushered in a new departure from the static tradition of Anglican plate. However, the usual vessels saw very little change in their basic shapes although decoration advanced along with the fashions of the times. In the hands of the best goldsmiths communion cups were sometimes better proportioned, were taller, and had smaller bowls. There are several made by Paul de Lamerie

35. Oman, *English Church Plate*, pl. 92.
36. Grimwade, *London Goldsmiths*, p. 462.

(1688-1751),[37] arguably the most distinguished Huguenot goldsmith of the second generation, which continue to use the old-fashioned knopped stem instead of baluster shapes.[38] Indeed, the latter feature was by no means universally adopted despite its obvious aesthetic appeal, which can be seen in the new Cathedral plate (see plate 12) made for Durham in 1766 by third-generation Huguenot goldsmiths Francis Butty (fl. 1757-76)[39] and Nicholas Dumée (fl. ca. 1758-76).[40] An interesting stylistic diversion of the rococo style was the exclusively British use of Gothic decorative motifs — these were deemed appropriate for locations with antiquarian associations, which of course included churches and chapels.

Perhaps the most complete and interesting set of eighteenth-century Anglican country house plate, however, is that ordered by George Booth, second earl of Warrington (1675-1758), for his house at Dunham Massey, Cheshire. Booth became a major client of the Huguenot goldsmiths and over a fifty-year period built up a store of over 26,000 ounces of plate, exclusively from the workshops of the émigré craftsmen.[41] His first acquisitions of new silver, after he had put his estates on a sure financial base, were for his new chapel.

Charles Oman suggests that this marked a change in the religious allegiance of the family, which until then had been Presbyterian.[42] The earl's grandfather had been a supporter of Cromwell during the Civil War, and the chaplain to the earlier household had been ejected under the Act of Uniformity. The new regime at Dunham Massey was unequivocally Anglican. Lord Warrington's own taste inclined for the most part to plain but exceedingly well-made and well-proportioned objects with an unusually heavy gauge of metal. Where appropriate, however, he was willing to order highly elaborate pieces, albeit sometimes in an old-fashioned style.[43] He was a generous subscriber to Huguenot charities and had an interesting library with a large theological and devotional section, including works by Jurieu, Claude, and Daillé.[44]

For his chapel silver (see plate 13) Lord Warrington went to Isaac Liger (fl. 1700-1730), probably originally from Saumur but from circa 1704 of Hemmings Row in the heart of the French community in the parish of

37. Grimwade, *London Goldsmiths*, p. 488.

38. Susan Hare, ed., *Paul de Lamerie: The Work of England's Master Silversmith* (exhibition catalogue, Goldsmiths' Hall, London, 1990), passim.

39. Grimwade, *London Goldsmiths*, p. 456.

40. Grimwade, *London Goldsmiths*, p. 497.

41. See John Hayward, "The Earl of Warrington's Plate," *Apollo*, July 1978, pp. 32-39.

42. Oman, *English Church Plate*, p. 184.

43. See James Lomax, "Parsimony by Candlelight: Lord Warrington's Silver Lighting Equipment," *Apollo*, April 1993, pp. 244-47.

44. John Rylands Library, University of Manchester, Dunham Massey archives, EGR 7/15 Catalogue of Books 1768.

32. Censer, silver,
London, 1732,
maker's mark for
Anne Tanqueray

Saint Martin's-in-the-Fields. Liger was Lord Warrington's favorite gold-smith until circa 1728 and provided his client with a wide variety of domestic pieces as well. In 1706 he supplied for the chapel: a communion cup and paten, an ewer, and a large alms dish. In 1716 came a pair of tripod candlesticks and a small alms dish. Like much of the Warrington plate, their appeal lies in their plainness and beautiful proportions.

Although these features may be said to characterize much of Lord Warrington's silver, there is one important exception among the chapel plate, namely, the large alms dish made by Liger but engraved and signed by Simon Gribelin (1661-1733). (It can be seen with the rest of the group in plate 13.) This is one of the most beautifully engraved pieces of early eighteenth-century English silver representing a Deposition after a composition by Annibale Carracci.[45] Gribelin was a Huguenot from Blois, recorded in England from 1681, a virtuoso whose decorative style became highly influential through his published designs.[46] Other objects made for

45. It is signed "An: Carr: fecit S G scupt." In fact, it does not appear to be based on an exact prototype by Carracci. The subject was treated many times by the artist, and the nearest composition to this would seem to be his *Christ of Caprarola,* the subject of a particularly fine engraving (Bartsch, vol. 18, p. 182, no. 4).

46. For example *A Book of Sevrall Ornaments* (London, 1682); *A Book of Ornaments Usefull to Jewellers, Watchmakers, and all Other Artists* (London, 1697); *A New Book of Ornaments Usefull*

33. Chalice, silver gilt, Strasbourg, 1779, maker's mark for Jean-Louis Imlin III

Lord Warrington and almost certainly engraved by Gribelin include a well-known tea canister of circa 1706 in the Victoria and Albert Museum.[47]

However, one should not be too pie-eyed about Lord Warrington and his patronage and support of the Huguenots. As we have noted, a considerable proportion of his plate was in a highly ornamental style, especially objects intended for the state bedroom. In addition to this there is the rather disconcerting fact that at least three of Lord Warrington's largest objects have been found to be "duty dodgers" with transposed marks (substituted from another piece of silver). These appear in the base of the giant sideboard fountain (1728), also by Liger, and a pair of jugs (1732) by Paul de Lamerie. The purpose of this highly illegal practice was of course to avoid paying tax of six pence per ounce, which on these heavy objects would have been considerable — the fountain weighing 575 ounces, the jugs 202 ounces. Warrington's subterfuge would have saved him nearly twenty pounds, or the equivalent of four months' wages for a skilled journeyman goldsmith.

Huguenot goldsmiths seem to have been equally detached in supplying liturgical plate for the English Roman Catholic community, for which there was a small market despite the official proscription of all Catholic practices. Most memorable are the thurible (see fig. 32) made in 1732 with the maker's mark of Anne Tanqueray (nee Willaume, 1691-1733)[48] and the holy water stoup of 1719 attributed to Joseph Barbut (fl. 1703-39).[49] In France, of course, Huguenots who had abjured continued to make sacred objects for Catholics: in 1719, for example, the Catholic goldsmiths of Saumur com-

---

to all Artists, Invented and Engraved by S. Gribelin (London, ca. 1702); and Livre d'Estampes de Sim Gribelin (London, 1722). See Sheila O' Connell, "Simon Gribelin (1661-1733): Printmaker and Metal-Engraver," Print Quarterly 2 (March 1985): 27-38.

47. J. F. Hayward, Huguenot Silver in England, 1688-1727 (London, 1959), pl. 46a.

48. Illustrated in Oman, English Church Plate, pl. 176; for biographical details, see Grimwade, London Goldsmiths, p. 676.

49. Oman, English Church Plate, pl. 186; biographical details in Grimwade, London Goldsmiths, p. 430. The interesting case of the new commission for a complete set of Catholic plate made for the Chapel Royal at Holyrood, Edinburgh, for James II in 1687 is discussed by Fenwick, pp. 1058-59. It appears to have been made in Edinburgh by Zacharius Mellinus, a Dutchman.

plained to Paris that not only the town's clergy but also the abbots and ab-besses of the region continued to give their work to "Protestant" gold-smiths.[50] Indeed, one of the most splendid examples of late eighteenth-century French ecclesiastical silver in the Victoria and Albert Museum is the gilt chalice (see fig. 33) of 1779 with the marks of the Strasbourg goldsmith Jean-Louis Imlin III, who came from a family of Protestants.[51]

The French Style

We should return to the mid–seventeenth century to consider the contrast-ing situations of the goldsmiths in both England and France. The earlier part of the century saw a considerable falling off of immigration into England on the part of the foreign goldsmiths, probably on account of increasing reli-gious toleration in both France and the Netherlands, and also because of the poor economic situation in England in the years leading up to the Civil War. With the Restoration of Charles II in 1660, however, and "the return of the politer way of living," this was to change. The English goldsmiths were to develop a number of new native forms — not least the two-handled cup — and to follow Dutch ideas of naturalistic ornament, usually with high relief embossing. In France the fortunes of the goldsmiths were improved with generally rising levels of prosperity and the encouragement of the luxury trades under Anne of Austria and Cardinal Mazarin.

It was, however, the assumption of personal rule by Louis XIV in 1661, together with the policies of his chief minister Colbert, which ush-ered in a twenty-year period of unprecedented growth and stability. The great policy of centralizing every facet of public life and making the country self-sufficient included Louis's plans to revolutionize and upgrade the lux-ury trades. With the establishment of the Gobelins factory one sees the de-velopment of a distinctive French baroque style, based ultimately on the classicizing trends of this style in Italy, but developed with a particular ele-gance and genius. So far as the work of the goldsmiths is concerned, it was characterized by a move toward applied decoration, rich classical moldings, and figurative castings. Shapes were based on classical prototypes — vases, balusters, and architectural motifs often derived from Renaissance sources. At its most splendid it was to be found in the silver furniture made for the Louvre, Fontainebleau, and Versailles, some of which can be glimpsed in contemporary illustrations, not least in the famous tapestry from the

---

50. Evans, p. 508, citing Henri Nocq, *Le Poincon de Paris* (Paris, 1926), vol. 4, p. 159.

51. Jean-Louis Imlin III in fact died in 1769, and his atelier was managed by Jacques-Henri Alberti (fl. 1764-95) until 1780 when Imlin's cousin Francois-Daniel (b. 1757) became master. Alberti was therefore responsible for this piece. R. W. Lightbown, *French Silver in the Victoria and Albert Museum* (London, 1978), pp. 92-93, cat. no. 85.

Histoire du Roi series which recorded the king's visit to the factory itself in 1667, or in some of the borders from *Les Mois* or *Les Maisons Royales*.[52] These are the work of master goldsmiths such as Alexis Loir (1640-1713), Claude de Villiers (fl. 1645-1705), Jacques Dutel (fl. 1667-80), Claude I. Ballin (1615-78), and, later, Nicolas Delaunay (1647-1727). Other pieces might be supplied by privileged goldsmiths with workshops in the Louvre: Louis Brunet (fl. 1672-77), Jacques Le Mire (fl. 1672-77), Jacques Pastor (fl. 1672-74), Claude Roussel (whose family occupied workshops here, 1657-1755), or Jean Veret (fl. 1674-77).[53]

Simultaneously, working alongside these were the *ornemanistes* who were evolving and adapting generally classical decoration for all aspects of the applied arts, in particular Jean Le Pautre (1618-82) and Jean Berain (1640-1711). For the goldsmiths the style became interpreted by a host of lesser *ornemanistes*, sometimes from the provinces. As we shall see, it was a diluted version of this style which was to filter down to every level of the crafts in France and, in a simplified form, to spread through Europe via the circulation of ornamental engravings, Louis XIV's expansionist policies, and his expulsion of the Huguenot craftsmen. It was to spread to Holland and thence to England, where it found its finest exemplar in the designs of Daniel Marot (1663-1752), architect to William III, and the subsequent work of the émigré craftsmen.[54]

As in so many other areas of economic life, Louis and Colbert pursued a relentless policy of interventionism in the goldsmiths' trade.[55] The economic theories of the time measured a country's wealth by the volume of precious metals it possessed. France, having none of its own, had to rely on imports mainly from America and had to watch carefully what happened to its specie, always attempting to increase its quantity. This meant having a favorable balance of trade and preventing the export of gold and silver at all costs. This could be achieved by limiting or preventing the import of foreign goods, and by developing the quality of native industries so

52. Frances Buckland, "Gobelins Tapestries and Paintings as a Source of Information about the Silver Furniture of Louis XIV," *Burlington Magazine* 125 (1983): 271-83.

53. See Tessa Murdoch, "A French Silversmith," *Country Life*, 13 November 1980, p. 1764.

54. Marot's chief designs for silver were published in his *Nouveau Livre d'Orfevrerie*, reissued in his *Oeuvres* (1703 and 1712); among other French ornamentalists working in London and publishing designs for goldsmiths were Simon Gribelin (see supra, n. 45), C. de Moelder (John F. Hayward, "A William and Mary Pattern Book for Silversmiths," *Proceedings of the Society of Silver Collectors* 2, no. 1 [spring 1970]: 18-21), and Cornelius Gole, *Book of Ornament* (London, 1712) (John Hardy and Adriana Turpin, "Cornelius Gole's 'Book of Ornament,'" *Apollo* 137 [January 1993]: 18-21).

55. See, for example, C. W. Cole, *Colbert and a Century of French Mercantilism* (London, 1939); Cole, *French Mercantilism, 1683-1700* (New York, 1965), pp. 224-27; and Warren C. Scoville, *The Persecution of the Huguenots and French Economic Development, 1680-1720* (Berkeley and Los Angeles, 1960), pp. 50, 57, 122-23, 130, 144-55, 321.

that they could hold their own against foreign competition. Goldsmiths' work was a great problem area, for the French, like many others, had often been tempted to hoard plate for use in times of emergency. But this instinct ran contrary to the economic theory which considered that precious bullion locked up in *objets d'art* or even useful utensils represented "dead" money which ideally should be in circulation.

In order to discourage this Colbert introduced a new tax in 1672, the *droit de marque*, which was doubled within two years and whose preamble justified its imposition by criticizing the luxury of gold and silver articles "which considerably diminishes trade among our subjects, for trade can only be carried on with an abundance of money in circulation." Typically, in England the government took a more pragmatic line in trying to stem this apparently unhealthy rush into luxury, and there was a considerable academic debate on the economic consequences of promoting the luxury trades.[56] In 1697 the New Standard Act decreed that all wrought plate should henceforth be of a higher standard, at 95.8 percent pure silver (the Britannia Standard), than the coin of the realm at 92.5 percent (Sterling Standard). (At the same time the entire silver coinage of the country was called in to be exchanged for new milled coins.) Whether this actually had the desired effect of reducing consumption in France or whether it caused any changes in style or design will be considered later.

Colbert's interventionism also targeted the guilds, which he saw as the ideal agents for change and improvement. He attempted to herd all craftsmen into these organizations, and to this end he supervised the incorporation of new crafts in the towns as well as great numbers of reforms in the ancient guilds, adding new privileges and setting new standards. During Colbert's lifetime, and until the crises of the late 1680s, the government probably genuinely thought this was the best way to "restore the quality of manufacture" to ensure that French products held their own against rivals in the Netherlands, Italy, and even England. Scoville has shown, however, that by the end of his reign Louis considered the guilds to be little more than moneymaking machines useful for raising additional revenues.[57]

The new and close supervision of the guilds was also a way of pursuing the government's anti-Protestant policy. Thus as early as 1667 Colbert attempted to limit the number of Huguenots entering the guilds in Languedoc to a maximum of one-third of the number in any one organiza-

56. See John Styles, "The Goldsmiths and the London Luxury Trades 1550-1750," in *Goldsmiths and Bankers: Innovations and the Transfer of Skill, 1550-1750*, ed. David Mitchell, Centre for Metropolitan History, Working Papers, no. 2, Institute of Historical Research, University of London, 1995, pp. 112-20. Also Julian Hoppit, "The Luxury Debate in Britain 1660-1790" (privately circulated paper delivered to an RCA/V&A symposium, Victoria and Albert Museum, 1989); Scoville, p. 331.

57. Scoville, pp. 397-99.

tion. How effective this was is doubtful, for up to 1684 they still outnumbered Catholics in several city guilds. In 1680 Louis had to remind the goldsmiths of Blois that their organizations still included too many Protestants.[58] In Paris the number of goldsmiths had been limited to 300 since the sixteenth century, thereby squeezing even further the chances of new Protestant masters. Thus in various ways the Huguenot goldsmiths felt the full impact of Louis's economic and religious policies.

It certainly appears that goldsmiths were one of the trades which contained more than the average number of Protestants. Exactly what proportion of the total they represented in the various cities depended on local traditions. At Lyon, for instance, there were 233 master goldsmiths noted for the whole of the seventeenth century, of which 53, or over 20 percent, were Protestant. Joan Evans stated categorically that of the 300 master goldsmiths of Paris at the time of the Revocation, 21 left the country, being Protestants and not prepared to abjure their faith, or at least intending to find new pastures abroad. How many of those who remained had previously been Protestant is not known, but those who became Catholics were later allowed special privileges. They were to be a cause of great resentment among the old established Catholic craftsmen, especially over orders for ecclesiastical plate. And, of course, in France exemptions under the law and anomalies are always to be found: Josias Belle, a favorite goldsmith of the king, managed to defy the religious laws and died a Protestant.

On the whole the evidence suggests that a high proportion of the goldsmiths reaching London after 1685 tended to come from the northern French provinces — Normandy, Brittany, Anjou, Touraine, Poitou — as well as from border country like Lorraine and Flanders.[59] This has been said to explain a certain provincial quality in the work of the refugees of the first generation.[60] However, the differences between silver made in the provinces and that made in the metropolis in France should not be exaggerated: the caprice of surviving evidence makes comparison difficult. Certainly in the next generation the work of the most accomplished Huguenots in England — Lamerie, Crespin, Willaume — can almost stand

58. Scoville, p. 50. The goldsmiths of Montpellier suffered numerous discouraging promulgations. See Jean Thuile, *L'Orfevrerie en Languedoc du XII au XVIII siècle* (Montpellier, 1964), vol. 1, p. 88. The position of the Huguenots in Normandy is discussed (inter alia) by Claude-Gerrard Cassan, *Les Orfevres de la Normandie* (1980), passim (for Bayeux, Saint-Lô, and Rouen).

59. Robin Gwynne, *Huguenot Heritage* (London, 1985), passim; Evans, passim; and Grimwade, *London Goldsmiths*, passim; P. A. S. Phillips, *Huguenot Goldsmiths in England Compiled from the Royal Bounty Lists, 1687-1737*, manuscript copies held by the Library of the Goldsmiths' Company and the Huguenot Society of London. The names of the refugee goldsmiths also appear with their towns of origin. See also Brian Beet, "Huguenot Silversmiths from Anjou: Amyraux, Guichardière, La Brosse and Michon," *Silver Society Journal*, no. 10 (1998, forthcoming).

60. Hayward, *Huguenot Silver in London*, p. 9, but see supra, n. 33.

comparison with that of the best Parisian masters. Even so, it is always true that, until the coming of neoclassicism in the 1760s, the work of English (or naturalized English) craftsmen who chose to work in a consciously French style lags behind that of their colleagues by at least five or ten years. When this is combined with a natural conservatism on the part of their English clients, it is easy to understand how some of the most accomplished and expensive new silver made in periods of transition (the 1730s, for example) might look somewhat *retardataire* in the eyes of Parisians.

The question arises as to why so many Protestants were attracted to this profession and why they were so good at it. Indeed, their disproportionate numbers in France are paralleled in parts of Germany. Of the leading 135 goldsmiths flourishing between the mid-sixteenth and the mid-eighteenth centuries in Augsburg (a notionally Catholic city), no less than 100, or 70 percent, were Protestant.[61] On the face of it there is no reason why this should be the case in France except for the negative one that Protestants were *not* expressly excluded from this vocation as they were from other occupations such as the civil service or the magistrature. But in fact there were few crafts or mercantile activities which were denied them, so it cannot really be argued that they were a repressed minority being squeezed into a marginal activity in which they excelled.

The answer is probably a combination of factors. Philip Benedict has suggested that in the sixteenth century the literate character of Calvinism had appealed particularly to the educated classes of town-dwelling artisans and craftsmen.[62] By the late seventeenth century the ever-higher standards of craftsmanship which were coming into force as a result of Colbert's policies probably encouraged even further the hereditary nature of the goldsmiths' craft in which grandfathers, fathers, and sons clung to the same profession. At the same time the Calvinist work ethic stressed that the conscientious fulfillment of one's secular vocation was part of a God-given task.[63] The fact that this involved the manufacture of objects in gold or silver, or jewelry, was no more a problem for Calvinists than the making of liquor or perfume in the monasteries of the Middle Ages. The same spirit promoted the desirability of long-term training, high skills, reliability, and honesty. Yet another factor may be that in France the Huguenot goldsmiths do not appear to have diversified

61. Annette Schommers, "Biographien de Augsburger Goldschmiede," in *Silber und Gold: Augsburger Goldschmiedekunst für die hofe Europas*, ed. Lorenz Seelig (exhibition catalogue, Bayerisches Nationalmuseum, Munich, 1994), pp. VIII-XXIX.

62. Philip Benedict, "Calvinism as a Culture: Preliminary Remarks on Calvinism and the Visual Arts," p. 36 in this volume.

63. Max Weber, *The Protestant Ethic and the Spirit of Capitalism* (London, 1930), pp. 352-69; Weber, *The Sociology of Religion* (London, 1963), pp. 220-21; John T. McNeill, *The History and Character of Calvinism* (New York, 1954), esp. pp. 221-25, quoting Calvin's *Commentary on 1 Corinthians 7:20*; *Inst.* 3.10.6.

into banking in the same way that many of their colleagues in England did throughout the seventeenth and early eighteenth centuries. As a result they were able to concentrate their efforts exclusively to perfecting their own craft instead of being tempted into possibly more lucrative sidelines.

The circumstances surrounding the Huguenot immigration into England from the 1680s were of course exceptional in producing a considerable number of refugees from well-bred backgrounds, even from the minor nobility. In their dire straits the most socially acceptable trade into which they could send their children to be apprenticed was that of the goldsmiths. According to R. Campbell, author of *The London Tradesman* (1747), it was "the most genteel in the Mechanic Way,"[64] especially if the more esteemed professions of the law, the church, and the army were out of the question. Thus for Paul de Lamerie's father, an army officer, it would not have been too *déclassé* to enter his son as an apprentice with a fellow countryman and in an occupation which could potentially reverse a family's fortunes. It would be extremely interesting to know whether the traditionally very high premiums — as much as one hundred pounds, or eighteen months' salary, for a qualified journeyman — which were paid by the parents of a goldsmith's apprentice at this time were sometimes reduced in view of the circumstances. Certainly the Huguenot goldsmiths did their best to promote their own status: they frequently corresponded with their clients in French and therefore presumably spoke to them in French as well.[65] It must have worked well, for the Ingram family of Temple Newsam, Viscounts Irwin, appear to have referred to their favored goldsmith of the early eighteenth century as "Mr." Willaume — a most important social nicety at the time.[66] The same Mr. Willaume was soon to retire from his successful business, acquire a country estate, and launch his family into the county squirearchy of Bedfordshire.[67]

A Mixed Reception

What were the prospects of a Huguenot goldsmith contemplating flight to England in 1685? On the one hand his technical and design skills were probably very much higher than those of his English counterpart. The restrained baroque classicism which had developed in France since the 1660s was almost unknown in England, which was still enjoying the last of the Dutch-inspired

64. R. Campbell, *The London Tradesman* (London, 1747), pp. 141-47.

65. For example, the invoice and receipt of 18 June 1712 from Jean Barbut to Lord Irwin, West Yorkshire Archive Service, Temple Newsam archives TN/EA 12/7.

66. "Mr Guilame ye Goldsmith" [*sic*]. Thomas Williams to Arthur Ingram of Barrowby, 8 September 1726. West Yorkshire Archive Service, Temple Newsam archives TN/EA/Correspondence Bundle 13, Letter 116.

67. Grimwade, *London Goldsmiths*, p. 704.

naturalistic style. Comparisons between English and French goldsmiths' work of this date are perhaps slightly unfair, but the point is easily made: it was no contest when a somewhat played-out style was matched against the sophisticated products of the French.[68] Thus a magnificent ewer by Charles Petit of 1674 (see fig. 34) shows a plasticity and confidence of form quite unlike its English counterpart — a sturdy flagon which performed the same function but whose shape had scarcely changed in England for a hundred years (see fig. 35). Examples of coffee-

34. Ewer, silver gilt, Paris, 1674, maker's mark for Charles Petit

pots by an English and a Huguenot goldsmith reveal the differences immediately; the former by George Garthorne and made in 1690 (see fig. 36) shows the early attempt to devise a receptacle for this new beverage in a tall tapering cylinder with a conical cover, while the later chocolate pot by Pierre Platel of 1708 shows the elegant resolution of the problem (see fig. 37).

Probably more than any other factor it was the superior training of the French goldsmiths which placed them in a different class from their English colleagues. On the evidence so far examined it seems that French apprentices had a highly regulated curriculum culminating in the presentation of a "masterpiece" to demonstrate their all-around skills — something long since abandoned by the English.[69] Furthermore, they were often taught draftsmanship and modeling as well as chasing, burnishing, and gilding. The sons of provincial goldsmiths were frequently sent to Paris to be apprenticed to celebrated masters and would then return to their home-town fully conversant with the metropolitan style. Yet others would travel to Rome for further training, on an equal footing with painters, sculptors, and engravers. Thus provincial goldsmiths' work in France is often as so-

---

68. Hayward, *Huguenot Silver in London*, pp. 2-4.

69. See Michele Bimbenet-Privat, "Goldsmiths' Apprenticeship during the First Half of the Seventeenth Century: The Situation in Paris," in *Goldsmiths and Bankers: Innovations and the Transfer of Skill, 1550-1750*, ed. David Mitchell, Centre for Metropolitan History, Working Papers, no. 2, Institute of Historical Research, University of London, 1995, pp. 23-31. In 1607 there had been an attempt to reimpose the production of a masterpiece on apprentices aspiring to the freedom of the London Goldsmiths' Company, but this appears to have been ineffective (W. S. Prideaux, *Memorials of the Goldsmiths' Company*, II [London, 1897], p. 363).

35. Flagon, silver, London, 1686, maker's mark "R" with a pellet below

phisticated as that of Parisian masters — again in contrast to the position in England.

But, on the other hand, there was no shortage of money and clients in England for high-quality luxury goods. It is a telling fact that Louis XIV's attempt to recover some of his gifted former subjects by sending the Marquis de Bonrepaus to England in the year following the Revocation with promises of toleration for those who returned fell on deaf ears since only 253 from the entire Emigration decided to go home.[70] Clearly, therefore, the refugees felt they had better chances in England than in their former homeland. Even so, they had to adapt to a certain degree to the habits and traditions of their hosts. Thus the goldsmiths embraced a new type of silver vessel, the two-handled cup and cover, which was previously unknown to them but was the standard English presentation or commemorative object. They proved extremely able in developing the inherent qualities of its shape and its potential for other purposes. Particularly fine examples on an almost miniature scale, intended as cups for a toilet service, are those made by an unidentified French goldsmith working in London circa 1695 known only by his initials, FSS (see plate 14). Conversely, their English clients seemed impervious to certain types of French objects, notably the *ecuelle,* which remains a type of considerable rarity.

To encourage their immigration the government's official policy toward the Huguenots was encouraging. As early as 1661 Charles II declared that he would protect the property and person of any Frenchman seeking refuge in England, and in 1681, shortly before the first *dragonnades,* he reiterated this with a promise to all Protestant immigrants that they could follow their professions without hindrance. After Charles's death in 1685 his Catholic brother James II was far less personally enthusiastic, but was obliged to bow to public pressure to confirm these privileges. With the arrival of William III and Mary II in 1688 the welcome became even more af-

70. Evans, p. 507; D. C. A. Agnew, *Protestant Exile from France in the Reign of Louis XIV* (London, 1871), p. 30.

36. Coffeepot, silver, London, 1690, maker's mark for George Garthorne

firmative. The crown was eventually able to raise the prodigious sum of ninety thousand pounds from the general public for the relief of the refugees, while in 1696 Parliament voted an annual relief fund of fifteen thousand pounds (although this was rarely distributed).

This official policy of welcome was certainly not matched by the London Goldsmiths' Company, however. The story of their opposition to this latest wave of foreigners has often been told but is central to this discussion.[71] As early as 1682 they refused admission to "an unnamed French Protestant" who had been recommended by the Lord Mayor and the Bishop of London, but later that year they were unable to resist a positive order read to their court requiring them to grant their freedom to him since he had "lately come from France to avoid persecution and lived quietly." This was in fact Pierre Harache (fl. 1682–ca. 1700), who was indeed one of the most successful of the early émigré craftsmen.[72]

Petitions to the court of the Goldsmiths' Company by native goldsmiths against the foreigners now followed: in 1682, 1683, and in 1697 when they complained that there were "above 800 able and substantial working goldsmiths" in London whose livelihoods were endangered by the newcomers. The figure is probably wildly overstated and must include the

71. Evans, pp. 504-7; Hayward, *Huguenot Silver in England*, pp. 15-22.

72. Grimwade, *London Goldsmiths*, pp. 533-34; Judith Banister, "The First Huguenot Silversmith," *Country Life*, 1965, pp. 1463-65.

37. Chocolate pot,
silver, London, 1708,
maker's mark for
Pierre Platel

great numbers of peripheral specialists who had grown around the core activity of goldsmithing: Campbell's *London Tradesman* (1747) lists them at that date as jewelers, snuffbox makers, tweezer-case makers, chasers, refiners, gold beaters, and even gold finders.[73] This diversification of skills — which was to become even more marked as the eighteenth century advanced — had grown up in England probably because, as we have seen, there had never been a very strong tradition of apprentices proving their all-around skills by producing a "masterpiece" (despite the Company's regulations governing this). In contrast, on the Continent, knowledge of all the processes used in the manufacture of wrought plate was often a strict requirement.

Another, more telling petition was submitted in 1711, signed by fifty-three of the most prominent working English goldsmiths.[74] This time they picked on the fact that these foreign craftsmen were diluting their work by using too much solder "to the wrong and prejudice of the buyer and the great discredit of the English workmen." This was obviously the result of the new fashion for cut-card work and the increasing use of cast ornament which required solder.

Their second complaint, though, specified their real grudge: "that by the admittance of necessitous strangers, whose desperate fortunes oblige them to work at miserable rates the representing members have been forced to bestow much more time and labour in working up their plate than hath been the practice of former times when prices of workmanship

73. Campbell, pp. 144-47.
74. Hayward, *Huguenot Silver in England*, pp. 20-21.

were greater." In other words, the foreigners were charging less for "fashion" — that crucial charge for added value for working up plate with decoration, chasing, engraving, and cast work — which, depending on the amount of work required on any particular piece, could be as much as double the price of the intrinsic cost of the metal itself (throughout the eighteenth century this stood at an almost constant price of five shillings and six pence per ounce).

Despite these petitions the Goldsmiths' Company appears to have permitted considerable numbers of Huguenots to register their marks at the Hall (often by specific order of the Lord Mayor), but without granting them admission to the Company as freemen, which entitled them to trade within the City of London (and two miles beyond) on their own account. This anomaly became irrelevant in 1725 when it was declared that the Company was henceforth obliged to mark all work submitted to them for assay.

With all these problems, how did the refugees manage to earn their own living? First, like all immigrant groups they sought mutual support by living and working within close physical proximity to each other. For the goldsmiths and several other groups involved in the luxury trades (but not the silk weavers who went to the East End at Spitalfields), it was in the newer residential areas of the West End, especially in the parishes of Saint Anne's, Soho, and Saint Martin's-in-the-Fields. At first this may have been because their existing churches at Hog Lane and the Savoy were nearby. It was an area which was declining in high fashion, since the aristocracy were moving out farther toward Saint James's and Mayfair. Nevertheless, for the supply of luxuries it remained an important hub, with Saint Martin's Lane remaining one of the best addresses for enterprising retailers and craftsmen. Later we shall see how this concentration of the Huguenots into a small geographical area might have had an effect on their styles and working practices.

Probably one of the principal ways in which they found ready work was to become a journeyman with one of their own number or with an established English goldsmith. Despite their public protestations to the contrary, it seems likely that any ambitious goldsmith would have been delighted at the opportunity of learning French styles and techniques at first hand and from a newcomer who was also an employee. There is plenty of evidence of this practice when one observes a sudden apparent change in an established goldsmith's style: Ralph Leeke in 1688 (with the Chelsea Hospital chapel plate, as we have seen), Anthony Nelme in about 1691, George Garthorne at about the same date, and Benjamin Pyne by at least 1698 when his workshop produced the superb chased dishes for Powderham Castle.[75] These "English" goldsmiths continued to make superb baroque plate for the rest of their careers: Anthony Nelme's huge pil-

---

75. Hayward, *Huguenot Silver in England*, pl. 61.

grim bottles at Chatsworth represent a new type of ornamental silver vessel for the English goldsmiths. The examples dating from 1715 (see plate 15) represent a development of the late seventeenth-century Continental type, also found at Chatsworth, by Adam Loofs, William III's favorite Dutch goldsmith who had spent many years training in Paris.[76]

Another way — which was centuries old — was for a Frenchman to have his own wares submitted for assay at Goldsmiths' Hall by an English freeman who would give the object his own mark. The result is again the appearance of some highly sophisticated pieces bearing the unlikely mark of a well-established and possibly otherwise old-fashioned English goldsmith.

Yet another way included claiming immunity from the guilds' restrictions by having premises in the ancient monastic Liberties of Blackfriars or Saint Martin le Grand in the City of London. However, these were finally declared to be invalid in 1697. Finally, there was the option to join one of the more easygoing guilds like the Butchers or Longbowstringmen, who did not inquire too deeply into the nature of one's trade, but whose freedom entitled one to set up shop.[77]

Before considering the development of a distinctive new style in English silver as a result of the arrival of these foreigners, it is necessary to bear in mind one additional factor which may have weighed with Huguenot goldsmiths before deciding to flee their homeland: the effects of the economic recession which is often considered to have started in 1683, and the subsequent sumptuary laws which hit their trade with great severity. By the time of the declaration of war in 1689 there was a desperate shortage of ready money in France, not helped by the smuggling of specie out of the country by the departing Huguenots. Over one million gold louis had been received by the London Mint alone by 1687.[78]

The first of the sumptuary decrees, that of 1689, severely restricted the weight of articles to be made in both gold and silver, and completely forbade whole new types of objects: tables, vases, chandeliers. Those possessing banned or overweight articles were to surrender them, and no bullion, except from abroad, was to be melted anywhere except at the mints. The king himself led the way by consigning the spectacular silver furnishings of the palaces, while the court followed suit. This appalling expedient was of course severely regretted later. Real efforts were made to enforce the new enactment by further legislation, and it was tightened up even fur-

76. E. A. Jones, "A Pair of Dutch Silver Gilt Bottles at Chatsworth," *Burlington Magazine* 76 (1940): 94-99.

77. For example, Thomas Jenkins, a fine goldsmith but a freeman of the Butchers' Company, took the Huguenot Jacob Margas as an apprentice in 1699. Paul Crespin was a freeman of the Longbowstringmens' Company. Grimwade, *London Goldsmiths,* pp. 478-590.

78. Scoville, pp. 331-32. See also Daniel Defoe, *Roxana* (London, 1724; Penguin Classics reprint 1987), pp. 37-38.

ther in 1700. Exceptions were only rarely made; for example, when some newly manufactured silver plates were seized in a goldsmith's shop in Paris as being overweight, it was discovered that they had been ordered by the exiled James II of England, and a personal dispensation from the king had to be obtained.[79]

The decrees must certainly have been effective, at least on the production of new plate if not on the handing in of old pieces. In 1709 a new "voluntary" campaign was dreamt up at court by the duchesse de Grammont, who was anxious to ingratiate herself with the king. Saint Simon provides an unforgettable account of her failure and the reaction of the court to this desperate attempt to remedy a chronic situation.[80]

Although only partially successful, the effect of these sumptuary laws obviously took its toll on the appearance of such new silver as began to be made in France in the years that followed. At court the new service ordered from de Delaunay for the king's use was altogether on a smaller scale than before, although there is evidence that certain larger pieces, albeit in a more restrained style, were partially revived. Generally speaking there was now more use of chasing and engraving rather than the expensive cast work of before. New types of objects, like the *surtout* or the tureen, were also evolving in these apparently lean years which also saw the advance of alternative materials — gilt bronze, faience and Oriental porcelain. In general, however, shapes became simpler, with more coherent and restrained classical ornament based on small-scale strapwork, medallions, lambrequins, shells, masks, guilloche bands, and, slightly later, diaper or "mosaic" grounds. The combination of these motifs is indeed the epitome of the style of Jean Berain, the master *ornemaniste* of the age. Cousinet's drawings of Delaunay's objects for the king's table,[81] as well as rare surviving pieces like the grand dauphin's *ecuelle* and the version of his gilt bronze *surtout de table*, show the elegant simplicity of the late Louis XIV style which was to develop in the course of time into that of the Regence.

Despite this, however, the evidence indicates that the tradition of grand ornamental pieces with richly cast figurative motifs continued, especially in Francophile foreign countries like Sweden and England where financial constraints were not so acute. Indeed, in England there is a group of exceptional pieces dating from as late as the 1720s and 1730s which appear to be entirely in the pre-1689 Versailles tradition.[82] This nostalgia for the masterpieces of the *grand siècle* is expressed in the portrait of the sec-

---

79. Cole, *French Mercantilism, 1683-1700*, p. 225.

80. See, for example, Lucy Norton, ed., *St Simon at Versailles* (London, 1985), pp. 153-57.

81. Some exhibited at *Les Tables Royales*, Musée National du Chateau de Versailles, 1994.

82. For example, the pair of gold mounted ewers sold from the Houghton Collection, Christie's, London, 8 December 1994, lot 94.

ond-generation Huguenot goldsmith Paul Crespin in which he proudly holds a gigantic vase — by implication his masterpiece — which is nonetheless a completely archaic vessel and entirely at variance with the then prevailing rococo style (see plate 16).

The New Clients

No better example of the translation of the late Louis XIV style to England can be found than the pair of decanters (see plate 17) made in 1697 by the same Pierre Harache who was the first Huguenot to be admitted to the Goldsmiths' Company in 1682. Its shape and style are closely related to the examples seen in an engraving of circa 1700 of Louis XIV's sideboard at Marly, showing pieces perhaps supplied by Delaunay.[83] These decanters are in effect French pieces of silver which just happen to have been made on English soil: nothing like them — in terms of their shapes — had ever been made by an English goldsmith before. They show many of the characteristics of contemporary French work: they are made from a heavy gauge of metal (over thirty-seven ounces each), have formalized leafy cut-card work, and are spectacularly engraved with the arms of their first owner, Charles Howard, third earl of Carlisle, the builder of Castle Howard.[84] They originally formed part of one of two garnitures of sideboard plate (one in silver gilt, the other in white silver) which adorned the two marble-topped side tables in the dining room of that most Francophile of English baroque houses.[85]

Indeed, this was one of the great features of the Huguenot goldsmiths — they quickly found their new clientele among the free-spending nobility who had by now become aware of the elegancies of French art and life. Many of these now traveled abroad as diplomats, or were used to foreign travel if only because of their own participation in Continental wars. As the eighteenth century advanced the English were to become seasoned and enthusiastic travelers in Europe, and the phenomenon of the Grand Tour was to have an enormous effect on upper-class life and culture. At this date, however, they must have been able to observe the new trends in etiquette and gastronomy which were also partly responsible for the development of new objects in silver for the dining room, including the sideboard and table, and also the dressing table. These included fountains for rinsing glasses (replacing old-fashioned English monteiths), wine coolers,

83. From Pierre Lepautre, *Livre de Tables qui sont dans les Apartemens du Roy sur lesquelles sont posee les Bijoux du Cabinet des Medailles*, illustrated by Peter Thornton, in *Seventeenth Century Interior Decoration in England, France, and Holland* (London and New Haven, 1978), pl. 19.

84. Lomax, *British Silver*, p. 59.

85. Inventory of plate, 1730, Castle Howard archives, Castle Howard, 2/4/2. The tables were sold Sotheby's, 11 November 1991, lots 22-23.

38. Ewer and basin, silver gilt, Lille, circa 1692, maker's mark for Elie Pacot.

tureens (for the new ragouts and stews), sauceboats, and *surtouts* or centerpieces. For the bedroom *levee* the essential accompaniment (for the nobility as well as monarchs) was of course the fully developed silver toilet service.

Any number of examples could be cited to illustrate this trend toward a more Francophile taste among the educated classes, avid for French fashions and works of art despite the recurring state of war and the presence of a Dutch king on the throne. Just one example of a spectacular piece of imported plate is the ewer and dish made by Elie Pacot of Lille in 1692, clearly always intended as ornamental pieces for the sideboard, and which must have been acquired by the Duke of Marlborough shortly after it was made, either in Flanders or soon after its arrival in England (see fig. 38).[86] The dish has a broad border of Berainesque ornament, with medallion heads, shells, and foliage, while the ewer has a characteristic helmet shape

86. Arthur Grimwade, "The Master of George Vertue: His Identity and Oeuvre," *Apollo* 127 (1988): 87-88; see also Nicolle Cartier and Isabelle Cartier, "The Elie Pacot Surtout," *Silver Society Journal* 6 (winter 1994): 296-307. Parts of the latter sold Sotheby's, New York, 21 October 1997, lot 138.

and has a sculptural demi-figure handle. Particularly interesting is the fact that the engraving of the cartouche (but not the central armorial, which was reengraved later) was almost certainly executed in England soon after its arrival by a French engraver, Blaise Gentot — probably a Catholic — active in London from the early 1680s until his return to France around 1701. Gentot was also responsible for the engraving on a spectacular silver-topped table at Chatsworth, and he is associated with some of the finest English and Huguenot goldsmiths of this time.[87]

Clearly, then, a certain number of grand objects were arriving in England in the baggage of sophisticated travelers and soldiers and were therefore becoming available for goldsmiths in London, English and Huguenot, to copy. Somewhat later in the eighteenth century it was to become almost commonplace for returning Grand Tourists to bring home one or more specially admired objects of French silver to have them copied into sets. Occasionally an English nobleman, like the duke of Kingston or the earl of Berkeley, might order a complete service from a Parisian *orfèvre*, but the expedient of acquiring a single piece as a model to copy would have saved the enormous costs of taxes and customs duty.

Another explanation for the appearance of "French" silver — in all but name — may have been through the use of imported lead or base-metal patterns especially for the making of decorative cast or chased component parts. These could often have a long life and pass through the hands of many different craftsmen, resulting in a certain degree of conservatism. Thus the toilet service made for the Fox-Strangways family (on loan to Hampton Court Palace, 1996) circa 1695 by Daniel Garnier includes decoration of mythological figures on the boxes which appear again over thirty years later in Lady Warrington's toilet service made by Isaac Liger.[88]

Indeed, this practice of the prefabrication of decorative moldings and castings by specialist makers was to become one of the new features of the trade. In many instances identical finials, terminals, leaf-capped handles, etc., can be seen on a wide variety of objects bearing different makers' and date marks, indicating that they were probably being turned out on an almost wholesale basis for assembly by the goldsmiths.[89]

87. Grimwade, "The Master of George Vertue," pp. 83-86.

88. Sotheby's sale, London, 12 May 1966, lot 113; an interesting discussion about a different toilet service can be followed in David Kaellgren, "French Influence in a Toilet Service by David Willaume," *Silver Society Journal* 4 (1993): 162-72. See also Lorenz Seelig, "The Importance and Functions of Models for Goldsmiths' Work and Jewellery," *Handbook of the International Silver and Jewellery Fair and Seminar* (London, 1991), pp. 23-30.

89. See Helen Clifford, "Paul de Lamerie and the Organization of the London Goldsmiths' Trade in the First Half of the Eighteenth Century," in *Paul de Lamerie: The Work of England's Master Silversmith*, ed. Susan Hare (exhibition catalogue, Goldsmiths' Hall, London, 1990), pp. 24-28.

Thus, even though the Huguenots were the leaders of the avant-garde in the first two decades after their arrival in England, they could become victim to the conservative instincts of their hosts. The magnificent center-piece made in 1731 by the workshops of the brother and sister team David Willaume and Anne Tanqueray in their premises next door to one another in Saint James's Street and intended for the earl of Coventry (see plate 18) is somewhat old-fashioned by French standards. Its ornamental repertory of chased medallions, geometric strapwork, and diaper "mosaic" back-grounds in a Marotesque style would have been out of date in Paris for at least ten years. Nevertheless this piece must have been highly prized, for when it was acquired secondhand a few years later the only alterations made by its new owner, Cholmley Turner of Kirkleatham, Yorkshire, were to replace Lord Coventry's armorials with his own and place them within more up-to-date rococo cartouches.[90]

Another reason which may account for the continued use and popu-larity of French fashions in English silver design, albeit with a time lag of up to twenty years, was the fact that the Huguenots in England managed to maintain their links with their former homeland. French books and pub-lications (including engravings) were available in Huguenot-owned book-shops, and there was even a certain amount of precarious travel by the craftsmen between the two countries. David Willaume, previously men-tioned, was sent back to Metz by his father in 1717 in order to reclaim an inheritance. This could of course be a risky business for former French-men, as the author of *A New Journey* (1714) related when he witnessed the interrogation at Calais of a Huguenot returning temporarily to France.

At the same time there was a certain amount of interchange between other French craftsmen and artists who were not necessarily Huguenots nor intending to remain in England permanently. The engraver Blaise Gentot has already been cited. Another highly influential figure of the next generation was Hubert Gravelot (1699-1773). A pupil of Francois Boucher, he arrived in 1733 and rapidly became part of the artistic circle associated with Old Slaughter's Coffee House in Saint Martin's Lane.[91] He became a celebrated drawing master and was involved in almost all the most avant-garde enterprises of the day. He returned to France in 1745-46, possibly because of temporary public resentment against his countrymen which oc-casionally prevailed at the height of the various wars throughout the cen-tury.[92] But those who returned were very much the exceptions.

90. Lomax, *British Silver,* pp. 87-91.

91. See Mark Girouard, three articles in *Country Life:* "Coffee at Slaughter's," 13 Janu-ary 1966, pp. 58-61; "Hogarth and His Friends," 27 January 1966, pp. 188-90; and "The Two Worlds of St Martin's Lane," 3 February 1966, pp. 224-27.

92. For anti-French movements and the Anti-Gallican Society, see especially Linda Colley, "The English Rococo," in *Rococo Art and Design in Hogarth's England* (exhibition cata-logue, Victoria and Albert Museum, London, 1984), pp. 14-17.

So far we have been discussing works produced in the high baroque style, mainly for the court and aristocracy over the years circa 1690 to 1725. But there was of course another style available for all classes of consumers, including the middle and professional classes. This was the plain style — long since christened by antique dealers as the "Queen Anne" style — in which the great majority of objects were produced at this time. It is characterized by simple shapes, fine proportions, and plain surfaces, and is particularly appropriate for small domestic objects connected with tea and coffee drinking or for pieces destined for the dressing table. Often these take the form of clear geometric shapes, frequently hexagonal or octagonal in section, perhaps enriched only by the flourish of a handle or an engraved armorial device. In the popular imagination the style has often been associated with the Huguenot goldsmiths since it has been thought to reflect their own as well as their clients' simple but elegant lifestyles.

While it is certainly true that the French immigrants excelled at work of this nature, as in most other things, it cannot be said that it was their invention nor that it has particularly religious overtones. Indeed, the use of carefully proportioned geometric shapes should be seen to be derived, at least in part, from the love of Oriental porcelain with its myriad of vessels in these forms. Thus the various shapes of silver teapots — pear shaped, bullet shaped or rectangular shaped — can be seen to echo porcelain equivalents for wine and tea. Likewise rectangular and cylindrical tea canisters closely reflect similarly shaped vases. "Salad" bowls with their scalloped borders are clearly derived from porcelain dishes with calyxes of lotus leaves.

At the same time there is considerable evidence that much of the work of the French provincial goldsmiths before 1685 was in a similar restrained style, and so naturally this was what they brought with them to England after the Revocation. But in any case Louis XIV's sumptuary laws obliged the goldsmiths to work in a less lavish style which they therefore developed within its limitations. In England it could also be argued that the new Britannia Standard, introduced in 1697, made the cost of silver slightly more expensive (five shillings and nine pence per ounce instead of five shillings and six pence), and this may have had the effect of simplifying the design of silver vessels.

But cost has never been a major consideration among those wealthy enough to order silver, for often we find that any savings which could have been made by choosing a plain style were obviated by its heaviness or by expensive engraving. Possibly the English have a natural predisposition toward enjoying simple geometric shapes. As Lady Caroline Fox wrote in 1764, "Tho' whims and fripperies may have a run, one always returns to what is really handsome and noble and plain."[93] Another explanation for this apparently strange coexistence of often highly elaborate pieces and rel-

93. *Rococo Art and Design*, p. 103.

atively plain objects in the same household is that the clients themselves had a sense of their appropriateness. What was suitable for staterooms and for public occasions was not so for the private apartments and more informal occasions.[94]

Even so, the English have always enjoyed the intrinsic quality and worth of silver — for whatever psychological reasons — and have always been prepared to pay for a heavy gauge of plate and also for beautiful engraving. Most of the cost of Lord Warrington's silver would have been contained in the bullion value of the metal itself (which would of course have been recoverable), although he would have paid considerably more for the fashioning of the numerous pieces, many of which were elaborately engraved, cast, and chased (for which he would never recover the expense).

Finally, what sort of silver was being ordered by the Huguenots for their own use in the early eighteenth century? We have already noted the liturgical vessels made for the churches, but what of domestic pieces? On the whole there is very little evidence that the Huguenots behaved any differently than anyone else at this time, and therefore ordered plate with a degree of fashion according to their own taste and pockets. Throughout society silver was considered as much a liquid asset as the coin of the realm or investments in government stock: its bullion value remained constant for almost the whole of the eighteenth century, and there is very little evidence that its possession violated any moral or religious code.

One has to look a short way down the social scale to discover the Huguenots' own attitude toward this subject since they were rarely among the highest nobility or the richest in the land, to whom lavish plate was an assertion of power and wealth. One of the most successful of the early immigrants was Sir John Chardin (1643-1712), who was born in Paris, became a wealthy jeweler and merchant, and traveled throughout the East. He came to England in 1681, where he became a jeweler to the court and created a baronet. His son, the second Sir John, displayed his own personal taste in the relatively plain pair of cups ordered from Paul de Lamerie, the first in 1718 and its twin in 1730 (see fig. 39).[95] Nevertheless, these would have been expensive objects, having been gilded and ornamented with heavy cast moldings.

On the other hand, to illustrate that these expatriate Frenchmen and Frenchwomen could be equally partial to domestic objects in the most up-to-date and fashionable style, one need look no further than the famous tea equipage (see plate 19) made (probably as a wedding present) once again by Paul de Lamerie in 1735 for his fellow countrymen and coreligionists

94. This can be substantiated by the evidence of the plate in a large number of noble households of the early eighteenth century; e.g., those of the dukes of Norfolk, Devonshire, and Portland; the earls of Carlisle and Warrington, Viscount Irwin. See Hartop, *passim*.

95. *The Quiet Conquest*, p. 238.

39. Two-handled cup and cover of Sir John Chardin, silver gilt, London, 1730, maker's mark for Paul de Lamerie

Jean-Daniel Boissier and Suzanne Berchère of London.[96] Suzanne's father was a banker and jeweler, and it was undoubtedly through his professional contacts that he and Paul de Lamerie were acquainted and that the order for this equipage came about.

Not only is this a fascinating document of social history, but it also reveals the subtleties of a moment of transition in the history of taste largely being brought about through the influence of the Huguenot goldsmiths themselves. For during the 1730s fashions were moving inexorably toward the rococo — year by year more and more asymmetries, curlicues, and naturalistic ornaments were to be found on even the humblest items of domestic silver.

By this date the Huguenots were merging imperceptibly into the mainstream of English life and beginning to lose the distinctive features which had marked out the early arrivals. However, their names still frequently occur among lists of goldsmiths right through to the end of the century. A final example of their agency in subconsciously promoting Francophile taste appears in their involvement with the Louis XVI–style subtheme in early neoclassical English silver. Many customers for new silver in the 1760s, 1770s, and 1780s disliked the new classicism of Robert Adam (1728-92) and James Wyatt (1747-1813), preferring instead the sinuous and elegant French version.

96. Lomax, *British Silver*, pp. 122-27.

The king's own architect, Sir William Chambers (1726-96), was a leading exemplar of this "alternative" taste.[97] His commission to provide bespoke silver to George, fourth duke of Marlborough, of which the tureen of 1769 (see plate 20) is one piece, is in a style owing much to that of Robert-Joseph Auguste. Chambers's own design was executed (via the retailers Parker and Wakelin) by yet more Huguenot goldsmiths — this time of the third generation: the brothers James and Sebastian Crespel (fl. ca. 1760–ca. 1806).[98] Indeed, this family were to continue as goldsmiths into the middle of the nineteenth century.

The Craftsmen and Their World

One of the most distinctive features of the Huguenot goldsmiths in London was the close family and professional relationships which existed between them. Well-known Huguenot names constantly cross-refer to each other in marriage and baptismal documents: Jean Chartier (fl. 1688–ca. 1731) married Suzanne Garnier; David Willaume (1658-1741) the elder married Marie Mettayer, daughter of the minister of the Church of La Patente, Spitalfields; Peter Courtauld (1690-1729) married Judith Pantin. Frequently apprentices married their master's daughters or widows: David Tanqueray (fl. 1708–ca. 1729) married Anne Willaume; Simon Pantin's daughter Eliza married Abraham Buteux (1698-1731), and, secondly, Benjamin Godfrey (fl. 1731–ca. 1741); and Jean Chartier's daughter married Peze Pilleau (1696-1776).[99]

Just as significant was the way in which Huguenot masters frequently took only apprentices from their coreligionists. Whole "family trees" of trade relationships could be drawn up, although by mid-century the trend fell away when English apprentices began to be taken on. One "line of descent" would start with Pierre Harache I (fl. 1682–ca. 1698), whose apprentices included his son Peter II (1653–ca. 1717) and Simon Pantin I (fl. 1700-1728). The latter was master to his own son Simon Pantin II (fl. 1717-33) as well as to Augustine Courtauld (1685–ca. 1750), who was master to his son Samuel Courtauld I (1720-65), who in turn was master to the Englishman George Cowles (fl. 1751-1811), who formed a business partnership with his master's widow Louisa (fl. 1749-1807). A second line begins with Louis Cuny (fl. 1697-1733) — who was endenizened on 8 May

97. Hilary Young, "Sir William Chambers and John Yenn: Designs for Silver," *Burlington Magazine* 128 (January 1986): 31-35; Young, "Sir William Chambers and the Duke of Marlborough's Silver," *Apollo* 125 (June 1987): 396-400; John Harris and Michael Snodin, eds., *Sir William Chambers: Architect to George III* (exhibition catalogue, London and Stockholm, 1996-97), pp. 149-62.

98. Lomax, *British Silver*, pp. 96-99.

99. Grimwade, *London Goldsmiths*, passim.

1697 alongside his fellow goldsmiths Pierre Platel (ca. 1664-1719) and Jean Chartier (fl. 1688-1731) — who was master to John Lesage (fl. 1708–ca. 1743), who in turn was master to Edward Wakelin (fl. 1730-84). A third important line began with the English master butcher Thomas Jenkins (fl. 1697–ca. 1708), who took on Jacob Margas (fl. 1699–ca. 1730), who in his turn was master to his brother Samuel Margas (fl. 1708–ca. 1751), who was master to Peter Archambo (fl. 1710-67), who was master to Thomas Heming (fl. 1738–ca. 1795).[100] Thus it is not difficult to find a certain consistency in styles, techniques, and working practices handed down from master to apprentice over numbers of years.

Is there any evidence that the training of Huguenot apprentices in London was any different from that of their English counterparts, and that this might account for their success? It is interesting that the author of *The London Tradesman* (1747) considered that a goldsmith should have the same "general" education as a notary public (a civil lawyer) and that, in addition, he "ought to be a good Designer, and have a good Taste in Sculpture . . . be conversant in Alchemy; that is in all the Properties of Metals . . . he ought to be possessed of a solid Judgement as well as a mechanical Hand and Head. His Education with respect to his Business, does not require to be very liberal; a plain *English* education will suffice. Designing is the chief Part of his early Study, previous to his Apprenticeship. . . ."[101]

Thus the desirable artistic qualities of a young goldsmith's education were skill in design (i.e., drawing) and a good sense of sculpture. So we find the sporadic appearance in the early eighteenth century of drawing and design academies mainly in Soho, now rapidly becoming the center of the avant-garde in London, and usually under the aegis of foreign masters. An early drawing master was John Baptist Gaspars (d. ca. 1692), who, according to Vertue, was "eminent for his Designs in Tapistry, having been an admirable Draftsman in the Academy."[102] In 1711 an academy of painting was set up by William III's court painter, the Dutchman Sir Godfrey Kneller (1646-1723), at which French artists were employed: Louis Laguerre (1663-1721) was one of the directors, as was the engraver Louis Dugenier (1687-1716), who arrived in London in about 1707. Another academy was established in 1720, although this may have been more a convivial dining society than a true place of study.[103]

History simply does not relate whether the pupils at these early establishments (or any of the other more ephemeral ones) included goldsmiths or their apprentices. But it would be inconceivable that Huguenots from any trade requiring skills in design would *not* have been found at the

100. Grimwade, *London Goldsmiths,* passim.
101. Campbell, p. 142.
102. George Vertue's Notebooks, *Walpole Society,* XX (1931-32), vol. 2, p. 135.
103. George Vertue's Notebooks, p. 126.

most celebrated academy of all — the Saint Martin's Lane Academy, established in their midst by Hogarth and where Hubert Gravelot was drawing master.[104]

Yet another academy was founded by George Michael Moser (1706-83), a chaser from Geneva. He arrived in England in 1726 and was first employed on furniture mounts by the furniture maker John Trotter (b. before 1730-99), and later worked with the Moravian goldsmith and chaser John Valentine Haid.[105] He then became manager and drawing master at the Saint Martin's Lane Academy, and his private pupils included no less a personage than the future King George III. Eventually he was to end his days as the keeper of the new Royal Academy of Art. His well-known drawing for a silver candlestick in the form of a Berniniesque *Daphne*[106] is a rare surviving example of a drawn design for goldsmith's work in rococo England (see fig. 40).

For the truth is that there was no tradition of draftsmanship or of goldsmiths' designs being committed to paper in England. Until this time craftsmen had worked entirely by eye. It was only with the arrival of the neoclassical architect-designers of the 1760s, together with the entrepreneurs of mass production, that the relatively new practice of drawn design began to overtake more traditional methods of transmitting and developing forms and ornament.

At the same time it is fascinating to look at the physical and geographical proximity of some of the Huguenots' workshops — so many of them were huddled together in the southwest corner of the parish of Saint Anne's, Soho, and in the adjoining parishes of Saint Martin's-in-the-Fields and Saint Giles. Indeed, the district was to become the natural hub of foreign life and a magnet for all French and French-speaking artists visiting the capital. It soon acquired a reputation as the artists' quarter. Saint Martin's Lane was its principal thoroughfare and most important shopping street, with the large premises of smart furnishers like Thomas Chippendale and John Channon, while the goldsmiths tended to be in the streets adjoining.

Soho and its environs must have presented a bewildering contrast to visitors to early- and mid-eighteenth-century London. On the one hand it was one of the centers of the luxury trades, and although it was not the fashionable residential area it had once been, it was very close to Mayfair and Saint James's, and it still contained some of the best shops in London. On the other hand its new inhabitants must have given it an atmosphere of

---

104. See Girouard, "Two Worlds," pp. 224-26.

105. J. C. Fuessli, *Geschicte der Besten Kunstler in der Schweits, nebst ihren Bildnissen,* 5 vols. (Zurich, 1769-79), vol. 4. I am grateful to Sarah Medlam for bringing this reference to my attention.

106. Illustrated, for example, in Susan Lambert, ed., *Pattern and Design: Designs for the Decorative Arts 1480-1980* (exhibition catalogue, Victoria and Albert Museum, 1983), pl. 51.

40. Design for a
Candlestick by George
Michael Moser

great sobriety as well as exotic charm. In 1739 it was said that "it is easy
for a stranger to imagine himself in France,"[107] and in 1748 a young diplo-
mat who was about to go abroad was described by a friend as "so busy going about the French that there is no getting a sight of him. He spends his
whole time in the neighbourhood of Soho amongst the French refugees."
Indeed, in 1711 a survey of the parish of Saint Anne's, Soho, found that
some 3,500 souls, or two-fifths of its total population of 8,133, were of

107. See *The Survey of London, XXXIII: The Parish of St Anne, Soho* (London, 1966), pp. 6-
10.

41. William Hogarth, *Noon*, first state, engraving, 1738

French extraction. Hogarth's engraving *Noon* (one of a set depicting the four times of day) (see fig. 41) shows the soberly dressed Huguenots leaving the Hog Lane church on a Sunday morning contrasted by a foppish and overrouged couple who walk by gesticulating but probably attired and equipped by the same hardworking folk behind them.

There are a small number of contemporary descriptions of life among the Huguenots in eighteenth-century Soho which are worth recalling in order to capture something of the frugal ambience of their working environment. The first was written by "a German gentleman" visiting the house of a shopkeeper in 1725: "Once on a Sabbath Day I was requested to dine with a Shopkeeper in this Parish: the Man's Income I believe amounted to about seventy Pounds per Annum, and his Family consisted of one Wife

125

and a Daughter of about eighteen; they were extraordinary Oeconomists, brewed their own Beer, wash'd at home, made a Joint hold out two Days, and a Shift three; let three Parts of their House ready furnish'd, and kept paying one Quarter's Rent under another. In such like circumstances they had gone on for some Years, and the Worst the world could say of them was, That they liv'd above what they had. . . ."[108]

As the years advanced, the distinctive flavor of Soho largely disappeared, although to this day it retains an air of Continental exoticism. While the families of the original refugees prospered, they dispersed and merged with the indigenous English. Their churches closed and their congregations dwindled. The philanthropist Sir Samuel Romilly vividly described the shabby and dispiriting condition of the churches of his youth in the 1760s.[109] Clearly by this date the cohesiveness of the original Huguenot community was in decline, and the next wave of immigration by French artists and craftsmen in the 1780s and 1790s was to be motivated by quite different factors — the patronage of the Prince of Wales and the Carlton House Set, and once again the unpropitious circumstances of the home market.

Thus it is difficult to find a directly religious motivation behind the work and styles of the Huguenot goldsmiths working in England. I would suggest that, like their fellow compatriots working in so many different trades, as far as their public lives were concerned they considered themselves Frenchmen-in-exile first, craftsmen second, and Protestants third. However, there is no denying that, as Daniel Defoe wrote of the Huguenot silk weavers in Spitalfields over on the other side of London, they were "men of exquisite art, clear heads and bright fancies in their business."[110] No wonder they were so successful.

Selected Bibliography

1. Reference

Evans, Joan. "Huguenot Goldsmiths in England and Ireland." *Proceedings of the Huguenot Society of London*, XIV (1930-33), pp. 496-554.
Grimwade, Arthur G. *London Goldsmiths, 1697-1837: Their Lives and Marks.* 3rd ed. London, 1990.

108. See *Survey of London*, pp. 6-10.
109. *Memoirs of Sir S. Romilly written by Himself,* I (London 1845), p. 15.
110. Daniel Defoe, *The Complete English Tradesman*, II (London, 1732), pt. 2, chap. 5, p. 154.

2. General

Campbell, R. *The London Tradesman.* London, 1747. David and Charles reprint, 1969.

Defoe, Daniel. *Roxana.* London, 1724.

Grimwade, Arthur G. *Rococo Silver, 1727-1765.* London, 1974.

Hartop, Christopher. *The Huguenot Legacy: English Silver 1680-1760 from the Alan and Simone Hartman Collection.* London: T. Heneage, 1996.

Hayward, J. F. *Huguenot Silver in England, 1688-1727.* London, 1959.

Murdoch, Tessa, ed. *The Quiet Conquest: The Huguenots, 1685-1995.* Exhibition catalogue, Museum of London, 1995.

Tait, Hugh. "London Huguenot Silver." In *Huguenots in Britain and Their French Background, 1550-1800,* edited by Irene Scouloudi, pp. 89-112. London, 1985.

3. Early Period

Glanville, Philippa. *Silver in Tudor and Early Stuart England.* London, 1990.

4. Church Plate

Jones, E. A. *The Old Silver Sacramental Vessels of the Foreign Protestant Churches in England.* London, 1908.

Oman, Charles. *English Church Plate.* Oxford, 1957.

5. Individual Goldsmiths

Beet, Brian. "Huguenot Silversmiths from Anjou: Amyraux, Guichardière, La Brosse and Michon," *Silver Society Journal* (London), no. 10 (1998, forthcoming).

Hare, Susan, ed. *Paul de Lamerie: The Work of England's Master Silversmith.* Exhibition catalogue, Goldsmiths' Hall, London, 1990.

Hayward, J. F. *The Courtauld Silver: An Introduction to the Work of the Courtauld Family of Goldsmiths.* London and New York, 1975.

Selected Collections Containing
Huguenot Goldsmiths' Work

England

Altrincham, Cheshire: Dunham Massey
Chatsworth, Derbyshire
Ickworth, Suffolk
Leeds, West Yorkshire: Temple Newsam
London: Victoria and Albert Museum, The British Museum (Wilding Bequest)
Manchester: Manchester City Art Gallery (Assheton Bennett Collection)
Oxford: Ashmolean Museum (The Farrer Collection)
Welbeck Abbey, Nottinghamshire
Woburn Abbey, Bedfordshire

U.S.A

Boston: Museum of Fine Arts
Colonial Williamsburg
New York: Metropolitan Museum of Art
Williamstown: Sterling and Francine Clark Art Institute

Canada

Toronto: Royal Ontario Museum

Discussion Following the Lomax Presentation

Gretchen Buggeln: My question concerns your use of the term "plain style" as applied to Queen Anne silver. From my (New World) perspective, Queen Anne does not appear plainer than its antecedents, although the English evidence you have presented supports the use of the term. I wonder if there is anything in the documentary realm to indicate that Englishmen who chose the Queen Anne style in silver were motivated by religious considerations or had any sense that in adopting the Queen Anne style they were moving in a new direction that might have consequences in terms of their religious identity?

James Lomax: In the inventory (1750) compiled by Lord Warrington, he distinguished between plain and chased candlesticks. He describes the differences quite deliberately, so there is in his mind a very conscious decision to buy objects in one or another category for a particular place in his house. But it is difficult to find documentary evidence that supports the choice of the plain over the more ornate, rococo style. I think these considerations were very much tied to the vagaries of a given client's tastes, and to considerations on the location(s) where a given object was intended to be exhibited. As for the function these objects were supposed to fulfill, silver was always a status symbol, very visible, objects designed to elicit the admiration of your peers, a way of advertising your wealth and place in the world by what you are able to show on your sideboard or dressing table. At the same time, chased or ornamental silver represented money that had been simply thrown away — above and beyond material costs, you would never be able to recover the labor costs for silver. This goes to the question of extravagance and luxury, an issue of public concern and public morality, an issue that was hotly debated in early eighteenth-century London. It would be interesting to know how this relates, if at all, with the choices made by Huguenot immigrants in London.

John Strang: Among the Huguenot goldsmiths who came to Bermuda and America there were evidently numerous women. Is there an English parallel?

James Lomax: When you encounter the mark of a woman who is an English goldsmith, she is always a widow, someone who has taken over her husband's business upon his death. Englishwomen were entitled to do this by law and were able to strike their own marks in their husbands' absence. We have no evidence that Englishwomen were the actual makers of individual pieces. Women in England would have had no training in this craft because the goldsmith's art was not considered a suitable occupation for women, nor does it become acceptable for women to participate in this kind of activity until much later in the arts and crafts movement. But women certainly functioned (often quite brilliantly) as the proprietors of goldsmith shops that they had taken over from their husbands. Anne Willaume Tanqueray (1691-1733) is an excellent example. She took over the business of her deceased husband, David Tanqueray (fl. London 1708?-1730; cf. *The Dictionary of Art* 30 [London and New York, 1996], s.v.; article by T. Schroder), and under her direction it was one of the smartest and most successful shops in London.

Raymond Mentzer: You seem to be presenting a case where the experience of being a minority in France, an experience that required skill and knowledge and social adaptability, served this community very well when they were forced to make the transition as refugees to London. Would you comment on this?

129

James Lomax: Yes. I think that the shared Huguenot experience in France helped to form a sense of social cohesion which carried over into England. This, I think, is beyond doubt. A map of Saint Martin's-in-the-Fields showing the location of Huguenot establishments might support this generalization. It would show how close all the Huguenot goldsmiths were to each other. Their common experience and their close interdependence thus acquires a graphic representation in the map of this London neighborhood, and this close interdependence continues for two or even three generations after the initial wave of immigration. Huguenot goldsmiths continued to be closely linked for much of the eighteenth century.

Reindert Falkenburg: I want to comment on the Hogarth painting (fig. 41) that you showed. It is sometimes suggested that the wearing of black garments was a Protestant (Calvinist) practice in the seventeenth century. But more recent work shows that this was not an expression of religious identity, the so-called Protestant plain style, but instead in early seventeenth-century Netherlands this was a custom introduced by the aristocracy and the haute bourgeoisie as a way of distinguishing themselves vis-à-vis people lower down on the rungs of the social ladder, people who dressed in bright colors, such as soldiers. Black silk became a symbol of elevated social and economic status but not of one's religious identity. This gives an example of luxury in conjunction with sobriety among the upper social classes, but this is in no way a reflection of religious identity.

James Lomax: Yes, in fact the black style which comes to England under Charles I is known as the "Spanish style." Later, Defoe's Roxana adopted it as a subterfuge, identifying it with the rich but sober Quakers with whom she sought refuge.

Hélène Guicharnaud: Can you tell us what are the geographical origins of the first generations of Huguenot goldsmith refugees who went to London?

James Lomax: They came from Normandy, Touraine, Flanders, Angou, Lorraine — all from northern France. Huguenot goldsmiths of southern French origin must have gone to Switzerland or Germany, but not to England.

FRANCE/SWITZERLAND

An Introduction to the Architecture of Protestant Temples Constructed in France before the Revocation of the Edict of Nantes

HÉLÈNE GUICHARNAUD

The establishment of Reformed worship in sixteenth-century France occurred according to a regular pattern. The earliest assemblies took place in private dwellings. Later, as Protestants became more powerful, they requisitioned public buildings and churches: the Church of Saint-Jacques at Montauban; the Observant Franciscan and Augustinian monasteries, and the Churches of Sainte-Eugénie and Saint-Etienne de Capduel at Nîmes; the Church of Saint-Fiary and the Dominican monastery at Agen; the Churches of Saint-Barthélemy and Sainte-Marguerite, the Saint-Yon temple in the remodeled refectory of the former Augustinian monastery, and the Salle Gargoulleau (previously a tennis court) at La Rochelle; the Chapel of Sainte-Colombe at Gap; and the Church of Nôtre-Dame at Montpellier. The Reformed community at Caen, much as its counterpart at Lyon in 1562, appropriated several churches for worship when the troops of the baron des Adrets occupied the city. This development occurred before the Edict of Pacification of Amboise (1563) assigned the Franciscan church and the Church of Confort to the Protestants while they awaited either the renovation of another structure or the construction of a wholly new building.

In 1598, the Edict of Nantes granted Protestants liberty of conscience

The author wishes to express her warmest thanks to Raymond Mentzer for his translation of this article.

and freedom of worship in those places where they had practiced their faith in 1596 and 1597. They were forbidden, however, to worship in Paris or within a radius of five leagues around the capital. Their temples,[1] moreover, were to be distinguishable from Catholic churches. Protestants could, within these limits, construct edifices dedicated exclusively to Reformed worship. The political stability of the early seventeenth century clearly promoted these Reformed building projects. More temples were erected during this period than in the years prior to the Edict of Nantes, when the destructive violence of the Wars of Religion frequently led to the ruin of the structures that had been built during those troubled times. It is hardly surprising that, without exception, the edifices that serve as the principal examples for the present study date from the era after the Edict of Nantes.

Several fundamental difficulties frame the subject of this essay and should be noted from the outset. The Protestant temples erected in France before the Revocation of the Edict of Nantes (1685) were destroyed within a few dozen years of their construction. As a result, it is impossible to examine them directly. They were, furthermore, rarely the object of artistic or architectural depictions, with the notable exception of the second temple of Charenton. The sources at our disposal are the contractual arrangements between the consistory, elders (anciens), and artisans (when they have survived), and the testimony of contemporaries or of members of the following generation who may have viewed the building and provided some description.

This evidence must be used cautiously. The writers, whatever their confessional stance, are likely to have been subjective. We have culled out comments that are patently tendentious. These are remarks issued by one side or the other to justify a posteriori the ideological climate and the Catholic coercion of Protestants, or, conversely, Huguenot statements destined to reaffirm their determination after the Revocation of the Edict of Nantes. There was the obvious overestimation of the capacity of the temples where the seditious Protestants assembled and, accordingly, confirmation of the essential danger of these meeting places. For example, according to François Farin,[2] the temple of Quevilly could accommodate nearly eleven thousand persons. For the Calvinists, the numbers became proof of

1. French Protestants, based on a reading of Scripture, labeled their houses of worship temples. The temple, in their understanding, was the physical structure in which the faithful gathered, while the church was the community of believers. The language also recalled the ancient temple of Jerusalem. Finally, the designation was an unambiguous way for Calvinists to distinguish their buildings from those of Catholic rivals. See Willy Richard, *Untersuchungen zur Genesis der reformierten Kirchenterminologie der Westschweiz und Frankreichs* (Bern: A. Franke, 1959), pp. 77-85.

2. François Farin, *Histoire de la ville de Rouen*, 6 pts. in 2 vols. (Rouen: Louis du Souillet, 1731), pt. 5, p. 146.

their membership in a much larger community, which could only serve to comfort them despite the terrible ongoing ordeal. Protestants sometimes even embraced disparaging comments about their temples. These unpleasant remarks can be found in some writings and must have been frequent in the age. The Huguenots turned the challenges and insults into badges of honor. The impoverished state of their temples, for example, occasioned comparisons to "barns" (*granges*) and even "rats' nests" (*nids à rats*), if we can believe the celebrated Reformed pastor Pierre du Moulin, who took up this theme in arguing the difference between Catholic and Protestant churches (App. 1, p. 156). It is true that Protestants sometimes gathered in refurbished barns. Still, the austerity of the Reformed temples must have struck, and undoubtedly shocked, contemporaries in an age when the Counter-Reformation deployed ornate ceremony and elaborate display. In the end, this sort of documentation should be generally avoided, especially when it proves too subjective to offer reliable evidence.

Accounts by contemporary foreign travelers such as Elie Brackenhoffer,[3] persons who were less involved in French religious affairs, are another source of credible, generally unbiased information. They typically wrote reports destined for what might be called "domestic consumption" — for relatives, friends, or even themselves. These observations appear in journals or domestic memoirs (*livres de raison*) and are quite different from the accounts discussed earlier, which people composed with the explicit aim of polemical publication and ideological propaganda. Finally, the work of later scholars, particularly those of the nineteenth century, cannot be ignored. These erudites had access to or themselves possessed documents which they used to good advantage in their publications. Some of the illustrations for the present essay derive from these sources. Obviously, these materials must also be used with some caution. Yet it is possible, despite the problems associated with the subject, to attempt an introduction to the architecture of the French Protestant temples built before the Revocation and to offer a number of conclusions.

Location

The terms of the Edict of Nantes determined the location of the temple. Though it was theoretically permissible to erect a temple in those towns where the Reformed religion had been practiced in 1596 and 1597, there were exceptions to the rule. The constraints were usually tied to the town's political past. For example, at Agen, which had been associated with the Catholic League, Protestant worship was prohibited within a half

3. Elie Brackenhoffer, *Voyage de Paris en Italie (1644-1646)*, trans. Henry Lehr (Paris: Berger-Levrault, 1927).

league of the town walls. Consequently, the temple was built at Boé between 1600 and 1606. Another restriction was likely brought to bear by what we would today call "public opinion." Article 5 of the Edict of Nantes, for example, authorized the Protestants of Dieppe to build a temple in the suburb of Le Pollet. Confronted by various problems associated with the proposed site, they agreed to construct their temple at Caudecot, which was a bit farther away.

In a general way, *Le voyage de France dressé pour l'instruction et commodité, tant des François que des estrangers,* a work that went through many editions,[4] provides a good notion of the state of affairs.

> The provinces of France where followers of the *Religion prétendue réformée* live in great numbers are Languedoc, Dauphiné, Guyenne, Saintonge, the pays d'Aulnois, Poitou, Normandy, the region of the Cévennes mountains and Vivarais where the exercise [of their religion] is allowed in the majority of towns. The region of Béarn also has many [Protestant] towns and inhabitants. The other provinces do not have the exercise [of Protestantism] in the towns themselves, but in the suburbs or in neighboring places.[5]

Plans

The structures varied depending upon place, capacity requirements, and economic imperatives. There was, in effect, no prototype temple or typical plan. The building designers, moreover, could have been local masons or architects from a variety of backgrounds. Still, the prohibition against any possible confusion between Catholic church and Protestant temple, and, above all, the needs of a Reformed worship that centered, especially during the early modern era, on the preaching of the Word, led to the adoption of plans that can be classified in two major groups: a basilican or longitudinal plan on the one hand and a centralized plan on the other.

The model and best example of the basilican type was the temple of Charenton designed by Salomon de Brosse. The engraving by Marot (see fig. 42; cf. fig. 48) (and by others depicting in particular the temple's destruction, a dramatic and emotional event from which the Protestants undoubtedly drew strength), the prominence of its architect (designer,

4. The first edition appeared at Paris: Olivier de Varennes, 1639; the second was in 1641, and so forth.

5. "Les provinces de France, où ceux de la R.P.R. sont en très grand nombre, sont le Languedoc, le Dauphiné, la Guyenne, la Saintonge, le pays d'Aulnois, le Poitou, la Normandie, les pays des Cévennes et Vivarais, où l'exercice est permis dans la plupart des villes. Le pays de Béarn en a aussi plusieurs villes et habitans. Les autres provinces n'en ont point l'exercice dans les villes mêmes, mais dans les fauxbourgs ou en quelques lieux voisins."

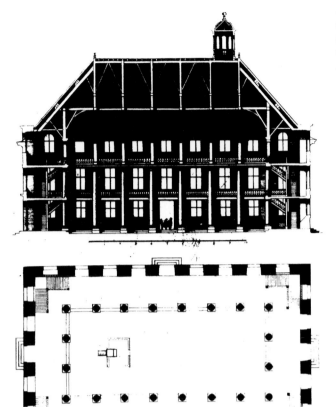

42. The temple of Charenton. Seventeenth-century engraving by Jean Marot

among other things, of the Luxembourg Palace for Marie de Medici), its symbolic place as the temple for the Parisian community, and the spread of the design beyond France assured the Charenton temple of enormous prestige and elevated it in some ways to the position of the ideal temple or, more appropriately, the ideal of the Protestant temple.

Yet remember that the temple designed by Salomon de Brosse was preceded by another structure constructed in 1607 by his uncle Jacques II Androuet du Cerceau.[6] Fire had destroyed this earlier building in 1621. Édouard-Jacques Ciprut,[7] who published the various construction contracts relating to the first temple, has correctly identified du Cerceau as the architect of the first temple. Scholars had traditionally attributed the earlier structure to Salomon de Brosse, architect of the second temple.

6. For the du Cerceau family, cf. Baron Henry de Geymüller, *Les Du Cerceau, leur vie et leur oeuvre* (Paris: J. Rouan, 1887).

7. Édouard-Jacques Ciprut, "Le premier grand temple de Charenton," *Bulletin de la Société de l'Histoire du Protestantisme Français* 114 (1968): 106-12.

Ciprut's welcome revision has corrected our understanding of the initial construction project.

The first temple of Charenton itself succeeded the temple of Ablon,[8] which Jacques II Androuet du Cerceau also built, at the very beginning of the seventeenth century. The Ablon temple, though entirely new, was destined to disappear when the "messieurs du Consistoire de Paris" — which is how the notarial acts identify them — arranged with various artisan guilds to dismantle and recover, as much as possible, the building materials, which the workers then utilized for Charenton. The contracts bear witness to the persistent concern of the consistory officials to reuse parts of the Ablon timbering, masonry, the roof down to the nails and lead, "iron fastenings and other iron fittings, all the doors, the windows,"[9] the dormer windows and balustrades. All were to be reutilized according to du Cerceau's instructions. The contracts clearly indicate that the new temple was to have a configuration analogous to that of the temple of Ablon. The precision of the contracts concerning this first temple[10] (signed, it should be noted, at du Cerceau's residence in Paris) allows us to grasp how much Salomon de Brosse was dependent upon his uncle.

The temple, about 33 meters long and 19.5 meters wide, was composed of nine bays unified by stone *chaînes*[11] that also served to underscore the corners of the structure whose walls were of good quarry stone, limestone and sandstone, and rough-cast limestone and sandstone. At each end of the structure, there was a large door, about six *pieds* (2 m.) wide; the arches of the doorways were in dressed stone. Another, small door three *pieds* by six or seven and one half *pieds* (about 1 m. by 2 or 2.5 m.) was envisaged. Within each bay, there was a window three *pieds* by four *pieds* (roughly 1.3 m. by 1 m.) "to illuminate the lower galleries."[12] Above, there were two dormer windows, of which the higher protruded through the roof. The arrangement was similar to the Ablon temple from which the windows had come.

The edifice, around which ran a large entablature designed to keep rainwater away from the base of the walls, was roofed with tiles taken from Ablon. At one end of the roof was a bell tower done in slate and lead. Inside the building, twenty posts set on stone bases supported the galleries,

---

8. The initial temple of the Parisian Reformed community was constructed at Ablon, near Fontainebleau.

9. ". . . lyens de fer et aultres ferrures, toutes les portes, les fenêtres. . ."

10. For additional details, see Ciprut.

11. *Chaînes* are vertical strips of rusticated masonry rising between horizontal string moldings and cornice. They divide a facade into bays or panels and were much used in seventeenth-century French architecture. John Fleming, Hugh Honour, and Nikolaus Pevsner, *The Penguin Dictionary of Architecture*, 4th ed. (London and New York: Penguin, 1991), pp. 87-88.

12. ". . . pour éclairer dans les galleries basses."

which were accessible by "four grand staircases *de pied droit*" (quarter-turned with landings) that were six *pieds* (1.92 m.) wide.

The descriptions provided in the contracts fit perfectly the documentary accounts of the second temple and, if we forget for a moment the 1621 fire, we might conclude that it was the same structure. It is quite different, in any event, from the description of the first temple as a "miserable edifice" that commentators contrasted and still contrast with the "splendid temple" of Salomon de Brosse. The sources for the second temple of Charenton (App. 2 and 3, pp. 157-59) and the depiction offered by the *Mercure galant* (App. 4, p. 160) confirm the similarities between the two buildings, including the dimensions.

The second temple of Charenton was then the heir, via the intermediary of the first, which burned in 1621, of the temple of Ablon, built by Jacques II Androuet du Cerceau at the start of the seventeenth century. The lineage of the three temples and their exceptional architectural quality deserve special emphasis if their designers, the most renowned architects of the age, are to receive proper credit.

Other temples adopted a longitudinal plan, too. At Claye, some twenty kilometers from Meaux to the northeast of Paris, the temple was an elongated rectangular building pierced by a row of windows. The temple of Saumur was a "long quadrangular form,"[13] nearly twenty-six by seven meters (App. 5, p. 161). The temple of La Calade at Nîmes, authorized by letters patent of Charles IX dated 13 March 1565, "was entirely finished toward the end of 1565, was comfortable and spacious . . . and . . . cost an enormous sum."[14] The temple was accessible by three doors of which the main one opened onto a *perron*,[15] or exterior platform with a staircase descending to ground level.[16] The *grand temple* at Montpellier, built at the initiative of François de Châtillon,[17] was also longitudinal, as were others built much later. The temple of La Villeneuve, constructed at La Rochelle

13. ". . . de figure carrée long."

14. ". . . fut entièrement fini vers la fin de l'année 1565, etoit commode et spacieux — et — coûta de grandes sommes." Léon Ménard, *Histoire des évêques de Nîmes où l'on voit ce qui s'est passé de plus mémorable . . .* , 2 vols. (The Hague, 1737), 1:332.

15. A *perron* is an exterior platform ascended by stairs to the building entrance. Also, it is the flight of steps ascending to the platform. Fleming, Honour, and Pevsner, p. 331.

16. The inauguration of the temple, even though it still lacked a pulpit, took place in January 1566. After having been set afire by Catholics on 5 September 1569 during the Wars of Religion, it was repaired and enlarged in 1601. Raoul Lhermet, *Nîmes, cité protestante* (Nîmes: Imprimerie Chastanier, 1959), p. 56. Pastor Viguié, quoting Borrel on the occasion of the dedication of the new temple on 29 November 1866: *Bulletin de la Société de l'Histoire du Protestantisme Français* 16 (1867).

17. Son of Gaspard II, admiral de Coligny, he was the governor of Montpellier in 1577. His motto, *Ex cinero vives colligo,* and his coat of arms adorned the grand arch of the temple. André Delort, *Mémoires inédits d'André Delort sur la ville de Montpellier au XVIIe siècle: 1621-1693* (1879; reprint, Marseille: Lafitte, 1980), pp. 106-7.

43. The temple of La Villeneuve at La Rochelle

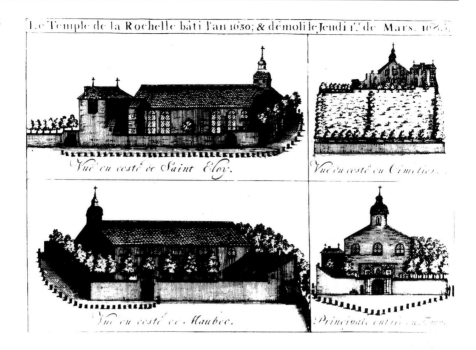

Le Temple de la Rochelle bâti l'an 1630; & démoli le Jeudi 1.er de Mars. 168.

Vue en costé de Saint Éloy.

Vue en costé du Cimetier.

Vue en costé de Maubec.

Principale entrée du Temple.

after the famous siege according to a longitudinal plan, did not follow a symmetrical design in its organization if the invaluable engravings depicting it are correct (see fig. 43). On the other hand, the strikingly simple temple of Pont-en-Royans (see fig. 44) near Grenoble in the province of Dauphiné offered an orderly design accented by arched windows. The façade had a principal door in the center with a smaller door to one side.[18] At Mens-en-Trièves, again in Dauphiné, the temple, destroyed in a fire that ravaged part of the town in 1650, was quickly rebuilt according to an elongated plan and roofed with slate. At Lasalle in the Cévennes a new temple was built between 1656 and 1659. Raised up on several steps, the longitudinal structure measured thirteen by seventeen meters. Three doors allowed access and twelve arched windows framed in stone let light into the interior. A tile roof covered the structure.

Each of these longitudinal temples had a great long arch on which the beams of the timbering rested. This was certainly the case at Montpellier where visitors repeatedly expressed admiration for the grand arch[19] made

18. Archives Nationales (Paris), TT 262/1162, 24 janvier 1682.

19. "On peut dire qu'on abattit un Temple dont le couvert étoit porté par un arc d'une longueur extraordinaire, fort dégagé, que tous les étrangers admiroient et disoient être le plus beau de l'Europe." Etienne Cambolive, *Histoire de divers événemens contenant en abrégé les persecutions exercées en France* (Amsterdam, 1698), p. 43. A Protestant manuscript cited by the nineteenth-century editor of André Delort's *Mémoires*, p. 106, adds that this arch was the object of admiring visits by "foreign" masons. "Foreign" in this instance refers to persons who lived outside the town or the region.

140

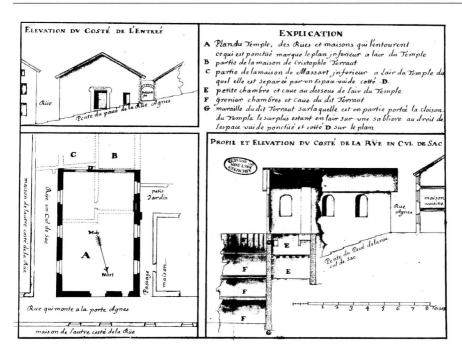

of stone quarried at Saint-Geniez. The same principle was applied at Orange, also in southern France; John Locke, for instance, took special note of it in 1675.

> 30 December [1675]. There are two Protestant churches in the towne. One we were in of a pretty sort of building, one long stone arch, like a bridg, running the whole length of the church, & supporting the rafters like the main beam of the building, a new but not incommodius way for such a room.[20]

The temple at Collet-de-Dèze in the Cévennes adopted a similar system. This design, which allowed the economic use of long beams, was the visible heir of a technique of rural roof construction; it was employed for barns in the region.

In their extreme simplicity, some of these structures can be effectively compared, if not to the "barn" so disdained by the Catholics, at least to models in use for local civil architecture and adopted to the needs of Protestant worship. Accordingly, we can distinguish a "popular" model, which followed the longitudinal plan and derived from the everyday experience of the masons (the temple of Pont-en-Royans in Dauphiné and the temples of southern France and their great long arches illustrate this type of construction), and a more learned model represented by the temples of Ablon and Charenton de-

20. John Locke, *Locke's Travels in France, 1675-1679, as Related in His Journals, Correspondence, and Other Papers*, ed. John Lough (Cambridge: Cambridge University Press, 1953), p. 11.

signed by Jacques II Androuet du Cerceau and Salomon de Brosse. An entire range of intermediary edifices existed between these two extremes.

A second major grouping consisted of centrally planned buildings. These have been the object of evolving and diverse interpretations. Even if it was not built expressly for use as a temple, it would be unthinkable to avoid mention of the *temple de Paradis* at Lyon, whose painting (see plate 21) is so often used to illustrate studies on French Protestantism. The building, located on the rue des Établéries, had been purchased in May 1564 to be refurbished as a temple; it was razed in August 1568. While its existence as a place of worship was brief, its disposition according to a centralized plan allows us to understand the interest in this type of building, which brought the pastor and congregation into close proximity for the sermon service.

Construction of the first temple at Dieppe in 1600-1601 took a full twelve months. Later, in March 1606, "a westerly wind storm, which was so violent that it uprooted trees,"[21] ruined the building. Undaunted, the town's Protestants once more set to work. The first temple, whose "walls were of brick, but too weak to support it,"[22] sat on a limestone foundation and had a two-tiered roof. The second temple was constructed

> of brick and wood . . . roofed with slate, in an oval shape, in the midst of which there were twenty-two wooden posts or pilasters divided into two rows that were ten *pieds* (3.2 m.) apart and which formed the body or nave of this building and supported the roof.[23]

The temple of Bourg-l'Abbé at Caen (see fig. 45), built in 1611-12,[24] had a two-tiered roof similar to that of the first temple of Dieppe. The structure followed a segmented centralized plan. A small tower, which housed a bell, sat on the roof, and there was a lantern *(pot-à-feu)* at each end. The depiction of the temple, which belonged to a Norman scholar at the end of the nineteenth century, has been frequently reproduced. It shows an elaborately conceived structure. Two bays flanked by colossal pilasters composed each of

21. ". . . par un orage de vent d'ouëst qui étoit si violent qu'il arrachoit les arbres." Michel Claude Guibert, *Mémoires pour servir à l'histoire de la ville de Dieppe,* with an introduction by Michel Hardy (Dieppe: A. Renaux, 1878), p. 204.

22. ". . . les murailles étoient de brique mais trop foibles pour le soutenir." Guibert, p. 203.

23. ". . . en brique et en bois, . . . couvert d'ardoises, de forme ovalle, au milieu duquel il y avoit 22 poteaux ou pilastres de bois partagez en deux rangs, distants de 10 pieds [3.20 m] l'un de l'autre, pour former le corps ou nef de ce bâtiment et en soutenir le comble." Guibert, p. 206.

24. The sale of the land where the temple was built occurred in 1611. The dates 1609 to 1612 proposed by Eugène Robillard de Beaurepaire, *Caen illustré, son histoire, ses monuments* (1896; reprint, Peronnas: Les Editions de la Tour Gile, 1994), p. 290, for the temple's construction are improbable and, in any event, contradicted by other sources.

142

45. The temple of Bourg-l'Abbé at Caen. From a nineteenth-century rendering

the shorter segments. An arched window pierced each bay. The principal façade, which faces the viewer, had five bays that repeated the order of the shorter segments, except for the central, larger bay that held the door, capped by an arched pediment that was itself crowned by a sort of lantern (*pot-à-feu*). The regular rhythm of the bays repeated itself on the second tier with two arched windows that recalled those of the lower level on a lesser scale. It is difficult to know precisely the number of sides to the building. Were there eight or twelve? Despite these admirable qualities, contemporary Catholics mocked the building. The unusual form of this house of worship undoubtedly astonished them. Simon de Marchand, a bourgeois of Caen, noted the following in his diary in 1612:

> The Huguenots have put up a building for their worship services; we call it "pie" (*godiviau*) because it is constructed in the shape of a pasty.[25]

This type of plan can also be found in Normandy, at Le Petit-Quevilly near Rouen, where the temple was a dodecahedron nearly thirty meters long and twenty-two meters at its maximum height, lighted by sixty openings — square double windows surmounted by a dormer window for each segment.

25. "Les huguenots ont fait faire une maison pour faire leur presche que nous appelons godiviau parce que il est fait en façon de un pastey." Mentioned by Sophronyme Beaujour, *Histoire de l'Eglise réformée de Caen* (Caen: Le Gost-Clerisse, 1877), citing a manuscript in the Bibliothèque Municipale of Caen.

143

46. The temple of Le
Petit-Quevilly near
Rouen (engraving)

[The Huguenots] had built a structure that was among the most peculiar in France; this was their temple *(Prêche)*. This edifice was dodecahedral, that is to say, of twelve equal faces; a three-story gallery ran around the inside; it [the building] had . . three double doors; it was illuminated by sixty windows . . . ; it was not supported by pillars, although it was entirely timberwork; the crown, at which all the timbers joined, enclosed the upper portion of the structure. Gigonday was the carpenter who contracted to do it; he began in 1600 and finished in 1601.[26]

As the engraving (see fig. 46)[27] shows, the walls of the structure, set upon a solid foundation, much as at Dieppe, were done in half timber.

The *grand temple* of La Rochelle was also part of this assemblage of polygonal edifices founded on a centralized plan. Although its construction had been decided already in 1577 and begun the same year, when Henry I

26. "[Les Huguenots] avoient bâti un ouvrage des plus curieux qui fut en France; c'étoit leur *Prêche*. Cet édifice étoit en dodécaèdre, c'est-à-dire, de douze pans égaux, autour duquel régnoit en dedans une galerie à triple étage; il avoit . . . trois portes à deux battants; il étoit éclairé de 60 fenêtres . . . ; il n'étoit soutenu d'aucun piller, quoiqu'il fut tout de charpente; une clef de bois, à laquelle toutes les autres venoient rendre, en fermoit le comble. Le Charpentier qui l'entreprit s'appeloit Gigonday; il le commença en 1600 et fut achevé en 1601." Farin, pt. 5, p. 146.

27. This print comes from Philippe Le Gendre, *Histoire de la persécution faite à l'Eglise de Rouën sur la fin du dernier siècle* (Rotterdam, 1704). The book also includes a plan of the temple. The latter illustration confirms that the structure was built according to a perfectly centralized plan.

144

of Bourbon, prince of Condé, laid the first stone, the temple was only a reality beginning in 1600 as proven by the contracts between the church elders and the stonecutters. The building, thirty *pieds* (9.6 m.) high, was girded inside and outside by an entablature in the form of a cornice. On each of the four principal sides were a door and two windows and, on each of the smaller sides, a window with a stone mullion. Three of the doors, twelve *pieds* high by seven *pieds* wide (nearly 3.9 m. by 2.25 m.), were framed by fluted pilasters crowned "by pedestals, molding and capitals, architrave, frieze, [and] cornice."[28] Access was by way of a perron, which was six *pieds* (about 1.9 m.) wide and seven *pieds* (2.4 m.) high. It formed a double stairway of seven steps with a *garde-corps*. The fourth and simplest door, because it faced the adjoining houses, was also the smallest: six and a half *pieds* by three *pieds* (a little more than 2 m. by nearly 1 m.). The windows, fifteen *pieds* high by six *pieds* wide (4.8 m. by about 1.9 m.), were raised twelve or thirteen *pieds* (3.85 m. or 4.14 m.) above the ground. The contractors committed themselves to completing the work at a cost of forty thousand livres (of which the lead roofing undoubtedly absorbed a major portion) in eight months. The first worship service, however, did not take place until 7 September 1603.

When Elie Brackenhoffer, a resident of Strasbourg, visited La Rochelle on 11 March 1645, the Catholics had taken over the temple after the siege and capture of the town.

> They [the inhabitants of La Rochelle] previously had a temple, which had cost about 100,000 *livres* (this I learned from an extremely old man who was in a good position to know); today they witness its occupation by papists.[29]

The alleged sum of one hundred thousand livres, at least two and a half times the actual cost, is highly revealing, especially in its excessiveness, of the importance attached to the temple. Above all, the Alsatian visitor has left us a fine description of the building and even a sketch of its plan.

> The most important of the churches is St. Barthélemy, which was formerly the temple. It is an octagon, yet irregular, because two of the faces are a little longer than the six others. There are no buttresses or pillars, but the (wooden) ceiling is a rounded vault, attached to the roofing. The roof is quite remarkable; it is entirely covered with lead. The rest of the building, the most stylish and prettiest in the world, is constructed of

28. ". . . de pieds d'estras [piédestals], bosse et chapiteaux, équitrave [architrave], frize, corniche. . ."

29. "Ils avaient autrefois un temple qui avaient coûté environ 100,000 livres (ce que je tiens d'un homme fort âgé et très bien placé pour le savoir); ils le voient aujourd'hui occupé par les papistes." Brackenhoffer, p. 91. After the siege of 1628, the temple fell to the Catholics and was set up as a cathedral. It was destroyed in a suspicious fire on 9 February 1687.

47. The *grand temple* of La Rochelle. From a nineteenth-century rendering.

beautiful dressed stone. There are doors and windows on four sides; there is also a spiral stone staircase, which provides access to a small lantern and from there onto the roof. After the capture of the town, Richelieu said the first mass there.[30]

The absence of interior pillars or supports drew the admiration of contemporaries, who frequently remarked upon this special feature.

Finally, the drawing of the elevation of the temple (see fig. 47), which has been reprinted many times, provides an opportunity to complete the description. Large double-fluted pilasters, raised on plinths, accentuated each corner. The arrangement recaptured and emphasized the order of the entry doors. Pilasters also framed the windows. A large sculpted frieze encircled the building and served as a window ledge. Another sculpted band

30. "La plus importante des églises est S. Barthélémy, qui était autrefois le *temple*. C'est un octogone, mais pas régulier, car des deux côtés, les murs sont un peu plus longs que les six autres. Il n'y a pas de contreforts ou de piliers, mais le plafond (en bois) est une voûte arrondie, appliquée sur le comble. Le toit est très remarquable; il est entièrement recouvert de plomb. Le reste du bâtiment est élevé en belles pierres de taille, le plus coquettement et le plus joliment du monde. Sur quatre côtés, il y a des portes et des fenêtres; quelque part, il y a un escalier de pierre en colimaçon, qui donne accès à un petite lanterne, et de là au toit. Après la prise de la ville, Richelieu a dit là la première messe." Brackenhoffer, p. 94.

146

encircled the upper part of the edifice; corbels or consoles crowned it at roof level. The physiognomy of the building, like the architectural and ornamental vocabulary employed here, derives from the Renaissance. Scholars have, without documentary proof, advanced the name of Philibert de l'Orme as the designer. Anthony Blunt, who refers to the artist in his study,[31] gives no hint about the source for his attribution. There was a noticeable stylistic lag between the architecture of the temple and the beginning of the seventeenth century when it was constructed. This proves little regarding the structure's attribution to Philibert de l'Orme, but may take account of an increasingly archaic architectural style or one drawing its forms from models that were no longer current, with frequent, unmistakable lags between Paris and the provinces.

The temple of Montauban was also built according to a centralized plan, although it is difficult to say whether it was polygonal or circular. The contract[32] signed in 1615 between the municipal consuls and the Toulousain architect Levesville (who was then working on rebuilding the town's central place, which fire had partially destroyed) reveals a building seven *cannes* (nearly 13 m.) high with two spiral staircases, twelve *palmes* (nearly 2.8 m.) wide set in turrets. Four doors, placed symmetrically two by two, offered access to the building. The principal entry had a grand doorway, partly brick, partly stone that was eighteen *palmes* high and eleven wide (about 4.15 m. by 2.5 m.); the three others were arched and measured ten *palmes* high by seven wide (2.3 m. by 1.6 m.). Pilasters with base, capitals, architrave, frieze, and cornice framed the grand doorway. These elements were themselves accentuated by the presence of monumental pilasters, each four *palmes* (0.92 m.) wide, which extended the entire height of the building and were in harmony with the vigor of the principal facade. Sixteen splayed windows, which allowed a maximum of light into the interior of the temple, were distributed around the structure. Their form was left to the discretion of the builder — "ovals or squares or the form that one will find the most agreeable."[33] As at La Rochelle, no interior pillars stood between pastor and congregation.

The temple of Grenoble, which the invaluable Brackenhoffer again described, was similar.

> The city has many monasteries and churches. . . . Of these churches, buildings or monasteries, the most beautiful of all is the Calvinists' temple and as I have heard said, it is the most beautiful church[34] in all of

---

31. Anthony Blunt, *Philibert de l'Orme* (London: A. Zwemmer, 1958).

32. For further details and the archival references, see Hélène Guicharnaud, *Montauban au XVIIe, Urbanisme et Architecture* (Paris: Picard, 1991), pp. 93-99.

33. ". . . en ovalles ou carrees ou de la forme que on trouvera estre plus agreable."

34. In this instance, the term "church" ought to be understood as a structure for worship. The temple is being compared here to churches and monasteries.

Dauphiné. It is constructed in the manner and style of the temple of La Rochelle — octagonal. It has no columns in the interior; the ceiling or roof is round, like a vault but it is done completely in wood.[35]

Materials

The geographic diversity of the examples we have considered suggests that the choice of structural materials depended greatly upon local tradition: quarried stone from the Île-de-France at Charenton; brick at Montauban; flint, brick, and wood at Dieppe and at Le Petit-Quevilly, for example. It was the same for the roof: slate at Mens-en-Trièves and Dieppe, tiles at Lasalle. La Rochelle, with its extremely costly leaded roof, opted for a patently luxurious solution.

Galleries

Whatever the type of plan adopted, one constant can be found throughout the kingdom, from north to south, east to west: the presence of galleries. It was not a question of balconies or triforia as in Catholic churches. These were actual galleries that rested on corbels and encircled the edifice, thereby increasing its capacity. Again, the Charenton temple of Salomon de Brosse (see fig. 48) is the best example with its elaborate two-story galleries. Still, Ablon and the first temple at Charenton had galleries too. They could be found as well in the temple of La Villeneuve at La Rochelle, the *grand temple* of Montpellier, in those of Dieppe, Le Petit-Quevilly, and Montauban. At Mens-en-Trièves in Dauphiné, they served to increase the seating capacity when the provincial synod decided to meet there in 1673.[36] The galleries could, as at Saumur (see fig. 49), vary in width (1.6 m. to 4.8 m.) and have differing numbers of rows of benches. A visitor's report (*procès-verbal de visite*) of February 1679 reported the arrangement in precise detail. Above and to the left, six rows of benches were arranged in amphitheatric fashion along the wall of the building, offering the best sight and hearing to the faithful seated in the back. Below in the center, two rows of benches were again placed in an amphitheatric order, and the pulpit, located on the north wall, was crowned by a canopy. Note that the galleries had an extremely varied and irregular arrangement. This arrangement,

---

35. "La ville a beaucoup de couvents et d'églises. . . . De ces églises, édifices ou couvents, le plus beau de tous est le temple des Calvinistes et comme je l'ai entendu dire, il serait la plus belle église de tout le Dauphiné. Elle est construite à la manière et sur le plan du temple de La Rochelle: octogone. Elle n'a pas de colonnes à l'intérieur; le ciel ou toit est de forme arrondie, comme une voûte mais tout est en bois." Brackenhoffer, p. 93.

36. At Mens-en-Trièves, where the temple was rebuilt after a fire in 1650, it was decided to enlarge it and construct a gallery to house the provincial synod of 1673.

148

48. The temple of Charenton, interior view. Seventeenth-century engraving by Jean Marot.

applied to longitudinal and centralized plans, assembled the maximum number of worshipers under optimal hearing conditions. No visual or acoustical obstacle stood between preacher and congregation. Brackenhoffer, the Strasbourg resident who visited Charenton in 1645, remarked in his travel notes that "in the center there are no columns; the central space is free and open; the faithful have nothing to block their view."[37]

Decorative Elements

Certain decorative elements completed the appearance of the temple in the seventeenth century. They were of both a civil and religious nature. The great arch of the *grand temple* at Montpellier bore the coat of arms and heraldic device of François de Châtillon, governor of Montpellier at the time of the temple's construction. The royal arms, a sure sign of Huguenot loyalty, adorned the two temples of La Rochelle, the temple at Marennes, and that of Montauban where the municipal coat of arms also appeared.

37. "au milieu il n'y a pas de colonnes, mais tout l'espace est libre et vide et les auditeurs n'ont rien devant les yeux."

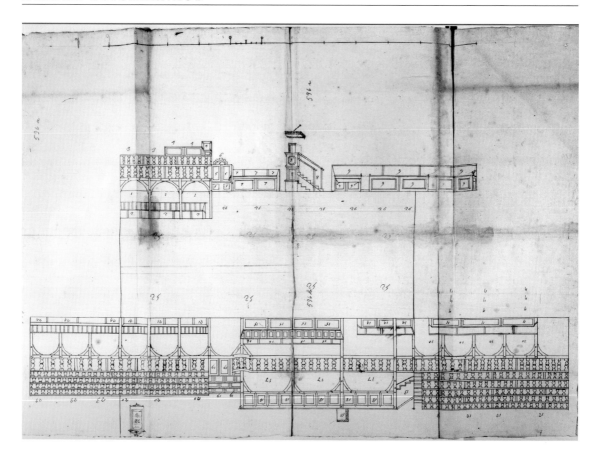

49. The temple of Saumur (a "flattened" interior view) ca. 1679-80.

On a religious plane, the tables of the Law occupied a prominent place. The *Mercure galant* indicated that at Charenton

> There was a great nave or ceiling on which were the Tables of the Old and New Testaments, written in gold letters on a blue background, and which had been painted directly on the ceiling paneling of the nave.[38]

At Poitiers, a contract dated 24 April 1600 between the consistory and the mason hired to whitewash the temple specified that this worker was obliged to reserve a space of one square *toise* (about 4 sq. m.) on the wall, which he was to coat with whitewash, so that the Commandments could be painted there. This directive in the text of the contract reveals the importance accorded to the presence of the Tables of the Law. Scriptural quotations composed in French and drawn from both the Old and New Testaments sometimes accompanied the Tables. These biblical verses were placed symbolically

38. "Il y avoit une grande nef ou plafond dans laquelle estoient les Tables du Vieux et du Nouveau Testament, écrites en lettres d'or sur un fond bleu, qui avoit été peint exprès sur les lambris de la voûte de ladite nef."

above the doors, the points of passage in and out of the temple. Again at Charenton, there were inscriptions above the two main doors.

> Quiconque veut venir après moi qu'il renonce à soi mesme, et qu'il charge sur soi sa croix et qu'il me suive; Si nous souffrons avec luy, nous règnerons aussy avec luy; Ne crains point petit troupeau, car le bon plaisir de vostre père a esté de vous donner le royaume; Mes brebis oyent ma voix et je les cognois et elles me suivent.[39]

At Montauban, inscribed in gilded characters on a black marble plaque, were the words:

> Ouvrez les portes de justice et j'y entreray et célebray l'Eternel; c'est la porte de l'Eternel, les justes y entreront.[40]

Sources and Innovation

These temples, as is well known, were rapidly demolished in the late seventeenth century. Two great successive waves of persecution during the 1660s and in the early 1680s, before the Revocation for the most part, led to the destruction of temples that had only been built several decades earlier.

If the Protestants did not create wholly new forms, they adopted plans inspired by antiquity and the high Middle Ages. These plans, basilican and centralized, were rediscovered and infused with new life by the architects of the Renaissance. Sebastiano Serlio's *Quinto libro d'architettura*, which Jean Martin had translated into French by mid–sixteenth century,[41] is especially eloquent on the subject. The author defines the principle of the architect-theoretician at the very beginning of the work.

> I shall design mine [temples, which must be understood here as "church" in a general sense] in the simplest manner possible, so that they can be built at the lowest cost and in the least amount of time.[42]

---

39. "If any man would come after me, let him deny himself and take up his cross and follow me" (Mark 8:34). "If we endure, we shall also reign with him" (2 Tim. 2:12). "Fear not, little flock, for it is your Father's good pleasure to give you the kingdom" (Luke 12:32). "My sheep hear my voice, and I know them, and they follow me" (John 10:27).

40. "Open the gates of righteousness, and I may enter through them and give thanks to the Lord. This is the gate of the Lord; the righteous shall enter through it" (Ps. 118:19-20).

41. Sebastiano Serlio, *Quinto libro d'architettura di Sebastiano Serlio Bolognese, nel quale se tratta di diverse forme de Tempii sacri secondo il costumo christiano, e al modo antico. Traduit en François par Jan Martin* (Paris: M. de Vascosan, 1547).

42. "Je disposeray les miens selon la plus simple maniere que possible me sera, a ce qu'on les puisse expedier a peu de fraiz et en la [*sic*] moindre espace de temps que faire ce pourra." Serlio, p. 3v.

151

The simplicity of the building plan facilitated construction and reduced costs. In addition, the architect goes on to propose a variety of structures based on a centralized plan and offers numerous examples with striking imagination. For the roofing, while Serlio recommends local materials, he does not hide his preference for lead.

> The roofing of this temple ought to be made from materials that will be easily found in the region where it will be built; still, lead would be better than any other material.[43]

And, after having offered many examples of centralized structures, he concludes:

> The preceding has treated the diverse forms of temples suitable to the customs among Christians such as ourselves in observing the manner of the ancients and without departing from the round or the square. But now I will specify several that better conform to use by the congregation.[44]

He then presents the more traditional plans.

Still, these two types of architectural plans, basilican and centralized, derived from antiquity and transmitted within a learned tradition, were adapted and modified for the construction of buildings suited to the Reformed worship service. If the Protestant temples, especially the most elaborate among them, were raised above ground level (access was by several stairs or a perron), the number of doors, which would facilitate the fluidity of movement for entry and exit, was important. The means of illuminating the interior of the structure should also be underscored. The windows were numerous, of substantial dimensions, and fitted with clear glass or occasionally stained glass that displayed the coats of arms of prominent members of the community. Nothing here compares with the stained glass windows of medieval and later Catholic churches, even if we recognize that beginning in the Renaissance clear glass was often used in Catholic churches. In addition, the temple windows sometimes had shutters, which could be closed.

As previously noted, the utilization of common local building materials was frequent. Finally, the ceiling differed from traditional methods of vaulting, both as an economy measure and because the system of tim-

---

43. "La couverture de ce Temple soit faicte de la matiere qui se trouvera plus commode au païs ou il sera basti: toutefois elle seroit meilleure de plomb que d'autre chose." Serlio, p. 4r.

44. "Cy dessus a esté traicté de diverses formes de Temples, accomodées a la coustume d'entre nous Chrétiens: en observant touteffois la maniere des antiques, et sans me departir du rond ou du quarré. Mais maintenant i'en specifieray quelques uns plus conformes a l'usance commune." Serlio, p. 25v.

bering (at Montpellier and Orange) or paneling (at La Rochelle, Montauban, Grenoble, and Charenton) allowed rapid construction. By way of proof, construction time was less than two years between the laying of the foundation stones and the inaugural sermon, assuming normal building conditions.

Conclusion

The various examples presented in this essay of Protestant temples constructed prior to the Revocation in France offer the opportunity for some final reflections. The first order of business for architects and contractors was to create a structural arrangement that would be well suited to the sermon service, that most important and elementary feature of Reformed worship. They strove to eliminate any possible obstacle between preacher and congregation. Visitors to the French temples, for instance, nearly always commented upon — and frequently emphasized — the absence of interior pillars. A related element and yet another distinctive feature of these buildings was the systematic use of galleries. Although galleries were usually one story, in some temples, notably Charenton, they were multistoried. Occasionally, such as at Saumur, the width of the galleries also varied. In every instance the presence of galleries allowed for a significant increase in the capacity of the temple.

If the Reformers enjoyed particular success in designing temples that were well adapted to the sermon service, they were not allowed nearly so free a hand in choosing the geographic locale for constructing their houses of worship. Site selection depended upon precise criteria contained in the Edict of Nantes. The Edict, moreover, stipulated that the Protestant temple must not be confused with the Catholic church. The Protestant edifices were required to conform then to certain internal requirements as well as the external demands of the crown. Still, the temples built prior to the Revocation of the Edict of Nantes offer a wide diversity, and the reasons for this variety are multiple.

The individual character of some temples — La Rochelle, Charenton, and Montauban, for example — was a function of their architects. The greatest architects of the time — Jacques II Androuet du Cerceau and Salomon de Brosse — designed the successive temples constructed at Charenton. These men were also employed for royal building projects. And when they erected the Protestant temples, Androuet du Cerceau, de Brosse, and others drew upon a learned or "savant" style of architecture, one closely connected to their culture. They created centralized plans at La Rochelle and Montauban, and a basilican plan at Charenton, which probably recalled the temple of Jerusalem, even if the reference is never made specific. Other temples represented the transposition (adapted, as always,

153

to the needs of Reformed worship) of "popular" architectural forms and were the work of local carpenters and masons. Naturally, there was a range of intermediary edifices between the extremes of these forms of architectural inspiration.

Whether the architect came from a learned tradition or not, the systematic utilization of local building materials is striking everywhere among French Protestants. The constant recourse to local and thus readily available materials allowed for rapid construction at the lowest cost. The temple decoration also possessed a number of local, civil elements. Decoration occasionally included the arms of the local élite, the municipal arms, or even the royal arms. The latter reaffirmed in visible fashion Reformed loyalty to the French monarchy. Many temples had a combination of these different decorative details. In addition, religious decoration such as biblical inscriptions was often affixed to the interior walls, and there was always a Decalogue Board.

In the end, the Protestant temples constructed in France before the Revocation of the Edict of Nantes provide an enormous architectural diversity. At the same time, many commonalities, traits shared by most all temples, attest their membership in a single Reformed community.

Selected Bibliography

Beaujour, Sophronyme. *Histoire de l'Eglise réformée de Caen.* Caen: Le Gost-Clerisse, 1877.

Benedict, Philip. "Rouen dans la tourmente (milieu XVIe siècle–milieu XVIIe siècle." In *Histoire de Rouen,* edited by Michel Mollat, pp. 179-203. Toulouse: Privat, 1979.

———. *Rouen during the Wars of Religion.* Cambridge: Cambridge University Press, 1981.

Biéler, André. *Liturgie et architecture. Le temple des chrétiens.* Geneva: Labor et Fides, 1961.

Borrel, Abraham. *Histoire de l'église réformée de Nîmes depuis son origine en 1533 jusqu'à la loi organique du 18 germinal an X.* 1844. 2nd ed. Toulouse: Société des livres religieux, 1856.

Brackenhoffer, Elie. *Voyage de Paris en Italie (1644-1646).* Translated by Henry Lehr. Paris: Berger-Levrault, 1927.

Bulletin de la Société de l'Histoire du Protestantisme Français (BSHPF). (1852-present).

Cambolive, Etienne. *Histoire de divers événemens contenant en abrégé les persécutions exercées en France.* Amsterdam, 1698.

Ciprut, Edouard-Jacques. "Le premier grand temple de Charenton." *Bulletin de la Société de l'Histoire du Protestantisme Français* 114 (1968): 106-12.

Coope, Rosalyn. *Salomon de Brosse and the Development of the Classical Style in*

French Architecture from 1565 to 1630. University Park: Pennsylvania State University Press, 1972.

Delort, André. *Mémoires inédits d'André Delort sur la ville de Montpellier au XVIIe siècle: 1621-1693.* Montpellier: C. Coulet, 1876, 1 vol.; J. Martel aîné, 1876-78, 2 vols.

Désert, Gabriel, ed. *Histoire de Caen.* Toulouse: Privat, 1981.

Farin, François. *Histoire de la ville de Rouen.* 6 pts. in 2 vols. Rouen: Louis du Souillet, 1731.

Guibert, Michel Claude. *Mémoires pour servir à l'histoire de la ville de Dieppe.* With an introduction by Michel Hardy. Dieppe: A. Renaux, 1878.

Guicharnaud, Hélène. *Montauban au XVIIe, Urbanisme et Architecture.* Paris: Picard, 1991.

Jourdan, Jean-Baptiste-Ernest. *La Rochelle historique et monumentale.* La Rochelle: A. Siret, 1884.

Le Gendre, Philippe. *Histoire de la persécution faite à l'Eglise de Rouën sur la fin du dernier siècle.* Rotterdam, 1704.

Lhermet, Pasteur Raoul. *Nîmes, cité protestante.* Nîmes: Imprimerie Chastanier, 1959.

Ménard, Léon. *Histoire des évêques de Nîmes où l'on voit ce qui s'est passé de plus mémorable . . .* 2 vols. The Hague, 1737.

Pannier, Jacques. *Un architecte français au commencement du XVIIe siècle: Salomon de Brosse.* Paris: Librairie Centrale d'Art et d'Architecture, 1911.

Perrot, Jean-Claude. *Cartes-plans, dessins et vues de Caen antérieures à 1789.* Inventaire de collections publiques françaises (extracted from the *Bulletin de la Société des Antiquaires de Normandie,* 1961-62).

Robillard de Beaurepaire, Eugène de. *Caen illustré, son histoire, ses monuments.* Caen: F. Leblanc-Hardel, 1896.

Rogère, Claude. *Dieppe.* Ingersheim: Editions S.A.E.P., 1972.

Saint-Blanquat, Agnès de. *Les protestants et les pouvoirs à Caen et en Basse-Normandie XVI-XVIIe siècles.* Exposition catalogue. Caen: Archives Départementales de Calvados, November 1972.

Travers, Emile. "Notes sur quelques temples de Basse-Normandie." In *Congrès archéologique de France,* pp. 270-94. Besançon, 1891.

Vitet, Louis. *Histoire de Dieppe.* Paris: C. Gosselin, 1864.

Appendix 1

"Les temples que Dieu aime ce ne sont point ces temples superbes dont les voûtes haut eslevées retentissent, qui sont soustenus de longs rangs de colomnes, dont le pavé reluit de marbre de diverses couleurs, et les murailles de dorures et d'images. C'est là où volontiers se nichent les diables. . . . De mesme nature sont les temples magnifiques où les âmes ne sont point repues et sustentées d'aucune nourriture spirituelle. . . . C'est une foible objection que nous font nos adversaires quand ils nous opposent la grandeur et beauté de leurs temples et comparent les lieux où nous preschons à des granges ou à des nids à rats. . . . L'Eglise est une imitation du ciel non à cause que les temples ont des voûtes azurées et marquetées d'estoiles mais à cause que le soleil de l'Evangile y reluit; . . . la verité n'est point attachée à des pierres et ne demande pas un grand lustre exterieur." Pierre du Moulin, *Décades de Sermons,* quoted in Jacques Pannier, *L'église réformée de Paris sous Henri IV* (Paris: Honoré Champion, 1911), p. 459.

Appendix 2

Although Rosalyn Coope, in *Salomon de Brosse,* takes note of the specifications for the masonry and timbering of the second temple of Charenton, she does not publish the documents. She also gives the wrong shelf mark. Under the circumstances, it seems advisable to summarize the first and more interesting of the two lists of specifications.

Paris, Archives Nationales, M.C., CV, 350, 27 juin 1623, *Devis des ouvrages de maçonnerie pour la construction du bastiment du temple a Charenton Saint Maurice:*

"Les fondations des murs du dehors et du dedans pour porter les colonnes seront démolies, en leur place sera posée une autre fondation à bon moellon chaux sable de rivière pour le grand mur du dehors de 4 pieds [1.28 m] d'épaisseur jusqu'à 4 pouces [10.8 cm] au-dessus du rez-de-chaussée. Les fondations intérieures pour porter les colonnes auront 2 pieds ½ [0.8 m] d'épaisseur.

"Sur la fondation de 4 pieds [c'est à dire la fondation du mur extérieur] sera élevé le corps du mur de 3 pieds 6 pouces d'épaisseur [1.12 m] en sa première assise sur 3 pieds [0.96 m] sous l'entablement. Ce mur aura 4 toises ½ [environ 8.8 m] de hauteur. Le pied de ce mur sera construit par le dehors de trois assises de pierre de taille, de pas moins de 12 pouces [32.4 cm] de haut chacune; leurs joints seront de qualité et chacune de ces assises aura 1 pouce ½ [4 cm] de retrait l'une sur l'autre. Les encoignures seront de pierre dure de 6.5 et 4 pieds de long [1.92 m; 1.6 m; 1.28 m] afin de pouvoir supporter le fardeau, résister aux poussées de la charpente.

"Toutes les portes, fenêtres, lucarnes, entablements, plinthes, voussures seront de pierre de taille. Le reste sera fait de bon moellon, chaux, sable de rivière, enduit par le dedans de plâtre; par le dehors aussi de chaux, sable de rivière.

"Les colonnes, à l'intérieur du temple, faites de pierre dure bien nette et bien taillée de 2 pieds [0.64 m] de diamètre à l'assise, seront posées sur la maçonnerie; elles auront une base naissante du sol et un chapiteau d'ordre dorique. Les colonnes et les autres ouvrages de pierre dure de taille seront bien assis, maçonnés, coulés de bon mortier.

"Il sera refait l'aire du temple et des galeries basses de grand pavé de pierre dure bien proprement taillée, assise garnie coulée. L'entrepreneur pourra se servir du vieux pavé pour enpaver autour des murs du temple. Si les marches des galeries basses se trouvaient brûlées, corrompues, gâtées, il en sera fourni de neuves, bonnes.

"Il sera fait deux planchers aux deux galeries hautes, qui seront tamponnés, ourdis de plâtres et enduits dessus et dessous. Les sabliers qui courront de long du mur seront portés sur des corbeaux de fer.

"Il sera fait quatre escaliers aux quatre angles du temple de plâtre, plâtras, enduits dessus et dessous; ils monteront jusqu'à la dernière galerie haute. Leurs quatre premières marches seront de pierre dure de largeur convenable.

"Les perrons de l'entrée du Temple seront refaits de bonne pierre dure, de celle qui y est maintenant ou d'autre si elle se trouve gâtée.

"Tous les ouvrages ci-dessus et le lambris de tout le plafond du comble sur lattes clouées seront faits par les entrepreneurs bien loyalement, gardant et observant soigneusement les épaisseurs, hauteurs, proportions. Les entrepreneurs sont tenus de travailler avec la plus grande diligence possible et 'la plus grande quantité d'ouvriers que faire se pourra' . . . 'qu'il sera rendu en estat pour y livrer le comble devant le present d'octobre.'

" 'L'entrepreneur prendra tous les matériaux du vieil temple dont il se pourra servir et ne pourra ny pretendre ny toucher aux desmolitions et matériaux des autres bastimens.' "

Appendix 3

Brackenhoffer, Elie. *Voyage de Paris en Italie (1644-1646)*. Translated by Henry Lehr. Paris: Berger-Levrault, 1927.

The Alsatian traveler Elie Brackhoffer, in the company of the baron of Rakonitz and his intendant, visited Charenton on Sunday, 15 January 1645. He described the temple as follows.

"Le premier des édifices, c'est l'église réformée, bâtie il n'y a pas longtemps. Elle est quadrangulaire, oblongue; elle repose sur vingt colonnes de pierre disposées tout autour, dont huit aux deux bouts, et six sur chacun des autres côtés. Par contre, au milieu, il n'y a pas de colonnes, mais tout l'espace est libre et vide, et les auditeurs n'ont rien devant les yeux. Le plafond, au-dessus, s'applique, tout ovale et rond, en comble, comme dans le temple de Grenoble.

"Tout autour, il y a deux galeries l'une au-dessus de l'autre, qui sont assez larges et munies de sièges. L'église ayant des fenêtres des quatre côtés, est très claire; elle a trois portes, de sorte qu'on peut y entrer par tous les côtés. Elle est toute blanchie au plâtre, et n'a pas d'autres ornements, en peinture et moins encore en sculptures qu'en haut, sur la voûte, l'une en face de l'autre, des tables où sont peints dans l'une *les dix commandements,* dans l'autre *le symbole des Apôtres et l'oraison dominicale.* . . . L'église est capable de contenir de 800 à plus de 1,000 personnes. . . . Aux deux portes principales de ce bel édifice, il y a deux belles incriptions. Sur la première on lit: *Quiconque veut venir après moi, qu'il renonce à soi mesme, et qu'il charge sur soi sa croix et qu'il me suive* Marc 8-34. Item: *Si nous souffrons avec luy, nous règnerons aussy avec luy* Thim. 2–12. Sur l'autre porte figurent ces deux passages: *Ne crains point petit troupeau, car le bon plaisir de vostre père a esté de vous donner le royaume* Luc 12–32. *Mes brebis oyent ma voix et je les cognois et elles me suivent* Jean 10–27."

Appendix 4

Mercure galant
February 1686

"Le plan de ce temple etoit un quarré long, percé de trois portes, sçavoir une à chaque bout, et une au milieu des grandes faces. Il estoit éclairé par 81 croisées en trois étages, l'une dessus l'autre, élevées de 27 pieds [8.64 m] jusqu'à l'entablement. Il avoit de longueur 104 pieds [33.28 m] dans oeuvre, et 66 pieds [21.12 m], aussi dans oeuvre. Les murs avoient 3 pieds ½ [1.12 m] d'épaisseur par le dedans. Il y avoit une grande nef ou plafond dans laquelle estoient les Tables du Vieux et du Nouveau Testament, écrites en lettres d'or sur un fond bleu, qui avoit esté peint exprès sur les lambris de la voûte de ladite nef, laquelle estoit de 74 pieds [23.68 m] de long sur 35 pieds [11.2 m] de large, et au pourtour de laquelle estoient 20 colonnes d'ordre dorique de 21 pieds [6.72 m] de haut et qui formoient trois estages de galeries, au pourtour desquelles on montoit par quatre escaliers qui estoient dans lesdits angles. La charpenterie du comble du temple estoit d'un fort bel assemblage, et les bois d'une considérable longueur. Il y avoit un clocher dans lequel estoit une cloche de 3 pieds [0.96 m] de diamètre qui pesoit deux milliers [une tonne] environ. La lanterne de ce clocher estoit revestue de plomb et tout le reste du comble couvert de thuiles en pavillon."

Appendix 5

On 21 February 1679 and for several days thereafter, Alphonse Dutertre, royal judge for the seneschalsy, town, and jurisdiction of Saumur, visited the city's temple and composed the following description.

". . . il est de figure carrée long et il a de longueur 13 toizes 1 pied [25.67 m] sur 5 toizes 3 pieds de large [6.81 m] par lededans entre les murs."

On the south, "le mur est garny de deux galleries l'une sur l'autre en forme de tribune de 6 pieds [1.92 m] de hauteur chacune sur la largeur de 6 piedz et demy [2.08 m] et de 5 toizes [9.75 m] de longueur. Le restant [of the wall] et le retour qui est au bout vers le couschant sont des galleries d'environ 7 pieds de hault et de 9 pieds de large [2.24 m by 2.88 m] sur lesquelles sont quatre rangz de bancs en forme d'amphithéâtre."

On the east, "dans toute la largeur du temple est une gallerie de 7 pieds de hault et de 15 pieds de large [2.23 m by 4.8 m] sur laquelle sont six rangz de bancs en forme d'amphithéâtre."

On the north, "joignant la gallerie qui est du costé du couchant, dans l'estendue de 3 toizes [5.85 m] il y a une gallerie de 7 pieds de haut et 5 pieds de large [2.24 m by 1.6 m] sur laquelle il y a deux rangz de bancz aussy en amphithéâtre et au bout d'ycelle une chaize en forme de faulteuil. Du même côté et au milieu est une chaize a deux estage d'un assemblage de menuizerie avec un daix audessus. Dans le bas le long du mur du mesme costé sont des bancz avec des dossiez et priedieu audevant de menuizerie avec une estrade au bas de 5 poulces [13.5 m] de haulteur." Paris, Archives Nationales, TT 266, 598 à 605.

Another description of the Saumur temple, dated 1680, specified that the door was six *pieds*, seven *pouces* wide and eight *pieds* high [2.11 m by 2.54 m]. The door opened to a square vestibule that was six *pieds en carré* [1.92 m]. From there, a stairway led to the galleries. Paris, Archives Nationales, TT 266, 616 à 624.

Calvinism and the Visual Arts in Southern France, 1561 to 1685

MATTHEW KOCH

On 28 March 1838 the "diligence" that was transporting Stendhal from Agen to Toulouse stopped at Moissac to change horses. Stendhal had found Agen unappealing, but reacted very differently to Moissac:

> Lovely houses in brick; I should think myself in my beloved Lombardy. . . . I am delighted. Handsome mouldings and window frames. . . . The brick begins to renounce Gaulish ugliness. Agreeable overhanging roofs. That is always wanting in France.[1]

Stendhal did not think he had left France by entering Moissac: he was echoing a long-standing practice of using the name of the kingdom as a whole to refer only to its northern segment.[2] This custom points to significant cultural differences between northern and southern France, and for Stendhal the architecture of the Toulousain Midi was more akin to that of the Lombard plain than what he had seen in the Île-de-France.

The contemporary traveler can experience this difference between north and south from another perspective by visiting Montauban, a short distance south and east of Moissac. Montauban is one of the cities of southwestern France in which brick has long been the building material of choice, but the facade of its cathedral is white stone and contrasts sharply with the red brick

---

1. "Belles maisons en briques; je me crois dans ma chère Lombardie . . . je suis charmé. Belles moulures et cadres des fenêtres. . . . La brique engage à se départir de la laideur gauloise. Saillie convenable du toit sur le mur. Cela manque toujours en France." Stendhal, *Voyage dans le Midi de Bordeaux à Marseille* (Paris: Encre, 1979), pp. 69-70.

2. Cf. Jean Baumel, *Montpellier au cours des XVIe et XVIIe siècles: les guerres de religion* (Montpellier: Causse, 1976), p. 231; Henri Polge, "La cathédrale d'Auch," *Congrès archéologique de France* 128 (1970): 353; and Robert Mesuret, *Toulouse: métropole artistique de l'Occitanie* (Lunel: Saber, 1986), p. 7.

employed liberally elsewhere in the city. Moreover, the cathedral occupies a prominent site, towering over the city as one crosses the fourteenth-century Pont Vieux[3] or walks south along the Tarn River. Completed in the early eighteenth century, the cathedral[4] was a particularly monumental witness to the Catholic reconquest of Montauban, one of the most redoubtable strongholds of French Protestantism in the sixteenth and early seventeenth centuries. Since the cathedral's appearance and design were so foreign to the region, however — its facade paralleling that of Notre-Dame de Versailles — it could also be seen as a visible affirmation of the triumph of a central government located in the north over some of its most recalcitrant southern subjects. A distinction between northern and southern France can also be observed in painting: arriving in Rome in 1728, the Languedocien painter Pierre Subleyras was criticized by partisans of the rococo, then the fashionable style at the French court, for his rather severe, classicist approach to portraiture, a style he had developed at Toulouse under the guidance of Antoine Rivalz, an admirer of Nicolas Poussin.[5]

The stylistic dividing line between northern and southern France, however, was not nearly so sharp as Stendhal's remarks could lead one to believe. In emulating Poussin, Rivalz and Subleyras were hardly perpetuating a specifically Languedocien aesthetic, but rather were demonstrating that they remained loyal to a style that had once been in royal favor but was now no longer in vogue at the court. Like many Languedocien and Provençal artists, Rivalz and Subleyras were more attracted to Rome than Paris, giving the lie to the portrayal of the "provincial" as desperately eager to imitate every facet of courtly or Parisian behavior, a notion widely accepted at Paris during the reign of Louis XIV;[6] however, the predilection for Rome had been commonplace amongst northern artists too when the seat of the papacy had been more important than the French court as a source of patronage and hence as a center of artistic activity.[7] In the late seventeenth century, Jean de Troy developed at Montpellier and Toulouse

3. On this bridge, considered "une grant et notable chose" by Charles VI, see Mathieu Méras, "L'architecture de brique à Montauban et dans sa région," *Revue du Tarn*, 3rd ser., 53 (1969): 111.

4. On the history of the design and erection of Montauban's cathedral, see Robert Neuman, *Robert de Cotte and the Perfection of Architecture in Eighteenth-Century France* (Chicago: University of Chicago Press, 1994), p. 168, and Madeleine Huillet d'Istria, "L'art de François d'Orbay révélé par la cathédrale de Montauban," *XVIIe siècle* 72 (1966): 3-47.

5. Christian Peligry, Jean Penent, and Jean-Pierre Suzzoni, *Le portrait toulousain de 1550 à 1800: exposition présentée au Musée des Augustins du 21 octobre 1987 au 7 janvier 1988* (Toulouse: Loubatières, 1987), pp. 105, 116, 130.

6. Alain Corbin, "Paris-province," in *Les lieux de mémoire*, ed. Pierre Nora, 3 vols. (n.p.: Gallimard, 1984-92), vol. 3, pt. 1, pp. 778-82.

7. Alain Mérot, *La peinture française au XVIIe siècle* (n.p.: Gallimard/Electa, 1994), p. 12, and Jacques Bousquet, *Recherches sur le séjour des peintres français à Rome au XVIIème siècle* (Montpellier: ALPHA, 1980), pp. 55-57, 62 n. Bousquet claims that in the first two-thirds of

an idiosyncratic style in portraiture that paid little homage to what was then Parisian convention, but his younger brother François followed a very different path, moving from Toulouse to Paris and securing there the patronage of a courtly clientele; his work was very much to the taste of the court and the Parisian nobility of the robe, and indeed played an important role in eliciting enthusiasm for portraits which presented their sitters as figures from ancient Greek mythology.[8] Few portraits proclaim the triumph of Louis XIV's centralizing policies more lavishly than Hyacinthe Rigaud's 1702 depiction of the "Roi-Soleil," and Rigaud was still more popular at the court than François de Troy, yet Rigaud hailed from one of the most southerly reaches of the Midi, having been born in Perpignan in 1659, the year it was formally ceded to France, and had studied at Montpellier.[9] The artistic communities of north and south interacted extensively during the early modern period, and this stylistic commerce was not restricted to southern copying of models developed at the capital and court. These complex exchanges render the identification of a specifically southern style or "artistic geography"[10] problematic, but the issue is of importance in considering to what degree French Protestants had developed a distinctive aesthetic, for although French Protestantism was hardly exclusively a southern phenomenon, the majority of French Reformed of the sixteenth and seventeenth centuries resided in the Midi.[11]

Two issues, then, are to be explored here: I want to consider what if any forms a distinctively southern French culture and aesthetic took by the outset of the sixteenth century, and to what extent that identity was re-

---

the seventeenth century "la quasi-totalité des artistes français . . . va se mettre à l'école d'Italie."

8. Peligry, Penent, and Suzzoni, pp. 92-93, 96, 108, 114.

9. Rigaud's teacher at Montpellier was Antoine Ranc; one of his sons married Rigaud's niece and became a court painter at Madrid. Baumel, pp. 309, 312; Mérot, p. 204; Anthony Blunt, *Art and Architecture in France, 1500 to 1700*, rev. ed. (London: Penguin, 1982), pp. 398, 400-401; and Claude Colomer, *La famille et le milieu social du peintre Rigaud* (Perpignan: Sinthe, 1973), pp. 11, 14, 16-17, 20, 25-26, 30.

10. "géographie artistique." For the concept, see Enrico Castelnuovo and Carlo Ginzburg, "Domination symbolique et géographie historique dans l'histoire de l'art italien," trans. Dario Gamboni, *Actes de la recherche en sciences sociales*, no. 40 (November 1981): 51; in France, however, centers of artistic activity were not able to impose their values on their hinterlands as readily as Castelnuovo and Ginzburg claim they could in the Italian context, and their portrayal of artists of the peripheries as intrinsically inclined to be lacking in creativity is highly problematic. Jean-Marie Pérouse de Montclos provides a more satisfactory framework for understanding the interaction of artistic centers and peripheries, presenting what he describes as a "géotypologie" of French architectural forms. Montclos, *L'architecture à la française: XVIᵉ, XVIIᵉ, XVIIIᵉ siècles* (Paris: Picard, 1982), pp. 76, 199.

11. Janine Garrisson, *Protestants du Midi 1559-1598* (Toulouse: Privat, 1980), p. 335, and Philip Benedict, *The Huguenot Population of France, 1600-1685: The Demographic Fate and Customs of a Religious Minority* (Philadelphia: American Philosophical Society, 1991), pp. 7-8, 10, 77.

flected in the attitudes toward the arts articulated and fostered by southern French Protestants over the subsequent two centuries. Shared language and creed are two common foundations for regional or national identities,[12] but in the decidedly particularist context of the Midi, neither played that role more than briefly or marginally. Despite, and indeed perhaps to some extent because of, southern France's relatively numerous Protestants, the Catholics of the Midi were wanting in neither religious fervor nor political clout.[13] Each of the southern cities that was the seat of a *parlement* remained under Catholic control in the sixteenth and seventeenth centuries; Aix-en-Provence and Toulouse proved to be particularly ardent supporters of the Counter-Reformation.[14]

Regional distinctiveness, then, was not manifested in adherence to a single confession, but the Occitan language offered a more promising basis for the articulation or maintenance of a regional identity, and proved to be a useful resource for aristocrats who sought to emphasize their autonomy from the crown. Thus Jeanne d'Albret followed her 1566 interdiction of Catholicism in the kingdom of Navarre with measures designed to ensure that the New Testament and the Psalms as well as Calvinist liturgical texts were available to her subjects in the local dialect of Occitan, and with such action sought to strengthen the cultural boundary between her tiny realm and that of her French cousin; in the early seventeenth century the dissident aristocrats Henry II de Montmorency and Adrien de Monluc became major patrons of Occitan writing.[15] Local particularism was one of the most salient features of Occitan literature of the sixteenth and seventeenth centuries: "every region of our Gascogny claims that it alone speaks good Gascon," observed the Gimontois poet Guillem Ader, who then asked: "how am I to write a poem that will please everyone?"[16] Occitan was still the mother tongue of the majority of the inhabitants of southern France in

12. On the importance of what Partha Chatterjee calls the "spiritual" in the development of nationalism, see his *The Nation and Its Fragments: Colonial and Postcolonial Histories* (Princeton: Princeton University Press, 1993), p. 6.

13. Regarding painting in Provence, Marie-Paule Vial suggests that "on pourrait . . . supposer que les conflits religieux ont pu entraîner pour la communauté catholique la nécessité de manifester sa présence avec plus d'éclat." Vial, "Etats des lieux," in *La peinture en Provence au XVIᵉ siècle*, ed. Marie-Paule Vial, Marie-Claude Leonelli, and Hélène Pichou (Marseille: Rivages, 1987), p. 30.

14. Claire Dolan, *Entre tours et clochers: les gens d'église à Aix-en-Provence au XVIᵉ siècle* (Aix-en-Provence: Edisud, 1981), p. 241, and Robert Alan Schneider, *Public Life in Toulouse, 1463-1789: From Municipal Republic to Cosmopolitan City* (Ithaca: Cornell University Press, 1989), p. 91.

15. Robert Lafont, *Renaissance du Sud: essai sur la littérature occitane au temps de Henri IV* (n.p.: Gallimard, 1970), pp. 57-58, and Schneider, pp. 139-40, 148.

16. "Touts lous locs de noste Gascouigne/Se disputen deu boun Gascoun/Coum haré jou que ma besouigne/Pousque este au grat de tout lou moun?" Ader, *Poésies*, ed. A. Jeanroy and A. Vignaux (Toulouse: Privat, 1904), p. 2.

this period, but by 1550 it had been replaced by French as the language of administration virtually everywhere in the Midi. Vigorous efforts were undertaken to preserve Occitan as a literary language, but in the name of one of its local dialects rather than as a manifestation of participation in a larger regional culture; a grammar which aspired to demonstrate the fundamental unity of these dialects would not appear until the nineteenth century. The poets Ader and Pey de Garros presented themselves as advocates of Gascon, but Pèire Godolin's frame of reference was still more geographically circumscribed: he was the champion of "moundi," the variety of Occitan spoken at Toulouse.[17]

Such preoccupation with the local community was hardly unusual among early modern Europeans, but it distinguished the culture of southern France from that of the north, which had long been more politically integrated and more inclined to accept the cultural and political authority of the crown.[18] Strong municipal governments were a long-standing tradition in the Midi, and the extensive rural areas governed by southern French consulates were evidence of their enduring power; that so many of the revolts that accompanied the growth of absolutism in the early seventeenth century occurred in southern France was no coincidence, but rather evidence of the degree of indignation that a new approach to governance inattentive to local demands could arouse in the Midi.[19] The governing elites

17. Janine Estèbe and Robert Lafont, "Cris, révoltes et fureurs 1515-1660," in *Histoire d'Occitanie*, ed. André Armengaud and Lafont (n.p.: Hachette, 1979), pp. 480-82; Schneider, p. 156; Lafont, pp. 66, 69, 78, 86, 233, 236, 238, 240-41, 245, 264-65; and Hélène Merlin, "Langue et souveraineté en France au XVIIe siècle: la production autonome d'un *corps de langage*," *Annales* 49, no. 2 (March-April 1994): 374.

18. This integration was more than a web of patron and client relations centered on the monarch. Benedict Richard O'Gorman Anderson provides considerable insight into the growth and consolidation of national identities, but he ascribes too much importance to what he calls "print-capitalism" in the development of national consciousness, overlooking the extent to which imagined communities were fostered before as well as after the widespread introduction of mechanical printing in Europe and elsewhere by common devotional practices, public rituals, and the replication of common points of reference by the visual arts. "Print-capitalism" was, given its capacity to disseminate dissent, potentially more subversive than the sustaining of national community. Cf. Anderson, *Imagined Communities: Reflections on the Origin and Spread of Nationalism*, rev. ed. (London: New Left, 1991), pp. 33-35, 44, 77; Michèle Fogel, "Naissance d'une cérémonie," "Questions d'interprétation," in *Les cérémonies de l'information dans la France du XVIe au XVIIIe siècle*, ed. Michèle Fogel (n.p.: Fayard, 1989), pp. 136, 138, 416-17, 421, 425, 427-28; Gerard Nijsten, "The Duke and His Towns: The Power of Ceremonies, Feasts, and Public Amusement in the Duchy of Guelders," trans. Arnold Kreps and Frank van Meurs, in *City and Spectacle in Medieval Europe*, ed. Barbara Hanawalt and Kathryn Reyerson (Minneapolis: University of Minnesota Press, 1994), pp. 262-63; Claudio Lomnitz-Adler, *Exits from the Labyrinth: Culture and Ideology in the Mexican National Space* (Berkeley: University of California Press, 1992), pp. 295-96; Clifford Geertz, *Negara: The Theatre State in Nineteenth-Century Bali* (Princeton: Princeton University Press, 1980), pp. 103, 107; and Chatterjee, p. 6.

19. Yves-Marie Bercé, *Histoire des Croquants: études des soulèvements populaires au XVIIe siècle dans le Sud-Ouest de la France*, 2 vols. (Genève: Droz, 1974), 1:186-205, 2:689; Garrisson,

of southern communities were jealous of their autonomy and confident that they should be entrusted with a wide range of powers; hence when these elites became convinced that the Catholic Church was beset with serious problems, they were quite prepared to accept theological positions which called for an expanded role for themselves in ecclesiastical governance, having long sought to enhance the devoutness of their communities by encouraging preaching and regulating the religious orders within their walls as well as scrutinizing the moral probity of the laity.[20] At the outset of the sixteenth century, the most powerful families of southern communities sought legitimacy for their position through consultation of the heads of household of their consulate, relying on local consensus rather than a hierarchical chain of command. These elites were inclined to favor artistic endeavors which confirmed their importance and affirmed the cohesive and orderly character of their communities.

Local particularism, then, was fundamental to the cultural identity of the Midi. The decentralized character of southern French culture and the rivalries of adjoining consulates did not efface regional commonalities,[21] but the local orientation of the region's inhabitants undermined the articulation of a common cultural outlook for an area which extended from the Atlantic Ocean to the Alps and from the Mediterranean to the Massif Central. Provençal communities shared the attachment to local autonomy that was a central feature of regional identity in Guyenne and Languedoc, but in many other respects Provençal culture had little in common with that of the other provinces in which Occitan was widely spoken: as the work of Pierre Puget,

---

Protestants du Midi 1559-1598, pp. 185, 220-21; Estèbe and Lafont, pp. 421-25, 448-50, 456; and René Pillorget, *Les mouvements insurrectionnels de Provence entre 1596 et 1715* (Paris: Pedone, 1975), pp. 76, 1008-9. Pillorget suggests that in the early seventeenth century "la Provence peut . . . être considérée comme un ensemble de 650 à 700 républiques autonomes." "Absolutism" is not an altogether satisfactory label for the Crown's commitment to centralizing power and imposing religious uniformity, as it can be interpreted as indicating that the central government was able to rule without compromise, without recourse to intermediaries, or only with the aid of royal officeholders. The only viable alternative that has been proposed, however, "administrative monarchy," is still less satisfactory, failing to capture the aggressiveness of the central government's response to dissent in the seventeenth century. Cf. James Collins, *The State in Early Modern France* (Cambridge: Cambridge University Press, 1995), pp. 1-3, 185.

20. On municipal governments' encouragement of preaching in the Toulousain Midi, see Marie-France Godfroy, "Le prédicateur franciscain Thomas Illyricus à Toulouse," *Annales du Midi* 97, no. 170 (April-June 1985): 101-14. On the moral paternalism of Toulouse's Capitoulat, see Schneider, pp. 63-64, 68, 73.

21. On the complexity of loyalties and rivalries in Cerdaña, see Peter Sahlins, *Boundaries: The Making of France and Spain in the Pyrenees* (Berkeley: University of California Press, 1989), p. 112. The consulates of the Midi were relatively powerful municipal governments, but the local community was also important in northern France: see Jean-Pierre Gutton, *La sociabilité villageoise dans l'ancienne France: solidarités et voisinages du XVIe au XVIIIe siècle* (n.p.: Hachette, 1979).

the annunciation relief of Aix-en-Provence's Andrettes chapel (see plate 22), the theatricality of the choir at Trets, and the high altar of Saint-Maximin's basilica attested (see fig. 50), the largely stone architecture of Provence developed a baroque, Italianate character[22] as the seventeenth century progressed that demonstrated little of the severity characteristic of southwestern French buildings, and Calvinism was much less successful in Provence than in neighboring Bas-Languedoc. In much of Guyenne and Languedoc, however, local architecture and painting pointed toward a shared predilection for austerity, the widespread use of common materials and styles, and the affirmation of the autonomy and importance of the community. These practices and values

50. High altar of Basilique Royale, Saint-Maximin

22. Jean-Jacques Gloton, *Renaissance et Baroque à Aix-en-Provence: recherches sur la culture architecturale dans le Midi de la France de la fin du XVᵉ au début du XVIIIᵉ siècle*, 2 vols. (Roma: Ecole Française, 1979), 2:274, 345-46, 397-98. Parisian claims concerning the slavish devotion of the "provinces" to the culture supported by the court notwithstanding, the dominant idiom of Provençal ecclesiastical architecture in the late seventeenth century was not that of the classicist work then endorsed by the crown.

were shared by Catholics and Protestants; the champions of the two confessions are depicted by the poet Ader transcending their differences in the defense of Gascon culture.[23] This regional identity was undermined in the seventeenth century by internal social tensions, the centralizing agents of the crown, and the allure the increasingly powerful court culture had for southern elites, but the triumphant advance of centralism never altogether eclipsed the distinctiveness of the region's culture.[24]

Common Styles and Materials: Elements of a Regional Aesthetic

Stendhal found the roofs of Moissac to his liking, and generally broad, low-pitched coverings of canal tile have long been characteristic of southern architecture, contrasting with the preference of northerners for much steeper roofs covered with flat tiles, slate, or thatch. The use in southern cities of steep roofs and flat tiles, slate, or tiles "varnished in black" to resemble slate measured the dissemination of interest in imitating northern building styles. In the late fifteenth and early sixteenth centuries roofing "in the style of France" was fashionable in Guyenne; in the late seventeenth century an attempt was made to introduce steep northern roofs at Beaucaire and Montpellier, though such coverings were unsuited to weathering the mistral, and two of them were replaced in the eighteenth century.[25]

Stone was the preferred building material at Montpellier, Nîmes, and in Provence. The widespread use of brick as a building material was common to Catholic as well as Protestant communities of the Toulousain Midi, contributing to the distinct character of the region's architecture. Brick had been used for construction in the area since the Romans had ruled Toulouse, and had acquired prestige because of its prominent utilization in many of the region's most admired Romanesque and Gothic cathedrals, churches, and monasteries. Though brick was much less costly than stone in this region, it was hardly inexpensive, and by the fifteenth century the great majority of Toulouse's structures continued to be timber-frame. As French cities grew in the fifteenth and sixteenth centuries, the continuing prevalence of wood as a build-

23. Ader, pp. 149-57, and Lafont, p. 237.

24. To the northeast of Provence, the mountains and valleys of the Dauphiné were home to a large proportion of France's Protestants, but the early modern architecture of this area has not been explored sufficiently to permit its adequate incorporation here. On the size of the Dauphiné's Protestant population, see Benedict, *The Huguenot Population of France*, pp. 10, 60.

25. Montclos, pp. 43, 51; Bernard Sournia and Jean-Louis Vayssettes, *Montpellier: la demeure classique* (Paris: Imprimerie Nationale, 1994), p. 19; and Paul Roudié, "Bordeaux et la région bordelaise," in *La maison de ville à la Renaissance: recherches sur l'habitat urbain en Europe aux XVe et XVIe siècles,* ed. André Chastel and Jean Guillaume (Paris: Picard, 1983), pp. 46-47.

ing material led to the possibility of fire damage on a scale previously unseen. Toulouse suffered from cataclysmic fires in 1442 and 1463; the latter conflagration lasted over a fortnight, and two-thirds of the city was destroyed. Responding with characteristic lethargy to the threat of a repeat of the 1463 catastrophe, Toulouse's municipal government slowly articulated a building code over the next century, insisting in 1528 that common walls be constructed of brick and deciding in 1550 that all new structures had to be constructed of either brick or stone. Nonetheless, much of the city's housing continued to be timber-frame into the seventeenth century, plaster serving to conceal this situation superficially from the municipal government and its agents.[26] Concerning nearby Montauban, the author of an anonymous account of the 1621 siege of that city, probably the pastor Hector Joly, noted that most of the Protestant community's "buildings & edifices" had been "reconstructed in brick" during the rather peaceful period in Montauban's history that roughly corresponded with the reign of Henry IV and the first decade of his son's rule.[27] Many of the bricks employed in this rebuilding were salvaged from demolished Catholic churches and monasteries.[28]

The prominence of brick in the Toulousain Midi did not fail to attract the attention of visitors of the late fifteenth through seventeenth centuries.[29] The skill demonstrated by Toulousain masons in the application of brick to a wide variety of uses was admired by these travelers; although, as

26. Yves Bruand, "Institutions, urbanisme et architecture," Bruno Tollon, "La ville de brique: du grand incendie de 1463 aux projets d'urbanisme du XVIIIᵉ," and Michèle Eclache, "L'îlot et l'hôtel particulier à l'âge classique," in *Toulouse: les délices de l'imitation*, ed. Maurice Culot (Liège: Mardaga, 1986), pp. 9, 31-33, 40, 44; Georges Costa, "Briques apparentes et enduits dans l'architecture traditionelle de la région toulousaine," *Revue de l'Art*, nos. 58-59 (1983): 115, 119; and Maurice Bastide, "Un exemple de reconstruction urbaine: Toulouse après l'incendie de 1463," *Annales du Midi* 80, no. 1 (1968): 8. Brick was a fashionable building material in the Ile-de-France in the sixteenth and for much of the seventeenth centuries, but was used in combination with much larger quantities of stone than in the Midi, a style known as "brique et pierre." In any event, the quantity and quality of brick available in the vicinity restricted its utilization at Paris. Marie-Jeanne Dumont and Bernard Marrey, "Les origines," "A Paris, la Renaissance," in *La brique è Paris*, ed. idem (n.p.: Picard, 1991), pp. 20, 22, 25; Hilary Ballon, *The Paris of Henry IV: Architecture and Urbanism* (Cambridge, Mass.: MIT Press, 1991), pp. 72-76; David Thomson, *Renaissance Paris: Architecture and Growth, 1475-1600* (Berkeley: University of California Press, 1984), pp. 140, 142, 144, 146, 148; and Nathalie Prat, "La construction en brique," in *Toulouse: les délices de l'imitation*, ed. Maurice Culot (Liège: Mardaga, 1986), p. 318.

27. *Histoire particuliere des plus memorables choses qui se sont passees au siege de Montauban, & de l'acheminement d'icelui* (n.p., n.d.), p. 34. This work was first published in 1622 at Montauban, in an edition which claimed to have been published in Holland; several other editions were produced, including the one cited here, bearing neither a place of publication, printer, nor date. See Emerand Forestié, *Histoire de l'imprimerie et de la librairie à Montauban* (Montauban: Forestié, 1898), pp. 107-8.

28. Henry Le Bret, *Histoire de Montauban*, ed. Abbé Marcellin and Gabriel Ruck, 2 vols. (1668; Montauban: Rethoré, 1841), 2:366-69.

29. Bruand, p. 10, and Tollon, "La ville de brique," p. 40.

Stendhal observed, brick was as characteristic of the Lombard plain as of the Midi, the soft Toulousain variety allowed the region's artisans to achieve considerable virtuosity in shaping them into the ornamentation that their northern Italian counterparts executed in terra-cotta.[30]

The distinctiveness of southwestern architecture was also delineated prominently by the region's church towers. Two styles predominated. Unable to undertake the expense of constructing an elaborate church tower, many southwestern parishes opted for the "clocher-mur," a wall erected above the facade or entry to the choir of their church that was pierced by one or more arcades, within which the parish's bells were hung. Such "clocher-murs" adorned Romanesque churches of the Quercy from the eleventh century, but continued to be erected six hundred years later. A census of the simplest of these "clocher-murs," provided with but a single arcade, has never been published for France as a whole, but over two-thirds of the more elaborate "church towers with a horizontal peak" and "church towers with triangular gable" still extant are found in the Midi.[31] Wealthier parishes could afford to build a church tower modeled after the kind whose first fully developed manifestation appeared at Toulouse's Jacobin church in 1299, a structure strongly reminiscent of the tower provided for that city's Saint-Sernin church in 1130; until the First World War, the builders of cathedrals and churches in Gascony, Haut-Languedoc, and the Quercy repeatedly emulated the style developed at Toulouse. The "clocher toulousain" is octagonal in shape and two to four stories high; each face of the octagon on each level is in most cases adorned with two bays (see plates 23 and 24), but the Franciscans of Lavaur, Pamiers, Toulouse, and probably also Montauban sought to demonstrate the intensity of their devotion to apostolic poverty by erecting "clochers toulousains" which had but one bay on each face, contrasting with the Dominican preference for paired bays; this simplified version cost less to erect, and hence was also adopted by a number of rural parishes.[32] Toulouse's Nôtre-Dame du Taur church was provided with a "clocher-mur" whose design incorporated features of a typical "clocher toulousain": it

30. Tollon, "La ville de brique," p. 34, and Prat, pp. 319-20.

31. Denise Jalabert, *Clochers de France* (Paris: Picard, 1968), pp. 64-65; Pierre Gayne, *Dictionnaire des paroisses du diocèse de Montauban* (Montauban: Montmurat-Montauriol, 1978), pp. 18, 20, 25, 31-32, 135-40, 169-70, 199-200, 242-43, 253, 257-59, 282-83; René Fage, "Les clochers-murs de la France," *Bulletin monumental* 81 (1922): 310, 321-22, 322-23 n, 325; and Archives Départementales de Tarn-et-Garonne, Montauban (hereafter cited as ADTG), Fonds Serr, 1², no. 10.

32. Jalabert, pp. 31, 54, figs. 58, 110-13; Gayne, pp. 12, 34-35, 38-40, 93-94, 147, 159-60, 167, 171, 191-92, 202-3, 289; Raymond Rey, "Les clochers toulousains," *Gazette des Beaux-Arts*, 5th ser., 16, no. 779 (July-August 1927): 30-31, 35, 35 n, 40; and Jean Coppolani, "Les clochers toulousains," *Mémoires de la Société archéologique du Midi de la France* 31 (1965): 60, 63-67, 71. On the many variants departing from the typical Toulousain style but sharing prominent features with it which appeared in the region, see Coppolani, pp. 63-70.

was decorated with diamond-shaped bays and each of its arcades was mitered. Several other parishes of the region adopted this hybrid design, particularly in the Lauragais.[33]

The adoption of the "clocher toulousain" or some of its characteristic features prominently demonstrated the dissemination of one facet of a regional culture centered on Toulouse. The design of a church tower was no indifferent matter to the denizens of medieval and early modern towns and villages, who rarely could afford to adorn their community with many more monuments of such prominence. Many believed their church's bells to be capable of preventing storms, and their importance as foci of communal identity was underlined by the crown's practice of destroying or removing the bells of communities which had participated in rebellions.[34]

Still more widely diffused than the "clocher toulousain" was the southern French variant of Gothic architecture. The "gothique méridional," like its northern progenitor, arose from a desire for lighter, more spacious structures, but the southern Gothic focused on creating vast, unified interiors of striking austerity rather than following the northern fascination with intricately dissecting an interior. In a northern Gothic cathedral or church, the choir, nave, and transept were elaborately distinguished from one another; patrons who adopted the southern Gothic style sought to create an interior in which such distinctions were minimized, and in which the dimensions and unity of the space enclosed by the vaulting and walls of the structure were emphasized. The impression of spaciousness conveyed by such structures was further enhanced by the absence of aisles in their naves and the fondness of southerners for flat, undecorated surfaces. The exterior of a southern Gothic cathedral or church was also characteristically much more austere than the exterior of its northern counterpart: in the north, an elaborate scaffolding of buttresses clings to much of the exterior of Gothic cathedrals, but in the Midi the buttressing was usually incorporated into or abutted directly against the walls of the structure, making flying buttresses unnecessary and giving the cathedral or church a much simpler appearance.[35]

The southern French variant of the Gothic style developed in the thir-

33. Rey, p. 41.

34. Bercé, 1:189-90.

35. Vivian Paul, "Le problème de la nef unique," in *La naissance et l'essor du gothique méridional au XIIIᵉ siècle*, ed. Marie-Humbert Vicaire (Toulouse: Privat, 1974), pp. 34, 38-39; Paul, "The Beginnings of Gothic Architecture in Languedoc," *Art Bulletin* 70 (March 1988): 104, 107; Gloton, 1:16-17; Jean Bony, *French Gothic Architecture of the Twelfth and Thirteenth Centuries* (Berkeley: University of California Press, 1983), pp. 305-6, 447-49; Jean-Louis Biget, "L'architecture gothique du Midi toulousain," *Revue du Tarn*, 3rd ser., no. 96 (1979): 507, 510, 525, 528, 533-34, 540-41; Biget, "La cathédrale Sainte-Cécile d'Albi: l'architecture," *Congrès archéologique de France* 140 (1982): 45, 47-48, 54; and Jacques Gardelles, *Aquitaine gothique* (Paris: Picard, 1992), pp. 7-8, 22, 32, 90, 109, 132, 148-50, 153-55, 192, 239, 259, 263, 279.

teenth century, and its emergence was associated with both the rapid growth in popularity and power of the new mendicant orders and the efforts of Catholic clerics directed toward the extirpation of Catharism. The austerity of the edifices demonstrated in the face of the Cathars' contempt for the material that orthodox Catholicism could welcome otherworldly asceticism. The severity of the original decor of the Cordelier and Jacobin churches of Toulouse and the Sainte-Cécile cathedral of Albi was in keeping with the mendicant orders' dedication to worldly poverty, reflecting their concern that worship not become confused with the ostentation of wealth and that worshipers not be distracted by "curiosities." The Dominicans prohibited vaulting in the naves of their churches in 1228; in 1243 crosses, coats of arms, and banners were removed from the Jacobin church at Narbonne.[36]

The absence of transepts and continuity between the choir and the highly unified space of the nave in southern Gothic cathedrals and churches facilitated a sentiment of participation in the mass for the worshipers in attendance, and helped as many of them as possible feel involved in the elevation of the host, a focus of Catholic militancy in a region where Cathars had been denying the incarnation. Jean-Louis Biget has argued persuasively that the austerity of these edifices encouraged spiritual introspection,[37] but the relative absence of worldly distractions combined with the size and unified space of these buildings also forcefully reminded the numerous faithful in attendance that they constituted a Christian community, a "miniature *corpus christianum*,"[38] and that as individuals their pursuit of Christian sanctity had to take account of this context. This powerful affirmation of attachment to a community could serve the needs of the faithful who attended mass at Toulouse's enormous Cordelier and Jacobin churches, all of whom had been drawn at least temporarily from their parish churches by the preaching of the mendicants, but was also appropriate for the parish communities served by Gaillac's Saint-Pierre, Gimont's Notre-Dame, and Montauban's Saint-Jacques.[39] The size of these buildings

36. Biget, "La cathédrale Sainte-Cécile d'Albi," p. 54; Benoît Montagnes, "L'attitude des Prêcheurs à l'égard des œuvres d'art," in *La naissance et l'essor du gothique méridional au XIIIe siècle*, ed. Marie-Humbert Vicaire (Toulouse: Privat, 1974), pp. 88-89, 92, 94, 96; and Richard Sundt, "*Mediocres domos et humiles habeant fratres nostri*: Dominican Legislation on Architecture and Architectural Decoration in the Thirteenth Century," *Journal of the Society of Architectural Historians* 46, no. 4 (December 1987): 396-99.

37. Biget, "La cathédrale Sainte-Cécile d'Albi," p. 54, and Biget, "L'architecture gothique du Midi toulousain," p. 511.

38. *"corpus christianum im kleinen."* Bernd Moeller, *Reichsstadt und Reformation*, rev. ed. (Berlin: Evangelische Verlagsanstalt, 1987), p. 49. Emphasis is in the original.

39. Marcel Durliat, "L'église de Gimont," *Congrès archéologique de France* 128 (1970): 256-57; Guy Ahlsell de Toulza and Daniel Cazes, "Le vieux Gaillac et l'église Saint-Pierre," *Congrès archéologique de France* 140 (1982): 263; Hélène Guicharnaud, *Montauban au XVIIe: 1560/1685* (Paris: Picard, 1991), p. 133; and Gayne, p. 149; cf. Pierre Bonnard, "L'ancienne cathédrale de Lectoure," *Congrès archéologique de France* 128 (1970): 213-14, 218.

enabled relatively large crowds to gather for services, an important consideration in the growing communities of the thirteenth-century Midi. Moreover, the relative simplicity of the southern Gothic style was conducive to its dissemination in an era when edifices which could be erected relatively rapidly helped the church keep pace with its growing flock.[40]

The enthusiastic response which Dominican piety and preaching ultimately elicited from the urban elite in the thirteenth and fourteenth centuries undermined the intensity of the order's commitment to austerity. In 1244 Innocent IV granted the Dominicans the right to perform burials in their churches, a change which was to transform the material circumstances of the order and affect the architecture of their churches significantly. At Toulouse, the city's wealthy families were increasingly generous in their contributions to the Dominicans as the thirteenth century advanced, and by the early fourteenth century Toulouse's mendicants were attracting donations from several powerful southern French prelates and the Avignonese papacy, who saw the order as an important bulwark of orthodoxy in the Midi. These resources placed the Dominicans of Toulouse in a position to take advantage of the relaxation of the rules governing building in their order to further enlarge and embellish their church; modifications included vaulting the nave, permissible from 1297, and erecting a four-story "clocher toulousain." Throughout the Midi cathedrals and parish churches as well as the mendicant orders added chapels to their naves in the fourteenth and fifteenth centuries as a response to the desire of the wealthy to establish more private devotional spaces for their families in prominent ecclesiastical edifices. The profusion of these chapels and the architectural changes they provoked detracted from the austerity and internal unity of southern French Gothic churches, but not to such a degree that the aspirations of the churches' founders were subverted fundamentally.[41]

40. Marie-Humbert Vicaire, "Le financement des Jacobins de Toulouse: conditions spirituelles et sociales des constructions," in *La naissance et l'essor du gothique méridional au XIIIe siècle*, ed. Marie-Humbert Vicaire (Toulouse: Privat, 1974), pp. 210-11, 226; Montagnes, pp. 95, 99 n; Biget, "La cathédrale Sainte-Cécile d'Albi," p. 25; Paul, "Beginnings of Gothic Architecture," p. 121; and Richard Sundt, "The Jacobin Church of Toulouse and the Origin of Its Double-Nave Plan," *Art Bulletin* 71, no. 2 (June 1989): 194. The relative simplicity of the southern Gothic was attractive to communities on which the Inquisition had imposed the obligation of erecting new churches rather quickly as penance for heresy; see Biget, "L'architecture gothique du Midi toulousain," pp. 515-17. As Richard Sundt demonstrates convincingly, the homogeneity of the interior of the Jacobin church at Toulouse has led some scholars to go too far in claiming that the edifice lacked any visible distinction between its choir and nave.

41. Biget, "La cathédrale Sainte-Cécile d'Albi," p. 51; Montagnes, p. 91; and Vicaire, pp. 237, 243-45.

Protestantism and Southern French Culture:
Reformation and Continuity

For Jean Calvin and his southern French followers, there was much that was profoundly misguided in the thinking of the mendicants, but the aesthetics of the Dominicans and the relative sobriety of the southern French Gothic were much more congenial to Calvinists than the exuberance of the flamboyant Gothic, the refined virtuosity of the mannerists, or the more elaborate and theatrical incarnations of the baroque. Achieving an understanding of the Calvinist reaction to the architectural traditions of southern France is complicated by the inability of many French Protestant communities to undertake the construction of churches due to their poverty or the brevity of their legal existence: few southern French Protestants launched building campaigns of any sort during the civil strife that engulfed France in the late sixteenth century, and although the peaceful interlude that followed the promulgation of the Edict de Nantes in 1598 made envisaging and beginning architectural projects easier, renewed and devastating conflict from 1621 to 1629 and the redoubled aggressiveness of the Counter-Reformation during the personal reign of Louis XIV discouraged new building ventures and destroyed much of what had been erected by Protestants.[42] Particularly because of the dearth of surviving archaeological evidence, the reflections of Calvinist theologians are of great importance in the reconstruction of southern French Protestant attitudes toward the arts in the sixteenth and seventeenth centuries.

Worship was a central concern of Calvin, because it was for him the requisite context for the only sort of spiritual commerce with the divine fallen humankind could hope to enjoy. Since any individual's knowledge of God was limited to the testimony of Scripture, any deviation from the approach to worship indicated by scriptural authority for Calvin necessarily led to the substitution of human invention for divine witness, which involved an idolatrous confusion of the material and spiritual realms.[43] The association of images that claimed to depict the divine with worship presented a temptation to supplement or alter the scriptural message that Calvin believed the corrupted wills of the worshipers were unable to resist; Calvin claims that "the spirit of man has always been and always will be a workshop for the forging of idols." This frailty makes the presence of any representations of the divine during worship a provocation to sin:

42. Louis Hautecœur, *Histoire de l'architecture classique en France*, 7 vols. (Paris: Picard, 1948-67), vol. 1, pt. 3, p. 599, and Janine Garrisson, *L'édit de Nantes et sa révocation: histoire d'une intolérance* (Paris: Seuil, 1985), pp. 126-27.

43. Carlos Eire, *War against the Idols: The Reformation of Worship from Erasmus to Calvin* (Cambridge: Cambridge University Press, 1986), pp. 197-201, 205-6, 208-10, 213-14, 217, and Francis Higman, *The Style of John Calvin in His French Polemical Treatises* (Oxford: Oxford University Press, 1967), pp. 143, 152.

as soon as there are images in a church, it is as if an ensign has been raised to rally men to idolatry. Because the folly of our reasoning cannot restrain itself from turning and running like water . . . to foolish rites.[44]

Calvin's concerns regarding the use of images in places of worship and the pervasiveness of idolatrous inclinations were shared by southern French Protestant theologians. In 1599 the Gascon Bernard de Sonis listed six reasons for which he believed the Catholic Church had to be condemned as idolatrous, including in his adumbration the nature of the sanctuaries in which Catholics celebrated mass.[45] The Dauphinois Daniel Chamier asserted in 1618 that any "Church that teaches & encourages the painting of God . . . teaches and encourages Idolatry," and added that to "paint God" is the "greatest devotional crime there can be."[46] The transplanted Glaswegian John Cameron, who for much of his career preached and taught in southwestern France, sought to achieve a somewhat more conciliatory tone than Chamier or Sonis when addressing Catholics, choosing to follow Calvin in insisting on the pervasiveness of the tendency to confuse the signifier and the signified, an inability or unwillingness "to distinguish the signs and seals of celestial things from the celestial things themselves." Explicitly including Protestants in his warning, he declared that "we must have a golden calf, we must have a God that we can see either in a painting or enveloped in accidents. . . . worldlings that we are, we must have a corporal presence."[47]

Such assertions, voiced repeatedly by Protestant preachers and theologians in the Midi, left little room for doubt concerning the Calvinist position on the appropriateness of images in churches, but often led to a reac-

44. "si tost qu'il y a des images en un temple, c'est comme une banière dressée pour attirer les hommes à idolatrer. Car la folie de nostre entendement ne se peut tenir qu'elle ne décline et découle comme eau . . . à sottes devotions." Calvin, *Institution de la religion chrestienne*, ed. Jean-Daniel Benoît, 5 vols. (Paris: Vrin, 1957-63), 1:129-30, 136.

45. Sonis, *Repliqve povr la response faicte à la declaration de fev Iean de Sponde* (Montauban: Haultin, 1599), p. 419. On Sonis see Michel Nicolas, *Histoire de l'ancienne Académie protestante de Montauban* (Montauban: Forestié, 1885), pp. 80-81, 85-90.

46. "plus grãd crime qui puisse estre en la Religion." Chamier, *La iesvitomanie* (Montauban: Heritiers de Denys Havltin, 1618), pp. 40, 42. On Chamier see Nicolas, pp. 114-28.

47. "il nous faut vn veau d'or, il nous faut vn Dieu que nous voyïons ou en peinture, ou enuelopé sous des accidens. . . . corporels que nous sommes, nous voulons vne presence corporelle." Cameron, *Sept sermons* (Saumur: Girard & de Lerpiniere, 1624), pp. 307-9. Cameron saw in the behavior of Amerindians evidence of humankind's naturally idolatrous tendencies: presented with "quelque riche tableau," he argued, the "pauvres Indiens" treated it as an object to be worshiped. Cameron, *Traicté avqvel sont examinez les prejugez de ceux de l'Eglise Romaine* (La Rochelle: Herbert, 1617), p. 6. For a summary of Cameron's career, see Brian Armstrong, *Calvinism and the Amyraut Heresy: Protestant Scholasticism and Humanism in Seventeenth-Century France* (Madison: University of Wisconsin Press, 1969), pp. 44-47, 56, 59-62, 70.

tion that much of the Protestant leadership found lamentable. In a work published in 1560, Pierre Viret had denounced idolatry as "the most hateful sin in God's eyes" and "spiritual fornication"; his preaching at Nîmes in 1561 was followed closely by iconoclastic outbursts.[48] Indeed, heated excoriation of Catholic idolatry from the pulpit frequently led to or served as a pretext for the destruction of religious art and the infliction of severe damage on ecclesiastical edifices. Calvin disapproved of any iconoclasm conducted without the consent of the legitimately constituted magistrates, arguing that *"God has never ordained the destruction of idols, except to each in his home, and in public to those whom he arms with authority,"* and Reformed consulates were also inclined to disapprove of the spontaneous and unruly destruction of religious images; nonetheless, Calvinism initially had a decidedly negative impact on the artistic heritage of the Midi.[49]

In many cases, these destructive outbursts were the result of a desire for booty or retribution cloaked rather transparently by a pretext of devoutness. However, the Calvinist suspicion of images in churches reflected a "longue durée" phenomenon of a southern French predilection for austerity in the precincts of worship that was more than four centuries old at the outset of the French Reformation.[50]

That pride in regional traditions was in the southern French context readily compatible with fervent attachment to Calvinism was evident in the work of the poet Guillaume de Saluste, seigneur du Bartas. In 1578 du Bartas wrote a poem which was to serve as part of the welcome offered to Marguerite de Valois on her entry into Nérac, then the seat of the court of her husband, the future Henry IV. Marguerite arrived in southern France during a period in which, following the Saint-Barthélemy massacres of 1572, the Protestants of the Midi had reacted by usurping the crown's au-

---

48. Robert Sauzet, "L'iconoclasme dans le diocèse de Nîmes au XVIe et au début du XVIIe siècle," *Revue d'histoire de l'église de France* 66, no. 176 (January-June 1980): 12-13, and Ann Guggenheim, "Calvinism and the Political Elite of Sixteenth Century Nîmes" (Ph.D. diss., New York University, 1968), pp. 265-66.

49. Sauzet, pp. 5, 7-10 (emphasis in original); Garrisson, *Protestants du Midi 1559-1598*, pp. 163-64; Marcel Durliat, "La Gascogne dans l'art," Paul Mesplé, "Marciac: église Notre-Dame," and Françoise-Claire Legrand, "L'Isle-Jourdain," *Congrès archéologique de France* 128 (1970): 21, 35-36, 265; Pierre Quarré, "L'église abbatiale de Saint-Antoine-en-Viennois," *Congrès archéologique de France* 130 (1972): 412; Paul Bergeon, "Eglise Saint-Jacques de Montauban: réexamen des dommages subis lors des guerres de religion," *Bulletin de la Société Archéologique de Tarn-et-Garonne* 101 (1976): 24; Guy Ahlsell de Toulza and Daniel Cazes, "L'église abbatiale Saint-Michel de Gaillac," and Georges Costa, "La cathédrale de Castres," *Congrès archéologique de France* 140 (1982): 223, 283, 288; Costa, "Pierre Levesville: l'œuvre d'un architecte orléanais dans le Midi de la France pendant le premier tiers du XVIIe siècle," *Actes du 96e congrès national des sociétés savantes, section d'archéologie et d'histoire de l'art* (1971), 2:316, 359-60; and ADTG, MS 3, pp. 214-15, 218, 235.

50. Some Calvinist divines embraced the Cathars as good Protestants who had been calumniated by Catholic propaganda. Jacques Solé, *Le débat entre protestants et catholiques français de 1598 à 1685*, 5 vols. (Paris: Amateurs des Livres, 1985), 2:569, 578.

thority in much of the region and adopting Henry as their monarch on his return from the royal court in 1576.[51] Du Bartas's poem presents the Midi as formidable, trumpeting regional pride and providing a warning to Marguerite's courtly companions, but he chooses as his vehicle for this gesture a trilingual debate between nymphs representing the French, Gascon, and Latin tongues concerning which of them should have the honor of welcoming Marguerite to Nérac. The Latin nymph claims seniority and characterizes the representatives of French and Gascon as barbarians, unable to match her in nobility of conduct or linguistic virtuosity; the French nymph argues that her language of "bards and druids" is older than Latin, and that the Muses have now abandoned Greek and Latin in favor of French. "If Cicero were to live again he would speak French," she boasts. The Gascon nymph is willing to concede that French and Latin have developed greater sophistication than her tongue, but only because Gascons have been more concerned with acting virtuously than with elegant diction: "if in the past," she claims, "our sons had held the pen as they did iron, I could compete, but hitherto Pallas has been dumb among them, because they have loved doing good more than speaking elegantly."[52]

Ironically, similar formulations had earlier been used to explain the putative weakness of French and Latin literature, by Joachim du Bellay as recently as 1549 in the French case.[53] However, instead of following du Bellay and calling on writers to improve the quality of their native speech and literature, du Bartas's nymph adds further criticism of the refinement of French and Latin that reflects the long-standing southern taste for austerity while echoing a Calvinist suspicion of human contrivance: "all your beauty is now but paint, mannerisms, trinkets, buckles, cosmetics," she concludes, "and my beauty has no other mother than nature, always more beautiful than art."[54]

Here the nymph endorses du Bartas's efforts to create a new kind of epic poetry of which Calvin could have approved, one in which human intervention is minimized and the gloriousness of God's creation is the central focus; du Bartas sought to follow the lead of Garros, also a Gascon Protestant, in composing poetry as free of pagan references as

51. Lafont, p. 87; Garrisson, *Protestants du Midi 1559-1598*, pp. 179, 220-22; and Archives Communales de Montauban, AA 2, fols. 177ff.

52. "S'en man nous hils avèn, lou tens passat, tengude/La plume coum lou hèr, iou pouiri rampela;/Mès entre ets dinquio ci Pallas s'es biste mude,/Car ets an mès amat plan hè que plan parla." Du Bartas, *Works*, ed. Urban Tigner Holmes Jr., Robert White Linker, and John Coriden Lyons, 3 vols. (Chapel Hill: University of North Carolina Press, 1935-40), 3:477-79, 481.

53. Du Bellay, *La deffence et illvstration de la langue francoyse* (Paris: l'Angelier, 1549), bk. 1, chap. 3.

54. "Toute boste beutat n'es are que pinture,/Que maignes, qu'affiquets, que retourtils, que fard:/Et ma beutat n'a punt aute mai que nature;/La nature toustem es mes bele que l'art." Du Bartas, *Works*, 3:478-79.

possible.[55] In a fashion reminiscent of English Puritans of the early seventeenth century, du Bartas censures the refinement of the court and contrasts it with the simple virtue of the "country," here Gascony.[56] To be sure, the wealthier Protestant nobility and urban notables were not as enthusiastic about repudiating courtly sophistication as du Bartas and others, reflecting a tension within French Calvinism that surfaced in 1584 when the pastor Michel Berauld barred the wife of a Calvinist noble from attending divine service because he deemed her coiffure to be lacking in modesty.[57]

A common inclination toward celebrating the merits of asceticism and simplicity was not the only manner in which Reformed religiosity found a responsive echo in the culture of the Midi. The priority of the local community in southern France prepared the region to listen with particular interest to Reformed preachers who placed the community at the center of their divine service and whose theology reflected its gestation in a context of autonomous cities and independent city-states.[58] The Reformed conception of worship was implicit in their practice of describing their devotional edifices as "temples": this custom was troubling to some English Protestants, who found it pagan,[59] but for the French and Swiss Reformed it indicated that the congregation hearing the gospel and partaking of the

---

55. Du Bartas, *La sepmaine,* ed. Yvonne Bellenger, 2 vols. (Paris: Nizet, 1981), 2:345-46, 353; Jan Miernowski, *Dialectique et connaissance dans "La sepmaine" de du Bartas: "discours sur discours infiniment divers"* (Genève: Droz, 1992), pp. 156, 310-13; and Lafont, p. 85. In a response to critics first published in 1584, du Bartas explains that he cannot be expected to follow the rules for epic poetry derived from Aristotle and Horace because his work is not "purement Epique, ou Heroyque," but also seeks to teach, praise God's creation, and spread the gospel. He apologizes for making some references to classical mythology, but claims that such allusions are so deeply embedded in the writing of epic that he has not been able to altogether free himself from contaminating his poetry with paganism; he expects a future poet will complete his work of cleansing French literature of these "monstreuses bourdes."

56. Cf. du Bartas, *La Judit,* ed. André Baïche (Toulouse: Publications de la Faculté de Lettres et Sciences Humaines, 1971), pp. 64-65, and Robert Ashton, *The English Civil War: Conservatism and Revolution, 1603-1649* (New York: Norton, 1979), pp. 22, 28-32, 35, 37-38, 42.

57. *Mémoires et correspondance de Duplessis-Mornay: pour servir à l'histoire de la Réformation et des guerres civiles et religieuses en France,* ed. P. Auguis and A. de la Fontenelle de Vaudoré, 12 vols. (Paris: Truettel et Würtz, 1824-25), 2:490-91, 493-94, 496-97. Cf. Philippe Chareyre, "'The Great Difficulties One Must Bear to Follow Jesus Christ': Morality at Sixteenth-Century Nîmes," trans. R. A. Mentzer, in *Sin and the Calvinists: Morals Control and the Consistory in the Reformed Tradition,* ed. Mentzer (Kirksville, Mo.: Sixteenth Century Journal, 1994), pp. 63-96. On early modern French clergymen and women's hair, see James Richard Farr, "The Pure and Disciplined Body: Hierarchy, Morality, and Symbolism in France during the Catholic Reformation," *Journal of Interdisciplinary History* 21, no. 3 (winter 1991): 391-414.

58. Moeller, pp. 36, 41-42, 49, 51, 59.

59. Keith Vivian Thomas, "English Protestantism and Classical Art," in *Albion's Classicism: The Visual Arts in Britain, 1550-1660,* ed. Lucy Gent (New Haven: Yale University Press, 1995), p. 225.

Eucharist were the body of Christ, constituting a "temple" that since Christ's crucifixion was no longer in the Reformed view the site of a sacrifice.[60] In the context of the fervent religiosity of sixteenth-century France, a more compelling case for the importance of the community could hardly have been imagined.

Pierre Levesville and Montauban: Innovation and Tradition

The career of architect Pierre Levesville suggests that southern French Calvinists hardly rejected the aesthetic traditions of the region. Levesville was the scion of an Orléanais family of architects; his brother Jean worked on the reconstruction of Orléans's cathedral, demolished by Protestants in 1568. How precisely Pierre achieved a high degree of architectural competence is unclear, but he quickly established himself in southern France as a master of completing and renovating Gothic structures, and probably developed this expertise through working on the early stages of the reconstruction of Orléans's cathedral, which in an assertion of the resilience of Catholicism was being rebuilt in the Gothic style. By 1604 Levesville was working as an architect in the Gévaudan, where he restored the Gothic rose window of the Mendois cathedral, another victim of Calvinist iconoclasm. In 1610 he was hired to repair Toulouse's Saint-Étienne cathedral, badly damaged in a fire of 1609. Levesville's work at this cathedral, an edifice of pivotal importance in the development of the southern French Gothic, won him a reputation throughout much of southwestern France as an accomplished architect, a result of the continuing cultural power of Toulouse in the region. His services were now sought by a wide variety of clients from an area extending almost to the Spanish border. He completed the Gothic cathedral at Auch, but did not refuse more modest contracts such as reconstructing the "clocher-mur" of the Haut-Languedocien village of Deyme or providing plans for a timber-frame house. The Calvinists of Montauban also employed him to direct two major projects, a new church and the reconstruction of two sides of their community's central square.[61]

---

60. Bernard Reymond, *L'architecture religieuse des protestants: histoire-caractéristiques-problèmes actuels* (Genève: Labor et Fides, 1996), p. 49.

61. Sournia and Vayssettes, p. 43, and Costa, "Pierre Levesville," pp. 314-18, 320-22, 328, 333, 354. Gothic architecture was sufficiently variegated that contradictory meanings were ascribed to it by its patrons. Deborah Howard observes that in Scotland, "where Gothic elements were revived in churches after 1620, this could express either a Laudian High-Anglican bias or, in more sober versions, the leanings of devout Covenanters." Howard, *Scottish Architecture: Reformation to Restoration, 1560-1660* (Edinburgh: University of Edinburgh Press, 1995), p. 219. On the continuing cultural authority of Toulouse, cf. William Beik, *Abso-*

Completed by 1617, the church Levesville designed for Montauban, known as the "temple neuf," was destroyed in 1664, at an early stage of Louis XIV's campaign of confessional cleansing. Much the largest of the city's two Reformed churches, it had been erected on land that had formerly belonged to the Catholic clergy, and consequently its demolition, eagerly sought by the leaders of Montauban's growing Catholic minority, was required by a judgment of the Conseil d'Etat. The poor and in some respects mutually contradictory quality of the surviving iconographic evidence concerning the Temple Neuf renders ascertaining some aspects of its design difficult, but the contract covering the project Levesville signed with Montauban's consulate has survived, providing considerable information regarding the intentions of the architect and his patrons.[62]

The Temple Neuf was large, striking, and unusual in its appearance. Montauban's political elite devoted much attention to its design and contributed substantially to covering the expense involved in erecting it; much urban pride was invested in the building, which displayed Montauban's coat of arms prominently over its elaborately decorated principal entrance.[63] An apothecary of Villefranche-de-Rouergue who visited Montauban in 1624 described the Temple Neuf as not only "very handsome and ably constructed," but also as having been erected "in the form of a synagogue," an observation he reiterated.[64] Why he insisted on this point is uncertain: the Temple Neuf may have reminded him of a synagogue he had seen personally or in an illustration, the comparison could have been his vehicle for labeling the building as exotic, or he may have been suggesting that if the building was intended to be a replica of the temple of Solomon, it was a less than successful effort. In any event, his comments are hardly evocative of a conventional structure in keeping with the architectural traditions of the region; throughout France architects serving Protestant patrons were encouraged to innovate because successive edicts of pacification in the sixteenth century had insisted that Protestant houses of worship not resemble Catholic churches, an expectation that French Calvinists did not find objectionable since they, like many other European Protestants, were eager to demonstrate their distinctness from Catholicism.[65] That the Temple Neuf was exotic in design is confirmed

---

lutism and Society in Seventeenth-Century France: State Power and Provincial Aristocracy in Languedoc (Cambridge: Cambridge University Press, 1985), p. 70.

62. Garrisson, L'édit de Nantes et sa révocation, p. 127, and Guicharnaud, p. 97.

63. "Relation de mon voïage à Montauban en l'année 1624," Recueil de l'Académie de Tarn-et-Garonne, 2nd ser., 15 (1899): 83; Henri de France, Le Temple Neuf de Montauban: étude historique et archéologique (Montauban: Forestié, 1881), pp. 34-37, 47, 52-59, 69-71; Garrisson, L'édit de Nantes et sa révocation, p. 127; and Guicharnaud, pp. 95, 97.

64. "Relation de mon voïage," pp. 81-82.

65. David Thomson, "Protestant Temples in France," in L'église dans l'architecture de la Renaissance: actes du colloque tenu à Tours du 28 au 31 mai 1990, ed. Jean Guillaume (Paris: Picard, 1995), p. 247; Reymond, p. 101; and Howard, pp. 177-78.

by a drawing of 1650, in which the church is surmounted by a dome which looks to be derived from an Ottoman or Russian model.[66] Other iconographic evidence suggests a less unusual building, although some representations leave open the possibility that the Temple Neuf's exterior walls were decorated with a sequence of columns or pilasters after the fashion that was thought by architectural theorists such as Sebastiano Serlio to be typical of early Christian martyrs' shrines.[67]

Levesville adopted a centralized plan for the Temple Neuf, a common choice for French Calvinist churches of the seventeenth century.[68] He could have been inspired to choose such a design by the example of other Calvinist churches, by considering Serlio's recommendations concerning the design of ecclesiastical edifices, or by observing Italian round or oval churches. The evidence concerning the appearance of the Temple Neuf that has survived suggests that Levesville may very well have been attempting to pattern his creation after the temple of Solomon as that edifice had been depicted in late medieval and early modern iconography: the divinely designed Solomonic temple was felt by many Catholics as well as Protestants to be the ultimate authority in ecclesiastical architecture. In drawing on sources such as Hartmann Schedel's *Liber cronicarum* or Sebastian Münster's *Cosmographia universalis*, Levesville would be relying on illustrations that confused the Islamic Dome of the Rock and the older Jewish structure, which would account for the idiosyncrasy of the Temple Neuf.[69] The religious fervor of Montauban's consistory combined with their urban pride and sense of themselves as a chosen people could have led them to conceive of their city as a new Jerusalem in the making.[70]

66. De France, pp. 49, 60, 66.

67. Guicharnaud, pp. 97-98; de France, pp. 52-53; and Serlio, *Architettvra* (Venezia: Combi e la Nou, 1663), pp. 375, 390-91; cf. Arnaldo Bruschi, *Bramante architetto* (Bari: Laterza, 1969), pp. 467-69, 491-92, 498.

68. Guicharnaud, pp. 98-99; Rosalyn Coope, *Salomon de Brosse and the Development of the Classical Style in French Architecture from 1565 to 1630* (University Park: Pennsylvania State University Press, 1972), pp. 184-85; Thomson, "Protestant *Temples* in France," pp. 249, 251-52; and Reymond, pp. 53, 101, 144-46.

69. Helen Rosenau, *Vision of the Temple: The Image of the Temple of Jerusalem in Judaism and Christianity* (London: Oresko, 1979), pp. 64-65, 71, 87, 91; Reymond, p. 54; and Thomas, pp. 231-32. Cf. Solange Deyon, "L'organisation des églises," in *Les huguenots: exposition nationale* (Paris: Archives Nationales, 1985), p. 82. A diagram of Solomon's temple constitutes one of the few illustrations included in a Genevan edition of the Bible of 1567. *La Bible* (Genève: Estienne, 1567), p. 176.

70. For the pastor Pierre Berauld, Montauban's victories over royal armies in 1562 and 1621 were indications of God's favor, and warnings to Louis XIII. Berauld, *La froissure de Ioseph* (Montauban: Coderc, 1622), pp. 11, 68. David Underdown argues that the "godly" of early seventeenth-century Dorchester sought to make of their community "a reformed city on a hill, a veritable new Jerusalem." Underdown, *Fire from Heaven: Life in an English Town in the Seventeenth Century* (New Haven: Yale University Press, 1992), p. 108. Cf. Sacvan Bercovitch,

Levesville visited Rome before establishing himself at Mende,[71] and his work at Montauban is reminiscent of Italian architecture of the sixteenth century. His additions to Montauban's Grand'Place, occasioned by a fire that destroyed two sides of the central square, are similar in some respects to works of Donato Bramante and Andrea Palladio. Here Levesville raised three stories over an arcaded ground floor, decorating and vertically dividing the facades with massive pilasters in a manner somewhat similar to that employed by Palladio for his Palazzo Valmarana;[72] Levesville's pilasters are interrupted by brick capitals, two of which on each pilaster are coordinated with lateral moldings to suggest architraves, creating facades which echo the lower court of Bramante's Belvedere project.[73] Levesville follows the lead of Michelangelo Buonarroti's Roman work and Palladio's Palazzo Valmarana in presenting pilasters which are not secondary or merely supportive of other architectural elements, but rather are foci of the design.[74]

Bramante probably was largely responsible for the design of the Piazza Ducale of Vigevano, a unified square surrounded by loggias that was begun in 1492 and completed two years later, a remarkably brief construction period for such an ambitious project. The arcades and symmetry of Vigevano's square are in keeping with the model of an ancient forum provided by Vitruvius and his Renaissance counterpart, Leon Battista Alberti. Squares were important to Alberti not only as a means of ordering the urban landscape, but also as structures which if properly designed could encourage achievement and virtue. Levesville's patrons at Montauban, the city's political elite, were very much concerned with preserving order and would have found any project which proposed to foster urban harmony at their community's commercial core an attractive one. Like Ludovico Sforza, the patron of the Renaissance renovation of Vigevano's square, Montauban's consulate was concerned to demonstrate its good taste and public utility in a highly visible location. Indeed, Levesville followed Alber-

"The Ends of American Puritan Rhetoric," in *The Ends of Rhetoric: History, Theory, Practice*, ed. John Bender and David Wellbery (Stanford: Stanford University Press, 1990), pp. 171-90.

71. Bruno Tollon, "L'architecte Pierre Levesville et les origines du style du XVIIᵉ siècle à Toulouse," in *Pèire Godolin 1580-1649: actes du colloque international*, ed. Christian Anatole (Toulouse: Université de Toulouse-Le Mirail, 1982), pp. 7-8, and Costa, "Pierre Levesville," p. 374.

72. Guicharnaud, pp. 48-49, 54, 57, 66; *Histoire particuliere*, p. 35; and "Relation de mon voïage," p. 83; cf. Lionello Puppi, *Andrea Palladio*, 2 vols. (Milano: Electa, 1973), vol. 1, pls. 213-14, 2:371, and Rudolf Wittkower, *Architectural Principles in the Age of Humanism*, 5th ed. (London: Academy, 1988), pp. 84-87.

73. Tollon, "L'architecte Pierre Levesville," p. 9, and Guicharnaud, pp. 54, 57; cf. Bruschi, pp. 344-55. The capitals of the Grand'Place are similar to the ones with which Inigo Jones decorated his Palladian Banqueting House of 1622. Peter Murray, "Il palladianesimo," in *Mostra del Palladio Vicenza/Basilica Palladiana*, ed. Renato Cevese, rev. ed. (n.p.: Electa, n.d.), pp. 160-61.

74. Cf. James Ackerman, *Palladio*, 2nd ed. (London: Penguin, 1977), p. 112.

ti and Vitruvius as closely at Montauban as Bramante had at Vigevano: though financial constraints limited him to replacing two sides of the Grand'Place, the consulate decided to follow the pattern he had established when in 1649 another fire destroyed most of the central square's remaining timber-frame structures (see plates 25 and 26).[75]

Levesville flattered the Montalbanais political elite by associating them and their city with the prestige of antiquity,[76] but he also created a square that reflected central preoccupations of contemporary urban planning in northern France. Like the Place Dauphine and Place Royale of Paris, Montauban's Grand'Place as renovated by Levesville was not designed to furnish an elegant setting for noble *hôtels particuliers,* but rather was to provide a context of distinction for mercantile activity, situating the shops of prosperous artisans in relatively prestigious brick edifices.[77]

The consuls of Montauban did not seek to encourage democracy by installing allusions to classical forums at the core of their city. Montauban had never been governed democratically, and in the late sixteenth century its municipal government, which had heretofore fostered a sentiment of participation in its decisions by consulting regularly with the Montalbanais heads of household in general assemblies, was becoming increasingly oligarchic. As the city grew, the political elite found canvassing a wide range of opinion increasingly unwieldy and difficult to manage. On the pretext that the Montalbanais were annoyed by the too frequent convening of general assemblies, in 1584 the consulate established a Conseil Ordinaire of twenty members which enabled them to govern without regular recourse to such gatherings. In 1627 the consulate sought to go further, abolishing general assemblies and replacing them with a council of ninety members renewed by co-optation; these reforms were annulled in 1628 through an armed uprising.[78] The conflict between consultative and oligarchic visions

75. Guicharnaud, pp. 54-56, 69-71; Bruschi, pp. 647-50; Alberti, *De re aedificatoria,* ed. Paolo Portoghesi, 2 vols. (Milano: Il Polifilo, 1966), 2:712-17; and Mark Jarzombek, *On Leon Baptista Alberti: His Literary and Aesthetic Theories* (Cambridge, Mass.: MIT Press, 1989), pp. 117, 177.

76. Christine Smith notes that Alberti and Leonardo Bruni had associated the quality of a city's built environment with the intelligence and virtue of its denizens; she adds that in the fourteenth and fifteenth centuries manuscripts of Augustine's *De civitas Dei* were illustrated with depictions of the city of God, demonstrating a concern to present virtue visually. Smith, *Architecture in the Culture of Early Humanism: Ethics, Aesthetics, and Eloquence, 1400-1470* (Oxford: Oxford University Press, 1992), pp. 11, 23-24.

77. "Relation de mon voïage," p. 83; Guicharnaud, p. 50; and Ballon, pp. 83, 104, 113, 115, 250, 252-55.

78. Archives Communales de Montauban, AA 6, fol. 79; "Documents pour servir à l'histoire des guerres civiles dans le Montalbanais," ed. M. Gandilhon, *Recueil de l'Académie de Tarn-et-Garonne,* 2nd ser., 20 (1904): 53-54; Jean-Ursule Devals, "Esquisses historiques," ADTG, Bibliothèque Serr 219, pp. 150-51, 153-56; and Pierre Berauld, "L'estat de Montauban depvis la descente de l'anglois en Ré," ADTG, MS 6, pp. 5, 15-16.

of how the city's government would best function was exacerbated from 1621 by the aggressive efforts of the crown to enhance its authority in the Midi: as in Montpellier and other southern Protestant communities,[79] at Montauban bellicose defenders of the community's autonomy clashed with a political elite unenthusiastic about incurring the cost of fighting the crown on the battlefield and concerned that their control of their city was being challenged profoundly.[80] In this context Montauban's consulate eagerly sought to enhance its prestige and encourage deference to its leadership by renovating the urban topography in a fashion that would promote a more deferential devotion to community.[81]

Montauban's Temple Neuf and the new facades of its Grand'Place broke with the prevailing and traditional architecture of southern France, serving as standing assertions of the city's autonomy. From Henry IV's entry into Paris in 1594 until the resumption of civil war in 1621, Montauban's political elite left their mark on their city, reshaping the urban landscape and proclaiming their domination over it. The structures they built and renovated during this period contrasted sharply with the visible remains of the vanquished Catholics, whose cathedral and churches in ruins served as arsenals, components of the city's defenses, and a garbage dump, resounding negations of the power of Catholicism.[82] Montauban was transformed profoundly during the interlude of peace, acquiring a Protestant university in 1597, replacing most of its timber-frame facades with brick, and erecting formidable and imposing fortifications[83] as well as financing the construction of a striking new church and reconstructing two sides of its central square with prestigious and architecturally sophisti-

---

79. Cf. Jean-François Bouyssou, "La composition sociale des révoltes de Rohan à Castres," *Revue de Tarn,* 3rd ser., 58 (1970): 156-57, 162-63, 166-67; Jack Alden Clarke, *Huguenot Warrior: The Life and Times of Henri de Rohan, 1579-1638* (Amsterdam: Nijhoff, 1966), pp. 123, 133, 160-62; and Steven Mark Lowenstein, "Resistance to Absolutism: Huguenot Organization in Languedoc, 1621-1622" (Ph.D. diss., Princeton University, 1972), pp. 118, 125, 133-34.

80. This concern was not unfounded: in 1625 and 1628 the consuls were overthrown by an alliance of artisans and soldiers. Berauld, "L'estat de Montauban depvis la descente de l'anglois en Ré," pp. 16, 33, and the anonymous work, *Histoire veritable de tovt ce qvi s'est fait & passé dans la ville de Montauban durant & du depuis les derniers mouuemens iusqu'à present* (n.p., 1627), pp. 13-14, 19, 29-44, 48, 59.

81. On the decline of communal solidarity at Aix-en-Provence during the sixteenth century, a transformation similar to that in progress at Montauban, see Claire Dolan, "Des images en action: cité, pouvoir municipal et crises pendant les guerres de religion à Aix-en-Provence," in *Les productions symboliques du pouvoir XVIᵉ-XXᵉ siècle*, ed. Laurier Turgeon (Québec: Septentrion, 1990), pp. 69, 73, 86. On the "cultivation of deference" in English towns through new town halls and other embellishments, see Robert Tittler, *Architecture and Power: The Town Hall and the English Urban Community* (Oxford: Oxford University Press, 1991), pp. 93, 106, 114-20.

82. Le Bret, 1:41, 102-3; ADTG, MS 3, pp. 264, 276; and Bergeon, pp. 26, 28.

83. Guicharnaud, pp. 26-27, 142.

cated edifices. Particularly when juxtaposed with the abandoned ruins of Catholic churches, these modifications of the city's physiognomy constituted a transformation of the city's identity according to the widespread contemporary tendency to define a city's singularity in terms of the more monumental features of its built environment.[84]

The realization of an ambitious program of urban renewal was facilitated greatly by the relative strength of Montauban's municipal government, which had recurrently imposed authoritarian measures on the Montalbanais during and since the civil wars whenever an insurrection or siege seemed imminent.[85] The consuls persuaded the administrators of Montauban's *hôpitaux* to provide the site of one of their buildings for the new Académie in 1597, and expropriated adjacent landholdings in order to provide adequate space for the new institution.[86] Impatient when confronted with disorder, the consuls also used expropriation to straighten or widen streets, and were not afraid to demand the alteration of building plans they found to be prejudicial to the quality of the urban environment. The successful completion of the restoration of the Grand'Place was made much more likely by a municipal government that was willing and able to compel the proprietors of the lots surrounding the square to rebuild in conformity with the program adopted by the consuls.[87] The interventionist vigor of Montauban's consulate contrasted sharply with the lack of engagement of the Toulousain Capitoulat in urban design: hobbled by an often meddlesome *parlement*, the *capitouls* left urban renewal largely to individual proprietors, and consequently no substantial attempt to transform the urban geography of Toulouse was realized until the eighteenth century.[88]

The capacity of Montauban's consulate to bring to fruition Levesville's reconstruction of the Grand'Place contrasted with the impotence of its Toulousain counterpart in comparable situations, but the projects designed by Levesville for Protestant Montauban displayed features of long-standing cultural inclinations common to much of southern France. Although the appearance of Levesville's Temple Neuf defied convention, its size, austerity, and interior simplicity recalled fundamental features of

84. Claire Dolan has traced the expression of this view of the specificity of the city in the genre of "antiquités." Dolan, "L'identité urbaine et les histoires locales publiées du XVIe au XVIIIe siècle en France," *Canadian Journal of History* 27, no. 2 (August 1992): 282-83, 292. An example of such a work from southern France is Jean Poldo d'Albenas's *Discovrs historial de l'antiqve et illvstre cité de Nismes* (Lyon: Roville, 1560).

85. ADTG, MS 3, pp. 247, 249, 270-71, 288.

86. Archives Hospitalières de Montauban, E2, 12 October 1597, and Guicharnaud, p. 142.

87. Guicharnaud, pp. 43-44, 69. "Ne nous leurrons pas," Hélène Guicharnaud comments, "si l'incendie de 1614 n'avait pas coïncidé avec une période de pouvoir politique tenu par une organisation unique et toute puissante, cette place, une des premières à programme, n'aurait pas vu le jour."

88. Bruand, pp. 6-12, and Tollon, "La ville de brique," pp. 29-30.

187

the southern French Gothic.[89] The inclination to regard the congregation in worship as the physical embodiment of a sanctified community was accommodated by southern French Gothic ecclesiastical architecture, and Levesville's Temple Neuf was still more in keeping with this communal ethos, its octagonal, oval, or round shape placing most of the large congregation opposite other believers during sermons instead of facing an isolated clergyman.[90]

The construction of the Temple Neuf was the culmination of a Calvinist reunification of Montauban's sacred spaces which had begun violently in 1561 with an iconoclastic assault on the city's churches and convents. In Catholic Montauban, before the Calvinist seizure of power, the local "corpus christianum" had been fragmented by fourteen churches and freestanding chapels, the largest of which further segmented the Christian community through the side chapels they contained and competed among themselves for preeminence in the city, thereby undermining the establishment of an orderly hierarchy of sacral spaces;[91] by a reduction of the number of sites of public worship serving the city from fourteen to at most three,[92] Montauban's ecclesiastical ge-

89. On the basis of eyewitness testimony, the seventeenth-century historian Elie Benoit said of the Temple Neuf that "il etoit malaisé de voir rien de plus propre dans une extrême simplicité." De France, p. 54.

90. Cf. de France, pp. 64-66. On the creation of "unified, open space" in German Protestant churches of the sixteenth century, see Thomas DaCosta Kaufmann, *Court, Cloister, and City: The Art and Culture of Central Europe, 1450-1800* (London: Orion, 1995), p. 135. David Thomson argues that "Protestant worship was incompatible with the compartmentalized spaces of Catholic churches." The Protestant architect Jacques Perret designed a church which could seat over nine thousand people. Thomson, "Protestant *Temples* in France," p. 247. The early eighteenth-century German architect Leonhard Christoph Sturm commented that "in Protestant churches one must ensure above all that a large crowd can see and hear a preacher clearly." Dieter Großmann, "L'église à tribunes et les tribunes des églises en Allemagne au XVIe siècle," in *L'église dans l'architecture de la Renaissance: actes du colloque tenu à Tours du 28 au 31 mai 1990*, ed. Jean Guillaume (Paris: Picard, 1995), p. 257. Cf. Reymond, pp. 79, 81.

91. Firmin Galabert and François Moulenq, *Documents historiques sur le Tarn-et-Garonne*, 4 vols. (Montauban: Forestié, 1879-92), 1:97-100, and Le Bret, 1:143-69. For the Calvinist theologian Sonis, the large number of devotional spaces with which Catholics invested their communities was evidence of their polytheistic idolatry: "il n'a bout de rue," he contended, "où on ne trouue temple, Chapelle, oratoire, couuent. Il ny a Carrefour, où il n'y ait croix: Porte de ville, où il n'y ait quelque Idole." Sonis, pp. 417-19.

92. From 1567 until 1600 Montauban was served by two Reformed churches; mass was unavailable. In the wake of a 1600 decision of the Conseil du Roi and under pressure from the crown, Montauban's Protestants allowed mass to be celebrated at the Saint-Louis church. Hostility to the Catholic presence was so intense, however, that the Catholic bishop and clergy left Montauban in 1603 and did not return until 1606. The renewal of civil war led to Montauban being deprived of its Catholic clergy from 1621 to 1623 and on two occasions from 1625 to 1629, but following the Paix d'Alès the number of Catholic churches in the city quickly increased. During the two decades of royally enjoined toleration of Catholics at Montauban that preceded the resumption of civil war in 1621, the practice of Catholicism was

ography was simplified greatly under Calvinist rule, and with the completion of the Temple Neuf was furnished with a clearly demarcated focus, providing a framework in which the interdependency and mutual obligations of the members of the urban community could be affirmed more readily and publicly.

Levesville's renovation of the Grand'Place also reflected local traditions. Montauban had been founded in 1144 as a "bastide," a community organized around a central square. At a fundamental level, then, the city was structured in a fashion which facilitated the harmoniousness achieved by Levesville's project; such "bastides" were a characteristic urban form of southwestern France.[93] Levesville strengthened the links between his renovation of the Grand'Place and customary building practices in the Midi by furnishing the arcades he reconstructed with rib vaulting, a characteristic feature of Haut-Languedocien Gothic structures.[94] In utilizing brick for virtually every aspect of the exterior of the renovation, including its massive pilasters and decorative details, Levesville and the Montalbanais continued a local tradition and provided another opportunity for local bricklayers to demonstrate their virtuosity. Moreover, although the Grand'Place was in many respects reminiscent of the architecture of the Italian Renaissance, there are considerable similarities between its facades and that of Toulouse's Hôtel de Clari, also a work of the second decade of the seventeenth century.[95] Levesville further tied his work on Montauban's Grand'Place to the architecture prevalent in the Toulousain Midi by endowing the two sides of the central square he renovated with a truncated fourth story adorned with arched windows, a feature suggestive of the galleries that Alberti, following Vitruvius, claimed

---

so hedged with restrictions that Catholic devotions served as an affirmation of Protestant hegemony: mass was to be delivered "à voix basse," and Catholics were only permitted to process in the immediate vicinity of the Saint-Louis church. Catholics who in the view of Protestant crowds were too visible were treated roughly: a 1607 Catholic burial procession was met with "grands cris" and a shower of mud and stones, one of which seriously wounded the bishop, and on returning from the burial the Catholics and their bishop were obliged to wait for an hour outside the city's walls while the consulate decided whether or not to readmit them to Montauban. The Catholic clergy were "très mal logés" and were disinclined to wander far from the Saint-Louis church, "les autres lieux publics leurs estant suspect for y estre mal traités." Bergeon, pp. 26-28; Guicharnaud, pp. 91-97, 106, 108, 111, 116; and ADTG, MS 3, pp. 268-69, 271, 273-74, 280-81, 291, 294, 302, 304; cf. Le Bret, 2:104-5. The chronicler Perrin de Grandpré believed that Catholics were but a tiny minority at Montauban at this point, but the number of Montalbanais who braved intimidation to attend mass during this period and the number who outwardly conformed to Protestantism while remaining attached to Catholicism have yet to be determined by historians.

93. Costa, "Pierre Levesville," pp. 371-72; Guicharnaud, pp. 47-48; and Ballon, p. 83.

94. Paul, "Beginnings of Gothic Architecture," p. 104, and Guicharnaud, p. 68.

95. Yves Bruand and Bruno Tollon, "L'architecture baroque toulousaine: mouvement original ou maniérisme prolongé?" *Gazette des Beaux-Arts*, 6th ser., 80, no. 1246 (November 1972): 263-64.

had surmounted ancient Greek forums,[96] but which also resembled the southwestern French practice of crowning buildings with an open gallery, known most commonly as a "mirande," but also as a "soulelhadou" in Languedoc and an "arrajadé" at Auch.[97]

Local Particularism, Southern Urban Elites, and the Renovation of Urban Space: Aix-en-Provence, Marseille, Moissac, Toulouse, and Montpellier

The strong municipal government which made possible the reshaping of Montauban's urban topography was not unique to the Bas-Quercinois city: indeed, in the southern French context the inertia of Toulouse was more exceptional than the dynamism of Montauban.[98] As the expansion of Marseille in the late seventeenth century and Aix-en-Provence's Quartier Mazarin development demonstrated, the comparatively modest and locally focused approach to urban design embraced at Montauban persisted in the Midi after celebrating the monarchy had become the central concern of most urban renovation projects in northern France. The Aixois and Marseillais expansions were facilitated by interventionist local governments; Marseille's *échevins* were particularly aggressive, in 1668 taking control of and enlarging greatly the expansion project originally undertaken by the crown, now to be centered on a "cours" along which the *échevins* enforced the use of common building materials and respect for a design for facades prescribed in detail. Although the newly developed area at Marseille provided the space necessary for some Marseillais to erect Parisian "hôtels entre cour et jardin," the expansion was dominated by housing for prosperous artisans; it was not a theater for the celebration of royal power, and many of the structures surrounding the new Cours de Marseille were

---

96. Alberti, 2:714-15.

97. Paul Roudié and J. Ducos, "Le château de Caumont," and Henri Polge, "La ville d'Auch," *Congrès archéologique de France* 128 (1970): 283, 340, 340 n; Henri Pradalier, "Le Palais de la Berbie," *Congrès archéologique de France* 140 (1982): 134; Tollon, "La ville de brique," pp. 35-36; Costa, "Pierre Levesville," pp. 336, 371; and Guicharnaud, p. 68.

98. The inertia of Toulouse was in large measure a result of the power struggle between the Capitoulat and the Parlement. At Bordeaux, too, the Parlement hobbled the municipal government. Newly created sovereign courts such as the ones established at Agen and Montauban in the seventeenth century, though adding to the burden imposed on hard-pressed taxpayers, were effective in the preservation of royal authority: their judges owed their positions to the crown, contributed handsomely to the royal coffers through the sums they paid for their positions, served as another arm of the royal bureaucracy, and could curtail municipal autonomy significantly. William Beik, *Urban Protest in Seventeenth-Century France: The Culture of Retribution* (Cambridge: Cambridge University Press, 1997), pp. 78, 260-61.

decorated in a style strongly reminiscent of Italian baroque, not French classicism.[99]

Despite paralyzing conflicts with other governing institutions, the Toulousain Capitoulat was insistent on asserting its autonomy and importance. The pride of the *capitouls* found expression in the group portraits of themselves they commissioned each year, a widespread practice in Languedoc.[100] Like southern French architecture, Toulousain painting was often austere in tone; this sobriety accorded well with the early seventeenth-century fashion for "nuits," artificially illuminated nocturnal scenes.[101] One of the more accomplished practitioners of this genre was the Provençal Trophime Bigot le Jeune, who was active and commercially successful at Rome between 1620 and 1634.[102] At Toulouse, the style was continued and invested with great emotional power by Nicolas Tournier, who had been born a Protestant but later converted to Catholicism; in his austere treatments of biblical themes darkness provides a stark setting, focusing attention on grave and pensive figures isolated from one another in contemplative silence, their expressions connoting an acute awareness of the profundity of the events in which they are involved (see plate 27).[103] Jean Chalette used the contrast provided by darkness with striking effectiveness in his 1622 portrait of the Toulousain *capitouls* (see plate 28): against a dark background he presents a crucified Christ, behind whom he depicts members of the Capitoulat kneeling before their prie-dieu and facing the viewer. Some art critics of the eighteenth

99. Gloton, 2:256, 269-72, 362, 371-73, and Béatrice Hénin, "L'agrandissement de Marseille," *Annales du Midi* 98, no. 173 (January-March 1986): 11-12, 14, 17, 19. Marseille's *échevins* insisted on taking control of their city's expansion from the crown despite Louis XIV's recently minted measures to curtail the city's autonomy dramatically, which included transforming consuls into *échevins* and subjecting their election to royal approval. The Aixois were able to bring the Quartier Mazarin project to a highly successful conclusion despite the repeated factional power struggles that marked the administrative center's history in the seventeenth century. On these conflicts see Sharon Kettering, *Judicial Politics and Urban Revolt in Seventeenth-Century France: The Parlement of Aix, 1629-1659* (Princeton: Princeton University Press, 1978), pp. 150-81, 251-328.

100. Several of the extant early seventeenth-century portraits of Montpelliérain consuls have been attributed to the Protestant painter Pierre Varin. In 1657 the Montpelliérain consuls paid native son Sébastien Bourdon 1,300 livres for a collective portrait and one of each of the consuls accompanied by his wife; Bourdon had been expelled from the city as a boy during the siege of 1622 as one of the "bouches inutiles." Baumel, pp. 310, 312.

101. Mérot, pp. 81-83.

102. Little documentation has been unearthed concerning this artist, described by Jacques Thuillier as "l'une des énigmes les plus singulières qui se soient proposées durant ces dernières années aux historiens de l'art du XVIIᵉ siècle." See Mérot, pp. 83-84, and Jacques Thuillier, " 'Trophime Bigot' " and "Le 'Maître à la Chandelle,' " in *La peinture en Provence au XVIIᵉ siècle*, ed. Henri Wytenhove (Marseille: Laffitte, 1978), pp. 3, 6.

103. Arnauld Brejon de Lavergnée and Jean-Pierre Cuzin, *Valentin et les caravagesques français* (Paris: Musées Nationaux, 1974), pp. 106, 118-19; Benedict Nicholson, *Caravaggism in Europe,* ed. Luisa Vertova, 3 vols. (Torino: Allemandi, 1990), vol. 2, pls. 610-11, 626-28, 630, 632; and Peligry, Penent, and Suzzoni, p. 74.

century were scandalized by the painting, claiming that not to portray the *capitouls* facing the suffering Christ was a sacrilegious departure from custom. Chalette's work did not give rise to such complaints in the early seventeenth century: although the artist allows himself an ironic comment on the preoccupation of the *capitouls* with making known their worldly status by placing at the foot of the crucifix a skull, familiar to contemporaries as a symbol of vanity, his painting was nonetheless a particularly forceful instance of a tendency of these portraits of the *capitouls* to present the municipal government as the principal guarantor of the preservation of proper devotion.[104] Chalette associates the *capitouls* with the crucifixion intimately, underlining their role as defenders of the faith.

This collective portrait shows Catholic consuls of the Midi ascribing to themselves a centrality in religious reform similar to the stance adopted by their Protestant counterparts. Indeed, an urban Counter-Reformation such as Moissac experienced in the early seventeenth century could closely parallel the earlier implementation of a Protestant Reformation elsewhere: like the Calvinists of nearby Montauban, the Moissagais elite sought a greater degree of responsiveness to the expectations of the laity from their church, including in their demands such Protestant themes as dedication to preaching and the assigning of local church revenues to schooling.[105] Montauban and Montpellier repudiated domination by Toulouse in adopting Protestantism; Moissac repudiated domination by Montauban in adhering to Catholicism,[106] but the Counter-Reformation at Moissac echoed the Reformation at Montauban by fashioning a church more responsive to the priorities of local lay elites. An attempt to refashion the local church radically had also been mounted at Toulouse in 1562, when a Protestant insurrection aimed at seizing control of the city was not opposed by the Capitoulat. But this initiative was brutally crushed by the church and its allies, the most important of which was the resolutely Catholic and royalist *parlement*.[107] In 1589 another effort was made at Toulouse to place the

104. Peligry, Penent, and Suzzoni, pp. 21, 50-52; Alain Mousseigne, *Jean Chalette* (Toulouse: Musée des Augustins, 1974), p. 46; and Christian Cau, *Les capitouls de Toulouse: l'intégrale des portraits des "Annales de la Ville"* (Toulouse: Privat, 1990), pp. 33, 35-36, 79, 93-95. Many more portraits of the Toulousain *capitouls* have survived than depictions of comparable figures for other early modern French cities and towns, rendering comparisons problematic; nonetheless, the surviving portraits of Parisian *échevins* of the seventeenth century do not allow themselves to ascribe the importance to their subjects attributed by Chalette to the *capitouls* of 1622. Cf. Mérot, pp. 196-97.

105. ADTG, G 575.

106. ADTG, MS 3, pp. 210, 212-13, 218; Le Bret, 2:11-12; and Arlette Jouanna, "La première domination des réformés à Montpellier," in *Les Réformes: enracinement socio-culturel,* ed. Bernard Chevalier and Robert Sauzet (Paris: de la Maisnie, 1985), p. 152.

107. Joan Davies, "Persecution and Protestantism: Toulouse, 1562-1575," *Historical Journal* 22, no. 1 (1979): 32-34, and Mark Greengrass, "The Anatomy of a Religious Riot in Toulouse in May 1562," *Journal of Ecclesiastical History* 34, no. 3 (July 1983): 382-83, 390.

church more firmly under the control of local elites by aligning the city with the Sainte Union, but nationally that movement proved to be unable to defeat Henry IV and his supporters, and hence collapsed.[108]

In the seventeenth century, the primacy of Toulouse as a center of government in Languedoc was rivaled increasingly by Montpellier. Though Montpellier became a bastion of absolutism, the "hôtels" erected by its wealthy denizens reflected the tenacity of regional culture in the city. The local social elite, representatives of the crown, and the Catholic Church made a sustained effort to introduce a more northern, classical building style to their city. This campaign was the result of a desire for a closer association with the culture of the Île-de-France in a city which had been a bulwark of Protestant resistance to the crown, but whose social elite in the wake of the siege of 1622 grew increasingly keen to demonstrate their fealty to the king: Louis XIII had not been able to subdue Montpellier during that siege, but the war had drained the resources of southern Calvinists, and in order to bring the conflict to an end they allowed the Montpelliérain consulate to be evenly split between Catholics and Protestants, ensuring that the city's government would be more friendly to the expansion of royal power, and also permitted a garrison of two royal regiments to be imposed on Montpellier in order to dismantle its recently erected defenses. By 1643, the year of Louis XIII's death, the black tiles of Montpellier's new Palais Royal towered over the pink roofs of the city, affirming the central government's presence in a highly visible manner; the king's power was asserted more aggressively by a formidable citadel which was built on a plateau overlooking the city to house its new garrison. Although Montpellier's social elite was eager to align itself with the crown, particularly since its members had had occasion recently to observe that their control over Montpellier was becoming difficult to maintain without royal buttressing, the propertied denizens of the city were limited in their capacity to transform their late medieval, Italianate, vertically oriented "hostals" into expansive Parisian "hôtels entre cour et jardin" by the small size of their lots. Moreover, most of these patrons of local architects retained some affection for the Gothic, and consequently a relatively modest and uniquely Montpelliérain style evolved that mixed elements of late medieval Mediterranean and French classical architecture (see fig. 51).[109]

Greengrass comments that "by appealing successfully to the powerful sense of corporate municipal identity in the city, typical of the French Midi generally, the [Protestant] revolt . . . became one in which the political rights of *capitouls* and *parlement* were a matter for dispute."

108. Schneider, pp. 122-28, 130-31, and Michael Wolfe, *The Conversion of Henri IV: Politics, Power, and Religious Belief in Early Modern France* (Cambridge, Mass.: Harvard University Press, 1993), pp. 164-80, 191.

109. Sournia and Vayssettes, pp. 18-19, 31-71.

51. Courtyard of the Hôtel de Sarret, Montpellier, renovated extensively in 1637 under the direction of Bertrand Delane, a Bayonnais architect. An elegant entrance to an interior stairway and the extensive use of rustication are in accord with contemporary northern tastes, but the contract for the renovations specified Gothic windows for two sides of the courtyard, largely effaced by subsequent changes.

Conclusion

At Montpellier some features of southern architecture proved resilient despite the city's important role as a center of the expansion of the absolutist state, but Montpellier's Protestants had been marginalized politically well before Louis XIV's criminalization of Protestantism in 1685.[110] Elsewhere, the survival of Protestant power into the late seventeenth century was compatible with the preservation of the region's architectural traditions. Protestant iconoclasm had damaged or destroyed many southern churches, paintings, tapestries, and sculptures, but this destructiveness reflected a suspicion of the ornate that, although evident in many geographic settings, had long been especially pronounced in the Toulousain Midi: where the visual arts were concerned, the centralizing culture patronized by the Bourbon state was more fundamentally at odds with traditional southern culture than with Calvinism. The only Protestant church in France dating from before 1685 that still stands and has not undergone major exterior renovations is that of Collet-de-Dèze, erected in 1646. Here, not far from Mende, where Pierre Levesville began to acquire a reputation among Languedocians as a man capable of successfully confronting the challenges posed by the restoration of Gothic churches, a small Protestant community erected a simple church surmounted by one of the "clocher-murs" typical of the region. Inside the small, simple church, the communal bond between the preacher and his flock is emphasized by a single longitudinal arch, which supports the building's roof.[111]

Here the southwestern inclination toward austerity was perpetuated, and the traditional understanding of the church as the public locus of the affirmation of community reaffirmed. The congregation of Collet-de-Dèze could not muster the financial resources at the disposal of the consistory and consulate of Montauban, and thus was unlikely to have been troubled by debates concerning what concessions to Italianate mannerism or classicism good Calvinists could make. Montauban's social elite were willing to associate themselves with innovative architecture, encouraging the dissemination of a more deferential attitude toward themselves and prominently announcing their distinctiveness, but nonetheless in many respects proved to be no less traditional than the denizens of Collet-de-Dèze, endowing their city with a grand but austere legacy of buildings erected with local materials and reflecting local traditions which asserted the cohesiveness of their community. Aesthetically as well as politically and spiritually, Calvinism was compatible with the culture of the Midi in rural as well as urban contexts.

---

110. Philip Benedict, "Faith, Fortune and Social Structure in Seventeenth-Century Montpellier," *Past and Present*, no. 152 (August 1996): 53, 75.
111. Reymond, pp. 49-50, 52-53.

Some Suggestions for Further Reading

Although problematic in some respects, Janine Garrisson's *Protestants du Midi 1559-1598* (Toulouse: Privat, 1980) continues to be an invaluable point of departure for any study of southern French Calvinism in the sixteenth century. Garrisson's *L'édit de Nantes et sa révocation: histoire d'une intolérance* (Paris: Seuil, 1985) provides a helpful narrative for the seventeenth century; probing analysis of developments over the same period is offered by Philip Benedict, *The Huguenot Population of France, 1600-1685: The Demographic Fate and Customs of a Religious Minority* (Philadelphia: American Philosophical Society, 1991).

The architecture of two cities of central importance in the history of southern French Calvinism has been the subject of two excellent, recently published studies, Bernard Sournia and Jean-Louis Vayssettes' *Montpellier: la demeure classique* (Paris: Imprimerie Nationale, 1994) and Hélène Guicharnaud's *Montauban au XVIIᵉ: 1560/1685* (Paris: Picard, 1991). A comprehensive study of the architecture of Nîmes in the early modern period is provided by Corinne Potay's "L'architecture de l'âge classique à Nîmes: fin XVIᵉ siècle-fin XVIIIᵉ siècle" (thèse de l'histoire de l'art, Université Lyon II-Lumière, 1991).

Jean-Jacques Gloton's *Renaissance et Baroque à Aix-en-Provence: recherches sur la culture architecturale dans le Midi de la France de la fin du XVᵉ au début du XVIIIᵉ siècle*, 2 vols. (Roma: Ecole Française, 1979) is fundamental for the study of Provençal architecture. Three catalogues provide a comprehensive overview of early modern painting in Provence: *La peinture en Provence au XVIᵉ siècle*, ed. Marie-Paule Vial et al. (Marseille: Rivages, 1987); *La peinture en Provence au XVIIᵉ siècle*, ed. Henri Wytenhove (Marseille: Laffitte, 1978); and Jean Boyer, "La peinture et la gravure à Aix-en-Provence aux XVIᵉ, XVIIᵉ, et XVIIIᵉ siècles," *Gazette des Beaux-Arts*, 6th ser., 78, nos. 1230-32 (July-September 1971): 1-188.

For an informative account of the early modern history of Toulouse, see Robert Alan Schneider, *Public Life in Toulouse, 1463-1789: From Municipal Republic to Cosmopolitan City* (Ithaca: Cornell University Press, 1989). Intelligent commentary on Toulousain painting is offered by Christian Peligry, Jean Penent, and Jean-Pierre Suzzoni, *Le portrait toulousain de 1550 à 1800: exposition présentée au Musée des Augustins du 21 octobre 1987 au 7 janvier 1988* (Toulouse: Loubatières, 1987). Much of value concerning Toulousain architecture can be found in *Toulouse: les délices de l'imitation*, ed. Maurice Culot (Liège: Mardaga, 1986). On Toulouse as a regional center of artistic endeavor, see Robert Mesuret, *Toulouse: métropole artistique de l'Occitanie* (Lunel: Saber, 1986).

On the history of Calvinism in Guyenne, two studies by Gregory Hanlon are valuable: *L'univers des gens de bien: culture et comportements des élites urbaines en Agenais-Condomois au XVIIᵉ siècle* (Bordeaux: Presses Universitaires, 1989) and *Confession and Community in Seventeenth-Century France: Catholic and Protestant Coexistence in Aquitaine* (Philadelphia: University of Pennsylvania Press, 1993). A good point of departure for studying the early modern history of printing in southwestern France is provided by Louis Desgraves, *Etudes sur l'imprimerie dans le Sud-Ouest de la France aux XVe, XVIe et XVIIe siècles* (Amsterdam: Erasmus, 1968). For Bordeaux, a good overview of the early modern period is offered by *Bordeaux de 1453 à 1715,* ed. Robert Boutruche (Bordeaux: Fédération Historique du Sud-Ouest, 1966).

For the best narrative of Montauban's history in this period see Garrisson, "La 'Genève française'" and "La reconquête catholique," in *Histoire de Montauban,* ed. Daniel Ligou (Toulouse: Privat, 1984), pp. 99-166; my forthcoming Johns Hopkins University at Baltimore doctoral thesis, "Community and Religious Reform in Montauban and the Bas-Quercy, 1547 to 1629," explores a number of the issues discussed in this essay at greater length. A good start on the complex history of Haut-Languedocien Calvinism can be made via R. A. Mentzer, *Blood and Belief: Family Survival and Confessional Identity among the Provincial Huguenot Nobility* (West Lafayette: Purdue University Press, 1994). On the early history of Calvinism in the Rouergue, see Nicole Lemaitre, *Le Rouergue flamboyant: clergé et paroisses du diocèse de Rodez* (Paris: Cerf, 1988).

An excellent analysis of the Calvinist seizure of power at Montpellier is provided by Arlette Jouanna, "La première domination des réformés à Montpellier," in *Les Réformes: enracinement socio-culturel,* ed. Bernard Chevalier and Robert Sauzet (Paris: de la Maisnie, 1985), pp. 151-60. A helpful narrative of the more tumultuous segments of the history of the city during the early modern period is offered by Jean Baumel, *Montpellier au cours des XVIe et XVIIe siècles: les guerres de religion* (Montpellier: Causse, 1976). The changing social structure of the city is explored in Frederick Irvine, "Social Structure, Social Mobility and Social Change in Sixteenth-Century Montpellier: From Renaissance City-State to *Ancien-Régime* Capital" (Ph.D. diss., University of Toronto, 1979), and Benedict, "Faith, Fortune and Social Structure in Seventeenth-Century Montpellier," *Past and Present,* no. 152 (August 1996): 46-78.

Several historians have explored the relatively ample documentation extant concerning Nîmes's Protestants in the sixteenth and seventeenth centuries; see Ann Guggenheim, "Calvinism and the Political Elite of Sixteenth Century Nîmes" (Ph.D. diss., New York University, 1968), and "The Calvinist Notables of Nimes during the Era of the Religious Wars," *Sixteenth Century Journal* 3 (1972): 80-96; Philippe Chareyre, "'The Great Difficulties One Must Bear to Follow Jesus Christ': Morality at Sixteenth-Century Nîmes," trans. R. A. Mentzer, in *Sin and the Calvinists: Morals Control and the Consistory in the Reformed Tradition,* ed. R. A. Mentzer (Kirksville, Mo.: Sixteenth Century Journal, 1994), pp. 63-94, and "Le consistoire de

Nîmes 1561-1685," 4 vols. (thèse de doctorat, Université Paul Valéry, 1987); R. A. Mentzer, "Ecclesiastical Discipline and Communal Reorganization among the Protestants of Southern France," *European History Quarterly* 21, no. 2 (1991): 163-83; and Sauzet, "L'iconoclasme dans le diocèse de Nîmes au XVIᵉ et au début du XVIIᵉ siècle," *Revue d'histoire de l'église de France* 66, no. 176 (January-June 1980): 5-15. On Calvinism in the Cévennes, see Didier Poton, "Aux origines du protestantisme en Basses Cévennes," *Bulletin de la Société de l'Histoire du Protestantisme Français* 129, no. 4 (1983): 469-88; Alain Molinier, "Aux origines de la Réformation cévenole," *Annales* 39, no. 2 (1984): 240-64; and R. A. Mentzer, "Le consistoire et la pacification du monde rural," trans. Elisabeth Labrousse, *Bulletin de la Société de l'Histoire du Protestantisme Français* 135, no. 3 (1989): 373-89.

On Calvinism in Provence, much can be gleaned from Marc Venard, *L'église d'Avignon au XVIe siècle,* 5 vols. (Lille: Université de Lille III, 1980), recently reissued with minor revisions as *Réforme protestante, réforme catholique dans la province d'Avignon au XVIe siècle* (Paris: Cerf, 1993). On the relatively numerous but historiographically neglected Protestants of early modern Dauphiné, see *Le protestantisme en Dauphiné au XVIIᵉ siècle,* ed. Pierre Bolle (La Bégude de Mazenc: Curandera, 1983); *Le protestant dauphinois et la république des synodes à la veille de la Révocation,* ed. Bolle (Lyon: La Manufacture, 1985); Elisabeth Rabut, *Le roi, l'église et le temple: l'éxecution de l'Edit de Nantes en Dauphiné* (Grenoble: Pensée Sauvage, 1987); Laurence Fontaine, "Affare di stato, affare di famiglie: politica anti-protestante, strategie private e vita comunitaria in una valle alpina nel XVII secolo," *Quaderni Storici,* new ser., 24, no. 3 (December 1989): 849-82; for some evidence concerning their reading habits, see Hubert Carrier et al., *Livres et lecteurs à Grenoble: les registres du libraire Nicolas,* 2 vols. (Genève: Droz, 1977).

The Reformed Churches of France and the Visual Arts

RAYMOND A. MENTZER JR.

The creative achievement of the French Reformed community during the sixteenth and seventeenth centuries was substantial and multifaceted as Calvinists throughout the kingdom repeatedly demonstrated rich and distinctive artistic talent, especially in the areas of literature and music. The poet Clément Marot's (1496-1544) rendering of some fifty psalms into metrical French[1] and their subsequent incorporation into the Calvinist liturgy are the best-known examples. Calvin himself took pleasure in music,[2] and composers such as Loys Bourgeois (ca. 1510–ca. 1560) and Claude Goudimel (ca. 1514-72) created tunes appropriate for congregational singing of the sacred verses. Even today, the Psalter[3] remains a familiar, engaging text for Reformed worshipers.

At the same time, gifted Calvinists realized important accomplishments in the pictorial arts and in architecture. The work of sculptors Jean Goujon (ca. 1510–ca. 1567) and Ligier Richier (ca. 1500-1567) and of painters Abraham Bosse (1602-76), Sébastien Bourdon (1616-71), and the Testelin brothers — Louis (1615-65) and Henri (1616-95) — attest the breadth and depth of artistic inspiration and ability within Protestant circles. Menna Prestwich[4]

---

1. The classic study is Orentin Douen, *Clément Marot et le psautier huguenot*, 2 vols. (Paris: Imprimerie Nationale, 1878-79).

2. Menna Prestwich, "Calvinism in France, 1559-1629," in *International Calvinism, 1541-1715*, ed. Menna Prestwich (Oxford: Clarendon Press, 1985), p. 75.

3. For the early printing history of the Psalter, see Eugénie Droz, "Antoine Vincent: le propogande protestante par le psautier," in *Aspects de la propogande religieuses* (Geneva: Librairie Droz, 1957), pp. 276-93. Francis Higman, *La diffusion de la Réforme en France, 1520-1565* (Geneva: Labor et Fides, 1992), pp. 120-32.

4. Menna Prestwich, "Patronage and the Protestants in France, 1598-1661: Architects

and Anthony Blunt[5] have taken special care to underscore the importance of Huguenot contributions in the architectural sphere. They point out that French Protestant capabilities were nowhere more apparent than in the work of Salomon de Brosse (ca. 1571-1626) or various members of the du Cerceau family, especially Jacques I Androuet du Cerceau (ca. 1520–ca. 1585), Baptiste Androuet du Cerceau (ca. 1545-90), and Jacques II Androuet du Cerceau (1550-1614).[6] Altogether, Calvinist participation in the arts, including architecture, was diverse, strong, and dynamic.

Still, much of the activity that historians have traditionally cited and examined, particularly for the visual arts, occurred only among the cultural and political elite, typically at Paris and with considerable aristocratic, often royal patronage. Less clear is the place of art and architecture in the provinces and at the local level — within the broader landscape of the ordinary faithful. How, for example, did Protestant townspeople and villagers understand the architectural imagination displayed in their temples? What, in their estimation, were appropriate decoration and ornamentation? What, above all, was the conjunction of art, worship, and everyday life? In exploring these and related issues, I wish to draw upon the deeply informative archival records of the local Reformed churches and their consistories. Attention to the activities of individual congregations and the temples that they built under the guidance of civic and religious leaders can identify and amplify a number of ideas, insights, and perspectives.

1. Architecture

French Calvinists, in their design and construction of buildings for worship, were keenly aware of the architectural requirements of Reformed religious services. The special weight placed upon the pastor's sermon and the faithful's vigorous participation in the liturgy through prayer and song prompted a reconsideration of building plans. The new structural arrangements, while drawing from established architectural traditions, sought to create an open auditorium where people could assemble and listen to the pastor announce the word of God. The goal was to allow the congregants to see, hear, and share in a corporate liturgical worship.

---

and Painters," in *L'Age d'or du Mécénat (1598-1661)*, ed. Roland Mousnier and Jean Mesnard (Paris: Editions du Centre National de la Recherche Scientifique, 1985), pp. 77-88.

5. Anthony Blunt, *Art and Architecture in France, 1500 to 1700*, 2nd ed. (Baltimore: Penguin, 1970), pp. 80-85, 94-104.

6. See, in addition, the remarks of Jean-Pierre Babelon, *Demeures parisiennes sous Henri IV et Louis XIII* (Paris: Le Temps, 1965), pp. 241-43, and Emile-G. Léonard, *Histoire générale du Protestantisme*, 3 vols. (Paris: Presses Universitaires de France, 1961), 2:124, 150-51, 315, 334-35.

The Calvinist redefinition and reconfiguration of sacred space is a good place to begin the discussion. Rejecting medieval sacramentalism, including the real presence in the Eucharist, French Reformers ceased to regard the church building as a holy and sacred place, a sanctuary in which God was manifestly present.[7] One of the by-products of this attitude was that they abandoned the cruciform church — the "temple of the idols," according to some Calvinist commentators[8] — in favor of longitudinal and centralized, frequently amphitheatric, assembly halls. The altar and "false service of the mass"[9] disappeared. The pulpit and communion table, representations of the Word and the sacrament, now occupied the central position.[10] Around them, the devout gathered to hear the pastor's sermons and partake of the Lord's Supper.

The replacement of the altar by the pulpit as the focal point of the worship also lent a more unified, spatially undifferentiated quality to the temple interior. The occasionally disjoined character of medieval church buildings — divided as they were into devotional side chapels and exhibiting multiple altars, choir stalls, and rood screens — gave way to a more integrated spatial arrangement.[11] Liturgical differences visibly transformed the character of buildings which the French Calvinists created for public worship. Finally, an austere, even ascetic view of proper Protestant worship, perhaps most dramatically displayed in the widespread aniconism — cult without images — associated with the Reformed movement, led to a "cleansing" of the interior, modifying the appearance considerably from the elaborate decoration of the pre-Reformation era. The Calvinist temples in France were modest, plain, relatively unembellished structures. Their aesthetic consists in an elegant simplicity.

The Calvinist penchant for redefining sacred space — evident in the design and function of the temple — extended to other areas of public life. The Reformed church of Nîmes,[12] for instance, redrew the community's religious boundaries, laying out supervisory districts for the elders of the consistory. Every local church had a consistory composed of one or

7. John Calvin, *Institutio Christianae Religionis . . .* (1559), 3.20.30, in *Ioannis Calvini Opera quae supersunt omnia* 2, ed. G. Baum, E. Cunitz, and E. Reuss, 59 vols. (Brunswick: C. A. Schwetschke, 1863-1900), 2:758-59. Bernard Reymond, *L'architecture religieuse des protestants* (Geneva: Labor et Fides, 1996), pp. 46-48.

8. Archives Départementales (hereafter cited as AD), Gers, 23067, 20 avril 1618.

9. AD, Gers, 23067, 20 avril 1618.

10. André Biéler, *Liturgie et architecture. Le temple des chrétiens* (Geneva: Labor et Fides, 1961), pp. 79-81. On Biéler and the "Protestant principle" in church architecture, see Paul Corby Finney, "Early Christian Architecture: The Beginnings," *Harvard Theological Review* 81 (1988): 325-27.

11. G. W. O. Addleshaw and F. Etchells, *The Architectural Setting of Anglican Worship* (London: Faber and Faber, 1948), pp. 15-22; Reymond, *L'architecture religieuse*, p. 101.

12. Philippe Chareyre, "Le consistoire de Nîmes, 1561-1685" (Thèse de doctorat d'Etat, Université Paul Valéry — Montpellier III, 1987), pp. 340-47.

more pastors and a dozen or so laypersons serving as elders and deacons. The members, in their weekly meetings, directed the religious life of the community and had primary responsibility for ecclesiastical administration, social welfare, and above all morals control.[13] The elders, in particular, watched over the behavior of the faithful. At Nîmes, each had charge over one of nine districts or *surveillances* into which the church had divided the city. These ecclesiastical supervisory districts, however, bore little resemblance to either the traditional municipal quarters or long-established medieval parishes. Their geography was new and distinctive. The situation differed from Geneva[14] and cities in other parts of Switzerland where the reformers tended to retain and adapt pre-Reformation civic forms, ecclesiastical buildings, and parish arrangements, including parish boundaries.

An immediate, troublesome obstacle to knowing in precise fashion the creative legacy of Protestant religious architecture in France is the absence of surviving structures. Louis XIV's officers pulled down nearly all the French temples as the crown moved toward the general proscription of Protestantism in 1685.[15] These royal Catholic counterreformers removed materially and psychologically the sites of what they considered repeated abomination and pollution.[16] Recovering the sparse details means sifting through ecclesiastical and municipal documents, a handful of sketches and plans, reports by contemporaries, and later scholarly descriptions, many of whose original sources have since disappeared. There are some exceptions, such as the second temple at Charenton, which served the Protestants of Paris and for which there is unusually rich documentation.

The temples of the Reformed churches of France stood at the center of a vigorous communal religious life. John Calvin, *Institutes* 4.1.9-10, identified what he believed to be the marks of the true church. He emphasized the pure preaching of the gospel and the right administration of the

13. By way of introduction to the Reformed consistory in France, see Raymond A. Mentzer, "*Disciplina nervus ecclesiae*: The Calvinist Reform of Morals at Nîmes," *Sixteenth Century Journal* 18 (1987): 89-115; Mentzer, "Organizational Endeavour and Charitable Impulse in Sixteenth-Century France: The Case of Protestant Nîmes," *French History* 5 (1991): 1-29.

14. For Geneva, see William G. Naphy, "The Renovation of the Ministry in Calvin's Geneva," in *The Reformation of the Parishes: The Ministry and the Reformation in Town and Country,* ed. Andrew Pettegree (Manchester and New York: Manchester University Press, 1993), p. 116; for Zurich, Bruce Gordon, "Preaching and the Reform of the Clergy in the Swiss Reformation," in *The Reformation of the Parishes,* p. 68.

15. The temple at the southern French town of Collet-de-Dèze, which was built in 1646, is the only one that has survived in its original state. Reymond, *L'architecture religieuse,* p. 52.

16. See, inter alia, Albert Colombet, "Les temples protestants en Bourgogne," *Pays de Bourgogne* 118 (1982): 1015-17; Suzanne Tucoo-Chala, "Un patrimoine méconnu des pays de l'Adour: les temples réformés XVIe-XXe siècles," *Revue de Pau et du Béarn* 18 (1991): 35-57.

sacraments.[17] To these, Reformers such as Martin Bucer,[18] Théodore de Bèze,[19] and John Knox[20] added discipline — the promotion of virtue and punishment of sin — as a third mark. Although Calvin and the others were referring in their discussions to the church as the body of believers, the French temple was very much an architectural expression of their concerns. It was the physical locus for the actions associated with the explicit underpinnings of the church noted by Calvin, Bucer, and other Protestant theologians. Here the pastors preached and taught true doctrine as found in Scripture; the congregation gathered for reception of the sacraments, namely, baptism and the Lord's Supper, as well as for the performance of other religious ceremonies, including daily prayer; and the consistory met regularly to administer the discipline that Calvin and his followers deemed essential for the pious conduct of the faithful.

French Calvinists, unlike followers of the Reformed movement elsewhere in Europe, tended not to appropriate Catholic churches for their places of worship, even in the towns that they controlled. During the earliest years of the movement, they frequently met in private dwellings or buildings converted from other public uses. The Nîmes congregation first met in houses belonging to the faithful, later in the former Franciscan monastery, and briefly in the cathedral and town hall before beginning construction of a temple in 1565. Protestants at neighboring Calvisson gathered initially in a mill. The *temple de Paradis* at Lyon was a private structure, which the Calvinists renovated in 1564. The earliest worship site at Montauban, known as the *Grande Boucherie,* had probably been a butcher shop or slaughterhouse before the Reformation.[21]

17. "Symbola ecclesia dignoscendae, verbi praedicationem sacramentorumque observationem posuimus." Calvin, *Calvini Opera*, 2:754. My thanks to Glenn S. Sunshine for allowing me to draw upon his fine unpublished paper "Discipline as the Third Mark of the Church: Three Views." In his 1539 debate with Cardinal Sadoleto, Calvin spoke of discipline. Addressing the apostolic model of a true church, he argued that "there are three things upon which the safety of the Church is founded, viz., doctrine, discipline, and the sacraments. . . ." John Calvin and Jacopo Sadoleto, *A Reformation Debate*, ed. John C. Olin (New York: Harper and Row, 1966), p. 63.

18. The many aspects of Bucer's ideas on discipline are summarized and analyzed by Amy Nelson Burnett, "Church Discipline and Moral Reformation in the Thought of Martin Bucer," *Sixteenth Century Journal* 22 (1991): 439-56; Burnett, *The Yoke of Christ: Martin Bucer and Christian Discipline* (Kirksville, Mo.: Sixteenth Century Journal Publishers, 1994).

19. ". . . en quelque lieu que la Parole de Dieu soit purement annoncée, les Sacramens purement administrez, avec la police ecclésiastique dressée conformement à la saincte et pure doctrine, là nous recognoisons l'Eglise de Dieu. . . ." Théodore de Bèze, *Confession de la foy chrestienne, contenant la confirmation d'icelle, et la refutation des superstitions contraires* (Geneva: Conrad Badius, 1559), pp. 156-57.

20. "The third marke of the church is ecclesiastical discipline, which standeth in admonition, and correction of fautes." John Knox, *The forme of prayers and ministration of Sacraments, etc. used in the English Congregation of Geneva* (Geneva: Jean Crespin, 1556), p. 39.

21. Chareyre, "Le consistoire de Nîmes," pp. 292-95; Hélène Guicharnaud, *Montauban*

Religious warfare and iconoclastic riots, moreover, had led to the severe damage of many ecclesiastical structures. Protestant mobs throughout France pillaged, and in some cases destroyed, medieval churches and monasteries. At the southern French town of Nîmes and in the surrounding area, for instance, popular violence erupted by summer 1561. Participants seized and sacked churches, pulled down statues and crosses, overturned altars, and drove out priests and monks.[22] The repair of these buildings would have required substantial financial effort. Here and elsewhere, other structures needed extensive remodeling to meet the distinct liturgical requirements of the Reformed congregations. Accordingly, Huguenots often preferred newly built facilities. The Protestants of Aimargues destroyed the church of the Sainte-Croix in 1572 and then put up an entirely new edifice for their temple.[23] At their Atlantic stronghold of La Rochelle, the Calvinists worshiped sporadically during the 1560s at the pre-Reformation churches of Saint-Barthélemy and Saint-Sauveur. The subsequent ruin of these churches during years of strife and warfare, however, forced Protestants to lease various buildings, a banquet hall and tennis court, for services. Still, the arrangements proved awkward and unsuitable. Eventually they began construction of a new temple.[24]

Equally important, French Calvinists were a minority whose relationship with the Catholic monarchy was always ambivalent and strained. The king typically forced them to return medieval churches and related structures to Catholic claimants. Huguenots at Sancerre worshiped in the church of Saint-Jean until 1573 when, following a long siege, Catholic troops captured the town. For many years thereafter, the Calvinists of Sancerre had no specific place where they could gather. Permission to build a temple came only with the promulgation of the Edict of Nantes in 1598. At Mas-Grenier, Protestants met in the wine cellar of the medieval monas-

---

au XVIIe, 1560-1685. Urbanisme et architecture (Paris: Picard, 1991), p. 91; Aimé-Daniel Rabinel, "Le temple de Calvisson (Gard)," Bulletin de la Société de l'Histoire du Protestantisme Français 112 (1966): 250 (this periodical will hereafter be cited as BSHPF).

22. Robert Sauzet, "L'iconoclasme dans le diocèse de Nîmes au XVIe et au début du XVIIe siècle," Revue d'histoire de l'Eglise de France 66 (1980): 5-15. On the general subject of iconoclasm and the French Reformation, see the study by Olivier Christin, Une révolution symbolique: l'iconoclasme huguenot et la reconstruction catholique (Paris: Les Editions de Minuit, 1991). A helpful recent examination of iconoclasm in the neighboring Swiss and German world is Lee Palmer Wandel, Voracious Idols and Violent Hands: Iconoclasm in Reformation Zurich, Strasbourg, and Basel (Cambridge: Cambridge University Press, 1995).

23. Philippe Chareyre, Extension et limites du dimorphisme social et religieux en Bas-Languedoc: Aimargues, 1584-1635 (Mémoire de maîtrise: Université Paul Valéry — Montpellier III, 1978), p. 144.

24. Etienne Trocmé, "L'Eglise Réformée de La Rochelle jusqu'en 1628," BSHPF 98 (1952): 137, 172-74; Louis de Richemond, Origine et progrès de la Réformation à La Rochelle, 2nd ed. (Paris: Sandoz et Fischbacher, 1872), pp. 63-65; Louis de Richemond, "Anciennes églises et lieux de culte des réformés à La Rochelle," BSHPF 44 (1895): 364-71.

tery — the town's church having been destroyed — until Catholics reclaimed it upon their return in 1600.[25] To varying degrees, French Protestants also regarded medieval churches and chapels as irreparably corrupted and defiled. They had long housed superstitious papal rituals — chief among them the "abuses of the mass"[26] — and idolatrous material objects such as statuary, paintings, and stained glass windows. As such, the medieval edifices could be deeply offensive to Huguenot religious sensibilities.

While the French temples conformed to no grand model and varied considerably from one locale to another, their essential plan was either centralized (typically polygonal) or longitudinal (basilican). In either case, energetic Huguenot architects looked to antiquity, both Christian and Roman, for inspiration. Martin Bucer, the Strasbourg reformer and mentor to John Calvin, remarked on what he believed both the primitive ecclesiastical precedent and the practical value of the centralized design.

> From the plans of the most ancient temples, and from the writings of the holy fathers, it is well known that among the ancients the position of the clergy was in the middle of the temples, which were usually round; and from that position divine service was so presented to the people that the things recited could be clearly heard and understood by all who were present.[27]

The reformers' infusion of new life into older forms, whether a longitudinal plan derived from the Roman basilica and adopted by early Christians or what men such as Bucer believed was the ancient model of a centralized temple plan, conformed to their objective of returning to the purity of the primitive church.

The very use of the term "temple" recalled the temple of Jerusalem and suggested the forceful biblical imagery, which French Calvinists found especially appealing. These reformers, drawing upon their understanding of Scripture, insisted upon calling their places of worship temples. For them, the temple was the physical structure in which the faithful assembled, while the church was the community of believers.[28] The nomenclature with its scriptural roots also conveyed a strong sense of Calvinist aims in reforming religion and society. Finally, the designation temple must

25. Jean-François Breton, "Mas-Grenier, place de sûreté protestante, 1576-1621" (Montauban, typescript, 1977), p. 169; Yves Gueneau, *Les protestants dans le colloque "de Sancerre" de 1598 à 1685* (Mémoire de maîtrise, Faculté des Lettres et Sciences humaines de Tours, 1970), pp. 108-9.

26. For example: AD, Gers, 23067, 2 avril 1603; 16 février 1606; 3 and 28 juillet 1606; 27 août 1606; 2 mars 1607; 4, 13, and 20 avril 1607; 26 décembre 1607.

27. Martin Bucer, *Scripta Anglicana fere omnia . . . collecta . . .* (Basel, 1577), p. 457. Quoted in Addleshaw and Etchells, p. 245.

28. Willy Richard, *Untersuchungen zur Genesis der reformierten Kirchenterminologie der Westschweiz und Frankreichs* (Bern: A. Franke, 1959), pp. 77-85.

have been an explicit and effective way for Protestants in France, who co-existed, though not always peacefully, with Catholics, to distinguish their buildings from those of their Catholic rivals.

Depictions of the interior of the Lyon *temple de Paradis* (see Guicharnaud, plate 21) or the modest exterior of the polygonal temple built at Caen (see Guicharnaud, fig. 45) typify the centralized plan. The *grand temple* of La Rochelle, begun in 1577 but unfinished until the early seventeenth century, had a comparable design (see Guicharnaud, fig. 47). The Temple Neuf at Montauban, completed in 1615, and the temple at Le Petit-Quevilly (see Guicharnaud, fig. 46) had centralized plans as well.[29]

Temples in other towns followed, perhaps more commonly, a longitudinal design and, in this sense, drew inspiration from the ancient Roman basilica. The acclaimed Huguenot architect Salomon de Brosse rebuilt the temple at Charenton (see Guicharnaud, fig. 42) in 1623, after the first, constructed in 1607 and designed by his uncle Jacques II Androuet du Cerceau, had burned.[30] The new temple, with its elegant symmetry, became a prized symbol of Huguenot artistic achievement.[31] Other temples, built before and after Charenton, adopted a longitudinal plan too, even if they were less celebrated. The *grand temple de la Calade* at Nîmes, constructed in 1565, and the *grand temple* of Montpellier, built in the mid-1580s, were similarly basilican. During the early 1620s, Protestants at Pau erected a middling-sized rectangular building surrounded by a walled courtyard.[32] The temple at Arnay-Le-Duc in Burgundy appears to have conformed to an analogous model. It occupied a considerable parcel of land, approximately twenty-two meters by twelve meters, and was said to have room for 250 worshipers.[33]

Whether centralized or longitudinal, these structures met the needs of a public meeting space, an element that historians have also stressed for England and North America. They were the places where people came together for common worship, especially for the sermon service, and toward this end the architects and designers developed elaborate plans to house and seat the persons in attendance.

---

29. Guicharnaud, *Montauban*, pp. 93-98; Reymond, *L'architecture religieuse*, p. 53; Trocmé, pp. 173-74.

The references to the Guicharnaud figures in this paragraph and the one following refer to her article in this volume, "An Introduction to the Architecture of Protestant Temples Constructed in France before the Revocation of the Edict of Nantes."

30. See the contribution of Hélène Guicharnaud in this volume. Babelon, pp. 242-43; Blunt, p. 101.

31. Henri Lehr, "Les deux temples de l'Eglise Réformée de Paris sous l'Edit de Nantes," *BSHPF* 2 (1853): 247-88; 3 (1854): 148-56, 418-72, 540-63; 4 (1855): 29-106, 476-96; 5 (1856): 162-78.

32. Tucoo-Chala, "Un patrimoine méconnu," p. 37; Tucoo-Chala, *Quatre siècles de Protestantisme à Pau* (Pau: J. & D., 1991), pp. 3-4, 6.

33. Colombet, p. 1017.

The French temples typically had galleries, which served to define further the interior space and enhance walls that were otherwise plain, bare, and frequently whitewashed.[34] The galleries also increased seating capacity for the many worshipers who came to hear the pastor explain God's Word. Protestant services in France tended to be crowded, especially as the seventeenth century wore on. The Protestant population seems to have grown, and the monarchy, during the same period, sought to restrict construction of new temples. As a practical matter, the elevated position of the gallery offered good acoustics and an unobstructed view of the pulpit. The large temple at Charenton even had a two-tier arrangement with a second gallery set above the first. Many churches took advantage of the segregation afforded by the galleries and reserved them for male congregants or persons relegated to the margins of the community. The well-known painting of the interior of the Lyon temple during the mid-1560s (see Guicharnaud, plate 21, in this volume) shows only men sitting or standing in the gallery. The church of Arnay-Le-Duc also set aside the gallery, which went around the perimeter of the temple interior, for men from the congregation.[35] Religious leaders confined women, who were commonly subject to stricter supervision than men, to the main floor. The church of Nîmes controlled access to the gallery in other ways. Officials, for a time, locked it off lest amorous couples take advantage of the relative seclusion that it offered. The closure took place in the early seventeenth century after the consistory censured two young women who had used the gallery for meeting with male friends. Perhaps the fear of illicit sexual encounters further explains the restriction of galleries to men at other churches. Even when the Nîmes gallery was open, the church imposed limitations. At one point, it reserved the gallery for visiting Catholics; at another time, for young unmarried women who were boarding at Nîmes and presumably required close watching.[36]

In all of this we ought not to forget the strong regional character and local focus of French Protestantism. Calvinists dubbed their organization *les Eglises Réformées de France*, purposefully using the plural. They thought of themselves as a federation and by that asserted the associative nature of their national union. The individual church and its consistory were the foundation of the system. Accordingly, much of the imagination, initiative, and responsibility for the affairs of the church resided at the local level. Among other things, the particular congregations shouldered enormous financial burdens for support of the clergy, provision of relief for the poor, and the construction and maintenance of temples. The results were cause for intense pride.

34. Elisabeth Labrousse, "L'Eglise Réformée du Carla en 1672-1673 d'après le registre des délibérations de son consistoire," *BSHPF* 106 (1960): 48.
35. Colombet, p. 1017.
36. Chareyre, "Le consistoire de Nîmes," pp. 298-99.

The rural community of Montagnac in Gascony labored for years to assemble the economic resources necessary to build a temple. The pastor and elders even went house to house soliciting financial subscriptions. The far larger and richer congregation at Nîmes was no less strapped by these construction projects. Building a small second temple in 1611 for the town's growing population proved a major financial undertaking. At Montauban, members of the consistory voiced concerns to the municipal council already in 1603. They decried the cramped quarters for worship and emphasized the need for a new temple. Construction costs, however, were substantial. Finally in 1609, the city consuls authorized the expenditure of nine thousand livres. A series of neighborhood collections to amass the funds then followed. The process took time, and the project did not get underway until 1615. Still, the community agreed to spend a significant sum — fifteen hundred livres — to hire a respected architect from nearby Toulouse.[37]

Much of the impetus for these building projects was overcrowding, a severe and continuing problem for the French Protestants, especially by the seventeenth century. The *grand temple* at Nîmes was likely among the largest in France. According to some reports, it measured forty-eight meters by thirty meters and held as many as five thousand worshipers. If true, it would have been comparable in size to the Charenton temple. Yet the Nîmes church found itself forced to build a second temple in the early seventeenth century to accommodate the increasing numbers of faithful.[38]

Small communities experienced similar difficulties. By the mid-1630s church officials at Durfort on the eastern fringe of the Cévennes realized that the existing temple was too small. It simply could not hold the town's faithful and Protestants from several neighboring villages who regularly attended services there. Evidence of the problem was continual. In 1643 the consistory allowed the captain Jacques Soulier to install a portable bench for himself and his family. Given the tight and confining conditions in the "very small" temple, however, his bench could be no larger than two seats and had to be stored elsewhere when not in use. Several years later, when the Durfort consistory acceded to Jean Cahours's request for a "more comfortable" bench, it stipulated that the new one must be the same length and width as the previous one.[39] Worshipers were tightly packed into the temple's close interior.

Civic and ecclesiastical leaders at Durfort saw a permanent solution

37. AD, Gers, 23015, 31 août 1614, 18 mai 1616, 29 septembre 1616, 20 novembre 1616, 2 février 1617, 5 septembre 1617, 29 novembre 1617. Chareyre, "Le consistoire de Nîmes," pp. 308-11; Guicharnaud, *Montauban*, pp. 92-94.

38. Chareyre, "Le consistoire de Nîmes," p. 303.

39. Mairie de Durfort, Registre des délibérations du consistoire de Durfort (1634-1667), fols. 36v, 52v; Béatrice Ducret, *Le consistoire et la communauté réformée de Durfort au XVIIe siècle (1634-1667)* (Mémoire de maîtrise, Université Sorbonne — Paris I, 1994), pp. 59, 70.

to the crowding in construction of a new temple. Yet the project proved far too ambitious, and officials gradually realized that the financial demands of a new building were well beyond their abilities. They resolved instead to enlarge the existing structure. The undertaking was very much a communal effort — the joint endeavor of municipal and religious authorities.[40] The town council attended to the financial arrangements and construction schedules while church officials directed the architectural design. The consistory, for example, requested the municipal consul Isaac Tresfon and the mason responsible for constructing the arch to visit the nearby town of Lasalle. It further instructed the pair to examine the temple door at Lasalle and the "small arch" that framed it, with the express purpose of reproducing the design at Durfort.[41] Although Durfort failed eventually to build a new temple and may not have even expanded the existing structure in exact accordance with the preferred model at Lasalle, the process suggests the aesthetic standard to which the community and, presumably, Calvinists most everywhere in France aspired. Simply put, the temple was a powerful measure of esteem and distinction.

As is evident from the Durfort experience, constructing a temple was often a cooperative project. The same was true in other locales. Town officials oversaw the construction of a new temple at Calvisson in mid–seventeenth century. They negotiated the financial arrangements, worked out the details of site selection, arranged for the purchase of materials, and contracted with the various builders. This was the case at Marsillargues and Montauban too. Municipal governments, when controlled by Huguenots, took the lead in planning and executing these projects.[42]

The French Reformed temple was very much a communal structure. It was, of course, the ritual locus for celebrating critical junctures in the life cycle: birth, marriage, and death. The faithful met twice a week for worship — a public and shared piety that centered on sermons and singing the Psalms. Four times annually they went to the temple for the Lord's Supper. They used it as well for daily common prayer and regular catechism lessons.

The temple was often the meeting place for the consistory, the body that attended to the moral and physical welfare of the community, counseled the faithful, and mediated their conflicts. The consistories of Castres and Saint-Amans regularly met in the temple. The pastor and elders of Mens-en-Trièves also assembled in the temple, usually on Sunday evening following the worship. The consistory bench in the Nîmes temple even had, at one end, a locked box in which the register of deliberations and

---

40. Ducret, pp. 59-60, 70.

41. Ducret, p. 60; Mairie de Durfort, fols. 58v-59.

42. Maurice Aliger, *La Réforme en Vaunage* (Nîmes: Bene, 1986), pp. 127-28; Rabinel, pp. 250-71; cf. Labrousse, "L'Eglise Réformée du Carla" (1960), pp. 44-46, 195-200.

Book of Discipline were kept. The same was true at Aimargues. In the seventeenth century the consistory of Durfort met ordinarily in the temple and exceptionally at the pastor's residence. Attached to the back of the temple at Montauban was a room where the consistory convened. The temples at Niort in Poitou and Brinon in the Nivernais also had small chambers which were set aside for the conduct of consistorial business. Protestants at Saint-Maixent purchased the building adjoining their temple for use by the consistory.[43]

Some temples, especially in small communities, also served as town halls, a French twist on the meetinghouse model. At Mas-Grenier, the municipal council generally met in the temple. The consuls of Marsillargues agreed to help pay for a new temple with the understanding that they, too, would hold their sessions in the building. The city council typically convened immediately following the worship service. Other features of the temple could possess civic purpose too. The bell at Pont-de-Camarès summoned congregants for worship and alerted the town consuls to their weekly meetings. At Aimargues and Le Vigan, a common bell served to strike the hour and announce Reformed services.[44]

In all of this, something of a functional explanation seems in order. Unlike the Catholics, who had a rich variety of vehicles to express their civic and religious identity, the minority Protestants had far fewer choices. The temple became, in many ways, the elementary symbol of the Reformed world.

These cultural creations, however, were rarely seamless garments, impervious to outside influences. Competitive borrowings and an interactive exchange certainly occurred between the Protestant minority and Catholic majority. The two spheres were more permeable, less rigidly separate and opposed to one another than is sometimes assumed. Now and again there was remarkable fluidity, even accommodation. Much as early Calvinists had occasionally appropriated Catholic churches, the reverse occurred in the seventeenth century. When the prince de Condé ousted Protestants from their temple at Saint-Amans in 1628, they built anew outside the walls. Meanwhile, Catholics took over the vacant structure. The populace dubbed it the *"temple servant d'église,"* thereby

43. AD, Gers, 23067, 8 décembre 1606. AD, Tarn, I 1; I 8. Solange Bertheau, "Le consistoire dans les Eglises Réformée du Moyen-Poitou au XVIIe siècle," *BSHPF* 116 (1970): 352-53; Pierre Bolle, "Religion et vie quotidienne à Mens-en-Trièves," in *Le Protestantisme en Dauphiné au XVIIe siècle*, ed. Pierre Bolle (La Bégude de Mazenc: Curandera, 1983), p. 41; Chareyre, "Le consistoire de Nîmes," p. 316; Chareyre, *Aimargues*, p. 145; Ducret, p. 45; Gueneau, pp. 113-14; Guicharnaud, *Montauban*, p. 97.

44. Bibliothèque de l'Arsenal, Ms 6563, fol. 34; Breton, p. 169; Chareyre, *Aimargues*, p. 117; Jean-Marc Daumas, *Marsillargues en Languedoc, fief de Guillaume de Nogaret, petit Genève* (Marsillargues: Studium Réformé Occitan, 1984), p. 50; Henri Gelin, "Les cloches protestantes," *BSHPF* 40 (1891): 603.

acknowledging the unique architectural form that Calvinists had created in the ecclesiastical sphere.[45]

Following the revocation of the Edict of Nantes, Catholics at Arthez in Béarn converted the Reformed temple for their own use, though they do not appear to have guarded the memory of its former function.[46] In any event, it remained a Catholic church until the Revolution. There were also less strident, more cooperative examples. As noted earlier, the city council at the Protestant stronghold of Montauban hired a Catholic architect from Toulouse to design a new temple in the early seventeenth century. The communal use of bells offers an even more stunning instance from the same epoch. When the bell for the Catholic parish church at Villemagne broke in early 1603, the town consuls agreed to have a new one cast at municipal expense with the understanding that it would serve the entire community, both Catholic and Protestant. The two religions thereafter shared a common bell, each ringing it to summon respective followers to mass or to sermon service.[47]

The centralized and longitudinal plans favored by French Calvinists for the construction of their temples drew upon their perception of Christian antiquity. Here, as elsewhere in the Reformation, Protestants sought a return to the pristine splendor of the early church. These architectural plans were also very much in accordance with a life of worship that actively engaged the body of the faithful. People seated on the main floor and in the galleries had a ready view of the pulpit, and the arrangement facilitated the congregational recitation of prayers and singing of the Psalms. Additional, nonliturgical features of the Reformed temple confirmed the shared experience that it represented. Planning and construction were frequently a community project, which involved the mobilization of scarce resources under the direction of civic as well as ecclesiastical officials. Some Protestant towns even used the temple as a gathering place for secular purposes. The temple was unquestionably the creation of the entire congregation. It was the visible, material expression of the Reformed community, and the faithful were extremely attentive to its aesthetic qualities.

2. Furnishings

The interior furnishings of the Reformed temples, much as their architectural plans, took fresh and imaginative direction. Beyond the removal of the statues, paintings, and ornate windows that adorned pre-Reformation

---

45. Jean Calvet, *Histoire de la ville de Saint-Amans* (Castres and Paris: Granier and Lechevalier, 1887), pp. 140-41.

46. Tucoo-Chala, "Un patrimoine méconnu," p. 38.

47. Archives Nationales (Paris) (hereafter cited as AN), 275 B, dossier 12, Contract du 23 juin 1603; "Correspondance," *BSHPF* 41 (1892): 54-56; Guicharnaud, *Montauban*, pp. 94-95.

churches, perhaps the most conspicuous change was the introduction of pewing. It was a brave and often frustrating endeavor to impose discipline by making people sit and listen attentively to the pastor's sermon. Other aspects of the furnishings had a similar instructive or didactic quality, in addition to their decorative function. Decalogue Boards and biblical inscriptions, for instance, appeared in most every temple to remind the faithful of religious obligations and to offer prescriptive counsel. Finally, some liturgical articles and related objects, though essentially practical in their purpose, displayed substantial artistic accomplishment. Pulpits and lecterns, silver plate and communion cups, and even temple bells lent distinction to an otherwise austere and simple worship.

Around the pulpit, the Calvinists placed benches or pews in concentric rings, amply displayed in the *temple de Paradis* at Lyon, or in extensive grids as is evident at Charenton. The seating, which varied from simple planks in rural villages to ornate, well-fashioned benches in the larger cities,[48] became critical when the minister's preaching replaced the mass as the principal feature of the new Reformed liturgy. Ideally, the officiating pastor was within easy sight and earshot of the congregants. The only columns were typically around the perimeter where they supported the gallery. Several times each week, the faithful sat attentively and orderly, listening to God's revealed truth as contained in Scripture and "Scripture alone." No longer did anyone dare to wander about as had been possible in the medieval church where seating was generally limited to bishops, canons, and a handful of persons from the social and political elite. Antoine Cathelan, a Catholic commentator, likened the Reformed arrangement to that of a "college or school." According to his description, the women and children gathered close to the preacher, while the men sat a bit further back.[49] Cathelan understood full well the pedagogical intent in this reorganization of the ecclesiastical interior.

Benches and pews were without doubt among the most significant and innovative elements of the Protestant liturgical furnishings. Yet their incorporation soon led to the establishment of visible distinctions within the congregation and incessant squabbling as old habits clashed with new ways. An elaborate temple such as *la Calade* at Nîmes had special pews reserved for the most eminent members of the congregation: municipal consuls, presidial judges, royal officers, lay members of the consistory, pastors, theology students, nobles, attorneys, and the highest bourgeois. Select seating along these lines was commonplace. Already in the mid-1560s, the church of Montauban set a bench aside for the municipal consuls. Later, these same

---

48. Addleshaw and Etchells, pp. 86-98; Breton, p. 169; Guicharnaud, *Montauban*, p. 90; Labrousse, "L'Eglise Réformée du Carla" (1960), p. 48.

49. Antoine Cathelan made the observation after staying seven months at Lausanne in the mid-1550s. Quoted in Henri Vuilleumier, *Histoire de l'Eglise réformée du Pays de Vaud sous le régime bernois*, 4 vols. (Lausanne: Editions La Concorde, 1927-33), 1:323-24.

212

civic leaders benefited from a private door that gave them direct access from outside the temple to their seats. The *grand temple* at La Rochelle had a "magistrates' bench" too. Temples elsewhere followed in similar, if more modest, patterns. The small church of Durfort even built a bench for the pastor's family by the mid-1660s. It had three seats and stood just below the local seigneur's pew. In some temples, Lyon for example (see Guicharnaud, plate 21, in this volume), the places of honor were turned so that the occupants faced the general congregation. The Lyon temple, moreover, accentuated these special benches by draping them in rich blue cloth, complete with fleurs-de-lis. The church of Le Carla in the Ariège also marked its select pew with fleurs-de-lis. Congregations could distinguish these elite benches in other ways too. The consistory pew at Castres had a small door to prevent persons "other than the elders" from entering.[50] These and related measures unquestionably lent vivid definition to the community's elite.

There was also common seating, segregated according to gender and available on a first-come, first-served basis. Churches tended to seat women and children in front, near the pulpit and just beyond the pews belonging to the civic and ecclesiastical dignitaries. Men settled along the sides, toward the back, and in the galleries. Still, people took matters into their own hands as they sought to validate spatially their perceived position within the community. Two women from the Nîmes municipal elite joined several benches together to create a larger, more splendid pew for themselves. A university professor from the same town demanded and received for himself and his wife the preferential seating, which he clearly believed they deserved. Indeed, the consistory agreed and gave him a place on its own bench, while providing his spouse a special seat among the women. Two women of Montauban nailed cushions to their favorite benches in an attempt to stake out territory. At Layrac in Aquitaine, members of one family attached a nameplate to the bench they considered theirs and then forcibly ejected anyone else who ventured to occupy the spot. The church of Castres, likely responding to similar incidents, found it necessary to issue a sweeping prohibition against persons who tried to retain a particular place in the temple.[51]

Eventually many Reformed churches, especially those in the larger towns, allowed individuals to have private pew space, thereby satisfying the desire of many to display rank and wealth. By the early seventeenth

50. AD, Tarn, I 2, pp. 68-69. Chareyre, "Le consistoire de Nîmes," pp. 400-401; Guicharnaud, *Montauban*, pp. 91, 95; Mairie de Durfort, fol. 79; Labrousse, "L'Eglise Réformée du Carla" (1960), pp. 25, 50; Gaston Serr, *Une église protestante au XVIe siècle, Montauban* (Aix-en-Provence: La Pensée Universitaire, 1958), pp. 149-50; Trocmé, p. 174.

51. AD, Gard, 42 J 29, fol. 375; 42 J 31, fols. 194-94v, 201. AD, Tarn, I 1, fol. 137; AD, Tarn-et-Garonne, I 1, fol. 332v; Gregory Hanlon, *Confession and Community in Seventeenth-Century France: Catholic and Protestant Coexistence in Aquitaine* (Philadelphia: University of Pennsylvania Press, 1993), p. 220.

century, nearly eight hundred persons occupied 242 "private" benches in the *grand temple* of Nîmes. The church soon developed a detailed inventory — a kind of seating map — to keep track of these arrangements. Some pews had family coats of arms attached to them, and more than a few individuals, upon dying, bequeathed their places in the temple to specific heirs named in last wills and testaments. Perhaps the most striking aspect of private pewing at Nîmes centered on so-called *cabinets*, small rooms attached to the outside of the temple walls. The church originally authorized construction of these exterior compartments to alleviate the chronic crush of worshipers. The occupants sat in relative comfort and isolation, watching and listening to the service through a window cut in the wall. The semidetached booths quickly became the places of choice for members of the aristocracy and municipal elite, who undoubtedly saw these "luxury boxes" as stunning reinforcement of status and recognition.[52]

The privatization of seating led inevitably to prolonged bickering. Some wished to extend use of personal, individual benches while others sought to limit or end the practice. The consistory of Nîmes never fully settled the issue. After years of struggle, the contending parties finally compromised and decided that the seating system would vary depending upon the occasion. The church of Castres had a similar heated dispute, involving both civic and ecclesiastical authorities, over the question of communal or private pews. At least one faction in the church wished to institute specific seat assignments. Officials, however, took a dim view of the initiative. The turmoil over pews sprang, in their opinion, from people's "fondness for certain seats" and notions that some benches were "more honorable than others." Ultimately, most French churches appear to have wrestled vigorously if inconclusively with the problem of seating privilege.[53]

The proprietary rights individuals attached to specific pews tended to confirm both collective and personal notions of prominence within the community. In 1597 the attorneys of Montauban requested an "elevated bench," set off by partitions. The pastor and elders denied the petition, arguing that the temple was simply too small. They added that in the thirty-two years since the temple had been established the attorneys had never asked for such "preeminence." The demand, apparently, was unseemly.[54] People everywhere could become irritated when they believed that their

---

52. Chareyre, "Le consistoire de Nîmes," pp. 299-300.

53. Chareyre, "Le consistoire de Nîmes," pp. 417-20. AD, Gers, 23016, 16 mai 1649; 23068, 20 décembre 1637. AD, Hérault, E Dépôt, Ganges GG 24, fol. 138v; AD, Tarn, I 1, fols. 1226-27, 1232-44; AD, Tarn-et-Garonne, I 1, fol. 332v; Bertheau, p. 547; Bolle, p. 43; François Martin, "Ganges. Action de son consistoire et vie de son église au 16e et 17e siècle," *Etudes évangéliques* (Revue de théologie de la faculté libre de théologie protestante, Aix-en-Provence) 2 (1942): 155-56. Cf. J. J. Scarisbrick, *The Reformation and the English People* (Oxford: Blackwell, 1984), pp. 164-65, 173-74.

54. AD, Tarn-et-Garonne, I 1, fol. 255; Serr, pp. 149-50.

status had not been properly recognized. In 1637 Mademoiselle de la Rouvière, daughter of a local notable at Durfort, complained that she had nowhere to sit because townspeople had taken over her father's bench. The local consistory agreed to provide her a small portable bench on condition that it be removed during times other than the worship service. About a decade later, when the pastor and elders questioned de la Rouvière about her repeated absence from services, she replied that "the sole cause" was other people's use of "her bench." The consistory reaffirmed the woman's "possession" of the bench, thereby tacitly acknowledging the slight. It also pointedly told her to be "more diligent" in future attendance.[55]

The characteristic Calvinist attempt to impose discipline and proper behavior at worship or during the administration of the sacraments repeatedly challenged common assumptions. Churches throughout France (and some English Puritan congregations) experienced endless fights over seating and related liturgical arrangements. People sought to retain or extend the honor, privilege, and position they had enjoyed "during the time of the papacy." At Chizé, for example, nobles had preeminent seating, and they preceded the elders in receiving the bread and wine at communion services.[56] These privileges inevitably led to problems. During the Christmas 1598 celebration of the Lord's Supper at Ganges, a town in the Cévennes mountains, a spectacular fracas erupted as the congregation, the men followed by the women, moved in a measured procession toward the communion table. The community's two most prominent noblewomen became engaged in a fierce shoving match, each trying to elbow her way ahead of the other and, presumably, establish superiority of social position. It was a battle for precedence, fought here in sacramental circumstances, between the leading families. A few months later, the two men who headed these honorable lineages scuffled at the temple door, vying for entrance to the sermon service. One angrily claimed that for the last three hundred years he and his ancestors had enjoyed the privilege of highest rank.[57] In the minds of many, these religious formalities, to include the order of reception for the Lord's Supper or seating patterns at worship,[58] announced and sustained an overall social order.

Two notaries complained bitterly to the consistory of Saint-Jean-du-Bruel in February 1596. Someone had hacked to pieces the pew belonging

---

55. Mairie de Durfort, fols. 18-18v, 39.

56. Bertheau, p. 547.

57. AD, Hérault, E Dépôt, Ganges GG 24, fols. 100, 101v, 106v-8v, 116v, 117v. For an examination of this and similar incidents, see Raymond A. Mentzer, "The Persistence of 'Superstition and Idolatry' among Rural French Calvinists," *Church History* 65 (1996): 220-33.

58. Churches in other communities experienced analogous fights over precedence. Gregory Hanlon, *L'univers des gens de bien: culture et comportements des élites urbaines en Agenais-Condomois au XVIIe siècle* (Talence: Presses Universitaires de Bordeaux, 1989), pp. 222-23; Hanlon, *Confession and Community*, pp. 74-75; Labrousse, "L'Eglise Réformée du Carla en 1672-1673 d'après le registre des délibérations de son consistoire," *BSHPF* 107 (1961): 248-49.

to their wives. Upon investigation, ecclesiastical officials learned that the bench, which had only recently been built and installed in the temple, deeply offended Mademoiselle de Capluc, a prominent member of the congregation. Her pew stood immediately to the right of the new one. More to the point, the carpenter had moved the bench on which Mademoiselle de Capluc's daughters sat in order to accommodate the notaries' wives. The perceived slight led to "highly passionate" exchanges and considerable murmuring around town. It so enraged mother and daughters that they arranged for the destruction of the upstarts' seats.[59]

Another mother and daughter, members of one of the foremost families at Aimargues, physically attacked the pastor's wife, whom they held responsible for moving their bench to a less prominent spot within the town's temple. The pair "rudely shoved and insulted" the minister's spouse and were accused of pulling her hair and scratching her throat and upper chest. The consistory, anxious to restore peace, called upon two pastors from neighboring towns to settle the quarrel and restore communal harmony. These mediators, following considerable posturing by both sides, eventually assigned the women to benches at opposite ends of the temple. It was years, however, before the two families could forget the various affronts and put their disagreement to rest.[60] In the mid-1650s, several judicial officers from Castres became entangled in a tiresome feud over who had priority in the seating that most every temple set aside for the community's elite. The consistory found the parties so intractable that it finally compelled them to submit to outside arbitration.[61]

Other aspects of the temple interior and liturgical furnishings elicited less controversy. At the same time, they underscore additional transformations and innovations in the Reformed approach to the place of the arts. Scriptural themes and subjects were prominent in the decoration. Most temples, for instance, displayed a Decalogue Board,[62] with its obvious didactic intent. A seventeenth-century watercolor depicting the interior at Charenton shows the tables of the Law placed conspicuously on the wall high above and behind the pulpit.[63] According to one account, this Decalogue Board had gilded letters set upon a blue back-

59. AN, TT 270, dossier 13, pp. 779-81.

60. Archives Municipales, Aimargues (conserved at AD, Gard), GG 57, fols. 66-77v, 86v-87.

61. AD, Tarn, I 1, fols. 1212-13.

62. See also figures 129 and 136 in James Tanis, "Netherlandish Reformed Traditions in the Graphic Arts, 1550-1630," in this volume.

63. Commissioned by Achilles Werteman de Basle in 1648, the watercolor is now in the collection of the Royal Library, Copenhagen. Alastair Duke, Gillian Lewis, and Andrew Pettegree, *Calvinism in Europe, 1540-1610: A Collection of Documents* (Manchester and New York: Manchester University Press, 1992), jacket notes.

ground.[64] Two tablets hung in the temple at Brinon. The Decalogue was inscribed on one, the Lord's Prayer on the other. Châtillon-sur-Loire and Sancerre possessed elaborate paintings of the Decalogue, complete with the figures of Moses, Joshua, and Aaron in the background.[65] Even a modest temple, such as that at Caveirac near Nîmes, had the tables of the Law.[66]

The fondness for biblical representations and references found its way into other aspects of ecclesiastical decor. An inscription on the temple at Calvisson, for instance, carried the words "Aime ton Dieu et ton prochain come toy même," a conflation of the words contained in Matthew 22:37-39, Mark 12:30-31, and Luke 10:27. The so-called Law of Love appeared in many temples. Although the Lyon *temple de Paradis* did not display the tables of the Law, the two commandments of the Law of Love — "Love the Lord thy God with all thy heart" and "Love thy neighbor as thyself" — flanked a large coat of arms that was affixed to the wall at the level of the gallery. At other temples, such as that of Châtillon-sur-Loire, the Law of Love was appended to the Decalogue.[67] Inscriptions appeared elsewhere too. A black marble plaque with gold lettering hung above the main door of the Montauban temple. The phrase came from Psalm 118:19-20: "Ouvrez les portes de justice et j'y entreray et célebreray l'Eternel; c'est la porte de l'Eternel, les justes y entreront."[68] The temple at Hastingues near Béarn had several inscriptions carved in the stonework. They included the words "La Parole de Dieu demeure éternellement" from Isaiah 40:8[69] and "Servir à Dieu, c'est régner."[70]

One or two additional architectural features bear mentioning. Windows, in keeping with Calvinist tradition, were usually clear,[71] although

64. The description comes from the *Mercure galant* (February 1686). See Appendix 4 of the article by Hélène Guicharnaud in this volume. Lehr, "Les deux temples," *BSHPF* 5 (1856): 169-70, has also published the text.

65. Gueneau, pp. 114-16.

66. Aliger, p. 128.

67. Philippe Chareyre, " 'The Great Difficulties One Must Bear to Follow Jesus Christ': Morality at Sixteenth-Century Nîmes," in *Sin and the Calvinists: Morals Control and the Consistory in the Reformed Tradition*, ed. Raymond A. Mentzer, Sixteenth Century Essays and Studies 32 (Kirksville, Mo.: Sixteenth Century Journal Publishers, 1994), p. 78; Gueneau, p. 114; Jacques Pannier, "Le baptême et la sainte cène au XVIe siècle, d'après trois représentations contemporaines," *BSHPF* 82 (1933): 236.

68. "Open the gates of righteousness, and I may enter through them and give thanks to the Lord. This is the gate of the Lord; the righteous shall enter through it."

69. ". . . the word of our God will stand forever."

70. "To serve God is to hold sway." Guicharnaud, *Montauban*, p. 95; Charles Blanc, "Le temple d'Hastingues," in *Réformes et Révocation de Béarn, XVIIe-XXe siècles* (Pau: J & D Editions, 1986), pp. 87-93; Tucoo-Chala, "Un patrimoine méconnu," pp. 38, 55.

71. Some poor rural churches could not afford glass for the windows. The consistory of Le Carla eventually purchased parchment to cover them. Labrousse, "L'Eglise Réformée du Carla" (1960), pp. 47-48.

they sometimes bore municipal coats of arms. At Nîmes, for example, the temple windows displayed a crocodile chained to a palm tree — the city's emblem. In addition, the windows of Nîmes appear to have had a fanciful, perhaps biblical armorial bearing that featured the sun and the moon. Reformers also fastened heraldic devices, presumably those associated with political authority and prominent local families, to the walls and atop the columns that supported the galleries. Armorial bearings were conspicuous, for instance, in the temples at Lyon and Calvisson. These decorative elements announced the communal nature of the church and its integration into the social groupings and political institutions that dominated civic life. By mid–seventeenth century, Reformed congregations found it increasingly important to create iconographic affirmations of political allegiance, especially to the monarchy. The temple of Montauban displayed the royal coat of arms in addition to that of the city. Protestants at La Tremblade placed a large round heraldic device containing no less than nine fleurs-de-lis above the doorway of their temple.[72]

Each temple possessed a communion table, which in the early years was usually portable and set up only on those Sundays when the communion service took place.[73] Larger churches such as that of Castres sometimes had two communion tables, one for men and another for women. The *grand temple* at Nîmes had several tables, while the small temple had but one. The Nîmes church owned a number of large shallow dishes — some fashioned from silver, others from pewter — for the bread in the communion service; there were, moreover, cups made of glass and silver for the wine. How elaborate and ornate was this plate? Unfortunately, the elders sold most of the silver in the decade or so before the Revocation. Churches in other communities also possessed silver plate for use in the Lord's Supper. On the other hand, the elders customarily supplied the tablecloths and napkins necessary for the service. Finally, the pulpit had the obligatory Bible, and a collection box was placed somewhere inside the temple. Often a lectern for the cantor (*chantre*) who led the congregants in singing the Psalms stood to one side of the pulpit.[74]

An almost universal and ever costly external feature of the temple was a bell and bell tower. It was an aesthetically pleasing and distinguishing detail, which emphasized the structure's character as a place of worship. Furthermore, unlike Dutch Calvinists, who frowned on bells as popish superstition, French Protestants willingly adopted them to "sound the

---

72. AN, TT 272, dossier 25; Chareyre, "Le consistoire de Nîmes," pp. 301-2; Guicharnaud, *Montauban*, p. 95; Pannier, pp. 234-37; Rabinel, pp. 253, 261-62; Bernard Reymond, "Les styles architecturaux du protestantisme: un survol du problème," *Etudes Théologiques et Religieuses* 68 (1993-94): 514.

73. Reymond, *L'architecture religieuse*, p. 165.

74. AD, Tarn, I 2, pp. 74, 127, 180, 224, 390, 400, 403; I 8, 6 septembre 1596. Chareyre, "Le consistoire de Nîmes," pp. 301-2, 311-14; Gueneau, pp. 111-13.

worship and assemble the faithful to hear the Holy Word."[75] The church of Pau, for example, took enormous pride in its bell, the instrument and symbol of the call to gather. There, as elsewhere, the bell regularly summoned the faithful to both Wednesday and Sunday services. For the principal Sunday worship at Montauban, the bell rang one hour in advance, as much to alert the pastor and lector as the congregants, and again immediately before services. The bell at the small town of Pont-de-Camarès rang three times for sermon services and twice on days when there was only a prayer service. It also called the members of the consistory for their weekly sessions.

Bells were a prominent part of Calvinist temples from the outset. The church of La Rochelle had a bell as early as mid-1563. The Protestants of Nîmes built an elaborate belfry with windows in 1581 and installed the bell in the following year. A number of temples, Charenton and Sancerre for example, had on the roof a lantern, which housed the bell. Others, such as Castres or Saint-André-de-Valborgne, had detached or semidetached towers.[76]

Reformed Christians regarded the use of bells as a reflection of dignity and honor. Nîmes commissioned a special bell cast by a foundry in the papal city of Avignon. In some communities the local lord donated the bell — leastways this was the gracious seigneurial gift at Durfort and Montagnac. The duc de Sully, Henri IV's finance minister and loyal adviser, gave the bell for the temple at Châtillon-sur-Loire. The municipal councils of both Calvisson and Caveirac agreed to bear the costs of having bells cast for their towns' temples. Just as often the elders canvassed the community for contributions. The faithful of Castres donated a hefty sum to build a new bell tower when the old one fell into ruin.[77]

Taken together, the various furnishings constitute a well-orchestrated artistic program. Pewing, Decalogue Boards, and various biblical inscriptions informed the very meaning of the temple. They reinforced Calvinist insistence upon the temple as the place where the faithful assembled to hear God's Word, offer prayer, and partake of the sacraments. Other elements — pulpits, communion plate, and bells — were perhaps a bit more

---

75. The consistory of Aimargues in 1633. Quoted in Chareyre, "Le consistoire de Nîmes," p. 306.

76. AD, Tarn-et-Garonne, I 1, fols. 58, 65-65v, 106, 318; Bibliothèque de l'Arsenal, Ms 6563, fols. 21v-22, 34; Bolle, pp. 43-44; Chareyre, "Le consistoire de Nîmes," p. 303; Gelin, "Les cloches protestantes," pp. 591-607, 652-64; Gueneau, pp. 4-5, 111-12; Lehr, "Les deux temples," *BSHPF* 5 (1856): 170-71, 174-78; Trocmé, p. 174; Tucoo-Chala, "Un patrimoine méconnu," p. 53.

77. AD, Gers, 23015, 23 janvier 1613, 12 janvier 1615, 12 février 1615; 23067, juin 1622, 20 août 1634; AD, Tarn, I 2, pp. 299-300, 323, 410-11; Aliger, pp. 127, 129; Chareyre, "Le consistoire de Nîmes," pp. 303-6; Daumas, p. 51; Ducret, p. 69; Gelin, "Les cloches protestantes," p. 596; Gueneau, p. 111.

functional than decorative. Yet here, too, artists applied their decorative talents. And while gilded tables of the Law, inscribed marble plaques, silver plate, bells, and related items were costly, the congregation willingly shouldered the expense for these details in the conviction that they manifested the worth and stature of their church.

3. Communion Tokens (Méreaux)

Another facet of the visual arts within the Calvinist tradition was the metal tokens (méreaux) that most French Protestant churches[78] used to control access to the Lord's Supper. The sacramental meal took place four times annually, on Easter and Pentecost, in early September, and at Christmastide. Given the crucial position that the Lord's Supper had in the spiritual life of the congregation, the token that offered admission to this shared celebration was, by association, a symbol of membership in the body of believers. Marked with various figural and nonfigural devices, the méreaux gave artists and craftsmen opportunities to fashion powerful religious and sacramental images. They created some with depictions of Christ as the shepherd with his flock, but more common were representations of graceful communion cups. Artisans also adorned the tokens with Scripture verses and abbreviated versions of the name of the local church. In each instance, the méreaux reinforced the notion of the Lord's Supper as the centerpiece of a collective religious experience to which the token bearer was now granted admittance.

Since the thirteenth century, religious chapters and collegial churches had employed elaborate counters and slugs in conjunction with the liturgy, devotional services, and poor relief. Later, Reformed Protestants found them equally practical. In January 1560, John Calvin and Pierre Viret urged adoption of a token system to regulate access to the communion service at Geneva. Although the Genevan ruling council rejected the idea, the Reformed churches of France, again at Calvin's prompting, readily embraced it. The churches of Le Mans and Nîmes were among the first to put méreaux into use, by late 1561.[79]

To avoid profanation of the Eucharist, the elders in their role as moral watchdogs distributed these entry counters to those members of

---

78. Méreaux do not appear to have been used by Calvinists in the regions of Touraine, Dauphiné, and Provence. Charles Delormeau, Les méreaux de communion des Eglises protestantes de France et du Refuge (Le Mas Soubeyran: Musée du Désert, 1983), p. 8.

79. Adrien Blanchet and A. Dieudonné, Manuel de numismatique française, 4 vols. (Paris: Auguste Picard, 1912-36), 3:511-23; E. Delorme, "Le méreau dans les Eglises réformées de France," BSHPF 37 (1888): 204-7; Delormeau, pp. 5-10; Henri Gelin, Le méreau dans les Eglises Réformées de France et plus particulièrement dans celles du Poitou (Saint-Maixent: Ch. Reversé, 1891), pp. 1-22.

the faithful whom they deemed qualified by virtue of correct belief and proper conduct. Protestant men and women usually had to attend catechism lessons in the several weeks preceding the Lord's Supper. Assuming they were otherwise well behaved, they subsequently received the required *méreaux*.

The custom at Montauban, for instance, was that all who wished to take communion were catechized, and afterward the elders distributed the tokens. The church of Montdardier, to cite another example, refused to give tokens to persons from outlying villages unless they had presented themselves for catechism at least once during the year. Each communicant then gave the token to a specially appointed elder when he or she approached the communion table. No one could receive without doing so, and the consistory severely censured persons who attempted to circumvent the procedure, such as Jacques de Leuzière at Saint-Jean-du-Gard.[80] The church of Mougon thought the control mechanism so helpful that it extended usage to baptism and marriage. At Mougon, no one could present an infant for baptism or obtain permission to marry without producing a *méreau* from her or his elder.[81]

The tokens[82] were cast mostly in lead, occasionally in a lead and tin alloy. In a few rare instances they were struck in brass or copper. The *méreaux* were almost always round. Exceptions were an oval example from Nîmes (see fig. 52) and an octagonal token from the church of Oberseebach in Alsace. Size varied a great deal. Tokens with fairly elaborate shepherd representations measured twenty-nine to thirty-four millimeters in diameter. Those displaying the communion cup ranged between nineteen and twenty-five millimeters. The designs were typically done in relief, and the artisans tended to be local metalworkers. The consistory of Nîmes hired one of the town's pewterers to make some tokens in 1581 and again seven years later.[83] Montauban contracted with a goldsmith to fash-

---

80. Bibliothèque de la Société de l'histoire du Protestantisme Français, Ms 554/4, 2 octobre 1606.

81. AD, Tarn-et-Garonne, I 1, fol. 358. AN, TT 237, dossier 13, fols. 786, 791, 795, 796, 799, 804; TT 268, dossier 9, fol. 647. Bibliothèque de l'Arsenal, Ms 6563, fol. 64; Bibliothèque de la Société de l'Histoire du Protestantisme Français, Ms 222/1, fol. 34v; Anjubault and H. Chardon, *Papier et registre du Consistoire de l'Eglise du Mans, réformée selon l'évangile, 1560-1561 (1561-1562 nouveau style)*, in *Recueil de pièces inédites pour servir à l'histoire de la Réforme et de la Ligue dans le Maine* (Le Mans: Monnoyer, 1867), p. 35; Delorme, p. 317; Ducret, pp. 77-78; Labrousse, "L'Eglise Réformée du Carla" (1961), p. 256; Labrousse, "L'ancienne Eglise Réformée de Montdardier," *BSHPF* 22 (1873): 67; Gelin, *Le méreau dans les Eglises Réformées*, pp. 23-28.

82. Among the best collections of *méreaux* are those at the Bibliothèque de la Société de l'Histoire du Protestantisme Français (54, rue des Saints-Pères, 75007 Paris), the Musée Protestant de La Rochelle (2, rue Saint-Michel, 17000 La Rochelle), and the Musée du Désert (Le Mas Soubeyran, 30168 Mialet).

83. Bibliothèque Nationale, Ms 8667, fol. 271; AD, Gard, 42 J 29, pp. 10 and 14.

52. Communion
token, lead,
23 mm. × 19 mm.,
Nîmes (Gard),
seventeenth century

53. Communion to-
ken, lead, 29 mm.,
Agenais, sixteenth
century

ion a "new" *méreau* in the late 1590s.[84] Churches within a given region often shared a single mold. Each then stamped the tokens with its own identifying mark.[85]

Méreaux bore various religious and, in the case of Nîmes and
Mazamet, civic motifs; occasionally there were biblical inscriptions. The
two most common devices were the shepherd summoning his flock and
the communion cup. The shepherd type was predominantly from the
southwestern portion of the kingdom in the regions of the Agenais, the
Bordelais, Lower Quercy, and Saintonge.

The obverse of a seventeenth-century token from the Agenais (see
fig. 53) shows a standing shepherd, a time-honored biblical symbol of
Christ as pastor and protector, facing right; he is dressed in an elegant

84. AD, Tarn-et-Garonne, I 1, fol. 313v.

85. These and related details are discussed at length in Gelin, *Le méreau dans les Eglises
Réformées*, chaps. 5 and 6.

222

54. Communion token, lead, 34 mm., Montauban (Tarn-et-Garonne), eighteenth century

doublet and holding a staff in the right hand, a horn *(bucina)* in the left. He sounds the horn to call his flock, the grazing sheep in the lower-right field quadrant. On the left a tree trunk and branches follow the rounded field perimeter, and in the right background we see a small stand of bushes. Above center, there is a levitating Greek cross with a banner flying in the wind. The reverse shows an open Bible and above it a radiant sun. The page on the left reads: "Ne crains point petit troup[eau]." The right page gives the locus: "St. Luc, C[hapitr]e XII, V[erse]t 32."[86] Other Reformed churches, among them Gemozac, La Tremblade, Montauban, and Sainte-Foy-la-Grande, repeated this pastoral depiction in modified fashion.[87]

An elaborate eighteenth-century token from Montauban (see fig. 54) shows on the obverse the shepherd at the center of the field with his staff in his right hand and horn in his left; there are flanking trees and sheep, and a bird, perhaps a dove, the symbol of peace and purity, in the field above. The reverse of another eighteenth-century *méreau* of Montauban displays an open Bible, again with the passage from Luke 12:32 and a radiant sun above. In addition, there are three stars on each side, slightly below the sun. To the left of the Bible are the letters "V.B." and on the right the

86. "Fear not, little flock" (Luke 12:32).

87. Blanchet and Dieudonné, 3:565; Delorme, pp. 323-24; Delormeau, pp. 12-16; Charles-Louis Frossard, "Description de quarante et un méreaux de la communion réformée," *BSHPF* 21 (1872): 239-41.

letter "M." Most likely, this token was used at Ville Bourbon, the principal suburb of Montauban — hence, V[ille] B[ourbon] M[ontauban].

The biblical inscription "Ne crains point petit troupeau" appears on other tokens, too. It covers both the obverse and reverse of an eighteenth-century *méreau* from Saverdun in the eastern Pyrenean region of Ariège. The iconographic accompaniment of the shepherd, however, is absent. Instead, the Saverdun token has on the reverse a small communion cup flanked by the letters "C S," probably an inversion of S[ainte] C[ène]. A small indistinct flower is in the field above the cup.[88] Tokens bearing the cup design, at least those that have survived, begin to appear in the eighteenth century and come mainly, though not exclusively, from the region of Poitou. Does this development suggest a more sacramental version of Calvinism in and around Poitou in the century following the revocation of the Edict of Nantes? Possibly.

A graceful communion cup with flanking rectangles — morsels of communion bread according to some scholars[89] — adorns a *méreau* from La Brousse (see fig. 55). On the reverse, the letters "A: P: D: F: D: L. B:" (Assemblée Protestante Des Fidèles De La Brousse) are arranged around an inner circle. A cup flanked by rectangles also appears on the slightly more elaborate token of Celles-sur-Belle. A string of twenty-four pearls decorates the surrounding border. A stippled sphere around which appear the letters "E. D. C. LE." (Eglise De Celles) graces the reverse. The church of Melle added roundels to the rectangles that flank the cup. On the *méreau*'s reverse, the letters "E. D. MLE." (Eglise De Melle) enclose a small circle. A token from the church of La Mothe-Sainte-Héraye also has rectangles and roundels flanking the cup; a third roundel is below the cup. The letters "E. D. L. M." (Eglise De La Mothe) are on the reverse. The church of Chenay (see fig. 56) added the date 1772 to the rectangles and roundels. In addition, the inscription on the reverse is somewhat more developed: "E. D. CHENAY" (Eglise De Chenay).[90]

The obverse of a token from the church of Saint-Sauvant (see fig. 57) has a small communion cup with two rectangles turned on end. The encircling letters are "St S. R. G. A. DIEV" (Saint Sauvant, Rendez Grâces A Dieu).[91] A small fleur-de-lis, separating the beginning from the end of the inscription, suggests the Reformed community's tacit submission to royal authority by the second half of the eighteenth century. A five-petaled flower occupies the center of the field on the obverse. Around it are the letters "PSLFICHTVA." Their significance, however, is far from clear. Henri Gelin[92] proposes to divide the letters — I CHT V A. P S L F — and offers the possi-

88. Blanchet and Dieudonné, 3:565; Delorme, pp. 324-25, 486-89; Frossard, p. 241.

89. See, in particular, the comments of Delorme, pp. 375-79.

90. Blanchet and Dieudonné, 3:566; Delorme, pp. 375-80; Frossard, pp. 287-88, 291-92.

91. "Give thanks to God."

92. Gelin, *Le méreau dans les Eglises Réformées*, p. 102.

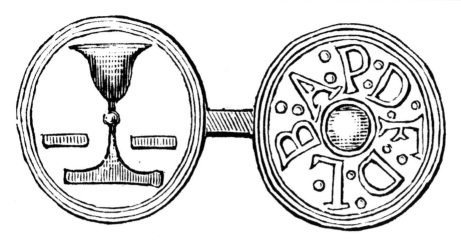

55. Communion token, lead, 21 mm., La Brousse (Deux-Sèvres), eighteenth century

56. Communion token, lead, 20 mm., Chenay (Deux-Sèvres), eighteenth century

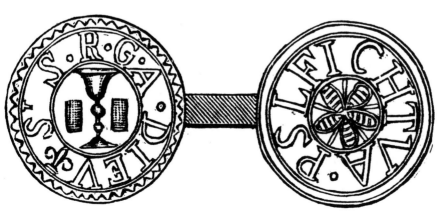

57. Communion token, lead and tin alloy, 24 mm., Saint-Sauvant (Vienne), eighteenth century

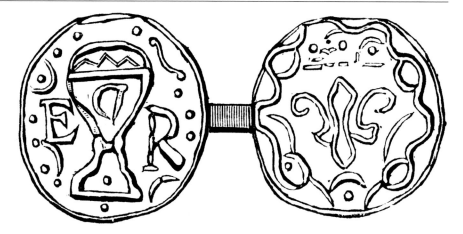

58. Communion token, lead, 24 mm., Régné (Deux-Sèvres), eighteenth entury

ble reading: "Iésus CHrisT Vous Appelle. . . . Pour Servir Lui Fidèlement."[93] The *méreau* of Sainte-Eanne displays the communion cup flanked by the letters "R G A D" (Rendez Grâces A Dieu). The reverse has a large circle, in the center of which is a flower with four petals. Circumscribing the outside of the circle are the crudely fashioned, inverted letters "SEAD REGNE" (Sainte Eanne. Dieu Règne).[94] A rough grid partitions the two groups of letters.[95]

The church of Régné adopted yet another variant of the cup design for its ornate token (see fig. 58). The communion cup with cover is done in a kind of line drawing, which the engraver had cut into the mold. The letters "E R" are to the left and right of the cup, respectively, while an inverted "D" is inside the cup. They undoubtedly stand for Eglise De Régné. The surrounding border has four crescents and a dozen dots or pearls. A fleur-de-lis, again a demonstration of eighteenth-century Huguenot loyalty to the crown, occupies the field on the reverse. Various dots, crescents, branches, and the like decorate the border.[96]

Devices on other tokens drew upon a variety of religious and, in at least two instances, civic motifs. A seventeenth-century Parisian *méreau*, unusual because it was struck in copper, has a rose surrounded by four fleurs-de-lis alternating with four stars. The words "Christ est le pain de vie," a slight rephrasing of John 6:35 and 48,[97] are on the reverse. Some scholars claim the church of Charenton used the token. Others argue that it came from the so-called Eglise de Madame, the private aristocratic exercise of Calvinism permitted Catherine de Bourbon, sister of Henri IV.[98]

Nîmes designed a distinctive oval token (see fig. 52) with its munici-

93. "Jesus Christ calls you . . . to serve him faithfully."
94. "God reigns."
95. Blanchet and Dieudonné, 3:565-66; Delorme, pp. 484-86; Frossard, pp. 294-95.
96. Delorme, p. 380.
97. In the scriptural text, Jesus says, "I am the bread of life."
98. Blanchet and Dieudonné, 3:563-64; Delormeau, pp. 18-20.

pal coat of arms on the obverse. It shows a crocodile chained to a palm tree and the inscription "Col(onia) Nem(ausensis)," recalling the city's Roman foundation by veterans of Octavian's Egyptian campaign (30 B.C.). This obverse design duplicates the reverse design of a common Roman provincial coin struck circa 27-23 B.C. at Nîmes under Augustus (formerly Octavian).[99] The reverse of the Nîmes *méreau* shows a radiant heart pierced by two swords. There is, in

59. Communion token, lead, 28 mm., Mazamet (Tarn), eighteenth century

addition, a cross centered on the heart. Around these elements is the inscription "Christ soleil de justice,"[100] an image taken from Malachi 4:2. The Hautpoul family coat of arms inspired the rooster or cock that dominates the *méreau* of Mazamet (see fig. 59). Part of the family name — *poul* — was the word for domestic fowl in regional dialect. The Hautpoul were a powerful, noble clan who acted as Mazamet's protectors. The letters "H" (Hautpoul) and "M" (Mazamet), along with six stars, complete the design. The reverse (not shown) is nearly identical. The only differences are that the cock faces left and the pearls, which decorate the border of the obverse, are absent.[101]

An eighteen-century token from the church of Saint-Maixent adopted a more austere design. A circle envelops the town's initials (S M) and a rough fleur-de-lis, while the reverse simply has two concentric circles. The Reformed communities at Aigonnay and Saint-Savinien cast equally modest *méreaux*. The token from the church of Aigonnay has the letters "E A" (Eglise Aigonnay), separated by a small dot, on the obverse. The reverse has a jumble of letters, "E A D," along with a reclining "D" below; it may be a crude attempt at Eglise D'Aigonnay. A token from the church of Saint-Savinien simply displays the letters "P C" with two dots between them. The letters stand for Port-Charente, which was the town's former name. The reverse is blank.[102]

Finally, Reformed groups outside France but with ties to those within the kingdom used *méreaux*. Although its Protestant community was largely

99. Andrew M. Burnett, Michael Amandry, and Père Pau Ripollès, *Roman Provincial Coinage* (London and Paris: British Museum Press and Bibliothèque Nationale, 1992), vol. 1, nos. 522-55.

100. "Christ sun of righteousness."

101. Blanchet and Dieudonné, 3:565-66; Delorme, pp. 371-73; Delormeau, pp. 21-22.

102. Blanchet and Dieudonné, 3:565-66; Delorme, pp. 374-75, 485, 488; Delormeau, p. 22.

Lutheran, there were several Reformed churches in Alsace, a province joined to France after 1648. The church of Oberseebach had an octagonal token, struck in brass on one side only (the obverse was blank). The field showed a communion cup, below which was a number that varied with each piece. Another Alsatian Reformed church, Bischwiller, struck a brass token with the letters "B K" (Bischwiller Kommunikant). Huguenots who fled France after the revocation of the Edict of Nantes in 1685 organized refugee churches, following the French model, in their host countries. They, too, adopted *méreaux*. The Reformed church of Erlangen, founded in 1689, created a round leaden token whose obverse featured a burning heart held between two hands. The encircling inscription read: "Venes avec foi, repentance et charité."[103] The Walloon church at Amsterdam, established by a much earlier religious emigration, had a small token, struck in lead, whose field displayed the church's emblem, two hands clasped on an anchor. To the left, in the border, was the date 1586. The obverse presented the municipal coat of arms.[104] As with the architectural plans of the temples, the designers of *méreaux* turned to Christian antiquity and, in this instance, appropriated images such as the shepherd and his flock or the dove. They were safe, long-accepted subjects within a religious tradition that generally shunned ornate depictions. To be sure, many tokens bore a simple cup or a series of letters that stood for the issuing church or perhaps some pious phrase. More than anything, the tokens underscored the central Christian ritual of the Lord's Supper. They allowed the holder to share in the sacrament and participate in the moral and social body of all believers.

Conclusion and Summary

Like the Reformation itself, the Calvinist artistic endeavor in France was vibrant, complex, and original. Its dynamics strongly paralleled changes in theology, the liturgy, and forms of piety. Artists, much as theologians, sought to restore and reclaim the beliefs and practices of the primitive church, even as they expanded their vision and pushed forward. Though Huguenots exhibited an incontestable aniconism, barring statues, stained glass, and paintings from the buildings in which they worshiped, they exercised enormously productive and innovative talents in the arts. These efforts meant the recovery of ancient architectural forms, whether the Roman basilica or what reformers such as Bucer believed was the early Christian model of a centralized temple plan. Additionally, Protestant architects redesigned the temple interior around pulpit and communion ta-

103. "Come with faith, penitence and charity."
104. Blanchet and Dieudonné, 3:564; Delormeau, pp. 23-30; Frossard, pp. 295-96.

ble and added new elements such as pews and galleries. Artisans created Decalogue Boards, set biblical inscriptions and civic coats of arms in windows and above doorways, fashioned silver communion plate, installed bells, and cast communion tokens with images of shepherds and communion cups. While some of these activities maintained and strengthened existing traditions, many were fresh and original.

Overall, the Calvinist artistic enterprise responded to particular communal circumstances as well as overarching theological concepts. Temples frequently blended local talents, financial resources, and building materials with national if not international ideas about the visual arts. Ordinary congregants, moreover, worked with the architects and artists, molding and shaping their achievements. Naturally, the minority status of French Calvinists deeply colored their creativity, often forcing them to rethink and restructure their activities. The confessional struggle was energizing and productive in some respects, emphatically undermining in others. And with the end of the intense violence that accompanied the Wars of Religion and the reduction of confessional stridence, Calvinist artistic and intellectual endeavors even had the occasional cooperative ring.

Is there room, finally, to underscore the ameliorating aspect of the competitive energies arising from religious rivalry? Local congregations clearly understood that their temples were at once a proud aesthetic accomplishment and a challenge to others. For both sides in the prolonged struggle that framed the Reformation, Huguenot temples and the array of artistic creations surrounding them symbolized the success of Protestantism as well as its defiant nature. Ultimately, the interface of Calvinist and Catholic along the innumerable fault lines of protest and rejoinder belied conventional notions concerning the destructiveness of religious rivalries. Far from ruinous, the struggle in the artistic and cultural sphere proved creative, imaginative, and enriching.

Bibliography

Biéler, André. *Liturgie et architecture. Le temple des chrétiens.* Geneva: Labor et Fides, 1961.

Blunt, Anthony. *Art and Architecture in France, 1500 to 1700.* 2nd ed. Baltimore: Penguin, 1970.

Chareyre, Philippe. "Le consistoire de Nîmes, 1561-1685." Thèse de doctorat d'Etat, Université Paul Valéry — Montpellier III, 1987.

Colombet, Albert. "Les temples protestants en Bourgogne." *Pays de Bourgogne* 118 (1982): 1015-17.

Delorme, E. "Le méreau dans les Eglises réformées de France." *Bulletin de la Société de l'Histoire du Protestantisme Français* 37 (1888): 204-13, 316-25, 371-81, 483-92.

Ducret, Béatrice. *Le consistoire et la communauté réformée de Durfort au XVIIe siècle (1634-1667)*. Mémoire de maîtrise, Université Sorbonne — Paris I, 1994.

Frossard, Charles-Louis. "Description de quarante et un méreaux de la communion réformée." *Bulletin de la Société de l'Histoire du Protestantisme Français* 21 (1872): 236-42, 286-96.

Gelin, Henri. *Le méreau dans les Eglises Réformées de France et plus particulièrement dans celles du Poitou*. Saint-Maixent: Ch. Reversé, 1891.

———. "Les cloches protestantes." *Bulletin de la Société de l'Histoire du Protestantisme Français* 40 (1891): 591-607, 652-64.

Gueneau, Yves. *Les protestants dans le colloque "de Sancerre" de 1598 à 1685*. Mémoire de maîtrise, Faculté des Lettres et Sciences humaines de Tours, 1970.

Guicharnaud, Hélène. *Montauban au XVIIe, 1560-1685. Urbanisme et architecture*. Paris: Picard, 1991.

Labrousse, Elisabeth. "L'Eglise Réformée du Carla en 1672-1673 d'après le registre des délibérations de son consistoire." *Bulletin de la Société de l'Histoire du Protestantisme Français* 106 (1960): 22-53, 191-231; 107 (1961): 223-72.

Lehr, Henri. "Les deux temples de l'Eglise Réformée de Paris sous l'Edit de Nantes." *Bulletin de la Société de l'Histoire du Protestantisme Français* 2 (1853): 247-88; 3 (1854): 148-56, 418-72, 540-63; 4 (1855): 29-106, 476-96; 5 (1856): 162-78.

Pannier, Jacques. "Le baptême et la sainte cène au XVIe siècle, d'après trois représentations contemporaines." *Bulletin de la Société de l'Histoire du Protestantisme Français* 82 (1933): 234-37.

Prestwich, Menna. "Patronage and the Protestants in France, 1598-1661: Architects and Painters." In *L'Age d'or du Mécénat (1598-1661)*, edited by Roland Mousnier and Jean Mesnard, pp. 77-88. Paris: Editions du Centre National de la Recherche Scientifique, 1985.

Reymond, Bernard. *L'architecture religieuse des protestants*. Geneva: Labor et Fides, 1996.

———. "Les styles architecturaux du protestantisme: un survol du problème." *Etudes théologiques et religieuses* 68 (1993-94): 507-35.

Tucoo-Chala, Suzanne. "Un patrimoine méconnu des pays de l'Adour: les temples réformés XVIe-XXe siècles." *Revue de Pau et du Béarn* 18 (1991): 35-57.

A Sixteenth-Century Limoges Enamel Tazza Illustrating the Judgment of Moses

BETSY ROSASCO

The Schultz *tazza*, or cup, consists of a shallow bowl (see fig. 60) 24.5 centimeters in diameter supported by a tapered foot 12 centimeters in diameter at its base (see fig. 61).[1] The two parts were not originally made for each other but were joined at a later date, most likely to salvage the intact portions of two damaged vessels. The bowl was executed in Limoges, in the workshop of Jean Court,[2] whose initials, "I.C.," appear within one of the four white, oval frames on the underside of the bowl (see fig. 62). As

---

I am grateful to Frederick H. Schultz, Jr., for permission to publish photos of the *tazza* in his collection and to P. Corby Finney for his generous help and advice during the research for and writing of this article.

1. Frederick H. Schultz Jr., Princeton class of 1976, received the *tazza* in 1994 as a fortieth birthday gift from his parents, who acquired it in the 1950s from a dealer in Lucerne, Switzerland. It bears a printed label beneath the foot that reads "Baron L. Rothschild." This is the only evidence of its earlier provenience. Goldsmiths invented this vessel form in the sixteenth and early seventeenth centuries; it then spread to artisans in other media, such as enamelers. The term *tazza* has no authority in Renaissance France; cf. Henri Havard, *Dictionnaire de l'ameublement et de la décoration depuis le XIIIᵉ siècle jusqu'à nos jours* (Paris, n.d.). It was applied retrospectively, on which see Carl Hernmarck, *The Art of the European Silversmith, 1430-1830*, 1 (London and New York, 1977), pp. 125-30. Hernmarck notes that Renaissance paintings sometimes show the *tazza* vessel form used as a drinking vessel, or to contain fruit or sweets, but he designates the type as "first and foremost ornamental."

2. On Jean Court, cf. Philippe Verdier, *The Walters Art Gallery: Catalogue of the Painted Enamels of the Renaissance* (Baltimore, 1967), pp. xv-xvi and catalogue entry no. 173 (a Court piece depicting Exodus 32:19: Moses destroying the tables of the Law); and Susan L. Caroselli, *The Painted Enamels of Limoges: A Catalogue of the Collection of the Los Angeles County Museum of Art* (Pasadena, 1993), pp. 156-58. The earliest dated work by Court is the portrait

60. Schultz *tazza*, bowl
interior. *Judgment of Moses,*
or *Counsel of Jethro,* by
Jean Court. Grisaille
enamel, flesh tones,
touches of color, and
gold on copper

232

with most of his works, Court did not date this bowl, but it must be situated within his years of productivity, which specialists in the field of Limoges enamels locate between 1555 and 1585.

The foot is signed with the initials "P.R." for Pierre Reymond,[3] and dated to the year 1546 (figs. 61 and 62). Reymond (1513-84+) was also an enameler in Limoges, and a near contemporary of Jean Court. Given the dates of Jean Court's activity, the bowl must postdate the foot, but by ex-

61. Schultz *tazza*, side profile, on the lower end of the tapered pedestal within a stylized *tabula ansata*, initials "P.R.": Pierre Reymond

of Marguerite de France in the guise of Minerva, dated 1555 (Wallace Collection). Court may have been painter to Charles Bourbon, prince de la Roche-sur-Yon, in 1553, and to the widowed Mary, queen of Scots, from 1562 to 1567; he was subsequently *peintre du roi* to Charles IX (died 1574). According to this latter interpretation, Court would have lived at the court while at the same time directing an enamel workshop in Limoges. Court was a Protestant and married the daughter of a Protestant goldsmith; cf. M. Cassan, *Le temps des guerres de religion: le cas du Limousin (vers 1530–vers 1630)* (Paris, 1996), p. 229 and n. 20.

3. On Reymond, cf. U. Thieme and F. Becker, *Allgemeines Lexikon der bildenden Künstler von der Antike bis zur Gegenwart* 27/28 (Leipzig, 1933-34; reprint, Munich 1992), pp. 213-14; Marvin Chauncey Ross, "Notes on Enamels by Pierre Reymond," *Journal of the Walters Art Gallery* 2 (1939): 78; Philippe Verdier, pp. xxiii-xxiv; Caroselli, pp. 80-83.

62. Schultz *tazza*, underside of the bowl showing the initials "IC" within a white oval frame

actly how much is not known. We also cannot determine the date when the component parts of the Schultz *tazza* were combined, but this probably took place in the nineteenth century when such works became sought-after collectors' objects (fortunately this has no direct bearing on the subject of this short essay, which concerns the iconography of the scene on the bowl interior).

The scene on the interior of the Schultz bowl illustrates Exodus 18:13-23. Moses sits on a throne at the center of the composition, facing forward, with his head turned to the right toward Jethro, his father-in-law. The biblical pericope concerns the establishment under Moses of an Israelite judiciary. The narrative depicts Moses as God's agent; he sits in judgment of the people, arbitrates their disputes, transmits God's laws to them, and instructs them in their statutory rights and responsibilities as God's people.

In verses 17 and 18, Jethro remonstrates with his son-in-law on the grounds that Moses has taken on a job that is too much for one man alone.

234

63. Woodcut illustrating Exodus 18 from Claude Paradin's *Quadrins historiques de la Bible, revuz and augmentez d'un grand nombre de figures* (Jean de Tournes, Lyons, 1558²)

In the following two verses, Jethro affirms Moses' role as chief judicial officer of the Israelites, but in verses 21-23, contemplating a strategy for diminishing the volume of cases brought before the central court system (thereby relieving the stress placed on its sole officer), he advises Moses to appoint deputy officers to preside at circuit courts set up on an ad hoc basis throughout the land:

21 You should look for able men among all the people, men who fear God, are trustworthy, and hate dishonest gain; set such men over them as officers over thousands, hundreds, fifties and tens.

22 Let them sit as judges for the people at all times; let them bring every important case to you, but decide every minor case themselves. So it will be easier for you, and they will bear the burden with you.

23 If you do this, and God so commands you, then you will be able to endure, and all those people will go to their home in peace.

Jean Court based the composition decorating the bowl of the *tazza* on an illustration (see fig. 63) executed in woodcut form by Bernard Salomon

235

("le petit Bernard") for Claude Paradin's *Quadrins historiques de la Bible* (Lyons, 1553).[4] In this octavo volume, epigrammatic verse (quatrains) based on biblical narratives appears under each illustration. Paradin's *Quadrins* covered only the Old Testament, but in 1554 there followed *Figures du Nouveau Testament*, with poems by Charles Fontaine (1515-88+)[5] and illustrations again by Bernard Salomon. For both of these volumes the publisher/printer was the well-known Lyonnais, Jean I de Tournes.[6]

The format of these volumes resembled the recently invented emblem books[7] of Andrea Alciati (whom Calvin came to know in 1529 at the University of Bourges and whom he much disliked),[8] as well as other contemporaneous books of personal "devices" (heraldic, chivalric figures combined with mottoes), and the idea of presenting visual vignettes taken from the Bible together with accompanying epigrammatic verse may have come from one or both of these emerging traditions. According to one analysis of this subject,[9] it was probably Jean I de Tournes, Paradin's printer/publisher, who thought up the project and asked Paradin and then Charles Fontaine to collaborate with him and his favorite illustrator, "le petit Bernard."[10]

4. For Claude Paradin (after 1510-73), see the introduction by Alison Saunders to a reprint of his *Dévises héroïques* (Aldershot, Hants., 1989). A canon of the church of Beaujeu, Paradin published *Dévises héroïques* (1551), *Quadrins historiques de la Bible* (1553), and *Alliances généalogiques des rois et des princes de Gaule* (1561) with the printer Jean I de Tournes. For further information about the Paradin family, see the introduction by Mathieu Méras to the journal of Guillaume Paradin, Claude's brother: *Le journal de Guillaume Paradin, ou, La vie en Beaujolais au temps de la Renaissance* (Geneva, 1986), pp. 3ff.

5. On Fontaine, cf. J. F. Michaud and L. G. Michaud, *Biographie Universelle Ancienne et Moderne* 14 (Paris, 1856), pp. 312-13.

6. The standard work on Jean I de Tournes, along with other members of his family, is Alfred Cartier, *Bibliographie des Editions des De Tournes, Imprimeurs Lyonnais* (Paris, 1937-38).

7. Still the basic introduction: Henry Green, *Andrea Alciati and His Books of Emblems: A Biographical and Bibliographical Study* (London, 1872; reprint, New York, n.d.). Thought to have been invented ca. 1522 in Milan by Alciati, this literary genre, which marries a short text with an image, first appeared in published form in 1531 at Augsburg; the genre quickly caught on, with many expanded editions and imitations following during the next decades.

8. Alciati was professor of Roman law at Bourges from 1529 to 1534; he lectured mainly on Justinian's *Code* and *Pandects* and gave his first lecture on Monday, 29 April 1529. Calvin, Melchior Wolmar, and Nicholas Duchemin went to Bourges to hear him. For Calvin, Alciati was too full of himself and too much the Milanese gourmand; cf. B. Thompson, *Humanists and Reformers* (Grand Rapids and Cambridge, 1996), pp. 478ff. Thanks to Corby Finney for this reference.

9. Alison Saunders, *The French Sixteenth-Century Emblem Book: A Decorative and Useful Genre* (Geneva, 1988); Saunders suggests that Paradin's *Quadrins* and Fontaine's *Figures* were intended for a "literate but not highly educated reading public"; she denominates them subliterary "para-emblem books," created in the orbit of emblem books and influenced by them. Other works that fall under this rubric include illustrated and simplified bestiaries based on Aesop's *Fables* and Ovid's *Metamorphoses*.

10. Despite his considerable influence on later Bible illustrations and other pictorial genres, Bernard Salomon (active 1540–died after 1561) is a shadowy figure among Renais-

Jean Court did not necessarily have to copy his composition directly from Paradin's *Quadrins*, however. Salomon's woodcuts for this highly successful publication, which appeared in different editions and languages, were later to become even more widely known through copies and reuse in illustrating different texts. For the present context, it is interesting to note that Jean I de Tournes reused the woodcuts to illustrate several Bibles. The most notable of these was a sumptuous Bible[11] in French, dated 1554, that had the appearance of a Catholic Bible but was actually based on the "Geneva Bible" of J. Gerard of 1540, with only some modifications, including the suppression of Calvin's preface. The publication of a vernacular Bible without Calvin's preface could be interpreted as a precautionary measure. Circumstantial evidence seems to suggest that Jean I de Tournes, who died a Protestant in 1564, may have converted to the new faith as early as 1545.[12]

In later years, Bernard Salomon's illustrations for the *Quadrins* were reused to illustrate at least twenty-one other publications.[13] The printer's son, Jean II de Tournes, also a Protestant, took over his father's publishing firm after the latter's death (1564) from the plague. In 1585 Jean II de Tournes fled Lyon for Geneva and took with him the woodblocks of Salomon's Bible illustrations.[14] Descendants of the family continued to use the plates as late as 1680, and in 1935 the surviving plates entered the *Musée d'art et d'histoire* in Geneva.

Whether Bernard Salomon was himself an evangelical,[15] or harbored clandestine Protestant sympathies, is difficult to determine. He drafted his

---

sance artists. He worked nearly exclusively for the printer Jean I de Tournes in Lyon. For his illustrations to the *Quadrins historiques* and *Figures du Nouveau Testament,* see Natalis Rondot, *Bernard Salomon: Peintre et Tailleur d'histoires à Lyon, au XVIe siècle* (Lyon, 1897), pp. 64-65, 75; also Herta Schubart, "Die Bibelillustration des Bernard Salomon" (diss., Hamburg University; defended 1929, published Amorbach, 1932); and particularly Renée Loche, *Bernard Salomon, Peintre et tailleur d'histoires: Illustrations pour l'Ancien Testament* (Geneva, 1969).

11. On *La Sainte Bible* (1554), cf. Cartier, vol. I, catalogue entry no. 266 (with 181 woodcut illustrations for the Old Testament, none for the New Testament), pp. 362-65. Previous, less elaborate Bibles by the de Tournes shop that utilized the woodcuts of "le petit Bernard" from the *Quadrins historiques* were: (1) *La Sainte Bible* of 1553, consisting of the five books of Moses, the book of Joshua, the book of Judges, the book of Ruth, with 75 woodcut illustrations (Cartier, pp. 343-45, cat. no. 240); (2) *Le Nouveau Testament de Nostre Seigneur Iesus Christ* of 1553, based for the first time in de Tournes's production on the third revision of Jean Calvin, and illustrated with 107 woodcuts (Cartier, p. 345, cat. no. 241); (3) *The true and lyuely historyke purtreatures of the vvoll Bible* of 1553, with 194 woodcut illustrations (Cartier, pp. 348-49, cat. no. 245); and (4) *Biblia Sacra* of 1554, with 198 woodcut illustrations for both the Old and New Testament (Cartier, pp. 361-62, cat. no. 265).

12. See Cartier, vol. I, pp. 122-23.

13. Cf. Loche, p. xiii.

14. Cf. Rondot, pp. 79-80; also Schubart, p. 12; and Loche, p. xiii.

15. N. Z. Davis, "Le milieu social de Corneille de la Haye (Lyon, 1533-1575)," *Revue de l'art* 47 (1980): 26: Davis suggests that Salomon, Pierre Eskrich, and Jean Perrissin gave up their evangelical adherence in 1559.

will[16] in 1559 according to conventional Catholic forms, but then sometime after 1561 he mysteriously disappeared from Lyon, in a manner some modern authors[17] want to connect with the pattern of flight typified by such Protestant artists as Étienne Delaune or Jacques Androuet du Cerceau. But Salomon was certainly working in a milieu with strong Protestant connections. Not only was Jean I de Tournes probably already a Protestant when he commissioned the text of the *Quadrins* from the Catholic author Claude Paradin, and the illustrations from Bernard Salomon, but it may be also argued, based on the book's contents, that this volume would certainly have appealed to Protestant sentiments.

The *Quadrins* contains 229 illustrations of Old Testament subjects, of which 172 (75 percent) were devoted to Genesis and Exodus, precisely the books that were of particular interest to Reformed Christians.[18] Moreover, the very idea of putting Bible stories into the vernacular and hence within the reach of less educated readers, and of joining biblical word and image, accords nicely with evangelical intents and purposes. Even a minimalist reading of the evidence reveals that the prototype Jean Court copied for his image of *The Judgment of Moses* (or *The Counsel of Jethro*) was invented and re-used several times over in an ambient conspicuous for its Huguenot and Reformed Christian associations.

It is also worth noting that Exodus 18 was seldom illustrated before the sixteenth century.[19] Suddenly a number of works in enamel illustrating

16. See H. L. Baudrier, *Bibliographie lyonnaise* 2 (Lyons, 1904), pp. 53-54.

17. For example, Jacques Thirion, "Bernard Salomon et le Décor des Meubles Civils Français à Sujets Bibliques et Allégoriques," in *Centre de Recherches d'Histoire et de Philologie de la IVe Section de l'Ecole Pratique des Hautes Etudes, VI. Histoire et Civilisation du Livre, 1. Cinque Etudes Lyonnaises* (Geneva and Paris, 1966), p. 57 n. 9.

18. Cf. Schubart, pp. 8, 30.

19. Under "Moses counselled by Jethro" the Princeton *Index of Christian Art* shows eleven entries extending from the ninth to the fourteenth centuries. Among the four monumental representations are a frescoed choir screen in Peterborough Cathedral (twelfth century), and windows in the apse of the upper Church of Assisi (thirteenth century) and at Canterbury Cathedral (twelfth- and thirteenth-century examples). The eight manuscript examples include a thirteenth-century Psalter in Brussels (Bibliothèque Royale 99612, fol. 24r°); a Bible at S. Isidoro in Léon, dated circa 1162 (Bible 3, I, fol. 40r°); a fourteenth-century Picture Bible in London (British Museum Add. 15277, fol. 11v°); a twelfth- or thirteenth-century Bible in Madrid (Real Academia de la Historia, Bible of S. Millán de la Cognolla, I, fol. 47r°); a Moralized Bible of the first half of the thirteenth century at Oxford (Bodleian Library, Bod. 270b, fol. 51v°); a ninth-century S. Parall. of John of Damascus in Paris (Bibliothèque Nationale, gr. 923, fol. 322 v°); a Moralized Bible of the first half of the thirteenth century in Paris (Bibliothèque Nationale, lat. 11560, fol. 40r°); and the Velislaus Miscellany from the fourteenth century in Prague (University Library, C.124, fol. 78v°). The manuscripts are all extensively illustrated, and the glass examples are parts of large cycles. The subject is obscure in Western art, a fact confirmed by its omission from standard iconographic handbooks, e.g., Louis Réau (*Iconographie de l'Art Chrétien*, 2 [Paris, 1956]) or A. Pigler (*Barockthemen: Eine Auswahl von Vorzeichnungen zur Ikonographie des 17. und 18. Jahrhunderts*, 1 [Budapest, 1974]).

the subject, all based on Bernard Salomon's woodcut, appeared in Limoges. Three of these works, all signed by Pierre Reymond, are dated.

1. A lidded *tazza*[20] in the Los Angeles County Museum, dated 1575. As in the Schultz *tazza*, the biblical scene appears on the interior of the bowl. The cover shows scenes inspired by Exodus 16 (the provision of food in the wilderness).
2. A plate[21] formerly in the Basilewsky Collection, now in the Hermitage Museum, showing the enthroned Moses surrounded by Israelites; the step of Moses' throne is inscribed "Moise/Exode XVIII" and dated 1572.
3. A dish[22] that T. H. Whitehead loaned to the South Kensington Museum, London, for an exhibition (1874) of enamels; it showed the judgment of Moses with two women and children, tents, and a landscape background and was initialed "P.R." (Pierre Reymond) and dated 1571.

Caroselli lists four additional examples in her Limoges enamel catalogue;[23] all the examples she cites are by Pierre Reymond and from his workshop and are based on the Bernard Salomon model.

None of the examples just cited exhibits precisely the same secondary motifs (the two children and the dog) that appear in the foreground of the bowl composition in the Schultz *tazza* (fig. 60). In the Los Angeles example, Caroselli offered an interpretation of a woman accompanied by two baby boys — a similar threesome appears elsewhere in Limoges enamel illustrations of the judgment of Moses — as possibly Moses' wife, Zipporah, with her sons Eliezer and Gershom. But in the Scultz *tazza* there is no obvious mother for the babies, and the one child wearing a dress is probably a girl. This leads me to suspect that the children and dog might be interpreted emblematically rather than as strictly narrative components drawn from the Bible — in sixteenth-century emblematic symbolism the dog represents fidelity, while the babies could be intended generically as the children of Israel.[24] This combination, then, would add up to a sort of hiero-

20. Caroselli, pp. 122-27, cat. no. 18.

21. A. Darcel and A. Basilewsky, *Collection Basilewsky: Catalogue Raisonné* (Paris, 1874), cat. no. 325.

22. *Catalogue of the Special Loan Exhibition of Enamels on Metal held at the South Kensington Museum in 1874* (London, 1875), p. 63, cat. no. 538.

23. Caroselli, p. 127.

24. In antiquity the dog was proverbial for its fidelity; cf. Pliny *Natural History*, VIII, 61; cf. A. Otto, *Die Sprichwörter und sprichwörtliche Redensarten der Römer* (Leipzig, 1890), s.v. "canis." Thanks to Corby Finney for this reference. Within emblem literature it appears in Alciati's "In fidem vxoriam" (cf. *Emblemata cum commentariis* [Padua, 1621; reprint, New York and London, 1976]), emblem CXCI, pp. 812-14; also see Cesare Ripa's image for *Fedeltà*, a woman accompanied

glyph, an emblem underlining the fidelity of God's chosen children to his laws. Within the de Tournes' milieu an interest in emblems goes back at least to 1547, the year in which Jean I de Tournes published a Latin edition of Alciati's *Emblems,* containing 113 woodcut vignettes executed by Bernard Salomon. The same illustrations accompanied a de Tournes French edition[25] of Alciati the following year.

Bernard Salomon's illustrations for the *Quadrins* became important models for sixteenth-century masters of various kinds of decorative arts. Besides the Limoges enamelers, who exploited many of the stories of the life of Moses in particular,[26] as well as other Old Testament subjects, the potters of Lyon faience exploited this same source,[27] as did the joiners who made wooden chests, armoires, and cabinets. In the scholarly literature on this latter subject there have been speculations about possible connections with Reformed ideology.

In an article focused on biblical iconography in the secular context of domestic furniture *(coffres, armoires, dressoirs),*[28] Jacques Thirion has explained the appearance of carved biblical reliefs by suggesting that they, like mythological stories, were popular and current reading matter for French sixteenth-century laypersons — they would know and feel at home with these narratives. Thirion suggested that some of the furniture decorated with reliefs illustrating biblical subjects could have ended up on display in ecclesiastical or semireligious settings, that they might have been

by a white dog, in C. Ripa, *Iconologia* (Rome, 1603; reprint, Hildesheim, 1970), s.v. "Fedeltà." Support for the interpretation of the children as the children of Israel is lent by the appearance of two otherwise unexplained children in a number of Bernard Salomon's illustrations for Exodus in *Quadrins historiques de la Bible,* beginning with Exodus 18 and ending with Exodus 32, the scenes designated as follows: Exodus 18, *Jethro Meets Moses in the Desert;* Exodus 19, *Moses Receives the Tablet;* Exodus 22, *The Worship of the Golden Calf;* Exodus 22, *Burnt Offerings Made to the Golden Calf;* Exodus 32, *The Feast before the Golden Calf;* Exodus 32, *Moses Breaks the Tablet;* Exodus 32, *Moses Burns the Golden Calf* (only one child is shown here).

25. Cartier, cat. nos. 72 and 107; cf. John Manning, "A Bibliographical Approach to the Illustrations in Sixteenth-Century Editions of Alciati's *Emblemata,*" in *Andrea Alciati and the Emblem Tradition: Essays in Honor of Virginia Woods Callahan,* ed. Peter Daly (New York, 1989), p. 141: "As in many cases, Bernard Salomon's design [for the emblems of Alciati] was the one that exerted the most lasting influence on the form of the emblematic *picturae* in all editions of the *Emblemata* of the last half of the sixteenth century."

26. See, for example, an oval platter in the Los Angeles County Museum by Jean de Court showing the destruction of the hosts of Pharaoh, after Bernard Salomon's illustration in the *Quadrins historiques* (Caroselli, pp. 166-69, cat. no. 27); two *tazze* in the Walters Art Gallery by Jean de Court, one with a design on the underside of the bowl much like that of the Schultz *tazza* (*Catalogue of the Painted Enamels of the Renaissance,* pp. 318-21, cat. no. 173) and the other with a different underside (pp. 316-17, cat. no. 172), both with Moses destroying the tablets of the Law, after the *Quadrins historiques* composition; and a *tazza* by Jean de Court in the Frick Collection with Moses striking the rock (François Verdier, *The Frick Collection, 6: Enamels, Oriental Rugs, and English Silver* [New York, 1977], pp. 194-97).

27. Rondot, p. 48.

28. Thirion, pp. 55ff.

commissioned by members of the clergy or by religious communities, and that many of the armoires exhibiting Old Testament subject matter could have been executed with Protestant intentions in mind. Thirion noted that the Protestant printers Jean I de Tournes and Gilles Corrozet had exhorted their readers to substitute biblical imagery for any and all mythological iconography on display in their homes. Indeed, in the 1553 *Dédicace* to Paradin's *Quadrins*, de Tournes advised his readers of the powerful effect of images on the viewer, and concluded:

> Donques, pour l'importance des Saintes Histoires, qui est si grande, qu'elles ne devroient estre ignorees de personne: nous avons choisi certeins adminicules de Peintures, accompagnez de *Quadrins Poëtiques*, tirez de la Bible, pour graver en la table des affeccions, l'amour des sacrees *Histoires*, à celle fin que un chacun fust induit à l'amour de ce *seul et unique necessaire*, qui est la sainte parole de Dieu.

And, in the 1558 introduction to *Figures de Nouveau Testament* (with poems by Charles Fontaine), de Tournes wrote a very provocative defense of the use of images, even going so far as to suggest that visual cognition was more powerful than auditory modes of knowing:

> Les choses d'instruccion qui sont representees à la veuë, & par icelle ont entree en l'apprehension, & de là en avat en l'entendement, & ouis en la memoire, esmeuvent & incitent davantage, & demeurent plus fermes & stables, que celles qui ont leur seule entree par l'oreille.[29]

Accordingly, biblical images, pedagogical subjects directed at viewers' eyes, should be construed not just as valid supplements to reading the Bible, but as even more powerful than words heard by auditors. By surrounding themselves in their secular and domestic settings with objects illustrating biblical stories, Reformed Christians could avoid Calvin's strictures against the use of sacred images in churches, while at the same time imbibing these very same images for their own spiritual edification.[30]

29. *Figures du Nouveau Testament* (Lyons, 1558), *Dédicace*. The dedication to Marguerite de France, duchesse de Berri, from Charles Fontaine, ends, "Recevez le dong, Lecteurs, pour recreacion à l'oeil, ayde à la memoire, & contentement à l'esprit, que Dieu vous vueille tousiours garder à son honneur & louange eternelle." For the argument that it was de Tournes and not Fontaine who composed the *Dédicace*, see Saunders, *French Sixteenth-Century Emblem Book* (supra, n. 9), and also Saunders, *The Sixteenth-Century Blason Poétique* (Bern, 1981), p. 187 n. 65.

30. For Calvin's dual stance on images, see the summary in Sergiusz Michalski, *The Reformation and the Visual Arts: The Protestant Image Question in Western and Eastern Europe* (London and New York, 1993), p. 70: "Calvinist churches were stripped of visual elements, only tablets with inscriptions from the Bible remaining. Though Calvin, somewhat contradictorily, allowed the keeping of holy images in private homes, his numerous negative pronouncements and the impact of his whole system predetermined their reduction in this case too. On the

Let us return to the Schultz *tazza*. Despite the fact that we cannot identify its first owners, like those of other related decorative objects exhibiting subjects drawn from the *Quadrins,* objects that are no longer preserved in their original contexts, a strong case can be made that this kind of subject matter would have resonated in the minds and imaginations of Reformed Christians, who saw their own identities very much in terms of Old Testament types and who, in matters of community organization, church polity, and rules and regulations governing the internal life of their communities, were eager to subscribe to Israelite models. There is no way to prove that the Schultz cup belonged to Huguenot owners, nor can we prove the opposite. But given the subject portrayed in the bowl of the cup, we can at least assert that this is an object which, based on its iconographic associations, would have appealed to Huguenot sensibilities.

---

other hand, he left an open field for narrative biblical scenes — especially from the Old Testament — and for secular art. Of decisive importance was the removal of works of art from the sacral sphere, from places of worship; in profane places an image took on an entirely different meaning." I thank Barbara T. Ross for this reference.

Calvin's Portrait: Representation, Image, or Icon?

MARY G. WINKLER

In 1577 a French physician named Jérome Bolsec published *Histoire de la vie, moeurs, actes, doctrines, constance et mort de Jean Calvin jadis ministre de Genève,* a work which portrays Calvin as ambitious, angry and filled with hatred, arrogant, bloodthirsty, conceited, covetous, cruel, extravagant, hypocritical, ignorant, stubborn to the point of intractability, vain, unchaste, vindictive, wicked, and a thoroughly intrusive personality who nosed about in other people's business. Bolsec clearly had a bit of a chip on his shoulder.

On the subject of Calvin's vanity and inordinate ambition and hypocrisy, he wrote the following words:

> Ie retourne au dire de Theodore de Beze en sa dicte preface[1] assauoir qu'il passera condamnation au moindre argument allegué de l'ambition de sondict maistre, pere & amy Caluin . . . ie demande si c'est signe d'humilité, & abiection de vaine gloire de se faire peindre, & permettre que son pourtraict, & image fut attachee en lieux publiques de Geneue, & portée au col de certains folz, & femmes qui en faisoyent leur Dieu? Si Beze ou autre de leur secte me respond que ledit Caluin n'en sauoit rien ie tesmoigne Dieu qu'ilz parleront contre vérité & leur conscience: car cela estoit tout commun & publiq en Geneue, et luy fut remonstré par parolles de gens de bien & authorité. Plus luy fut mandé par lettres qu'ayant condamné, & faict abbatre les images de Saincts, de la vierge Marie, & de Iesus-Christ mesme ce ne luy estoit honneur de laisser

---

1. Bolsec is referring to the preface of Théodore de Bèze's *Ioannis Calvini Vita . . . accurate descripta . . . ,* which appeared at Geneva in three editions: 1564, 1565, 1575. It is probable that Bolsec composed his *Vie de Calvin* in response to the 1564 edition; see P. C. Holtrop, *The Bolsec Controversy on Predestination from 1551 to 1555* (Lewiston, N.Y., 1993), pp. 785ff.

dresser la sienne en publiq & porter au col: Et que pour le moins Iesus-Christ le valloit bien. . . .

[I return to the saying of Théodore de Bèze who in the Preface lets it be known that he will condemn the slightest allegation of ambition to his so-called master, his (spiritual) father and friend, John Calvin. I ask, is it a sign of humility, a rejection of vanity, if one allows one's portrait to be painted? Or if one permits one's portrait to be hung in the public places of Geneva? Or if one allows one's portrait to dangle around the necks of certain fools and women who have made Calvin their God? If de Bèze or anyone else among the Calvinist sectarians responds by saying that Calvin knew nothing about this, I swear by God that they are lying and going against their own consciences, for in fact, these were common and public practices in Geneva. And good people, including the municipal authorities, criticized Calvin (for these practices). Furthermore, since Calvin had issued a written mandate condemning and calling for the destruction of saints' images along with those of the Virgin Mary and Jesus Christ himself, it could hardly be construed as an honor to Calvin to allow his portraits to be set up (and displayed) in public places or worn around (some fool's) neck. At the very least Jesus Christ is fully worthy (of being venerated in this manner).]

Bolsec's *Vie* is a bald invective (λόγος/*vituperatio*), and hence on the details of Calvin's life and personality the document's reliability is at the very least problematic. But we do know that Calvin's portrait was painted in Geneva during his lifetime. What Calvin thought about this is not entirely clear, but the least that can be said is this: Calvin must have agreed to have his portrait painted. It is also possible that he took a more active role, that he approved of the process and perhaps even encouraged it.

Correspondence (24 January 1555) between Pierre Viret and Guillaume Farel reveals that there was some uneasiness about the existence and possession and distribution of portraits depicting evangelical leaders.[2] When a colleague took portraits of Calvin, Viret, and Farel to Berne, some people accused the three of having their portraits painted as objects of adoration. Five years earlier, the request of a young Englishman for portraits of Zurich's reformers had led to an exchange of letters concerning the acceptability of portraits within evangelical Reformed circles.[3] The young man, Christopher Hales, responded to reservations about

2. "Scriptum est ad me Orba, vulgo iactare Zebaedeum cum alio quodam Bernam proficisci ac eo ferre Calvini, tuam et meum imaginem, nimirum quia nos pingendos curavimus ut adoraremur quemadmodum quidam nos calumniantur." Pierre Viret to Guillaume Farel. *Carpuo Reformatorum, Ioannis Calvini Opera*, vol. 15, ed. Wilhelm Baum, Edward Cunitz, and Edward Reuss (Braunschweig: C. A. Schwetschke and Sons, 1876), p. 395.

3. Mary G. Winkler, "A Divided Heart: Idolatry and the Portraiture of Hans Asper," *Sixteenth Century Journal* 18 (1987): 213-30. The correspondence can also be found in *Epistolae*

owning portraits: He has not asked for the portraits to open "a window to idolatry" [quod periculum sit ne in posterum idololatriae fenestra patefiat], nor does he want the men portrayed to be accused of vainglory. No. He wants the portraits to "adorn his library" [ut et Bibliothecae ornamento essent] so that the "worthy faces pictured as in a mirror might be seen by those who, due to distance, are hindered from seeing the Reformers with their own eyes" [et vestrae imagines effigies in tabella quasi in speculo conspicerentur iis, qui loci intercapedine prohiberentur, quo minus vos coram cerner possent]. Hales ends with a firm assertion that he has no intention whatsoever of setting up the images as idols.

Any iconophobic movement must (if it allows *any* representational images at all) make distinctions between pictures that are acceptable and those that are not. The presence of portraits of the evangelical leaders within the Zurich and Geneva communities may reveal an inconsistency in Reformed practice and perhaps in Reformed image theory. Why, for instance, may one own a portrait of a religious leader, but not the image of a saint? Is the portrait in any way like an idol? Although never central to theological discussions about the right uses or abuses of images, portraits nevertheless present a potential danger. As Calvin observed, ". . . man's nature, so to speak, is a perpetual factory of idols" [Unde colligere licet, hominis ingenium perpetuam, ut ita loquar, esse idolarum fabricam] (*Inst.* 1.11.8).[4] Yet portraiture is a genre that we customarily associate not just with Protestantism in general, but more specifically with the Calvinist or Reformed branch of Protestantism.[5] Indeed, portraiture fits neatly within the category of acceptable subjects for Calvinist art. Calvin would not allow that anyone should imagine him "gripped by the superstition of thinking absolutely no images permissible" [Neque tamen ea superstitione teneor ut nullas prorsus imagines ferendas censeam] (*Inst.* 1.11.12). Indeed, he countered, the ability to make art, along with the art objects themselves, is a gift of God. But these gifts have legitimate and proper uses. Calvin implied that artists should avoid attempts to represent those mysteries that are beyond sensory perception when he argued that artists

---

Tingurinae, Parker Society publication (Cambridge, 1848), p. 126. Paul Boesch, "Der Zürcher Apelles," *Zwingliana* 9 (1949): 16ff.

4. All quotations from the *Institutio Christianae Religionis* are from *Corpus Reformatorum, Ioannis Calvini Opera Quae Supersunt Omnia*, vol. 2, ed. Wilhelm Baum, Edward Cunitz, and Edward Reuss (Braunschweig: C. A. Schwetschke and Sons, 1864).

5. See, for example, Emil Doumergue, *L'Art et la Sentiment dans L'Oeuvre de Calvin*, reprint of the 1902 edition (Geneva: Slatkine Reprints, 1970); and Peter-Klaus Schuster, "Abstraktion, Agitation, und Einfühlung, Formen protestantischer Kunst in 16. Jahrhundert," in *Luther und die Folgen für die Kunst*, ed. Werner Hoffmann (Munich: Prestel Verlag, 1983), pp. 204-10. This catalogue for an exhibit held in Hamburg in the Hamburg Kunsthalle (November 1983–January 1984) places portraits in the category of Protestant genres.

should use their gifts to produce histories and events, aspects of nature, "images and forms of bodies without any depicting of past events" [In eo genere partim sunt historiae ac res gestae, partim imagines ac formae corporum, sine ulla rerum gestarum notatione]. Let them paint for the edification of the viewer or to give chaste pleasure. But let them paint or sculpt only those things "which the eyes are capable of seeing" [Restat igitur ut ea sola pingantur ac sculpantur quorum sint capaces oculi: Dei maiestas, quae oculorum sensu longe superior est, ne indecoris spectris corrumpatur] (*Inst.* 1.9.12). The portrait clearly falls under this latter rubric — it is something the eyes can see. And thus we must ask, was it only a few earnest young men, disaffected citizens, or perhaps overly scrupulous iconophobes, perhaps even rigoristic iconoclasts, that concerned themselves with the idolatrous associations of the Reformed portrait? Were the uses of the Renaissance portrait genre so harmless that the Reformers found themselves either indifferent to the genre or embracing it in some greater or lesser degree?

Portraiture was a well-established genre long before the Reformation. Nearly all of the portrait types attested for the sixteenth century were in existence at least a century earlier.[6] The list includes portrait series (illustrations of illustrious persons living or dead, genealogies, monarchs, and aristocrats); group portraits (often showing some corporate activity or underscoring some group affiliation); double portraits (often of spouses); single portraits; portrait drawing for albums; portrait miniatures to be kept in a private place or worn on one's person. All of these types are attested in sixteenth-century contexts under Protestant patronage. Lest we forget, Bolsec's complaint draws attention to "certains folz, & femmes" who wear miniature portraits of "their God" around their necks. As to the other categories of portraiture, we have abundant extant pictorial evidence to support the inference that the new evangelicals were happy to embrace the several variant manifestations of the genre.

The uses of the portrait genre and the meanings attributed to individual portraits had remained more or less constant throughout early modern Europe. The portrait is an exercise in empiricism,[7] a kind of visual report about a particular individual, and Renaissance patrons used portraits in much the same way we use photographs — as family documents to record marriages, births, the rise of family fortunes, the loss of family members.[8]

6. Lorne Campbell, *Renaissance Portraits: European Portrait Painting in the Fourteenth, Fifteenth, and Sixteenth Centuries* (New Haven and London: Yale University Press, 1980), pp. 41ff.

7. John Pope-Hennessy, *The Portrait in the Renaissance* (New York: Pantheon, 1966), p. 94.

8. Diane Owen Hughes, "Representing the Family: Portraits and Purposes in Early Modern Italy," in *Art and Art History: Images and Their Meaning,* ed. Robert I. Rotberg and Theodore K. Rabb (Cambridge: Cambridge University Press, 1988). See, also, Campbell, pp. 193-225.

Portraits were visual evidence of appearance and demeanor. Holbein's "fact-finding" missions for Henry VIII resulted in his well-known portraits of Henry's prospective brides; and Renaissance parents and grandparents were as eager as we are to possess portrait records of a child's growth. This sweet letter from the six-year-old duke of Longueville to his mother, Mary of Guise, reveals both the evidentiary and affective uses of the portrait:

> My lady granny will send me to my lady the Queen, but painted on a canvas and as big as I am and I am so pretty now that I have my hair cut like my uncle's.

> [Madame grant mamen me envoyra a la Roynne Madame, mais que je soy pinct en une toille et sy grant que moy et suis tant jolly que je suis tondu comme mes oncles.][9]

The above suggests the affective pull of the portrait as a symbolic evocation of the absent. The portrait "stands in" for the absent or departed friend, lover, or family member. Leon Battista Alberti made this aspect explicit when he praised the portraitist's skill. "The painter," he wrote, "possesses the truly divine power in that not only does he make what is absent present (as they say of friendship), but he also represents the dead to the living many centuries later" [Tiene in sé la pittura forza divina non solo si dice dell'amicitia, quale fa li huomine assenti essere presenti ma più i morti dopo molti secoli, essere quasi vivi].[10]

Christopher Hales's letter is useful here. In his letter to Rudolf Gwalther he defended his desire for portraits of Zurich's reformers by arguing that he wanted to possess their likenesses — appearing as if in a mirror — as an aid to those who due to distance are prohibited from beholding with their own eyes.[11]

Hales is clear about two uses of portraiture. One is commemoration: his portrait brings the absent friend to mind and holds him near in imagination. The other is emulation — a concept that is closely tied to commemoration.

For example, in Thomas More's *Utopia* statues of "distinguished men who have served their country well were erected in the marketplace to preserve the memory of their good deeds, and to spur on citizens to emulate the glory of their ancestors" [Ideoque statuas viris insignibus et de republica praeclare meritis in foro collocant, in rerum bene gestarum

---

9. *Foreign Correspondence with Marie de Lorraine, Queen of Scotland from the Originals in the Balcarres Papers, 1537-1548,* ed. M. Wood, Scottish History Society Publications, 3rd ser., IV (Edinburgh, 1923), pp. 81-82. Cited in Campbell, p. 196.

10. Leon Battista Alberti, *Della Pittura,* II.25, ed. Luigi Malle (Florence: G. C. Sansoni, 1950), p. 76; *On Painting* II.25, trans. Cecil Grayson (London, 1991).

11. Winkler, p. 223.

memoriam simul ut ipsorum posteris maiorum suorum gloria calcar et incitamentum ad virtutem sit].[12]

In Renaissance portraits of heroes, philosophers, and humanists, interest in psychology coincided with the artists' attempts to explore character and emotion in the countenance.[13] The humanist belief that history can teach ethics thus supported the portraitist's pursuit of illustrious men.

What Hales refuses to acknowledge, however, is the peculiar, almost magical, hold a portrait can exert on the viewer's emotions — especially if the image portrays a beloved object. At the time Alberti wrote of the painter's power to bring the absent near, Leonardo Giustinian (1387/88-1446) wrote this poem to his beloved:

> I' t'ho dipinto in su una carticella
> come se fusti una santa de Dio.
> Quando mi levo la mattina bella
> ingenocchion mi butto con desio.
> Sì t'adoro, e poi dico: chiara stella,
> quando farai contento lo cor mio?
> Bàsote (= ti bacio) poi, e stringo con dolcezza:
> poscia mi parto, e vòmen a la messa.

> [I have painted you on a little (holy) card
> as if you were one of God's saints.
> When I rise early in the morning
> I throw myself to my knees (filled as I am) with desire.
> Yes, I worship you, and then I utter (as if in prayer): O bright star
> When will you satisfy my heart?
> Then I kiss you and embrace you tenderly:
> after which I depart and betake myself to mass.][14]

Giustinian makes explicit the emotional connection in the viewer between the beloved and her portrait.

Giustinian might also be cited as an example of the dangers inherent in emotional attachment to images in general, and portraits in particular. The lover's response suggests a parody of the mass. He kneels in desire for communion with the source of his longing, he speaks to the portrait in a

---

12. Thomas More, *Utopia, Latin Text and English Translation,* ed. George M. Logan, Robert M. Adams, and Clarence H. Miller (Cambridge: Cambridge University Press, 1995), pp. 194-95.

13. Francis Haskell, *History and Its Images: Art and the Interpretation of the Past* (New Haven and London: Yale University Press, 1993). Haskell offers a lengthy discussion of portrait anthology. Many portraits, however, were not true likenesses but imaginative reconstructions of historical figures. The aim was to depict the *persona* of the individual.

14. *Antologia della Letteratura Italiana* 2, ed. M. Vitale (Milano, 1966), Leonardo Giustinian, s.v. (Strambotto III).

form of prayer, takes it to his mouth in a kiss. During these devotions he blurs the distinction between his painted card and the distant woman ("Then I kiss you and embrace you tenderly"). This veneration of his own private icon precedes the poet's discharge of his regular orthodox religious duties (". . . I depart and betake myself to mass").

This fifteenth-century example of image worship belongs to a context which Calvin and the other reformers deplored and despised. Of course, the whole poem is a charming conceit; but the conceit derives its charm from its placement within well-established religious practices — images of saints were set up in private shrines as well as in churches. The lover treats the lover "as if" she were a saint — and treats her portrait as if it were a saint's image.

It is quite clear that even before the Reformation there was a relatively broad range of applications and responses to portraits. Some of these were indistinguishable from common responses to religious portraits. The truth is that the portrait is surrounded with dangers intrinsic to its very nature: It represents an individual in his or her particularity. It is a likeness, and as a likeness it may evoke the selfsame emotions associated with the person represented. The above may, in fact, be true of all Renaissance uses of portraiture. To use a portrait as an *exemplum* or a memorial will, after all, remind the viewer of the characteristics of the individual portrayed. Even the pictorial report aims at conveying something of the elusive personal nature of the sitter. Finally, it could be argued that the lover's "adoration" of his beloved's portrait represents a version of idolatry.

In view of these considerations, it is not surprising that there should have been some uncertainty and anxiety surrounding the uses of portraits depicting evangelical notables. In fact, the expression of such concerns is comparatively rare and is commonly countered with asseverations that no improper use is intended. The debate between Christopher Hales and another English exile, John Burcher,[15] is illuminating. Burcher seems to have argued that no pious man would allow his portrait to be painted. In fact, Burcher would allow *no* images of any sort. Hales responds that he sees no harm in images provided their emplacement does not promote abuse. A library is not a church, and a portrait in a "museum" is not an idol. Hales argues that there is no wrongdoing in hanging a portrait that "mirrors" the aspect and characteristics of a distant friend or hero.

This essay began with the quotation in which Bolsec accuses Calvin of vainglory and ambition and hypocrisy. He attacks Calvin as the destroyer of religious images and as the hypocrite who replaces traditional Christian iconography with his own portrait. Perhaps Bolsec's accusations should be dismissed as the ravings of an angry man, but at the same time it seems there are contradictions in the Calvinist approach to portraiture. Calvin

15. Winkler, p. 223.

himself observed that human nature is a "perpetual factory of idols." As we have also seen, the Renaissance portrait could be interpreted at multiple levels, including idolization — Renaissance patrons often regarded portraits as a palpable presence, a physical and quasi-magical substitute for the portrayed subject. Furthermore, the accusation of vainglory and self-admiration *should* have troubled Protestant sensibilities. Even the accepted practice of contemplating images of the illustrious or virtuous men and women should have raised some doubts. After all, to the evangelical sensibility fame and virtue are good only insofar as they reveal God's grace. As fallen humans our works are full of uncleanness:

> There is no doubt that whatever is praiseworthy in works is God's grace; there is not a drop that we ought by rights to ascribe to ourselves. . . . To man we assign only this: that he pollutes and contaminates by his impurity those very things which were good. For nothing proceeds from man, however perfect he be, that is not defiled by some spot.

> [Gratiam Dei esse non dubiam est quidquid in operibus est quod laudem meretur; nullam esse guttam quam proprie nobis adscribere debemus. . . . Tantum hoc homini assignamus quod ea ipsa, quae bona erant, sua impuritate polluit et contaminat.] (*Inst.* 3.11.3)

Yet a portrait is also an image of our neighbor whom we are commanded to love. When Christians meet a stranger they are to say: "He is contemptible and worthless; but the Lord shows him to be one to whom he has deigned to give the beauty of his image" [Dic contemptibilem ac nihili: at eum Dominus esse demonstrat, quem imaginis suae decore dignatus sit] (*Inst.* 3.7.6). It is the image of God in each of us that should incline us toward each other in love and service. Thus we should forgive the evil intentions of others, as we ourselves are not without taint. Rather, we should "look upon the face of God in them, which cancels and effaces their transgressions, and with its beauty and dignity allures us to love and embrace them" [Si meminerimus non hominum malitiam reputandam esse, sed inspiciendam in illis Dei imaginem; quae inductis ac obliteratis eorum delictis, ad eos amandos amplexandosque sua pulchritudine ac dignitate nos alliciat] (*Inst.* 3.7.6).

Leonardo da Vinci's painter's dictum may have some significance in the present context: "The good painter has to paint two principal things, that is to say, man and the intention of his mind" [Il bono pittore ha à dipingere due cose principali cioe l'homo è il concetto della mente].[16]

---

16. Leonardo da Vinci, *Treatise on Painting*, vol. 2, facsimile, trans., and ed. A. Philip McMahon (Princeton: Princeton University Press, 1956). Also in *Leonardo on Painting*, ed. Martin Kemp, trans. Martin Kemp and Margaret Walker (New Haven and London: Yale University Press, 1989), p. 144.

Leonardo's statement is the product of the Renaissance "pneumatic physiology"[17] which considered the body to be animated by the soul. On this theory one could read the contours of the soul through an observation of the body. As one contemporary scholar puts it: "The viewer of the Renaissance portrait was assumed to see, by means of the painting, the spirit of the sitter, and inevitably the spirit of the painter."[18] When Calvin wrote of the "beauty and dignity" observable in our neighbors, he was thinking primarily of spiritual dignity. Although we may see God's glory in the form of "the outer man," according to Calvin, "there is no doubt that the proper seat of his image is in the soul" [Quamvis enim in homine externo refulgeat Dei gloria, propriam tamen imaginis sedem in anima esse dubium non est] (*Inst.* 1.15.3). Despite belief in the soul's invisibility, Renaissance medical theory and art doctrine suggested that something essential and true could be glimpsed in the shape and movement of the body parts, but especially in the contours of a person's physiognomy. In short, disclosures of the soul were to be found in the outer man.

If we review the evidence for and against a proper Calvinist approach to portraiture, we find a paradox. On the one hand, the portrait is clearly realistic, and therefore may be acceptable. Moreover, there is surprisingly little debate about the affective or superstitious use of the portrait image. In this context the situation of the portrait is crucial: images in churches are suspect or forbidden — images in libraries are not. On the other hand, it is clear that within the Protestant community there was awareness of the self-aggrandizing motives of many sitters. Accusations about vainglory and ostentation are not inconsistent with Calvinist theology or anthropology. Calvin's observation that "there is nothing that man's nature seeks more eagerly than to be flattered" [Siquidem nihil est quod magis appetat humanum ingenium quam blanditiis demulceri] (*Inst.* 2.1.2), is both pithy and apropos. No doubt many sitters *were* vain and lacking in proper humility. Perhaps the most intriguing aspect, finally, is the role of the portraitist. As interpreter and revealer of the individual's soul, the painter created both "a window to idolatry" and opportunities to see in our neighbors the image of God and to look on them with love.

17. David Summers, *The Judgment of Sense: Renaissance Naturalism and the Rise of Aesthetics* (Cambridge: Cambridge University Press, 1987), p. 110. Summers begins his discussion from an observation of Michael Baxandall in *Painting and Experience in Fifteenth Century Italy* (Oxford: Oxford University Press, 1972), p. 60. Baxandall observed that Renaissance discussions of expression in art are difficult for us to comprehend "because we no longer believe the old pneumatic physiology through which they are rationalized."

18. Summers, p. 111.

A Note on de Bèze's Icones

PAUL CORBY FINNEY

In her contribution to this volume, Mary Winkler draws attention to an intriguing excerpt (cf. p. 243) from chapter 12 of Bolsec's *Histoire de la Vie . . . de Iean Calvin*. Unfortunately, with the noteworthy exception of Holtrop's excellent study,[1] scholarship on Bolsec is riddled with denominational bias and is thus mostly unedifying. There is also no doubt, as remarked by Winkler, that Bolsec's *Vie* is itself a work of bias; *Vie* has all the hallmarks of heresiology, a diatribe exposing Calvin as the Antichrist. It is also clear that Bolsec had good reason to impugn his former mentor and friend: in 1551 at Geneva Calvin had betrayed Bolsec in a manner best described as despicable. But none of this directly affects the subject at issue here; namely, the manufacture, distribution, and reception of Calvin portraits during and immediately after the Reformer's lifetime.

Bolsec identifies two kinds of Calvin portrait applications: images exhibited "en lieux publiques" and those "portée au col." This is the full extent of Bolsec's portrait typology; the two types might be subsumed under the rubrics public and private. Bolsec does not specify technical or historical details, for example, in what medium the Calvin portraits that he had seen were executed or where, when, under what circumstances, and by whom they had been executed. He had no reason to bother with these details. After all, Bolsec had but one overarching purpose, namely, to expose Calvin as an ambitious rogue, and given that purpose, it was sufficient simply to record as fact that Calvin allowed his portrait to be made and exhibited in both public and pri-

---

For permission to photograph the 1580 de Bèze portraits and for numerous other courtesies, I want to extend my sincere thanks to William O. Harris, the Librarian for Archives and Special Collections, Speer Library, Princeton Theological Seminary Rare Books Collection.

1. P. C. Holtrop, *The Bolsec Controversy on Predestination from 1551 to 1555* (Lewiston, N.Y., 1993).

vate venues. Having once established this fact (as he believed he had done), Bolsec could then invite his readers to draw the appropriate conclusions.

As far as statements of fact are concerned, there is nothing in the external record to contradict Bolsec's claims that Calvin allowed public and private applications of his portrait. From 1535 onward we have surviving portraits of Calvin, as a young man, and in his forties and fifties; the portraits are in enamel and in oil, on canvas and on wood. We also have sixteenth-century Calvin miniatures[2] executed in a medallion format, in precious and base metals (both struck and cast); miniatures are also attested on canvas stretched over a small wooden flan as well as painted directly onto a wooden flan — under the latter rubric there is the very good (Doumergue[3] to the contrary notwithstanding) Rillet miniature (diameter 12.5 mm.; whereabouts unknown) on cedar.

But what we do not know about all of these Calvin portraits is their original application: how they were exhibited is unclear. Nothing forbids the possibility that some of the oils could have been displayed in Geneva's "lieux publiques." Nor does anything (beyond Bolsec's report) demand it. The same is true for the medallions: Calvin's followers (Bolsec's "folz & femmes") could have carried miniature portraits of their hero on their persons, perhaps even displaying them in the manner of pendants or brooches; however, given the contemporaneous Catholic practice of wearing objects such as scapulars, medals, and crosses on one's person, and given Calvin's relentless opposition to idolatry, it is perhaps stretching the case to imagine that Calvin would have allowed his followers to indulge in adulation of this sort. It seems more probable that Bolsec was simply smearing Calvin with a little of his own idolatry-bashing medicine. But this still leaves unanswered the question of how sixteenth-century Calvin medallions were exhibited, when and where and by whom. New studies of both the portrait genres just mentioned (oil paintings and miniatures) are now long overdue; Doumergue's treatment of this subject was acceptable for its own time, but by present standards it is uncritical and antiquated and needs to be updated.

In addition to oil paintings and miniatures, there is still a third category of Calvin (and Calvinist) portraiture that Bolsec does not mention; namely, graphic renderings that were based on woodblock (less commonly on copper-plate) prototypes and published in portrait anthologies. Of all the visual media pressed into service by sixteenth- and seventeenth-century Protestants (especially within the Reformed wing), this was the genre that had the widest circulation, hence at the level of reception it might well be argued that this portrait type had the greatest impact. Within the Reformed community, as elsewhere, this is clearly a genre of portraiture that was targeted to an audi-

2. General introduction to the subject of sixteenth-century French portrait miniatures: L. R. Schidlof, *The Miniature in Europe*, I (Graz, 1964), pp. 9ff.

3. E. Doumergue, *Iconographie Calvinienne* (Lausanne, 1909), p. 60, pl. 9.

254

ence at the upper rungs of the socioeconomic ladder: the prosperous bourgeoisie (with some leisure time on their hands along with spare cash for the
acquisition of books) and the educated nobility. The Reformed *pièce de
résistance* within this genre is Théodore de Bèze's portrait anthology, entitled
*Icones: id est verae imagines virorum doctrina simul et pietate illustrium, quorum
præcipuè ministerio partim bonarum literarum studia sunt restituta, partim vera religio
in variis orbis Christiani regionibus, nostra patrumque memoria fuit instaurata: additis
eorundem vitæ & operæ descriptionibus, quibus adiectæ sunt nonnullæ picturæ quas
emblemata vocant,* which appeared in Geneva under the Jean de Laon imprint in
1580, sixteen years after Calvin's death. In 1581 a second, expanded vernacular version of de Bèze's *Icones,* translated by Simon Goulart[4] and entitled *Les
vrais pourtraits des hommes illustres en piete et doctrine . . . ,* appeared in Geneva,
once again under the de Laon imprint. At the end of the century, another
slightly less well-known Protestant portrait anthology appeared in the Netherlands — under a general print privilege[5] granted by the States General,
Hendrick Hondius published his own version of the genre based on a new set
of plates and entitled *Icones virorum nostra patrumq. memoria illustrium, quorum
opera cum literar. studia, tum vera religio fuit restaurata* (The Hague, 1599). There
are numerous surviving seventeenth-century exemplars of yet other Reformed portrait anthologies (including a 1672 reprint of the 1581 French edition of de Bèze's *Vrais pourtraits . . .*).

The sixteenth-century portrait anthology[6] has a humanist pedigree, and
its literary roots are ancient. Pliny (*NH* 35.2.11) says Varro published seven
hundred portraits of famous men *(inlustrium)* in his biographical *Imagines.* In
Plutarch scholarship since Weiszäcker (1930),[7] a distinction is drawn between chronology and eidology, the former concerning the narration (in a linear sequence) of events in a man's lifetime, the latter consisting in thematic
clusters (presented in a nonlinear arrangement) of deeds, events, habits, and
sayings which disclose a man's character — εἶδος in this context corresponds
to what we in English would call a person's nature or character, defined primarily by moral nomenclature (generosity, integrity, honesty, courage, etc.).
Plutarch, who had a profound effect on sixteenth-century humanism, was a
lifelong believer in the power of physiognomy, including the portrait genre; he
believed that gifted portraitists could discern and represent a person's character through their scrutinization of the face, especially the eyes.[8]

---

4. L. C. Jones, *Simon Goulart, 1543-1628. Étude biographique et bibliographique* (Geneva,
1917), passim, esp. pp. 570-71.

5. On print privileges, cf. N. Orenstein, "Prints and the Politics of the Publisher: The
Case of Hendrick Hondius," *Simiolus* 23 (1995): 242 n. 7.

6. P. O. Rave, "Paolo Giovio und die Bildnisvitenbücher des Humanismus," *Jahrbuch der
Berliner Museen* 1 (1959): 119-54.

7. A. Weiszäcker, *Untersuchungen über Plutarchs biographische Technik* (Berlin, 1930).

8. . . . οἱ ζωγράφοι τὰς ὁμοιότητας ἀπὸ τοῦ προσώπου καὶ τῶν περὶ τὴν οἶ ὄψιν εἰδῶν, οἷς
ἐμφαίνεται τὸ ἦθος . . . ; *Vitae Parallelae,* ed. C. Sintenis (Leipzig, 1891): *Alexander* I.16ff.

In ancient biography we can discern multiple literary/rhetorical strands and influences, but one of the most conspicuous is the epideictic tradition of *encomium*,[9] the praise of a biographical subject for his accomplishments, his goodness, his integrity and honest character. Sixteenth-century portrait anthologies clearly reflect the influence of Plutarchian eidology and encomiastic biography. Lest we forget, thanks to the agency of the print medium, the texts of Greek and Latin biographers (including Plutarch, Varro, Nepos, Suetonius, Jerome) were available to European humanists on a fairly broad scale during the entire sixteenth century.

As for visual models, it is extremely improbable that the sixteenth-century humanists who drafted portrait anthologies had access to ancient book portraits; more likely they drew their immediate visual prototypes from the hands of contemporaneous coin and medal illustrators,[10] for example, Guillaume du Choul,[11] Andrea Fulvio,[12] Hubert Goltzius,[13] Guillaume Rouillé,[14] and Jacopo Strada,[15] to name only a few of the better-known sixteenth-century numismatic/medallic book engravers. In de Bèze's world (which consisted in south-central France, the Rhineland, and northern Switzerland) the most important book event that is likely to have stimulated his decision to publish his own illustrated, Protestant equivalent of a humanist *de viris illustribus* was the appearance (1575/77) at Basel of Paolo Giovio's portrait anthology,[16] illustrated with the splendid woodcuts of Tobias Stimmer[17] and under the imprint of the Italian Protestant Pietro Perna (born in Lucca, emigrated to Basel).[18]

De Bèze published his portrait anthology (see Appendix) in February 1580. He dedicated the volume to James VI of Scotland (b. 19 June 1566),

9. L. Pernot, *La rhétorique de l'éloge dans le monde gréco-romain*, II, Collection des Études Augustiniennes: Série Antiquité 138 (Paris, 1993), pp. 674ff.

10. As observed by F. Haskell, *History and Its Images* (New Haven and London, 1993), pp. 13ff. (with the literature cited there).

11. *Discours de la religion des anciens romains escript par noble seigneur Guillaume du Choul . . . et illustré d'un grand nombres des médailles . . .* (Lyon, 1556).

12. *Illustrium Imagine Imperatorum: & illustrium uirorum ac mulierum uultus ex antiquis nomismatibus expressi* (Rome, 1517).

13. *Vivae Omnium fere Imperatorum Imagines . . . ex antiquis veterum numismatis . . . adumbratae* (Antwerp, 1557); Goltzius, *C. Julius Caesar sive historiae Imperatorum Caesarumque Romanorum ex antiquis numismatibus restitutae* (Bruges, 1563).

14. *La première — la seconde partie du promptuaire des médailles des plus renommées personnes qui ont esté depuis le commencement du monde* (Lyon, 1553).

15. *Epitome Thesauri Antiquitatum . . .* (Lyons, 1553); translated (1553) by Jean Louueau d'Orléans as *Epitomé du Thrésor des Antiquitez . . . Pourtraits des vrayes Medailles des Empp. . . .*

16. Linda S. Klinger, "The Portrait Collection of Paolo Giovio" (Ph.D. diss., Princeton, 1991) (with the literature cited there).

17. U. Thieme and F. Becker, *Allgemeines Lexikon der bildenden Künstler von der Antike bis zur Gegenwart*, 32 (Leipzig, 1938), s.v. "Stimmer, Tobias" (article by F. T. Schulz).

18. D. M. Manni, *Vita di Pietro Perna, Lucchese, diligentissimo impressore in Basilea* (Lucca, 1763).

64. James VI of Scotland, reprinted from de Bèze's *Icones* (1580)

who at the time was a mere lad of thirteen years. From 1603 to 1625 he reigned as James I, England's first Stuart king. Although he vigorously opposed an attempt by certain Presbyterian ministers to challenge the Scottish monarchy on theocratic grounds, James remained steadfast throughout his lifetime in his attachment to Presbyterian theology and doctrine. In other words, he was a friend of the Reformed cause. De Bèze placed a profile portrait (see fig. 64) of the teenage James opposite the frontispiece of his *Icones*.

De Bèze's anthology contains portraits of other political notables,[19] including Francis I (see fig. 65),[20] king of France from 1515 to 1547, and his sister Marguerite (1492-1549) (see fig. 66),[21] who was devoted to her brother throughout his lifetime. Francis was a refined and chivalrous personality, in many respects more medieval than modern; he was a distinguished patron of humanist scholarship and of the arts, including poetry,

19. For example, under the German leaders, Duke George of Anhalt-Dessau in Saxony is included; see Appendix.

20. *The Oxford Encyclopedia of the Reformation* (hereafter: *OER*), ed. H. J. Hillerbrand (New York, 1996), s.v. "Francis I" (article by R. J. Knecht).

21. *OER*, s.v. "Marguerite" (article by P. Sommers).

65. Francis I, king of France, reprinted from de Bèze's *Icones* (1580)

music, architecture, and painting. Under the latter rubric, for example, the French portrait genre flourished thanks to Francis: François Clouet (ca. 1510-72) worked for the king, as did Corneille[22] de Lyon for Francis's second wife, Eleanor of Portugal. Francis remained a Catholic throughout his lifetime, but his sister Marguerite (also a Catholic) along with his mistress was a sympathetic supporter of the Reformed cause, and together they attempted (and mostly succeeded) in exerting a moderating influence on Francis's treatment of the Protestants within his realm. Marguerite was an exceedingly important person in her own right, an author and poet, a mordant satirist with a strong reformist agenda, a patroness of artists and humanist scholars, a protector of the rights of religious minorities (including Huguenots) — in short, an independent thinker of exceptional stature.

Most of the thirty-eight portraits in de Bèze's 1580 edition of the *Icones* illustrate either leaders who are Protestant insiders or reformist outsiders, the latter group consisting in men whose approach to learning and religion

---

22. *The Dictionary of Art,* ed. J. Turner (New York, 1996), s.v. "Corneille" (article by P. Rouillard; with the literature cited there).

66. Margaret of Angoulême, reprinted from de Bèze's *Icones* (1580)

de Bèze could harmonize with his own explicitly Reformed convictions. For de Bèze the real inner circle consisted in Calvin (see fig. 67), Farel (see fig. 68),[23] Viret (see fig. 69),[24] and of course himself. In addition, within the Francophone wing of the magisterial reform, de Bèze illustrated portraits of the Hellenists Guillaume Budé,[25] Jacques Lefèvre d'Étaples,[26] James Tussan (1498–ca. 1547), and Melchior Wolmar (de Bèze's childhood tutor); of the Hebraist François Vatable; of Francis I's "valet de chambre" and translator of the Huguenot psalter, Clément Marot;[27] of King Charles's chancellor Michel de l'Hôpital[28] (present with de Bèze at the Colloquy of Poissy, con-

23. Guillaume Farel (1489-1565); cf. *OER*, s.v. "Farel, Guillaume" (article by F. Higman).

24. Pierre Viret (1511-71); cf. *OER*, s.v. "Viret, Pierre" (article by R. L. Linder).

25. Guillaume Budé (1468-1540); cf *OER*, s.v. "Budé, Guillaume" (article by D. O. McNeil).

26. Jacques Lefèvre d'Étaples (ca. 1455-1536); cf. *OER*, s.v. "Lefèvre d'Étaples, Jacques" (article by Guy Bedouelle).

27. Clément Marot (ca. 1496/97-1544); cf. *Die Musik in Geschichte und Gegenwart* 8, ed. F. Blume (Kassel, 1960), s.v. "Marot, Clément" (article by P.-A. Gaillard; with the literature cited there).

28. Michel de l'Hôpital (1505?-1573); cf. *OER*, s.v. "L'Hôpital, Michel de" (article by S.-H. Kim).

67. John Calvin, re-printed from de Bèze's *Icones* (1580)

vened 9 September 1561);[29] of Augustin Marolat; and of Francis I's royal printer/publisher, the very distinguished Robert Éstienne,[30] who in the year of his death (1559) brought out the famous edition of the *Institutes*.

In addition, *Icones* contains portraits of leaders within the German and Swiss wings of the Reformation, and there are also images of John Knox,[31] John A'Lasco, Juan Diaz, Erasmus, Jerome of Prague, and Girolamo Savonarola of Ferrara.[32] Throughout the entire work de Bèze's purpose is the same; namely, to commemorate, honor, and praise the leaders of the Protestant cause along with their reform-minded sympa-

29. D. Nugent, *Ecumenism in the Age of the Reformation: The Colloquy of Poissy* (Cambridge, 1974); also see D. Willis-Watkins, "The Second Commandment and Church Reform: The Colloquy of St. Germain-en-Laye, 1562," *Studies in Reformed Theology and History* 2.2 (1994): 1 n. 4.

30. *OER,* s.v. "Éstienne, Robert" (article by F. Armstrong).

31. C. Borgeaud, "Le 'vrais portrait' de John Knox," *Bulletin de la Société de l'Histoire du Protestantisme Français* 84 (1935): 11-36.

32. Girolamo Savonarola (1452-98); cf. *OER,* s.v. "Savonarola, Girolamo" (article by L. Polizzotto); also see *Girolamo Savonarola: Piety, Prophecy, and Politics in Renaissance Florence,* ed. D. Weinstein and V. Hotchkiss (Dallas, 1994).

68. William Farel, re-
printed from de Bèze's
Icones (1580)

thizers insofar as they are persons of distinction. De Bèze's language is
consistently and unabashedly encomiastic — there is no doubt that this
is a book that bespeaks pride in the emerging Reformed tradition. This
handsome book was designed for the praise and propagation of the
Protestant cause.

The *Icones* portraits are not signed, and thus we do not know whom
de Bèze chose as his engraver. Bernard Salomon (d. ca. 1561)[33] had
been dead for nearly twenty years. Tobias Stimmer was active in his profession until his death in 1584, but there is neither internal nor external
evidence to support his participation in the project. Claude Woeiriot,[34]
who may have executed an unsigned copperplate engraving of de Bèze,
is a remote possibility. Corneille de Lyon, based on his style and the
known circumstances of his life,[35] is even more remote. There are dozens of other possible woodcut engravers whom de Bèze might have en-

33. Thieme and Becker, *Allgemeines Lexikon*, 29 (1935), s.v. "Salomon, Bernard."

34. Thieme and Becker, *Allgemeines Lexikon*, 35/36 (Leipzig, 1992), s.v. "Woeiriot,
Claude."

35. N. Z. Davis, "Le milieu social de Corneille de La Haye," *Revue de l'art* 47 (1980): 21-
28.

69. Peter Viret, re-printed from de Bèze's *Icones* (1580)

gaged,[36] but based on the direct stylistic evidence (derived from the Fontainebleau school) of his signed work and the indirect evidence of his life circumstances, Pierre Eskrich (ca. 1518/20–after 1590)[37] is still a good choice as the probable portrait engraver of the *Icones*. We know that in Geneva between 1561 and 1563 Eskrich executed portraits of several Protestant reformers for the *Mappemonde papistique*. Eskrich was also the engraver of the forty-four emblemata appended to de Bèze's portrait anthology, and it is clear that he was on close personal terms with de Bèze. But ultimately this is a question that art historical scholarship will need to resolve, hopefully in a definitive manner: Was Eskrich the engraver of de Bèze's *Icones* portraits?

In summary, de Bèze's portrait anthology marks the Reformed Protestant beginnings of participation in a pictorial genre that was widespread in

36. For a list of fifty-nine woodcut engravers working in Lyon between 1550 and 1600, see N. Rondot, *Graveurs sur bois à Lyon au seizième siècle* (Paris, 1898), pp. 111-13.

37. Thieme and Becker, *Allgemeines Lexikon* (Leipzig, 1928/29), s.v. "Eskrich, Pierre" (article by E. Vial; with the literature cited there). Eskrich was probably born in Paris; he was the son of engraver Jakob Krug of Freiburg im Breisgau. Eskrich is known by various surnames, including the gallicized equivalents of Krug: Cruche and du Vase. He also used the pseudonym Jean Moni.

the sixteenth century, a genre that had humanist, classicizing, and antiquarian roots, and that was conceived first in Italy to lionize great men, including politicians, military and literary figures, benefactors, scholars, and reformers. In addition to the two other genres (oil and miniature painting) that Bolsec mentioned in connection with Calvin, this third genre, the portrait anthology, constitutes the third important branch of Protestant (and specifically Reformed) iconography that circulated widely in the sixteenth and following centuries. This third genre of Protestant portraiture was targeted to an audience made up of noblemen, bureaucrats, and related persons in high places, along with prosperous commoners; in short, it was a genre aimed at the high culture of sixteenth- and seventeenth-century Europe. The effectiveness of this genre (its reception) as a medium for propagating the Protestant cause has never been fully evaluated. Portraiture within the German Lutheran wing of the Reformation circles has long been the object of scholarly investigation;[38] it is now time to take a look at the several Reformed versions of this same subject.

38. H. Preuß, *Lutherbildnisse* (Leipzig, 1913); D. Koepplin and T. Falk, *Lukas Cranach — Gemälde — Zeichnungen — Druckgraphik. Katalog zur Ausstellung im Kunstmuseum Basel 1974* (Basel and Stuttgart, 1974); *Luther im Porträt. Druckgrafik 1550-1990* (Bad Oeynhausen, 1983); also see R. W. Scribner, *For the Sake of Simple Folk* (Oxford, 1994[2]), p. 259 n. 24.

Appendix: Icones Contents

ICONES id est VERAE IMAGINES VIRORUM DOCTRINA SIMVL ET PIETATE
ILLVSTRIVM . . .
Theodoro Beza Auctore.

APVD IOANNEM LAONIVM. M.D.LXXX.

SEX GERMANIÆ EXIMII MARTRYES

HENRICVS ZVPPHANIENSIS . . . . imago omissa
WOLFGANGVS SCHVCVS . . . . imago omissa
LEONARDVS CÆSAR . . . . imago omissa
GEORGIVS CARPENTERIVS . . . . imago omissa
PETRVS FLISTEDIVS ET ADOLPHVS CLAREBACHIVS . . . . imagines
omissae

PRÆCIPVI INSTAVRATORES RESTITVTI NOSTRA MEMORIA IN HELVETIA

HVLDRICHVS ZVINGLIVS . . . . imago
IOANNES OECOLAMPADIVS . . . . imago
BERTHOLDVS HALLERVS . . . .
FRANCISCVS KOLBIVS . . . . imagines
omissae
IACOBVS MEIERVS . . . . imago omissa
AMBROSIVS BLAVRERVS . . . . imago
HENRICVS BVLLINGERVS . . . . imago
LEO IVDÆ . . . . imago omissa
SIMON GRYNÆVS . . . . imago
CONRADVS PELLICANVS . . . . imago omissa
PETRVS MARTYR . . . . imago
IOSIAS SIMLERVS . . . . imago
IOCHIMVS VADIANVS . . . . imago
PETRVS CHOLININVS . . . . imago omissa
SEBASTIANVS MVNSTERVS . . . . imago
CONRADVS GESNERVS . . . . imago
IOANNES CALVINVS . . . . imago
GVILLELMVS FARELLVS . . . . imago
PETRVS VIRETVS . . . . imago
IOANNES FROBENIVS . . . . imago omissa

ILLVSTRES GALLI

FRANCISCVS I . . . . imago
MARGARETA VALESIA . . . . imago
GVLIELMVS BVDÆVS . . . . imago
FRANCISCVS VATABLVS . . . . imago
IACOBVS TVSSANVS . . . . imago
MICHAEL HOSPITALIVS . . . . imago
IVLIVS CÆSAR SCALIGER . . . . imago omissa
MELIOR VOLMARIVS . . . . imago
IACOBVS FABER . . . . imago
IOANNES MERCERVS . . . . imago omissa
ROBERTVS STEPHANVS . . . . imago omissa
CLEMENS MAROTVS . . . . imago
IACOBVS PAVANAS . . . . imago omissa
IOANNES CLERICVS . . . . imago omissa
LVDOVICVS BERQVINVS . . . . imago omissa
IOANNES CADVRCVS . . . . imago omissa
ALEXANDER CANVS . . . . imago omissa
IOANNES MASSO . . . . imago omissa
IOANNES BORDELLVS, MATTHÆVS VERMELLIVS,
PETRVS BVRDO . . . . imagines
omissae
ANNAS BVRGIVS . . . . imago omissa
AVGVSTINVS MARLORATVS . . . . imago
ΠΟΛΥΑΝΔΡΙΟΝ ΚΕΝΟΤΑΦΙΟΝ (Waldensian martyrs) . . . . imago omissa

265

266

GERMANY

Observations on the Arts of the Huguenots in Brandenburg-Prussia

SIBYLLE BADSTÜBNER-GRÖGER

After the Revocation (1685) of the Edict of Nantes, it was not so much art as technical skill and craftsmanship that the *réfugiés* from France and Switzerland brought to Brandenburg-Prussia. With certain qualifications, one could argue that an explicitly Huguenot form of art never really developed in Brandenburg-Prussia. At the same time, artists of Huguenot origin were active participants in the art and cultural life of Brandenburg-Prussia, and there can be no doubt that they exercised a decisive influence within these realms. Among French, Rhenish-Palatinate, and Swiss refugees who settled in Berlin and the electorate, both before and after the Edict of Potsdam[1] (issued by decree of Frederick William the Great Elector on 29 October 1685)[2] there were relatively few practitioners of what today is denominated under the rubric "fine arts": architecture and, especially, painting and sculpture.

Instead, the first generations of immigrants consisted mainly of preachers, scholars, military personnel, physicians, attorneys. Laborers and factory workers were also present, along with farmers, military architects, canal builders and bridge builders, tapestry weavers, wallpaper manufacturers, silk embroiderers, metalsmiths and chasers and foundry laborers, gunsmiths, cabinetmakers, manufacturers of paper, specialists in miniature painting, clock makers and watchmakers. Statistics based on a colony inventory taken in 1700 show that in Berlin, Cölln, and the suburbs there were two architects and engineers, one engraver, only one sculptor, and six painters, but fifty-two

---

1. J. Wilke, "Berlin zur Zeit des Edikts von Potsdam. Das Edikt und seine Bedeutung," in *Hugenotten in Berlin*, ed. G. Bregulla (Berlin, 1988) (hereafter cited as *Hugenotten in Berlin*), pp. 13-53.

2. This is the Julian reckoning which was observed in Brandenburg-Prussia; it represents 8 November of the same year according to our Gregorian calender.

jewelers.[3] In other words, from the beginning of the Protestant colony's history under the protectorate of Brandenburg-Prussia, the arts represented tended toward those that served an immediate practical purpose, arts commonly classified in English under the rubrics "craft" (Kunstgewerbe) and "applied" arts (angewandte Künste), in contrast to the "fine" arts which normally are thought to serve no practical purpose. What the immigrant Huguenot artisans and craftspeople encountered in Prussia was a cultural and economic backwater, an underdeveloped territory that had been severely damaged by the ravages of the Thirty Years' War (1618-48). In populating the marches of Brandenburg, they were able to stimulate its economy and elevate the standards of education and the territory's overall cultural life.

Protestant craftspeople introduced such new branches of industry as tobacco farming, silkworm breeding, and wool manufacturing; gradually over time these industries matured and contributed to the economy. Furthermore, the Huguenots also stimulated and enriched the luxury market that was defined by the court and the nobility. They furnished palaces with fine silks and fabrics (see fig. 70), wall tapestries, wallpaper, mirrors and elaborately wrought glass artifacts, and porcelains. Articles of the nobleperson's attire, including jewelry and shoes, fine fabrics and buttons, were also under Protestant manufacture within the electorate, and merchants were able to distribute these items at retail prices that undercut the import market. The elector granted privileges to his industrious Protestant subjects, including monetary grants for the creation of new factories, land grants to farmers, and exemption from certain conditions of free and common socage land tenancy, including up to ten years' exemption from land taxes. For a German Reformed Court intent on guaranteeing tolerance in religious matters, it followed as a matter of course that the elector would also grant unrestricted freedom of worship — these privileges, exemptions, and guarantees were repeatedly renewed and ratified by later generations of Prussian monarchs. As a consequence, due to their industry and hard work combined with a favorable economic and political climate, many of the Protestant réfugiés became householders and managed to achieve considerable personal success and prosperity.

Huguenots in Brandenburg-Prussia clearly influenced the intellectual standards of the burgeoning electorate. By situating themselves at the very center of the social order, they managed for example to exercise an important pedagogical role, providing tutors and governesses to no less than five Prussian kings.[4] And even if it is difficult to detect any direct Huguenot in-

---

3. E. Muret, *Geschichte der Französischen Kolonie in Brandenburg-Preußen* (Berlin, 1885), pp. 317-19; on the individual crafts and the branches of industry: Muret, pp. 41-50; also *Hugenotten in Berlin*, Anhang/Tabelle 4, pp. 478-79.

4. Marthe de Rocoulle (b. 1659, d. 1741 Berlin), who from 1685 lived as a *réfugié* in Berlin, was the governess of Frederick William I and of his son Frederick II. Also among Frederick William's tutors were Alexander von Dohna and Jean Philippe Rebeur from Switzerland.

1. *Above:* Old Meetinghouse at Horningsham in Wiltshire
2. *Below:* Walpole meetinghouse

3. *Above:* Interior view of Walpole meetinghouse

4. *Below:* Rivington Chapel

5. *Above:* Old Meetinghouse, Norwich
6. *Below:* "The Octagon Chapel" in Norwich

7. *Right:* Portrait of William
   Huntington

8. *Below:* Pulpit and table pew at
   Jireh Chapel

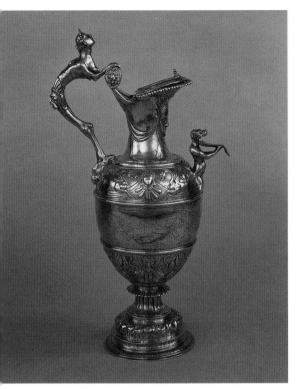

9. *Above Left:* The Wyndham Ewer, silver gilt, London, 1554, mark: intersecting triangles

10. *Above Right:* The Mostyn Flagon (one of a pair), silver gilt, London, 1603, made by John Acton

11. *Left:* Communion cup and paten cover from Saint Mary Aldermary, London, silver gilt, London, 1549, mark: "W."

12. *Above:* Altar plate from Durham Cathedral, silver gilt, London, 1766, makers' marks for Francis Butty and Nicolas Dumée

13. *Below:* Chapel plate from Dunham Massey Hall, Cheshire, silver gilt. London, 1706: cup paten, flagon, alms dish, maker's mark: Isaac Liger. London, 1716: dish and candlestick maker's mark: Isaac Liger.

14. *Above:* Pair of toilet cups and covers, silver gilt, London, circa 1695, mark: "FSS."

15. *Left:* Pair of bottles, silver, London, 1715, maker's mark for Anthony Nelme

16. Portrait of Paul Crespin, oil on canvas, artist unknown, early eighteenth century

17. *Left:* Pair of decanters, silver gilt, London, 1697, maker's mark for Pierre Harache

18. *Below:* The Kirkleatham Centrepiece, silver, London, 1731, makers' marks for David Willaume and Anne Tanqueray

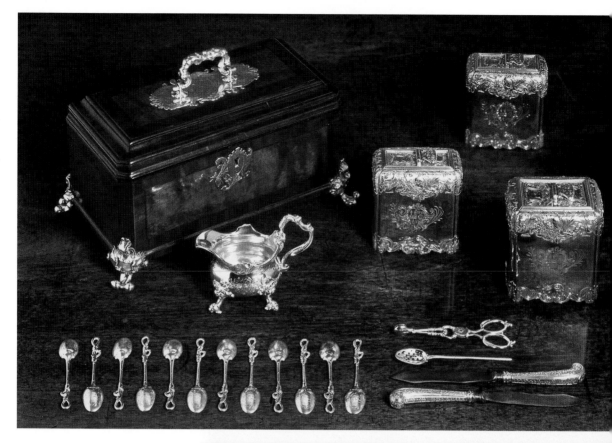

19. *Above:* Tea equipage of
Jean-Daniel Boissier and
Suzanne Berchère, silver,
London, 1735, maker's
mark for Paul de Lamerie

20. *Right:* Tureen made for
the fourth duke of Marl-
borough, silver, London,
1769, makers' marks for
John Parker and Edward
Wakelin (made by
Sebastian and James
Crespel; designed by Sir
William Chambers)

21. The *temple de Paradis* at Lyon

22. Relief surmounting entrance to the choir, Andrettes chapel, Aix-en-Provence

23. "Clocher toulousain"
of Saint-Jacques
church, Montauban

24. Detail of "clocher toulousain," Saint-Jacques church, Montauban

25. *Above:* Northwest corner of Grand'Place (now Place Nationale), Montauban

26. *Left:* East side of Grand'Place (now Place Nationale), Montauban. It was renovated 1656-1708 following the design provided by Levesville

27. Nicolas Tournier,
    Entombment of Christ,
    Musée des Augustins,
    Toulouse

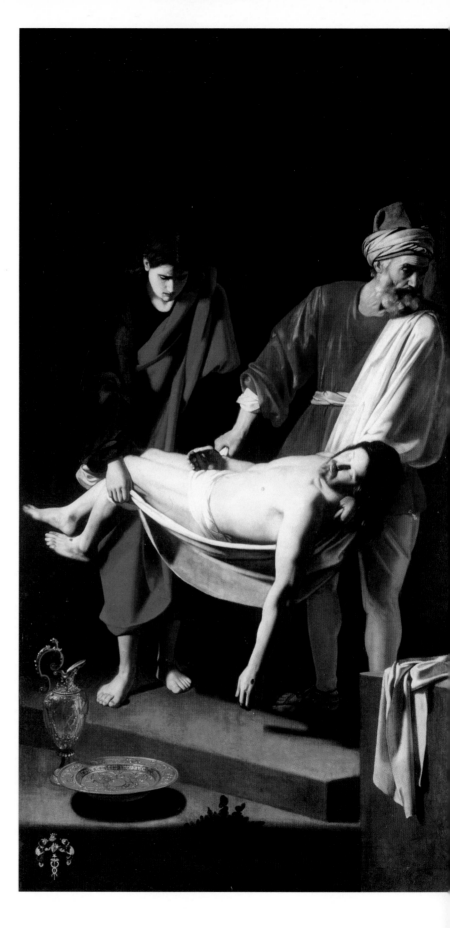

28. Jean Chalette, *Christ on the Cross and the Capitouls of 1622-1623*, Musée des Augustins, Toulouse

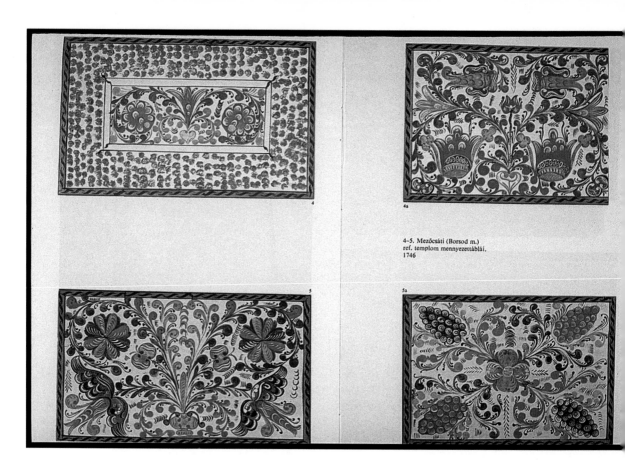

4–5. Mezőcsáti (Borsod m.)
ref. templom mennyezettáblái.
1746

29. Painted wooden ceiling-panels, Mezőcsát, 1746

30. Szenna, 1787, interior

31. Aladár Kriesch, *Eagles above the Hero's Grave,* 1918, tapestry

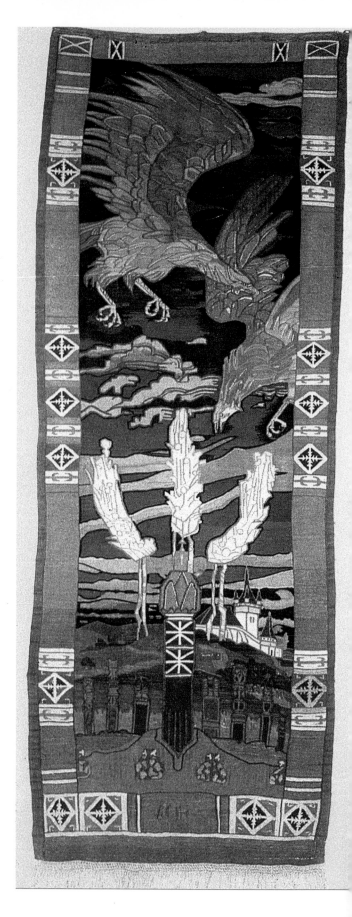

32. *Left:* Turkish shawl, Tordos, seventeenth century

33. *Below:* Aladár Árkay, 1911-13, Pest church, detail of tiles surrounding main entrance

34. Ferdinand Bol, *Joseph Selling Corn in Egypt*, 1669, canvas, 157 cm. × 171 cm.,
Stichting De Nieuwe Kerk, Amsterdam

35. Adriaan Gerritsz. de Vrije after a design by Joachim Wtewael, *The Triumph of Freedom of Conscience*, 1595-97, detail of stained glass window in St. Janskerk, Gouda

36. Adriaan Gerritsz.
de Vrije, *King David
and the Christian Knight*,
1595-97, stained glass
window in St. Janskerk,
Gouda

37. Pieter de Grebber, *Elisha Refusing the Gifts of Naaman*, 1637, canvas, 120 cm. × 185 cm., Frans Halsmuseum, Haarlem

38. First Congregational Church, Hartford, Conn.

39. *View of the City*, Hartford, Conn. (ca. 1824), anonymous painting (oil on canvas) in the collection of the Connecticut Historical Society. The First Congregational Church is the large building to the left. The spire to the right is the old building of the South Congregational Society, replaced with the present building in the 1820s. Note the rural character of Hartford, and the central importance of the Connecticut River.

40. First Congregational Church, Hartford, Conn., detail of portico capitals and cornice molding

41. First Congregational Church, Hartford, Conn., interior view

42. Rocky Hill Meetinghouse, Amesbury, Mass., 1785, exterior

43. Rocky Hill Meetinghouse, Amesbury, Mass., 1785, exterior

44. Rocky Hill Meetinghouse, Amesbury, Mass., 1785, interior

45. Rocky Hill Meetinghouse,
    Amesbury, Mass., 1785,
    interior

46. Rocky Hill
    Meetinghouse,
    Amesbury, Mass.,
    1785, interior

70. Daniel Chodowiecki, *Les Réfugiés Francois établissent des Fabriques dans le Brandenbourg,* title engraving for Erman and Reclam, *Mémoires,* vol. 4

fluence on the aesthetics and general taste of their court and its arts, there can be no doubt that the princes were educated in accordance with Huguenot virtues: loyalty to the state, a strong sense of duty, as well as committments to pragmatic and practical leadership combined with thrift.

On the aesthetic side, the Huguenot influence may be said to have been indirect, as is demonstrated for example in the realm of secular architecture. One of the trendsetters within the late eighteenth- and early nineteenth-century electorate was David Gilly (1748-1808),[5] a second-generation Huguenot whose family had come from Provence. He established the theory and practice of rural architecture in Brandenburg-Prussia; functionality and utility were the paradigms by which he designed buildings. Through his son Frederick (1772-1800), Gilly influenced the famous romantic-classicist Karl Friedrich Schinkel (1781-1841)[6] and his school.

Even before the enactment of the Edict of Potsdam, the elector had called to Berlin several Calvinist architects and artists from the Netherlands. They had a lasting influence on artistic development in Brandenburg-Prussia and set the cultural and artistic scene for the Huguenots. Even after 1700, Frederick I continued to draw Netherlanders and Frenchmen to the Prussian court, though not all of them were of Huguenot origin. Especially those painters and architects who came from the Calvinist Netherlands[7] (or had been trained there) exercised a formative influence

---

Jacques Egide Duhan de Jandun (1685-1746), who was born in Sedan, was engaged for Frederick the Great; after 1736 he was attended by, among others, Charles Etienne Jordan (1700-1745), from a *réfugié* family, who in 1740 became *Kurator der Universitäten* and in 1744 vice president of the Akademie der Wissenschaften. Like Heinrich August de la Motte Fouqué (1698-1774), he belonged to the "Rheinsberg Circle," later also joined by Oberst Karl Theophil Guichard, called Quintus Icilius, a second-generation Huguenot from Magdeburg (1724-75). Frederick William II (1744-97) was advised by de la Haye de Launay and the Swiss Nicolas de Béguelin, a preacher and, from 1747, a member of the Akademie der Wissenschaften. The French preacher Guillaume Moulines was tutor to Frederick William III (1770-1840), and Jean Pierre Fréderic Ancillon (1767-1837), a descendant of David Ancillon, who later became a minister of state, was Frederick William IV's (1795-1861) tutor from 1810. Cf. *Das Edikt von Potsdam 1685: Die französische Einwanderung in Brandenburg-Preußen und ihre Auswirkungen auf Kunst, Kultur und Wissenschaft* (exhibition catalogue, Potsdam-Sanssouci, 1985), pp. 56-59; C. Grau, "Die Berliner Akademie der Wissenschaften und die Hugenotten," in *Hugenotten in Berlin*, pp. 327-62; also K. Steiner, "Das Schulwesen," in *Hugenotten in Berlin*, pp. 206-26.

5. Cf. David Gilly, *Handbuch der Land-Bau-Kunst vorzüglich in Rücksicht auf die Construction der Wohn- und Wirtschaftsgebäude für angehende Cameral-Baumeister und Oeconomen I & II* (Berlin, 1797 and 1798); M. Lammert, *David Gilly: Ein Baumeister des deutschen Klassizismus* (Berlin, 1964).

6. See W. Büchel, *Karl Friedrich Schinkel* (Hamburg, 1994); *Karl Friedrich Schinkel 1781-1841* (exhibition catalogue, Berlin, 1982).

7. H. Börsch-Supan, *Die Kunst in Brandenburg-Preußen* (Berlin, 1980), passim. A. Terwesten (b. 4 May 1649 Ouwerkerk, d. 21 January 1711 Berlin), electoral court painter in Berlin from 1692, *Akademiedirektor* from 1698; C. Ryckwaert (b. before 1640 Holland, d. 9 November 1693 Küstrin), 1667-70 fortress engineer in Brandenburg service: designs for Berlin,

on Protestant sacred and profane architecture, and perhaps also Protestant portraiture. Their number included the painter August Terwesten and the architects Cornelius Ryckwaert, Gregor Memhardt, Rutger Langerveld, and Arnold Nering, as well as the partly Huguenot architects Jean-Baptiste Broebes, Philippe de la Chièze, Louis Cayart, Abraham Quesnay, and, later, Karl von Gontard.

Their numerous buildings, sketches, and idealized plans for castles in Berlin, Potsdam, and the surrounding area, as well as for urban projects, inspired the native architecture of Brandenburg-Prussia, even though only a few of their design conceptions were ever realized. The special skills and knowledge of the immigrant Huguenot artists and architects lay in the area of functionally defined construction: defense complexes and fortresses, canals and bridges, eleemosynary and educational institutions such as hospitals, poorhouses, orphanages, and schools. As Francophones, the Huguenots spoke the *lingua franca* of the European courts and thus had direct access to patronage from the pan-European high culture, including that of Brandenburg-Prussia. This not only made their reception and assimilation in foreign countries much easier, but it also enabled them to influence the development of the Prussian economy, along with its art and scholarship.

In the early stages of the Huguenot colonies in Berlin and Brandenburg, tightly organized and inward-looking parishes were the centers of

---

Schwedt, Zerbst, Oranienbaum, et al.; G. Memhardt (b. Linz, d. around 1678), in Brandenburg service from 1640: buildings in Potsdam, Oranienburg (1673), design of the Friedrichswerder; A. Nering (b. 13 January 1659 Wesel, d. 21 October 1695 Berlin), from a family of Dutch immigrants, trained as a fortress architect in 1676, collaborator of M. M. Smids, appointed *Kurfürstlicher Oberingenieur* in 1684, *Oberbaudirektor* in 1691, numerous castles, churches, and residential buildings in Berlin and its environs; R. Langerveld (b. 15 February 1635 Nijmegen, d. 5 March 1695 Berlin), painter and architect, appointed electoral mathematician and architect on 25 March 1689, involved in the building of Köpenick castle, the Dorotheenstädtische Kirche in Berlin, etc.; J.-B. Broebes (b. ca. 1660 Paris, d. after 1720 Barby), probably Huguenot, *Ingenieurhauptmann* in Berlin from 1692, appointed professor of architecture in 1696: collection of engravings *Vue des Palais et Maisons de Plaisance de S. M. le Roy de Prusse* (1733) with idealized plans and views of Oranienburg, Friedrichsthal, Köpenick, Bornim, Glienicke, etc.; J. de Bodt (b. 6 May 1670 Paris, d. 3 January 1748 Dresden), Huguenot, in Berlin starting in 1698: supervision over the building of castles and military installations, collaboration in the building of the armory and the Stadtschloß Potsdam (1701), Wesel fortress, in Dresden from 1728; Ph. de Chièze (b. 25 December 1629 Amersfoort, d. 1673 Berlin), probably Huguenot, moved to Berlin in 1660 after a stay in Sweden, *General-quartiermeister*: extension of the castles in Caputh and supervision of electoral buildings (after 1662), Klein Glienicke and Potsdam, among others, involved in the laying out of the "Neuer Graben" close to Müllrose (1662); reports on the fortresses in Küstrin, Stargard, Kolberg, and Berlin; J.-L. Cayart (b. 1645 La Capelle, d. 30 April 1702 Berlin), *réfugié*, in electoral Brandenburg service from 1687, fortress architect in Küstrin, Kolberg, and Wesel; A. Quesnay (b. 7 February 1666 Rouen, d. 14 September 1726 Berlin), *réfugié*, attested in Berlin from 1698; K. von Gontard (b. 13 January 1731, d. 23 September 1791), from a Huguenot noble family that immigrated to various countries, in 1763 called from Bayreuth to the court of Frederick the Great as architect. Cf. n. 30 below.

71. Title engraving for
Charles Ancillon,
*Histoire de
l'etablissement des
Francais Réfugiés,*
G. van der Gouwen
after G. de Lairesse
(1690)

G. de Lairesse delin.   G. vander Gouwen sculp.

Protestant spirituality. Only after 1700 did these communities gradually
begin to open their doors to the outside world; the boundaries which this
immigrant community had so carefully constructed and maintained slowly
began to disappear. It is at this point that the Huguenots began to exercise
a broader influence beyond the boundaries of their colonies, as mediators,
for example, between French and German culture.

In 1690 Charles Ancillon (1659-1715) wrote an important history
outlining the settlement of the *réfugiés* in Brandenburg-Prussia.[8] The

8. *Histoire de l'etablissement des Francais réfugiés dans les États de Brandenbourg* (Berlin,

book's frontispiece (see fig. 71), engraved by G. van der Gouwen after a design by G. de Lairesse, shows Frederick William, the founder of Brandenburg-Prussia; personifications of the allegorized virtues Faith, Hope, and Charity flank the Great Elector, and in the background one sees Apollo and Mars, signifying war and peace. Ancillon praised Frederick's Edict of Potsdam, dubbing it "Neues Evangelium" (the new gospel) — on the level of political ideology here rendered iconographically, this is a good example of what one might judge to be a typical Huguenot intermingling of secular themes with sacred paradigms. Thanks to Frederick, their liberator and patron, the French exiles were free to live and prosper under the protections accorded by the Edict, which had become the basic law governing the French colonies in Brandenburg-Prussia.

Ancillon also alludes to the building projects that the Huguenots had introduced under Frederick, projects, he notes, that were motivated primarily by the social necessities of immigration: churches, hospitals, and factories. In this manner, Huguenot art and especially architecture came to be praised under a common set of epithets that were popularly thought to typify the Calvinist *ésprit:* practical and functional, simple and economical, realistic in conception and execution.

Huguenot Church Building

Huguenot religious architecture in the Brandenburg colonies is characterized by familiar pan-Reformed attributes: simplicity and usefulness. Lack of money helped contribute to the formation of these virtues. The Huguenots undertook the construction of new church buildings only very rarely; instead they took over and adapted already-standing buildings, mostly monasteries, hospital churches, and town halls, which had been abandoned during the Thirty Years' War. They preferred modest structures whose appearance could be harmonized with Huguenot intents and purposes, and they altered the interiors of such buildings for worship according to principles of economy and usefulness. The reconfiguration of a standing building was conceived and executed along lines that would allow the easiest and most economical architectonic solutions.

Building materials were sought and often obtained free of charge; as an alternative they were paid for out of offertory monies. Thus, in Angermünde, Prenzlau, Bernau, and Magdeburg, the medieval hospital churches destroyed in the Thirty Years' War were given to the newly

---

1690). Ancillon (1659-1715) composed two additional treatises important to the French Protestants in Brandenburg-Prussia: *A l'occasion de la première pierre posée au temple de Frédérikstadt, pour les réfugiés francais* (Berlin, 1701); *Discours sur la statue érigée sur le pont neuf de Berlin à l'électeur Frédéric-Guillaume* (Berlin, 1703); see *Edikt von Potsdam* (1985), p. 63.

72. The former
Französische Kirche in
Frankfurt an der Oder

founded Huguenot colonies. In Frankfurt an der Oder (see fig. 72) and
Magdeburg, the Huguenots obtained monastery churches and transformed
them into community houses of worship;[9] the Walloons who since 1691
had resided in Strasburg (Uckermark) (see fig. 73) received a burnt-out

9. Cf. Muret, pp. 185-282: in Angermünde (pp. 185-87), the Hl.-Geist-Kapelle (four-
teenth/fifteenth centuries) was given to the Huguenot colony founded in 1698; the Prenzlau
parish (pp. 259-63), founded in 1687 by Frenchmen from the Pfalz, initially used the hospital
church; the Bernau colony (pp. 194-96), founded in 1699 by Swiss *réfugiés*, received the hospital church St. Georg (fifteenth century); of the two great colonies in Magdeburg (pp. 236-45),
both founded in 1686, the Walloons used the Augustinian church, the French, St.
Gertraudenkapelle, until a large new building was constructed in 1705-10 (it burned in 1804
and was replaced by a new classical building in 1806); in Frankfurt an der Oder (pp. 213-17),
the colony, founded in 1686, used the Franciscan church, together with the German Reformed
(only in 1736 did they begin a new building at the tower of the German Reformed church, ultimately demolished in 1866).

73. Französische
Kirche in the eastern
part of the town hall
in Strasburg/
Uckermark, eighteenth
century

town hall which they rebuilt as a worship space.[10] New construction was undertaken only after the colonies in Magdeburg, Frankfurt an der Oder, Müncheberg, and Prussian Königsberg had been consolidated[11] — this occurred in the wake of Protestant prosperity, which was the product of tobacco and vegetable farming, silkworm breeding, glass and textile manufacture. The names of the architects involved in this new construction are not recorded. Most of these churches no longer survive. In rural environs they disappeared mostly as a consequence of the demographic decline among eighteenth-century Protestant parishioners. Only the urban church buildings in Potsdam (see fig. 74) and Schwedt, as well as the Berlin Französische Friedrichstadtkirche (see fig. 75), have been preserved. Although their architects are known, only those who designed the Berlin

10. Cf. Muret, pp. 271-74.

11. Cf. Muret: on Magdeburg and Frankfurt an der Oder, cf. n. 6; in Müncheberg (pp. 248-50), where a colony existed from 1697 to 1805, the church was finished in 1710 and demolished in 1826 because it had become dilapidated; in Königsberg (pp. 227-30), the great colony at the *Freiheit* "Neue Sorge" had been promised a church building by the Great Elector as early as 1687. A medallion struck in the same year shows the planned building; as the elector died, however, the church was not built until 1733, and then with a different appearance.

277

74. The Französische
Kirche in Potsdam,
built after plans
of G. W. von
Knobelsdorff
(1750-53)

building were Huguenot in origin. The other two, Georg Wenzeslaus von
Knobelsdorff (Potsdam) and Georg Wilhelm Berlischky (Schwedt), designed the buildings for the French colonies on the instructions of their respective courts.

At the time of the founding of the colonies and before embarking on
their own separate and independent building program, the Huguenots in
Berlin entered into formal agreements (the so-called *Simultaneen*) with
other Prussian Protestants for the joint use of the same church building.
The Berlin Huguenots ratified *Simultaneen* with both Lutherans and the
German Reformed. Furthermore, when the Huguenots did undertake to
build their own ecclesiastical structures *de novo*, a specifically Huguenot
style of church architecture never really developed within Brandenburg-
Prussia. External simplicity joined to interior functionality, the rational ex-
ploitation of unadorned interior spaces, was already characteristic of the

278

75. Französische Friedrichstadtkirche, copperplate engraving by J. D. Schleusen, circa 1760

other Protestant traditions within this realm. In this sense participation in the *Simultaneen* may have contributed to the lack of a distinctive architectural style within the Huguenot communities of Brandenburg-Prussia.

The two churches in Potsdam and Schwedt constitute something of an exception due to their close connections to eighteenth-century court architecture. The French Reformed colony in Potsdam was founded in 1720. Its church, a centrally planned structure with a shallow vaulted cupola, was built 1750-53 by Johannes Boumann after designs executed by Georg Wenzeslaus von Knobelsdorff.[12] King Frederick II called for the construction of this church, and the imperial treasury underwrote its costs. The entrance features a neoclassical portico with four columns supporting an entablature; the real wall of the portico is pierced with pendant *aediculae* that frame sculptural personifications left and right of the large main door. In 1832-33, the church's interior gallery, altar wall, and pulpit were reconfigured and refurnished according to designs supplied by Karl Friedrich Schinkel.

It is important to note that even before construction of the Französische Friedrichstadtkirche tower in Berlin, and hence prior to its rather elaborate sculptural program, the exterior of the Potsdam church, at the king's request, had been fitted out with its own architectural sculp-

12. Cf. Muret, pp. 256-59; *Edikt von Potsdam*, pp. 14-17, 69f.; Badstübner-Gröger (1988), pp. 172-76. The renovation of the church was mostly complete by 1996.

tures. As just noted, the *aediculae* cut into the rear wall of the portico house sculptural personifications executed by Johann Georg Glume: *Spes* (left) and *Caritas* (right). As we have seen, these allegorical figures had already appeared in a Huguenot graphic format and had been published (1690) as pendants framing the Great Elector on the frontispiece of Ancillon's *Histoire* (see fig. 71). In both settings the figures are meant to embody theological virtues exemplified by the immigrant community. In addition, on the registers above the sculptural personifications in the Potsdam portico are reliefs exhibiting two familiar Gospel pericopes, the cleansing of the temple (Mark 11:11, 15-19 par.) and the tribute money (Mark 12:13-17 par.) — both are representative subjects within Reformation iconography.[13]

The church in Schwedt (1779), a centralized building over a lengthened oval ground plan, is the work of Georg Wilhelm Berlischky. The building had originally been planned as the burial place for the margraves of Schwedt, but it was given to the Huguenot congregation upon its completion.[14] Following the style of the Berlin school of baroque architecture, the church is distinguished by high rounded and arched windows, plaster pilasters, and portals; the architectonic space was vaulted by a domed roof surmounted by a modest lantern.

The city of Berlin, which contained the largest Huguenot colony, had a number of places of worship in different parts of town — parishes utilized these places either jointly or on their own. The first services of the *réfugiés* in what was then the center of Berlin took place close to the *Schloß* in the royal stables and later in the *Dom*.[15] In the Dorotheenstadt, the *réfugiés* were given joint use (1688) and later joint possession (1698) of the Dorotheenstädtische Kirche, which had been built for the German Reformed and Lutheran congregations, probably after designs of Rutger von Langerveld and Michael Matthias Smid (following a Netherlandish model that was completed in 1687).[16] In the former Electoral "Long Stable"

13. *Art and the Reformation: An Annotated Bibliography*, ed. L. B. Parshall and P. W. Parshall (Boston, 1986), pp. 145ff.; W. Velten, "Die bildlichen Darstellungen der Gleichnisse Jesu in den Niederlanden und in Deutschland im 17. und 18. Jhdt" (diss. theol., Halle, 1996); see also Lucas Cranach, *Passional Christi vvnd Antichristi* (Erfurt, 1521).

14. Cf. Muret, pp. 263f. The church in Schwedt was built as a burial place for the margraves Friedrich Wilhelm (d. 1771) and Friedrich Heinrich (d. 1789). Until 1794 their coffins stood in the crypt; later they stood next to the altar, to the annoyance of the French congregation. After the destruction of the city in the Second World War, the church was renovated and is now used, not for worship, but as a concert and exhibition hall.

15. Cf. Muret, pp. 85-88.

16. The model, apart from the polygonal eastern apse, was Hendrik de Keyser's Noorderkerk in Amsterdam (1620-23): a cross-shaped, vaulted building with a tower above the crossing and low buildings in the angles of the cross-arms. Cf. Muret, pp. 107f.; W. Henckel, *Geschichte der evangelischen Dorotheenstädtischen Gemeinde und ihrer Kirche im ersten Vierteljahrtausend 1687-1937* (Berlin, 1937); R. Stechow, *Geschichte der Dorotheenstädtischen*

(Langer Stall) on the Friedrichswerder, which was converted (1701) into a double church, separate worship spaces were granted to both the French and the German Reformed congregations. In connection with the conversion of this building, we hear the name of the architect Jean de Bodt, of Huguenot origin.[17] At the same date as the alteration on the Friedrichswerder, a barn in the Luisenstadt was made into a makeshift church for French refugees from Switzerland.[18]

In 1701 the *réfugiés* began the construction of their first independently planned church (see fig. 75), situated by decision of King Frederick I in a prominent open piazza (Friedrichstädtischer Markt) in Friedrichstadt within Berlin; the military architects Louis Cayart and Abraham Quesnay designed the building, which was financed by offertory monies, lotteries, and donations from Protestant states and cities all over Europe; King Frederick I also donated a large sum of money to cover the cost of building materials and for the beautification of the building site (now denominated Gendarmenmarkt). The laying of the building's foundation stone took place on 1 July 1701 in the presence of the crown prince, Frederick William; François de Repey gave the festive dedicatory speech to the text of Ezra 3:10-11. And the consecration of the completed structure roughly four years later on 26 February (= 1 March of the new calendar) 1705 took place in the presence of King Frederick I, who invited the well-known theologian/pastor Jacques Lenfant to give the dedicatory sermon.

The Friedrichstadt church was constructed on a slightly modified rectangular plan. The building lacked a bell tower. The corners on the short sides were slightly curved. There were double registers of superimposed windows, those above extending nearly the entire vertical height of the upper register. The church's interior consisted of a surrounding gallery, a parquet, and a pulpit chair that was originally on the northern, short side of the worship space. This congregation's object was to create a building redolent of the famous Huguenot temple at Charenton, destroyed in 1685 after the repeal of the Edict of Nantes.[19] The years 1721-26 saw the construction of a new French church in the Klosterstraße, and

---

Kirche und Gemeinde: Zur Feier des 200jährigen Kirchenjubiläums (Berlin, 1887); Badstübner-Gröger (1988), pp. 136f.

17. Cf. F. Hartung, *Kurze Nachricht von der Erbauung der Friedrichs-Werderschen Kirche* (Berlin, 1801); Muret, pp. 109-15; L. Giese, *Schinkels architektonisches Schaffen, Entwürfe und Ausführungen, Bd. 1: Die Friedrichs-Werdersche Kirche zu Berlin* (Berlin, 1921); Badstübner-Gröger (1988), pp. 138-42.

18. Cf. Muret, pp. 120-23; E. Mengin, *Die Französisch-reformierte Luisenstadtkirche zu Berlin 1728-1928: Festschrift zum 200jährigen Bestehen* (Berlin, 1928); Badstübner-Gröger (1988), pp. 166-69.

19. Cf. Muret, pp. 128-34; Badstübner-Gröger (1988), pp. 142-55, and (1996) with further bibliography; see also n. 31.

in 1727-28 a modest new chapel replaced the makeshift church in the Luisenstadt.[20]

Overall the Reformed structures are characterized by a lack of architectural adornment, a large open interior on a rectangular/oval plan, a surrounding gallery (or galleries), a parquet, and a pulpit and communion table positioned normally along one of the long sides of the building. Unfortunately, little or nothing survives of the original churches and their modest furnishings. Because of Reformed opposition to images within worship spaces, there was probably very little or no pictorial iconography in these church interiors. A single painted Decalogue Table (dated 1748, executed by Eleazar Laurent at Stettin) has survived — it was originally exhibited in the church of Groß Ziethen and is now in the collection of Berlin's Hugenottenmuseum.[21] Only in recent times did paintings and reliefs depicting the history and the anniversaries of the Huguenot immigrants find their way into the interiors of Reformed churches.[22]

Huguenot Educational and Social Buildings

The French colonies in Berlin and in the districts of Cölln, Friedrichswerder, Dorotheenstadt, and Friedrichstadt kept growing in numbers during the eighteenth century. In 1700, it is estimated that approximately 5,500 Huguenots were living in these places.[23] Not only did they oversee the occasional new construction and the more common reconfiguration of already standing buildings that were adapted as places of worship, but also the *réfugiés* were involved at various levels in the creation of more purely functional buildings, including schools and educational institutions, eleemosynary foundations such as poorhouses and orphanages, and hospitals.[24] It appears that the actual design and exe-

20. Cf. Muret, pp. 120-23, 169-72; see n. 14. The Französische Kirche in the Luisenstadt was in the Kommandantenstraße. The church in the Klosterstraße was abandoned in 1923 in favor of a theater and later demolished. Cf. Badstübner-Gröger (1988), pp. 169-71.

21. *Zehn-Gebote-Tafel* by E. Laurent, opaque water colors on parchment (Stettin, 1748), Hugenottenmuseum, Berlin; cf. M. Welge, "Die Französische Kirche zu Berlin," in *Hugenotten in Berlin*, pp. 117-18.

22. Paintings depicting the history of the Huguenots and their reception in Brandenburg-Prussia, e.g., by Carl Wendling, 1878, in the possession of the French Reformed parish in Berlin; bronze reliefs by Johannes Boese, 1885, showing the welcoming of the Huguenots by the Great Elector, formerly on the Französische Kirche, Klosterstraße, since 1983 in the southern portico of the Französischer Dom, Berlin; relief depicting Calvin, George Morin, 1935, French Reformed Friedrichstadtkirche, Berlin.

23. Wilke, p. 66.

24. On the individual foundations, cf. Muret, pp. 85-184; see also M. Welge, "Die Armenfürsorge," in *Hugenotten in Berlin*, pp. 177-205, and Steiner, pp. 206-26.

cution of such buildings was rarely the responsibility of Huguenots alone, but at the same time Huguenot conceptions in laying out the form and organization of these service institutions became paradigmatic for similar foundations and their buildings within eighteenth-century Brandenburg-Prussia.

The buildings in question were normally long, two or three stories high, with plaster or stucco exteriors. The king frequently supplied the basic (usually simple) building materials gratis. Exterior demarcations indicating the floor levels of such buildings were clearly defined; the doorways were commonly highlighted, as was the roofline projecting out over the high rectangular windows — these were often the only distinguishing features of the facades. Buildings that served a charitable, educational, or medical purpose and that date from the period of Frederick the Great have basically the same appearance as other kinds of public buildings. Most or all of these structures were demolished or rebuilt in the course of the nineteenth century; the rest were destroyed during the Second World War.

The earliest building in this group, the Französisches Gymnasium (Le Collège), dating to 1689, followed the model of the Huguenot academy in Sedan.[25] Louis Cayart is said to have participated in the planning of the double buildings and their two double staircases. The French court held its sessions in this building, and it was from here that the Consistorium[26] ruled over the colony for 170 years. In 1720, the foundation stone of an orphanage (Französisches Waisenhaus)[27] designed by Abraham Quesnay was laid in the Berlin Friedrichstadt, and in 1729 the poorhouse named Maison de Refuge received a modest new building.[28] In 1732-34, the earlier building in front of the Oranienburg gate was replaced by the new French hospital, an impressive building designed by the engineer Magister, with three wings, a chapel, and a children's hospital (Petit Hospital).[29] In

25. Cf. Muret, pp. 135-47. The buildings, at Niederlagstraße 1/2, were rebuilt in 1786 with royal support.

26. On the role of the consistory, cf. Welge, "Die Französische Kirche zu Berlin," pp. 88f. (esp. pp. 100-108, "Die Struktur der Französische Kirch zu Berlin im 18. Jhdt").

27. Cf. Muret, pp. 152-57. The foundation stone was laid at the corner of Charlottenstraße and Jägerstraße; on 16 May 1725 the orphanage was opened, and in the 1780s Frederick the Great changed it into a three-story corner building (proportion of axes, 9:7) with clearly defined division between the stories and highlighted portals.

28. Cf. Muret, pp. 115-26. The site had been bought by the Consistorium as early as 1699. The Maison de Refuge is a two-story corner building (proportion of axes, 9:11).

29. Cf. Muret, pp. 92-99. The old hospital, at Friedrichstraße 129, had been built in 1686 as the first foundation of the parish. In 1779, the Petit Hospital was built on its site; cf. Muret, p. 103. In 1730, a new hospital building was planned; in 1732-34, the three wings were built, and on 14 June 1733 the hospital chapel was consecrated. The second and third buildings were finished in 1805-6 and 1878. The *Armenbäckerei* (bakery for the poor, founded 1699) was temporarily part of the building complex — it moved there in 1779 from the corner of Charlottenstraße and Französische Straße and was put into Mauerstraße 45 in 1781 — as was the soup kitchen *La Marmite*; cf. Muret, p. 105.

1747, Jean-Henri-Samuel Formey opened the École de Charité at Jäger-straße 63. This long, two-story school was designed to accommodate one hundred poor children.[30] Since the Prussian public schools were distin-guished by their exceptionally low standards, the foundation of this emi-nent educational institution was an event of considerable cultural impor-tance. Connected with the school was the teachers' seminar, the so-called *Pépinière*, founded in 1779.[31] Other charitable buildings included the new Maison d'Orange (begun in 1792), a common residential building for the Huguenots expelled from the Orangeois,[32] and the Fondation Achard, an endowment for the colony's poor.[33] The latter began as a humble construc-tion which, however, in the years 1777-85 Frederick the Great upgraded into a splendid, three-story edifice.

Architects and Artists of Huguenot Origin

Among the considerable achievements of Huguenot architects in the employ of the Brandenburg electors and the Prussian kings, the design of military structures and related defensive installations including fortresses, bridges, and canals figures prominently. One of the early arrivals under the fortress architecture rubric was Philippe de la Chièze, who came to Berlin before 1685 and was favored with a string of imperial appointments, including chamberlain, *Generalquartiermeister,* and *Oberingenieur.* Chièze presided over numerous projects, including an extension of the Neuer Graben, the canal between the Oder and the Spree next to Müllrose; in riverine Berlin he pre-sided over the construction of new locks, and in revenue-hungry Berlin he was involved in the building of a customhouse next to one of the locks. For a time he also supervised the construction of fortresses at Küstrin, Stargard, Kolberg, and Berlin. His designs for the initial erection of the Potsdam Stadtschloß (see fig. 76) and for Caputh castle are also extant; in addition, Chièze supervised the building of Klein Glienicke castle.[34] As early as 1666, the Great Elector had appointed Chièze "managing director of all Berlin de-fensive installations" (Generaldirektor der Berlin Fortifikationsanlagen).

---

30. Cf. Muret, pp. 157-66. In 1760 152 boys and 128 girls attended the school; later a girls' school, Maison du Cloitre, was opened at Klosterstraße 43.

31. Cf. Muret, pp. 168f.

32. Cf. Muret, pp. 147-52. This residential building for 1,600 Huguenots was situated at Dorotheenstraße 26. After it had become dilapidated, a new building (proportion of axes, 7:12) was erected in 1792-94, and it survived until 1884.

33. Cf. Muret, pp. 179-81. The widow of the preacher Achard had left the simple houses at Friedrichstraße 40/41 to the Consistorium. After 1777, Frederick the Great ex-tended them into a splendid corner building (proportion of axes, 13:3) on Markgrafenstraße 53/54 and Französische Straße 40/41. They were replaced by a new building in 1863.

34. Cf. n. 7 supra.

After Chièze, Jean de Bodt came to Berlin in 1698; he had already proven himself as a skilled engineer and dike builder, and in consequence of these achievements had received an invitation to preside over the entire construction industry within Brandenburg-Prussia. De Bodt was a Huguenot who in 1685 had emigrated to Holland via Brussels. In 1689 he followed William of Orange to England. In Berlin, along with Arnold Nering and Andreas Schlüter, de Bodt played a decisive role in the completion of the Berlin armory situated on Unter den Linden. In addition, King Frederick I contracted with de Bodt to supervise the building of the Potsdam Stadtschloß (1700-1701). He built a number of palaces in Berlin, for example, for the counts Podewils (1701-4) and Schwerin (1704), as well as residences for *réfugiés* at the Stechbahn.

76. Potsdam Stadtschloß, Potsdam, after plans of Philippe de la Chièze, Joh. Gregor Memhardt, Jean de Bodt, and A. Nering, copperplate engraving by Petrus Schenck (1700-1701)

In 1713, together with Arnold Nering and Martin Grünberg, de Bodt contributed to the design of the Protestant *Parochialkirche* bell tower. However, of special importance for the development of architecture in Brandenburg-Prussia were his many unexecuted architectural designs, into which he incorporated Netherlandish, English, and also Italian features. In 1715, de Bodt was appointed major general, and in 1719 he became commander of the fortress Wesel and was temporarily involved in the fortress-building projects of Magdeburg, then part of Prussia. It is interesting to note that de Bodt took part — through his design for the bell tower — in the conversion of the Friedrichswerder *Langer Stall* into a church. In 1728, he left Berlin and went to the Saxonian court at Dresden.[35]

35. Augustus the Strong in Dresden, too, appointed him *Generalintendant der Zivil- und Militärgebäude* (general intendant of civil and military buildings). In 1738 he became *Direktor*

The third noteworthy fortress architect within this first wave of Huguenot immigrants was Louis Cayart, who in 1686 came to Berlin from Metz, together with the family of the preacher David Ancillon. He had received his training as a military architect from S. de Vauban, and he entered the service of the Brandenburgs in 1687. First he supervised the building of the fortress at Küstrin, where he replaced Cornelius Ryckwaert in 1693. Later he worked on the reinforcement of the fortresses at Wesel and Peitz (1695), Driesen (1697), and Kolberg (1698). Only foundation walls have survived for most of these buildings. Cayart worked intermittently on commissions granted by the city of Berlin, the Lange Brücke (1692-95) for example, which he designed with Arnold Nering, but Cayart was continuously in the employ of the French colony.

Cayart's design for the first independent Huguenot church building in the Friedrichstadt is particularly important. As noted above, construction was begun in 1701 and completed (following Cayart's death in 1702) by Abraham Quesnay in 1705. As also noted above, this church was conceived to replicate the Charenton "temple," but perhaps more in a symbolic than literal sense: like Charenton the Friedrichstadkirche was to function as the primary architectural marker of the French colony's identity within Brandenburg-Prussia.[36] As was true for many Huguenot architects, Cayart was also interested in architectural theory, and in 1699 he submitted a comprehensive plan for the reorganization of the electoral building industry, but this did not come to fruition.

In addition to Cayart, Abraham Quesnay, a Rouen *réfugié*, was also involved in the design and construction of the Französische Kirche. He evidently arrived in Berlin before 1696, since he assisted in the construction of the Großes Waisenhaus; work on this structure had begun in 1696 following designs executed by Martin Grünberg and Philipp Gerlach.

---

des Zivilbauwesens (director of civilian architecture), and in 1741, infantry general. De Bodt had great influence on Saxonian architecture as well, especially on Pöppelmann, Leplat, and Knöffel. Cf. *Edikt von Potsdam*, pp. 54-56; see also n. 7.

36. Cf. nn. 14 and 19; A. Werner, *Der protestantische Kirchenbau des friderizianischen Berlin* (Berlin, 1913); K. Manoury, *Die Geschichte der Französischen Kirche zu Berlin 1672-1955* (Berlin, 1955); H. Reuther, *Barock in Berlin* (Berlin, 1969); S. Badstübner-Gröger, "Der hugenottische Kirchenbau in Berlin und Potsdam," in *Hugenotten in Berlin*, pp. 142-54; Badstübner-Gröger, *Der französische und deutsche Dom in Berlin* (Berlin, 1996³). The church was placed opposite the German Reformed church on the Friedrichstädtischer Markt. In 1780-85 both were provided with towers. There were various changes in the course of the eighteenth and nineteenth centuries. During the Second World War, the buildings were destroyed by air raids (1943-44). The rebuilding of the Französische Kirche, which took the renovation of 1905 as a model, was completed on 17 April 1983, while the Deutsche Kirche was finished only in 1996. The rebuilt Französische Kirche was given two stories and double stairs on the west side. The tower is used as an observation tower and contains not only the collections of the French parish (archives, libraries, and the Hugenottenmuseum), but also a restaurant. The renovated Deutsche Kirche and tower will have a modern interior; they are planned as an exhibition center.

77. The Great Elector, by Abraham Romandon, Berlin, Charlottenburg castle (ca. 1688)

Quesnay is also said to have designed and built the Französisches Waisenhaus (French orphanage).[37]

Under the Great Elector and his successors, resident aliens consisting of French (and Netherlandish) artists and craftsmen had a profound effect not only on the architecture of Brandenburg-Prussia, but also on its crafts and fine arts. Only a few of the artists so far attested for the period were of Huguenot origin, although historical/archival scholarship of this subject needs more work before we can evaluate the period accurately. Among the first wave of Huguenot immigrants, for example, were the well-known portraitists Abraham (d. 1687) and Gedeon Romandon (1667-97), father and son, who arrived in Berlin in 1685; shortly afterward (1687) they received appointments as court painters to the elector along with a yearly salary of 500 Imperial taler. They painted portraits (see fig. 77), especially of court personalities, and their paintings reflect not only a considerable degree of portrait realism, but also the coloristic drama of the Italianate palette characteristic of the portrait genre in its

37. Cf. n. 27 supra.

southern Mediterranean setting.[38] Gedeon was initially engaged as supervisor of the electoral painting collection; in 1696 he received an appointment (along with a salary of 1,000 taler) as professor at the newly established Akademie der Künste. Further research on the older and younger Romandons is needed; their influence on the portrait genre within Brandenburg-Prussia has yet to be determined. In connection with the Romandons and the portrait genre, one should also mention the miniaturist tradition, consisting in the production of miniature portrait medallions painted in enamel. The *réfugiés* were distinguished practitioners of this exquisite art form, which they introduced into Brandenburg-Prussia. Two of the most prominent and accomplished French enamelists were the Huguenot brothers Jean-Pierre and Amy Huaut from Geneva, who on 18 May 1686, just a short time after their arrival in Berlin, received appointments as painters to the elector.[39]

An event of special importance for the electoral court was the 1686 arrival in Berlin of the *réfugié* Pierre Mercier, a tapestry manufacturer from Aubusson.[40] In November of the year, the Great Elector Frederick William appointed him tapestry weaver and carpet manufacturer to the court and granted him an incredibly generous line of credit of 2,400 Imperial taler. Thanks to this impressive patronage granted by the court, Mercier was able to establish himself in Berlin and create a manufacturing center for the production of the highest-quality tapestries that were sought after throughout Europe. Mercier's factory remained in Huguenot hands until 1787; after Mercier's departure, it was run by Jean Barraband the Elder and his son, Jean II, who from 1720 shared the management with the *réfugié* Charles Vigne.[41]

38. A. Romandon (born in Tournon, died 1687 Berlin?), *réfugié*, came from Paris to Berlin in 1685 and was appointed court painter on 21 February 1687. His son Gedeon (b. in Venice, d. 1697/98 Berlin) was appointed court painter on 7 April 1687 and professor in 1696. Cf. Börsch-Supan, p. 48; *Edikt von Potsdam*, pp. 34, 72, 76. Compare the portraits of the Great Elector (ca. 1688), the electors Frederick William (ca. 1687/88) and Frederick III (ca. 1688), and Joachim Ernst von Grumbkow (ca. 1690).

39. Cf. Muret, p. 45; *Edikt von Potsdam*, pp. 76ff. The brothers Huaut, Amy (1657-1724) and the more important Jean-Pierre (b. 28 July 1655, d. 6 February 1723), worked together in Berlin in 1698-99. They came from Geneva, to which they returned in 1700. Jean-Pierre, who was called to the Berlin court in 1686, received the title of court painter on 18 May 1686, while another brother, Pierre II, was appointed court miniaturist on 16 September 1691. His widow was identified as *réfugié* in 1698-1700. Cf. H. Clouzot, "Les Frères Huaut," *Revue de l'art ancien et moderne* 22 (1907): 293-306; Clouzot, "Artistes Huguenots — Les Frères Huaut," *Bulletin de la Société de l'Histoire du Protestantisme Français* 55 (1906): 182-91.

40. Pierre Mercier (d. 22 June 1729 Dresden) went to Berlin in 1686 and founded the tapestry manufactory; he went to Dresden in 1714 as *Inspecteur* of the tapestries of Augustus the Strong. Cf. Muret, pp. 46-48, on the production of wallpaper and tapestries; *Edikt von Potsdam*, pp. 80-87; Wilke, pp. 232-50.

41. Jean Barraband, tapestry manufacturer from Aubusson and *réfugié*, went to Berlin in 1685; his son Jean II (d. 7 August 1725) founded the joint enterprise together with Vigne in

78. Tapestry after motifs of Nicolas Lancret, textile factory of Charles Vigne the Elder, Berlin, Charlottenburg castle (ca. 1749)

Under Vigne's direction the tapestry factory begun by Mercier reached its apogee (see fig. 78). Vigne employed forty-five weavers, most of them residents of the French colony; 210 loom assistants from Berlin city were also on the payroll. Markets for these tapestries were found throughout the court culture of European royalty, and the export of these products continued unabated until tapestries went out of fashion — Mercier's original foundation remained preeminent to the end and was never superseded within Prussian territory. Initially, the manufacture of these products was targeted only to the local markets, satisfying the needs of the Brandenburg-Prussian court and producing hangings for their imperial properties within Berlin and Potsdam. But in 1690 an important imperial commission brought international attention to the Mercier factory; it consisted in eight tapestries entitled *Actiones von dem höchstseeligen Churfürsten Friedrich Wilhelm* (1693-99) — produced on instructions given by Elector Frederick III and intended to be exhibited in the picture gallery

---

1720. In 1725, Vigne (d. 1751 Berlin) became the sole owner of the factory, which was subsidized by the state. It supplied the courts in Sweden and Russia; there are series (by Vigne and others) on Italian comedy (Charlottenburg castle), the history of Psyche (former Berlin castle), Don Quixote, Molière's comedies, and the myths of Odysseus and Helen. Cf. Muret, pp. 46-48; Börsch-Supan, pp. 73f., 96; *Edikt von Potsdam*, pp. 80-87; see also n. 38.

of the Berliner Schloß; six are presently on display in Schloß Charlottenburg.[42]

The *réfugiés* also played an indispensable role in the design and manufacture of imperial weaponry and miscellaneous luxury items (precious metals, glyptics, glass) that were desired by the court. The list of *réfugié* masters who supplied the court with finely cast and chased luxury items in precious metals is long. The glyptic arts and glass engraving also flourished at the elector's court thanks to the wizardry of French stonecutters and engravers. One of the most distinguished metal chasers whose work was sought after at the court was Pierre Froméry from Sedan, a man of great versatility who was known for his virtuoso engraved pieces that included weapons, clocks, vessels, jewelry, furniture with engraved overlays, and small engraved boxes. In 1687 Froméry received an appointment to the court as *Hofbüchsenmacher* (imperial box maker), and in the same year he was nominated *Hofwaffenschmied* (imperial armorer).[43]

The elector Frederick III (later King Frederick I) was a great lover of luxury arts, and it was he who retained numbers of silk embroiderers to work on the embellishment of the imperial thrones and the official imperial robes and gowns and related costumes. By imperial exemption some of these embroiderers were counted among the domain's "free" artists, meaning they were exempted from the *Zunft* (textilers' guild); the French colony lists three such persons in Berlin in 1700 and a fourth in Brandenburg. Among them were the families of the brothers Pavret and Elie Pally. Elie (1664-1751) came from Sedan and in 1724 was given a license to embroider ribbons for imperial decorations. Other French Protestant silk embroiderers who served the crown included Jacques Hurlin (d. 1722) and Jean Barez (1694-1782), the latter from the Champagne region and the father-in-law of Daniel Chodowiecki (1726-1801), who was of Huguenot extraction on his mother's side.[44]

On one level it is clear that Chodowiecki's popular copperplate engravings and etchings were intended to give pleasure to their viewers, but on still another level they can be submitted to a traditional "Calvinist" interpretation; one can analyze these visual materials for their practical and pedagogical purposes. With his calendar and book illustrations, Chodowiecki raised commercial graphic art to a new level, and in his depictions of past and current events, literature and life, he strove for objective representations and a kind of documentary realism. He was active in the service of the colony; not only did he preside over traditional honorific offices, but he also was a working artist who labored for the benefit of the

---

42. Cf. Börsch-Supan, pp. 73f.; H. Göbel, *Wandteppiche*, T. 3, Bd. 2 (Berlin, 1934); H. Huth, "Zur Geschichte der Berliner Wirkteppiche," *Jahrbuch der Preußischen Kunstsammlungen* 56 (1935): 80-99. The *Actiones* were woven according to the designs of various artists, including Rutger von Langerfeld (size 405 cm. × 423 cm.).

43. Cf. Muret, pp. 44f.; *Edikt von Potsdam*, pp. 77-80; Wilke, pp. 254-64.

44. Cf. Muret, pp. 43f.; *Edikt von Potsdam*, pp. 87-91.

Huguenot congregation. For example, he illustrated the nine-volume *Mémoires pour servir à l'histoire des réfugiés dans les Etats du Roi* of Jean-Pierre Erman and Pierre Christian Fréderic Reclam (Berlin, 1782-99), and he created frontispieces for hymnals and for a variety of compositions that advanced or otherwise documented the Huguenot cause. Chodowiecki provided designs for numerous commemorative bronze medallions and, last but not least, drew the red chalk cartoons (see fig. 80) for the architectural sculpture of the Französischer Turm.[45]

The Französischer Turm and Its Sculptural Program

Like Chodowiecki, the Huguenot sculptor Emanuel Bardou[46] (b. 1744 in Basel) was active in Berlin starting in the 1770s. A member of the French colony, of its church and its consistory, he not only acted in an advisory capacity but was also an active participant in the execution of the sculptures that adorn the exterior of the Französische Kirche. It was only recently (1983-85), during the restoration of the tower and its sculptures, that the initials "EB" were discovered on the figure of the Evangelist Mark — it might be a reasonable inference to suppose that Bardou sculpted all four Evangelists. Bardou was also involved in the architectural decoration of the Brandenburg Gate. His most impressive works, however, are his realistic portrait busts of Frederick the Great, Chodowiecki, and Immanuel Kant, along with his double portrait of the preacher Friedrich Roloff and his wife in Berlin's Marienkirche. Bardou was one of the first Berlin sculptors to design a monument of the still-living King Frederick the Great posed on horseback and dressed in the costume of the day. Bardou should be regarded as a precursor of the Berlin school of sculpture which Johann Gottfried Schadow founded at the end of the eighteenth century and which Goethe[47] dismissed on the grounds that it betrayed

---

45. Cf. *Edikt von Potsdam*, pp. 59-62, 64f.; S. Badstübner-Gröger, "Der Anteil Daniel Chodowieckis am Bildprogramm des Französischen Domes in Berlin," in *Chodowiecki und die Kunst der Aufklärung in Polen und Preußen*, ed. H. Rothe and A. Ryszkiewicz (Köln/Wien, 1986), pp. 75-98; S. Badstübner-Gröger, "Daniel Chodowieckis Arbeiten für die französische Kolonie in Berlin," in *Hugenotten in Berlin*, pp. 435-71; T. John, "Der Turm der Französischen Kirche in Berlin und die von Daniel Chodowiecki überlieferten Entwurfszeichnungen" (master's thesis, Stuttgart, 1995). See also n. 48.

46. On Emanuel Bardou, cf. S. Badstübner-Gröger, "Schweizer Künstler in Berlin und Potsdam in der zweiten Hälfte des 18. Jahrhunderts," in *Schweizer im Berlin des 18. Jhdts.*, ed. M. Fontius and H. Holzey (Berlin, 1996), pp. 159-98, esp. pp. 168ff.

47. "In Berlin scheint, außer dem individuellen Verdienst bekannter Meister, der Naturalismus, mit der Wirklichkeits- und Nützlichkeitsforderung, zu Hause zu seyn und der prosaische Zeitgeist sich am meisten zu offenbaren. Poesie wird durch Geschichte, Character und Ideal durch Portrait, symbolische Behandlung durch Allegorie, Landschaft durch Aussicht, das allgemein Menschliche, durchs Vaterländische verdrängt." J. W. Goethe, *Propyläen. Eine Periodische Schrift* 32 (Tübingen, 1800), p. 167.

79. The Französischer Dom on the Gendarmenmarkt in Berlin, after plans of Karl von Gontard (1780-85)

an excessively "prosaic" spirit — in other words, its tendency to realism did not satisfy the romantic expectations which Goethe sought in the plastic arts.

The process of conceiving, drawing, and executing the architectural sculpture for the Französische Kirche posed a great challenge to the French parish. On principle and in fact, Calvinists were opposed to the presence of religious images, especially three-dimensional images, inside or on the exterior of their church buildings. In this respect they stood apart from the two other major branches of the magisterial reform, the Lutherans and the Anglicans. But it was Frederick the Great's wish to decorate the two similar towers with architectural sculpture. In a sense Karl von Gontard (of Huguenot ancestry) had already prepared the way; in 1779-85 he had erected towers in front of the modest churches (see fig. 79) on the

Gendarmenmarkt in order to embellish and enhance the architecture of the square.[48]

For the sculptural program of the French tower a special committee[49] was convened, its members including Pastor Jean Pierre Erman; Daniel Chodowiecki and Emanuel Bardou; the director of the Academy, Christian Bernhard Rode; along with selected parishioners and other artists. Rode was also responsible for drafting the sketches of the architectural sculpture on the Deutscher Dom. Both the program in its written form and Chodowiecki's designs were changed at the request of Gontard, who objected especially to the fact that Chodowiecki dressed his subjects (Calvin, Zwingli, Oecolampadius, de Bèze, Hus, Wycliffe) in the contemporaneous preacher's costume, consisting in a loose-fitting, hooded cloak. In contrast to Chodowiecki, Rode designed Old Testament biblical figures, namely, prophets, for the main facade of the building, and it was these figures that won the day. But in place of New Testament subjects (notably Christ's miracles), allegorical figures embodying virtues were chosen. The program that had been put forward by the Consistorium (namely, statues of Reformers dressed according to contemporaneous standards) reveals a typical Enlightenment consciousness of history and historicity on the part of the Berlin Huguenot community. If this original conception for the sculptural program of the tower had come to fruition, it would have constituted the earliest public iconographic program within Brandenburg-Prussia presenting the dramatis personae of the Reformation.

In content the program that was chosen had its foundation in a variety of classical Reformed sources: Calvin's biblical exegesis, his moral and constructive theology (the latter embodied in the *Institutes*), Huguenot martyrological[50] treatises, and de Bèze's forty-four *Emblemata* which he published as an addendum to his famous illustrated portrait book (*Icones* [Geneva, 1580]) of Protestant notables. Formal models were also subscribed from other sources, including the graphic materials (woodcuts and etchings) and printers' marks[51] (*Druckerzeichen*) that had become a part of

---

48. Cf. P. Goralczyk, *Der Platz der Akademie* (Berlin, 1987) (Ph.D. thesis, 1984); L. Demps, *Der Gend'armenmarkt: Gesicht und Geschichte eines Berliner Platzes* (Berlin, 1987).

49. Cf. n. 45. The program is described in K. L. von Oesfeld, *Umständliche Beschreibung der beiden neu erbauten Türme auf dem Friedrichs-städtischen Markte zu Berlin, welche seine K. M von Preussen in d. J. 1780-1785 daselbst haben ausführen lassen* (Berlin, 1785). Cf. S. Badstübner-Gröger, "Zur Ikonographie der Bauplastik am Französischen Dom in Berlin," in *Von der Macht der Bilder: Beiträge des CJHA-Kolloquiums "Kunst und Reformation,"* ed. E. Ullmann (Leipzig, 1983), pp. 429-39; Badstübner-Gröger, "Zur Ikonographie der Bauplastik am Französischen Dom in Berlin," in *Acta historiae artium* 29 (1983): 105-16.

50. E.g., Jean Crespin, *Acta martyrum, eorum uidelicet, qui hoc seculo in Gallia, Germania, Anglia, Flandria, Italia, constans dederunt nomen Euangelio, idque sanguine suo obsignarunt: ab Wicleffo & Husso ad hunc usque diem* (Geneva, 1556).

51. S. Badstübner-Gröger, "Zur Ikonographie der Bauplastik am französischen Dom in Berlin," *Acta Hist. Art. Hung.* 29 (1983): 116 nn. 18, 19.

the book industry controlled by Reformed publishers/printers. For the representation of allegorized virtues, clearly one of the models was Karl Wilhelm Ramler's *Allegorische Personen zum Gebrauche der bildenden Künstler* (Berlin, 1788)[52] — this is a work that had evoked a good deal of discussion in Berlin academic circles.

As shown by Chodowiecki's red chalk drawings (see fig. 80, rediscovered in 1995), the reliefs on the three large tympana depicted Christ teaching and proclaiming the ideals of a virtuous Christian life. The subjects represented included the Sermon on the Mount (see fig. 81), Christ and the Samaritan woman, the journey to Emmaus. The portico on the eastern main facade exhibits figures of the prophets of Israel (instead of the Protestant Reformers as originally planned) — these Old Testament types point to the birth of Christ. The reliefs above show scenes from the life of Christ and contain references to baptism and communion. Above the portico pediments stand the allegories of the Christian virtues: Faith, Hope, and Charity; Patience, Compassion, Kindness, Gratitude, Beneficence, and Temperance. Next to them are the seated figures of the four Evangelists. More allegories of virtues are depicted in the relief fields atop a row of six apostles on the tower walls: Innocence, Worship, Devotion, Brotherly Love, and Bliss, all virtues that go back to Calvin's interpretation[53] of Saint Paul at Galatians 5:22, where they are praised as characteristic of the disciples. On top of the entire sculptural program, as a pendant to Virtue Victorious, the cupola figure of the Deutscher Dom, we see Religion Triumphant, the symbol of true bliss. Chodowiecki designed this sculpture following the emblems in de Bèze's *Icones* along with the iconographic tradition of Huguenot printers' marks. Holding the gospel and the palm of victory, Religion stands on a skull that is itself placed atop a die. Both skull and die must be understood as referring to Christ and to victory over death through true faith in the gospel.

In conclusion, the French and Swiss *réfugiés* who were received in Brandenburg-Prussia at the German-Reformed court under the Great Elector found a culture dominated by Protestant Netherlandish influences, hence a culture whose basic concepts and premises were familiar to them. In architecture, the *réfugiés* promoted the familiar Reformed virtues: usefulness, functionality, thrift, sobriety; in craftsmanship also they took a largely utilitarian point of view. Rather than developing their own specifically Huguenot style of art in Brandenburg-Prussia, they followed the major stylistic trends of the seventeenth and eighteenth centuries. In the late

52. The copperplate engravings for this volume were executed by Christian Bernhard Rode: cf. S. Badstübner-Gröger, "Karl Friedrich Ramlers Schrift 'Allegorische Personen zum Gebrauch der bildenden Künstler,'" in *300 Jahre Akademie der Künste — Hochschule der Künste* (Berlin, 1996), pp. 87-90.

53. *Ioannis Calvini opera . . . omnia* 50, ed. G. Baum, E. Cunitz, and E. Reuss (Braunschweig, 1893), ad loc.

80. Religion Triumphant, red chalk sketch by Daniel Chodowiecki for the dome figure of the Französischer Dom, private collection, Berlin (after 1780)

81. Tympanum relief depicting the Sermon on the Mount. Main facade of the Französischer Dom, Berlin, probably by Heinrich Föhr after a design by Daniel Chodowiecki (1780-85).

eighteenth century, for example in the design of the French Tower, the Berlin Huguenots[54] appear to have been espousing many of the same attitudes toward history and art that are found elsewhere in Enlightenment Europe.

Bibliography

Das Edikt von Potsdam 1685: Die französische Einwanderung in Brandenburg-Preußen und ihre Auswirkungen auf Kunst, Kultur und Wissenschaft. Exhibition catalogue. Potsdam-Sanssouci, 1985.

Erman, J. P., and P. C. F. Reclam. *Mémoires pour servir à l'histoire des réfugiés dans les États du Roi.* 9 vols. Berlin, 1782-99.

Hugenotten in Berlin. Edited by G. Bregulla. Berlin, 1988.

Jersch-Wenzel, S. *Juden und Franzosen in der Wirtschaft des Raumes Berlin/ Brandenburg zur Zeit des Merkantilismus.* Berlin, 1978.

Manoury, K. *Die Geschichte der französisch-reformierten Provinzialgemeinden.* Berlin, 1961.

54. In this context one should mention the *réfugié* Alphons de Vignoles (1649-1744), mathematician, member of the Akademie der Wissenschaften in Berlin, and preacher in Brandenburg town. He compiled one of the first inventories in Brandenburg-Prussia, listing the burial monuments in Brandenburg's churches before they were demolished; cf. *Edikt von Potsdam*, p. 59.

Muret, E. *Geschichte der Französischen Kolonie in Brandenburg-Preußen*. Berlin, 1885.

Savage, P.-P. *Berlin und Frankreich: 1685-1871*. Berlin, 1980.

Discussion Following
Sibylle Badstübner-Gröger's Presentation

Paul Corby Finney: The materials you have shown us present the first instance we have seen of sculpture in a Calvinist Reformed setting for worship. Could you comment on this?

Sibylle Badstübner-Gröger: The sculptors commissioned for the Berlin project accommodated to the demands of the state, which was their patron. Since they were loyal to the state, they honored their commitments to their patron, even though in their personal convictions they were opposed to the use of sculpture in a Reformed worship setting. It was Frederick the Great's desire that the Berlin tower be decorated with sculpture, and the sculptors simply acceded to the demands of their patron. The artists in question wanted to present sculptural representations of several of the Reformers, but this intention never came to fruition, mainly because they could not come to agreement on the matter of how to represent their costume.

James Lomax: I am very interested in the international quality of French Huguenot art as we see it in so many manifestations outside of France, for example in Brandenburg-Prussia. There is one particular artist who I think typifies the diaspora of Huguenot artists, a most interesting character, namely, Philippe Mercier (cf. *The Dictionary of Art* [London and New York, 1996], s.v.; article by J. Ingamells), who was born in Berlin (1689 or 1691), perhaps the son of Pierre Mercier (who came to Berlin in 1686 as a *réfugié*), the tapestry designer whom you have mentioned. Philippe trained in Berlin, traveled to Italy and France and Hannover, thence to London, where in 1729 he became the Principal Painter to Frederick, the Prince of Wales (who had come from Hannover to London a year earlier). In 1730 Philippe became Keeper of Frederick's library. In 1739 Philippe moved to York; in 1747 he visited Ireland; in 1750 he was in Edinburgh. Philippe painted portraits and conversation pieces entirely in the French style, the so-called *fête galante* style. When (1736) he then fell out of favor with Frederick and moved to Yorkshire, he worked for a decade painting portraits of the nobility — we have in Temple Newsam House about ten of his pictures, all in a soft French style, but very much adapted to the English sensibility. He then (1752) took up with certain Yorkshire merchants who sent him to Portugal, where he then executed portraits of the English expatriate community

297

in Oporto (Porto); later he returned to London. After his death, his wife fell on hard times, and she became the recipient of Huguenot charity in London. In addition to Mercier, there is Jean de Bodt, who also came to Yorkshire, who worked there for the nobility and built one of the biggest houses in Yorkshire at Wentworth Castle. So what we are witnessing here is a very broad picture of the mobility and freedom of certain artists and architects within a period that is frequently depicted as being rather socially restricted and closed.

Sibylle Badstübner-Gröger: A similar pattern of far-flung international connections (Venice, Berlin, London) is attested for the two Romandons, Abraham (d. Berlin 1687; cf. U. Thieme and F. Becker, *Allgemeines Lexikon der bildenden Künstler von der Antike bis zur Gegenwart,* 28 [1934], s.v. "Romandon, Abraham"; article by C. F. Foerster) and his son Gedeon (d. Berlin 1697 or 1698).

HUNGARY

Art and Architecture in the Hungarian Reformed Church

GEORGE STARR

Within the Hungarian Reformed church there gradually evolved an architecture appropriate to the community it served; its salient features emerged during difficult times for the church, in the course of the seventeenth and eighteenth centuries, and fell into disuse as the church thrived in the nineteenth century. In the decades preceding World War I, this style was seized upon as expressing the very essence of the Hungarian nation; the resulting revival has had a decisive influence on twentieth-century Hungarian architecture, inspiring not only handsome Reformed churches but outstanding secular work as well.

The discussion that follows will therefore consider the reception as well as the origins of Reformed art and architecture in Hungary. The impact of this material, long after its creation and far beyond the Reformed community, is a significant part of Hungarian cultural history. In what might be called its twentieth-century afterlife, this idiom has achieved a vitality, both political and aesthetic, equal to that of the earlier building types and decorative styles on which it was based.

The present essay will begin by sketching briefly the situation of the country when the Reformation reached it, and the vicissitudes of the Reformed church since the sixteenth century. It will then chart the changes and innovations that eventually gave the spatial arrangements, the accoutrements, and the surroundings of Reformed churches their distinctive character. Among the features to be surveyed are the panel paintings on wood that decorate many ceilings, pews, and pulpits; the shingled timber bell towers adjacent to many churches; the *fejfák*, or wooden head posts and headboards, that serve as grave markers in Reformed cemeteries; and the textiles that adorn the Lord's Table. Along with these accounts of specific genres will be remarks on the interior spaces and floor plans of Reformed churches, with some attention to the consequences, social and psychological as well as theological, of the removal of altars, the obliteration of wall paintings, the insertion of pews and galleries, and (perhaps most crucial of all) the location, size, and structural elaboration of pulpits.

*   *   *

Between the Turkish defeat of a Hungarian army at Mohács in 1526 and the expulsion of the Turks at the end of the seventeenth century, what was once a single nation became but three fragments: Upper Hungary, nearly coextensive with present-day Slovakia, ruled by the Hapsburgs; Transylvania, now part of Romania but then ruled by Hungarian princes, more or less independent vassals of the Turks who were often at war with the Austrians; and the remainder of the country, roughly corresponding with post-1919 Hungary, which was occupied by the Turks.[1]

When the Reformation reached Hungary in the 1530s, the country was in a defeated, divided, demoralized, and (particularly in the Turkish areas) depopulated condition. Its initial, Lutheran phase took hold rapidly in the towns of Upper Hungary, inhabited largely by ethnic Germans, and in the countryside as well as the towns of southeastern Transylvania, populated almost entirely by "Saxons," who in fact had come from other parts of Germany besides Saxony. In the later sixteenth century the Reformed church displaced Catholicism throughout the Turkish-occupied lands, the bulk of Transylvania, and rural Upper Hungary. By 1600 Hungary as a whole is estimated to have become 80 to 85 percent Protestant.[2] The last

1. Hungary's changing borders during this period are traced in Paul R. Magosi's *Historical Atlas of East Central Europe* (Seattle and London, 1993), maps 14 and 15, pp. 46-50. Among sources for the historical information in the next three paragraphs, the following are most accessible: R. J. W. Evans, "Calvinism in East Central Europe: Hungary and Her Neighbours," in *International Calvinism, 1541-1715*, ed. Menna Prestwich (Oxford, 1985), pp. 167-96; David P. Daniel, "Calvinism in Hungary: The Theological and Ecclesiastical Transition to the Reformed Faith," in *Calvinism in Europe, 1540-1620*, ed. Andrew Pettegree, Alastair Duke, and Gillian Lewis (Cambridge, 1994), pp. 205-30; Winfried Eberhard, "Reformation and Counterreformation in East Central Europe," in *Handbook of European History, 1400-1600*, ed. Thomas Brady Jr., Heiko A. Oberman, and James D. Tracy, 2 vols. (Leiden and New York, 1995), 2:551-84; Imre Révész, *History of the Hungarian Reformed Church*, trans. (and abridged by) George A. F. Knight (Washington, D.C., 1956). Good general surveys are to be found in chapters 7-9 of *A History of Hungary*, ed. Peter F. Sugar (Bloomington and Indianapolis, 1990), pp. 83-137: Ferenc Szakály's "The Early Ottoman Period," Katalin Péter's "The Later Ottoman Period," and Peter F. Sugar's "The Principality of Transylvania." Challenging the traditional view that Ottoman rule reduced Hungary to a wasteland, Vera Zimányi offers a picture of agricultural progress alongside urban decline in *Economy and Society in Sixteenth and Seventeenth Century Hungary (1526-1650)* (Budapest, 1987).

2. This figure is Katalin Péter's: see page 161 of her chapter, "Hungary," in *The Reformation in National Context*, ed. Bob Scribner, Roy Porter, and Mikulas Teich (Cambridge, 1994), pp. 155-67.

decades of the century, before the Counter-Reformation had marshaled its forces, marked a period of struggle among Protestants: at this time the most acrimonious debates appear to have been not between Lutherans and Calvinists but between both and the Unitarians, especially in Transylvania.[3]

During the seventeenth and most of the eighteenth century, Protestantism was on the defensive against the Counter-Reformation, which succeeded in reclaiming most of Upper Hungary to Catholicism by the end of the seventeenth century. In the Transylvanian and Turkish territories, where Catholicism was not backed by Hapsburg power, the Counter-Reformation made only limited inroads in the seventeenth century. Under Turkish domination, the Reformed community was impoverished but its faith flourished; when this portion of Turkey-in-Europe became in effect an Austrian province, its material condition improved but its religious autonomy was put under great pressure. In the eighteenth century, the process of Counter-Reformation was not as heavy-handed as it had been in Upper Hungary in the 1670s and 1680s — Reformed ministers were no longer imprisoned, condemned to galley slavery, or martyred — but by various means, Hapsburg rule managed to restore Catholic dominance over much of the area. On the eastern flank of present-day Hungary and in much of Transylvania, the Counter-Reformation was less successful. Aside from a small Unitarian minority, the Saxon districts remained Lutheran; in other parts of Transylvania and eastern Hungary the Reformed church retained a significant role but not, in most areas, its former numerical superiority.

Throughout the Reformation era the country was in turmoil, and although intellectual and spiritual ferment can sometimes be exhilarating and productive, the prolonged conflict, the privation, and the insecurity afflicting Hungary tended to discourage artistic creativity. Under such unpromising circumstances, it is hardly surprising that no new Reformed churches were built. Had the country been peaceful, prosperous, and growing in population, Reformed congregations might have required new churches. But even if they had been needed, new facilities could not have been built, owing to economic and demographic decline, especially in the Turkish-occupied regions. In fact, the transition from Catholicism to Reformation was so swift and complete that in most communities an existing church stood ready to hand. For these reasons new buildings were not called for, and in those taken over by Lutherans not much change was necessary to accommodate the old church to the new service.

For Calvinists inheriting places of worship, the situation differed mainly in degree. The obligation to reform Catholic spaces did not demand radical reconstruction, yet significant shifts in orientation and emphasis

---

3. See the chapter on Unitarianism in Transylvania in George H. Williams, *The Radical Reformation*, 3rd ed. (Kirksville, Mo., 1992), pp. 1099-1133.

303

were in order. Hungarian Reformed architecture sought to adapt older Catholic churches to a new set of relationships between congregation, clergy, and God, and to new patterns of worship that expressed these changed relationships.

First and most obvious was the removal of altars. In Catholic worship, the congregation's attention had been fixed on the actions of a single man at the eastern end of the church: through priestly celebration of the mass, the old religion had mediated between believers and God. Calvinists condemned this mode of worship. They required the elimination of anything that might obstruct or deflect the individual's access to saving truth, understood as the word of God. The pulpit therefore took over the crucial role formerly played by the altar, both in the worship service and in the visual dynamics of the church's spatial arrangement. But in assuming the paramount position previously occupied by the altar, the pulpit did not move to the altar's vacated location. Instead it remained where it always had been — usually at some point on the long north wall of the church, closer to its east end than its west end, often just outside the arch (if there had been one) dividing chancel from nave. In the longitudinal plan that had long prevailed, everything tended to be oriented eastward, so imbalance between the eastern and western parts of a church had posed no problem. But the removal of the altar threatened to introduce an element of spatial confusion, especially where the chancel had been articulated as separate from the body of the church. Similarly, the placement of the pulpit was liable to appear somewhat random. Only in the last two centuries, and only when building anew, have Hungarian Reformed churches put pulpits either in the chancel or at the center of the long north wall.

Until the end of the seventeenth century new building was out of the question, and even the work done on Romanesque and Gothic churches appropriated for Reformed worship seems to have consisted, apart from repairs, mainly of subtraction rather than addition. The whitewashing of medieval frescoes, many of which have reemerged in the course of modern restorations, may suggest the overlaying of one tradition with another, with the church becoming a kind of palimpsest. Gradual, piecemeal accretion does seem to have occurred in the late seventeenth and eighteenth centuries. But in its initial phase, the Hungarian Reformation was more concerned to purify than to beautify, to rectify old abuses than to create afresh. At the same time, iconoclasm could not simply efface what had gone before. More was removed than replaced, but the resulting blanks and gaps must in their own way have been rather eloquent, creating a kind of aesthetic of absence. They served as mute reminders of a prior state of things, not quite visible vestiges of a past that might be deplored rather than regretted, but always threatening to reemerge. To be sure, the passage of time would have obliterated not only many physical traces of the pre-Reformation past, but the very memory of that past. Within a generation or two, people with no experience to the contrary would come to assume that church walls are white and unadorned, always and everywhere.

As we shall see, neither walls, ceilings, nor the floor space once occupied by altars remained bare or empty. Although various Reformed churches built around 1800 have the cool, spare, understated quality that we associate with their American counterparts from the same era, these may represent a lapse or aberration in the history of Hungarian taste, which abhors anything approaching a vacuum. Once altars had been removed from the former chancels, for example, they were usually replaced with pews facing westward, toward the pulpit. At the western end of a typical church, the formal options depended on whether there was a narthex, and whether the ceiling or roof was sufficiently high to admit a balcony; the height and width tended to be those of the nave, nor were there the windows, or the irregularities of plan or vaulting, often found in the chancel. When organs began to be installed early in the nineteenth century, western galleries became organ lofts; their predecessors are sometimes referred to as choir lofts, but most seem to have served as simple galleries, particularly in smaller churches.

Distinctions between seating areas seem to have been along social and gender lines. Local luminaries and church officers were adjacent to or opposite the pulpit; unmarried young men occupied galleries, married men sat in inherited family pews to one side of the pulpit, with married women and girls together on the other side. Thus the construction of pews in the former chancels and the erection of galleries changed the character of Reformed churches dramatically; they made for a communal intimacy and mutual visibility that was undoubtedly valuable, socially as well as spiritually, although they could also create unwelcome imbalances, both visual and acoustic.

An even more distinctive characteristic of Reformed churches, as they underwent repairs and refurbishings in the course of the seventeenth and eighteenth centuries, is the elaborate and colorful ornamentation of the available surfaces, particularly those made of wood. There are a few surviving wall-paintings, such as the delightful specimens at Csaroda (see fig. 82), dating from 1642.[4] But Reformed frescoes appear to have been uncommon, whereas nearly every church made some effort to decorate its ceilings, pews, or galleries. We know from documentary records that there had been paneled and coffered wooden ceilings in late medieval and Renaissance Hungarian buildings, both religious and secular, but all the surviving examples are from the

---

4. At Csaroda there is both a tower over the western end of the church and a freestanding wooden bell tower: see Nándor Gilyén, Ferenc Mendele, and János Tóth, *A Felső-Tiszavidék Népi Építészete* (Folk architecture of the Upper Tisza Region) (Budapest, 1975), pp. 129, 152, 153. Csaroda is extensively illustrated in Balázs Dercsényi, Gábor Hegyi, Ernő Marosi, and Béla Takács, *Calvinist Churches in Hungary* (Budapest, 1992), pp. 4-9, figs. 7-26.

82. Wall painting,
Csaroda, western
gallery, 1642

mid–seventeenth through the mid–nineteenth century.[5] A curious specimen
of 1676, from Tancs in Transylvania (see fig. 83), has caused disagreement

5. See Ilona Tombor, *Magyarországi Festett Famennyezetek és Rokonemlékek a XV-XIX.
Századból* (Hungarian painted wooden ceilings and related monuments from the fifteenth to
the nineteenth century) (Budapest, 1968), passim; Ilona Tombor, *Old Hungarian Painted Woodwork, Fifteenth–Nineteenth Centuries* (Budapest, 1967), contains illustrations in color but a
much abbreviated text.

306

83. Painted wooden ceiling panels, Tancs, 1676

among commentators, owing to the prominence of human figures and secular mythology among its subjects: in the decoration of Reformed churches, both tendencies are rare.[6] One hypothesis is that these scenes were derived from some illustrated Russian chronicle or liturgical book; another conjecture is that the painter had worked previously in Greek Orthodox churches and was not restrained by Reformed puritan scruples, which would in any case have been set aside after the Turkish and Tatar raids around 1660. Whether the painter understood the classical *topos* of the deified ruler ascending to heaven

6. Tombor, *Magyarországi Festett Famennyezetek és Rokonemlékek a XV-XIX. Századból*, pp. 88-89.

307

is doubtful: in fact, the subject of this primitive apotheosis, Alexander the Great ("Sándor"), is mounted not on an eagle but on a fat Hungarian crow. In what appears to be a similarly ironic vein, the occupant of the next panel is not the Bacchus we might expect but a mere private ("Baka") astride a barrel. Some of the other motifs of the Tancs ceiling, such as the siren or mermaid, recur elsewhere, but seldom are the decorations this insistently figural, or this crudely executed.

At Zubogy, the 1726 ceiling is composed of continuously patterned planks rather than separate rectangular scenes.[7] Some of the panels executed at Noszvaj in 1734 by Imre Asztalos of Miskolc are entirely floral, others contain storks and snakes (see fig. 84) and the pelican feeding its young.[8] A ceiling of the following year from Megyaszó is also the work of Imre and István Asztalos of Miskolc; its iconography is less figural, but its elaboration of pomegranates and other floral motifs is similarly ingenious.[9] Kraszna has a ceiling of 1736 replete with a many-headed beast, a Jonah, an angel, a peacock, and other fauna commoner in picture books than in the Transylvanian countryside.[10] A ceiling of 1740 from Tök, near Budapest, the work of a team operating from Komárom, exhibits grapes, tulips, roses, and carnations in quite abstract patterns.[11] A similar tendency is present in a ceiling of 1746 from Mezőcsát (see plate 29), executed by the same group of Komárom artisans.[12] Of the same year, but from Magyarókereke in Transylvania, are some panels by Lőrinc Umling, narrower in palette but unusually vigorous in pattern.[13] This is also true of the work done in a quite different style two decades later at Maksa, also in Transylvania.[14] Dating from the same year, 1766, the work of Ferenc Lándor at Tákos, in northeastern Hungary, shows how forceful these designs can be, especially when seen at close range in the smaller churches and when carried through from ceilings to galleries, pulpits, and pews.[15] The work of János Nagyváti at Szenna (1787) also achieves this coherence of effect on an intimate scale (see plate 30).[16]

7. For the Zubogy ceiling of 1726, see Tombor, *Old Hungarian Painted Woodwork*, pl. 20.

8. Tamás Hofer and Edit Fél, *Magyar Népművészet* (Hungarian folk art) (Budapest, 1975), fig. 26.

9. See Hofer and Fél, figs. 30, 33-36, and György Domanovszky, *A Magyar Nép Díszítőművészete* (Decorative art of the Hungarian people), 2 vols. (Budapest, 1981), 2:362-63.

10. Tombor, *Magyarországi Festett Famennyezetek és Rokonemlékek a XV-XIX. Századból*, table 50.

11. Domanovszky, *A Magyar Nép Díszítőművészete*, 2:364; this ceiling has been housed in the *Iparművészeti Muzeum* (Museum of Applied Art, Budapest) since 1900.

12. See Domanovszky, *A Magyar Nép Díszítőművészete*, 2:348-49.

13. See Hofer and Fél, fig. 38, and Tombor, *Old Hungarian Painted Woodwork*, p. 35.

14. See Tombor, *Old Hungarian Painted Woodwork*, p. 41.

15. See József Várady, *Tiszántúl Református Templomai* (Reformed churches east of the Tisza), 2 vols. (Debrecen, 1991), 2:910; also Attila Komjáthy, *Felső-Tisza-Vidéki Templomok I* (Churches of the Upper Tisza Region I) (Budapest, 1983), figs. 34-40.

16. See Tombor, *Old Hungarian Painted Woodwork*, pl. 1; cf. also Ernő Marosi, *Magyar*

84. Painted wooden ceiling panels, Noszvaj, 1734

These painted panels have long been objects of appreciative attention: toward the end of the last century, the documenting and restoring of older Reformed churches became a subject of interest not only to their

Falusi Templomok (Hungarian village churches) (Budapest, 1975), pl. 64, a curious Szenna scene of a crowned mermaid bearing both a sword and a scimitar.

congregations and to other Calvinists, but also to historians, ethnographers, artists, and architects of other denominations. A Museum of Applied Art was founded at Budapest in the 1890s and began collecting such material from churches being modernized or razed. Much of value has been gathered, preserved, and exhibited; an additional challenge, however, has been the taxonomic question posed by such material.

Most commentators have classified it as folk art, which is to say that it has aroused great admiration, but from a certain social distance that is analogous to the affectionate yet patronizing manner in which pastoral poetry tends to treat its rustic subject matter. A good deal of the paneling in Hungarian Reformed churches is known to have been made, painted, and signed by trained professionals, associated with well-organized workshops, who executed similar commissions over a wide area.[17] But because much of the work was done in the provinces, and seems to modern urbanites naive in conception and unpolished in execution, the "folk" rubric persists.

The European discovery and celebration of folk art around the turn of this century also encouraged the classification of these monuments under that rubric. This entire exercise of identifying and glorifying folk art has had very mixed results, however, in the artistic as well as the political realm.[18] Fascist glorification of folk culture and *Heimat* was no doubt the nadir of this movement. Within Hungary an infatuation with the peasantry and peasant culture has often served questionable purposes, although it might be argued that at times an interest in folk culture may have done Hungarian art and architecture more good than harm. (It should perhaps be noted that, as does the German language, Hungarian uses the same word — *nép* — to signify both "folk" and "people," so there may be a stronger suggestion than in English that a certain class embodies the nation at its truest and best; negative connotations belong entirely to a cognate — *népies* — the equivalent of our "folksy.") At all events, it is not at all clear that the ceiling panels in question were in fact made by folk artists; one senses that those who commissioned and executed this art regarded themselves as a cut above peasant culture.

"Vernacular" might be a better label than "folk" for this art. This term would have the advantage of diminishing the class associations of "folk" nomenclature; at the same time, this term would strengthen the associa-

---

17. See Tombor, *Magyarországi Festett Famennyezetek és Rokonemlékek a XV-XIX. Századból.*

18. Dezső Malonyay's monumental *A Magyar Nép Művészete* (The art of the Hungarian people), 5 vols. (Budapest, 1907-12), illustrates the close linkage between artistic and ethnographic research and attempts to construct and celebrate a Hungarian national identity. In the series of special numbers of *The Studio*, edited by Charles Holme and published in London before World War I — *Peasant Art in Sweden, Iceland, and Lapland* (1910); *Peasant Art in Austria and Hungary* (1911); *Peasant Art in Russia* (1912); and *Peasant Art in Italy* (1913) — the function of folk art is less to inspire patriots than to gratify collectors and connoisseurs.

tion between these works of art and the larger program of the Reformed church, which was to reestablish a vital linkage between religion and the community, defined in terms of national language and culture. Hence the importance assigned not only to biblical translation, but to the availability in Hungarian of sermons, commentaries, and other edifying literature. From this perspective, the interior decoration of Reformed churches can be regarded as a close analogue in the visual realm to the well-known Reformed emphasis on the vernacular in the linguistic realm — an equivalent expression of the insistence that Reformed worship work with indigenous materials.

It might also prove useful to position this art in relation to the concept of the "regional," which suggests an art rooted in its own geographical locale. Working out the possibilities of an inherited idiom with unselfconscious relish, regional art can appear to possess a special appropriateness to its setting, and for this reason has often been regarded as a wholesome alternative to artistic internationalism or cosmopolitanism. But whatever the most appropriate terminology may be, whether "folk," "vernacular," or "regional," there can be no doubt that these painted panels develop a set of stylized motifs with extraordinary verve. What any one of them lacks in originality, it tends to make up for in artful elaboration: resourcefully improvising on well-defined themes, this art is at once firmly grounded and richly inventive.

$$*\quad*\quad*$$

A second feature that gave Reformed churches their distinctive character was the wooden bell tower (see fig. 85), sometimes built over or contiguous with the west end, more often a separate structure. Most extant examples date from the later seventeenth and eighteenth centuries, but many of these are enlarged or restored versions of earlier prototypes. In the absence of pre-seventeenth-century specimens, there is some question about the origins and early evolution of this genre.

There are earlier wooden churches in eastern Christendom, with many impressive examples, including towers, in Russian and Greek Orthodox corners of today's Slovakia, Ukraine, and Romania.[19] It seems reasonable to suppose that the shingled timber bell towers in northeastern Hun-

19. The broadest treatment of this material is David Buxton's *The Wooden Churches of Eastern Europe: An Introductory Survey* (Cambridge, 1981). More detailed and sympathetic accounts of the Hungarian towers are to be found in Hélène Balogh, *Les Édifices de Bois dans l'Architecture Religieuse Hongroise* (Budapest, 1941), and in publications on the historical monuments of specific areas, such as György Domanovszky's *Magyarország egyházi faépítészete: Bereg megye* (The religious wooden architecture of Hungary: Bereg County) (Budapest, 1936). For good photographs, elevations, cross sections, and plans of a number of bell towers, see Gilyén et al., pp. 151-79.

85. Wooden bell
tower, Mezőcsávás,
late sixteenth century

gary and Transylvania owed something to these models from farther north
and east. But stylistically their sources are Western. They are usually freestanding, rather than being built over the nave as in most Orthodox
churches, and the shapes of steeples (and of the often-present ministeeples
mounted at their four corners) appear to have been inspired by medieval
Germanic traditions, not Eastern exemplars from beyond the Carpathians.

If we pay attention to the lookout gallery, which is a regular feature of

312

these towers along with the careful walling, gating, and in some cases subtowering of the cemetery or church precinct that is associated with many of them, we are reminded not only of the spires of Bavaria or Bohemia, but also of the dozens of fortress-churches of Saxon Transylvania. In these watchtower bastions, often constructed entirely of stone except for the steeple, form may have been dictated less by ecclesiastical or aesthetic considerations than by defensive function. These are not Transylvanian castles that happen to have a church inside, but fortified precincts in small Germanic towns and villages, with the church itself usually as the stronghold; they have been Lutheran or Unitarian since the sixteenth century, and their main contours are often quite well preserved.[20] Without contending that wooden towers standing adjacent to Reformed churches a bit farther west are just like them, or derived from them, one can recognize interesting affinities between them, not only stylistic but practical. The ecclesiastical is not compromised by the secular, but the distinction between these realms tends to collapse, as I believe happens in other aspects of design (and life) in the Hungarian Reformed church.

But even if one doubts that these towers were built with enemies in mind, or that they would have been of much use in the face of Mongols, Tatars, or Turks, they clearly exceed the functional requirements of mere belfries. In any case, for more than a century an air of exoticism and mystery has surrounded these towers.[21] Although some are modest in scale, many dwarf their nearby churches and are elegantly detailed, achieving in their own idiom the monumentality of a classic campanile. Yet their wooden fabric must always have given them a contrary aura as well, of plainness, simplicity, and impermanence.

*   *   *

This is to shift our focus, however, from the genesis of buildings to their effects — from the motives and rationale of their design and construction to their impact on actual users and observers over the years. Such an approach seems legitimate, and can be extended to another distinctive category of Hungarian Reformed art, the grave markers found in Calvinist cem-

---

20. A useful study of these (mostly Lutheran) fortified precincts is Hermann and Alida Fabini, *Kirchenburgen in Siebenbürgen* (Wien, Köln, Graz, 1986). Cf. also Tibor Szentpétery and Terézia Kerny, *Az Olttól a Küküllőig: Erdélyi Szász Erődtemplomok* (From the Olt to the Küküllő: *Transylvanian Saxon Fortified Churches*) (Budapest, 1990); and especially János Gyöngyössy, Terézia Kerny, and József Sarudi Sebestyén, *Székelyföldi Vártemplomok* (Eastern Transylvanian Fortress Churches) (Budapest, 1995), with excellent maps, diagrams, photographs, and bibliography, and brief summaries in German and Romanian.

21. Typical of the twentieth-century mystique of the Transylvanian bell tower is the rendering of Ketesd by László Debreczeni, *Erdélyi Református Templomok és Tornyok* (Transylvanian Reformed churches and towers) (Kolozsvár, 1929), p. 48.

313

86. *Fejfák* (wooden head posts)

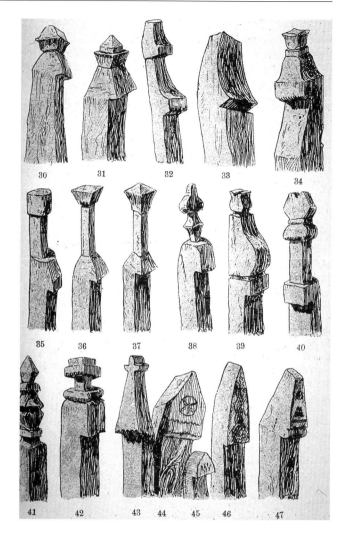

eteries (see fig. 86).[22] These head posts and headboards are found throughout the country in Reformed cemeteries, but not in those of other denominations. (In many villages different denominations have in fact shared cemeteries since the eighteenth century, but occupy distinct areas within them.) Both Roman and Greek Catholic graves (the latter mostly those of ethnic Romanians) are marked by crosses of stone or wood, varying in form and elaborateness; Lutheran cemeteries, like Lutheran

22. For photographs of Calvinist head posts and headboards, see those by József Hapak accompanying Béla Takács's essay, "A református temetők fejfáinak népi ornamentikaja" (Folk ornamentation of headboards in Reformed cemeteries), in *Vallási Néprajz* (Religious ethnography), ed. Imre Dankó and Imola Küllős, 2 vols. (Budapest, 1985), vol. 1, pls. 1-38. But stylistic variations can be traced better through drawings, such as Dezső Nagy's in "A magyar fejfák és díszítményeik" (Hungarian headboards and their decoration), published as vol. 2 of *Folklór archívum* (1974), and József L. Novák's (fig. 86).

churches, also admit crosses, although they tend to be less ornate; but there are no crosses in Reformed cemeteries. In their place are stone or more often wooden headboards, either rectangular or with arched tops, bearing simple inscriptions but not much ornamentation apart from tree-of-life motifs. More interesting are the head posts, usually with no inscription whatsoever but varying greatly in the kind and amount of their carving. Most are square, with more or less complicated designs executed uniformly over all four surfaces. Some, found chiefly in Transylvania, have in effect a front and a back and eschew overall patterns for simpler, bolder carving, often quite primitive or modern in spirit. (Whether the sculpture of Constantin Brancuşi is formally indebted to traditional Transylvanian head posts is a question that does not seem to be addressed in standard English works on Romania's most important twentieth-century artist, but the similarities are rather striking.)[23]

In their stark way these head posts are powerful works of art, and part of their power is owing to their enigmatic shapes, highly abstract yet suggestively anthropomorphic. But the origins of these strange objects are as mysterious as their forms. There is nothing like them in traditional Catholic funerary art. They do bear some resemblance to Turkish head posts, with which it seems plausible to link them on historical, chronological, and geographical grounds. But most Hungarian commentators balk at the idea that Calvinists could have owed anything of value to the Turks; they tend to favor a theory, on the face of it rather farfetched, that these head posts hark back to Hungary's pagan past, before the Magyars were converted to Christianity.[24] According to this interpretation, the Reformed church not only rejected as idolatrous the veneration of crosses, but also revived the use of funerary monuments from the nation's heroic age.

This thesis bears all the earmarks of an invented tradition[25] — a way of bestowing on recent or artificial developments an aura of antiquity and naturalness as part of a nation's effort to define, justify, and aggrandize itself.

23. The affinities are strongest with Brancuşi's *Exotic Plant* and some versions of his *Endless Column* and *Cock:* these works are reproduced in Sidney Geist, *Brancusi: The Sculpture and Drawings* (New York, 1975), pp. 101, 100, 116-17. Cf. also Sidney Geist, *Brancusi: A Study of the Sculpture* (New York, 1968), and Friedrich T. Bach, Margit Rowell, and Ann Temkin, *Constantin Brancusi, 1876-1957* (Cambridge, Mass., and London, 1995).

24. See Ernő Kunt, *Folk Art in Hungarian Cemeteries* (Budapest, 1983), p. 15 and passim. László Novák acknowledges that "in the development of the decorative features Turkish influence predominates," but maintains that the headposts "have an archaic stratum too," and that their "form points to an even more ancient heritage," harking back to Magyar "cultic custom" prior to their arrival in the Carpathian Basin ("A Duna-Tisza köze Temetőinek Néprajza" ["The Ethnography of the Cemeteries of the Region between the Danube and the Tisza Rivers"], *Cumania* 5 [Kecskemét, 1978]: 219-305, with excellent drawings and photographs and an extensive summary in English).

25. See *The Invention of Tradition,* ed. Eric Hobsbawm and Terence Hanger (Cambridge and New York, 1983).

This is not to suggest that the Hungarian reformers, in adopting a style of grave markers that may or may not be of much earlier origin, were themselves engaged in this process; their intentions on the subject, apart from a determination to avoid idolatry, can only be surmised. The point is rather that around 1900 these homely monuments were seized upon as links with a legendary past, and that it was precisely because of their picturesque inscrutability that they lent themselves so well to the invention of tradition — to nation building based on poetic make-believe, not on historical fact.

Renderings of head posts by turn-of-the-century artists demonstrate the quasi-historical, quasi-mythological romanticizing tendencies that have shaped the interpretation of these objects. *Eagles above the Hero's Grave* (see plate 31) is a tapestry of 1918 designed by Aladár Kriesch (1863-1920), woven by Rózsa Frei: here the mythical overtones are pagan, but the head posts differ little from those that Kriesch grew up among in Transylvania, and in the background is a stylized version either of Körösfő or Magyarvalkó.

In Kriesch's tapestry we find an element of nostalgia for a larger-than-life legendary past, a tendency expressed on a much grander scale in his murals for the cultural palace at Maros-Vásárhely. But the head post could also lend itself to more domesticized, sentimental longings, as in a book illustration (see fig. 87) by Károly Kós (1883-1977) that may be more playful than solemn, or another (see fig. 88) by Lajos Kozma (1884-1948) for a poem entitled "Vergődés" (Writhing), where the head posts are engulfed not so much by vegetation as by a proliferation of sheer pattern.

Kós's relish for the Transylvanian landscape[26] gives way in Kozma to a more somber symbolism, and Álmos Jaschik (1885-1950) pushes still further in this direction in a 1912 illustration (see fig. 89). Here the setting is that of nightmare, with monstrous head posts threatening the puny human figures — the "you" and "I" of the poem, weary and dispirited wanderers — rather than embodying, as they do for Kriesch, a heroic past that can inspire the living. For Kriesch, the hovering eagles seem to be totemic figures, linking the primitive hero and his tribe to the forces of nature. But in the illustrations of Kozma and Jaschik, nature gradually disappears and the Transylvanian countryside is transformed into the dark, troubled landscape of the modern psyche.

Nor were these the only ways that twentieth-century artists have interpreted head posts. In the decade after World War I, bucolic images such as László Debreczeni's *Kalotaszegi Fejfák* (Kalotaszeg head posts) (see fig. 90), along with various engravings by Kós, registered (and perhaps intensified) Hungarian regret for the loss of Transylvania. Thus in the decades

---

26. Similar in spirit to Kós's treatment of the Transylvanian heritage (and like Kós's spanning the fields of architecture, furniture design, and graphics) is the work of Ede Wiegand (1869-1945); cf. his rendering of a head post in the final picture of *Hajdonába régösrégön . . .* (Once upon a time long ago . . .) (Budapest, 1917), pl. 16.

around World War I, the image of the Calvinist head post could lend itself to various artistic projects and moods: that it could elicit such different readings, and be put to such diverse uses, can be regarded as evidence not only of its provocative impassivity and muteness, but of its symbolic richness for artists and other cultural commentators.

It is also worth noting the high degree of anonymity of most of these monuments. In recent centuries, the funerary art of most Christian denominations has sought to commemorate the deceased by identifying them as fully as possible, given the constraints of space, material, and expense — as if people's value were a function of their uniqueness, which survivors must try to capture through a design or (more commonly) an inscription. Sometimes this individualizing gesture has been limited to a bare notation of name and dates; the further it goes beyond this, the greater the risk of its becoming an exercise in familial vainglory rather than

88. Lajos Kozma, *Vergődés* (Writhing), 1908, book illustration

piety. Moreover, the imagined beholder/reader is a stranger, lacking information that the monument must provide.

Over against such assumptions, the nameless Calvinist head post can be thought of as an expression of community, in which there is no need to specify, let alone trumpet, who's who. From the fact that the grave marker is anonymous, it may not follow that individual uniqueness is not recognized or prized in life; the implication may be rather that in death, these and other earthly distinctions lose their importance. Nor does anonymity entail uniformity: within a large repertory of motifs there is room for endless recombinations and improvisations, so that even in the absence of inscriptions there is considerable variety. As with the interior furnishings of Reformed churches, one can say that the head posts reveal an interest in creating sturdy, handsome objects; although they vary in complexity of shape and surface design, even the plainest of them seem products of a keen if somewhat austere artistic sensibility, not of indifference or hostility toward art.

318

89. Álmos Jaschik, *Az óriások temetője* (The cemetery of the giants), 1912, book illustration

*   *   *

Although the filiation of Calvinist head posts from Turkish models is an unpopular line of inquiry among Hungarian historians, in the area of textiles it has long been recognized that the Reformed church adopted Turkish material extensively and unashamedly. On the eve of the Reformation, every church would have had one or more altars in its sanctuary and any other chapels, each of which would be furnished during the celebration of mass not only with the necessary utensils but with various fabrics. Woven into them or embroidered onto them, throughout Catholic Europe, would be scenes or symbols objectionable to Calvinists on the same grounds that wall paintings were. But after altars and their accoutrements were banished, there was a need for comely and appropriate decorations for the Lord's Table, and among the most treasured textiles that have been preserved in Reformed churches since the seven-

90. László Debreczeni,
Kalotaszegi Fejfák
(Kalotaszeg head
posts), 1929, book
illustration

teenth century there is a significant number of Turkish embroideries (see plate 32 and fig. 91).[27]

Why Turkish? It could be maintained that they are more beautiful than Hungarian work of the time, and that the Calvinists were sensible and modest enough to be able to see that this was so and implicitly acknowledge it. Hungarian embroidery both before and since has many charms, but seldom the sophisticated coherence and continuity of overall design present in old Turkish work. Instead of a flowing, linear structure, Hungarian embroidery tends to be built up from internally elaborate but more or less self-contained components. In both traditions, carnations, roses, tulips, pomegranates, and

27. The fullest account available to me was Gertrud Palotay, *Oszmán-Török Elemek a Magyar Himzésben (Les Elements Turcs-Ottomans des Broderies Hongroises)* (Budapest, 1940), with text in French and Hungarian; most of the specimens discussed and illustrated are from Calvinist churches. Cf. also Béla Takács's *Református templomaink úrasztali teritői* (Tablecloths for the Lord's Table in Our Reformed Churches) (Budapest, 1983).

other stylized flower and fruit motifs provide the basic vocabulary (see figs. 92 and 93). Even when represented most realistically, such subject matter posed no threat to Calvinists, since it was not liable to be mistaken as an object of worship, and since various flowers and fruits retained in Reformed settings their traditional iconographic functions.

*   *   *

Far from being proscribed, visual symbolism of certain kinds was recognized as legitimate and flourished in Hungarian Reformed churches. The sounding boards over most pulpits were topped with elaborate crowns, at the peak of which was often a sculptured pelican, piercing its breast with its beak. This emblem of extreme maternal solicitude, nourishing one's brood with one's own blood, has a long figurative history, with Christ's sacrifice as its chief referent. But like the lamb, of which there are also pictures in Hungarian Reformed churches, this symbolism did not violate Calvinist principles: designed to stimulate pious contemplation rather than adoration, such images were not forbidden by the Second Commandment.

 As to the pulpits themselves, they displace the Catholic altar as the focal point, both visual and ideological, of the Reformed service, even though their actual position within the church from the sixteenth through the eighteenth century is seldom central in any literal, spatial sense. Perhaps partly to counteract any instability that might result from these *a*symmetrical, *de*centered rearrangements, and perhaps partly to compensate for the absence of an altar, no longer there but a worrisome shadow-presence lurking in the spatial confusions and awkwardnesses caused by its removal, the Reformed pulpit was made as monumental as possible. This objective, whatever the theological or psychological imperatives that lay behind it, is pursued in at least three ways: through sheer magnification, the height and mass of the pulpit of-

92. Hungarian table-cloth (detail), Magyarkirályfalva, seventeenth century

ten dominating, if not overwhelming, its surroundings; through formal articulation, with stairs, supporting members, surrounding panels, and overhead crown often making up a composition structurally more complex and visually more interesting than anything else in the church; and through sheer profusion of surface ornament.

For instance, during the first century and a half of the Hungarian Reformed church, it seems that the only stone carving, apart from a few memorial slabs containing inscriptions and the coats of arms of princes or great magnates, was devoted to pulpits. The most impressive works in this medium are the pulpit (see fig. 94) executed in 1646 for a church in Kolozsvár, under the patronage of Prince György Rákóczi I, and the pulpit made around 1680 for the church in Fogaras, also in Transylvania.[28] In the case of the Kolozsvár pulpit, we know who carved the alabaster panels around the pulpit, and who did the lower panels and the rest of the stone structure; anonymous local craftsmen are credited with the work at Fogaras. In both instances — or rather in all three, since the styles of the two parts of the Kolozsvár pulpit are quite distinct — there is a degree of formality and a level of finish seldom found in other Reformed decoration of this period. This is ascribable in part to the sophistication of Rákóczi and the Kolozsvár cultural milieu at the time, but it

28. Although there are good photographs of a few of these pulpits, their design and ornamentation can be rendered more fully and legibly by careful drawings: see Katalin B. Murádin's excellent *Faragott Kőszószékek Erdélyben* (Carved stone pulpits in Transylvania) (Budapest and Kolozsvár, 1994), with thirteen-page English summary.

322

93. Hungarian table-cloth, Nagyvarsány, seventeenth century

may also owe something to the nature of the medium, and to the conservatism of those working in it. Thus the rigidly composed, lateral symmetry of the panels, involving realistically rendered fruit suspended by drapery from metal rings, would not be out of place in high-Renaissance Hungarian work of a century and a half earlier.[29] Yet what seems most noteworthy about such work is that it draws on images of beauty and richness in the natural world to heighten a sense of all being derived from, dependent on, and referring back to the life-giving word. (Although the bunches of grapes, the pomegranates, and so on are rendered realistically, their inclusion is probably owing to traditional iconographic associations — as in the cases of pelicans, lambs, and ships — with Christ or the church; that such a program is at work is borne out by the presence, on the central panel of the Kolozsvár pulpit, of the two tables of the commandments, also a frequent and prominent feature of Reformed church interiors.) The Kolozsvár pulpit may be atypical in its costly medium, its ornateness, and the representational realism of its decor — elsewhere in Transylvania, pulpits with painted paneling are more common[30] — yet it springs from, and in its own way effectively carries out, the scheme of every such pulpit: to give palpable expression, through scale, structure, surface

29. Compare the similar lower side-panels of the Nagyrév tabernacle in the inner-city church of Pest, carved between 1503 and 1506, illustrated in Rózsa Tóth Feuer, *Reneszánsz Építészet Magyarországon* (Renaissance architecture in Hungary) (Budapest, 1977), pl. 60.

30. See the photographs of painted wooden Transylvanian pulpits from Kalotadámos and Bogártelke in Tombor, *Magyarországi Festett Famennyezetek és Rokonemlékek a XV-XIX. Századból*, pls. 45 and 47.2, and from Kispetri (1715) in Domanovszky, *A Magyar Nép Díszítőművészete*, 2:374.

94. Pulpit, Kolozsvár, 1646

treatment, and sometimes location as well, to the centrality of the word and its preaching in the Hungarian Reformed church.

*   *   *

Although surviving evidence of the painted ornamentation of town halls, castles, burghers' houses, and other secular interiors is much more fragmentary than that from churches, it suggests continuity, if not identity, between ceiling treatments in these different settings. Where there were already Gothic vaults, these were merely whitewashed, or painted with stars, crescents, stylized flowers, or cartouches framing texts. Otherwise, from the Renaissance on, there were usually either coffered ceilings or continuous panels. In either case the flat coffer or panel surfaces were regarded as calling for decoration.

In each of these areas of Reformed church design — painted paneling, towers, head posts, and pulpits — there is enormous artistic variety but no clear stylistic taxonomy: continuity seems more pronounced than change, with variations appearing to be as much individual or regional as temporal. Perhaps this constancy owes something to a principled resistance to faddish innovation — an equivalent in the visual realm of the social and doctrinal tenacity that characterized these much-tried, much-tempted communities.

In the later eighteenth and nineteenth centuries, however, there is evidence that Reformed congregations did not simply resist the baroque, rococo, or neoclassical innovations of their Catholic neighbors. On the contrary, there are specimens of work in each of these modes which suggests that neither unawareness of new developments nor sheer hostility to them can quite account for the persistence of older styles. In addition to redecoration using baroque elements, there was new construction of a number of churches, including some very substantial ones, in the neoclassical style. But most of these seem to have been built in cities and larger towns, not in remoter villages. In the seven decades between the death of Maria Theresia (1780) and the revolutions of 1848, when the rigors of the Counter-Reformation were somewhat relaxed and the Reformed church operated under fewer official restrictions and disabilities, Calvinists in the more urbane and prosperous parts of the country wished to demonstrate that they were in step with the times, abreast of the progress of civilization.

Various churches of the early nineteenth century express this mood, on a grand scale and in the new idiom of neoclassicism. The earliest and most famous of these is the Great Church of Debrecen, built to replace an earlier structure destroyed by fire. Mihály Péchy, whose background was in military engineering, initially explored a ground plan that does not seem to have found favor but would have marked a sensational new departure in Calvinist architecture had it been carried out: the panopticon would have been ideally suited to the Reformed service (see fig. 95). But the only Reformed church that actually utilizes a round plan, a small neoclassical building at Szilvásvárad, places the pulpit not in the center but against the wall.[31] A dif-

31. For good exterior and interior views of the round church at Szilvásvárad of circa 1820, see Marosi, *Magyar Falusi Templomok*, figs. 84, 85. But this church is said to have been originally Catholic (Anna Zádor and Jenő Rados, *A Klasszicizmus Építészete Magyarországon* [The architecture of classicism in Hungary] [Budapest, 1948], p. 191); and although a number of neoclassical Catholic churches, chapels, and mausoleums were round (Zádor and Rados, pls. 38, 41-44), there do not seem to be other Reformed specimens of this building type. Therefore Szilvásvárad probably does not belong in the present survey.

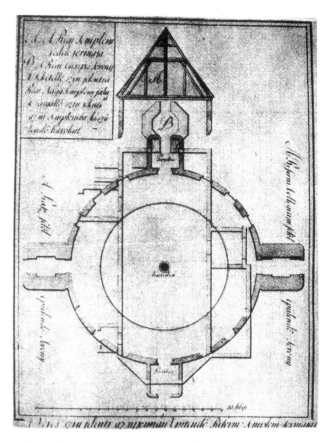

95. Mihály Péchy,
1802 panopticon plan,
Debrecen

ferent scheme of Péchy's, with a columned portico but without the great drum and cupola he also envisioned (see fig. 96), was carried out after his death in 1807 (see fig. 97).

The chaste, severe structures at Debrecen and elsewhere, which the Reformed church did not inherit but designed and built from the ground up, are in fact the first to express in formal terms a linkage between Calvinism and architecture. Here at last we find buildings laid out in a way that reflects what actually goes on within them, the arrangement of which makes transparent the roles of preaching, communion, and baptism in Reformed worship. In other words, what is innovative and important about Reformed neoclassicism is not so much its facades, which resemble Catholic cathedrals of the same era, but its floor plans and distribution of space, particularly those of the Great Church of Debrecen (see fig. 98) and of the very similar Magyar Street church in Kolozsvár (1829-51).

These buildings make a positive program out of a practice that had been an often-awkward accommodation for more than two centuries. What happened in these churches was that a de facto transverse plan, which had been imposed with mixed results on axially conceived spaces, could for the first time assert itself freely and capaciously as an appropriate

response to the demands of the Reformed service and community. Although there might be no virtue in symmetry for its own sake, this plan could more effectively express and facilitate the centrality of preaching. If we visualize the resulting space as a variant on the ancient cruciform plan, both nave and sanctuary have been collapsed, with the pulpit assuming what had been the altar's position and the congregation occupying both arms of a greatly expanded crossing. It could be objected that one thrust of this arrangement is to prevent our thinking of the newly redefined space in such terms, insofar as laying out churches in the form of crosses is redolent of Byzantium or Rome. But these churches appear to respond actively

327

97. Debrecen, Great
Church, elevation as
actually built

and critically to the traditional Catholic layout, with a different arrangement that invites, perhaps even assumes, the drawing of comparisons.

Even though these buildings avoid lavishness and pretentiousness, their monumental facades and sheer scale may make them suspect as embodiments of the actual situation of the Hungarian Reformed church. In the rapidly growing cities of later nineteenth-century Hungary, Catholics and Jews may have poured more resources into their building programs, judging by the number and splendor of their edifices, but Calvinists were not exempt from a competitive mania. Much of the new construction sought conspicuousness without being very venturesome; it cultivated an air of respectability by producing ever grander versions of currently fashionable revival styles. Some critics were disturbed by the prevailing derivativeness and eclecticism, and particularly by its lack of any identifiably national character.

Measured against developments in western Europe, the literature,

328

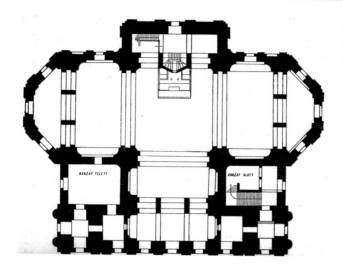

98. Debrecen, Great
Church, plan as
actually built

painting, and architecture of Budapest seemed distressingly belated and derivative. Such reflections stimulated a search for homegrown movements that could be nurtured and elaborated into an authentic national style. Unflattering comparisons with England, France, and Germany played a part, but so also did concerns closer to home: the desire, for example, to minimize dependence on Austria, and the wish to justify and reinforce Magyar hegemony over the various national minorities within Hungary, such as Slovaks, Romanians, Serbs, Croats, and Slovenians. Yet the search for cultural originality and authenticity was as much backward-looking as forward-looking: with their country undergoing rapid but uneven development, Hungarians scrutinized their past for bulwarks against modernity, traces of living at a more tolerable pace, on a more meaningful scale, to a more humane purpose, than seemed possible in contemporary factories and cities.

One phase of this process, linking the recovery of a usable past with the creation of significant new works, is familiar in the West through the activity of Bartók and Kodály in collecting folk music and reworking its traditional themes in new compositions. An analogous development took place in architecture. Even before the turn of the century there had been attempts, pioneered by Ödön Lechner (1845-1914), to adapt folk motifs to modern urban settings, but Lechner's experiments in this direction were largely confined to surface ornamentation. The results were colorful and exotic but had a mixed reception: when a critic referred to Lechner's Museum of Applied Art as the palace of the gypsy baron, these were by no means terms of praise but were meant to suggest tastelessness, garishness, and excess.

A few years later, however, a group of student architects aroused great interest with a series of designs evocative of the Reformed churches of seventeenth- and eighteenth-century Transylvania. The work of Károly Kós, Lajos Kozma, Dénes Györgyi (1886-1961), and Dezső Zrumeczky

329

(1883-1917) was published in a leading architectural monthly;[32] they and others in their circle were called upon, while still students, to design bookplates, book illustrations, and covers for major journals. The initial influence of these young architects was greatest through their graphic work, in which certain scenes are elaborated so as to become emblematic not only of Reformed architecture, or even of Transylvania, but of Hungarianness itself — motifs that seemed to capture what this generation thought of as most essential and most creditable to the national character.

If we ask why this earlier body of vernacular building and decoration should have inspired new work around the turn of the century, there are several answers. One has to do with an interest all over Europe in rediscovering (or inventing) distinctive national or regional styles. This concern was fostered by the aspirations of competing groups within the multidenominational and multinational European empires before World War I; by nostalgia for the supposed wholesomeness of a less urbanized, less industrialized society; and not least by world's fairs, which required participating countries to erect stylistically "authentic" national pavilions. Hungarian experimentation in a national style is by no means a unique response to these demands: the architecture of Sonck, Saarinen, and others in Finland at the turn of the century represents an analogous development, drawing on vernacular traditions to assert cultural independence from Russia, much as Hungary sought to distinguish itself from Austria.[33]

Another reason for a revival of this particular material was that amidst the stylistic-ideological contests of the day, motifs drawn from earlier Reformed church architecture enjoyed great rhetorical advantages, owing as much to the historical associations of Hungarian Calvinism as to purely aesthetic considerations. Whether or not Catholicism was compromised by the connection between the Counter-Reformation and Hapsburg power, there is no question that the Reformed church had long stood for Hungarian resistance to Austrian hegemony in political as well as religious spheres. Furthermore, it represented the most purely Magyar element in the population, both ethnically and linguistically: it had many fewer members of German, Slovak, Croat, or Slovene stock than the Catholic Church, and there was a much higher percentage of Hungarian monoglots in the Reformed church than in any other denomination. To outsiders these might not all seem matters to boast about, yet they help to explain why the

---

32. Béla Málnai, "A Fiatalok: Építészeti hallgatók kiállítása" (The youngsters: Architectural students' exhibition), *Magyar Építőművészet* (Hungarian architecture) (hereafter cited as *MÉ*) 6, no. 2 (1908): 21-26.

33. Hungarian interest in Finnish developments can be gauged by the entire number of *Magyar Iparművészet* (Hungarian applied art) (hereafter cited as *MI*) devoted to the subject (vol. 11, no. 1 [1908]: 1-56), and by the translation and publication of a 243-page, illustrated monograph, János Őhquist's *A Finnek Művészete Ős Időktől Maig* (The art of the Finns from primitive times to today) (Budapest, 1911).

Reformed church should have come to be thought of as the *Hungarian* church, and why motifs strongly associated with it, such as those discussed in this essay, should have taken on patriotic as well as artistic resonance.

Finally, Transylvanian Reformed church material lent itself to turn-of-the-century revival because it exemplified so fully the ideals of the international arts-and-crafts movement, as it had been developed most influentially through the writings and artistic practice of John Ruskin, William Morris, and Walter Crane, who were well known in Hungary.[34] The Ruskinian ethos need not be recapitulated here, beyond noting the insistence that ornament be the product of craftsmen who labor with zest and joy, free to improvise rather than executing totally prescribed tasks, and therefore liable to create objects that are technically imperfect but have character because they reveal some of the individuality of their makers.[35] It should by now be clear that the material under consideration richly fulfills Ruskin's requirements, and that young architects in Hungary sympathetic with his, Morris's, and Crane's aims naturally turned to it as a source and model for their own kindred efforts at cultural renewal.

Typical of their early work are many stylized renderings of the Reformed church in Magyarvalkó: among the more noteworthy are an etching of 1908 by Sándor Nagy (1869-1950) (see fig. 99), magazine covers of the same year by Károly Kós and Lajos Kozma (see fig. 100), and another Kós title page of the following year (see fig. 101).[36] The young architects' student exercises are similar in spirit: good instances are Dénes Györgyi's *Small Village Church* of 1907, a *Church and School* of 1908 by Valér Mende (1886-1918), and Dezső Zrumeczky's *Village Church and Minister's House* of 1909.[37] But their efforts

34. Walter Crane visited Hungary in 1900: there was a major exhibition of his work at the Museum of Applied Art, and an issue of *MI* consisted of articles by and about him (vol. 3, no. 4 [1900]: 149-208). The artist Aladár Kriesch published a book on Ruskin and the Pre-Raphaelites and wrote an essay on Morris and his reform endeavors in *MI* 9, no. 1 (1906): 15-20. For further discussion and references see Katalin Keserü, "Art Contacts between Great Britain and Hungary at the Turn of the Century," *Hungarian Studies* 6, no. 2 (1990): 141-54.

35. For the notion that ornament can express delight in God's work, see *The Works of John Ruskin*, ed. E. T. Cook and Alexander Wedderburn (London, 1903-12), 8:218; 9:70, 253, 264, 310, and passim.

36. Magyarvalkó continued to be a popular subject; among postwar engravings, see Debreczeni, pl. 28, and Kós's illustration from *Kalotaszeg* (Kolozsvár, 1932), reproduced in *Kós Károly Képes-Könyv* (Karoly Kos picture book), ed. Péter Sas (Budapest, 1985), p. 81. For photographic views of Magyarvalkó, cf. Péter P. Várady and Anikó Borbély, *Erdély Magyar Templomai: Kalotaszeg* (The Hungarian churches of Transylvania: Kalotaszeg) (Budapest, 1991), pl. 75; J. István Kováts, *Magyar Református Templomok* (Hungarian Reformed churches), 2 vols. (Budapest, 1942), 1:229; Ottó Szőnyi, *Régi Magyar Templomok* (Old Hungarian churches) (Budapest, n.d.), p. 136, figs. 215-16.

37. For Dénes Györgyi's small village church of 1907, see "A Fiatalok," *MÉ* 6, no. 2 (1908): 26; Valér Mende's project for a church and school is in "Fiatal Építészek" (Young architects), *MI* 11, no. 3 (1908): 117; Dezső Zrumeczky's village church and minister's house are in *A Ház* 2 (1909): 276.

99. Sándor Nagy,
Magyarvalkó cemetery,
1908, etching

were not confined to the graphic arts, or to projects on paper: they were able to build, and they were able to retain in the work they executed, much of the visionary (or perhaps merely fanciful) quality of their drawings. In their hands this mode is never a simple revival like those of the nineteenth century, but an imaginative attempt to invest recognizably modern buildings with powerful associations, drawn from the Transylvanian Reformed church repertory.

Among the resulting structures, the most striking is a church Aladár Árkay (1868-1932) did in Pest between 1911 and 1913.[38] The link with Kós and Kozma is clear in one of Árkay's sketches (see fig. 102); the actual

38. A detailed and well-illustrated account of this project is to be found in Péter Farbaky, "A Fasori Református Templom" (The Reformed church in the [Gorki, now Városligeti] Fasor), *Ars Hungarica* 12, no. 2 (1984): 255-69, pls. 31-56.

100. Lajos Kozma, Magyarvalkó, 1908, cover for journal *A Ház* (The house)

building, although on a grand scale and urbane in its interior layout and detailing, nevertheless plays up its vernacular heritage. The facade is strongly asymmetrical (unlike the interior); the tower is not detached but notably overscaled; the roof (and the exterior generally) is picturesquely incidented. The zones of iridescent ceramic tile around the main door employ motifs of folk derivation, but in abstracted, modernized versions, and in places where they never occur in earlier churches (see fig. 103 and plate 33). In other words, rather than seeking simply to reconstitute a prestigious past, Árkay's church ingeniously alludes to it.

A similar allusiveness can be found in other works that apply traditional idioms of rural religious architecture to modern, urban, secular purposes. In the case of a school in Buda that was one of Kós and Györgyi's early commissions, a stylistic vocabulary derived from old Transylvanian churches is drawn upon to make a large city school romantic and inviting rather than massive and forbidding. This adaptation of originally religious

333

101. Károly Kós,
Magyarvalkó, 1909,
cover for journal *A
Ház*

motifs to secular purposes is carried even further in work by Kós and
Zrumeczky that is contemporary with Árkay's church. Among their buildings for the Budapest zoo are a couple that brilliantly combine the new and
the old: thus the severe modern geometry of triangular clerestory windows
is akin in shape but remote in source and connotation from the central
steeple of the bird house (see fig. 104).[39] Nor were Kós and Zrumeczky being merely playful in transplanting such a form to such a setting; they set
themselves the serious task of exploring the kinds of intellectual and emotional resonance a familiar form can take on when lifted out of its ordinary
context and thrust into a different one. Both Árkay and the Kós/
Zrumeczky team are visually witty, but by no means frivolous or trifling.

39. Illustrations of various zoo buildings of 1909-13 are to be found in Pál Balázs, *Kós
Károly* (Budapest, 1983), figs. 10-20, and accompanying Kós's essay "Nemzeti Művészet"
(National art), *MI* 13, no. 3 (1910): 141-61.

334

102. Aladár Árkay, circa 1911, Pest church, sketch

The richness and adaptability of this style can be illustrated from the work of various architects who continued to draw on it for new Reformed churches up to World War II. Over the years Kós produced designs for various churches, but of those actually built the most important is probably the Kolozsvár church of 1912-13, where he effectively incorporates traditional materials and rustic motifs into modern urban spaces.[40] During the interwar period, a number of architects produced variants of this style; among the more interesting is a Buda church of 1929 by István Medgyaszay (1877-1959).[41] Although Bálint Szeghalmy (1889-1963) built six Re-

40. Attractive sketches for churches at Csucsa (1911) and Barót (1927) are reproduced in *Kós Károly Képes-Könyv,* pp. 34, 72; exterior views and interior details of the church in Kolozsvár are published by Pál Balázs in *Kós Károly,* fig. 34, and in *Kós Károly Képes-Könyv,* pp. 154, 40.

41. For illustrations, see Dercsényi et al., p. 123, figs. 344-45; for a description of the project, which included an adjacent apartment house on either side, see András Ferkai, *Buda*

103. Aladár Árkay,
1911-13, Pest church,
main entrance

formed churches in the 1930s, some of his work involves a certain confusion of idioms. His 1938 church at Miskolc is built of logs, as was once common in parts of Transylvania, but in Eastern Orthodox rather than Reformed churches; the pronounced longitudinal arrangement of its interior seems out of keeping with the Reformed service, and with most other Hungarian Reformed churches of all periods.[42]

Two other churches from the interwar period deserve mention, if only because both are in important Pest locations and depart markedly from the pattern I have been tracing. One stands in imposing isolation overlooking the Danube, on Pozsonyi út in Újlipótváros, and was built between 1936 and 1940 (see fig. 105).[43] The other, built in the same

Építészete a Két Világháború Között (The architecture of Buda between the two world wars) (Budapest, 1995), pp. 197-98. As a young man in 1904, Medgyaszay had made excellent drawings of Transylvanian churches such as those at Körösfő and Bánffyhunyad, reproduced in *MÉ* 7, no. 5 (1909): 9; and 7, no. 4 (1909): 13. His career is surveyed in Imre Kathy, *Medgyaszay István* (Budapest, 1979).

42. Szeghalmy's Miskolc church is illustrated in Dercsényi et al., pp. 78-79, figs. 225-31; for documentation on his other churches of the 1930s, see János Gerle, Attila Kovács, and Imre Makovecz, *A Századforduló Magyar Építészete* (Turn-of-the-century Hungarian architecture) (Budapest, 1990), p. 185.

43. The architects were Imre Tóth and Jenő Halászy; see Nóra Pamer, *Magyar Építészet a két Világháború között* (Hungarian architecture between the two world wars) (Budapest, 1986), pp. 147, 155.

104. Károly Kós and Dezső Zrumeczky, 1910, bird house, Budapest Zoo, sketch

years and also large but less monumental, stands at the edge of Szabadság tér with the National Bank and the former Stock Exchange among its more grandiose neighbors (see fig. 106).[44] The first uses an arcade to yoke its modern tower to a massive neoclassical block, which has less in common with Hungarian neoclassical precedents, such as the Great Church of Debrecen, than with contemporary work in Rome and Berlin. The other church, which at first glance might be mistaken for an upscale office or apartment building, combines well-thought-out modern spaces with handsome traditional detail in its interior. It is in fact a more interesting building than the other, in part because it is more in keeping with Calvinist tradition, paradoxical as this may sound. As a very contemporary structure, vernacular yet dignified, it stands in a relation to the surrounding community which Reformed churches have always sought: not set apart by any supposedly sacred character, yet possessing an air, at once concentrated and composed, of attending to people's vital concerns.

*   *   *

This essay has touched on many but by no means all of the artistic media and genres that have found a place in and around Hungarian Reformed churches during the past four centuries. Nothing has been said about the

44. The architects were József Győri and Gyula Halász; the interior was by Karoly Bodon. See Antal Kampis, "A Szabadságtéri református templom" (The Freedom Square Reformed Church), *MI* 43 (1941): 109-16, with good interior photographs. Pamer (p. 147) assigns this work to *Géza* Halász and *Sándor* Győri.

105. Imre Tóth and Jenő Halászy, 1936-40, Pest church, Pozsonyi út

cups and plates used in the Lord's Supper, although a number of such vessels survive from the seventeenth and eighteenth centuries and have been well documented, both in the large-scale surveys of historical monuments published since World War II and in more specialized monographs.[45] Nothing has been said about the physical appearance of books published by or for members of the Reformed church, or about the vigorous if homely manuscript illustrations found in eighteenth- and nineteenth-century Reformed documents such as parish registers, in which the human figure appears to be more common than in the decoration of churches,

45. Ida Bobrovszky provides a well-illustrated analysis of much of this material in *A XVII. századi mezővárosok iparművészete (Kecskemét, Nagykőrös, Debrecen)* (The applied art of seventeenth-century country towns [Kecskemét, Nagykőrös, Debrecen]) (Budapest, 1980). Reformed church plate from other parts of the country is catalogued and illustrated in surveys of the historical monuments of various counties, such as *Szabolcs-Szatmár Megye Műemlékei* (Historical monuments of Szabolcs-Szatmar County), ed. Géza Entz (vols. 10-11 of *Magyarország Műemlékei Topográfiája* [Topography of Hungary's historical monuments], ed. Dezső Dercsényi), 2 vols. (Budapest, 1986-87), 1:106, 222, 379, 402, 410; 2:26 and passim.

106. József Györi
and Gyula Halász,
1936-40, Pest church,
Szabadság tér

where it is rare.[46] Nor has much been said about Reformed churches erected in the late baroque style of the eighteenth century or the Gothic-revival styles of the nineteenth century: some of these churches are attractive, but they are examples of building types that do not originate in the Reformed church, are not peculiar to it, and are not especially well adapted to its requirements. For the same reason, discussion of Reformed churches in the neoclassical style has focused largely on the transverse plans of some of them, because these have proved ideally suited to the structure of the Reformed service; less has been said about the restrained decor of such churches, partly because this was the tendency of neoclassical Catholic churches as well, and partly because such restraint has not in fact been characteristic of Reformed church interiors before or since. A certain austerity has no doubt been an important feature of traditional Hungarian

46. For charming specimens of watercolor illustrations from title pages of early eighteenth-century parish registers, see *Szolnok Megye Népművészete* (Folk art of Szolnok County), ed. Tibor Bellon and László Szabó (Budapest, 1987), figs. 134-39.

339

Calvinism, and has found expression in political as well as moral and spiritual rigorousness. But far from eschewing church decoration as a threat to the decorum or discipline of a godly community, the Reformed church has preferred colorful profusion to drab sparseness, celebrating (and in the process adding to) the plenitude of creation.

NETHERLANDS

Calvinism and the Emergence of Dutch Seventeenth-Century Landscape Art — A Critical Evaluation

REINDERT L. FALKENBURG

Conventional wisdom holds that during the first decades of the seventeenth century landscape art in the northern Netherlands developed into a genre with a marked indigenous character that differed radically from earlier landscape art. It was especially in Haarlem that between 1615 and 1630 a group of talented young artists — among them Claes Jansz. Visscher (1586-1652), Esaias van de Velde (1590-1630), Jan van de Velde II (1593-1641), Pieter Molijn (1595-1661), Jan van Goyen (1596-1656), and Salomon van Ruysdael (1600/1603-1670) — turned away from the traditional mosaic-like idiom of sixteenth-century Flemish landscape art and developed a manner of landscape printing and painting that is generally called "realistic." The older idiom has often, rather negatively, been dubbed "mannerist," in order to denote the highly faceted, heavily detailed, and rather stereotypical compositions produced by landscapists such as Joachim Patinir (ca. 1485-1524), Herri met de Bles (active ca. 1530-60), and their followers (see fig. 107). Among the refugees from the southern Netherlands who had fled Antwerp after the conquest of the city by the Spanish in 1585, several artists settled in Amsterdam in the beginning of the seventeenth century, where they continued the Flemish manner. Among them were Gillis van Coninxloo (1544-1607) (see fig. 108) and David Vinckboons (1576–ca. 1632). Other, younger artists belonging to the generation of Esaias van de Velde and Jan van Goyen

---

I would like to express my gratitude to Sam Herman and Gerbrand Kotting for their assistance in the preparation of this article.

107. Joachim Patinir, *Landscape with St. Jerome,* Paris, Musée du Louvre

(see fig. 109) — some of them (sons of) refugees — moved to Haarlem and around 1615 started to produce a new landscape idiom based on the direct observation of the natural surroundings of their new habitat. Compared to the earlier Flemish landscape manner, landscape prints and paintings in this new manner offered a higher degree of compositional and spatial unity, an attunement of color values in an overall atmospheric tonality, more austerity in the use of narrative details (especially in the depiction of the human staffage), and the sense that the image had been made from the artist's first-hand impression of nature.

This is the standard view of the rise of realistic Dutch seventeenth-century landscape painting and printmaking, which dates back to the nineteenth century.[1] Also conventional is the belief that this realistic genre reflects a new, secularized interest in nature and in the aesthetic qualities of the world as it presents itself to the eye. This, it has been suggested, is why during the first decades of the seventeenth century the new Dutch landscape idiom abandoned the biblical or allegorical staffage of sixteenth-century Flemish landscape painting and freed landscape of all religious and literary content. As a result, for the first time in Western art history, landscape became an autonomous genre, portrayed for its own sake, i.e., expressing the personal "feeling" or "mood" of the artist for nature.

It is only in recent years that the latter part of this view has been challenged. In 1982 the Dutch art historian Maarten de Klijn remarked that it

1. Cf. Stechow 1966; Briels 1987, chap. X.

344

108. Gillis van Coninxloo, *Landscape with the Prophet Elias,* Brussels, Musées Royaux des Beaux-Arts de Belgique

was not a secular "l'art-pour-l'art" mentality that determined the rise of a realistic landscape genre in Dutch seventeenth-century art, but, on the contrary, Calvinism.[2] According to de Klijn Calvinism in the sixteenth and seventeenth centuries viewed nature, i.e., Creation, as the "second book" of God (the Bible being the other book), reflecting the omnipotence, wisdom, goodness, and grace of God. Nature should, therefore, be studied and praised as a manifestation of the beauty and reflection of the godly order since its fruits may be enjoyed and properly used for the needs of man. Calvin himself, in his *Institution de la Religion Chrestienne* (Geneva, 1545), had already licensed the depiction of landscape — "animals, towns, countryside" — as an innocent subject that "serves purely for pleasure."[3] Therefore, landscape was a perfect subject for a Protestant painter. De Klijn relates, accordingly, the rise of realistic landscape painting during the first decades of the seventeenth century directly to the theocentric view of nature in the emerging Calvinist culture of the northern Netherlands. Not only does the general

2. De Klijn 1982.

3. J. Calvin, *Institution de la Religion Chrestienne* (Geneva, 1545), vol. I, chap. XI, para. 12 (ed. J.-D. Benoit [Paris, 1957], p. 135): "Quant à ce qui est licite de peindre ou engraver, il y a les histoires pour en avoir mémorial, ou bien figures, ou médales de *bestes, ou villes, ou pais.* Les histoires peuvent profiter de quelque advertissement ou souvenance qu'on en prend; touchant du reste, ie ne voy point à quoy il serve, sinon à plaisir" (my italics).

345

109. Jan van Goyen, *Village near the Beach*, 1631, Carcassonne, Musée des Beaux-Arts

interest in and exploration of visual reality in early Dutch landscape art originate from Calvinist thinking, so too, and more specifically, does the change in pictorial idiom from "mannerism" to "realism" in the works by (Reformed) artists such as Gillis van Coninxloo and Esaias van de Velde. Fidelity to nature, naturalness in the rendering of space, atmospheric and compositional unity, the reduction of the dimensions of the human staffage and its integration in the landscape, a coherent color palette: these are the values which de Klijn links with a Calvinist view of the world and which he contrasts with mannerist landscape conventions.[4] This becomes explicit in de Klijn's description of Esaias van de Velde's *Landscape with a Ferry* (1622) in the Amsterdam Rijksmuseum (see fig. 110):

> Here is no interesting sum of details, no mythological or biblical story which needs to be illustrated, no fantasy and no dream which has to compensate for the lack or loss of literary subject matter; here is a synthesis of reality, as it appears in actual daily life — a reality which is characterized by inner peace and contented industry. This is a landscape in which it is a blessing for man to stray, a pleasure for his eyes — and perhaps even a place that reflects God's grace.[5]

4. De Klijn 1982, pp. 49ff. — hereby implying that mannerist landscape painting was non-Calvinist.
5. De Klijn 1982, p. 53 (my, rather paraphrased, translation).

346

This view formed the basis in a recent article by Boudewijn Bakker for an interpretation of a series of landscape prints made in the 1610s by Claes Jansz. Visscher (1586-1652) which are generally considered to be crucial for the rise of the realistic Dutch landscape idiom.[6] Visscher was an active member of the Reformed church and a prolific printmaker, specializing in, among other things, cartographic, topographic, and emblematic depictions of the new Dutch Republic. According to Bakker, Visscher's landscape prints, along with his interest in topography and cartography, can be seen as expressions of his desire to study Creation, the "book of nature," directly from life ("naar het leven").

Around 1612 Visscher issued a series of twelve landscape etchings depicting the surroundings of Haarlem which are based on drawings, made from life about 1607. The title page shows an emblematic picture of the city arms of Haarlem against the background of a sun-lit dune landscape (see fig. 111). The sun itself, in the upper-left corner of the print, contains the Hebrew signs for JHWH. Bakker explained this image of the name of God as a reference to the "Sun of Salvation," the Creator and Lord of heaven and earth, which shines over Haarlem and bestows on the city the light of His grace.[7] The next — also introductory — print (see fig. 112) shows a coastal view, seen through the opening of a stone niche portraying

110. Esaias van de Velde, *Landscape with a Ferry,* 1622, Amsterdam, Rijksmuseum

6. Bakker 1993.
7. Bakker 1993, pp. 103, 110.

347

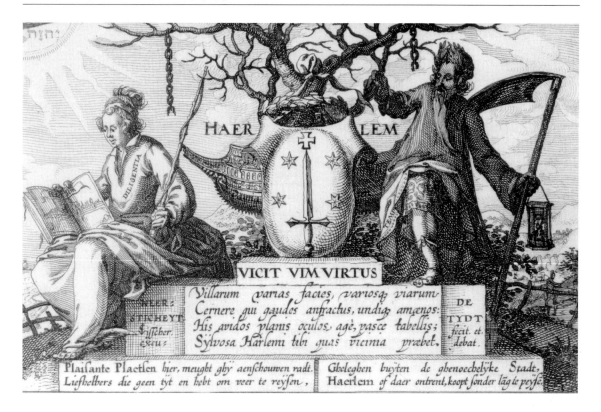

111. Claes Jansz. Visscher, title print from the print series *Plaisante plaetsen* (ca. 1612), Amsterdam, Rijksprentenkabinet

on the bottom slab a variety of objects used in artistic professions (including books; writing, etching and painting utensils; and a map). Among the etching utensils is a plate or sheet revealing the contours of a church; discernible in the coastal scene in the background are a group of fishermen. In Bakker's view these details have a symbolic value, referring to the name and the profession of the artist (*Visscher* = fisherman) as well as to his piety and his artistic ambition to render nature as God's Creation.

Bakker argues that there is a second element to this religious program which is revealed on the title page and the tablature under the niche in this second print. Here the artist has included a few lines in Latin and Dutch, which refer to the pleasure which the series will give to the eye of the beholder who has no time to actually travel and enumerate the names of the "pleasant spots" (*Plaisante plaetsen*) rendered in the following twelve landscape prints.[8] Bakker interprets these texts as an expression of

8. The Latin text runs: "Villarum varias facies, variosque viarum/Cernere qui gaudes anfractus, undique amoenos:/His avidos planis oculos, agè, pasce tabellis;/Sijlvosa Harlemi tibi quas vicinia praebet." The Dutch lines read: "Plaisante Plaetsen hier, meught ghij aenschouwen radt./Liefhebbers die geen tijt en hebt om veer te reijsen,/Gheleghen buijten de ghenoechelijke Stadt,/Haerlem of daer ontrent, koopt sonder lang te peijsen." De Groot 1979, sub fig. 23, gives as a translation for the Latin text: "You who enjoy the varied view of country houses and the surprising turns in ever delightful roads: come, let your eager eye roam these

NAMEN DER VOLGEN

t'Amsterdam, Gedrukt, by
Klaes Ianſſ Viſſcher wonede inde
Kalverſtraet inde Viſſcher

DE LANDTSCHAPIENS

2. Vierbake t'Sandtvoordt.
3. Sandtvoordt.
4. Paters herbergh.
5. Potjes herbergh.
6. Aende Wegh na Leyden.
7. Onder wegen Heemſtee.
8. Blekeryen door den Houdt.
9. Laſery van Haerlem.
10. Plaiſante plaets aёde duy kāt.
11. Blekeryé aёde duyne gelegen.

12. t'Huys te Kleef.

Visscher's "Calvinist" cartographic interests in the surroundings of Haarlem and an allusion to the theme of wandering (with the eye) through God's Creation.

Bakker contrasts his interpretation with the opinions of two other researchers who have recently discussed the intellectual content of Dutch seventeenth-century landscape art. He cites with approval the 1980 study by David Freedberg, who first suggested the idea of Dutch landscape prints as a pleasant playground for viewers to wander with their eyes through depictions of nature.[9] Bakker criticizes Freedberg, however, for playing down the interrelation between the aesthetic enjoyment and the religious contemplation of nature.[10] He also cites Bruyn's thesis of a fundamentally "scriptural" reading of Dutch seventeenth-century landscape painting, which Bruyn based on the popularity, especially in pietistic circles, of the

112. Claes Jansz. Visscher, *Beacon-Light near Zandvoort*, no. 2 from the print series *Plaisante plaetsen*, Amsterdam, Rijksprentenkabinet.

open vistas offered by the sylvan surroundings of Haarlem" — and for the Dutch text: "The pleasant spots here you can contemplate with ease, devotees who have no time to travel far. Situated outside the agreeable city of Haarlem or thereabouts. Buy without thinking for long."

9. Freedberg 1980.
10. Cf. Bakker 1993, pp. 111-12 (and n. 34), and Freedberg 1980, pp. 14-15.

113. Jan van Goyen, *Landscape with Dilapidated Farmhouse*, 1632, Hamburg, Kunsthalle

allegory of the pilgrimage of life through this sinful world.[11] According to Bruyn, this allegory is the main theme of Dutch seventeenth-century landscape art, as expressed in the often recurrent motif of a wanderer who seems to be heading for a distant church or castle, or halting at a roadside chapel. He symbolizes the true pilgrim who ignores the temptations of this sinful world and heads for the heavenly Jerusalem. These temptations and the sheer vanity and idleness of earthly existence are symbolized by ruins, barren trees, waterfalls, taverns, dilapidated houses, and peasants who laze away the day (see fig. 113). Bakker criticizes this interpretation, among other things because it implies a negative view of the world and its pleasures. Bakker claims that, on the contrary, Calvinist artists such as Visscher, but also other Dutch landscape painters and printmakers, are singing songs of praise of the Lord and His Creation. Their landscapes show a positive approach toward nature and the pleasures it offers to the eye.

Although Bakker and Bruyn fundamentally differ on this point, they agree that Dutch seventeenth-century landscape art reflects a basically reli-

11. Bruyn 1987/88, following Wiegand 1971 and Raupp 1980.

350

gious worldview. I would like here to give a short critical assessment of this idea, more especially of the suggested relation between Calvinism and the rise of realistic Dutch landscape painting and printmaking in the first decades of the seventeenth century. I shall discuss a few prints and paintings by Claes Jansz. Visscher, Esaias van de Velde, and Jan van Goyen in some detail in order to test the validity of the arguments of de Klijn, Bakker, and Bruyn. In addition, I shall comment on the — rather limited — possibilities of identifying one specific denomination as the underlying force behind the rise of the realistic Dutch landscape idiom. In conclusion I shall offer some suggestions for further research in this matter, concentrating on the meaning and function of the human staffage in early Dutch landscape.

Let us start by taking a closer look at Visscher's print series of *Plaisante plaetsen*. Following the introductory lines on the title page of the series,[12] there can be little doubt that the primary function of the prints was to please the eye of the viewer with characteristic scenes of the country around Haarlem. As Bakker and others have pointed out,[13] people would often take a stroll outside the city walls, as contemporary literary witnesses testify. Many of these poems and songs refer to the pleasures offered by these surroundings as an interplay of stimuli for different senses. Not only does nature delight the senses of sight and smell, for example by the beauty of trees and the sweet smells of flowers, but the sense of touch too. Often these writings refer to the amorous activities of young people in the woods and fields. The countryside near the "Huys te Kleef" was a well-known spot for lovers taking a walk, merry companies riding in a cart, and other tourists taking a day off from work.[14] It is this spot which is depicted in the last print of Visscher's series of *Plaisante plaetsen* (see fig. 114). The staffage in this print conforms exactly with the tourists and amorous adventurers in these contemporary songs and poems — among them a couple walking in the ruins to the left and a charabanc with day-trippers towards the right. Another print, *Potje's Inn* (see fig. 115), contains the same figure types: a pair of lovers, a woman leaving the inn with a jug in her hands, and a couple making their way into a cornfield in order to make love.

Whereas the pleasurable aspect of these activities is readily apparent, the idea that they are an expression of a Calvinist outlook on the world is rather less evident. To my mind the kind of pleasure which is offered to an eye sensitive to the beauty of the countryside is of a very different, i.e., aesthetic, order than the worldly pleasures which are depicted by Visscher — I even suspect that the latter are rather at odds with Calvinist ethics. These

12. Cf. n. 8.
13. See also Leeflang 1993.
14. Leeflang 1993, pp. 29-32.

114. Claes Jansz.
Visscher, *Kleef Manor*,
no. 12 from the print
series *Plaisante plaetsen*,
Amsterdam,
Rijksprentenkabinet

activities do not seem to be attempting to arouse admiration and praise for
the Lord and His Creation. On the contrary, strict Calvinists would probably have associated them with the Fall of man.

Does this prove that Calvinist thinking has no bearing on Visscher's
landscape prints at all? No, but it puts Bakker's interpretation into perspective. If there is any relation between this series and Calvinist thought,
it is certainly not direct; one should not approach these prints from the
perspective of Calvinist dogma, as a theologian might do. Although
Visscher's interest in the natural surroundings of Haarlem may have been
based on a personal (Calvinist) view of nature as the second book of God,
the semantic value of his staffage figures certainly points in a different direction, where religious connotations seem to be absent.

In a recent publication Huygen Leeflang reinterpreted Visscher's series to show that Calvinist thought and allusions to amorous activities are
only two of several possible associations which these series may have en-
gendered in a contemporary audience.[15] In his approach Leeflang follows
the "association method" of Haverkamp-Begemann and Chong, who argued that one should investigate the whole range of semantic relations
which the public may have attached to landscape images, instead of focus-

15. Leeflang 1993.

352

ing on a single meaning that an artist may have wished to communicate programmatically to his audience.[16] This implies a shift from production-focused to reception-focused analysis of meaning. Although I have criticized the "association method" in the past,[17] I have come to realize its usefulness in analyzing the frame of reference — the general reception "attitude" — of the audience of landscapes, especially if one takes into account ideas about reception theory that were developed in the 1970s by literary historians in Germany.[18] In the light of these ideas it appears that pictorial content, in a landscape painting or print which is not dependent on literary iconographic conventions but which is primarily based on visual reality, is not something which is inherently fixed in the image but consists of a "field" of semantic potential which is "triggered" by the image as well as by the expectations and experiences of the audience. Depending on the cultural background and the experience of (looking at) art of the individual viewer, each "act" of reception and interpretation realizes only part of the total semantic potential of the image.

One cannot decide, therefore, on the basis of Visscher's landscape

115. Claes Jansz. Visscher, *Potjes Inn*, no. 5 from the print series *Plaisante plaetsen*, Amsterdam, Rijksprentenkabinet

16. Haverkamp-Begemann and Chong 1985.
17. Falkenburg 1989.
18. Cf. Jauss 1970 and Iser 1972.

353

116. Claes Jansz. Visscher, *The Lepers' Asylum near Haarlem,* no. 9 from the print series *Plaisante plaetsen,* Amsterdam, Rijksprentenkabinet

prints alone, whether an impetus to praise the Lord of Creation will have prevailed over other thoughts and associations that may have arisen in the minds of seventeenth-century viewers. It follows, then, that it is not possible to show, as Haverkamp-Begemann, Chong, Schama, and others have suggested, that a positive, secular attitude toward nature, or feelings of pride in the new Republic and its economic prosperity, were the dominant associations in the minds of the artist's public.[19] But neither can one say with any certainty that religious thoughts, whether relating to the sinfulness and vanity of the world or to visual reality as a mirror of the omnipotence of the Lord, prevailed in their perception of these landscapes.

Even in the individual motif and the individual print there is no way of determining what triggers a particular association and the possible order of precedence of any such associations. *The Lepers' Asylum near Haarlem* (see fig. 116), for example, which shows the inmates wandering around, seems to defy any sense of *Plaisante plaetsen* or glorification of God at all. Is it the stag hunt which is the dominant factor in evoking associations in a *Pleasant Spot near the Dunes* (see fig. 117), or are these primarily determined by the (to my eyes rather nondescript) geography and vegetation of the spot? What is the value in this context of the small rabbits to the right, and what

19. Cf. Haverkamp-Begemann and Chong 1985; and Schama 1987/88.

354

about the two equestrians, the lonely wanderer, the person resting, and the peasants working in the field? There seem to be reasonable grounds for suspecting certain amorous connotations in the day-trippers in some of Visscher's *Plaisante plaetsen*. But are we justified in thinking that these or other connotations came to mind each time travelers are depicted — notice, for example, the tiny carriage in the back of the village in the *Zandvoort* print (see fig. 118)? How unspecific can a motif be and yet still evoke definable associations? How are we to decide whether the motif of a man urinating in the *Potje's Inn* (see fig. 115) may have evoked, or enhanced, thoughts of indecent behavior in the mind of a — perhaps religious, perhaps Calvinist — onlooker and/or may have evoked a feeling of license? We could refer, in this case, to the pictorial tradition of urinating and defecating men in sixteenth-century Flemish landscape paintings.[20] These figures have their antecedents in a repertoire of motifs portraying the "world turned upside down" in marginal decorations of late medieval manuscript painting.[21] In this tradition men urinating and defecating have a negative connotation with sinful and antisocial behavior. We do not know, however, whether Visscher referred to this tradition programmati-

117. Claes Jansz. Visscher, *Pleasant Spot near the Dunes,* no. 10 from the print series *Plaisante plaetsen,* Amsterdam, Rijksprentenkabinet

20. Falkenburg 1988, p. 99.
21. Falkenburg 1994; Falkenburg 1998.

355

118. Claes Jansz. Visscher, *Zandvoort*, no. 3 from the print series *Plaisante plaetsen*, Amsterdam, Rijksprentenkabinet

cally, and if so, how he wanted his audience to relate it to the other motifs in the image.

I am inclined to conclude that the lack of thematic specification is no accident, and that the semantic openness of the prints is programmatic. There is a clue to this in the Latin text on the title page — it reads: "You who enjoy the varied view of country houses and the surprising turns in ever delightful roads: come, let your eager eye roam these open vistas offered by the sylvan surroundings of Haarlem."[22] Variety, surprising views, and an eager eye; these are the key terms which suggest the state of mind of a traveler exploring the countryside for the unexpected. If Visscher had wanted to anticipate this state of mind with his designs as well, he could have done so by deliberately creating a high degree of semantic indeterminacy in various individual motifs. This does not mean, as will be clear by now, that he has left his audience without any guide in the title page about the directions in which to look for associations. A feeling of "pride of place" (Schama) is only one *aegis* among many under which viewers may set out on their visual journey through the landscape, as is the benign presence of the Lord, indicated by the symbol of His Name. But there is no compelling reason for identifying the word JHWH exclusively with a Calvinist pictorial program.

22. Cf. n. 8.

356

One element in Visscher's prints defies one of the postulates of de Klijn regarding the difference between the new realistic landscape idiom and earlier mannerist landscape conventions. This is the supposed insignificance, in the new idiom, of the individual motif, integrated as it is in the compositional and spatial unity of the landscape as a whole. It is interesting that a tiny detail such as the carriage in the background of the *Zandvoort* print (see fig. 118) is only found if one allows the eye to roam eagerly in the spirit of the text on the title page of this series. The existence of motifs such as these in Visscher's series undermines the "holistic" concept of visual reality which lies at the heart of de Klijn's thesis. This concept is governed by formal characteristics such as spatial unity, clarity of compositional arrangement, the reduction and visual merging of ("mannerist") narrative details, especially of the staffage, in the landscape as a whole. Since these characteristics are related to a Calvinist view of nature as the well-structured, orderly Creation of the Lord, it is much harder than de Klijn assumed to associate early seventeenth-century Dutch landscape art with Calvinist influence, if this art continues to show the "mannerist" characteristics it is supposed to have overcome. As I have argued elsewhere, many seventeenth-century Dutch landscape paintings continued to show tiny narrative details, which lie concealed in the background of the landscape or in the margins of the composition.[23] These would encourage a specific way of looking at a painting: one which stimulates the viewer to look for interesting vistas and individual motifs with specific semantic values in the countryside depicted. This weakens de Klijn's thesis — at least in the way he has formulated it — as does the fact that de Klijn relies entirely on an aesthetic conception of landscape art which had already been defined in the nineteenth century as being rooted in a postmedieval, secularized "Weltanschauung."[24]

It is also necessary to analyze de Klijn's premise in more general terms, that it was primarily Calvinist artists who developed the new realism in landscape art. It appears that painters only rarely felt that their denomination urged them to paint exclusively "religiously correct" subjects. An example is perhaps the Calvinist Jan Victors, who refused to paint God the Father and Christ.[25] Generally, Protestant artists worked equally for a Catholic audience and vice versa, and were willing to depict subjects which were frowned on in their own denominational iconography.[26] Protestant artists illustrated Catholic Bibles, just as Catholics produced illustrations for Protestant Bibles.[27] This lack of denominational dogmata in artistic matters is also true of the Calvinist Esaias van de Velde, who, in addition

---

23. Falkenburg 1989, pp. 143ff.; cf. Falkenburg 1998.
24. Cf. Falkenburg 1988, pp. 2ff.
25. Manuth 1993/94.
26. Tümpel 1991; Pastoor 1991.
27. Cf. Van der Coelen 1991.

to many landscapes, painted a number of church interiors, some of which unmistakably show Catholic themes such as a priest saying mass.[28] The same is true of the Calvinist painter Gillis van Coninxloo. Some of his landscapes show stories from Scripture, for example, stories from the lives of Old Testament prophets (see fig. 108), which are iconographic novelties and seem to point to a personal, Calvinist predilection for certain themes. There is even a landscape with the story of the Good Samaritan, attributed to van Coninxloo, which shows the indifferent priest who passes by the wounded traveler, dressed as a Roman Catholic priest — a downright anti-Catholic image.[29] Other landscapes by van Coninxloo, however, incorporate religious staffage which can only be imagined as being favored in a Catholic *milieu,* such as landscapes with the temptation of Saint Anthony, or Saint Anthony and Saint Paul in the desert.[30] Jan van Goyen, on the other hand, the most prolific propagator of the new realism, appears to have been a Catholic;[31] yet he never seems to have painted a single religious figure in the more than 1,200 landscapes that are known. This leads to the conclusion that, generally, the rise of the new idiom in Dutch seventeenth-century landscape is not specifically connected with the religious convictions of the artist. But what about the religious ideas of the audience?

Study of Delft and Amsterdam inventories from the period 1620-79 has led Montias to the conclusion that, generally, there was an equal preference for landscapes in Roman Catholic and in Protestant households of modest financial means.[32] In wealthier households, however, the number of landscapes owned by Protestants during the period 1620-49 was twice as high as the number owned by Catholics. In the period 1650-79 interest in landscapes among Catholics grew and almost reached the level of the numbers owned by Protestants, who appear to have retained a constant appetite for landscapes throughout the century. Catholics owned a higher proportion of religious pictures than Protestants. Moreover, during the first half (especially the first decades) of the seventeenth century the market was, quantitatively, dominated by the enormous output of realistic landscape paintings by artists such as Esaias van de Velde, Jan van Goyen, Pieter Molijn, and Salomon van Ruysdael; these pictures fetched comparatively low prices.[33] Although artists had developed greater stylistic and thematic variation by 1645, a general tendency emerged toward a more refined style of landscape painting, including the "Italianate" idiom of painters such as Jan Asselijn (ca. 1615-52), Jan Both (ca. 1618-52),

28. Keyes 1984, pp. 94-95.
29. Sale cat. Sotheby's, London, 13 November 1968, no. 83.
30. See Briels 1987, fig. 435.
31. Cf. Beck 1972, p. 17 n. 2.
32. Montias 1991.
33. Cf. Chong 1987/88.

358

Nicolaes Berchem (1620-83), and Adam Pijnacker (ca. 1620-73) — see figure 119. Works in this refined fashion, although fewer in number, fetched higher prices than those in the indigenous mode and were collected by wealthier persons.

119. Jan Both, *Italian Landscape*, Kopenhagen, Statens Museum for Kunst

　　These facts may be explained in several ways. One possibility is that Protestants were indeed more open to realistic landscape painting than Catholics because of its appeal to a Calvinist view of nature as the "second book of God." Or perhaps Protestants were more open to landscape, regardless of its mode or idiom, because it was a relatively new genre which had no ties with traditional Catholic belief and iconography. Catholics, on the other hand, may have been less open to the new genre because their needs could still be easily fulfilled by traditional iconography. If well-to-do, they may not have been keen to buy an art form which, judging from the low prices fetched by landscapes in the realistic "tonal" mode, may have been considered of modest artistic quality. In addition, the rise in interest in landscape among Catholics after 1650 may have been caused by a growing "Salonfähigkeit" of landscape art (made in the more polished style), which could now be collected for primarily aesthetic reasons — or there may have been other reasons as well, beyond our present understanding.

359

In any case, one should never be too hasty in jumping to general conclusions regarding a direct connection between the religious convictions of people buying landscapes in the first decennia of the seventeenth century and the emergence of the new realistic idiom. The historian Spaans has shown that around 1620, i.e., during the period in which the new landscape idiom crystallized in the work of Esaias van de Velde, Pieter Molijn, Jan van Goyen, and other artists active in Haarlem, only a fifth of the city's inhabitants were members of the Reformed church, 14 percent were Anabaptist, 12.5 percent Catholic, 1 percent Lutheran, and 1 percent Walloon Reformed; at least half the population had no specific denominational ties.[34] In the first place, these figures put Montias's statistics into perspective: focusing on Protestant and Catholic art owners, those statistics appear to relate to the denominational affiliations of only a minority of the population. Moreover, these figures show that it is unlikely, from an economic point of view, that landscape artists created their new idiom with an especially Calvinist audience in mind: if they were to have done so, they would have rigorously and willfully reduced their sales potential. On the contrary, the fact that these artists began to serve a large anonymous market so soon and successfully and stopped depicting religious stories as staffage, may point to a conscious avoidance of possible denominational associations in their landscapes.

If one were to explore possible connections between Calvinism and the rise and spread of realistic landscape painting in the northern Netherlands, one obvious focus of attention would be the evolutionary process along which the predominantly religious iconography of the staffage in sixteenth-century landscapes gave way to the semantic openness of seventeenth-century landscapes in the realistic idiom. If we are to assume that this idiom was related in a particular way to Calvinist convictions, this hypothesis has to answer the objection that of all the narrative details, the religious staffage, which could have been so useful in expressing Calvinist thought (as seems to have been the case in some paintings by van Coninxloo), was abandoned.

Since Bruyn's "scriptural reading" of Dutch seventeenth-century landscape art relies heavily on an allegorical interpretation of secular staffage figures and on the persistence of late medieval modes of pictorial expression into the seventeenth century, the continuity of meaning in pictorial traditions over long periods of time, which this hypothesis implies, deserves more thorough investigation. Here, however, matters do not look very promising, as two examples illustrate.

Jan van Goyen's *Landscape with a Village Scene* (1625), in Bremen (see fig. 120), shows a rowing boat in the foreground right, carrying a merry company including a man smoking a pipe, a lute player and a violin player,

34. Spaans 1989, esp. chap. 3.

360

120. Jan van Goyen, *Landscape with a Village Scene*, 1625, Bremen, Kunsthalle

a blind man and an amorous couple. These figures have been interpreted as personifications of the Five Senses.[35] Let us suppose that this interpretation is correct — correct not only in the sense that this is a reasonable reading on the part of the viewer, but also because this reading was programmed by the artist. These figures, then, allow the viewer to see the whole scene in the perspective of sensual pleasure — with all the (morally) negative associations that could feasibly accompany it. According to Raupp, the peasants on the left who are on their way to the market, laden with the produce of their labor, represent a positive alternative: the "vita activa." Bruyn, on the other hand, referring to Raupp's own reading of sixteenth-century prints of peasants symbolizing sinful behavior, interprets the peasants in van Goyen's landscape as negative types. Whatever the "correct" reading, this example clearly shows that pictorial traditions do not produce standardized readings and do not, by themselves, allow interpretations along lines of "fixed" meaning during long periods of time.

An example of an apparent change of meaning in a single, frequently recurring motif is the figure of a man standing on his hands.[36] This motif harks back to marginal illustrations in late medieval manuscript painting, in which it symbolizes the topsy-turvy world. It occurs again with a similar

35. Raupp 1980, pp. 101-2; Bruyn 1994, pp. 71-73.
36. Cf. Falkenburg 1994, pp. 185ff.; and Falkenburg 1998.

121. Anonymous sixteenth-century Antwerp artist, *Landscape with Moses and the Burning Bush,* Napels, Pinacoteca

meaning in sixteenth-century landscapes by Joachim Patinir and his followers, for example in an anonymous *Landscape with Moses and the Burning Bush* in Naples (see fig. 121). In this painting the figure of the man standing on his hands is combined with a cart with revelers from the city passing by. This figure underscores the purport of the main scene by way of exaggeration and opposition. Moses is shown removing his shoes on God's demand, because, as the Bible indicates (Exod. 3:5), the ground on which he stands is holy. The man standing on his hands, with his feet off the ground as well, echoes the sense of the biblical injunction, but, at the same time, parodies it. He turns Moses' gesture of respect into a jest. The fact that his performance is aimed at the passing day-trippers suggests that, in this context, their pastime has a pejorative connotation.

The same combination occurs in several landscapes by Esaias van de Velde, Jan van Goyen, and Salomon van Ruysdael. In the case of Esaias's

362

Landscape with the Abspoel Estate (1619) in Minneapolis (see fig. 122), it is an august company which, after leaving the estate for a ride, passes by a buffoon. Since one of the gentlemen is offering the humble family of the acrobat alms — and since there is no religious story that could offer an antipode to the man standing on his hands — there is no reason to suppose a moral opposition in the social disparity between the noble company and the troupe. Here, it seems, the buffoon is simply underscoring the pleasures which go along with a ride in the countryside. Even more "innocent" in meaning is the combination of a buffoon standing on his hands and an approaching merry company in a pleasure cart in landscapes by Jan van Goyen and Salomon van Ruysdael of 1646, 1648, and 1658.[37]

These examples suggest that, with the course of time, a "strong" reading of individual motifs as pictorial symbols for specific moral concepts seems to become less suitable than a "weak" reading of these motifs as pleasant narrative details. Taken as a whole, they seem to illustrate what has been called the "wearing out" of meaning in seventeenth-century realistic painting.[38] Perhaps the phrase "wearing out" is a little unfortunate — a growing tendency toward "semantic openness" might be more appropriate. This development is already manifest before 1620,

122. Esaias van de Velde, *Landscape with the Abspoel Estate*, 1619, Minneapolis, Minneapolis Institute of Art.

37. Beck 1973, cat. nos. 1153 and 1157; sale cat., Christie's, London, 7 July 1995, no. 42.

38. Cf. De Vries 1977.

123. Salomon van Ruysdael, *Landscape with the Pilgrims to Emmaus*, 1659, location unknown.

that is, even before the realistic idiom had fully crystallized in Dutch landscape painting and printmaking — Visscher's series are an example of this development. It is, therefore, unclear to me how this general tendency toward more "semantic openness," which manifests itself so early, connects with the supposedly predominant allegorical content of landscapes after 1620, and with the suggestion that specific Calvinist ideas were an important impulse for the rise of realistic landscape painting in the northern Netherlands.

I am therefore inclined to conclude that the development toward a realistic idiom and secular staffage in early seventeenth-century Dutch landscape is, as a general principle, not likely to be connected with a religious, and more specifically Calvinist, view of nature. In individual cases, however, a connection of this kind may have existed. If there is a chance of finding a more specific relation between individual landscape paintings and a specific denomination, pictures with a religious staffage are obviously the best candidates. Contrary to general belief, landscapes with a religious staffage continued to play a role in Dutch landscape painting well into the second

364

half of the seventeenth century, although it should be added that they formed only a small part of the total production. I have tried to make a case for eight landscapes by Salomon van Ruysdael (who was an Anabaptist himself), all showing the pilgrims to Emmaus (see fig. 123), by arguing that they were possibly connected with Anabaptist spirituality and interest in the Emmaus story as an example of the spiritual pilgrimage of life.[39] But whereas Salomon rarely painted any other religious story, Esaias van de Velde, for example, painted at least fifteen landscapes with religious staffage, twelve of them on different themes — five from the Old Testament; six from the New Testament; and one saint.[40] These simple figures already illustrate important differences among the first generation of painters of the realistic landscape idiom with respect to religious staffage. Indeed, Jan van Goyen never appears to have painted religious figures in his landscapes at all. An extensive and comparative investigation of the narrative content of the human figures, including the religious staffage, in landscapes by Esaias van de Velde, Jan van Goyen, Salomon van Ruysdael, and their fellow artists is required if speculations on the possible ties between certain landscapes and Calvinism, or other denominations, are to be substantiated in any way.

Literature

(Bakker 1993) — B. Bakker, "Levenspelgrimage of vrome wandeling? Claes Janszoon Visscher en zijn serie 'Plaisante Plaetsen,'" *Oud Holland* 107 (1993): 97-115.

(Beck 1972) — H.-U. Beck, *Jan van Goyen, 1596-1656. Ein Oeuvreverzeichnis,* I (Amsterdam, 1972).

(Beck 1973) — H.-U. Beck, *Jan van Goyen, 1596-1656. Ein Oeuvreverzeichnis,* II (Amsterdam, 1973).

(Briels 1987) — J. Briels, *Vlaamse schilders in de Noordelijke Nederlanden in het begin van de Gouden Eeuw, 1585-1630* (Antwerpen, 1987).

(Bruyn 1987/88) — J. Bruyn, "Toward a Scriptural Reading of Seventeenth-Century Dutch Landscape Painting," in P. C. Sutton et al., *Masters of Seventeenth-Century Dutch Landscape Painting* (Amsterdam-Boston-Philadelphia, 1987/88), pp. 84-103.

(Bruyn 1994) — J. Bruyn, "Le paysage hollandais du XVIIe siècle comme métaphore religieuse," in *Le paysage en Europe du XVIe au XVIIIe siècle. Actes du colloque organisé au musée du Louvre par le Service culturel du 25 au 27 janvier 1990* (Paris, 1994), pp. 67-88.

(Chong 1987/88) — A. Chong, "The Market for Landscape Painting in Sev-

39. Falkenburg 1990b.
40. Cf. Keyes 1984, pp. 119-23.

enteenth-Century Holland," in P. C. Sutton et al., *Masters of Seventeenth-Century Dutch Landscape Painting* (Amsterdam-Boston-Philadelphia, 1987/88), pp. 104-20.

(Van der Coelen 1991) — P. van der Coelen, "Thesauri en trezoren. Boeken en bundels met oudtestamentische prenten," in Chr. Tümpel et al., *Exh. cat. Het Oude Testament in de Schilderkunst van de Gouden Eeuw* (Zwolle-Amsterdam, 1991), pp. 168-93.

(Falkenburg 1988) — R. L. Falkenburg, *Joachim Patinir: Landscape as an Image of the Pilgrimage of Life* (Amsterdam-Philadelphia, 1988).

(Falkenburg 1989) — R. L. Falkenburg, "De betekenis van het geschilderde Hollandse landschap van de zeventiende eeuw: een beschouwing naar aanleiding van enkele recente interpretaties," *Theoretische geschiedenis* 16 (1989): 131-53.

(Falkenburg 1990a) — R. L. Falkenburg, "Antithetical Iconography in Early Netherlandish Landscape Painting," in exhibition catatogue *Bruegel and Netherlandish Landscape Painting from the National Gallery Prague* (Tokyo-Kyoto, 1990), pp. 25-36.

(Falkenburg 1990b) — R. L. Falkenburg, "Landschapschilderkunst en doperse spiritualiteit in de 17de eeuw — een connectie?" *Doopsgezinde Bijdragen*, n.r. 16 (1990): 129-53.

(Falkenburg 1994) — R. L. Falkenburg, "Randfiguren op het toneel en in de schilderkunst in de zestiende eeuw," in B. A. M. Ramakers, ed., *Spel in de verte. Tekst, structuur en opvoeringspraktijk van het rederijkerstoneel (Jaarboek De Fonteine, 1991-92)* (Ghent, 1994), pp. 177-99.

(Falkenburg 1998) — R. L. Falkenburg, "Marginal Motifs in Early Flemish Landscape Painting," in J. H. Marrow, ed., *Proceedings of the Herri Bles Colloquium, The Art Museum Princeton, 14-15, Oktober 1995* (Turnhout, 1998), in press.

(Freedberg 1980) — D. Freedberg, *Dutch Landscape Prints of the Seventeenth Century* (London, 1980).

(De Groot 1979) — I. de Groot, *Landschappen. Etsen van de Nederlandse meesters uit de zeventiende eeuw* (Maarssen, 1979).

(Haverkamp-Begemann and Chong 1985) — E. Haverkamp-Begemann and A. Chong, "Dutch Landscape Painting and Its Associations," in H. R. Hoetink, ed., *The Royal Picture Gallery Mauritshuis* (Amsterdam, 1985), pp. 56-67.

(Iser 1972) — W. Iser, *Der implizite Leser. Kommunikationsformen des Romans von Bunyan bis Beckett* (Munich, 1972).

(Jauss 1970) — H. R. Jauss, *Literaturgeschichte als Provokation* (Frankfurt a/M, 1970).

(Keyes 1984) — G. Keyes, *Esaias van den Velde 1587-1630,* with a biographical chapter by J. G. C. A. Briels (Doornspijk, 1984).

(De Klijn 1982) — M. de Klijn, *De invloed van het Calvinisme op de Noord-Nederlandse landschapschilderkunst. 1570-1630* (Apeldoorn, 1982).

(Leeflang 1993) — H. Leeflang, "Het landschap in boek en prent. Perceptie en interpretatie van vroeg zeventiende-eeuwse Nederlandse landschapsprenten," in B. Bakker and H. Leeflang, *Nederland naar't leven. Landschapsprenten uit de Gouden Eeuw* (Zwolle-Amsterdam, 1993), pp. 18-32.

(Manuth 1993/94) — V. Manuth, "Denomination and Iconography: The Choice of Subject Matter in the Biblical Painting of the Rembrandt Circle," *Simiolus* 22 (1993/94): 235-52.

(Montias 1991) — J. M. Montias, "Works of Art in Seventeenth-Century Amsterdam: An Analysis of Subjects and Attributions," in *Art in History/History in Art: Studies in Seventeenth-Century Dutch Culture*, edited by D. Freedberg and J. de Vries (Santa Monica, 1991), pp. 331-72.

(Pastoor 1991) — G. Pastoor, "Bijbelse historiestukken in particulier bezit," in Chr. Tümpel et al., *Exh. cat. Het Oude Testament in de Schilderkunst van de Gouden Eeuw* (Zwolle-Amsterdam, 1991), pp. 122-33.

(Raupp 1980) — H.-J. Raupp, "Zur Bedeutung von Thema und Symbol für die holländische Landschaftsmalerei des 17. Jahrhunderts," *Jahrbuch der Staatlichen Kunstsammlungen in Baden-Württenberg* 17 (1980): 85-110.

(Schama 1987/88) — S. Schama, "Dutch Landscapes: Culture as Foreground," in P. C. Sutton et al., *Masters of Seventeenth-Century Dutch Landscape Painting* (Amsterdam-Boston-Philadelphia, 1987/88), pp. 64-83.

(Spaans 1989) — J. Spaans, *Haarlem na de Reformatie. Stedelijke cultuur en kerkelijk leven, 1577-1620* (Leiden, 1989).

(Stechow 1966) — W. Stechow, *Dutch Landscape Painting of the Seventeenth Century* (London, 1966).

(Tümpel 1991) — Chr. Tümpel, "De Oudtestamentische historieschilderkunst in de Gouden Eeuw," in Chr. Tümpel et al., *Exh. cat. Het Oude Testament in de Schilderkunst van de Gouden Eeuw* (Zwolle-Amsterdam, 1991), pp. 8-23.

(De Vries 1977) — L. de Vries, "Jan Steen, 'de kluchtschilder'" (diss., Groningen, 1977).

(Wiegand 1971) — W. Wiegand, "Ruisdael-studien. Ein Versuch zur Ikonologie der Landschaftsmalerei" (diss., Hamburg, 1971).

Selective Bibliography

B. Bakker, "Levenspelgrimage of vrome wandeling? Claes Janszoon Visscher en zijn serie 'Plaisante Plaetsen,'" *Oud Holland* 107 (1993): 97-115.

J. Bruyn, "Toward a Scriptural Reading of Seventeenth-Century Dutch Landscape Painting," in P. C. Sutton et al., *Masters of Seventeenth-*

Century Dutch Landscape Painting (Amsterdam-Boston-Philadelphia, 1987/88), pp. 84-103.

R. L. Falkenburg, "De betekenis van het geschilderde Hollandse landschap van de zeventiende eeuw: een beschouwing naar aanleiding van enkele recente interpretaties," *Theoretische geschiedenis* 16 (1989): 131-53.

M. de Klijn, *De invloed van het Calvinisme op de Noord-Nederlandse landschapschilderkunst. 1570-1630* (Apeldoorn, 1982).

W. Stechow, *Dutch Landscape Painting of the Seventeenth Century* (London, 1966).

Netherlandish Reformed Traditions in the Graphic Arts, 1550-1630

JAMES R. TANIS

In a land where Calvinists gained notoriety for their violent destruction of religious imagery, Protestant artists nonetheless produced hundreds of graphic images of religious subjects, and in every medium of the day — woodcuts, etchings, and drawings. Were the artists of such works necessarily Reformed or Calvinist? Can all prints of a religious nature by Calvinist artists be considered Calvinist prints? Among artists, some of whose works will be discussed in detail, are Hendrick Goltzius (1558-1617), a non-Calvinistic Protestant; Hendrik Hondius (1573-1649), a committed Calvinist; and the very young Rembrandt van Rijn, a confessing member of the Reformed Church, though a person of broad religious convictions. This paper seeks to investigate the characteristics of a Reformed as well as, more specifically, a Calvinist print.

This seminar has raised concerns about the term "Calvinism" in the Netherlandic context, particularly for the period prior to the Synod of Dort (1618-19). Far more viable is the more inclusive word "Reformed." In the Netherlands an indigenous Reformation was under way well before Jean Calvin turned from Catholicism to Protestantism. In the early years of the sixteenth century the reforming movement in the Netherlands was fed by local theologians — Erasmus not least among them — then informed by other theologians, particularly Martin Luther. By the mid-1520s the movement was supported in its sacramental theology and its view of the church and the arts by the Swiss theologian Ulrich Zwingli (1484-1531), the East Frisian pastor Georgius Aportanus (ca. 1495-1530), and others.[1] Thus, dis-

---

1. For further clarification, see Charles Garside Jr., *Zwingli and the Arts* (New Haven: Yale University Press, 1966), and James Tanis, "East Friesland and the Reformed Reformation," *Calvin Theological Journal* 26 (1991): 313-49.

tinctly Reformed theological structures were established in the northern Netherlands several decades before Calvinism invaded the southern Netherlands (today's Belgium) in the 1540s, 1550s, and 1560s. As much as possible the term "Calvinist" will be restricted to those works specifically so informed, though the use of the term "Reformed" will necessarily often directly or indirectly include Calvinistic elements.

The topic will be approached from the viewpoint of a cultural historian and a theologian, not an art historian. This will no doubt have disadvantages, but it will also have advantages. Though artistic issues might better be left to art historians, it may be useful to distinguish between certain categories of prints (not all of which we will have time to treat): propaganda prints, anti-Catholic broadsides, illustrations of books (such as Théodore de Bèze's emblems, though de Bèze himself later backed off from the genre), illustrations of biblical subjects, and other such religiously or theologically oriented portrait prints and historical views.

The flowering of Netherlandic Reformed iconography in the 1560s followed that of German Lutheranism by three to four decades. This is in part attributable to the Reformed bias against forms of imagery which might become objects of devotion and, in greater part, to the underground nature of the Reformed movement, which mitigated against its printing in any public form in its early years. It was only in the 1560s that Calvinists began to appear openly. Clandestine printing in the northern and southern Netherlands was important, but by its nature very limited. In 1528 the first Reformed confession of faith was published in nearby East Friesland, where the new religious movement had free rein under the protestantizing Count Edzard.[2] The first public Calvinist statement of faith in the Netherlands itself came thirty-three years later when the Confession of Faith written by Guido de Bres in 1561 was tossed over the wall of Margaretha of Parma's Brussels palace.

A remarkable print (see fig. 124) had appeared meanwhile in the late 1550s. Even more remarkable, in the absence of a body of early Netherlandic Protestant art, is the fact that the print derives from a drawing created already in the mid-1520s in the circle of the Flemish artist Barent van Orley.[3] The drawing's anticlericalism and its critique of the Catholic Church were more heavily indebted to indigenous humanist and reformist thinkers than to Lutheran or other Protestant literature smuggled into the southern Netherlands. Though the message conveyed by the image stemmed from the opening years of the still very fluid Reformation, the later issuance of the engraving was the result of growing local movements, almost surely Reformed, if not specifically Calvinist.

2. See Tanis.

3. James Tanis and Daniel Horst, *Images of Discord: A Graphic Interpretation of the Opening Decades of the Eighty Years' War* (Bryn Mawr, Pa., and Grand Rapids, 1993), pp. 5-6.

The print speaks eloquently for a whole genre of religio-political engravings that were to follow, accompanying the spread of Calvinism and its increasingly open appeal. One of numerous such prints in this category is a contemporary depiction (see fig. 125) of the infamous *beeldenstorm*, the "storming of the images," which took place in 1566 in both the northern and southern Netherlands (see fig. 126). The fury spread from town to town, beginning in western Flanders and ending in Friesland, and destroyed sculptures and paintings wherever local priests and officials had not moved quickly enough in hiding them away. In this engraving the *beeldenstorm* is depicted in the background while the foreground depicts the Calvinist attitude toward Catholic ceremonial, with the devil carrying off its altar adornments.[4] Both engravings were necessarily anonymous, for this was a time when the death penalty would have been meted out to a heretical artist or publisher.

The fact of the *beeldenstorm* and the earlier de-sanctifying of religious imagery has blinded many to the importance of the arts in the early Reformed tradition, though that importance lay in their didactic and aesthetic power rather than their devotional appeal. For example, it

124. School of Barent van Orley, *Concerning Contempt for the World (De contemptu mundi)*, circa 1550-60, engraving, 61 cm. × 67.5 cm. (plate 47 cm. × 67.5 cm.), Stichting Atlas Van Stolk, Historisch Museum, Rotterdam

4. Tanis and Horst, pp. 38-39.

TIS AL VERISREN · GHEB·E·ON · OFT · GHESCHETEN
ICK · HEB · DE · BESTE · CANSE · GHESTREKEN
1566

AET ONS VEL BIDDEN SONDER OPHELDEN | LÆT ONS RAS KEREN EN WORDEN NIET MOE~
OCH DAT ONS HEILCDOM TE MEER MACH GEIDEN | WANT ÆLIE DEES CREMEKIE HOORT DEN·DVVEL TOE

125. Anonymous, *The Iconoclasm*, 1566, engraving, 17.8 cm. × 22 cm., Rijksprentenkabinet, Rijksmuseum, Amsterdam

is sometimes hard to appreciate that at the very time Zwingli was having the pipe organs removed from the churches of Zurich, he was regularly playing in a small instrumental group — and writing music as well. Similarly, when the paintings and sculptures were being removed from Swiss churches, Zwingli illustrated the title pages of his tracts on the Lord's Supper with instructive wood engravings. He was not opposed in principle to art or the arts (which he personally enjoyed and in which he participated); he was against the adoration and sanctification of works of art.[5]

The early Reformers sought purification, a spiritualization of religion. The Reformed sought to put the arts in "their proper place." Visual biblical imagery was for instruction and delectation, not for adoration or even religious ceremonial. The didactic use of art had occasionally been employed

5. Lee Palmer Wandel, "Envisioning God: Image and Liturgy in Reformation Zurich," *Sixteenth Century Journal* 24 (1993): 21-40.

372

126. Map of *beeldenstorm* from James Tanis and Daniel Horst, *Images of Discord: A Graphic Interpretation of the Opening Decades of the Eighty Years' War*

in the pre-Reformation church, but there it was buried in its elaborate ecclesiastical functions.

Unfortunately, as Reformed ecclesiastical traditions became separated from the arts, later generations tended to lose touch with the arts in a religious context — in strong contrast to the Lutheran tradition. The visual arts were not only secularized but their didactic element became increasingly more literal, both to the detriment of art and theology. (It is little wonder that many Dutch artists turned to landscapes and still-life paintings in the seventeenth century.)

Initially, a goal of this essay was to try to determine which sixteenth- and early seventeenth-century artists were Reformed or, more specifically, Calvinist. Though that is a useful and necessary exercise, it is imprecise at

373

127. Hendrick Goltzius, *Willem van Oranje*, 1581, engraving, 26.5 cm. × 18.1 cm., Stichting Atlas Van Stolk, Historisch Museum, Rotterdam

best. It does open doors and raise fundamental questions; hence an artist's religious stance is a question we will continue to ask. Answers to that question, however, even if discernible, are no guarantee of the religious orientation of a given artwork, especially of a commissioned work. In order to establish a working paradigm, one could ask which basically nonbiblical print could be termed unambiguously Reformed, even Calvinist. The first to spring to mind, oddly enough, is Hendrick Goltzius's 1581 portrait of Willem of Orange (see fig. 127).

Since Goltzius (1558-1617) was certainly not a Calvinist, what would qualify this as a Calvinist print? Its subject was the leader of the Netherlandish forces for religious and political freedom from Spain and from Catholicism. Nine years before Goltzius painted his portrait, in 1572, Willem had openly accepted Calvinism, though he was never a zealot on its behalf. In fact, one could say that he was hugely motivated to change his religious affiliation by a painful awareness of the political realities of his

374

situation. In 1575 he married Charlotte de Bourbon, a former nun, indeed an abbess turned Huguenot. Goltzius also engraved her portrait to accompany Willem's.[6]

Portraits of the popular, even idolized, Willem were eagerly sought out, so it was not surprising that numerous artists, regardless of their religious orientation, sought to cash in on the market. Goltzius's print of Willem, however, was not simply a handsome portrait of a popular personage; it had an added religious dimension in both its surrounding iconography and accompanying texts. Here Willem becomes Moses. His portrait is accompanied by analogous vignettes of Moses receiving the Ten Commandments and being led by the pillar of fire by night and the pillar of cloud by day. Though Mosaic imagery was common to Christian art generally, it was particularly important in the Reformed tradition. In all three of these mini-scenes God the Father is represented by the Tetragrammaton rather than the old, long-bearded man in the sky, whose image was such an offense to Calvinists. Goltzius had, however, depicted God the Father in several other works.

A revealing sketch for the composition of Willem's portrait print (see fig. 128) survives in the museum in Darmstadt. The frame as originally conceived reflected Goltzius's own, more typical iconographical inclination. In it he introduced four allegorical female figures which he later replaced with the Old Testament scenes which gave the print its specifically Calvinist appeal. The four women were *Verbum Dei, Fidelis Custodia, Sollicita Gubernatio,* and, though undesignated, possibly *Humana Auctoritas. Pura Religio* also appears in the frame.[7] These terms would have been reasonably congenial to Willem's Calvinist supporters, although the allegorical points of reference were very much broader than the Mosaic analogues actually employed.

Little is known with certainty of Goltzius's actual religious views, though they are probably summed up accurately by Walter L. Strauss: "We have no positive indication that Goltzius took a definite stand on religious issues of his day, except that he probably was greatly influenced by [Dirck Volckertsz.] Coornhert's views."[8] That Goltzius's liberal-minded teacher Coornhert had this impact on his pupil's theological views is further confirmed in published attacks on Coornhert and Goltzius and their spiritualizing and de-historicizing Christology. That position is epitomized in the statement "that the ground of our salvation does not consist in the knowledge of the crucified Christ at Jerusalem . . . but in the divine being that is planted in all people. . . ."[9]

6. Tanis and Horst, pp. 23-24.

7. E. K. J. Reznicek, *Die Zeichnungen von Hendrick Goltzius* (Utrecht, 1961), vol. 1, pp. 369-70; vol. 2, pl. 28.

8. Walter L. Strauss, *Hendrik Goltzius, 1558-1617: The Complete Engravings and Woodcuts* (New York, 1977), vol. 2, p. 416.

9. Lawrence W. Nichols, "Hendrick Goltzius: Documents and Printed Literature Concerning His Life," *Nederlands Kunsthistorisch Jaarboek* 42/43 (1991-92): 86-87.

128. Hendrick Goltzius, *Willem van Oranje*, 1581, drawing, 27.1 cm. × 18.1 cm., Hessisches Landesmuseum, Darmstadt

Among Goltzius's several religious prints are those geared to a Reformed audience, while others reflect more traditional views. Following the removal of religious paintings from the churches, Calvinists sometimes hung in their stead large Decalogue Boards, emphasizing the importance of the call to holiness and sanctification. Typical of the genre is an anonymous board from the Rijksmuseum Het Catharijneconvent in Utrecht. For the devout Calvinist home Goltzius created this print (see fig. 129) of a Decalogue Board held in place by Moses. Interestingly, the main text is in German, though the "sum of the law" at the bottom of the sheet is in Dutch and the personifications of *Pietas* and *Charitas* are labeled in Latin. This elaborate print was created in 1583 from three separate plates, which would have made it possible to insert a Dutch or Latin text in place of the German. Among its border decorations are depictions of the Good Samaritan and the sacrifice of Isaac, popular stories among the Reformed.

376

129. Hendrick Goltzius, *Moses with the Tables of the Law*, 1583, engraving, 59.4 cm. × 42.3 cm., Stichting Atlas Van Stolk, Historisch Museum, Rotterdam

   The last of Goltzius's works to be discussed here is actually one in a series of twelve early prints, from about 1578, entitled *Allegories of Faith*. These prints were published in Antwerp when he was about twenty years old, and their imagery is heavily indebted to earlier Antwerp artists, including Catholic artists. Of the series only *Christ's Fulfillment* (see fig. 130) is inscribed by Goltzius, and it may be the only one

377

130. Hendrick Goltzius, *Christ's Fulfillment,* circa 1578, engraving, 24 cm. × 18.7 cm., Rijksprentenkabinet, Rijksmuseum, Amsterdam

actually engraved by him rather than by another artist in his workshop.[10]

For our purposes one important aspect of this set is the fact that the budding young Calvinist artist and print publisher Hendrik Hondius, at the age of twenty, republished the prints in 1594. Hondius appears to have acquired the copper plates and chosen this series for his first venture in publish-

10. *The Illustrated Bartsch,* vol. 3, ed. Walter L. Strauss (New York, 1982), p. 71.

378

131. Hendrick Goltzius, modified by Hendrik Hondius, *Christ's Fulfillment*, circa 1578, modified 1594, engraving, Department of Prints and Drawings, Metropolitan Museum of Art, New York (The Elisha Whittelsey Collection, The Elisha Whittelsey Fund, 1951)

ing.[11] Though Goltzius's several prints include some imagery more at home in the Catholic tradition, only the print *Satisfactio Christi,* which depicted God the Father (in the upper left-hand corner), was sufficiently offensive for Hondius to dramatically alter the plate for his Calvinist clients. In the altered state (see fig. 131) only the hands of the Almighty remain. Actually the divine hand was frequently used in place of the Tetragrammaton. Hondius's modification reveals a heavy-handed amateur at work, both aesthetically and techni-

11. Strauss, *Hendrick Goltzius,* vol. 1, p. 124.

cally, but it clearly makes its dogmatic point: God — that is, God the Father — is not to be depicted.

Turning from Goltzius to Hondius typifies the move from prints done by non-Calvinist artists for Calvinist purchasers to works by artists who were themselves Calvinists.[12] Hondius was born in Duffel, near Antwerp, and studied in Brussels and Antwerp before moving north to the United Provinces of the Netherlands. By 1597 he was living in The Hague, where he produced several prints in support of the ruling House of Orange. He was the first Dutch artist and print publisher to receive the general privilege from the government of the United Provinces, the equivalent of a copyright for a work of art. Graphically, the most arresting of the Calvinistic prints he produced in his early years was his *Piramide Papistique* (see fig. 132). Snakes wearing bishops' and cardinals' hats are entwined around a large snake, the Antichrist. This large snake, wearing a papal tiara, constitutes the pyramidal frame. The Word of God strikes the Antichrist in divine lightning bolts from the clouds; the whole is explicated in Dutch and French rhymes at the bottom and Bible verses from Daniel and the Revelation on the borders. Obviously a good seller, the print (see fig. 133), first published in 1599, was reissued with anti-Jesuit modifications in 1612.

A pair of prints (see figs. 134 and 135) published by Hondius at about the same time contrast the Reformed Church, "the true apostolic church," with the decaying Catholic Church. The foundation of the Reformed Church is Christ. Worshipers gaze up through the bright cupola in the ornate ceiling, kneeling in prayer and praise. The Roman Church, on the other hand, is in a ruinous state with the pope enthroned on the platform of *Ambitie* (ambition). In addition to his propagandistic Calvinistic prints, Hondius produced a number of biblical prints, both in designs he borrowed from other artists as well as many he created himself. He also produced a Decalogue Board (see fig. 136), with a somewhat more cluttered assemblage of favorite Reformed texts and images than Goltzius had employed. At the bottom of the print he added one further encouraging touch: a gaping hell for those who did not obey the ten injunctions above.

In 1604 Hondius reissued a series of twelve religio-political prints with a bitingly anti-Catholic thrust. They had been the work of Goltzius's teacher Dirck Volckertsz. Coornhert (1522-90) after designs by Adriaan de Weert (ca. 1510–ca. 1590). De Weert, who fled the religious persecutions in Brussels in 1566, went to Cologne, where he met the exiled Coornhert. The series, which was first issued in Cologne in the 1570s, included a popular image, entitled *Testimonium Scripturae*, of

12. Nadine Orenstein, "Prints and the Politics of the Publisher: The Case of Hendrik Hondius," *Simiolus* 23 (1996): 240-50. See also Orenstein, *Hendrik Hondius*, vol. 3 of *The New Hollstein Dutch and Flemish Etchings, Engravings, and Woodcuts, 1450-1700* (Roosendaal, the Netherlands, 1994).

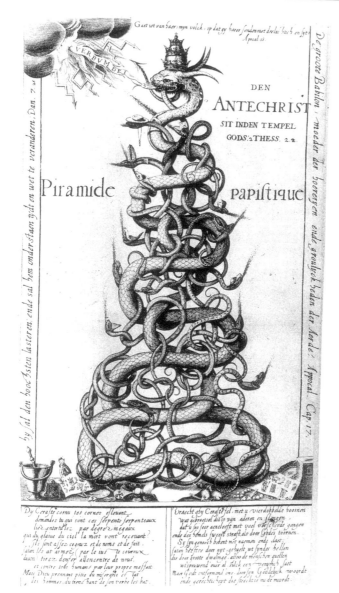

132. Hendrik Hondius, *Papist Pyramid*, circa 1599, engraving, 33.2 cm. × 18.3 cm., Konigelige Kobberstiksamling, Statens Museum for Kunst, Copenhagen

Luther bearing a flaming torch. With torch in hand, Luther lifts the pope's robes, and so reveals the demonic characters hidden beneath his garments. On the print's right a farmer studies the Bible, and in the background Erasmus uncovers the wolf in sheep's clothing. Although Coornhert rejected the full-blown theology of Luther and Calvin, he witnessed to the power of Scripture to expose the "dark ignorance of the papacy." The anti-Catholic message of the prints, aimed at the ecclesiology of the Catholic Church rather than its theology, was enough to prompt the ardent Calvinist Hondius to republish the prints.

133. Hendrik Hondius, *Papist Pyramid*, circa 1599, modified in 1612 (Atlas Van Stolk copy, reproduced here, has date altered to 1652), engraving, 33.2 cm. × 18.3 cm., Stichting Atlas Van Stolk, Historisch Museum, Rotterdam

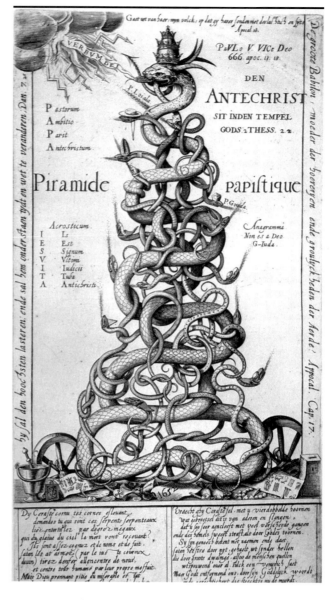

Hence we see the way in which images by an artist who was opposed to Calvinism (in this case Coornhert) could become tools of the Calvinist forces in their battle against Catholicism.[13]

Dirck Barendsz. (1534-92) belonged to a group of painters who provided images for several printmakers; but, unlike Goltzius, they did not themselves engrave or etch, as far as we know. A near contemporary of Goltzius, Barendsz. was born a Catholic but appears to have joined the Re-

13. Tanis and Horst, pp. 68-73.

134. Hendrik Hondius, *The True Apostolic Church,* circa 1599, engraving, 32.3 cm. × 21 cm., Stichting Atlas Van Stolk, Historisch Museum, Rotterdam

formed Church about the time of the Alteration of Amsterdam in 1578, when the city turned from Catholicism to Protestantism. Some of Barendsz.' early work is known to have been destroyed in the *beeldenstorm*. It is difficult to imagine an artist embracing a new religious tradition which was so directly involved in the destruction of some of his own most significant creations. Nonetheless, he was able to transcend the emotional impact that such acts must have had and to embrace and help develop the new iconography.

Barendsz.' Calvinistic perspectives are especially reflected in the series of four prints on New Testament subjects engraved by Jan Sadeler I (1550-1600). Most remarkable is the depiction (see fig. 137) of "Father, Glorify Thy Name," a subject handled, it seems, by no other artist of the period. His interpretation attempted to combine "self-denial typical of Calvinism but

135. Hendrik Hondius, *The Roman Catholic Church,* circa 1599, engraving, 32.3 cm. × 21 cm., Stichting Atlas Van Stolk, Historisch Museum, Rotterdam

also the stress upon the glory of God."[14] Judson's monograph on Barendsz. draws extensively on Calvin's writings to elucidate the text (John 12:28) on which Barendsz. based this and other pictorial images. The series may also have been influenced by Philips Marnix van Sint Aldegonde (1538-98), a close friend of Barendsz. and a leading Calvinist propagandist for Willem the Silent. (Hondius later engraved Marnix's portrait.)

Antwerp had become a center for the production of sixteenth-century religious art, but the fall of Antwerp to the Spanish forces under Alexander Farnese in 1585 had monumental effects on both religion and art. Though most people did not realize it at the time, following Farnese's long, grueling, and eventually successful siege of Antwerp, the permanent division of north and south had, in fact, taken place. Protestants were given two years to be

14. J. Richard Judson, *Dirck Bartendsz.* (Amsterdam, 1970), pp. 62, 78-79, 125-26, 131-32.

384

136. Hendrik Hondius, *Moses with the Tables of the Law*, 1598, engraving, 41.4 cm. × 30.6 cm., Rijksprentenkabinet, Rijksmuseum, Amsterdam

"reconciled" to Catholicism or leave the country. Among the Protestants was a high percentage of the city's artists and artisans. In the course of a few years the population of greater Antwerp fell from 82,000 to 42,000. Many, like artist and art critic Karel van Mander (1548-1606), had already left before the siege of the city. Other departing artists or artists-to-be included Frans Hals (1584-1666) and Hercules Seghers (ca. 1590–ca. 1640). Seghers was the most creative Dutch engraver before Rembrandt, indeed one of the most imaginative and inventive printmakers in all Dutch art.[15]

By the time of the Twelve Years' Truce (1609-21) between Spain and the United Provinces, the majority of artists in Amsterdam were former Flemings. Haarlem, the center of Dutch art at the end of the sixteenth and the beginning of the seventeenth century and the city in which van Mander settled, also had a determinative Flemish contingent. The locus of Calvinist artistic activities had completely moved from south to north.[16]

15. E. Haverkamp-Begemann, *The Complete Etchings of Hercules Seghers* (Amsterdam, [1973]).

16. Frans Baudouin, "1585, een belangrijke datum voor de geschiedenis der beeldende

137. Jan Sadeler I, after Dirck Barendsz., *Christ Praying: "Father, Glorify Thy Name,"* early 1570s, engraving, 26.3 cm. × 21 cm., Rijksprentenkabinet, Rijksmuseum, Amsterdam

PATER CLARIFICA NOMEN TVVM. Ioã.xɪɪ

In 1630, the closing year of this study, the twenty-four-year-old Rembrandt van Rijn was just a promising young artist in Leiden, though he had already been at work on his own. He was raised in a devout Reformed home, in which the reading of Scripture played a conspicuous role. This is reflected in his prints and paintings as well. His parents had been married in the Reformed Church where Rembrandt was baptized.

kunsten te Antwerpen," in *Antwerpen en de Scheiding der Nederlanden,* ed. Francine de Nave (Antwerp, 1986), pp. 103-18. Useful in this and in several other parts of this discussion is Robert P. Zijp's "Polemische Kunst in der Niederländischen Reformation," in *Von der Macht der Bilder,* ed. Ernst Ullmann (Leipzig, 1983), pp. 367-75.

Both parents, however, came from old Catholic families, most of whose members had remained faithful to the old church. In 1634 he married Saskia van Uylenburch, who had been raised in a strict Reformed family. Indeed, his marriage to Saskia probably had greater impact on his involvement with Calvinists than any other factor.[17] Both families appear to have sided with the Calvinist wing of the church during the Remonstrant controversy with the followers of Jacobus Arminius. Also in 1634, Rembrandt etched the portrait of Domine Jan Cornelis Sylvius, the Calvinist minister who married them, who was the godfather of their first child, and who later baptized their daughter. In 1646 Rembrandt etched a posthumous portrait of Sylvius with descriptive verses by two Remonstrant poets. Though Calvinist by confession, Sylvius appears to have had close ties to the Remonstrant community as well.

138. Rembrandt, *The Three Crosses*, etching (dry-point), 1653; fourth state, 1660 or 1661, 38.7 × 45 cm., Rijksprentenkabinet, Rijksmuseum, Amsterdam

17. Gary Schwartz, *Rembrandt, His Life, His Paintings* (London, 1985), pp. 161-62, 185. Also important are Ludwig Münz, *Rembrandt's Etchings*, 2 vols. (London, 1952); W. A. Visser 't Hooft, *Rembrandt and the Gospel* (London, 1957); and R. B. Evenhuis, *Ook dat was Amsterdam II. De kerk der hervorming in de gouden eeuw* (Amsterdam, 1967).

139. Rembrandt, *The Rest on the Flight into Egypt*, circa 1626, etching, 21.7 cm. × 16.5 cm., Rijksprentenkabinet, Rijksmuseum, Amsterdam

No artist more than Rembrandt so effectively points to the problem highlighted at the outset of this paper, that of distinguishing Calvinists among the Reformed. Since the word "Reformed" remained with the Calvinist branch after the Synod of Dort, rather than with the Remonstrant branch, there developed an unfortunate equating of Reformed and Calvinist. In fact, however, the Remonstrant position was closer to the indigenous Reformed tradition of the Netherlands than was the Calvinist orthodoxy imported from the southern Netherlands.

388

140. Lucas van Leyden, *The Rest on the Flight into Egypt*, by 1508, engraving, 16 cm. × 14 cm., Rijksprentenkabinet, Rijksmuseum, Amsterdam

Schwartz sums up the problem thusly: "Outside the hard dogmatic core of each party, however, most people in those confused times, no matter what their church, tended towards a middle-of-the-road religiousness with elements of all the prevailing religions, in varying degrees."[18] He adds: "The reader will undoubtedly be confused by the complexities and ironies of these relationships. Well, so is the author, and so were the people who were trapped in this mire of politicking, masquerading as religion."[19] That Rembrandt, too, was mired in the middle of this struggle is reflected in the fact that his first commissioned paintings were

18. Schwartz, p. 14.
19. Schwartz, p. 31.

141. Rembrandt, *The Circumcision*, circa 1626, etching, 21.4 cm. × 16 cm., Rijksprentenkabinet, Rijksmuseum, Amsterdam

"two large history paintings . . . with a Remonstrant political message."[20]

A few years earlier, in 1626, Rembrandt's experimentation as a graphic artist was just beginning. His earliest surviving etchings already revealed his fascination with biblical themes: the earliest known plates are *Rest on the Flight into Egypt; Circumcision; Peter, John, and the Cripple at the Gate of the Temple; Flight into Egypt; Jesus Disputing with the Doctors;* and *Presentation in the Temple* — all depicting themes to which he would return in later

20. Schwartz, p. 33.

390

142. Jan Sadeler I,
after Martin de Vos,
The Circumcision,
1581, engraving,
19 cm. × 13 cm.,
Rijksprentenkabinet,
Rijksmuseum,
Amsterdam

*Et poſtquàm conſummati ſunt dies octo vt circuncideritur puer. vocatum
est nomen eius Iesus, quod vocatum eſt ab angelo prius quàm in vtero cōciper:*

etchings. In spite of the long evolution in conception, design, technique, and emotional power among these six prints, worked by the end of 1630, and the dramatic magnificence of his last prints, Rembrandt evidenced in these early efforts the marks which he would gradually bring to incomparable fulfillment, epitomized some thirty years later by the fourth state of his massive *Three Crosses* (see fig. 138). In addition to the actual etching process, by careful wiping of the copper plate Rembrandt employed surface

391

tones to produce "a dramatic darkness, which intensifies the harshness of the tragedy."[21] Although this study focuses on the first years of Rembrandt's etching, this climactic work from his last years is included lest we lose the long-range focus while looking at his earliest work.

Before examining individual prints, a further commentary on Rembrandt's much debated religious position may be helpful. Claims of Roman Catholic sympathies have been effectively refuted,[22] but his Mennonite sympathies, particularly in the agonizing 1640s, were affirmed by a Reformed theologian who is historically informed on art, W. A. Visser 't Hooft, and recently reconfirmed by the careful research of Gary Schwartz. Rembrandt seems to have been sustained in his crisis years by friends in the Mennonite congregation of Amsterdam. The impact of the Mennonite emphasis was on the inner spiritual life, which already increasingly informed his biblical interpretations, rather than the ecclesiastical organization, which was, in fact, more rigid and judgmental than the Reformed Church to which he belonged.

His portrait prints and paintings in this earlier period reflect the breadth of his friendships, including not only Calvinist and Mennonite pastors but Remonstrant clergy as well. That he was to feel cut off from these Protestant roots after the anguishing debates with the Reformed Church council in 1654 concerning the complications of his relationship with Hendrickje Stoffels is perhaps reflected in the fact that after that agonizing experience he neither etched nor painted any further portraits of Protestant religious leaders. His penetration and portrayal of the biblical narratives, however, continued to deepen in both prints and paintings, and in both Old and New Testament subjects. Indeed, the first three states of the *Three Crosses* were completed in 1653, the year "the financial side of Rembrandt's life turned sour."[23]

At a time when many Protestant artists in the Netherlands, having lost ecclesiastical patronage, had in large measure turned aside from depicting religious subjects, Rembrandt's biblical etchings accounted for nearly a quarter of the approximately three hundred prints he produced and just more than a third of his fifteen hundred surviving drawings. The large number of his drawings (the most intimate of media) is all the more revealing of his sense of personal involvement with the men and women of the Bible. As Visser 't Hooft summed up the situation, "We must conclude from all this that Rembrandt's Christianity cannot be defined in terms of the Church, but is the result of his personal encounter with the Bible."[24]

21. *Rembrandt: Experimental Etcher,* ed. Eleanor A. Sayre and Felice Stampfle (New York, 1988), p. 11.
22. Evenhuis, pp. 293-99.
23. Schwartz, p. 283.
24. Visser 't Hooft, p. 70.

143. Rembrandt,
*Christ Disputing
with the Doctors*,
1630, etching,
10.9 cm. × 7.8 cm.,
Rijksprentenkabinet,
Rijksmuseum,
Amsterdam

The conception or general structure of *The Rest on the Flight into Egypt* (see fig. 139) reveals Rembrandt's personalizing of the traditional iconography. He appears to draw on an engraving (see fig. 140) by his Dutch forebear Lucas van Leyden (1494-1583), but he transforms Lucas's traditional picturing of Mary breast-feeding the infant to an informal family group. Here Joseph warms the food and holds the plate from which Mary spoons

393

the food for baby Jesus. Though the print leaves much to be desired technically, Rembrandt established in this, his first surviving etching, the Reformed rejection of traditional religious art, with its heavy theological load, in favor of works which instruct by their naturalism.

The second plate (see fig. 141), the more finished *Circumcision*, invites us to share in the event, to join the onlookers in the balcony.[25] The emotions, though still roughly detailed, are those of the moment, from the anguish of Mary and the crying of the baby to the empathic eyes of grandmother Anna. The almost "snapshot" quality of the etching is all the more effective when it is compared with Rembrandt's immediate prototype (see fig. 142), the carefully engraved 1581 print of Jan Sadeler I after Maerten de Vos (1532-1603), and even with the master prototype, Albrecht Dürer's woodcut of the circumcision.

Of the remaining four early subjects, we will last examine Rembrandt's *Christ Disputing with the Doctors* (see fig. 143). Though Rembrandt had experimented with light and darkness to some degree in each of the other prints, here he clearly sets the boy Jesus in the light which pours in from the upper left. The massing of light and dark is stronger in the first state, but the overall impact of the work is more telling in the cut-down plate of the third state (see fig. 144). This third state is compositionally stronger, and the added figures behind the table create a far more lively narrative than the figures he cut away from the left side of the larger first state. The searching figures of Mary and Joseph approaching in the distance on the right also assume a more integral place in the depiction. There is no known prototype among earlier treatments of this subject, though some design elements may have been borrowed from portrayals of other subjects.

With the creation of this third state, Rembrandt displayed his ability to penetrate the biblical narrative with perception, imagination, and empathy. If a chief goal of Reformed art was to bring the Bible to life for the viewer, tying past to present and turning the viewer into a participant, then Rembrandt presaged in his earliest prints the inner spiritual power that was to develop in his later work. A son of the Reformed Church, he was to go far beyond the theological conceptualizations of his tradition and to lead the Reformed from their earlier years of groping with the dichotomy of art and faith to the deeper understanding of art as an expression of faith.

Much has been said of the primacy of the "word" in the Reformed tradition. The greater emphasis in Calvinism, however, has been on the Word

25. The catalogue of Rembrandt's etchings by Christopher White and Karel G. Boon, *Rembrandt's Etchings: An Illustrated Critical Catalogue* (Amsterdam, 1969-70), vol. 1, p. 165, notes that *The Circumcision* was "rejected by Hind and all earlier catalogues, except for Gersaint, but [is] now generally accepted as the work of Rembrandt." Gary Schwartz, and Ludwig Burchard before him, consider it Rembrandt's first published etching. Schwartz, p. 25.

144. Rembrandt, *Christ Disputing with the Doctors,* circa 1630, etching, 8.9 cm. × 6.6 cm., Rijksprentenkabinet, Rijksmuseum, Amsterdam

made flesh. Implications of incarnational theology for the arts gradually emerged in the graphic arts of the period under review. Popular Dutch art of the seventeenth century, drawing on both religious and secular subject matter, was a natural evolution, developing because of the Reformed tradition, not in spite of it.

Bibliography

Dawn of the Golden Age, Northern Netherlandish Art, 1580-1620. Edited by Ger Luijten and associates. Amsterdam, 1993.

Duke, Alastair. *Reformation and Revolt in the Low Countries.* London, 1990.

Marnef, Guido. *Antwerp in the Age of Reformation.* Baltimore, 1996.

Orenstein, Nadine. *Hendrik Hondius.* Vol. 3 of *The New Hollstein Dutch and Flemish Etchings, Engravings, and Woodcuts, 1450-1700.* Roosendaal, the Netherlands, 1994.

Schwartz, Gary. *Rembrandt, His Life, His Paintings.* London and New York, 1985.

Protestantism and the Arts: Sixteenth- and Seventeenth-Century Netherlands

ILJA M. VELDMAN

In the past a number of stereotype views have been aired on the influence that Calvinism (or Protestantism in a broader sense) had on the visual arts in the Netherlands. One of the clichés is that Calvinism had a destructive effect on art. In 1964, for instance, the psychologist A. Chorus wrote that "Calvinism often acted as a brake on culture, on the one hand due to the system's inbuilt defence against the 'the world', which included music and theatre, in brief almost all the fine arts, everything that embellishes and adorns life."[1] Chorus attributed the flowering of the arts in the Golden Age, a phenomenon that he could hardly ignore, to the cultural influence of the southern Netherlands. Even a historian like Huizinga believed that painting did not owe much to the Protestant faith, and even less to Calvinism in particular.[2]

Others, though, felt that Calvinism had in fact made a positive contribution to art. Hegel, for example, considered that there was a clear connection between Protestantism and genre, that typically Dutch branch of painting in the seventeenth century: "By faith — this aspect is of great importance — the Dutch were Protestants, and Protestantism alone enjoys the distinction of infiltrating the prose of life, validating it entirely on its own, independently of any relations to religion, allowing it to develop in unbound freedom."[3]

---

1. A. Chorus, *De Nederlander uiterlijk en innerlijk. Een karakteristiek* (Leiden, 1964), p. 78.

2. J. Huizinga, *Nederland's beschaving in de zeventiende eeuw* (Haarlem, 1941), pp. 97-98.

3. G. W. F. Hegel, *Aesthetik*, ed. G. Lukács (Berlin, 1955), p. 562. The quotation and translation are from G. Schwartz, "The Destigmatization of Art Geography: A Preliminary to the Study of the Dutchness of Dutch Art," *Utrechtse Historische Cahiers* 14, no. 4 (1994): 1-14.

The fact is that very little well-founded research has yet been done on the relationship between Protestantism and the visual arts. It is only recently that the subject has attracted the interest of scholars, and their publications reveal a far subtler picture than the one painted in the past.

In this article I will start by examining the influence of the Reformation on Netherlandish art in the second and third quarters of the sixteenth century, before going on to discuss the relationship between religion and art after 1572 under the headings of art for churches, public buildings, and private individuals, and some Calvinist attitudes toward the visual arts.

The Reformation and the Visual Arts before 1572

In contrast to Germany, where Lutheranism played an important role in political developments, the Reformation in the Low Countries had only an unobtrusive effect on the visual arts. This was due both to the severity with which the central government suppressed attempts at reform, and to the fact that until around 1566 there was a diversity of doctrines which cannot easily be distinguished one from the other. Initially the new teaching was based mainly on Luther, and was disseminated mainly from Ghent and Antwerp. In addition to the influence of the Christian humanism of Erasmus, there was a strong spiritualistic current that originated in Switzerland and southern Germany. At first the Anabaptists were the only well-organized group, but from 1535 they were persecuted relentlessly. Many people who hoped for a reform of the Catholic Church did not, initially, wish to leave it.[4]

The visual arts in general underwent certain changes under the influence of humanism and the Reformation. A decline in devotional images went hand in hand with a demand for illustrations of biblical texts, mainly those devoted to Jesus' life on earth, his sayings (especially the parables), and Old Testament stories of a moral nature. One expression of this new attitude to religion was a booklet by Willem van Branteghem entitled *Dat Leven ons Heeren* (The life of our Lord) (Antwerp, 1537) — a Gospel harmony with more than two hundred woodcuts by the Ghent artist Lieven de Witte.[5] According to the foreword, the book was intended as a guide to help the reader apply the Gospels to everyday life. The purpose of the illus-

4. A. Duke, *Reformation and Revolt in the Low Countries* (London and Ronceverte, 1990); for the Reformation in Flanders, see J. Decavele, *De dageraad van de reformatie in Vlaanderen (1520-1565)*, 2 vols. (Brussels, 1975). See also P. Mack Crew, *Calvinist Preaching and Iconoclasm in the Netherlands* (Cambridge, 1978).

5. For the book and its illustrations, see I. Veldman and K. van Schaik, *Verbeelde boodschap. De illustraties van Lieven de Witte bij "Dat leven ons Heeren" (1537)* (Haarlem and Brussels, 1989).

dxvi   **Jesus leert**

145. Lieven de Witte, *Jesus Teaching in the Temple*, woodcut from Willem van Branteghem, *Dat Leven Ons Heeren*, Antwerp, 1537, Royal Library, The Hague

trations was to explain the content of the Gospels to those who could not read or whose work prevented them from listening to the sermon in church on Sundays. Lieven de Witte depicted the Gospel stories strictly according to the letter of the Bible, even down to Jesus' more abstract pronouncements, which had never been visualized before. An example is the woodcut *Jesus Teaching in the Temple* (see fig. 145), illustrating John 7:14-24. Represented is how Jesus went up into the temple and explained that his teachings were not his, but they were the doctrine of God. The Dutch edition of this book is featured several times around 1540 in lists of suspect works that were confiscated from reformists, the reason being that it could give readers the impression that salvation could be achieved by faith alone and not through the sacraments of the church or the performance of good works. Another reformist aspect of the book is the way in which Lieven de Witte scrupulously avoids portraying God the Father in human form. The introduction contains a reference to the first commandment accompanying a woodcut of the tetragrammaton, which in Germany was only customary in Reformational circles.

Lieven de Witte was brought before the Inquisition on several occasions, but unlike book printers, few artists were ever prosecuted for holding unorthodox views. Such charges as were brought against them were based on their actions, not their work. De Witte was arrested and convicted because he had associated with people suspected of heresy. In 1527,

399

the Brussels painter Barent van Orley was called to account for listening to a Lutheran sermon in his own house.[6]

Despite the vigilance of the Inquisition, a few depictions of Reformational views did make their appearance. They dealt with the new thinking on salvation, which Protestants achieved through faith and grace and not through the church's means of grace or the performance of good works. Those depictions, which can be regarded as personal, visual professions of faith, were restricted to unsigned drawings, painted glass panels, and prints. In many cases their iconography was derived from German Reformational imagery.

One recurrent theme was that of the true believer who imitates Christ and rejects the Catholic Church as an intermediary. A drawing of *Christ as the Light of the World* (see fig. 146; ca. 1530) was inspired by a woodcut by Hans Holbein the Younger.[7] In both the drawing and the woodcut Christ draws the attention of true believers to a huge candlestick, the symbol of his light, which is decorated with the figures of the apostles and the symbols of the four Evangelists. The subject is based on various biblical passages like Luke 11:33 and Matthew 4:16, but above all on John 8:12: "I am the light of the world; he that followeth me shall not walk in darkness." This extract from Jesus' dispute with the Pharisees was interpreted by Protestants as the new light that the Gospels shed in the darkness created by the Roman faith. On the right of the drawing and the woodcut, spiritual and temporal leaders who have turned away from the light are tumbling into a pit, led by the pope and other clerics. The believers who have turned toward the light are simple townsfolk and peasants. This is an allusion to the distinction between the "true church" (an invisible, spiritual congregation of the faithful) and "the church of Satan, antiChrist or the pope." The drawing is attributed to Lucas Cornelisz Cock, the son of the Leiden painter Cornelis Engebrechtsz, who fled to England after 1542 and thus probably had Protestant sympathies.

The painter Jan Swart van Groningen, who designed the woodcuts in the so-called Vorsterman Bible (Antwerp, 1528), also deals with the contrast between true and false believers. Two drawings, *The Broad Way* and *The Narrow Way* (see figs. 147 and 148), probably datable to the 1530s, are based on Matthew 7:13-14: "Enter ye in at the strait gate: for wide is the gate, and broad is the way, that leadeth to destruction, and many there be which go in thereat. Because strait is the gate, and narrow is the way, which leadeth unto life, and few there be that find it." These drawings make it abundantly clear that the established temporal and ecclesiastical

6. J. Decavele, "Vroege reformatorische bedrijvigheid in de grote Nederlandse steden: Claes van Elst te Brussel, Antwerpen, Amsterdam en Leiden (1524-1528)," *Nederlands Archief voor Kerkgeschiedenis* 70, no. 1 (1990): 13-29.

7. K. G. Boon, *The Netherlandish and German Drawings of the Fifteenth and Sixteenth Centuries of the Frits Lugt Collection*, 3 vols. (Paris, 1992), vol. 1, no. 133.

146. Lucas Cornelisz Cock, *Christ as the Light of the World*, drawing, Fondation Custodia (Coll. F. Lugt), Institut Néerlandais, Paris

powers have taken the broad way to destruction, and that only the community of simple, anonymous believers knows how to find the difficult path to heaven. On the broad way (see fig. 147) a long cavalcade is descending into hell, led by a flute-player and a drummer. At the head of the cavalcade are a pope and a cardinal, followed by other churchmen and a king. Death and the devil hover overhead. In the other drawing (see fig. 148), the righteous (who are indeed far fewer in number) are climbing a steep, narrow path

147. Jan Swart van Groningen, *The Broad Way*, drawing, Kupferstichkabinett, Berlin

leading to heaven, with a Tetragrammaton going before them. Snakes, fiendish monsters, and thorns hinder their passage. The "true believers" are all adults and come from humble, industrious groups of the population. Before undertaking their journey they are baptized by an angel with a pitcher containing water from the pool behind him. The hands clasped or

402

148. Jan Swart van Groningen, *The Narrow Way*, drawing, Kupferstichkabinett, Berlin

folded across the breast are also standard gestures in baptismal scenes. If there is one work of art that illustrates the central tenet of the Anabaptists, namely, adult baptism, it is this drawing — a point that has hitherto been overlooked in most literature.[8]

8. For the drawing see C. Tümpel, "Die Reformation und die Kunst der Niederlande," in exhib. cat. *Luther und die Folgen für die Kunst*, ed. W. Hofmann (Hamburg and Munich, 1983-84), p. 310, figs. 2-3; exhib. cat. *Kunst voor de beeldenstorm. Noordnederlandse kunst 1525-1580*, ed. J. P. Filedt Kok, W. Halsema-Kubes, and W. Th. KLoek (Amsterdam and The Hague, 1986), pp. 245-46, no. 125.1-2; and F. Muller, "Les premières apparitions du tétragramme dans l'art

149. Frans Hogenberg, *Christ's Prophecy of the End of the World*, etching, Rijksprentenkabinet, Rijksmuseum, Amsterdam

The depiction of specific Calvinist doctrines like predestation is extremely uncommon. One of the few scenes that does so, I believe, is a rare print by Frans Hogenberg, who was banished by the Duke of Alba and settled in Cologne. His *Christ's Prophecy of the End of the World* (see fig. 149), which he executed circa 1560 when still in Antwerp, is based on Matthew 24, where Christ describes the disasters that will befall the world before his second coming. In the foreground are famine and plague, in the middle ground people gather around two false prophets, with one man trying to restrain another while a third one walks away in horror. Depicted in the background is the culling described in Matthew 24:40-41: "Then shall two be in the field; the one shall be taken, and the other left," as the Latin inscription reads in translation, and "Two women shall be grinding at the mill; the one shall be taken, and the other left." The elect on the land and by the mill are being gathered up by the angel mentioned in Matthew. This seems to me to

allemand et nierlandais de débuts de la Réforme," *Bibliothèque d'Humanisme et Renaissance* 56 (1994): 336-39 (recognizing the Anabaptist tenet).

404

150. Dirck Crabeth, *Allegory of the Fight of the Reborn Christian*, drawing, Fondation Custodia (Coll. F. Lugt), Institut Néerlandais, Paris

be an unmistakable reference to predestination. Hogenberg became an active adherent of the Augsburg Confession in Cologne, and was twice arrested for this adherence. Perhaps he abandoned Calvinism and joined the Lutherans, because Lutherans in that city were in a better position.[9]

Another artist who produced Reformational images was Dirck Crabeth, best-known for his stained glass windows for St. Janskerk (the Church of St. John) in Gouda. Despite working for the Catholic church in Gouda for many years, Crabeth displayed distinctly unorthodox tendencies in his drawings and designs for small painted glass panels. In the lower

9. I. M. Veldman, "Keulen als toevluchtsoord voor Nederlandse kunstenaars (1567-1612)," *Oud Holland* 107 (1993): 34-58, esp. 42-46.

part of the drawing *Allegory of the Fight of the Reborn Christian* (see fig. 150; ca. 1560) man's struggle against the power of the devil has been depicted. The theme is based on Ephesians 6:10-18, where the "reborn man" is urged to fight against the wiles of Satan with the shield of Faith, the helmet of Salvation, and the sword of the Spirit, which is the word of God. To the left, the figure of Faith prevents the "old Adam," who is not yet freed from sin, from joining the struggle. Only after the resurrection of the spirit man is freed from earthly bonds, and if he has fought and suffered with Christ, he can enter into the Kingdom of God. That is illustrated in the upper part of the drawing, where Death is holding a crown and Christ with the cross is pointing to the Holy Spirit and God the Father. On the verso of the drawing is written a quatrain in Dutch, which says (in translation): "Than he perceives a constant struggle within himself: the Old Adam revolts in his mind, Christ with bodily death frees him from all oppression and summons him into His Kingdom."[10]

The drawing belongs to a group of related works by Crabeth or his circle that deal with the road that the true Christian takes to reach heavenly bliss. The series shows how man, enslaved by sin, is tormented by his conscience and despair, despite the good works he does. He then receives grace from the Holy Spirit, which enables him to acknowledge his sins, abandon good works, and elect for Christ's teaching, which brings him to the Gospels, where he is delivered from sin through Christ's death on the cross.[11]

In the illustrations in Netherlandish Bibles from the first half of the sixteenth century one finds very little difference between the Catholic and Reformed versions. Illustrations are lacking, however, in the translations of a more obvious Protestant stamp printed in Emden: the Bieskens Bible published from 1558, and the Deux-Aes Bible of 1561-62.[12] The absence of illustrations in these Bibles seems to reflect the growing belief in reformist circles that images should be banned from religious worship, the argument being that they encouraged idolatry, and that the faithful should pray to God without the mediation of images, saints, or relics. The most outspoken of these critics was, of course, Calvin, who interpreted the prohibition of graven images in Exodus 20 and Deuteronomy 5 as the subject of the Second Commandment, and likened the Christian veneration of images to

---

10. Boon, *Netherlandish and German Drawings*, vol. 1, no. 63, quoting the original Dutch verses.

11. K. G. Boon, "De glasschilder David Joris, een exponent van het Doperse geloof. Zijn kunst en invloed op Dirck Crabeth," *Academiae Analecta. Mededelingen van de Koninklijke Academie voor Wetenschappen, Letteren en Schone Kunsten van België* 49 (1988): 117-37. For a related print series see D. Horst, "Een zestiende-eeuwse reformatorische prentenreeks van Frans Huys over de Heilsweg van de mens," *Bulletin van het Rijksmuseum* 38 (1990): 3-24.

12. B. A. Rosier, *The Bible in Print: Netherlandish Bible Illustration in the Sixteenth Century*, 2 vols. (Leiden, 1997), pp. 116-22.

idolatry. According to Calvin, the divine could not be described, and should therefore not be depicted in material form.[13]

One book that had considerable weight in the Netherlands was *Der Leken Wechwyser* (The layman's guide) (Amersfoort, 1554) by the theologian Anastasius Veluanus. The author maintained that all images should be removed from Reformed churches and that the interior should be adorned solely with sayings from Holy Scripture or illustrations of Old Testament stories.[14] In the 1560s the discussion about the use of images in churches reached a climax, and in 1566 the first Iconoclasm erupted. Churches were looted and many of their artworks destroyed.[15] Philip II responded by dispatching the Duke of Alba to the Netherlands. His reign of terror made the Dutch Revolt a fact, and from then on scenes attacking Alba and the Catholic Church usually had a political purpose.[16]

Art and Religion after 1572

After the successful uprising, the States Assembly of 1573 proclaimed Calvinism as the official state-sanctioned religion in the northern Netherlands. The Reformed service was the only one that could be celebrated in public; other forms of worship were formally proscribed but tacitly tolerated. Dutch Calvinism may not have had the status of a state church, but it was nevertheless an important social and political force in that it became difficult for people of other faiths to hold certain public offices. With the fall of Antwerp in 1585, Spain reestablished its control over the southern Netherlands, many of whose artists emigrated to the north.[17] But does this all mean that Calvinism also placed a distinctive stamp on the visual arts? Before answering that question it is necessary to consider another: Just how Calvinist were the northern Netherlands?

During the last quarter of the sixteenth century the Calvinists were a tiny minority. Reformed preachers did soon draw hordes of sympathetic listeners, who were known as "the lovers of the true religion." A large proportion of the population, however, remained Catholic, and a smaller num-

13. M. Stirm, *Die Bilderfrage in der Reformation* (Gütersloh, 1977), pp. 161-222; C. M. N. Eire, *War against the Idols: The Reformation of Worship from Erasmus to Calvin* (Cambridge, 1986), pp. 195-233; G. J. M. Weber, *Der Lobtopos des "lebenden" Bildes. Jan Vos und sein "Zeege der Schilderkunst" von 1654* (Hildesheim, Zürich, and New York, 1991), pp. 68-69.

14. G. Morsink, *Joannes Anastasius Veluanus. Jan Gerritsz. Versteghe. Levensloop en ontwikkelingsgang* (Kampen, 1986), pp. 50-51.

15. For a survey see D. Freedberg, "Art and Iconoclasm," in exhib. cat. *Kunst voor de beeldenstorm*, pp. 69-84.

16. See J. Tanis and D. Horst, *Images of Discord: A Graphic Interpretation of the Opening Decades of the Eighty Years' War* (Bryn Mawr and Grand Rapids, 1993).

17. See J. Briels, *Vlaamse schilders in de Noordelijke Nederlanden in het begin van de Gouden Eeuw, 1585-1630* (Haarlem, 1987).

ber were Mennonite. The pluriformity of religious persuasion around 1620 is illustrated by Joke Spaans in analyzing the situation in Haarlem. Political control of the city passed to the Reformed community in 1572, but roughly fifty years later only 20 percent of the population was Calvinist. Mennonites accounted for 14 percent, Catholics for approximately 10 percent, and Lutherans (and Walloons) for 1 percent each. The remainder, in other words half the population, did not belong to any church at all.[18] The city authorities went out of their way to avoid creating tension between the different religious groupings, and strove above all for a tight-knit urban community.[19] The same was true of tolerant Gouda.[20] The administration of Amsterdam had been in the hands of the Calvinists since 1581, but in the first quarter of the seventeenth century the oldest and most respected families were still predominantly Catholic.[21]

The attitude that the city governments adopted toward denominations other than the recognized Calvinists was thus moderate and tolerant. An added factor here is that the Protestants were engaged in bitter factional struggles of their own. The dispute between the Remonstrants and Contra-Remonstrants over the Calvinist doctrine of predestination was decided in favor of the orthodox Contra-Remonstrants at the National Synod in Dordrecht in 1618-19. At the same time, Catholicism actually spread. In 1592 the Vatican had made a Delft priest apostolic vicar, and from then on it regarded the Dutch Republic as missionary territory. A number of new seminaries had trained some 500 active priests by around 1650, compared to 70 in 1602. A report from the apostolic vicar in 1656 stated that approximately one-third of the country's population had been "saved" for Catholicism.[22] Pieter van Thiel accordingly concluded in 1990 that "anyone who equates 17th-century Holland with Calvinism not only underestimates the religious diversity of the nation, but also misunderstands the position of the Catholic Church in that society."[23]

Despite Samuel van Hoogstraten's assertion in 1678 that there were few professional openings for Catholic painters after the Reforma-

18. See J. Spaans, *Haarlem na de Reformatie. Stedelijke cultuur en kerkelijk leven, 1577-1620* (The Hague, 1989), p. 104. For a recent publication on the position of Calvinists see J. J. Woltjer, "De plaats van de calvinisten in de Nederlandse samenleving," *De Zeventiende Eeuw* 10 (1994): 3-23.

19. Spaans, chap. 4.

20. See C. C. Hibben, *Gouda in Revolt: Particularism and Pacification in the Revolt of the Netherlands, 1572-1588* (Utrecht, 1983).

21. L. J. Rogier, *Geschiedenis van het katholicisme in Noord-Nederland in de zestiende- en zeventiende eeuw*, 2 vols. (Amsterdam, 1949), 2:360.

22. Rogier, 1:347-417, 2:1-66 and 115, and J. A. de Kok, *Nederland op de breuklijn Rome-reformatie; numerieke aspecten van protestantisering en katholieke herleving in de Noordelijke Nederlanden 1580-1880* (Assen, 1964), pp. 54-55.

23. P. J. J. van Thiel, "Catholic Elements in Seventeenth-Century Dutch Painting, Apropos of a Children's Portrait by Thomas de Keyser," *Simiolus* 20 (1990-91): 39-62, esp. 49.

tion,[24] they in fact had a very important share in the production of art in the Republic. Famous painters like Hendrick Terbruggen, Gerard van Honthorst, Dirck van Baburen, Jan van Bijlert, Abraham and Hendrick Bloemaert, Pieter de Grebber, Jan de Bray, Jan Miense Molenaer, and many other painters made paintings for clandestine Catholic churches.[25] Painters like Willem van der Velde the Elder and the Younger, Jan Steen, Johannes Cornelisz. Verspronck, Nicolaas Berchem, Willem Heda, Cornelis Saftleven, Jan van Ravesteyn, and Jan van Goyen were also probably Catholics.[26] Johannes Vermeer, who was born into a Protestant family, became a Catholic convert.[27]

The religious convictions of patrons or artists seem to have played little part in the award of commissions.[28] What counted was the painter's skill. The Remonstrant Thomas de Keyser of Amsterdam painted the portraits of the children of a Catholic family, and gave his picture a fitting iconography.[29] Rembrandt, who probably was not an official member of the Calvinist church (as has been supposed for a long time), but a so-called "liefhebber" of the Calvinist church,[30] portrayed people of every persuasion. Among the Catholic painters who worked on the decoration of the Oranjezaal in Huis ten Bosch (1648-52) for Amalia van Solms, the widow of the Calvinist stadtholder Frederik Hendrik, were Theodoor van Thulden, Gerard van Honthorst, and Pieter de Grebber.[31] Hendrick de Keyser, the architect of new Reformed churches in Amsterdam (the Westerkerk, Noorderkerk, and Zuiderkerk), was commissioned to make statues for the rood loft in the Catholic St. Jan's Cathedral in Den Bosch in 1610. (The designer of that loft, Coenraedt van Norenberch, had designed

24. Samuel van Hoogstraten, *Inleyding tot de hooge schoole der schilderkonst* (Rotterdam, 1678), p. 257.

25. Van Thiel, p. 54. For recent articles about Catholicism and the arts, see also R. Schillemans, "Schilderijen in Noordnederlandse katholieke kerken uit de eerste helft van de zeventiende eeuw," *De Zeventiende Eeuw* 8 (1992): 41-52, and X. van Eck, "From Doubt to Conviction: Clandestine Catholic Churches as Patrons of Dutch Caravaggesque Painting," *Simiolus* 22 (1993/94): 217-34.

26. Van Thiel, p. 55 nn. 72 and 73. See also S. Slive, "Notes on the Relationship of Protestantism to Seventeenth Century Dutch Painting," *Art Quarterly* 19 (1956): 3-15, esp. 7-9.

27. J. M. Montias, *Vermeer and His Milieu: A Web of Social History* (Princeton, 1989). For the research into the religion of artists in the Delft Guild of St. Luke, see also J. M. Montias, *Artists and Artisans in Delft: A Socio-Economic Study of the Seventeenth Century* (Princeton, 1982), pp. 153-60.

28. For a recent survey see V. Manuth, "Denomination and Iconography: The Choice of Subject Matter in the Biblical Painting of the Rembrandt Circle," *Simiolus* 22 (1993/94): 235-52.

29. Van Thiel, pp. 39-62.

30. A. Th. van Deursem, "Rembrandt and zijn tijd: het leven van een Amsterdamse burgerman," in exhib. cat. *Rembrandt: de meester & zijn werkplaats. Schilderijen*, ed. Ch. Brown, J. Kelch, and P. van Thiel (Amsterdam and Zwolle, 1991), pp. 40-49.

31. H. Peter-Raupp, *Die Ikonographie des Oranjezaal* (Hildesheim and New York, 1980).

a Protestant church shortly before.) De Keyser, incidentally, was able to complete only one statue, a *John the Evangelist,* because the consistory of the Reformed church in Amsterdam forbade him to do any more work on statues that would be used "for idolatrous purposes."[32] One could deduce from this that Dutch Calvinists had no objection to images as such, only to images that played a part in religious worship.

The Decoration of Calvinist Churches

It was for this reason that the establishment of the official Reformed faith had a far-reaching effect on the interior of Dutch churches. The earlier recommendations of reformist theologians were carried out: the walls were whitewashed and the altarpieces that had survived Iconoclasm were removed. They were not destroyed, however, but were treated as part of the nation's cultural heritage and moved to public buildings like the town hall, where they took on a new function.[33]

The painted altarpieces were replaced by beautifully calligraphed and decorated guild boards and panels with biblical texts, chief among them the Ten Commandments, such as the Ten Commandments panel by an unknown artist in the church of Schoonhoven (1612-14; see fig. 151).[34] Those panels were associated with the liturgical function of the church and reflected Calvin's view that Holy Scripture was the sole source and norm for the believer. Again, it seems there was no objection to images as such, only to images that played a part in religious worship. There were paintings in other parts of the church; vestries and churchwardens' rooms were often hung with pictures. In 1669, for example, Ferdinand Bol painted a *Joseph Selling Corn in Egypt* for the warden's room in Amsterdam's Zuiderkerk (see plate 34). This choice of subject was quite deliberate, for Joseph, who had stored up grain during the years of good harvests so as to be able to

32. J. Z. Kannegieter, "Het St. Jansbeeld van het Bossche Oxaal," *Oud Holland* 59 (1942): 110-11.

33. For the value that the Haarlem city government attached to the art owned by the churches, see G. van Bueren, *Tot lof van Haarlem. Het beleid van de stad Haarlem ten aanzien van de kunstwerken uit de geconfisqueerde geestelijke instellingen* (Utrecht, 1993), pp. 232-58. However, the consistories were not always very consistent in their elimination of Catholic decoration. The sculpted choir-stalls by Jan Terwen Aertsz in the Grote Kerk in Dordrecht (1538-40) are showing (still today) such typically Catholic subjects as *The Redemption, The Martyrs of the Catholic Faith, The Church Militant Trampling Heresy Underfoot,* and *The Triumph of the Catholic Church.*

34. See C. A. van Swigchem, T. Brouwer, and W. van Os, *Een huis voor het Woord: het protestantse kerkinterieur in Nederland tot 1900* (The Hague and Zeist, 1984), pp. 269-83; C. A. van Swigchem, "Kerkborden en kolomschilderingen in de St.-Bavo te Haarlem," *Bulletin van het Rijksmuseum* 35 (1987): 211-23; C. A. van Swigchem, *"Een goed regiment": het burgerlijk element in het vroege gereformeerde kerkinterieur* (The Hague, 1988).

151. Anonymous artist, *Painted Panel of the Ten Commandments*, 1612-14, Hervormde Kerk, Schoonhoven

feed the Egyptian people during the lean years that followed, was regarded by the churchwardens as an ideal example of the wise administrator who did not set out to enrich himself.[35]

Although paintings were banned from the main body of the church, the interior was nevertheless enriched with ornate choir screens, pulpits,

35. Exhib. cat. *Het Oude Testament in de schilderkunst van de Gouden Eeuw*, ed. C. Tümpel (Amsterdam and Zwolle 1991), no. 16.

411

and tombs. In addition, costly stained glass windows that had not served a liturgical purpose were retained, provided they did not contain any overtly Catholic motifs. In the Church of St. Bavo in Haarlem, the glass panels depicting the Trinity and the donor, Joris van Egmond, bishop of Utrecht, were removed from the large window designed by Barent van Orley. In or after 1595 they were replaced by a scene illustrating an episode from Haarlem's history: the augmentation of the city's coat of arms by Emperor Frederick II in recognition of Haarlem's part in the conquest of Damietta in Egypt (a totally fictive event, as it happens).[36]

Commissions for new windows demonstrate that Calvinists took not the slightest exception to stained glass with figurative scenes. St. Janskerk in Gouda provides a good example of this. When the Protestants took over the church in 1573 it had an entire stained glass cycle, with the apostles, and scenes from the life of Christ and the life of John the Baptist in the choir. None of the windows was removed, despite the fact that the large ones in the transept appeared to defend the legitimacy of the Catholic Church by combining scenes from the Old and New Testaments. Depictions of the Trinity were removed, but the many Catholic donors, priests among them, were left in peace.[37] From 1594 to 1603 the glazing in the ambulatory and nave was continued. Instead of ecclesiastical or temporal authorities it was now friendly towns or influential civic organizations that donated windows. These windows — of course — present an iconography divergent from the subject matter chosen during the Catholic period of worship. The new political constellation of proud cities and government bodies is reflected in the themes chosen for these later windows. Except for two biblical stories (*Christ and the Woman Taken in Adultery* and *The Pharisee and the Publican in the Temple*), the scenes were mainly illustrating the virtuous rule of the authorities. The States of Holland donated a *Triumph of Freedom of Conscience* (1595-97; detail, see plate 35), an allegory designed by the Calvinist Joachim Wtewael of the victory of religious self-determination after the lifting of the Spanish yoke.[38] The personification of Freedom of Conscience is shown on a triumphal carriage. Her left hand rests on a book, undoubtedly the Bible. Seated beside her is Protection of Faith, who protects her with shield and sword. The carriage is drawn by

36. A. van der Boom, *Monumentale glasschilderkunst in Nederland* (The Hague, 1940), pp. 127-32; Van Bueren, pp. 221-22.

37. A. A. J. Rijksen, "Veranderingen in de zeventiende eeuw krachtens gereformeerde opvatting in drie van de Goudse glazen. Gedeeltelijk herstel in de twintigste eeuw," *Zuid-Hollandse Studiëen* 1 (1950): 40-52. The Gouda stained glass windows are reproduced in R. W. Bogtman et al., *Glans der Goudse glazen. Een geschiedenis van behoud en beheer* (Gouda, 1990). An extensive catalogue of all the windows will be published in three volumes of the *Corpus Vitrearum: The Netherlands*, vol. 1 (Amsterdam, 1997); vols. 2 and 3 (forthcoming, 1999).

38. For the iconographic analysis see C. Janson, "Presenting the Word: Wttewael's Freedom of Conscience Window at Gouda," *Konsthistorisk Tidskrift* 57 (1988): 18-29.

the personifications of Love, Justice, Loyalty, Concord, and Steadfastness. Tyranny is being crushed beneath the wheels of the car, and his weapons and instruments of torture smashed. It is clear who the authors of this victory were: the towns whose coats of arms frame the scene, but above all the province of Holland and Stadtholder Maurits, whose arms are borne by angels above the gate. The verse below the window ends with the line, in translation: "Happy are the lands where the virtues reign."

The towns of the "Northern Quarter" of the Netherlands presented the church with a *King David and the Christian Knight* (1595-97; see plate 36), designed by Adriaan de Vrije. The inscription states that those who, like David, repent of their sins will receive "the crown of life" and will always be ready to take up the weapons of faith as Christian knights (compare Eph. 6:16-17). David is presented as both the model of a good ruler and an example of the weak man whose remorse earns him God's forgiveness.[39] The window donated by Dordrecht was *The Maid of Dordrecht* (1595-97) surrounded by the four cardinal virtues — an allusion to the fact that the virtues also ruled in that city. It was made by Gerrit Gerritsz. Cuyp. Haarlem gave Willem Thybaut's *Capture of Damietta* (1595-97), exemplifying courage and strength in the religious war against the Saracens. The gift that the city of Leiden presented to the church was not a window with its own famous relief from the Spaniards in 1574, but an Old Testament scene, *The Relief of Samaria* (1598-1601), designed by Isaac Claesz. van Swanenburgh. The inscription shows, however, that the biblical history, in which God intercedes to save the chosen people, should be seen as prefiguring the more contemporary event: the struggle of the people of Israel is thus likened to the Netherlands' fight for independence, which was won with God's aid. However, when it was the turn of the city of Delft to present a window, they felt free to order from van Swanenburgh the depiction of the contemporary theme, *The Relief of Leiden in 1574* (1600-1604).[40]

The new decorative programs stressed not only freedom of conscience in the shape of the triumph of the new faith, but above all the political independence of the Netherlands, which was expressed in national and urban pride, and the protection that the authorities gave their citizens. In short, the government was portrayed as the upholder of a Christian body politic. This is hardly surprising when one remembers just how much say the civil authorities had in ecclesiastical affairs. They provided the churches for the faithful and supplied the furnishings and the trappings of religious worship. The churchwardens were laymen, not clerics, and when there were disputes with ministers it was the civil power that had the last word.[41]

39. C. Janson, "Warfare with the Spirit's Sword: The *Christian Knight* Window at Gouda," *Sixteenth Century Journal* 21 (1990): 235-57.

40. See Bogtman et al., pp. 55, 9, 83, and 81.

41. Van Swigchem, *"Een goed regiment,"* pp. 8-9.

The Decoration of Public Buildings

The same tendency to stress the importance of good government is evident in the commissions that the new class of Calvinist regents awarded for the adornment of public buildings. One major project was the extensive decoration of the Amsterdam Town Hall (now the Royal Palace on Dam Square), which began in 1656. As van der Waal and Albert Blankert have demonstrated, events from both classical history and the Old Testament served as prefigurations of the contemporary state of affairs: the moral embodied in the stories depicted was explicitly applied to the rulers of Amsterdam.[42] In 1658, Govaert Flinck painted a *Solomon Praying to God for Wisdom* for the Council Chamber. The poet Joost van den Vondel (who was himself a Catholic, by the way) provided an inscription, the last line of which runs (in translation): "The state triumphs where wisdom has a voice."[43] For the Treasury Ordinary the city fathers chose the theme of *Joseph Selling Corn in Egypt* painted by Nicolaas van Helt Stockade. This was a subject as applicable to public servants as it was to churchwardens, for the wise Joseph was a role model for officials, reminding them to think of the future when administering the city's finances. In 1656, Ferdinand Bol painted a *Pyrrhus and Fabritius* and Govaert Flinck a *Marcus Curius Dentatus Refusing the Gifts of the Samnites* for the Burgomasters' Chamber, both of which were intended to exhort the city fathers to act as fearlessly, simply, and incorruptibly as their predecessors, the consuls of Rome, which is again confirmed by Vondel's verses on the two pictures.[44] In the Magistrates' Chamber Ferdinand Bol painted a *Moses as the Representative of the Law,* a scene which Jan Vos and Vondel interpreted respectively as meaning that "A free state is possible when the people respect the laws" and "Virtue prevails where the laws are wise."[45] Other parts of the building were decorated with scenes of the Batavian revolt against the Romans — an allusion to the successful uprising against Spanish rule.

Paintings of fitting subjects were also made for other public buildings. The Calvinist regents of the Haarlem Leperhouse saw themselves as the moral heirs of the selfless prophet Elisha, and in 1637 commissioned a painting of *Elisha Refusing the Gifts of Naaman* (see plate 37).[46] The prophet

---

42. H. van der Waal, *Drie eeuwen vaderlandsche geschied-uitbeelding 1500-1800,* 2 vols. (The Hague, 1952), 1:215-38; A. Blankert, *Kunst als regeringszaak in Amsterdam in de 17e eeuw* (Amsterdam, 1975). See also M. Huiskamp, "Openbare lessen in geschiedenis en moraal. Het Oude Testament in stadhuizen en andere openbare gebouwen," in exhib. cat. *Het Oude Testament,* pp. 134-55.

43. J. W. von Moltke, *Govaert Flinck* (Amsterdam, 1965), p. 71; Blankert, *Kunst als regeringszaak in Amsterdam in de 17e eeuw,* fig. 20.

44. Blankert, *Kunst als regeringszaak in Amsterdam in de 17e eeuw,* pp. 11-16, figs. 5 and 7.

45. Blankert, *Kunst als regeringszaak in Amsterdam in de 17e eeuw,* p. 35 and fig. 31.

46. Exhib. cat. *Het Oude Testament,* no. 31.

had cured the commander of the army of the king of Damascus of leprosy but declined to accept any reward, because he had carried out the cleansing in the service of God. Ferdinand Bol painted the same subject for the Amsterdam Leperhouse in 1661.[47]

Paintings for Private Individuals: Attitudes to Images

Now that ecclesiastical art had ceased to provide a living for most artists, and since commissions for town halls and the court were limited, painters turned to the private sector. Inventories show that most seventeenth-century homes were full of paintings, not just those of the rich townspeople (regents and patricians) and members of the middle classes (merchants), but humbler abodes as well, although in the latter case they were of lower quality and fewer in number. The subjects were biblical scenes, allegories, episodes from mythology, still-lifes, landscapes, portraits, and genre pieces. The popularity of the history painting declined markedly in the second quarter of the century, its place being taken by portraits and landscapes.

In a study of domestic inventories, Montias examined the types of subject represented in Catholic and Reformed households in Amsterdam between 1620 and 1679.[48] As for biblical themes, there is hardly a convincing evidence that any one denomination privileged certain religious themes. The fact that Protestants owned numerous paintings seems to indicate that in the private sphere, too, they had little against art. It is therefore worth taking a look at what theologians and other writers had to say on the subject.

One person who adopted an extreme standpoint was Johannes Geesteranus in his polemic manuscript *Idolelenchus* (before 1622), which was translated and annotated by his friend the poet and Remonstrant theologian Dirck Camphuysen: *Tegen 't geestig-dom der schilder-konst* (Amsterdam, 1647).[49] Although trained as a painter himself, Camphuysen expressed his heartfelt detestation of painting, which according to him merely cost money. Invoking

47. Amsterdam's Historisch Museum. See A. Blankert, *Ferdinand Bol, 1616-1680: Rembrandt's Pupil* (Doornspijk and Groningen, 1982), pp. 94-95, no. 14, fig. 41; see also Blankert, *Kunst als regeringszaak in Amsterdam in de 17e eeuw*, pp. 41-46.

48. J. M. Montias, "Works of Art in Seventeenth-Century Amsterdam: An Analysis of Subjects and Attributions," *Art in History, History in Art: Studies in Seventeenth-Century Dutch Culture*, ed. D. Freedberg and J. de Vries (Santa Monica, 1991), pp. 331-72.

49. G. M. C. Pastoor, "Bijbelse historiestukken in particulier bezit," in exhib. cat. *Het Oude Testament*, pp. 122-33, esp. p. 127, with a reference to D. Camphuysen, *Tegen 't geestig-dom der schilder-konst, straf-rymen ofte anders idolelenchus* (Amsterdam, 1647), pp. 215-30. See also Weber, pp. 86-87.

the second commandment, he dismissed it out of hand as mere sham and vanity, and complained that his depraved contemporaries had turned painting into a passionate appeal to the eye. He was particularly vexed by nudes and erotic subjects from the Bible (Eve, Lot and his daughters, Judith, David and Bathsheba, Susanna and the elders).

This total aversion to images was exceptional, however. The attitude of a Geesteranus or Camphuysen was even more radical than that of Calvin himself. Calvin believed that spiritual things should not be depicted. God was not to be portrayed, because it was impossible to capture him in visible bodily form and he could not be perceived by the human eye. Artists were only permitted to paint subjects that were perceivable to the eye, such as stories and events that serve some educational or cautionary purpose, and scenes without any historical content, such as portraits and genre pieces.[50]

This is echoed in the views of most Dutch theologians. In his *Beschryvinge ende lof der stad Haerlem in Holland* (Description and eulogy of the city of Haarlem in Holland) (Haarlem, 1628), the Haarlem minister Samuel Ampzing spoke out against the depiction of God the Father, a crucifix or other portrayals of "God's essence," but became enthusiastic over still-lifes and portraits. The scenes, though, had to be seemly. He branded the nude, mythological pictures made by his fellow citizens Hendrick Goltzius and Cornelis van Haarlem as lascivious and unchristian.[51] This criticism of erotic images was shared by other writers. Jacob Cats warns the readers of his *Houwelijck* (Marriage) (Amsterdam, 1625) against unchaste history paintings, whose lustful images have a pernicious influence on the viewer. The Dordrecht physician Johan van Beverwijck also said that looking at such pictures easily leads to unchaste behavior.[52]

A treatise on drawing of 1636 by Cornelis Pietersz. Biens, a poet of Enkhuizen and deacon and elder of the Calvinist church there, is an unalloyed defense of images. It is true that he starts by warning against depicting exalted subjects, namely, the divine, on the authority of the second commandment, but he goes on to point out that God's guidance can enable the human spirit to produce great works, and that the artist can imitate the Creator by mimicking reality. The image itself is not forbidden. The visual arts are delightful and useful, both a pleasure to the eye and an exercise for the

---

50. Manuth, pp. 240-41, 246, with a reference to Johan Calvin, *Institutio Christianae Religionis* 1.11.12. See also M. de Klijn, *De invloed van het Calvinisme op de Noord-Nederlandse landschapschilderkunst 1570-1630* (Apeldoorn, 1982), p. 45, and Weber, p. 68.

51. Van Bueren, pp. 15-17.

52. Pastoor in exhib. cat. *Het Oude Testament*, p. 127. Nevertheless, van Beverwijck's own domestic inventory shows that he possessed a painted copy of a *Susanna and the Elders* by Rubens. It is not known precisely which version he owned, but one thing is certain: all of Rubens's Susannas are equally erotic.

intellect.[53] Here he appears to be taking as his text Horace's well-known saying from the *Ars Poetica* (line 343): "Omne tulit punctum qui miscuit utile dulci" (he has won every vote who has blended profit and pleasure).[54]

For Calvin, Holy Scripture was the only source and norm. Earlier reformers, though, also regarded the Old Testament, in particular, as a fund of moral *exempla* from which people could learn how they should and should not behave.[55] This preference for the Old Testament was not restricted to Protestants, incidentally: half of the Catholic Pieter Lastman's paintings are of Old Testament subjects. Although interest in biblical themes waned in the course of the sixteenth century, staunch Calvinist painters remained wedded to the Old Testament. This is well illustrated by the *oeuvre* of Jan Victors, as Volker Manuth has recently demonstrated. Victors's daughter was baptized in 1645 by the strict and militant Calvinist preacher Petrus Wittewrongel, a champion of pietistic orthodoxy. Victors only depicted Old Testament stories, and often ones that had never been portrayed before, such as *Hannah Presenting Samuel to Eli* (1645), *Boaz Purchasing the Estate of Elimelech and His Sons,* or *Abraham and Isaac before the Sacrifice.*[56] Victors honored the Second Commandment strictly, and one never finds depictions of God the Father in his work. He also avoided nude figures or overtly erotic subjects. Other painters were less consistent in observing the ban. Rembrandt, Victors's teacher, and Arent de Gelder, for instance, did portray God the Father.[57]

Claes Jansz. Visscher: A Calvinist Print Publisher

The Amsterdam engraver and print publisher Claes Jansz. Visscher as well typifies the seventeenth-century Calvinist view of the importance and usefulness of biblical scenes. Visscher was a member of the Reformed church and a deacon of the Nieuwe Kerk, a bastion of strict orthodoxy. The political prints that he published show that he was a bitter opponent of the Remonstrants.[58] Visscher was clearly convinced that images were a powerful way of helping people arrive at a knowledge and understanding of the word of the Bible, and in using them he departed totally from the line of unillustrated Protestant Bibles of the second half of the sixteenth century. From 1639 he published several editions of the *Theatrum Biblicum,* an an-

53. E. A. de Klerk, "De *Teecken-Const,* een 17de eeuws Nederlands traktaatje," *Oud Holland* 96 (1982): 16-56, esp. 21-22 and 48-49.

54. Horace, *Satires, Epistles and Ars Poetica,* trans. H. Rushton Fairclough (London and Cambridge, Mass., 1947), p. 479.

55. See I. M. Veldman, "The Old Testament as a Moral Code: Old Testament Stories as Exempla for the Ten Commandments," *Simiolus* 23 (1995): 215-39.

56. Manuth, pp. 245-48, fig. 2, and exhib. cat. *Het Oude Testament,* figs. 60 and 24.

57. Manuth, pp. 244-45, figs. 5 and 6.

58. B. Bakker, "Levenspelgrimage of vrome wandeling? Claesz Janszoon Visscher en zijn serie *Plaisante Plaetsen," Oud Holland* 107 (1993): 97-116, esp. 105.

152. Cornelis Cort after a design by Maarten van Heemskerck, *The Lord Commanding Noah to Build the Ark,* engraving no. 1 from the series *The Story of Noah,* in the edition by Claes Jansz. Visscher, Rijksprentenkabinet, Rijksmuseum, Amsterdam

thology of prints illustrating the most important stories from the Old and New Testaments in chronological order. Most were restrikes from sixteenth-century plates, but Visscher was not in the least bit bothered by the fact that they had been made by Catholic artists. For instance, he reprinted or made copies of a large numbers of prints by Maarten van Heemskerck. Naturally enough, though, he did heed the Second Commandment, replacing depictions of God the Father with the Tetragrammaton, as in Heemskerck's *Story of Noah* (see fig. 152).[59] He also made a few changes if he thought that certain motifs were not represented entirely in accordance with the Bible. A case in point is his simplification of Noah's ark, which is a more fanciful vessel in Heemskerck's original version. Visscher also labeled the prints in his edition with the relevant biblical reference.

Just how easy it was to make sixteenth-century Catholic images suit-

59. I. M. Veldman, *The New Hollstein Dutch and Flemish Etchings, Engravings, and Woodcuts. Maarten van Heemskerck,* pt. 1 (Roosendaal, 1993), nos. 2-7. Cf. also *The Story of Gideon,* no. 80.

418

PANEM   NOSTRVM   QVOTIDIANVM   DANOBIS   HODIE.

able for a seventeenth-century Calvinist public with just a few modifications can also be seen in Heemskerck's print series of *The Lord's Prayer* (1570).[60] Heemskerck's illustration of the fourth entreaty, "Give us this day our daily bread," takes the form of a congregation listening to a sermon — the bread of the spirit (see fig. 153). In the background is a man at table giving thanks for the real bread. The action is set in a Catholic church, complete with an altar in the background where the priest is celebrating Holy Communion. Visscher added Heemskerck's entire series to his stock and needed to make only a few changes to remove objectionable motifs. In a few of the copper plates he replaced the image of God the Father with a tetragrammaton, and in the scene of the fourth entreaty (see fig. 154) he turned the Catholic altar

153. Jan Wierix after a design by Maarten van Heemskerck, *Give Us This Day Our Daily Bread*, engraving no. 4 from the series *The Lord's Prayer*, 1570, first edition, Rijksprentenkabinet, Rijksmuseum, Amsterdam

60. I. M. Veldman, *The New Hollstein Dutch and Flemish Etchings, Engravings, and Woodcuts. Maarten van Heemskerck*, pt. 2 (Roosendaal, 1994), nos. 321-28.

419

PANEM   NOSTRVM   QVOTIDIANVM   DANOBIS   HODIE *Matt. 6. 11.*

154. Jan Wierix after a design by Maarten van Heemskerck, *Give Us This Day Our Daily Bread*, engraving no. 4 from the series *The Lord's Prayer*, 1570, in the second edition by Claes Jansz. Visscher, Rijksprentenkabinet, Rijksmuseum, Amsterdam

into a communion table with a plain wall behind it. A minister is administering communion to the same people who were seen receiving the host in earlier editions of the print.

Visscher's prints were used again in the print Bible of the Mennonite Philip Schabaelje: the *Grooten Figuer-Bibel* of 1646. In his foreword Schabaelje vigorously defended the validity and usefulness of depictions of scenes from the Scriptures, and gave detailed commentaries on the prints.[61]

So Calvinism certainly did not impede the flowering of seventeenth-century art in Holland, nor did it ever intend to do so. Calvinists were opposed to religious altarpieces and representations of anything associated with the divine, which they had banished from their own circles. Notwithstanding the

61. P. Visser, *Broeders in de geest. De doopsgezinde bijdragen van Dierick en Jan Philipsz. Schabaelje tot de Nederlandse stichtelijke literatuur in de zeventiende eeuw*, 2 vols. (Deventer, 1988), 1:382-84 and 390-409; see 2:301-62 for a list of the prints and pages with text.

objections of a few theologians, the stained glass windows in Calvinist churches and the paintings in town halls and other public buildings were seen as a perfect way of teaching standards and values — those of the burgher society of the Dutch Republic. The flourishing market in art for private individuals was legitimized by the classical and Renaissance concept that the useful function of art was reinforced by its pleasing aspect. That, too, fitted in with Calvin's view that it was permissible to paint anything that was perceptible to the human eye. This attitude may even have fostered the characteristic realism of Dutch seventeenth-century painting and given that art such a manifestly secular and bourgeois character. It appears that one cannot speak of a specifically Calvinist choice of subject matter. During the period of religious strife, art was a way of expressing one's Protestant convictions, but after Protestantism had triumphed it seems that such proclamations were no longer considered necessary.

Discussion

George Starr (addressing Reindert Falkenburg): I am curious about the Visscher title page (Falkenburg, fig. 111). It strikes me that the figure of Diligence could be read ironically, for though she has the staff that is presumably for weaving or spinning, she is in fact not weaving or spinning. Instead she is looking at a picture book, and seems to be engaging in leisure, not work. And on the other side of the page, perhaps I was not paying enough attention to the scythe and the lantern, but I thought the label said Temporentia rather than Tempora. I wonder if instead this is supposed to be a figure not of Time but of Temperance, though the two concepts are clearly related. I would say that these do indeed introduce a kind of reading, but it is an ironic reading in which traditional iconography invites a quite different response to this world of plentitude or abundance, a world in which people are going off rather capriciously and self-indulgently in all their own little tangential directions.

Ilja Veldman: Diligence has the whip as her attribute — this is her traditional attribute during the whole sixteenth century. So there is no doubt that this figure is indeed Diligence. And Time is Time because he also has his traditional attributes. As far as traditional attributes are concerned, it is easy to identify the familiar sixteenth-century motifs. What is more difficult is to identify the meanings, whether attributed or intended or whatever, that are supposed to accompany landscapes.

Egbert Haverkamp-Begemann: I think the one Visscher frontispiece personification is Diligence, and I also think its pendant is Time. There is no other possibility, I think, in the reading of these allegorical figures. But I

421

think we have to read the title page more specifically, because in this title page we see the *Damiatschip*, the ship of Damiat which refers to the victory of Haarlem. There is also the barren tree in the distance. This can signify two things: the impermanence of nature as God's creation and everything on earth, but more specifically the barren tree was associated in Haarlem with the devastation wrought by the Spaniards when they besieged the city. In addition, there are all the ruins, which to a large extent were brought about by the Spanish army. So I think that Diligence and Time refer to Haarlem as having freed itself from the Spaniards and as it had demonstrated its greatness and its smooth functioning thanks to hard work, or diligence. The title page carries a more pointed allegorical meaning than do the rest of the pages in the series. The title page does not have much to say about just walking around and enjoying your time — obviously the series overall has this meaning, and this can be brought into comparison with other prints in other series where it is clearly stated that you can sit at home and you do not need to travel and yet you can enjoy all these wonderful sights. Which brings me to a point that I wanted to make; namely, that these prints are enormously complex and many-sided and point in so many directions. They can be read by different people in different ways and are so intended. They will not satisfy every taste and every viewer. For example, a person who loves ruins can find pleasure in these prints. And other viewers who love farm buildings and little animals like rabbits can also take their pleasure in these prints. Or a viewer can construe these prints more broadly as images of God's creation; one can even read them as symbolizing the destruction of humankind. These prints are in fact multidirected and multivalent, and they reflect a semantic openness. In addition, I think that later (seventeenth-century) paintings consciously address the viewer in different ways and also can be read on different levels.

The latter point of view is, I think, particularly clear in the work of Jacob Ruysdael (1628 or 1629–1682). It is not the case in Ruysdael's work that every castle on a mountain signifies the end of the narrow road to God or to virtue. But nevertheless, anyone who is particularly religious and who is really keen on interpreting the created order through the eyes of belief may very well do just that — this attribution of meaning is in a certain sense included in the picture, it is not excluded. Whether Ruysdael always intended that this subject be interpreted in one or another way is a different issue.

And in the case of the sketchiness of Jan van Goyen's (1595-1656) landscapes, it has been suggested that this was simply a matter of practicality: in order to make more paintings and thus dominate the market he needed to work quickly. I do not think that is the entire explanation, although it is perhaps part of the whole. One encounters the same stylistic sketchiness in drawings and etchings where there is no economic motivation. And the subject matter in these paintings which have been quickly executed will always underscore multivalent meaning; for example, a farm building which has been destroyed in part by time, whether it is carefully and in great detail or hastily represented, conveys the same message of impermanence to the viewer.

Daniel W. Hardy (addressing Reindert Falkenburg): On the question of the Calvinist implications of the pictorial evidence you have presented, it seems to me there is a kind of danger in the analysis you are offering in that Calvinism may be treated in a rather doctrinaire form. Is it not multivalence and semantic openness that is taking place exactly in the Calvinist view of faith, amongst other things a learning to read in an open semantic field which is nonetheless somewhat constrained by the authorial intentions of those who have produced the texts one attempts to read? In this sense the purpose of the exercise that is involved in being a Calvinist requires learning to read the abundance of God (on the example of the Visscher prints and by implication in nature).

Egbert Haverkamp-Begemann (responding to all three presentations on Netherlandish subjects): First I want to say it is such a good idea to raise the question of relations between Calvinism and the visual arts, and it is especially appropriate to include Dutch art under that rubric. This effort is long overdue, and we are very grateful to CTI for making this possible.

What we have heard so far are various approaches to the question of Calvinism or (to my mind more preferable) Protestantism and Dutch art. We have heard specific approaches to particular prints and artists and their relationship to Reformed beliefs in the sixteenth century — I am referring here to James Tanis's fine presentation. It is very difficult to make the connection between art and denomination, because, as we have heard, the artists' personal convictions and the art they were commissioned to make often diverge. That simple fact brings us into all sorts of considerations on the complexities of the work of art. And that, I think, is one of the key principles that makes it so very difficult to achieve a satisfactory answer on the relationship of Calvinism to Dutch art. These works of art are so complicated; they fulfill certain functions; they have a certain audience; they have certain patrons; only to a limited extent in the sixteenth and seventeenth centuries does Dutch art reflect the personal convictions of the artists involved. This is not a period of expressionism, or of romanticism, wherein a work of art is a blueprint or a clear reflection of artists' personal convictions. The work of art in this period is so complicated due to a host of factors; namely, the varying demands of different patrons, the differences of media, the varieties of viewers and audiences — given these complexities one has to search out very specifically Calvinist and Protestant prints, and that is what James Tanis has done, and he has come up with some fine examples, particularly in the prints of Hendrik Hondius.

Ilja Veldman has broadened our understanding of this subject; partic-

423

ularly in her very welcome presentation of the stained glass windows in Gouda she has raised a number of issues that are crucial to the understanding of the role of religious art, Old Testament art, New Testament art, allegory in the decorations of a church. It is indeed a remarkable phenomenon that all of these large windows which could easily have been destroyed have in fact survived. I have a feeling that in this case tradition plays a role. Sculpture lends itself so much more easily to veneration and idolatry than other works of art. Books in the sixteenth- and seventeenth-century Netherlands were not destroyed by iconoclasts. Books were for learning, and as we know, in medieval art stained glass windows were intended to facilitate the understanding of the Bible, in lieu of the printed word. This was no longer the case in the sixteenth century, but nevertheless I think that stained glass windows still intuitively filled the function of a pedagogical medium, a source for churchgoers to learn about the Bible. The combination of secular subject matter and allegory with religious subjects is really a remarkable phenomenon; one realizes that civic authorities exploited various opportunities presented by these glass windows to inculcate the meaning of secular power and of moral and religious concepts.

Finally, Reindert Falkenburg has underscored the multiplicity of attributed meanings that can be seen in landscape, their so-called multivalence, and that is a fundamental lesson for Dutch landscapes in this period. It is also especially important because this is a reaction (which he omitted to mention) to the interpretation of landscape painting that was conspicuous in a recent catalogue of Dutch landscape art (Peter Sutton, *Masters of Dutch Landscape Painting* [Boston, 1987]). This catalogue stressed the religious meaning and message of landscape painting, especially in the essay by Joshua Bruyne ("Toward a Scriptural Reading of Seventeenth-Century Dutch Landscape Painting," in Sutton, pp. 84-103). Others, for example Hans Joachim Raupp ("Zur Bedeutung von Thema und Symbol für die holländische Landschaftsmalerei des 17. Jhdts.," *Jahrbuch des Staatlichen Kunstsammlungen in Baden-Würtemberg* 17 [1980]: 85-110), have underscored similar attributed meanings. Falkenburg gives a more comprehensive overview. His interpretation does not exclude the attributed meanings offered by Bruyn and Raupp; it stresses certain continuities with these more symbol-specific interpretations. But at the same time Falkenburg points to the complexity and the open-ended character of the landscape work of art, the heterogeneous nature of its subject matter, the pure enjoyment of nature versus the more didactic attributions of pictorial narrative. All these issues are very complex and place the question of the influence of Calvinism on art in a much more tentative light than perhaps we originally expected. The complexity of the work of art; the complexity of the Reformed religion; the development of the work of art, its traditions, its continuities and discontinuities; the audience and the various possibilities of interpretation that the audience brings to the work of art — all of this

424

makes it extremely difficult to identify the impact of Calvinism on art. This contradicts what we have learned when art history was a younger discipline. And when we looked to the nineteenth and early twentieth centuries, it was once clear that Dutch Protestant art was demonstrably different from Catholic art, and the explanation of the difference lay in Calvinism. We find it more difficult today to accept this view, even though we have not yet reached a full definition of all the aspects of this problem.

But I think there is another element that contributes to our difficulties in interpreting this art and establishing a clear line of influence from one realm of thought and life (religion) to the other (art). In our day and age we are less willing to accept clear and distinct cultural identifications; this brings me back to the question of culture and to Philip Benedict's discussion of Hegel and Gombrich. I couldn't help but think that culture is something we want to avoid as the sole defining element with regard to the characteristics of a particular group. After all, we should really overcome our tribal instincts. At the same time, there is truth in the claim that one group is culturally different from another in its outlook on life, its habits, its general behavior, and thus one can talk about an English or a German approach to life. Or for that matter the Flemings and the Dutch are really quite different groups of people, culturally speaking. Hegel is now out of fashion; Gombrich is in. What it boils down to, however, is that one realizes there are certain cultural phenomena that different groups have in common. They are a kind of common denominator of different ethnic groups, but we are disinclined to accept these commonalities as the sole or more important factors in delineating the borderlines of a given group. And in a certain sense we are free of the nineteenth century. We do not believe in the sole validity of taxonomy, nor do we believe that anyone can give the ultimate definition of certain groups in their simplicity and clarity. We are more sophisticated and are now ready to look beyond the confusing and enticing simplicity of the concept of art influenced by culture — for example, the influence of Italy on Dutch art. This subject is far more complicated than we once thought. As a matter of fact, those Dutch artists who went to Italy to paint landscapes brought along their own Dutch sensitivities toward light and atmosphere and applied these sensitivities to the Italian countryside. The Italians did not paint their own landscape in the manner of Poelenburgh (Cornelius van Poelenburgh [1594/95-1667]; see Sutton, pp. 402-3) or Breenbergh (Bartholomeus Breenbergh [ca. 1598/ 99–ca. 1657]; see Sutton, p. 283). The situation is much more complicated. In a similar manner the case for Calvinist influence on Dutch art is also more complicated than was once thought. And that, I think, is the great benefit of the lectures just offered (Tanis, Veldman, Falkenburg) on Dutch art; namely, that they give us a sense of just how complicated our subject actually is.

THE NEW WORLD

Elegance and Sensibility in the Calvinist Tradition: The First Congregational Church of Hartford, Connecticut

GRETCHEN TOWNSEND BUGGELN

Ecclesiastical buildings embody religious meanings, and we can assume that the architectural manifestations of Calvinist communities will reflect their theology. But churches carry a variety of other attributed meanings and purposes as well. They can, for example, be arenas for subtle political and cultural contests between denominations, municipalities, or even nations. Churches can also embody a community's wealth and history. There may be no way to isolate the various needs that overtly religious artifacts serve. Yet by recognizing their multivalent character and sifting through their many uses, we are able to catch a glimpse of how religion and society interact. Reading church buildings univocally as religious artifacts is misleading; seeing them instead as the products of dense and rich historical circumstances can tell us much about the way belief shapes a community and the community, in turn, shapes belief.[1]

In December of 1807, the members of the First Congregational Society of Hartford dedicated a new building, the earliest "modern" brick church in Connecticut. This well-documented structure reflects the complex interaction of a new national identity, a growing urban prosperity, an appeal to refinement, and a strong Calvinist tradition (see plate 38).[2] Hart-

---

1. For a more thorough treatment of this topic, see Gretchen C. Townsend, "Protestant Material Culture and Community in Connecticut, 1785-1840" (Ph.D. diss., Yale University, 1995).

2. For the best summary of this building and the history of the congregation, see

ford, with just under six thousand inhabitants in 1807, was small by the standards of the early republic's larger urban areas. In regional terms Hartford was booming (see plate 39). In the next thirty years the city's population doubled in size. Hartford's site on the west bank of the navigable Connecticut River made it ideal for trade, and the agricultural products of the fertile Connecticut River Valley flowed into Hartford markets and out to the West Indies. Proud Hartford citizens felt their increasing importance in the worlds of commerce and government, and it was in these early decades of the nineteenth century that Hartford became the insurance and banking capital it still is today. In politics, Hartford was largely conservative — a Federalist enclave in a Federalist state — the "Land of Steady Habits," as Connecticut natives smugly dubbed their home.

First Society, Hartford's oldest and most socially prominent ecclesiastical society, had an enviable pedigree. Founded in 1636 by Thomas Hooker and a small group of Puritan emigrants from the Massachusetts Bay Colony, the society and its various buildings had been, for nearly two centuries, central to Hartford life. The year 1774 marked the beginning of the tenure of a very popular and effective minister, the Reverend Nathan Strong, a Connecticut native and Yale graduate, who served the Hartford congregation until his death in 1816. Strong earned a reputation as a revivalist, leading several awakenings in Hartford between 1798 and 1815.[3]

Under Strong's direction, the ranks of the congregation grew, and by 1804 it was clear that a new house of worship was necessary. In December of that year, First Society appointed a committee of nine men "to consider whether it be expedient for this Society to build a new meeting house."[4] The old and much-repaired meetinghouse was crowded and no longer sturdy enough to support regular, heavy use. Three months later the committee returned with its recommendation that the society build a brick church, capped by a slate roof, having the dimensions of 102 feet deep by 64 feet wide, over twice the square footage of the old meetinghouse. This new building, the committee estimated, would cost from eighteen thousand to twenty thousand dollars, a substantial expense. As for style, the committee suggested something "simple and decent."[5] After hearing the committee's

J. Frederick Kelly, *Early Connecticut Meetinghouses*, 2 vols. (New York: Columbia University Press, 1948), 1:191-203.

3. Not coincidentally, more people confessed their belief and joined the church during those Strong years, notably 88 who joined in 1808, and another 128 who joined as a result of the 1813-14 revival. See George Leon Walker, *History of the First Church in Hartford, 1633-1883* (Hartford: Brown & Gross, 1883), p. 356. Membership, of course, was not the same as attendance, and probably many more people worshiped in the church than the numbers of church members indicate.

4. Hartford First Congregational Society Records, 11 December 1804, microfilm, Connecticut State Library (hereafter noted as CSL mf.).

5. Hartford First Congregational Society Records, 22 March 1805, CSL mf.

proposal, the society voted "by more than two thirds parts" to proceed with the building project and appointed five of its men to the building committee. This committee, also known as the "contractors," would oversee the project to the end, promising the society that it would manage both construction and fund-raising, and take responsibility for any debt.[6]

Such vague and general references to procedure, style, and form typify the terse documentary record of period church building. Of what must have surely been more lengthy, detailed conversations between congregation and builders, nothing remains. Yet we can compile an understanding of this structure by looking carefully at what does exist: documents describing financial arrangements, the work and payment record of the builders, Nathan Strong's dedication sermon, and, of course, the fabric of the building itself. By taking this specific information and locating it in the context of early nineteenth-century Hartford's religious and social climates, it is possible to approach a textured understanding of this building. What is the relationship between this architecture and Calvinist theology? This is the pertinent question. But first, some underlying historical questions demand attention. Who paid for the building, and what were their intentions? Who designed and built it? To what other cultural forces was this architecture a response? To what extent, finally, was this building a manifestation of theological intent as opposed to a reflection of local taste and period style?

First Church had no one architect, no detailed blueprint for design. Instead, its form and style were the result of undocumented interaction between the society's building committee and the master builders. George Goodwin, Aaron Cook, Richard Goodman, Peter W. Gallaudet, and James Hosmer made up the committee. At the time Cook, Goodman, and Goodwin were sixty-two, forty-four, and forty-eight, respectively; all of them were established Hartford businessmen.[7] These men represented the congregation in all negotiations with the suppliers of building materials and with the builders themselves. Because the church membership records are incomplete, it is difficult to know the committee members' exact relationship to the worshiping congregation, although they were clearly involved with the business of the ecclesiastical society and were not members of any other.

There is an important distinction to be made between membership in the ecclesiastical society and membership in the church proper. New Englanders, until disestablishment, were taxpaying members of a Congregational ecclesiastical society unless they petitioned for membership in another legally recognized society.[8] The ecclesiastical society was the body

---

6. Hartford First Congregational Society Records, 22 March 1805, CSL mf.

7. Ages are not available for Gallaudet and Hosmer. See n. 9 below.

8. The State of Connecticut formally disestablished the Congregational Church in 1818.

that took care of a congregation's business. Not all ecclesiastical society members were covenanted church members. Church membership, or full communion, was contingent on a profession of faith that involved the relation of a conversion experience. There is no evidence that the five members of this building committee, although obviously important to the congregation, had joined the church prior to the building. The wives of Hosmer and Gallaudet, however, were members by 1807, and Richard Goodman himself joined in 1822, at age sixty-one.[9] We can assume that these men were actively involved in the life of the congregation and absorbed the teaching of the minister, although, not being church members, they would not have taken communion.

The building committee faced the task of financing this enormously expensive endeavor, a task made increasingly difficult by a competitive religious climate. For, despite First Society's claim to preeminence, by 1804 it was hardly the only religious option in town, even for Calvinists. The Second, or South, Society, formed in 1670, worshiped in its own decaying, 1752 building. Episcopalians held services in the newest religious structure in town, a 1791 church with Gothic detail. Quakers, Baptists, and Methodists also worshiped regularly in the Hartford area. This competition had severe implications for the financial stability of congregations and naturally impinged on the construction of new churches, the largest financial commitment a congregation could make. By original design, Connecticut's Reformed congregations relied on mandatory taxation of the members of the ecclesiastical society to cover operating expenses. Such simple taxation, however, had in fact long been inadequate to support expensive building projects, and congregations learned to rely on additional voluntary giving, usually in the form of an organized subscription.[10]

By 1804, it was clear that even taxation and subscription combined would not meet the needs of the Hartford building project, and the committee was thus driven toward a more complex method of financing. Hartford's citizens were willing to contribute to religion and church building, but they preferred to do so on terms that gave them free choice and something in return — pew rental or ownership. Pew rental schemes were becoming common in Connecticut's churches as a means of inveigling funds out of capitalist pockets. First Church's building committee thus designed to pay for the church through a combination of loans, subscriptions, and,

9. These figures have been determined from a reconstituted membership roster in the Society Records which lists, for some members, date of death and age at death. The roster is found in the microfilmed church records.

10. For the changing relationship between towns and religious societies, see Kevin M. Sweeney, "Meetinghouses, Town Houses, and Churches: Changing Perceptions of Sacred and Secular Space in Southern New England, 1720-1850," *Winterthur Portfolio* 28, no. 1 (spring 1993): 59-93. Regarding the colonial period, see Ola Winslow, *Meetinghouse Hill* (New York: W. W. Norton, 1952; 2nd ed. 1972).

especially, advance pew sales. Potential customers had the choice of buying a pew in "fee simple," that is, outright, or buying for a period of thirty years, after which the society would reclaim the pew. By March of 1809 (over a year after the completion of the building) the committee had raised $27,723 from pew rentals and sales, but final building accounts totaled a hefty $31,927. After accounts were settled, the committee still owed nearly $2,000, a burden it struggled for years to shake.

The committee and congregation had been overly sanguine in their fund-raising expectations. But it was not a simple case of overenthusiastic spending. As the future architectural history of Hartford shows, other Congregational and Episcopal congregations also took giant leaps of faith to build impressive buildings, and in a similar manner many of them found themselves encumbered by debt. This seems highly improper for Calvinists who historically shunned expensive churches or meetinghouses as a misappropriation of funds, funds better directed, for example, to the poor. Yet such sentiments do not appear among Connecticut's Congregationalists, at least until church debt becomes an aggravating problem at mid-century. Instead, we find these Calvinists congratulating each other for their generosity toward the building project.

What seems an incongruity between theology and behavior may be partly explained by two functions the Hartford building was expected to serve. First, a church was not just a building, it was also an advertisement for a congregation — an investment in the future of the society. A new building could attract style-conscious worshipers, and was therefore an important means of perpetuating the body of believers. Connecticut's Congregationalists struggled to maintain their presence in an increasingly complex religious atmosphere, and asserting preeminence architecturally was a means of ensuring the endurance of their theology and their community of believers. Part of the Congregationalist building strategy was that their buildings should be among the most beautiful, modern, impressive structures in town. Second, under a system of pew rental that was rapidly becoming the norm for Connecticut's churches, the building itself literally became the capital on which the congregation subsisted. As taxation declined, and before voluntary giving took its place, the revenue from pew rental served even to pay the minister's salary. Churches with a greater quantity of desirable pews earned larger dividends.[11]

Persons who purchased or rented pews made a financial investment, for pews could be bought and sold like any other real property equity. At the same time, they made a sound investment in the future of the body of Christ. This intermingling of spiritual and civic purposes in the new building is clear in the accounts of who purchased pews. Although church mem-

11. See figures 162 and 163 of James F. White, "From Protestant to Catholic Plain Style," in this volume.

bership rosters of this time reveal an increasing preponderance of women, the financial business of the society was the purview of men.[12] Ninety-six of the ninety-nine pew owners in the new Hartford church were men, yet only twenty of them were church members by the end of 1808. Twenty more had wives who were members of the church. On the other hand, fourteen of these men joined the church after 1808, and at least seven were involved in other ways, such as serving as society clerk. This suggests that many men played an active role in congregational life without feeling the call to join the church or even, perhaps, to worship regularly.

One such man was Daniel Wadsworth. Wadsworth's grandfather pastored Hartford's First Church from 1732 to 1747, a time of great revival, and preached the dedication sermon in the 1739 meetinghouse. His father was the wealthy Jeremiah Wadsworth, who died in 1804, leaving Daniel a sizable fortune and a family tradition of community leadership. In 1807, at age thirty-six, Wadsworth purchased the most expensive pew in the new church, a large box in the corner to the left of the pulpit, for $1,100. He also purchased eight other pews and slips valued at over $1,000 additional, either for an investment or to support the building project.[13] In February of 1815, Daniel Wadsworth became a covenanted member of Hartford's First Church. His wife, Faith (Trumbull) Wadsworth, was overjoyed. She recorded in her journal, "Blessed be God For his unspeakable mercies. This day I have had the long wish'd for comfort of seeing my husband profess his faith in our Lord Jesus Christ, and join himself in full communion with the visible church in Hartford."[14] From this we know that Wadsworth felt some sort of spiritual connection with the congregation. Yet, as a community leader, his interest in the building project also included a practical concern for the stability of his religious tradition.

Those who paid for the building, even Wadsworth, probably had relatively little to do with the building's specific architectural detail. Far more important in this regard were the many workmen who laid the foundation, raised the walls, and executed the carved and cast details of the structure.[15] Because of an extraordinarily complete building record left by the

12. See Mary Ryan, *Cradle of the Middle Class: The Family in Oneida County, New York, 1790-1865* (New York: Cambridge University Press, 1981); Nancy Cott, *The Bonds of Womanhood: "Woman's Sphere" in New England, 1780-1835* (New Haven: Yale University Press, 1977); Barbara Welter, "The Feminization of American Religion, 1800-1860," in *Clio's Consciousness Raised: New Perspectives on the History of Women*, ed. Mary Hartman and Lois Banner (New York: Harper & Row, 1974), pp. 137-57.

13. Wadsworth became one of the great benefactors of Hartford, particularly in his founding leadership and support of the Wadsworth Atheneum, an important early cultural institution devoted to the arts and history. Because of his reputation and involvement in the church, the architecture of the 1807 building has often been erroneously attributed to him.

14. Faith Wadsworth, *Journal of Faith Trumbull Wadsworth*, 5 February 1815, Wadsworth Family Papers, Manuscripts and Archives, Yale University.

15. J. Ritchie Garrison has noted the predominant role of the craftsman in not just the

society treasurer, Peter Gallaudet (one of the building committee), we know far more about the construction of this Hartford building than we know about most of its contemporaries. This account tells us not only the cost of materials and labor, but the work schedule, and it reveals in many cases the relationship between the craftsmen and the ecclesiastical society. No master builder emerges from the record, but we do know that the master mason was James Lathrop, a member of the society, and the master carpenter was David Wadsworth. Wadsworth (a very distant relation to Daniel) was apparently not a covenanted church member, but he did take as payment seven pews in the new church, and the death of his infant child was recorded in the records of the First Society in 1798, indicating that he at least was part of the religious society. Lathrop joined the church after an 1808 revival.

Some of the other craftsmen were members of the religious society or of the church proper. Deacon Aaron Colton, an established Hartford cabinetmaker, turned newel posts. Society member Daniel Danforth did the glazing, contracting with the building committee "to set the glass for the windows of the new meetinghouse at nine cents pr. light the glass to be bedded in putty & fastened in with tin, the sashes to have two coats of white lead painted — & to be finished in time for the building, the paint & putty I am to find & engage to have them well done."[16] Danforth later joined the church in an 1814 revival. Abel Buel carved the four large wooden capitals on the entrance portico and molded and cast smaller capitals for the embellishment of interior elements. Peter Thatcher and Solomon Taylor, two joiners who led crews of workmen, were both church members prior to 1807.

That a good share of the most important workmen had a relationship to the society suggests that the society preferred its own. One advantage to hiring its members either to work on the building or to furnish supplies was that the society could negotiate pew space in lieu of a cash payment. Daniel Danforth" contracted to do the windows for two hundred dollars, agreeing "to take the balance" of his payment "in a slip he shared with Edward Danforth" (possibly a brother). Alfred Bliss, who joined the church in August 1808, negotiated with the committee for "Plastering one Half the Meeting house." Bliss applied his payment of two hundred dollars toward the purchase of slip thirty-eight. Of a total of fifty-seven men and two "boys" whose names appear on the work records, however, the majority have no documented relationship to the society. Many other crew members remain anonymous.

---

dissemination but also the invention of regional style. See Garrison, "Tramping and the Transformation of Early New England Architecture" (unpublished paper delivered at the Asher Benjamin Symposium, Deerfield, Mass., November 1993), and forthcoming publications on the Stearns family of builders in western Massachusetts.

16. Peter Gallaudet's Account Book, section 1, p. 6, entry dated 28 July 1806, CSL mf.

155. *First Congregational Church,* Hartford, Conn., line drawing on paper, in the collection of the Connecticut Historical Society. Rendering of the 1739 meetinghouse of the First Congregational Society.

1739

These men worked on the building, sometimes sporadically, over the course of three years. On Tuesday, 10 December 1805, after a formal leave-taking by the congregation, Hartford First Society's 1739 meetinghouse was demolished (see fig. 155). During the winter of 1805-6, the building committee began gathering materials at the site, roughly the same lot in the commercial center of Hartford, on Main Street, where the old meetinghouse had been. The exterior walls would be brick, but an abundance of wood of different lengths and types was needed for the roof structure, the interior woodwork, and the scaffolding for the masons.

Work began on the new Hartford church with the laying of "the stone work for the foundations" on Thursday, 6 March 1806. As the building gradually rose from the ground, the carpenters worked alongside the masons, constructing scaffolding and laying floor joists. The greatest amount of concentrated work seems to have taken place in the summer of 1807, af-

436

ter the masons had finished the walls, the roof was on, and the floors were in place. At this time Wadsworth's crew, five other teams of workmen, and two individuals were at work on architectural details such as the portico and inside finish work. Just before the Thursday, 3 December, dedication, the pace of work increased, especially among the painters. Work on the building, including the construction of the steeple, was not finally completed until the following October.

The church, 102 feet by 64 feet as the society originally agreed, appears today very much as it did in 1808. Despite alterations, the majority of the original work, inside and out, remains. First Church is hardly a masterwork of architecture. Even contemporaries were occasionally puzzled by the curious arrangement of steeple stages and the apparent lack of coherent design. Timothy Dwight, onetime president of Yale College and a New England booster if there ever was one, was traveling through Hartford soon after the building was finished. Dwight, a practiced architectural critic, famous for his pithy observations, found fault with the odd geometric panels composed of architectural moldings and the steeple's "interesting but not altogether happy composition of five stages."[17] We can compare Hartford's First Church to the fourth building of New Haven's United Congregational Society, built ten years later (see fig. 156). The latter building was lauded for its elegant neoclassical design — it exhibits an overall design integrity, including the harmonious arrangement of individual features that are lacking in the blocky Hartford church and its overwrought tower.[18]

First Church may not be a monument to architectural genius, but it is important nonetheless as a harbinger of a crucial transition in New England ecclesiastical architecture (see White, plates 44-46, in this volume). The old building that the congregation left behind, the society's third structure, was a typical eighteenth-century Congregational meetinghouse: a rectangular block having a distinct, domestic cast. Many such meetinghouses had steeple or bell towers, but these were tacked on to the side rather than fully integrated into the design. Inside, the congregation sat in high-walled box pews surrounding a lofty pulpit. That pulpit was directly across from the main entrance in the middle of the long facade. Galleries at the sides and rear often made a U-shaped second story for additional seating.

These meetinghouses traditionally have been seen as one of the pur-

17. Timothy Dwight, *Travels in New England and New York* (New Haven, 1822; London, 1823), vol. 1, pp. 235-36.

18. In the case of the New Haven church, there was an architect — Peter Banner of Boston — and the builder was the well-known David Hoadley of the Connecticut River Valley. The best source on United Church is Elizabeth Mills Brown, *The United Church on the Green, New Haven, Connecticut: An Architectural History* (New Haven: United Church, 1965), although Brown does not recognize Banner as the architect.

156. *View of the Three Houses for Public Worship*, Amos Doolittle (1754-1832), hand-colored engraving, collection of New Haven Colony Historical Society. In the center is the First Congregational (Center) Church, designed by Asher Benjamin and completed in 1816. On the right is the United Church (Congregational), designed by Peter Banner and completed in 1816. The Gothic building to the left is Trinity Episcopal Church, completed in 1817.

est expressions of the Reformed tradition in architecture — buildings that shunned ecclesiastical fashion in favor of the simplicity of the "plain style." Stripped of extraneous ornament, and carefully avoiding any iconographic representation of divine things, these buildings seem to be a material embodiment of the purifying impulse of the Reformation. The work of English architects such as Christopher Wren had long influenced, directly and indirectly, colonial Anglican builders. But Congregationalists for the most part stuck with their familiar meetinghouse plan through the eighteenth century.

After the Revolution, these same Calvinist congregations wholeheartedly cast off the old-style meetinghouse. Hartford's new building, with its central steeple and Ionic-columned portico, is a provincial manifestation of the Wren-baroque style common in English church building. Orderly, stylish, and "churchly," First Church signaled Hartford's contribution to what scholars have dubbed the "meetinghouse to church" transition in New England.[19] This transition involved two elements: a reorientation of space and the application of neoclassical design features. Inside the Hartford church, movement now flowed along a central longitudinal axis from the

19. See Edmund Ware Sinnott, *Meeting House and Church in Early New England* (New York: McGraw-Hill, 1963); Kelly; James F. White, *Protestant Worship and Church Architecture: Theological and Historical Considerations* (New York: Oxford University Press, 1964), pp. 109-10; Peter Benes and Philip D. Zimmerman, *New England Meeting House and Church: 1630-1850* (Boston: Boston University for the Dublin Seminar for New England Folklife, 1979), pp. 28-35; Sweeney.

main portico entrance to the pulpit (see figs. 157 and 158). The First Church interior is not quite what it was in 1807. Alterations and additions in 1835 and 1851 lowered the pulpit and added a pulpit recess (1851) and a rear choir/organ gallery (1835). Traditional box pews under the galleries were later replaced with bench pews, or slips (see White, see figs. 162 and 163, in this volume). And, in the mid–nineteenth century, the ceilings were coffered and decorative details were enhanced. But the overall impression, particularly the axial orientation, is as it was. In 1807, neoclassical detail appeared in the form of narrow recessed arches, delicate moldings, geometric panels, and details such as urns. With this building the First Society threw off its New England Puritan habit and put on something much more in line with current transatlantic fashion. The multipurpose meetinghouse, a site for political and social as well as spiritual gatherings, gave way to the distinctive "church."

What are we to say about this significant change, a transformation experienced by literally hundreds of New England Calvinist congregations following the Revolution? As described above, numerous material and social causes begin to explain this shift. Many churches had, all at once, both the need and the means to build. Following the revolutionary era's spiritual dry spell, religious enthusiasm — loosely termed the Second Great Awakening — brought more people into the churches. Regional economic

157. First Congregational Church, Hartford, Conn., interior view

439

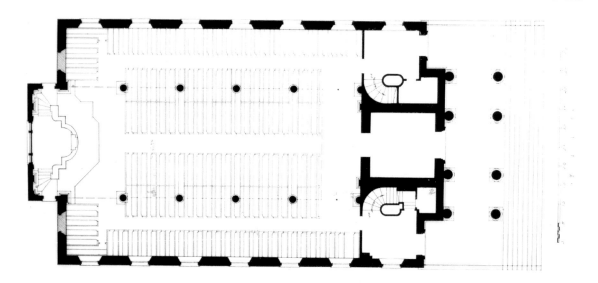

158. First Congregational Church, Hartford, Conn., plan of the first floor

recovery and growth created the capital necessary to rebuild decaying religious structures. *Stylistic* choice also had some practical causes. For instance, the long benches, or "slips," commonly used in new churches provided more seating space than did box pews. And an emerging generation of professional architects received commissions from congregations that wanted to rebuild in the contemporaneous fashion. The well-known regional architect Asher Benjamin (1773-1845), for example, published and circulated his designs, which included suggestions for church building.[20]

These explanations, however, can go only so far toward making sense of buildings like First Church. They fall short in their failure to answer one question: Why did these congregations, supposed inheritors of the Puritan "plain style" tradition, so swiftly and with virtually no protestation, accept these changes? Can we find a spiritual or theological dimension to this major reconceptualization of Calvinist religious space?

This significant change might suggest that Calvinism declined in presence and force. On the surface this would fit squarely with declension models so assiduously applied to New England Puritan history by mid-twentieth-century historians.[21] Yet the declension model, as the more recent work of historians demonstrates, is problematic.[22] Although weak-

20. Benjamin published seven builder's guides (1797-1843) directed at an American audience. The sixth edition of *The American Builder's Companion* contained three influential designs for churches.

21. See, for example, Perry Miller, *The New England Mind: From Colony to Province* (Cambridge, Mass.: Harvard University Press, Belknap Press, 1953); Kenneth Lockridge, *A New England Town: The First Hundred Years* (New York: W. W. Norton, 1970).

22. See, for example, Harry S. Stout, *The New England Soul: Preaching and Religious Culture in Colonial New England* (Oxford: Oxford University Press, 1986); Robert G. Pope, *The Halfway Covenant: Church Membership in Puritan New England* (Princeton: Princeton University Press,

ened in some quarters, New England Calvinism was not a casualty of the American Revolution. Unitarians on the one hand, and Baptists and Methodists on the other, did press into the territory of the ancient orthodoxy, but Congregationalists retaliated with a vital evangelicalism. Rev. Nathan Strong was among many charismatic revivalists stirring up Christians in southwestern New England. Strong was one of a group of Yale-educated, so-called New Divinity ministers, with the "new" in New Divinity indicating not theological innovation but temperamental distance from the "old" tired and wooden Congregationalism. By calling themselves "Consistent Calvinists," these preachers tell us bluntly where their loyalties lay. At least in the Connecticut congregations building these neoclassical churches, Calvinism, in the tradition of Thomas Hooker and Jonathan Edwards, was alive and well.[23]

By shedding the "plain style," were these congregations simply severing the connection between Calvinism and its architectural expression? On the surface, this seems plausible. As did Anglicans and Unitarians, Calvinists now uniformly turned to neoclassical motifs and current European architectural taste when designing new buildings. Rather than maintain "plain style" meetinghouses while their congregations grew more genteel and their cities more gracious, Calvinists chose to allow architecture that would seem inconsistent with "plain style" principles. Other urban congregations built neoclassical churches that argue for the popularity and endurance of this new taste. New Haven's United Church and its neighbor, First Church, built between 1814 and 1817, both seem to embrace aggressively this new style.

Rural congregations, such as that of Salisbury, responded to this aesthetic impulse as well (see fig. 159). These rural buildings were simpler and cheaper but fundamentally on the same new plan. So, if we continue with the assumption that the clearest expression of Calvinist theology *is* a "plain style" meetinghouse, we will have trouble finding that theology in these new, neoclassical, early nineteenth-century churches. In fact, neoclassical architecture has often been associated with Enlightenment ideas antithetical to Calvinism. At least as far as their buildings were concerned, Calvinists sold out to fashion, or so it appears.

I am suggesting a different way of looking at these buildings. My contention is that when choosing the Wren-Gibbs model, congregations continued a tradition of appropriating architectural style for their own purposes, an element of which was always spiritual. Meaning, in other words, was found as much in the congregation's *use* and *interpretation* of style as in

---

1969); Sacvan Bercovich, *The American Jeremiad* (Madison: University of Wisconsin Press, 1978).

23. See David Kling, *A Field of Divine Wonders: The New Divinity and Village Revivals in Northwestern Connecticut, 1792-1822* (University Park: Pennsylvania State University, 1993).

159. Congregational
Church, Salisbury,
Conn., 1800

a style itself. This argument requires, first, a reassessment of the supposed theological content of the eighteenth-century "plain style." How strong was the tradition of deliberately "simple" religious architecture? This style may not have been as closely regulated by theology as we have assumed, especially by the eighteenth century. Finally, we need to recognize how these new neoclassical buildings had specific spiritual meaning for their congregations as they served to enhance the sentimental and emotional side of Calvinist religious experience. These buildings mark not a disregard for Calvinist doctrine but a *change in emphasis.*

The New England meetinghouse had its roots in Reformation England. As we have seen, sixteenth- and seventeenth-century English Calvinists wanted their buildings to avoid the excesses that had captured the state church. To them, stripping altars of misleading representations and letting in the light of clarity succinctly demonstrated their commitment to revolutionary, unveiled truth. But, although there was clearly a deliberate "plain style" as applied to preaching and rhetoric, the application of that concept to the Puritan-built environment is more problematic.

It is difficult to tell how much New England's Puritans looked to Calvin and how much they relied on their own interpretation of doctrine in the creation of their religious spaces. Their belief that there was nothing sacred about a place of worship, as well as issues of economy and practicality, led them to conceptualize a central community building, a "meetinghouse," as a place where large groups could gather for both spiritual and secular occasions. These buildings are, from our perspective, plain. They were definitely not Anglican parish churches; they followed the forms of dissenters' buildings in Europe. To what degree that material reality was the direct result of a *theological* intent, a deliberate "Puritan plainness," is difficult to know, however, and is certainly not self-evident. Meetinghouses were among the most carefully crafted buildings in a town, and displayed a high degree of stylistic flourish. These buildings were not void of significant, and costly, ornament — an expensive quality that would not have been lost on contemporary viewers. Rather than pictorial decoration, beauty was in the form and details of the woodwork: elaborate paneled pulpits, cornice moldings, turned columns, and newel posts (see White, plates 44-46, in this volume). Even first-generation, seventeenth-century meetinghouses display the best that colonial craftsmen had to offer, as Robert Trent argued in his provocative analysis of fragments of seventeenth-century meetinghouse interiors.[24]

By the eighteenth century, the homelike place of worship reflected a local design integrity that had much to do, simply, with what looked "right," and with what was familiar to builders. As productions and representatives of a comfortable cultural majority, meetinghouses lost their original punch of visible dissent. One looks in vain for any expression of doctrinal guidance or intention in the building records of Congregational societies. Building committees, consisting of lay leaders, most frequently asked their builders to copy local designs, leaving the details to the builders' vocabulary. The building committee for the Salisbury meetinghouse of 1800, for instance, was operating in this customary manner when it asked the local carpenter Thomas Dutton to build "in the *modern* stile . . . after the Model and with as good workmanship as the Meeting House in Rich-

---

24. See Robert F. Trent, "The Marblehead Pews," in *New England Meeting House and Church: 1630-1850*, ed. Peter Benes (Boston: Boston University, 1979), pp. 10-11.

mond lately built is done."[25] By the time a few generations separated New England congregations from the English landscape, Reformation iconoclasm and Calvin's injunctions against excess ceased to be motivating factors for those who designed, built, and paid for these buildings. They simply worked in the tried-and-true local idiom.

What this apparent dilution of theological meaning as found in architecture meant for the quality of spiritual experience of worshipers is unclear. Several scholars, most notably Kevin Sweeney, have argued — and so far, very tentatively — for a growing "sacramentalism" in New England Puritanism as early as the second decade of the eighteenth century.[26] Rituals such as marriage and burial began to take on an increasingly ceremonial character, definitely not in line with the practices of the New Englanders' Puritan ancestors. Sweeney suggests that this may be a means by which orthodoxy attempted to reinvigorate waning cultural power in an era of increasing pluralism and sometimes shocking secularism. This remains to be proven, however, and we may as well find the impetus for this among a *laity* hungry for a certain kind of spiritual experience.

In the broadest terms, this "sacramentalization" appears to have come from the desire to reassert a spiritual element in a range of human experiences. In the small, virtually theocentric communities of seventeenth-century New England, a Puritan tone to life was so inescapable that colonists had limited spiritual or social need to reify the sacred in specific things, places, or times. Probably, as James Walsh has argued, in reality they did assign an unusual sanctity to certain times and places (such as the Sabbath, or the meetinghouse), yet all the while refusing to acknowledge that they did so.[27] In any case, there was no overt need to extract the sacred out of a secular landscape. But this was not a state of affairs that could last for long. Puritan leaders, while yet highly visible and influential, lost their *exclusive* hold on both politics and culture, and many aspects of life for the laity — not simply economics and politics, but their very understanding of the social organism — moved rapidly away from their seventeenth-century, essentially premodern, vision. So where, then, was religious experience to be found? This was no longer clear. Seen in this light, the construction of "churches" in the nineteenth century might be evidence not of the decline of Puritan orthodoxy and the corruption of pure Calvinism, but of an unexpected reassertion of the connection between theology and religious architecture.

Recall that when the building committee of the Hartford Society described what it wanted in a building, it specifically asked for something

25. Salisbury Town Records, 8 January 1798.

26. See Sweeney.

27. James P. Walsh, "Holy Time and Sacred Space in Puritan New England," *American Quarterly* 32 (spring 1980): 79-95.

"simple and decent."[28] What relationship did the ensuing highly fashionable and monumental building have to contemporary notions of "simplicity" and "decency"? Here is the problem of context. In order to understand, we must see these terms as relative rather than absolute. Calvin advocated no one particular style, but he did stress *moderation* in all things. "All things," he repeated over and over again, must be "done decently and with becoming dignity."[29] His prime directive was that Christian lives and Christian worship be pleasing to God, and that worship direct the believer to Christ. This goal did not change for Connecticut's early nineteenth-century Calvinists. The manner in which they sought to achieve it, however, did. Expressive yet tasteful — elegant — was how they came to understand the proper style of their faith. That, to them, was theologically appropriate.

Two theological ideas in the forefront at this time contributed specifically to the meaning of religious space. The Calvinism current among revivalists in western Connecticut was what David Kling calls a "sensual spirituality," an Edwardean "religion of the heart" that stressed the cultivation of piety.[30] An emphasis on aesthetic sensibility and religious feeling, particularly in public worship, heightened the potential of a church building to contribute positively to religious experience. The second theological tenet, related to the first, involves conversion and the value of preparation, or putting oneself in a position where one might be likely to receive the gift of salvation. While ministers in the Calvinist tradition stuck closely to the sovereignty of God and the sufficiency of grace alone, other cultural forces pointed repeatedly to the ability of individuals to influence their own destinies. If worshiping in a church increased one's receptivity to spiritual experience, and if God made a church his special home, could the building itself be an instrument of grace? Ministers never answered these questions in distinctly theological terms, but clergy and laity alike recognized the emotional and spiritual power of a place of worship.

It is impossible to understand the relationship between people and art or architecture in this period without acknowledging cultural developments that valued heightened emotions. Readers who devoured sentimental novels learned to crave a certain kind of emotional experience, and such cultural trends worked their way into religious practice. Calvinism, of course, had never been devoid of intense emotional experience. Puritans learned to listen very carefully to their emotions, even to relish the melancholy experience of a "Slough of Despond" that promised spiritual ecstasy on the other side.[31] Eighteenth- and nineteenth-century Calvinists not

28. Hartford First Congregational Society Records, 22 March 1805, CSL mf.

29. For example, see Calvin, *Inst.* 4.10.28.

30. See Kling, pp. 241, 243.

31. See Colin Campbell, *The Romantic Ethic and the Spirit of Modern Consumerism* (Oxford: Basil Blackwell, 1987).

only flocked to sentimental and romantic ideals but were instrumental in their creation.

Overblown sensibility eventually found its critique among the enlightened European upper classes, who in reaction turned to a neoclassical aesthetic of logic and restraint. Yet their criticism was not leveled against feeling per se, but against false sensibility, emotion purely for the sake of emotion. Eventually, sensibility and neoclassicism were able to bind in a more restrained emotionalism that accepted feelings as vehicles of moral insight yet tolerated no effusion. Putting these two things together, we have a culture that valued harmony and proportion, yet also yearned for emotional experience. That character is revealed in accounts of evangelical revival in these Connecticut churches. "Everything has been regular, grave, and solemn," wrote one newspaper correspondent of the 1808-9 revival in New Haven. "There has been nothing light, nothing ludicrous, nothing extravagant. Nothing incompatible with refinement of manners, delicacy of feelings, or sobriety of deportment."[32] Yet participants in such revivals remembered them, as did one woman who wrote of her "great" emotion: "Tears flowed without control. The language of my heart was, O my dear Savior, come, and take everlasting possession of my soul."[33] This refined yet sentimental neoclassicism became the dominant mode of cultural expression in early nineteenth-century America, and is reflected in Connecticut's nineteenth-century church buildings.

The spiritual meaning of these religious spaces, as we might expect, became a tricky puzzle for Congregationalists and other inheritors of Puritan iconoclasm. As I have suggested, nineteenth-century Christians inhabited an increasingly complex, market-driven world, where it was more and more difficult to sense the presence of God. They desired, consequently, to make worship space special in both design and function — a place where they could inevitably feel God's presence. In official doctrine ministers insisted that God was present in believers, not in buildings, and consequently there was no physical place that God would call his home on earth. Yet it is evident that many worshipers, and clergy, too, saw church buildings as the house of God and the place he was most likely to meet his people. For them, the idea of a transcendent, omnipresent God and an emotional insistence on "sacred" qualities of worship space could be held simultaneously only in a kind of tension.

This situation is illuminated in the brilliant balancing act performed by ministers in their dedication sermons. While insisting that God was no more present in one place than another, ministers freely used Old Testament imagery to suggest that their new churches shone with the glory of the temple. Dedication services regularly brought out local clergy and hun-

32. *Connecticut Evangelical Magazine* 2 (March 1809): 98.
33. *Connecticut Evangelical Magazine* 6 (May 1806): 431.

dreds of congregants and curious onlookers. The Reverend Thomas Robbins of Norfolk, Connecticut, was present at the dedication of Hartford's First Church in December of 1807, and he recorded it in his diary as "One of the most solemn and affected scenes I have ever witnessed . . . a very great collection of people."[34] Reverend Strong seized this opportunity to express his ideas about congregational vitality, right worship, and the nature of worship space. Looking down at an unusually large audience sitting in a sanctuary that still smelled of fresh paint and sawdust, he began to preach. As his text, he selected an Old Testament passage, Psalm 93:5: "Holiness becomes thine house, O Lord, forever." There should have been no question as to what Reverend Strong was going to say.[35]

Strong used this occasion to drive home two main points: the "holiness" of the beautiful building and the importance of sincere, heartfelt worship. He asked his audience to approach the dedication "with reverence, and fervent prayer." "There is a sanctity in the place where God reveals himself," Strong declared, where "we draw near to him in the duties of devotion."[36] In houses of worship Christians assembled in the fellowship of saints, "which raiseth them above the power of temptation and the afflictions of the world." Here God heard them, guided them, strengthened them, protected them, blessed them, and, finally, sanctified them. Strong insisted that the house of God demanded diligent attendance with "deep mourning on account of sin."[37] "Whoever comes with a light mind into the place where God is usually worshipped, or a heart filled with the pleasures or enmities of the world," Strong threatened, "doth not know how glorious Jehovah is." The Christian's attitude in church must be a resolute singleness of purpose.[38] Although Strong believed that his God was everywhere, he also was firmly convinced that God was more someplace than another, and this required a bit of rhetorical dexterity. God has "promised a special blessing," Strong stated, "in the sanctuary where he meets us to hear our prayer and praise."[39]

It was completely inappropriate, Strong claimed, that churches should be used for other than worshipful ends. "The house of God is not a place for us to mingle earthly and holy joys," he warned, "for they are not in their nature capable of being united." He made direct reference to New England's multipurpose meetinghouses, claiming "the impropriety of ap-

34. For a firsthand account of the dedication, see the Reverend Thomas Robbins, *Diary of Thomas Robbins, D.D.*, ed. Increase Tarbox, 2 vols. (Boston: Beacon Press, 1886), 3 December 1807.

35. Nathan Strong, "A Sermon Delivered at the Consecration of the New Brick Church in Hartford. December 3, 1807" (Hartford: Hudson & Goodwin, 1808), p. 5.

36. Strong, "A Sermon," p. 5.

37. Strong, "A Sermon," p. 7.

38. Strong, "A Sermon," p. 6.

39. Strong, "A Sermon," p. 14.

plying our churches, as is the custom in many places, to other uses besides the worship of God. Thus mingling things holy and unholy has a powerful influence to destroy Christian reverence."[40] Strong ventured to use the word "holy" to describe the church itself: this should shock a Calvinist. But Strong's use of the term was relatively innocuous; "when applied to inanimate things" it meant not a sacred quality inherent in the object but the condition that the object be restricted for "use in the worship and service of God."[41] Strong's comments suggest that while God may not have needed churches to make himself known, the sanctuary was of crucial necessity to *worshipers*.

The outcome of devotion should be that the Christian possessed "a conformity of the will and affections to the moral character of God." Only the Holy Spirit was capable of making such a transformation in people in their "natural state," but this change was always worked with the assistance of various "means" — the very greatest of them being worship in the sanctuary. And, as Strong noted, worship was less effective a means if intrusions were allowed that tended to "destroy Christian reverence." Concentration on right feelings was essential. The sinner, argued Strong, must take on a "holy disposition" in preparation for eternal life, and worship was a key way to ensure the development of such a character.[42] Strong's sermon, and the new building itself, reminded people of the duty of consistent Christian worship and encouraged them toward that end. The ability of church buildings to be a "means" not only to devotion but to salvation itself depended on their success at arousing the required emotions. Strong preached that "our weakness is such that we need every assistance in devotion. We are so affected by sensible things, that without their aid we fail in that warmth of the affections which is due a great subject."[43] If devotion and "warmth of affections" were so valued yet at the same time fragile and elusive, it is no wonder that ministers and worshipers sought to create a worship environment conducive to heightened emotion.

In his dedication sermon, representative of many others, Reverend Strong skillfully combined a plea for true worship and glorification of God with a promise of spiritual satisfaction. The new building of First Church, in his mind and presumably in the minds of his audience, was a perfectly appropriate place to pursue these several ambitions. As Strong understood it, he was preserving Christian reverence. He was reclaiming ecclesiastical space for the work of God. It was this same impulse, in effect, that had driven Puritan iconoclasts of previous centuries. In her recent book *Voracious Idols and Violent Hands*, Lee Wandel investigated the meaning of icono-

---

40. Strong, "A Sermon," pp. 8, 10.
41. Strong, "A Sermon," p. 9.
42. Strong, "A Sermon," p. 12.
43. Strong, "A Sermon," p. 9.

clasm for Calvinists in Reformation Europe with a special mission to un-cover what those destructive actions meant for the inarticulate laity.[44] She argued that for many, iconoclasm was a means of recapturing the presence of Christ. Although there was nothing inherently wrong in much of the art — and particularly in church plate, candlesticks, and more apparently func-tional objects — these were dangerous because of their history of use, because of the confusing, wrongheaded associations they conveyed. It was precisely because of the spiritual power of these objects that the icono-clasts destroyed them. Objects might have a positive spiritual role, but not *these* objects, which smelled of sulfur because of where they had been. Purifying the churches of such corrupted material accumulations allowed sixteenth-century Calvinists to direct their souls to the worship of God. Although Wandel's Zurich or Strasbourg and nineteenth-century Hartford are many historical and cultural miles apart, there are certain instructive similarities. In both cases an attitude toward objects was conditioned by historical circumstances and the need to move on to something more meaningful, something more conducive to true worship. In the first in-stance this happened by stripping the church down, in the second it came by making the church a special place.

How did a religious space thus conceived look, and how did it shape worship? Outside, First Church was impressive and, to the eyes of towns-people, enormous (see plate 38). Careful Flemish and running bond brick-work dignified the exterior walls. Fine woodworking, such as Abel Buel's Ionic capitals, and a bold, denticulated cornice molding added elegant touches (see plate 40). Inside, delicate neoclassical plasterwork, pale col-ors, finely articulated columns and capitals, geometric panels, egg and dart moldings, gracefully arched ceilings hanging like the canopy of heaven over the congregation — all helped create an atmosphere of awe and reverence (see plate 41). From the street, buildings that were churches and nothing *but* churches reminded Christians of a sovereign God who was greater than the perplexing concerns of their rapidly changing society. Shortly after Hartford's First Church dedicated its 1807 building, the congregation voted that "it is the opinion of this society that the Meeting house belong-ing to this society should not be appropriated to any other use than that of religious worship."[45] Strong's reservations about the secular uses of churches had not gone unheeded. The congregation subsequently used the church for worship and sacred concerts, but not, generally, for community business.

Interior church furnishings also reflected this new sensibility. Edward Kendall, a traveler visiting First Church in 1809, was struck by the quality of

44. Lee Palmer Wandel, *Voracious Idols and Violent Hands: Iconoclasm in Reformation Zurich, Strasbourg, and Basel* (Cambridge: Cambridge University Press, 1995).

45. Hartford First Congregational Society Records, December 1807, CSL mf.

pulpit textiles. "[W]hat is still more modern, and still more worthy of regard," Kendall remarked, was that "this Puritan church contains a pulpit of which the furniture is of green velvet, with cords of green and gold, fancifully entwined round the supporting columns."[46] What Kendall noticed stunned him because of his preconceptions about "Puritan" worship space. He failed to note, however, that this decoration was not only "worthy of regard," but becoming integral to Congregational spiritual experience. In the years following 1807, many other Congregational societies throughout Connecticut and New England incorporated these changes into their own new buildings. Neoclassical worship space was soon made even more conducive to heartfelt worship by lowering pulpits to a more personal level and adding organ and choir lofts to enhance the musical portion of worship.

The idea of "elegance" describes many of these changes, and was in fact a word that appeared with remarkable frequency in period documents. "Elegance" described both persons and objects, high style and simple, complex and plain.[47] The power of "elegance" rested in the way it was able to temper "luxury" and make it compatible with Christian virtue. "Elegance" implied a fashionable richness but also a proportion and balance, one quite in keeping, conveniently, with the new geometric, relatively restrained, neoclassical style. By 1807, Hartford's citizens were accustomed to this new style: it appeared in the 1796 statehouse as well as their homes, in architecture as well as furniture, ceramics, and clothing.[48] "Ele-

46. Edward Kendall, *Travels through the Northern Parts of the United States in the Years 1807 and 1808,* vol. 1 (New York: I. Riley, 1809), pp. 131ff.

47. Hartford cabinetmakers Samuel Kneeland and Lemuel Adams, for example, advertised that they had "an elegant assortment of cabinet furniture," and "Elegant Looking-Glasses," clearly in the neoclassical style, in the *American Mercury,* 14 October 1793. Cited in Nancy Richards, "Furniture of the Lower Connecticut River Valley: The Hartford Area, 1785-1810," *Winterthur Portfolio* 4 (1968): 8-9. The furnishing of the 1796 statehouse prompted competition among Hartford craftsmen and work in the latest style. Hartford's cultural ties were strongest with New York City because of water navigation and trade patterns. Some of the most prominent citizens purchased furniture from New York City. See Richards, "Furniture," pp. 2, 25. Richards also notes that former New Yorker William Flagg set up shop on Main Street, Hartford, and advertised his goods as "all made in the neatest New-York fashions." Richards, "Furniture," p. 15, from the *Connecticut Courant,* 4 July 1796.

48. See Richards, "Furniture," pp. 1-25; also Richards, *The Great River: Art and Society of the Connecticut River Valley, 1635-1820* (Hartford: Wadsworth Atheneum, 1985). Richards notes that the study of Hartford furniture craftsmen in this era is made difficult by the lack of documentary sources. See also Frank Futral, "Early Neoclassical Furniture in Hampshire Co." (unpublished Historic Deerfield Summer Fellowship Paper, 1993). Although Futral's paper addresses primarily western Massachusetts, he does discuss the early emergence of the neoclassical style in Hartford furniture. One of his key documents is a 1792 Hartford cabinetmaker's price list revealing the variety of forms cabinetmakers produced at that time. Futral links forms such as "bureau" and "Pembroke table," and features such as "swell'd front," to the new neoclassical style. Interestingly, the cabinetmakers met in the home of Aaron Colton, who later worked on the Hartford church.

450

gance" was not a set of unchanging visual characteristics but a proper relationship between people and things, a combination of rationality and sensibility.

The church allowed such an encroachment of worldly stylishness, or "elegance," in part because it was useful. Congregationalists were fighting a battle against a spirit of overblown religious enthusiasm on the one hand, and secularism and vice on the other. Refined worship space was intended to shape Christian behavior. Ministers and laity alike had complained about a perceived decline in the seriousness with which worshipers approached the house of God and hoped that special spaces would teach their congregations how to worship. In an 1818 dedication, the Reverend Elisha Atkins described his ideal house for Presbyterian worship:

> There ought to be not only room and convenience to accommodate the worshipers, but also dignity & elegance to assist devotion, and to express a respect for Divine institutions. . . . He who formed man with a taste for beauty, a love of order, and an admiration of grandeur, well knew that these properties, in the place and utensils of worship, contribute to inward piety and devotion; while, on the contrary, inelegance & disorder naturally tend to damp the fervor of devotion, and to repress the emotions of piety.[49]

Reverend Strong himself had preached that inelegant surroundings could "destroy Christian reverence." This was not merely a strategy to help congregations worship — it was a crusade to make them refined. Refinement, as Richard Bushman has shown, became not only legitimate for Christians, but an essential element of their spirituality, even a sign of sanctification.[50] Refinement was something sought by the old order, a controlled dignity that would separate them from fanatics and pagans both.[51]

In its elegance, and in its magnificence, the sanctuary of the First Congregational Society served both spiritual and social purposes. What is most extraordinary about buildings such as First Church, Hartford, is that they played so many roles so well. They served the practical needs of congregations, both financial and social, without compromising their spiritual needs. With these structures, Calvinists found ways to adapt and interpret the latest fashions to suit their purposes. As such, these buildings tell us not so much about Calvinism as a rigid theology but about Calvinism as a

---

49. Elisha Athins, "A Sermon Delivered November 18, 1818, at the Dedication of the Congregational Meeting House in the North Parish of Killingly," pp. 10-11.

50. Richard L. Bushman, *The Refinement of America: Persons, Houses, Cities* (New York: Knopf, 1992). See especially chap. 10, "Religion and Taste."

51. At the Calvinism and the Visual Arts conference, John Cook made the pertinent observation that the old "plain style" meetinghouse architecture is at the same time being adopted by (at that time) culturally radical groups such as Methodists and Baptists — another reason for Congregationalists to find a new style for their own buildings. It may be that the

culture, persistent because of its adaptability. Meaning was not inherent in the new style, but the new style presented an occasion to redirect worship and theological emphasis. It was a way to stress inner piety yet make it congruent with the growing wealth and respectability of the community. Calvin's very reticence on matters of buildings for worship allowed his followers in early nineteenth-century Connecticut to express their faith architecturally as local circumstances directed.

Connecticut's Calvinist worship spaces thus became "elegant," not quite sacred but reserved, nonetheless, for special, spiritual purposes. In this way ministers such as Reverend Strong assuaged a need for emotional worship experience. While an omnipresent God needed no special place to make himself known, the church nonetheless was a locus of special grace. The laity, however, at least in their romantic imaginations, might have crossed over the line. A hymn written for dedication ceremonies, appearing in the 1810 *Hartford Selection,* proclaimed with awe the mystery of a house of worship:

> And will the great eternal God
> On earth establish his abode?
> And will he from his radiant throne
> Avow our temples for his own?
> These walls we to thy honor raise,
> Long may they echo with thy praise;
> And thou descending fill the place
> With choicest tokens of thy grace.[52]

Worshipers belting out these stanzas, whether they realized it or not, were declaring that their church had a unique purpose as God's house.

Suggested Reading

Benes, Peter, and Phillip D. Zimmerman, eds. *New England Meeting House and Church: 1630-1850.* Boston: Boston University for the Dublin Seminar for New England Folklife, 1979.

Bushman, Richard. *The Refinement of America: Persons, Houses, Cities.* New York: Knopf, 1992.

Campbell, Colin. *The Romantic Ethic and the Spirit of Modern Consumerism.* Oxford: Basil Blackwell, 1987.

---

true "plain style" is by necessity an architecture for outsiders, which Congregationalists most definitely were not in New England.

52. "On Opening a New House of Worship," hymn no. 343 in Nathan Strong, *Hartford Selection of Hymns,* 3rd ed. (1799; Hartford: P. B. Gleason, 1810). Perhaps ironically, Reverend Strong himself might have written the words to this hymn.

Kelly, J. Frederick. *Early Connecticut Meetinghouses.* 2 vols. New York: Columbia University Press, 1948.

Kling, David W. *A Field of Divine Wonders: The New Divinity and Village Revivals in Northwestern Connecticut, 1792-1822.* University Park: Pennsylvania State University Press, 1993.

Purcell, Richard. *Connecticut in Transition: 1775-1818.* 1918. Reprint, Middletown, Conn.: Wesleyan University Press, 1963.

Sweeney, Kevin M. "Meetinghouses, Town Houses, and Churches: Changing Perceptions of Sacred and Secular Space in Southern New England, 1720-1850." *Winterthur Portfolio* 28, no. 1 (spring 1993): 59-93.

Discussion

John Cook: First, does the issue of historicism (neoclassicism applied with some regularity across all of Connecticut) elicit any interest among Reformed Christians in European precedents within the worship realm, an interest in spirituality and true forms of worship however they might be defined? And secondly, regarding the curriculum which Nathan Strong studied at Yale, is there any evidence that this curriculum emphasized the classical tradition in and around early Christianity or its expressions culturally?

Gretchen Buggeln: In the documentary record I have not found anything positive said about European traditions. If and when I encounter references to European architecture, for example, it is usually a statement to the effect that ours are not so magnificent but in some way or other we are better, truer, more authentic; in other words, I do not see any evidence of direct and conscious copying of European precedents. As for Strong's training, I do not know what the Yale curriculum was at his time. But we have a tendency when we encounter neoclassical architecture to think Enlightenment and rationalism; this is certainly not the right connection in the case of these meetinghouses, because what is happening on the inside of these buildings is certainly not an Enlightenment form of religiosity. On the other hand, in some instances, as for example within Unitarian meetinghouses, the worship form is indeed driven by Enlightenment ideology. As a consequence of the great variety of attributed meanings in the early nineteenth century, I am reluctant to infer meaning based on architectural style alone. Instead one needs to consult the relevant documentary sources to determine what meanings Reformed Christians were associating with the buildings in which they worshiped.

James Tanis: In the decade before the Hartford meetinghouse was built, the churches of New England were troubled with Unitarianism. At the same time one of the most popular prints in circulation showed City Hall in New York with the inauguration of George Washington taking place within a classical portico, not unlike the portico in Hartford. In developing meetinghouses like the ones in Hartford or New Haven, was there a feeling that we Puritans have lost our hold on the political scene in America, which we once controlled, which indeed we founded, and maybe one way we can recover our lost place in the community is to pick up on the classical note? Do you find any evidence of political longing to recover a lost past, a longing that might have shaped architectural decisions within Reformed communities at this time?

Gretchen Buggeln: Yes, but the answer to this question is very complicated. Political considerations are a major factor in this period; for example, in New Haven there were Federalist congregations and Republican congregations in competition with one another, and in part their competition took place within an architectural framework. Also there is the example of Timothy Dwight, who at one point warns that we are losing our young people, we have to make worship more exciting for them, and one way to do that is to change the shape of our meetinghouses. Connecticut was a relatively stable environment; Unitarians were an insignificant minority in Connecticut during this time. The situation in Massachusetts was obviously very different. How this might have affected Reformed architecture there is a subject that deserves looking into.

Philip Benedict: The building of the Hartford meetinghouse represents a substantial cash outlay; as you point out, it was a costly undertaking. If we think of this building in the light of Calvin or Zwingli, a potential critique of this kind of expenditure is that money is being wasted on this building, money that could be given to the poor or to other good and useful social works. Is that a reproach that would have been made at the time the Hartford meetinghouse was constructed? Would the works of Calvin in particular have been important in the formation of the Connecticut ministers at the end of the eighteenth and beginning of the nineteenth centuries? In what degree did the then-current theological curriculum involve the active reading of Calvin's works? A similar question could be put in terms of the sanctification of the place of worship. Again, one can construct a mental image of the sixteenth-century Reformers, and one can hear them say, "Wait, hold on, here is an example of just the kinds of false forms of worship that have led to corruption and idolatry in the past." I wonder if Reformed Christians in early nineteenth-century Connecticut would have been capable of making this same critique? At the same time you indicated they asked for a meetinghouse that was "simple" and "decent." Perhaps they saw this not as representing a greater expenditure of money, but this is just what one would spend on an ordinary church at this time, in which case this becomes much more the reflection of the greater wealth of the community than anything else.

Gretchen Buggeln: The use of "decent" and "simple" is confusing language, difficult for us to comprehend, since the Hartford building was, comparatively speaking, far from simple. I am not sure what these words meant to the Reformed Christians of Hartford at the beginning of the nineteenth century. As to the question of money, it appears that there was no objection to the spending of substantial sums of money on church buildings until the middle of the nineteenth century, at which time churches were beginning to find themselves in financial straits. When debt becomes a problem, as it does toward the middle of the century, then I find people beginning to talk about the problem of spending money on church buildings, but not before that time. There may well have been some earlier, principled Reformed opposition to the expenditure of money on a church building, but if there was, I have not found it. As for the correspondence between Calvin's theological thought and architecture, I doubt the connection at this time in New England or at any other time; I can see the connection between Calvinism or Reformed Christianity understood as a culture and architecture, but to phrase the relationship in terms of Calvin's writings and architecture is, I think, too narrow. As for the language of sanctifying space or consecrating a building, the Hartford community trod a very thin line, but they never crossed over it. Yes, it is true they used this language, but they did not construe this language in a Catholic or an Anglican manner. They never say that the church building is a holy place; their language becomes a somewhat problematic indicator of what they actually meant; they are really pushing the boundaries and limits of what is meant under the traditional language of consecration.

Daniel W. Hardy: It seems to me that during much of this symposium, including in your paper, we have seen a great variation of styles determined by local and regional political and economic and social considerations. It strikes me there is something very important about the Reformed tradition in that respect; namely, the freedom of this tradition to express itself in a multiplicity of styles determined at the local and regional level. This, I think, goes to the heart of the Reformed tradition and its relationship to the world of the arts; namely, it is a tradition that makes claims for the sovereignty of God and the fullness of God's salvation — of course, not yet visible in the present moment. But it is this belief which provides the freedom to experiment in local and regional styles and to change from one style to another. The search for new ways to exemplify that freedom artistically in local terms is clearly a major and continuing aspect of the Reformed tradition overall.

James Lomax: On the question of historicism and the romantic movement in the so-called age of sensibility, the matter of associational qualities of architecture interests me. Here at Hartford we have a style that you keep on calling neoclassical, and yet the most conspicuous feature of these meetinghouses is the great steeple, which is really baroque, the reflection of the Wren and Vanbrugh (Sir John Vanbrugh, 1664-1726) style. This is a style that is associated historically with Roman Catholicism. I wonder if this association worried Reformed Christians in the early nineteenth century, or were they even aware of it? I also wonder at what point Gothic became an acceptable building style for Reformed Christians in the New World?

Gretchen Buggeln: It is true that the New England steeple is a remnant of a Catholic baroque style, but this is not the association drawn by Reformed Christians in the New World. There are many American poetic evocations of the symbolic significance of the church steeple in the vast landscape of North America. I think the steeple has something to do in the American popular mentality with the ability of people to locate the religious in an unfriendly or unknown place.

Peter Williams: There is a kind of crossing of curves as the Gothic ascends during the later nineteenth century in its various Americanized modes while Calvinism is on the decline; by the later nineteenth century when you see all kinds of churches almost promiscuously adopting Gothic, most of them have lost their Calvinism in any meaningful sense of that word.

John Cook: In showing the contrast between the eighteenth- and the early nineteenth-century Hartford meetinghouses, you implied there was some corrective in going to the new style. Have you run across anything in the documentary record that implies that the plain style became associated with an indecent emotionalism? If this were the case, the new style might have been associated with a correction of old errors.

Gretchen Buggeln: This is an interesting and important point. What we think of as the real plain style, barnlike structures devoid of embellishments — in fact, Methodists were building in this plain style at the same time. And in fact in New Haven there was considerable controversy centering on whether Methodists would be allowed to build in the older plain style on the New Haven Green at the same time that the three other, more elegant structures were being built. So there is no doubt that at this time Reformed Christians were separating themselves from the older, more inelegant style.

From Protestant to Catholic Plain Style

JAMES F. WHITE

All Western church buildings, both Catholic and Protestant, consist in up to six kinds of worship spaces: congregational space (proportionally the largest), movement space, gathering space (vestibule or narthex), choir space, baptismal space, and altar-table space (the sanctuary). Four or five centers of liturgical action are present typically in Western churches: the pulpit, the altar-table, the baptismal font (or pool), the presider's chair, and perhaps a lectern or reading desk. We shall be looking at the way in which these worship spaces and liturgical centers function in the life of Reformed communities. Due to the nature of Reformed worship, much of our attention is directed to congregational space and to the pulpit as the focus of the worshiping community.

1. The Principles of Reformed Architecture

A good place to begin this discussion is Calvin's important but often neglected remarks (*Inst.* 4.10.30) regarding form and content in matters of Christian worship:

> God did not will in outward discipline and ceremonies to prescribe in detail what we ought to do (because he foresaw that this depended upon the state of the times, and he did not deem one form suitable for all ages [. . . neque iudicaret unam seculis omnibus formam convenire . . .]); here we must take refuge in those general rules which he has given, that whatever the needs of the church (necessitas Ecclesiae) will require for order and decorum should be tested against these. Lastly, because he has taught nothing specifically, and because these things are not necessary to

salvation, and for the upbuilding of the church ought to be variously accommodated to the customs of each nation and age, it will be fitting (as the advantage of the church will require) to change and abrogate traditional practices and to establish new ones. Indeed, I admit that we ought not to charge into innovation rashly, suddenly, for insufficient cause. But love will best judge what may hurt or edify. . . .

Calvin was clearly interested in distinguishing between worship forms instituted by humans versus those thought to be of divine origin. Unfortunately, with their insistence on finding biblical warrants for every detail of worship, the English Puritans ignored Calvin's sensible advice on this subject. They were conspicuously remiss in observing the last line just cited: "Sed quid noceat uel aedificet, charitas optime iudicabit." Calvin's overall reflection points to a kind of cultural and artistic contingency, a healthy dependency on time and place and circumstance. Rather than the biblical literalism endorsed by English Puritans, what Calvin suggests is that the form and content of Christian worship be guided by principles of flexibility and adaptation to local conditions. Time and place should determine the details of worship — in each age and nation the arts surrounding Christian worship should reflect these principles, and it might be said that at its best Reformed worship has managed to embody this principle.

Much of this resembles contemporary debates over inculturation in worship.[1] Calvin's approach underscores the present *necessitas Ecclesiae*, from which one might infer that neither the practices of the early church nor those attested in the Bible are to be mindlessly imitated. Calvin was convinced, for example, that the laying on of hands in ordination (*impositio manus*) was a liturgical act that had biblical and apostolic authority, but he also thought it best to avoid imitating this practice because it was likely (given his sixteenth-century time and place) to produce superstitious abuses. In short, Calvin felt it was the historical context that should determine the form of worship.

He wrote little specifically about church architecture. He thought it a good idea for the baptismal font to be located near the pulpit so that the words of initiation could be heard throughout the building. Here function takes precedence over the symbolic emplacement of fonts at the entrance to the church building. Most medieval fonts were located at the main entrance because part of the rite took place in the church porch so as to symbolize baptism as an act of entrance. But, for Calvin, the church is the people, not the building, and hence baptism needs to be proclaimed in the midst of the congregation.

In similar fashion, Calvin conducted most of the Genevan service

---

1. Anscar J. Chupungco, *Liturgical Inculturation: Sacramentals, Religiosity, and Catechesis* (Collegeville, Minn., 1992).

from the pulpit, and hence the latter became the chief liturgical center for all worship. Preaching was essential to all Reformed worship, but the pulpit was also the locus of reading and prayer. The Lord's Supper became a quadrennial event when Calvin lost his campaign for a weekly Eucharist, and when the communion service was performed in the setting of Reformed worship the faithful sat on benches around a moveable table.[2] But in both theory and practice, the Reformed service was nonsacramental in character, emphasizing the pulpit as the principal visual and liturgical focus within the space of the worshiping community.

In order to underscore that focus, the worship space must be free of images, hence the iconoclastic imperative. Reformed Christians were also concerned to counter ostentatious display, the same concern that motivated Zwingli in his campaign against church music in Zurich, where two rival choirs vied with each other for musical prominence. Gifts of images involved considerable expenditures of money and were often little more than a strategy for a rich patron to show off his wealth. Money spent on images could be better directed to caring for the poor. The stripping bare of churches, the substitution of simple liturgical furnishings for gold and silver, the creation of a kind of visual and material asceticism within places of worship are all important historical statements about the Reformed Christian identity. Underlying the rejection of hallowed vessels (and sacramentals in general) is the intention to sacralize all of life, including the most mundane elements of everyday life. It is just possible that the visual impact of the Reformed wooden trencher and cup (Zwinglian innovations) at the communion meal said more to the faithful than the new words of the Reformed rite. In other words, a new locus of the sacred was being forged, not in the remote, the expensive and precious, the inaccessible, but in the ordinary things of everyday life. In this sense, Rembrandt's grasp of the sacred in the ordinary is the expression of a quintessentially Reformed aesthetic. It should come as no surprise that Reformed places of worship often resemble houses — the interpenetration of sacred and domestic (or sacred and secular) is a veritable leitmotif within the Reformed tradition.

2. A Critique of the So-Called Protestant Plain Style

In recent times it has become fashionable to invoke the term "plain style"[3] as a label that describes New World meetinghouses from the seventeenth to the mid–nineteenth century. The usefulness of this term is

2. George Hay, *The Architecture of Scottish Post-Reformation Churches, 1560-1843* (Oxford: Clarendon Press, 1957), pls. 25 and 26; see also figure 24 in James Lomax, "Huguenot Goldsmiths in England," in this volume.

3. A. Garvan, "The Protestant Plain Style before 1630," *Journal of the Society of Architectural Historians* 9 (1950): 5-13.

questionable. In point of historical fact, it is only the Shakers who deliberately sought plainness as an end in itself, avoiding all things "meretricious." But in the New World as elsewhere, the Reformed principle of architectural design, rather than consisting in plainness, is better described as consisting in a set of attitudes that evaluates priorities and elevates what is functionally necessary and desirable while at the same time eliminating the dross.

Many churches were remodeled in Reformed countries during the sixteenth century. The challenge was to reconfigure and adapt existing churches to Reformed worship rather than building new ones. A parallel process was taking place in Roman Catholic churches, as is evidenced in the removal of rood screens.[4] In Milan, Charles Borromeo drew up a whole scheme of meticulous changes, including such then-novelties as communion rails and confessional booths.[5] As the sixteenth century wore on, new Reformed churches were built to replace those that had been destroyed. These began to appear in the Netherlands, France, and especially Scotland. Though stylistically different, they all show some common liturgical features.

The first of these changes involves the prominence of the pulpit, rather than the altar, as the chief liturgical center. The second is the move to centralized rather than longitudinal space. Third is the almost universal introduction of a balcony or balconies to gather as many people as possible as close as possible to the chief liturgical center. Fourth is the great concern about optimum acoustics. And fifth is the aniconic nature of these buildings, with the total elimination of traditional Christian iconography.

The Scottish church at Burntisland (1592) is a good example. Here is a totally new kind of church, designed as a square with the pulpit at one of the central piers. Balconies surround the central space on all four sides. No one is far distant from the pulpit. And it is a clear, well-lighted space devoid of representations of the deity, although the various trades are represented by symbols. George Hay calls it "a sturdy home product," not an imitation of Dutch or other models.[6] What does all this mean? A church has been built for the Reformed liturgy, in this case John Knox's *Book of Common Order* (1564), based on his prototype in Geneva.[7] The priorities are clear: everything focuses on the Word of God, read, preached, and prayed from a prominent pulpit. Everyone present can both see and hear the preacher, and there is nothing to distract their attention. Knox's service is

4. F. Bond, *Screens and Galleries* (London, 1908), p. 141.

5. Evelyn Carole Volker, "Charles Borromeo's *Instructiones Fabricae et Supellectilis Ecclesiasticae 1577*" (Ph.D. diss., Syracuse University, 1977).

6. Hay, pp. 32-33, pl. 2. Also Ian G. Lindsay, *The Scottish Parish Kirk* (Edinburgh: St. Andrew Press, 1960), p. 40.

7. William D. Maxwell, *The Liturgical Portions of the Genevan Service Book* (Westminster: Faith Press, 1965).

460

about as didactic as any has ever been; even the Lord's Prayer is prayed in commentary. If the building has many of the characteristics of a schoolroom, it is no accident. Here is a consistent and positive statement about the nature of Reformed worship, which always seems the most cerebral tradition of all.

In many of the Scottish churches, ingenious devices were made for communion pews so that the people could sit about the Lord's Table when communion was served. Everything in worship was to be both visible and audible. What a different world from the medieval church where Bishop Stephen Gardiner could argue "it was never meant that the people should indeed hear the Matins or hear the Mass, but be present there and pray themselves in silence."[8] Reformed churches are not built for private devotions but for common worship, especially preaching and communion services.

These same factors are present in the Dutch churches of the sixteenth and seventeenth centuries. Beginning with the octagonal church at Willemstad (1596-1607), they exhibit free and exuberant forms. The wealth of the culture is reflected in magnificent brass chandeliers and ornate pipe organ cases. The octagonal churches the Dutch erected in America have all disappeared. But other central plans evolved in the Netherlands: the dumbbell, two sets of shallow transepts intersecting a rectangle; the square; the Greek cross; and the "T" shape.[9] Frequently, medieval Netherlandish churches were remodeled with magnificent pulpits with large sounding boards halfway down the nave, the congregation circling this liturgical center. These pulpits are elaborate and far from plain. They deliberately catch the eye and focus on the essential item in worship, the Word of God. Many of these buildings were recorded by seventeenth-century Dutch painters, both remodeled churches and new.[10]

In France, all Reformed churches were destroyed after 1685. But the famous temple at Charenton,[11] built in 1623, shows the same arrangements as those we have witnessed. Two rows of balconies on all four sides gathered the maximum number of worshipers close to the tall, freestanding pulpit. The temple in Lyon, named "Paradise," had a single balcony en-

8. *The Letters of Stephen Gardiner,* ed. James A. Muller (New York: Macmillan, 1933), p. 355, spelling modernized.

9. See James F. White, *Protestant Worship and Church Architecture* (New York: Oxford University Press, 1964), pp. 89-91.

10. *Saenredam 1597-1665, Peintre des Églises* (Paris: 1970); *Perspectives: Saenredam and the Architectural Painters of the Seventeenth Century,* ed. Jeroen Giltaij and Guido Jansen (Rotterdam: Museum Boymans-van Beuningen, 1991), pp. 112 and 120; Gary Schwartz and Marten Jan Bok, *Pieter Saenredam: The Painter and His Time* (New York: Abbeville Press, 1989), pls. 103 and 228.

11. See figure 42 in Hélène Guicharnaud, "An Introduction to the Architecture of Protestant Temples Constructed in France before the Revocation of the Edict of Nantes," in this volume.

circling the whole building. The tall pulpit with sounding board had an ominous hourglass suspended. The only ornaments were coats of arms and monuments to the dead, which reflect the social hierarchies of the time.

I cite these European examples only to show a consistency in purpose in producing liturgical architecture for a totally new vision of what the liturgy consisted of, a focus on the service of the Word reinforced occasionally by the service of the table and baptism. All of these aspects of worship were seen as forms of proclamation. Calvin's plea for a weekly Eucharist went unheeded. Protestants expect to be edified in worship, Catholics to be sanctified. The purpose of these buildings is not plainness for the sake of plainness; instead the goal is to enable all to participate in the liturgy instead of being distant onlookers to an unheard mass. The medieval notion of participation as seeing was being replaced by the concept of participation by hearing.[12] In this sense, Reformed churches are "auditory churches," as remarked by Christopher Wren. But preaching also has a visual component, hence care was taken that the preacher be seen as well as heard.

Some appreciation of the Reformed aesthetic is provided by the Puritan William Dowsing, parliamentary visitor for East Anglia working in Cambridgeshire and Suffolk in 1643-44.[13] Dowsing's task was to purify the churches he visited of any relics of popery or superstition yet remaining. It may seem surprising that any of these was left after nearly a century of reformation, especially given the massive iconoclasm under Edward VI (1547-53). But Dowsing was energetic and found a number of things that even Roman Catholics were to proscribe such as figures of the Trinity in human form. There were still plenty of tombs with inscriptions of "Ora pro Nobis" that had to go as well as myriad angels and images of the saints. And he kept a careful journal of everything he saw and smashed.

Dowsing's agenda was strictly a theological one; he was destroying whatever would mislead the illiterate and unwary. In the parish church of Ufford, Suffolk, Dowsing paused to admire "a glorious cover over the Font" which is still there today, complete with the image of a pelican picking its breast.[14] Dowsing had no desire to demolish something because it was beautiful, only if it was not theologically correct. Plainness was not his agenda at all. And fortunately from our perspective, he must have taken an occasional bribe to spare windows in some of the Cambridge colleges.

North America was to provide the greatest laboratory for the design and execution of buildings for Reformed worship. Every village in New England had to have a meetinghouse; even today there are over five hundred

---

12. M. Miles, *Image as Insight* (Boston, 1985), pp. 95-125.

13. James F. White, "A Good Word for William Dowsing," *Theology Today* 18 (July 1961): 180-84.

14. Francis Bond, *Fonts and Font Covers* (London, 1908), p. 280.

churches and meetinghouses built before 1830 still standing in New England.[15] Most of them were built by Congregationalists; there is said to be a Congregational church in every inhabited town in Vermont. The Dutch Reformed built in the Hudson Valley, on Long Island, and in New Jersey. Presbyterian churches were scattered from New England to Georgia. Most of the Huguenots became Anglicans, although the French Huguenot Church (1845) remains in Charleston, South Carolina.[16]

The earliest building type in New England was the pyramid, of which a single example remains today, namely, the Old Ship Church (1681) (see fig. 160) in Hingham, Massachusetts.[17] Although much restored (and added onto in 1729 and 1755), Hingham has all the earmarks of Puritan liturgical architecture.[18] Balconies on three sides surround a beautifully paneled pulpit with a large sounding board over it, topped by a turned finial. There is nothing plain about the pulpit. Its woodworking is as elegant as anything possible in the colony at the time. Behind it are two round-headed pulpit windows, and in front of the pulpit is a pew with a hinged table leaf for the Lord's Supper. Between the two windows are fluted pilasters. The whole ensemble is an elaborate piece of woodworking. Otherwise the building has few ornaments other than the turned spindles on top of the box pews, each with a paneled door.

What is going on here? Obviously considerable ornamentation has been lavished on the chief liturgical center, the pulpit, with its elegant wineglass shape. One has only to compare it with domestic architecture of the time to see that this is the finest work of which colonial craftsmen in the Bay Colony were capable. At Hingham great care was lavished on the house of worship. The communion table, which folds down when not in use, was put into service only once a month, but the pulpit was used for Sunday sermons and weekday lectures. From every pew one has a view of the pulpit, which is raised enough so that those in the balcony can see the preacher. In short, everyone present in this elegant worship space is capable of both hearing and seeing the man in the pulpit.

It is intriguing to note that there are more extant and intact Quaker meetinghouses (Third Haven, Easton, Maryland [1684]; Flushing, New York [1694]; Portsmouth, Rhode Island [1700]) than Puritan meetinghouses dating to the seventeenth century. These buildings belonging to the

---

15. Edmund Sinnott, *Meetinghouse and Church in Early New England* (New York: Bonanza Books, 1963), appendix, pp. 211-39.

16. Preservation Society of Charleston, *The Churches of Charleston and the Low Country* (Columbia: University of South Carolina Press, 1994), pp. 9-11.

17. M. C. Donnelly, *The New England Meeting Houses of the Seventeenth Century* (Middletown, Conn.: Wesleyan University Press, 1968), pp. 121-30.

18. Horton Davies, *The Worship of the American Puritans* (New York: Peter Lang, 1990), pp. 233-50.

160. Old Ship Church,
Hingham, Mass.,
1681, exterior

Society of Friends have remained largely untouched down to the present due to the fact that Quaker worship has not changed substantially for the past two hundred years.[19]

Orientation to the long side of the worship space dominated Reformed meetinghouses during the eighteenth century in New England. Some notable examples survive of eighteenth-century Reformed meetinghouses. Several of the best examples are not far from the Massachusetts–New Hampshire border near Lawrence, Massachusetts. Amesbury, Massachusetts, boasts the Rocky Hill Meetinghouse of 1785 (see plates 42-46).[20] Here the pulpit dominates both the main floor and the balcony on three sides. The pulpit exhibits elegant raised panels, half a wineglass

19. Kenneth L. Carroll, *Three Hundred Years and More of Third Haven Quakerism* (Easton, Md.: Third Haven Meeting of Friends, 1984).

20. Carroll, pp. 54-55.

shape, and dentillations. A large sounding board surmounts the round-headed pulpit window, which is framed by marbleized, fluted pilasters. No pains were spared to make this an elegant focal point within the overall interior of the building.

Across the state line in New Hampshire there are marvelous meetinghouses in Danville (1760) and Sandown (1774) and somewhat less exciting examples in Hampstead (1745), now the town hall, and Fremont (1800).[21] Sandown is especially fascinating; reduced in scale, it could easily pass for a house. The building has elegant doors fitted out with pediments and pilasters. The interior pulpit is much like its counterpart at Amesbury with a round-headed pulpit window. Other examples remain in New England: Wethersfield, Connecticut (1764); Farmington, Connecticut (1771);[22] Walpole (1772) and Harrington (1772), both in Bristol, Maine; Alna, Maine (1789); and Rockingham, Vermont (1787). One of the more interesting meetinghouses is in Brooklyn, Connecticut (1771),[23] where a stair tower has been added at one end and crowned by belfry, lantern, and spire. Old Tennant Church in Tennant, New Jersey (1751), is a well-preserved meetinghouse with the pulpit on the long side. Scattered around New England are other eighteenth-century meetinghouses that were later reoriented to one of the short ends of the building; included are the buildings at Thetford Hill (1787) and Townshend (1790), both in Vermont.[24]

This reorientation happened in a church of somewhat different structure, the stone Fort Herkimer Reformed Church in New York's Mohawk Valley. This church was built by Reformed settlers from the German Palatinate and was originally oriented to a long side. Construction may have started in 1753, but due to the French and Indian War was not complete until 1767. A rebuilding occurred in 1812 in which the worship space was reoriented and the walls raised eight feet to accommodate a balcony. The Fort Herkimer meetinghouse possesses one of the most distinctive pulpits in North America. Flanked by stairs, it rises twelve feet from the floor. Its octagonal shape is reflected in a massive sounding board crowned by a decorative urn. The height of the pulpit is partly due to the need for eye contact with those sitting in the balconies. But it does provide a magnificent setting for Reformed worship with every eye focused on the place for preaching God's word.

There is an interesting parallel between the reorientation of meetinghouses and that of barns in the early nineteenth century. The earlier, so-called English barn had its entrance in the middle of a long side; ex-

21. Sinnott, pp. 56-65.

22. Frederick Kelly, *Early Connecticut Meetinghouses* (New York: Columbia University Press, 1948), vol. 1, pp. 157-69.

23. Kelly, vol. 1, pp. 36-43.

24. James F. White, "Landmark Churches," *Vermonter: Burlington Free Press,* 2 October 1977, pp. 4-8.

tant examples include medieval tithe barns in places such as Bradford-on-Avon or near Tewkesbury. But the so-called American barn which became dominant in the nineteenth century has the entrance in one of the short ends. And one of the causes of the change is the result of the move from wheat to dairy farming in the New World setting.

In many of the New World meetinghouses, the visual focal points important for worship — namely, the pulpit, the pulpit window, and the sounding board — are far from plain. Though he is speaking of the seventeenth century, Robert F. Trent underscores the fact that "such meetinghouse fixtures as survive are fashioned with a degree of ornamental detail and finish not inconsistent with high quality joinery intended for domestic interiors."[25] This is also true of the exterior woodwork. The denticulated cornices and the pedimented doorways bear comparison with the fine domestic structures of the eighteenth century such as those in Portsmouth, New Hampshire, Salem and Old Deerfield, Massachusetts.[26] Pulpit windows, sometimes doubled, are a lovely feature, as are finely wrought sounding boards, pulpit stairs, and the wineglass or tub-shaped pulpits.

In summary, we must conclude that "plainness" is not the right word. Instead, what is at stake in the first two centuries of American meetinghouses is a focus on the essentials of Reformed worship. The worship spaces and the architectural ornament declare the hierarchy of Reformed priorities culminating in the preaching of the Word of God. These buildings are splendid reflections of the worship purposes for which they were built.

3. Nineteenth-Century Reversals

Unfortunately, most books on New World Reformed architecture terminate the story around 1830 or 1840, the period of the Greek revival here exemplified by Congregational churches in Madison, Connecticut (1838) (see fig. 161), and Nantucket, Massachusetts (see figs. 162 and 163). By this date most Federal-period meetinghouses had been oriented to a short side, but the liturgical priorities remained the same as when the orientation had been to a long side. The neoclassical revival had a chastening effect in terms of standardizing the white painted exterior of the typical New England Congregational meetinghouse. Before that time, "colors were overwhelmingly more popular than plain white lead or stone color,"[27] and

25. Trent, "The Marblehead Pews," in *New England Meeting House and Church: 1630-1850*, ed. Peter Benes (Boston: Boston University Scholarly Publications, 1979), p. 103.

26. Hugh Morrison, *Early American Architecture* (New York, 1952), pp. 471-502.

27. Peter Benes, "Sky Colors and Scattered Clouds: The Decorative and Architectural Painting of New England Meeting Houses, 1738-1834," in *New England Meeting House and*

161. Congregational
Church, Madison,
Conn., 1838, exterior

records exist of churches painted blue, brown, yellow, and ochre. The familiar white church on the green, the faux marble New England temple, reflects a fascination with Greek culture and democracy in the early decades of the nineteenth century.

Major changes took place within Reformed communities in the decades after 1830s; they were particularly motivated by three factors: revivalism, the Sunday school movement, and romanticism. These three

Church: 1630-1850, ed. Peter Benes (Boston: Boston University Scholarly Publications, 1979), p. 59.

467

162. First Congrega-
tional Church,
Nantucket, Mass.,
interior

brought major disruptions in the configuration of worship space — the
latter had been upheld for more than two centuries despite changing
tastes in architectural style. A paradigm of this tumultuous period can be
seen in one of the most widely admired nineteenth-century meetinghouses, namely, the Litchfield, Connecticut, Congregational Church.[28]
The old parish church, where Lyman Beecher was the pastor, had stood
on the green. After the Connecticut disestablishment of Congregationalism in 1818, the congregation moved off the green and in 1829 built an

28. Frederick Kelly, *Early Connecticut Meetinghouses*, vol. 2 (New York: Columbia University Press, 1948).

468

163. First Congregational Church, Nantucket, Mass., interior

elegant, Federal-style building. But forty years later, the people of Litchfield found this building ugly and utterly without grace. So they abandoned it and built a Gothic building which they used for about sixty years; in 1929 the tower was removed and it was turned into a movie theater. In the same year, the Federal-style meetinghouse was restored, reflecting yet again the ephemera and vagaries of more recent Reformed taste shaping worship space.

469

Revivalism brought a major change to the worship of many Protestant traditions.[29] New methods were developed, often on the frontier, bringing Christianity to a largely unchurched population. The techniques elaborated in frontier camp meetings in the early 1800s were brought back east and domesticated in the major cities of the East Coast in the 1830s. Only the Anglican and Anabaptist traditions escaped much change. The frontier tradition became a liturgical black hole which drew the other Protestant worship traditions, even the Quakers, out of their accustomed orbits.

Soon a standard type of service evolved; it can be seen on television any Sunday. It consists of three parts: prayer and praise (largely music), fervent preaching for conversion, and the harvest of those converted. The role that music plays in the worship service grew enormously thanks to revivalism. Churches that had shunned the very notion of choirs now found themselves with quartets, octets, and full-blown choirs. To accommodate these, new spaces were necessary. A significant event in this evolution was the building of Broadway Tabernacle in New York City, in 1836.[30] Charles G. Finney, the pastor, had done more than anyone else to spread and domesticate the frontier tradition in worship in the East.

Several changes became imperative as the frontier tradition increasingly came to prevail among Congregationalists and Presbyterians. The pulpit was replaced by a platform with a desk pulpit on it. The more emotional and vigorous preachers needed more space, such as they had had on the rude platforms of the camp meeting. They, too, were joined by visiting preachers and song leaders. For the first time, clergy seating became prominent, resulting in the three pulpit chairs (for visiting preacher, minister, and song leader) which became so dominant as the century wore on.

Space had to be found for the musicians, now a major part of the worshiping community. Usually a concert stage arrangement was adopted so that the choir faced the congregation. And pipe organs began to sprout up — these were unthinkable within the Reformed tradition of earlier centuries. Balconies still abounded, but sloping floors eventually were introduced to improve sight lines. And acoustics became a major concern, especially as the scale of buildings increased.

The changes in Reformed churches were simply a reflection of the new worship. Whereas the Puritan tradition had once insisted on freedom to follow the Word of God in ordering worship, now the emphasis came to be freedom to do whatever worked well in worship. This meant a blithe disregard of tradition of any sort in favor of a pragmatic approach. What

29. James F. White, "The Frontier Tradition," in *Protestant Worship: Traditions in Transition* (Louisville: Westminster/John Knox Press, 1989), pp. 171-91.

30. See unpublished article by Jeanne Halgren Kilde on this church: "Charles Finney, the Free Church Movement, and the Transformation of American Protestant Architecture."

worked was whatever could be exploited to produce converts and rekindle the flames of devotion among the already converted. Obviously the new techniques worked. A whole continent was converted, but hardly by means that Calvin or Knox would have recognized. The process continues today and can be seen on Sundays on television.

The second factor which caused material changes in Reformed church architecture was the advent of the Sunday school. The founding (1824) of the American Sunday-School Union marks an important step in what was rapidly becoming a major part of parish church life. In time, denominations set up boards and agencies to promote Sunday schools in every congregation.[31] The whole process evolved, in many ways paralleling developments in public education. Graded curricula became standard, and this brought the need for separate classrooms for each grade level, often with boys and girls separated. Classroom time was usually prefaced by "opening exercises" which necessitated a large assembly room. The Sunday school became an important pedagogical tool, an integral part of evangelism. By the late nineteenth century, insiders claimed that 80 percent of new church members had come via the Sunday school route.

Consequences followed for the design of worship spaces. For example, multiple small classrooms arose around the perimeter of an assembly space. Many churches in New England accommodated the need for instructional space by simply jacking up the church and running another story underneath it — a good example of this expedient is the meetinghouse in North Montpelier, Vermont. Still another common solution was that of flooring over the church at the balcony level — examples can be found in the meetinghouses at Townshend and East Poultney, Vermont. Solutions like these compromised the worship space but enhanced the use of the building as an instructional center. This development had the collateral effect of causing the redefinition of the meetinghouse from a place of worship to a multipurpose building.

Larger churches solved the Sunday school problem in other ways. Very popular during the years after 1870 was the so-called Akron plan,[32] which combined worship space with Sunday school space via the introduction of moveable doors. This made major expansion for important events possible. The Sunday school unit often consisted in individual classrooms arranged on a main floor with a horseshoe balcony above surrounding an assembly space. Some communities introduced the so-called church plant

---

31. Anne M. Boyland, *Sunday School: The Formation of an American Institution, 1790-1880* (New Haven: Yale University Press, 1988), and Robert W. Lynn and Elliott Wright, *The Big Little School: Two Hundred Years of the Sunday School* (Birmingham: Religious Education Press, 1980).

32. Marion Lawrence, "The Akron Plan — Its Genesis, History, and Development," *Thirty-Second Annual Report of the Board of Church Extension of the Methodist Episcopal Church, South* (n.p., 1914), pp. 270-71.

paradigm, involving the intermingling of educational, social, office, and worship spaces.

Romanticism was the third factor affecting church design in the nineteenth century — with its broadly based appeal this movement caused a stylistic redefinition of the meetinghouses under a wide variety of types. There seems to be no compelling reason based on the principles of Reformed worship why a Presbyterian church in Nashville should be built in an Egyptian style, just as there are no convincing reasons why thousands of nineteenth-century Reformed churches should have been constructed to resemble Romanesque, Gothic, and Spanish mission churches.

Beginning in the 1830s, the first Gothic revival swept America. Popularized by figures like Bishop John Henry Hopkins of Vermont,[33] it soon became the almost official style of the Episcopal Church. But the darling of this stylistic fad, architect Richard Upjohn,[34] was eventually hired to produce the Congregational Church in Brunswick, Maine (1846) — the latter was built at the same time as his Trinity Episcopal on Wall Street.[35] Soon pointed windows, blank arcades, and sharp finials came to be standard details within Reformed structures — in structures built of wood most of these details made little sense.

In the 1880s the Gothic style gave way to flirtations with the Romanesque, particularly in affluent urban congregations where there was sufficient money to build in stone. The appeal of the Romanesque soon waned, and toward the end of the century a new eclecticism set in, offering a stylistic hodgepodge which arguably found its culmination in the Mormon tradition.[36] What was happening within Reformed communities was the surrender of traditional worship principles — nostalgia and romanticism took their place. Gothic churches were longitudinally planned spaces with chancels and transepts — the Reformed tradition had rejected much of this in the sixteenth century. Gothic churches featured stained glass windows, interior relief, three-dimensional wood and stone, and painting — indeed, a variety of pictorial arts. Reformed communities viewed this religious art under the rubric "decoration," and hence judged that this art did not constitute the kind of idolatrous threat that William Dowsing so dreaded.

The climax of these diversionary developments came in the second Gothic revival during the first decades of the twentieth century. Gradually

33. James F. White, "Theology and Architecture in America: A Study of Three Leaders," in *A Miscellany of American Christianity* (Durham: Duke University Press, 1963), pp. 362-71.

34. Everard M. Upjohn, *Richard Upjohn: Architect and Churchman* (New York: Da Capo Press, 1968), pp. 78-74.

35. Upjohn, pp. 45-67.

36. L. A. Andrew, *The Early Temples of the Mormons* (Albany, 1978).

the high priest of the neo-Gothic, architect Ralph Adams Cram,[37] managed to mesmerize congregations within the Reformed tradition. Cram remarked with delight that his East Liberty Presbyterian Church in Pittsburgh "could be prepared for a pontifical High Mass" in a few minutes. He rejoiced: "It would have surprised and even horrified Doctors Calvin and Knox in their day, but we are permitted to believe they are better informed now!"[38] That judgment remains to be seen.

For those congregations that could not afford neo-Gothic construction, neo-Georgian became an alternative. But despite the copybook details, the worship space of Reformed buildings in this style was configured with disregard of the relevant eighteenth-century models. Easily the dominant neo-Georgian advocate during the first forty years of this century was Elbert M. Conover, who presided over the Interdenominational Bureau of Architecture begun in 1934.[39] Conover had one credo: a Reformed church must have a chancel with a pulpit on one side, a lectern on the other, and a prominent altar at the back — not a table but an altar, and please, no conspicuous clergy chairs. The Reformed tradition of a congregation gathered about a central pulpit went out the window. And neo-Georgian Reformed buildings dating to the first half of this century are legion. It appears that in this century Reformed principles in the design of worship space have been smothered in an avalanche of romantic revivals of which the medieval and neo-Georgian re-creations play the most conspicuous role.

4. Roman Catholic Appropriations

The greatest irony in all this is that many of the liturgical and architectural principles of Reformed worship reappeared in the second half of this century at a very unexpected place, namely, among Roman Catholics. A Catholic liturgical movement had been underway since the 1830s,[40] and it, too, was fueled by many of the same romantic instincts that inspired Reformed Christians. In Catholic France, Dom Prosper Guéranger revived medievalism in all its forms, including the liturgy and its architectural setting. Until the middle of this century the Catholic liturgical movement remained essentially restorationist in character, oriented to recapturing past glories, but after World War II the monastic communities at Maria Laach and Saint

37. Douglass Shand Tucci, *Ralph Adams Cram: American Medievalist* (Boston: Boston Public Library, 1975).

38. Ralph Adams Cram, *My Life in Architecture* (Boston: Little, Brown, 1936), p. 255.

39. Elbert M. Conover, *Building the House of God* (New York: Methodist Book Concern, 1928), and *The Church Builder* (New York: Interdenominational Bureau of Architecture, 1948).

40. James F. White, *Roman Catholic Worship: Trent to Today* (Mahwah, N.J.: Paulist Press, 1995), pp. 69-114.

John's Abbey embarked on a new path which was more reformist than restorationist.

After 1945 the Catholic liturgical movement began to adopt a quasi-Reformed Protestant liturgical agenda. It sought to move the experience of Roman Catholic worship away from devotions performed by individuals apart from the body of the congregation to a communitarian liturgy in which all found "full, conscious, and active participation."[41] And it sought to achieve these goals by many of the same means that Calvin and others had introduced in the sixteenth century: a vernacular worship service, a strong emphasis on reading and preaching, a simplification of rites, congregational song. My late colleague Mark Searle used to say that what Vatican II decided was that "it was okay to be Protestant when it came to worship." In the years since the Council, Protestants have returned the compliment by adopting many of the post–Vatican II Roman Catholic reforms, notably the Sunday mass lectionary.

It did not take long for the changes in the liturgy to spark massive architectural changes. The first noticeable change was an *Instruction*[42] in September 1964 mandating moving the altar away from the wall so the celebrant could stand behind it facing the people. This had long been the Reformed tradition until the nineteenth-century stylistic revivals undermined basic principles. As the changes increased, moving the mass from being an occasion for devotions to a genuine liturgy (work of the people) caused the acceleration of architectural transformations. Objects that had once been the center of Catholic devotions began to disappear. The old "his and her" altars were displaced by a single altar. Images were carted off by the truckload. No one called this iconoclasm, but William Dowsing would have rejoiced. Stations of the cross, where they survived, were diminished or relegated to side chapels. Given the number of churches built and/or reconfigured in both Europe and America after 1945, it might be argued that more iconoclasm occurred in the 1960s than in the 1560s.

Much reordering went on in the years that followed. The twofold division between clergy space and people space was drastically reduced. The leading guide to liturgical architecture was *Art and Environment in Catholic Worship*. It states: "Among symbols with which liturgy deals, none is more important than this assembly of believers. . . . There is no audience, no passive element in the liturgical celebration."[43] Calvin did not say it any better.

The emphasis was on "simplicity and commonness." Ironically, the first illustration in *Art and Environment in Catholic Worship* was a Shaker interior. The word "plain" does not appear, but the results could easily be

---

41. *Constitution on the Sacred Liturgy* (Collegeville, Minn.: Liturgical Press, 1964), p. 13.

42. *Instruction for the Proper Implementation of the Constitution on the Sacred Liturgy* (Vatican City: Typis Polyglottis Vaticanis, 1964), p. 47.

43. *Art and Environment in Catholic Worship* (Washington: National Conference of Catholic Bishops, 1978), pp. 18-19.

called "Catholic plain style." But more importantly, what has happened is a clear focus on the essentials of worship. This has concentrated on four items: altar-table, pulpit, font, and presider's chair. It is also interesting to note the aniconic nature of splendid Catholic structures such as the Church of Saint Elizabeth Seton in Carmel, Indiana, or the Church of Saint John the Baptist in Hopkins, Minnesota. Here there are no images within the worship space, only liturgical centers. Even the altar-table has shrunk to very modest size, no bigger than the presider's outreached hands.

Another parallel with Reformed tradition is the Roman Catholic interest in centralized plans. This has meant just about any shape except a long rectangle with a chancel tacked on to one end. Indeed, the disappearance of the once-common longitudinal plan has provoked a considerable rethinking and reordering of worship space within the Catholic tradition. A good example would be Saint Peter's, Saratoga Springs, New York, as redesigned by Frank Kacmarcik. This was a traditional Gothic revival building of the 1920s. Now the chancel has been walled off as a weekday chapel. The altar-table, pulpit, and presider's chair have been placed in the middle of a long wall. The congregation gathers on three sides of the liturgical center. It is basically the same arrangement as the eighteenth-century Puritan meetinghouse. There is one exception: balconies are not convenient in a church where most people receive communion frequently.

Within the Catholic tradition we now see churches built to focus entirely on the essentials of the liturgy with the full participation of the congregation. The ministry of the Word has become a central focus in the Roman Catholic service, and the pulpits, sometimes containing a throne for the Bible, proclaim this fact. The altar-table is a central feature with the people gathered around it; communion rails have all but disappeared. At the present moment Roman Catholics seem well on their way to rediscovering baptistries for immersion, as are found in every Baptist church. And the presider's chair implies that the priest sometimes sits down and delegates leadership to someone else, be it reader or musician. In short, Reformed principles in the design of church architecture live on but now in a different community — Presbyterians seem to have forgotten these principles while Roman Catholics have appropriated them!

Bibliography

Benes, Peter, ed. *New England Meeting House and Church: 1630-1850*. Boston, 1979.

Benes, Peter, and Philip D. Zimmerman. *New England Meeting House and Church: 1630-1850*. Boston, 1979.

Donnelly, Marian Card. *The New England Meeting Houses of the Seventeenth Century*. Middletown, Conn., 1968.

Hay, George. *The Architecture of the Scottish Post-Reformation Churches, 1560-1843*. Oxford, 1957.

White, James F. *Protestant Worship and Church Architecture*. New York, 1964.

Discussion

Victor Nuovo: Regarding your opening remark about Calvin's sacramental theology and his desire to celebrate the Lord's Supper once weekly, I wonder what would have been the consequences, architecturally speaking, if he had had his way. Do you think that Reformed buildings would have had permanent tables along with pulpits rather than just the permanent pulpit?

James White: Hinged altar-tables at Hingham and Amesbury, I think, are indicative of the Reformed mentality: these are occasional liturgical centers, whereas the pulpit is always an invariable liturgical center. But if Calvin had got his way, presumably the table for the Lord's Supper and its benches would have played a much more prominent and fixed role in the overall liturgical furnishings of Reformed houses of worship.

George Hunsinger: I have a footnote on this subject. In the 1536 edition of the *Institutes* (*Opera selecta* I, ed. P. Barth [Munich, 1926], IV.140, p. 161), Calvin made a statement which was repeated in all subsequent editions all the way through to 1559. The Lord's Supper, he claimed, should be celebrated *at least* once a week: "Quantum ad sacram coenam attinet, sic administrari decentissime poterat: si saepissime et singulis ad minimum hebdomadibus proponeretur ecclesiae." This was reaffirmed in 1559 (*Inst.* 4.17.43). Can you comment on this?

James White: The average for late medieval Catholics was reception of the Eucharist *at the most* four times a year, so when Zwingli adopted a calendar of quarterly annual communion (at Christmas, Easter, Pentecost, September), he was basically saying no communion, no Eucharist, but he was in fact acting very conservatively by reinforcing the already existing Catholic practice. Calvin thought he could get away with requiring communion fifty-two times a year, but that was far too radical for the burghers of Geneva, and he failed to get his way. He went on record saying that our present practice is defective, but he had to yield to the magistrates on this point.

James Lomax: It seems to me that one of the conspicuous features of the plain style is the obsession with the intrinsic material quality of fittings, expensive mahoganies and other hardwoods, expensive brass chandeliers and fittings, expensive communion silverware, and so on. I wonder if this is not a psychological response which is perhaps typically Anglo-Saxon and is also typical of this period and is reflected in the whole English and New England set of attitudes not just to places of worship but also to domestic settings? It seems that these people just liked this style of furnishings. And what they liked in the way of decorative arts in the domestic sphere seems to have simply carried over into the sacred sphere. Can you comment?

James White: This is why I began with the Calvin quote to the effect that everything is culturally contingent, except for the general rules which God lays down in Scripture. In their decoration of their houses of worship, Reformed Christians in the New World simply went with the tastes of time. They did not have one particular style that they espoused or wanted to promote. But the Shakers, by contrast, did get into the bind of prescribing a style; Moses Johnson built most of the surviving buildings himself. The Shakers did legislate to preserve a distinctive style, as if an angel had brought down the design archetype from heaven: How could one dare to change or try to improve on such an archetype? But Reformed Christians simply went with whatever styles were current.

Metamorphoses of the Meetinghouse: Three Case Studies

PETER W. WILLIAMS

The *locus classicus* of the Anglo-American Calvinist (or Reformed) attitude toward the material setting of worship is chapter 21 of the Westminster Confession (1646), which stipulates:

> Neither prayer nor any other part of religious worship is now under the gospel, either tied unto or made more acceptable by any place in which it is performed, or towards which it is directed.[1]

Implicit here is the Calvinist premise that God manifests himself only through his Word, and that the ongoing communication of that Word is the only basis for Christian worship. The statement excludes and forbids the concept of "sacred space." Earthly "place," including space and the objects that inhabit space, cannot become sacred, nor should it ever be viewed as such. Instead, the physical setting for worship can only provide the material infrastructure through which the elect can continue to receive God's Word through the preaching and the orderly administration of the sacraments.

Phenomenologist Harold Turner captures this same dichotomy by contrasting the typology of the *domus dei* (house of [the] god) found in many ancient and modern religions with that of the *domus ecclesiae* (house of the congregation [or the church]), which was first formulated in third-century Christianity and was later adopted by the Reformation churches.[2] Although this dichotomy is too sharply drawn to account for the manifold varieties of attitudes toward worship space and its furnishings, it does of-

---

1. *Creeds of the Churches*, ed. J. H. Leith (Garden City, N.Y., 1963), p. 217.

2. H. W. Turner, *From Temple to Meeting House: The Phenomenology and Theology of Places of Worship* (The Hague, Paris, New York, 1979), pp. 11-12.

fer a useful contrast between two diametrically opposed attitudes that are often attested in Christian worship — the *domus ecclesiae* rubric may be invoked as an accurate paradigm of Calvinist attitudes toward the architectural setting of Reformed worship.

The development of that family of churches that came to be known as the Reformed tradition in North America has not been a simple or linear process. At different times and places, the fundamental Calvinist posture toward the spatial and material bases of worship as expressed in the Westminster Confession has undergone adaptations, transformations, and repristinations, all of which might be summed up in our title: "metamorphoses of the meetinghouse."

In the remainder of this essay, I would like to take a look at three examples of North American Christian communities rooted in the Calvinist tradition. In their creation of distinctively built environments, landscapes, and material cultures, all three have woven interesting variations on the core motif of the meetinghouse or *domus ecclesiae*. These include New England Puritan Congregationalism from the early seventeenth to the mid–nineteenth century; Welsh Calvinistic Methodism in southeastern Ohio in the nineteenth and early twentieth centuries; and Southern Baptists in southwestern Ohio in the later twentieth century.

The attitude of the New England Puritans, the main transmitters of Calvinism to New World shores during the earlier colonial period, toward sacred space seems to have been so deeply ingrained by the time of their arrival in the New World, and so little challenged prior to the arrival of an Anglican governor late in the seventeenth century, that it apparently received little attention in their voluminous writings. Thomas Shepard wrote that "under the New Testament, all places are equally holy," and a later writer, seemingly paraphrasing the words of Westminster, declared that "There is now *no place* which renders the worship of God more acceptable for its being there performed."[3] The fundamental posture toward holy places was developed theologically for the first time on the Continent and was then transferred to and applied in Britain; in New England it became a commonplace that inspired little reflection or reiteration. It was this fundamental theological assumption that gave rise to that most distinctive feature of the paradigmatic New England worship space, namely, the seventeenth-century meetinghouse.

A further theological consideration that needs to be invoked in the case of the early settlement of New England involves the land itself. These British Calvinists viewed the little-known land for which they were departing as a "wilderness," a place linked in their imagination typologically with

3. J. P. Walsh, "Holy Time and Sacred Space in Puritan New England," *American Quarterly* 32, no. 1 (spring 1980): 84; Ola Elizabeth Winslow, *Meetinghouse Hill* (New York, 1972), p. 52.

that prior wilderness in which the children of Israel were consigned to wander prior to their eventual admission into the Promised Land of Canaan. This "errand into the wilderness" — the phrase Perry Miller appropriated as the title for his classic essay on the American Puritans — was at first supposed to be a temporary expedient, ordained in God's providence as a means to demonstrate to the recalcitrant English what a "city set upon a hill" might look like once realized in the free atmosphere of the New World.[4] Even the third-generation Cotton Mather returned repeatedly to the wilderness motif, long after it had become evident that the Puritan sojourn in America was for the long haul.[5]

The first generation of New England Puritans thus viewed the land they had come to claim through a whole set of cognitive filters. First, they saw themselves as voluntary exiles, painfully forsaking their homeland for a new place full of danger and menace. Second, they legitimated this abandonment of England by interpreting it as a necessary response to a call from God, who was constituting them as a new Israel with a mission to the entire world that could only be realized through their relocation. Third, they brought with them an ambivalence toward the structures of English society, and were at once contemptuous of the Stuart regime (begun in 1603) but also hopeful that the polity of both their ancestral state and its established church might yet be reformed through their example. Fourth, they saw their stay in New England as most likely temporary, a mere act in a larger drama that would culminate in the return of the Church of England to biblical principles and the return of the reformers out of their wilderness to a newly purified state and, with it, a repristinated established church.

Two factors thus conspired against the investment of an unambiguously positive religious meaning in *place:* the rejection of the possibility of sacred space together with the idea that the land on which they were settling was a place to which they had been called for a temporary sojourn. This carried with it an ambiguous religious charge — it was the dwelling place of demonic aborigines and a biblical place of trial and testing. As circumstances changed — as, in Perry Miller's phrase, a revolution was transformed into an administration, and charisma became routinized with the passage of generations — both a positive attachment to the land and the erosion of the ideal of the meetinghouse as pure *domus ecclesiae* — a neutral, functional space set aside for but not restricted to the purposes of congregational assembly for worship — began to develop together as consequences of the same broad pattern of social and cultural change. A growing

4. P. Miller, *Errand into the Wilderness* (Cambridge, Mass., 1956).

5. G. H. Williams, "The Idea of the Wilderness of the New World in the *Magnalia*," in Cotton Mather, *Magnalia Christi Americana, Books I and II*, ed. K. B. Murdock (Cambridge, Mass., and London, 1977), pp. 49-58. See also B. C. Lane, *Landscapes of the Sacred: Geography and Narrative in American Spirituality* (New York and Mahwah, N.J., 1988), chap. 4.

sense of fondness for place can be seen by the late seventeenth century in writings such as Samuel Sewall's *Phaenomena*, which includes a lyrical evocation of the beauties of Plum Island:

> And as long as Plum Island shall faithfully keep the commanded post, notwithstanding all the hectoring words and hard blows of the proud and boisterous ocean; as long as any salmon or sturgeon shall swim in the streams of Merrimac, or any perch or pickerel in Crane Pond; as long as the sea-fowl shall know the time of their coming, and not neglect seasonably to visit the places of their acquaintance; as long as any cattle shall be fed with the grass growing in the meadows which do humbly bow down themselves before Turkey Hill; as long as any sheep shall walk upon Old Town hill, and shall from thence pleasantly look down upon the river Parker and the fruitful marshes lying beneath; as long as any free and harmless doves shall find a white oak or other tree within the township to perch or feed or build a careless nest upon, and shall voluntarily present themselves to perform the office of gleaners after barley harvest; as long as nature shall not grow old and dote, but shall constantly remember to give the rows of Indian corn their education by pairs; so long shall Christians be born there, and being first made meet, shall from thence be translated, to be made partakers of the Inheritance of the saints in light.[6]

These processes of tentative resacralization of both houses of worship and the landscape reached their fulfillment during the early nineteenth century, when a domesticated and eventually romantic vision of the New England landscape emerged simultaneously with the completed metamorphosis of meetinghouse into church. The first places for worship in Puritan New England were temporary sites, sometimes called "pulpit rocks" or "bethels," outdoor expedients that sufficed until something more permanent might be erected. A few, such as Bethel Rock, a natural stone pulpit in Woodbury, Connecticut, still survive.[7] By the middle of the seventeenth century, however, the "classical" shape of the Puritan meetinghouse had emerged, which clearly embodied the ideal of the *domus ecclesiae*. Visually prominent, in fact, was this very *domestic* aspect implied in Turner's phrase, evocative of the "house churches" of the earliest Christian communities. The meetinghouse was deliberately fashioned not in the Gothic style associated with Catholic churches, nor yet in the neoclassicism that was beginning to emerge as the English response to the Renaissance revival of the aesthetic modes of antiquity. Rather, it stood in continuity with the British tradition of secular building which the Puritans brought with

6. P. Miller, ed., *The American Puritans, Their Prose and Poetry* (Garden City, N.Y., 1956), pp. 214-15.

7. Federal Writers Project, *Connecticut: A Guide to Its Roads, Lore, and People* (Boston, 1938), p. 384.

them and utilized in both their domestic and public structures. One architectural historian, Marian Card Donnelly, has argued suggestively though not perhaps definitively that the English town market hall may have been the principal prototype.[8]

The typical seventeenth-century New England meetinghouse was of frame construction, and either square or rectangular in shape. When rectangular, the principal entrance was located on one of the long sides, in direct repudiation of the model that had emerged as definitive in Western Christendom during the medieval centuries. Inside, one would find box pews,[9] allocated to families on the basis of community standing, and galleries for the socially marginal, such as slaves, Indians, or the poor, who could not afford or were not otherwise entitled to pews of their own. The visual center was no longer the altar, which had now been diminished to a simple domestic-style communion table or just a wooden flap attached by hinges to the pulpit or wall for occasional communion use. Rather, it had become the massive pulpit with overhead sounding board (see White, plates 44-46), the dramatic and practical setting for the proclamation and exposition of the Word of God.

Architecturally, the meetinghouse was unprepossessing; the only surviving seventeenth-century example, the now Unitarian-Universalist Old Ship Church (see fig. 160) in Hingham, Massachusetts, resembles a good-sized house. Postcolonial neoclassical additions serve only imperfectly to mask its fundamental and intentional lack of ornament and any but the most vernacular sort of styling. Geographical isolation from a mother country torn by civil war, relative scarcity of means, and a firm theological commitment that was aniconic in its rejection of the notion that God could be imagined or in any sense confined within an earthly space all combined to produce a provincial austerity in the service of the preached Word.[10]

The seventeenth-century meetinghouse, however, was not simply a place for worship, although that was its primary function in a community for which worship was a central, informing activity. Since priority was given to the erection of the meetinghouse in the realm of public building, it often served a multiplicity of functions until social life became complex enough and economic means sufficiently plentiful to provide for a differentiation of function. Meetinghouses could be and thus were utilized for a variety of purposes, including schooling, the conduct of town meetings for governance, and defense against hostile Indians. Since the building itself

---

8. M. C. Donnelly, *The New England Meeting Houses of the Seventeenth Century* (Middletown, Conn., 1963), pp. 94ff.

9. See figures 162-63 in James F. White, "From Protestant to Catholic Plain Style," in this volume.

10. E. W. Sinnott, *Meetinghouse and Church in Early New England* (New York, 1963), p. 15; W. H. Pierson Jr., *American Buildings and Their Architects, Vol. 1* (Garden City, N.Y., 1970), pp. 55-58.

164. King's Chapel,
Boston, Mass., 1749

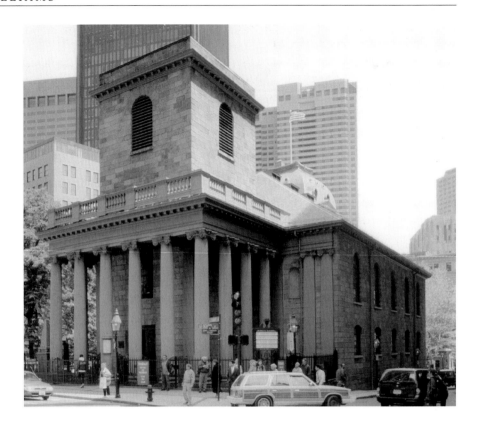

could not be sacred, all of these uses were religiously legitimate, especially in a community in which church and state, though formally separate, were nevertheless regarded as dual means to a common supernatural end.

The meetinghouse was also important in another way, ostensibly geographical and latently religious as well. Although practice may well have strayed from the norm, the Puritan ideal was for the meetinghouse to be sited on raised ground at the center of each of the new towns which were rapidly being founded to the west as the original Boston settlement of 1630 overflowed its bounds. A 1635 Massachusetts Bay Ordinance, for example, provided that "hereafter no dwelling house shall be built above half a mile from the meeting house, in any new plantation, granted at this court," and a document of the same period entitled *Essay on the Ordering of Towns* spoke of "the meetinghouse, the which we shall suppose to be the center of the whole circumference [of the town]."[11] Whatever actual practice may have been in particular cases, it seems clear that the meetinghouse functioned as an *axis mundi,* a necessity for turning a mere aggregate of buildings into a *cosmos* in a manner reminiscent of the Spanish ordi-

11. Donnelly, pp. 16-17.

484

nances for the settlement of their own New World empire in the name of a very different church.[12]

The meetinghouse as a social institution developed and flourished during an era of political and cultural isolation, but was hard-pressed to survive in pristine form after the British decided to rein in the virtual autonomy that the Puritans had enjoyed during their early decades. The establishment of an effective imperial presence in Boston brought with it an end to Congregational religious hegemony, and introduced the despised Church of England into New England precincts in the form of King's Chapel (see fig. 164) and, most significantly for our purposes, Christ Church (see fig. 165). "Old North," as it is popularly called thanks to the Paul Revere legend, is still a functioning Episcopal parish in Boston's North End now shared by Italian Americans and young urban professionals.[13]

Built in 1723, Old North Church in fact shared many characteristics with Hingham's Old Ship and with other Puritan meetinghouses: galleries, box pews, and a prominent pulpit with the mandatory sounding board. Aesthetically, it would have appeared awkwardly provincial to contemporary London sophisticates. However, it very definitely embodied two qualities lacking in Hingham: Old North was designed in a "high style," and it was a *church,* not a meetinghouse. Though conceived and executed by a local builder with limited resources, it follows the by now nearly normative plan for Anglican churches created by Christopher Wren in his campaign of rebuilding London's ecclesiastical fabric following the Great Fire of 1666. It is rectangular in shape, with the principal entrance on a short side — the west, as it turns out, thus properly orienting it with the altar at the east end. Though it boasts a prominent pulpit, the axial internal arrangement places the primary sight line on the altar-table, thus asserting the traditional Anglican emphasis on sacrament *together with* Word in the scheme of salvation. Colors are light and windows are clear, reflecting an Enlightenment emphasis on clarity.

Finally, the Old North architectural and ornamental schemes are neoclassical, exemplified in the four-stage brick frontal tower capped by a steeple composed of belfry and lantern and culminating in a spire and weather vane. Christ Church was definitely not a medieval survival; Old Ship, in fact, stood more in continuity with pre-Reformation building practice, reflecting both practical necessity and a Puritan nostalgia for "the world we have lost," at least in some of its social dimensions.[14] Nor, however, was it a Puritan meetinghouse, since it consisted in a worship space that was at once sacramental and attentive to the dictates of fashion. What

12. J. R. Stilgoe, *Common Landscape in America, 1580 to 1845* (New Haven and London, 1982), pp. 34-35 and 48.

13. Pierson, *American Buildings and Their Architects* (1970), pp. 98-100.

14. See Peter Laslett, *The World We Have Lost* (New York, 1966).

485

165. Old North
(Christ) Church,
Boston, Mass., 1723

it represented was something distinctively Anglican, drawing on both Catholic and Protestant emphases in its contours and accoutrements, and exemplifying a concern with fashion and style, a concern characteristic of the English establishment.

The Puritan reaction was rapid but equivocal. By the end of the decade, in 1729, Old South Meetinghouse (see fig. 166) had appeared in Boston in a form that at least superficially resembled its Anglican rival. Now preserved as a museum, Old South is visually identifiable by its Wren-like tower, steeple, and spire amid the welter of winding streets that makes up the modern city's commercial district; it is the first surviving instance of such features appearing within the architectural vocabulary of New England Puritanism. On closer examination, however, the results are somewhat less dramatic. The main entrance is still located on one of the building's long sides, despite the apparently conflicting visual clue given by the tower — which seems, from this perspective, an asymmetrical add-on rather than an integral part of the building. (There is, in fact, a frontal entry passage through the tower which is now used by the stream of tourists who regularly pay admission to peruse its exhibits.) On the inside, the dominant central pulpit is aligned axially with the main entrance, and box pews and galleries complete the standard seventeenth-century Reformed liturgical arrangements.[15]

Another challenge to Puritan hegemony during the eighteenth century came from within rather than without. Beginning in the late 1730s, the revivalist preaching which had only occasionally characterized the pulpits of New England and the Middle Colonies took on a new direction and intensity through the work of figures such as Jonathan Edwards and George Whitefield. Edwards worked largely within the Congregational Calvinist establishment, but Whitefield, a friend of John and Charles Wesley from their Oxford days, was something of a wild card. Like Wesley, Whitefield was an ordained priest of the Church of England; like Edwards, he was a Calvinist in theology. Like Wesley and unlike Edwards, he refused to be content with established ecclesiastical structures, acquiring the nickname of the "Grand Itinerant" during his preaching tours of the British Isles and, most particularly, the American colonies, where he eventually found his final rest.

During his early days of colonial preaching, Whitefield was invited to share pulpits in churches of a variety of denominations. As the radical implications of his medium and message became more apparent, however, such invitations dwindled, and other expedients became necessary. When possible, Whitefield preached to vast multitudes in the open air, inspiring Benjamin Franklin's admiration at the carrying power of his voice though not of his message.[16] Also, in Franklin's Philadelphia, Whitefield's pros-

15. Pierson, *American Buildings and Their Architects* (1970), pp. 102-5.
16. B. Franklin, *Autobiography and Other Writings,* ed. Russel Nye (Boston, 1958), pp. 97-100.

166. Old South Meeting-
house, Boston, Mass.,
1729

perous admirers erected in his honor a large structure that would serve as an auditorium for his preaching, the first in a long line of architecturally nondescript and liturgically nontraditional structures that would be utilized by latter-day urban evangelists such as Dwight L. Moody, Billy Sunday, Aimee Semple McPherson, and Billy Graham.

In the ad hoc shelters of these evangelists we encounter an architectural type we might call, in keeping with the Latinate usages of Mircea Eliade and Harold Turner, the *tabernaculum*[17] — a place for religious worship that is purely occasional and functional, with no fixed physical setting and deriving its sacred character from its very transiency. The historical and theological roots of the tabernacle — the portable "tent of meeting" containing the ark of the covenant — are clearly in that same Old Testament which had provided the Puritans with their providential self-interpretation. One significant factor in the context of its emergence is that the itinerants who in one form or another utilized this concept were united by a commonality not of theology but rather of practice. Though Wesley was an Arminian and Whitefield and many of his colonial imitators Calvinists, the principle of preaching outside a fixed ecclesiastical setting, whether church or meetinghouse, united them in a common rejection of structures. In the long run, this is arguably more significant than their theological differences.

It should be noted first that a major part of the impetus behind the practice of preaching outdoors or in improvised structures was practical rather than theoretical. However, it is clear that there is a correlation between the implicit attack on ecclesiastical structures, whether Anglican or Puritan, contained in the evangelists' message and work, and their indifference to the physical settings in which their preaching — the medium that in many ways was also their message — was staged. Itinerancy became a major feature of the early American Methodism commissioned by Wesley and his immediate disciples, as well as of the tradition of Calvinistic revival preaching that had begun with Whitefield.

This exemplification of the ritual principle of what Victor Turner has called *antistructure* has played an important role in the subsequent unfolding of an Anglo-American pattern of religious activity — including the British Isles and Canada — during the nineteenth and twentieth centuries, and this tradition has invoked the term "tabernacle" (as well as the biblically less appropriate "temple") in preference to the term "church."[18] But actual patterns of usage also reveal something of an indifference to usage, as in

---

17. On the Israelite models of the "tent sanctuary . . . the visible sign of Yahweh's presence . . . ," cf. R. E. Friedman, "Tabernacle," *Anchor Bible Dictionary* (New York, 1992), vol. 6, pp. 292-300. On relevance to American evangelicalism, see B. C. Lane, "Mythic Landscapes: Liminal Places in the Evangelical Revival," in *Landscapes of the Sacred* (New York, 1988), pp. 152-60.

18. V. Turner, *The Ritual Process: Structure and Anti-Structure* (Chicago, 1969).

Chicago's Moody Memorial *Church* and McPherson's Angelus *Temple* in Los Angeles.

It is also significant that in the United States especially, the lines between Reformed and Wesleyan traditions have become blurred in popular evangelical building patterns, so that revivalists and more settled congregations of both Baptist and Pentecostal provenance have espoused common patterns during the twentieth century. In both cases, the operative structuring principle is that of the *tabernaculum*. Structured architectural space is rejected or ignored in favor of temporary or easily rearrangeable facilities which showcase the charismatic character of the preaching and/or the congregational testimonies that constitute the "hot" part of worship. The "cooler" forms of liturgical worship — to invoke the vocabulary of the media analyst Marshall McLuhan[19] — that require structure are no longer in evidence. Although there are clear affinities with the *domus ecclesiae* model exemplified in the colonial Puritan meetinghouses, the *tabernaculum* is a distinct variant on that theme.

By the early nineteenth century, the New England meetinghouse had completed yet another metamorphosis into the white-painted neoclassical structure that has since become a veritable icon of regional culture. Part of this change was stylistic and reflected especially the influence of James Gibbs, whose Saint Martin's-in-the-Fields and other high-style British churches added features such as massive columned porches to the basic Wren model. Gibbs's designs became widely known in the colonies through pattern books, and were exemplified in churches ranging from Boston's King's Chapel (see fig. 164) to Charleston's Saint Michael's.[20] The elegance of American churches of the federal period — that is, the decades immediately following the Revolution — reflected the work not only of Gibbs but of the Adam brothers as well, manifested primarily in a greater refinement of proportion and detail.[21]

This new style of meetinghouse reflected the triumph of high style among urban New England Congregationalists, who could no longer be called Puritans except in the spirit of nostalgia. The Puritan ideal of a holy commonwealth informed by divine laws and guided by divine providence had been gravely undermined by the First Amendment and the religious pluralism and ideological shifts that had given rise to it. The Puritan version of Calvinism, moreover, had been significantly revised by Edwards and his followers from one direction, and by the 1820s its central premises were eroding rapidly through challenges from revivalists such as the Presbyterian Charles Grandison Finney and from liberals such as Unitarian William Ellery Channing within its own ranks.

19. M. McLuhan, *Understanding Media: The Extensions of Man* (New York, 1964).
20. Pierson, *American Buildings and Their Architects* (1970), pp. 131ff.
21. Pierson, *American Buildings and Their Architects* (1970), pp. 218ff.

Rural communities, to be sure, often adjusted to changing fashions without new building — many simply shifted their internal arrangements by ninety degrees and eliminated the door on the long side. For the wealthier urban congregations in emerging cities such as Hartford and New Haven, however, the *meetinghouse* had been in effect transmuted into a *church* in its basic structure and design and eventually even in name, if not entirely in function. The gradual erosion of Calvinism, which eventually collapsed like the senior Holmes's "wonderful one-hoss shay," may well have been a factor. More important, though, was the shift in social function.

Beginning early in the eighteenth century, many New England towns began to erect separate "town houses" for the conduct of public business, leaving meetinghouses free not only for worship but for other, previously secular (if that word can be applied to any aspect of Puritan life) functions such as weddings and funerals.[22] Although one would have been hard-pressed to find a Congregationalist who would admit that a house of worship might aptly be called a *sacred* space, it was nevertheless becoming clear that such houses were being conceived and built as *special* places, differentiated in function, design, and quality from "secular" buildings. The main difference, as Gretchen T. Buggeln has argued, lay in the cult of religious feeling that had emerged in evangelical Protestantism by the early nineteenth century. If not intended to accommodate the presence of God, these structures were at least set apart to nurture appropriate and distinctive *feelings* in the worshiper.[23]

By the time of the last major phase in the stylistic evolution of the meetinghouse, the separation of church and state had become formally complete throughout New England, culminating in definitive Massachusetts legislation in 1833. By this time the Greek revival (see White, plate 46) had become the dominant national fashion for all manner of buildings, from the U.S. Treasury Building (see fig. 167) to countless private homes, including meetinghouses, churches, temples, and cathedrals across the entire American denominational spectrum. Although what might by now be properly called the Congregational *churches* of New England often dominated New England's townscapes, they now had to share their roles with other groups, as exemplified in the erection of the Gothic revival Trinity Episcopal Church on the New Haven Green — standing next to not one but two Congregational churches, a visually compelling reminder of the schisms of the Great Awakening.[24] In the campaign of building that em-

22. Sinnott, pp. 72ff.; K. M. Sweeney, "Meetinghouses, Town Houses, and Churches: Changing Perceptions of Sacred and Secular Space in Southern New England, 1720-1850," *Winterthur Portfolio* 28, no. 1 (spring 1993): 59-93.

23. Gretchen Carol Townsend, "Protestant Material Culture and Community in Connecticut, 1785-1840" (Ph.D. diss., Yale University, 1995), pp. 174ff.

24. W. H. Pierson Jr., *American Buildings and Their Architects: Technology and the Picturesque: The Corporate and Early Gothic Styles* (Garden City, N.Y., 1978), pp. 136ff.

167. United States
Treasury Building,
Washington, D.C.,
1836-42

braced the Greek temple mode as an iconic embodiment of the spirit of the new democratic republic, a leveling took place in the prestige previously enjoyed regionally by the Congregational churches — expressed in Lyman Beecher's plaintive lament over disestablishment in Connecticut.[25] Also, though church and state were now formally separate, the various denominations, including Jews and Catholics, hastened to embrace the architectural fashion that established their identity as Americans, taking their place with the institutions of civil government as pillars of the Republic.

A final phase in meetinghouse design, which might be described as "Puritan rococo," was the fad of the Gothic revival that graced not only countless Protestant houses as the appropriate iconography for the "Christian home" advocated by the Beecher sisters, but Congregational churches as well.[26] Notable among these is First Parish Church (see fig. 168) in Brunswick, Maine, which stands catty-corner from the Bowdoin College campus. Designed by Richard Upjohn, the Anglican immigrant architect who virtually invented the fashion that evolved into "carpenter Gothic," First Parish Church visually symbolized the end of the Puritan revulsion

25. B. M. Cross, ed., *The Autobiography of Lyman Beecher* (Cambridge, Mass., 1961), vol. 1, pp. 251-53.

26. C. E. Clark Jr., *The American Family Home, 1800-1960* (Chapel Hill and London, 1986), pp. 65ff.

492

168. First Parish Church (UCC), Brunswick, Maine, 1845-46

from at least the outward and visible signs of the medieval *domus dei,* as well as the end of a tradition of vernacular building that had evolved into a regional high style that finally exhausted its creative impulse.

In November of 1944, as the Second World War was approaching its climax, *Life* magazine chose for its cover a photograph of a typical colonial New England meetinghouse — which, upon closer examination, turns out not to be colonial, nor a meetinghouse, nor in New England. First Congregational Church (see fig. 169) in Tallmadge, Ohio — now a suburb of Akron — was built in the 1820s by a group of displaced Connecticut folk taking part in the settling of their native state's Western Reserve, granted by the federal government as compensation for losses due to British depredations during the Revolution. These Yankee émigrés thus took their place among the first settlers of a state that would become synonymous with Middle America. Ohio attracted such a mixture of immigrants that none exercised a clear enough majority or even plurality to become culturally dominant, except at the local level. Though Germans eventually constituted the largest ethnic stock, their impact is best seen regionally, in enclaves such as Cincinnati's Over the Rhine, Columbus's German Village, and the Catholic farm settlements of Greene, Mercer, and Auglaize counties in the west.

With the exception of the Dutch, who settled to the north in western Michigan, Ohio became a microcosm of the Reformed tradition during the nineteenth and twentieth centuries. In addition to the Congregationalists of the Western Reserve in the northeast, Presbyterians were among the pi-

493

169. First Congrega-
tional Church (UCC),
Tallmadge, Ohio, 1821

oneering elite of the Cincinnati region in the southwest. These descendants of British Calvinists, however, were beginning to lose their traditional theological identity to the pragmatic and Arminian incursions of
revivalism, as indicated by the 1835 heresy trial of Lyman Beecher, the
president of Cincinnati's Lane Seminary. Similarly, the impact on the landscape of these incipient post-Calvinists was not distinctive; they chose to

494

build rather in the Greek revival, Richardsonian Romanesque, Gothic revival, and other styles that were nationally popular and not identified with any particular denominational cluster.

One interesting partial exception is Covenant-First Presbyterian Church (see fig. 170) in downtown Cincinnati, a building that stands back-to-back with the Plum Street temple, the "mother temple" of Reform Judaism in America. Covenant-First, which in the later twentieth century was experiencing the rapid decline in membership characteristic of downtown congregations, is interesting in that its interior worship space, configured in the auditorium style popular in the Victorian era, is turned at a ninety-degree angle from its external axis — on the pattern, its historical brochure informs us, of Scottish tithe barns, an interesting linkage with a branch of British tradition.

German Reformed churches in Cincinnati, as elsewhere in the area, tend toward the standard architectural vocabulary employed by German Catholics and Lutherans, especially the *Rundbogenstil*. An interesting example of this nineteenth-century Italian-influenced German variant on the Romanesque is the 1890 Phillipus Church (see fig. 171) at the north end of Cincinnati's Over-the-Rhine neighborhood, which boasts a golden hand pointing upward in place of a cross at the apex of its spire.[27]

One area where Ohio can claim innovation in the built environment of the Reformed tradition is in the Welsh settlements in Gallia and Jackson counties, in the state's southeastern Appalachian region, contiguous with West Virginia across the Ohio River. In 1850 the Welsh constituted, respectively, 57 percent and 74 percent of these counties' population by birth. Although Welsh Quakers had played a major role in settling the Philadelphia area in the days of William Penn, this new wave of early middle nineteenth-century migrants came largely in quest of land.[28]

The later Welsh migrants were primarily dissenters, many of them Baptists and Congregationalists. Distinctive among them, however, were large numbers of Calvinistic Methodists, a seemingly oxymoronic designation derived from their origins in the revivals stimulated in Wales by the "Grand Itinerant" George Whitefield in the 1740s. Although they followed Whitefield's Reformed theology, their early organizational forms were strongly influenced by the connectional system associated with John Wesley and utilized by Whitefield himself as he organized fellowship groups among the Welsh. As in the England of William Blake's "dark Satanic mills," the evangelization of Wales took place during a time of profound economic transformation, as agriculture yielded to the mining of the coal

27. J. Clubbe, *Cincinnati Observed: Architecture and History* (Columbus, 1992), pp. 46, 234.

28. M. T. Struble and H. G. H. Wilhelm, "The Welsh in Ohio," in *To Build in a New Land: Ethnic Landscapes in North America*, ed. A. G. Noble (Baltimore and London, 1992), pp. 79-81.

170. Covenant-First
Presbyterian Church,
Cincinnati, Ohio, 1875

171. Phillipus Church
(UCC), Cincinnati,
Ohio, 1891

that would fuel England's furnaces. During the nineteenth century, dissent became nearly as synonymous with Welsh national feeling as did Roman Catholicism for the Irish. "Chapel" or "church" became a binary choice of identity, and neoclassical chapels, often humble, began to dot the landscape in contrast with the Gothic revivalism favored by the Anglican Church in Wales.[29]

Welsh Calvinism began with domestic meetings for worship, and the spirit of itinerancy associated with Whitefield informed the early years of the movement before it began to coalesce into denominational forms and more permanent buildings. When transplanted to southeastern Ohio's rolling hills, which vividly evoked the Welsh landscape, the immigrants found themselves without any establishment against which

29. D. J. Williams, *One Hundred Years of Welsh Calvinistic Methodism in America* (Philadelphia, 1937), pp. 1-3.

497

to define themselves, but their scattered farmsteads did prolong the need for itinerancy. The resultant decentralization was reflected in a polity which, though modeled on the Presbyterian form, was in fact closer to congregational in that the *seiat,* or fellowship meeting, was a much more powerful vehicle for governance than its Scottish American counterpart, the session. The *seiat,* which arose in the eighteenth-century Awakening in Wales, was comprised of all communicants, including children, and its presiding officer, the elder, was a layman elected democratically. Part of this meeting was set aside for congregational business, with the rest devoted to worship, which included children reciting Scripture and adults giving testimonies.[30]

The first Welsh settlers in Ohio and elsewhere in America were not accustomed to a settled ministry, an issue which in later decades would be the source of generational conflict as the Calvinistic Methodist Church became gradually Americanized and moved toward its eventual merger with the Presbyterian Church, USA, in 1920. Preachers in the old country were able to deliver the same sermons frequently from different pulpits, a considerable aid to their reputations for eloquence. In the United States, the first Welsh preachers had been born and trained in the old ways in Wales, and generally farmed or conducted small businesses on the side. The results of this pattern, which resembled early Methodist practice more closely than Presbyterian, led to some interesting and even unique architectural innovations.[31]

After the log-cabin stage had passed, the earliest Welsh churches in the Gallia-Jackson region date from the 1840s and, not surprisingly, are vernacular Greek revival in style. As did contemporary Presbyterian and other churches, most had two symmetrically placed doors through which men and women would respectively enter. (An interesting exception is Horeb Chapel, patterned on the Welsh barn chapel, a vernacular expedient that had originated in Wales in the late eighteenth century.)[32] Internal arrangements are similar to those of other evangelical churches of the period, with a small, central pulpit or lectern. They bear either biblical names, such as Bethel, Horeb, Nebo, and Sardis, or descriptive Welsh names such as Tyn Rhos, or "house on the moor" — a nomenclature similar to that of their earlier New England counterparts, implying both a biblical self-identification and a rejection of the concept of sacralized space in the Roman or Anglican manner.[33] Worship was in the Calvinist tradition, with strict observance of the Sabbath. Several of

30. D. J. Williams, pp. 8-11.

31. D. B. Rees, *Chapels in the Valley* (Upton, Wirral, Merseyside, 1975), pp. 66ff.

32. M. T. Struble, "Horeb Chapel: The Evolution of a Welsh Barn Chapel upon the American Landscape," *Pioneer America Society Transactions* 25 (1993): 37-45.

33. E. D. Davis, ed., *Our Heritage: Early History of Tyn Rhos Welsh Congregational Church and Its Neighborhood* (n.p., 1979).

498

these churches, which dotted the rural landscape far from the small towns that eventually developed, have been restored and now alternate as sites for the annual *gymanfa ganus,* or preaching and hymn-singing festivals, which are held annually by nostalgic and mainly elderly Welsh Americans who tend to be Presbyterian.

Unique to the Gallia-Jackson region, however, is the *ty capel,* or "house chapel," which arose in response to the circumstances of itinerancy that characterized the early decades of Welsh American religious life. Since the churches were scattered far and wide in rural Appalachia, clergy were hard-pressed to serve them, and were at first forced to carry their own provisions. To help alleviate the stresses and strains wrought on their clergy, around 1860 church members began to build small outbuildings adjoining the churches to provide a place where the ministers might rest and eat. They consisted of two or three rooms, including kitchen, parlor, and sometimes a small bedroom. In conjunction with this institution, the practice of *cado y mis,* or "keeping of the month," originated, in which different families rotated responsibilities for the upkeep of both the *ty capel* and the minister it had been built to serve.[34] The *ty capel* was also used for congregational meetings as well as schooling. In addition to Sunday school classes — a popular Welsh institution — "secular" instruction was also provided here when public education had not yet become available.[35] The Reformed emphasis on literacy was certainly manifest among the Ohio Welsh.

Another distinctive regional practice was the *gymanfa ganu,* already mentioned as a present-day vehicle for ethnic and rural nostalgia. (The term "gymanfa," which means "assembly," was also used in Calvinistic Methodist polity for the body that paralleled the Presbyterian synod; with the *seiat,* it was the most important organ of that polity.) Every two years the regional *gymanfa* would be held at Moriah Church, the "mother church" of the Gallia-Jackson area; the service itself, though, would be held outside from a platform and pulpit built especially for the occasion since the church itself was far too small for the three thousand to six thousand participant-observers. Local choirs led their hymn-loving coreligionists in singing at the occasion.[36]

Although Welsh Calvinistic Methodism overall can be said to have espoused the *domus ecclesiae* ideal in its worship, one might argue that the *tabernaculum* motif makes an appearance here as well. The resistance of Welsh American itinerants to the coming of a settled ministry may have had practical, economic bases, but it seems likely that the concept of *unsettledness*

---

34. M. T. Struble, "Ty Capels and the Residual Patterns of Welsh Settlement upon the Landscape of Southeastern Ohio," *Pioneer America Society Transactions* 12 (1989): 21-27; D. J. Williams, pp. 150-51.

35. Interview with Prof. Howell Lloyd, Miami University Department of Geography, spring 1995.

36. D. J. Williams, pp. 137-42.

— a form of antistructure — may have exerted a deep resonance for those who harbored ancestral memories of the excitement of the early revival days. Similarly the *gymanfa ganus,* though perhaps as routinized as the Methodist camp meetings of the same era, nevertheless served as a kind of Durkheimian corroboree, in which a collective effervescence manifested itself that was necessarily grounded in the very transience of the occasion.[37] Finally, although we do not possess sufficient information to speak with certainty on the matter, it is possible that the testimonials at the *seiat,* if more spontaneous than formulaic, contributed yet another element of what Victor Turner has called "spontaneous communitas" to the Welsh experience.[38]

Although Calvinism has become an endangered theological species by the later twentieth century in the United States, one of the loci where it has been experiencing a revival in the 1990s has been among the Southern Baptists.[39] In the past two or three decades, the Southern Baptist Convention, like country music, has become an export commodity, and the once firmly regional denomination has now taken on a national profile and sphere of influence. For an even longer period Appalachians, primarily from Kentucky, have been crossing the Ohio River and seeking work in the Cincinnati-Dayton metropolitan area, including Butler County's industrial centers of Hamilton and Middletown. For some time the religious "growth industry" of southwestern Ohio has centered in both the Holiness-Pentecostal cluster on the one hand and the Southern and Independent Baptists on the other. It is worth noting that there is little difference in their basic liturgical patterns, and it is not easy to differentiate their worship facilities on the basis of external evidence. The fundamental requirements are congregational seating facing a platform or stage with pulpits and/or lecterns, often of Lucite; seating for officiants and musicians; and musical instruments, including a piano and percussion. All of this is clearly in the *domus ecclesiae* realm, with Pentecostals approaching the *tabernaculum* variant.

The first stage of congregational development consists of what one might call the "house church," a modest one-level building that resembles a large ranch house (see fig. 172) in its basic contours. These are usually sited on state or local roads, at the edges of urban areas or farther out amid farmlands, continuing in the pattern of "ribbon development" that has woven the entire region into a pattern of uneven but virtually continuous settlement. Such churches usually have ample parking, since they are built on agricultural rather than commercial property, and often have open outbuildings that can be used for the Southern-style "homecomings" held during the summer months.

37. E. Durkheim, *The Elementary Forms of the Religious Life* (New York, 1965), pp. 245ff.
38. V. Turner, chap. 4.
39. B. Leonard, "Seminary Crackdown," *Christian Century* 112, no. 16 (10 May 1995): 500-501.

172. First Baptist
Church, Somerville,
Ohio, circa 1990

The next step up is the neocolonial suburban church, such as the Richmond Road Baptist Church near Hamilton, Ohio. Clearly housing a more affluent congregation, such a church presents itself to the public through visual associations with the Wren-Gibbs tradition — at times unkindly characterized as "phony-colony" — through devices such as columned porches or porte cocheres; broken pediments, such as that which frames its plastic moveable-letter sign; and, of course, an at least vestigial steeple and spire, often mass-produced of plastic. It stands in dramatic contrast with its country-cousin neighbor, the Richmond Road Pentecostal Church.

Another variety of latter-day evangelical built environment, which may or may not represent a logical progression from the earlier-mentioned forms, is what might be called the "interstate temple," given the siting of these massive structures near the exit ramps of the federal divided highways that unite this region. One good example of this genre is the Far Hills Baptist Church (see fig. 173) in the Dayton suburb of Kettering, Ohio, one of the largest in the area, which features prominent speakers such as former vice president Dan Quayle. Located about half a mile from the exit ramp of I-675, which bypasses Dayton in linking I-70 with I-75, the church is basically a large auditorium on the nineteenth-century "opera seating" plan, with a large stage, elaborate musical equipment, and dramatic banners offering a new iconography of American "civil religion" to replace that rejected by the Reformation. Although Far Hills Baptist's plant is the largest of a series of increasingly more ample buildings, plans were afloat at this writing (mid-1990s) for a still larger structure. Its affluent setting also belies the stereotype that fundamentalists are recruited chiefly from the ranks of the "disinherited."

Another regional example is the older Landmark Baptist Temple along I-75 in Cincinnati, whose fleet of school buses emphasizes the transparochial outreach of this operation; its nondescript, warehouse-like plant expresses an

501

173. Far Hills Baptist Church, Kettering, Ohio, 1977

indifference to aesthetics and tradition, suggesting a linkage with the *tabernaculum* theme. At the other end of the stylistic spectrum is the somewhat "postmodern" interpretation of neoclassicism exemplified in Calvary Temple (see fig. 174), near the intersection of I-70 and I-465 at the northern fringes of Indianapolis, where affluence combines with vast scale as indicated by the large parking lot and inevitable fleet of buses. Note also the choice of the term "temple" as the self-designation of both of these congregations — an unintentionally ironic evocation of the *domus dei* type, given the meaning that the word invariably carried in both Hebrew and classical antiquity.

A suitable concluding example is a mid-1990s Southern Baptist Church in Butler County, Ohio, sited on U.S. 27 between the hamlets of Millville and McGonigle in the area between Hamilton and Oxford. The sign that appeared at its front while the church was under construction in 1994 — "GOD! MADE THIS BUILDING POSSIBLE" — is interesting in itself as a reminder of the notion of providential direction that informs the congregation's theology. The building follows plans provided by the denominational office in charge of such matters, and its interior combines a standard worship space, with platform and fairly elaborate central pulpit, at one side, together with offices and Sunday school facilities at the other. What is interesting from the exterior is that, while at first glance the church appears to be cast in the mold of countless other such structures, there is a subtle but important difference. While the vestigial steeple and spire rest at the short end of the church that fronts the highway, the main entrance is in the middle of one of the long sides. The tensions that informed the design of Old South Meetinghouse in Boston

502

nearly three centuries ago have never been fully resolved, and appear to be with us to this day.

 This tour of the descendants of the Calvinist impulse through several temporally, spatially, and culturally diverse North American loci illustrates first the premise that the development of a religious tradition is seldom linear and, consequently, not often predictable. What seems to be at work here are two tendencies. First, throughout Western religious history there has been a continual tension between the drive — perhaps innate in *homo religiosus* — to sacralize the material realm and the opposed reformist drive to banish this particularization of the divine from earthly precincts. This tension is certainly intrinsic to the classic Protestant-Catholic dichotomy, but continues to manifest itself *within* as well as between each of these two religious camps, as exemplified also in post–Vatican II Roman Catholic church design.

 Secondly, the experience of all three strains of North American Calvinist communities explored here requires a reevaluation of the dichotomous way of contrasting "secular" or "profane" with the "sacred" that has characterized the typological study of religious phenomena from the days of Émile Durkheim and Rudolf Otto through the epoch-making work of Mircea Eliade.[40] One might suggest, for example, that the very rejection of

174. Calvary Temple, Indianapolis, Ind., 1991

40. Colleen McDannell, *Material Christianity: Religion and Popular Culture in America* (New Haven and London, 1995), pp. 4-8.

sacrality inherent in earthly places and material objects expressed classically in the Westminster Confession might be interpreted as an *overt* rejection of the category of *positive* sacred space, but simultaneously a *covert* affirmation of *negative* sacred space — that is, space which acquires a sacral power when prescribed activities are performed in the *absence* of certain material accoutrements. The sacred here might thus be better defined as *relational* rather than absolute. Similarly, the development of the nineteenth-century Congregational church from the colonial meetinghouse is not so much a matter of an absolute change from profane to sacred space, or from *domus ecclesiae* to *domus dei*, but rather from one definition and experience of space to another along a continuum of theological and phenomenological possibilities. Much work still needs to be done in exploring and articulating the nuances of this continuum.

Bibliography

Brereton, Joel P. "Sacred Space." In *The Encyclopedia of Religion,* edited by Mircea Eliade, vol. 13, pp. 526-35. New York and London: Macmillan, 1987.

Donnelly, Marian Card. *The New England Meeting Houses of the Seventeenth Century.* Middletown, Conn.: Wesleyan University Press, 1963.

Knowles, Anne Kelly. *Calvinists Incorporated: Welsh Immigrants on Ohio's Industrial Frontier.* Chicago: University of Chicago Press, 1997.

Lane, Belden C. *Landscapes of the Sacred: Geography and Narrative in American Spirituality.* New York and Mahwah, N.J.: Paulist Press, 1988.

Sinnott, Edmund W. *Meetinghouse and Church in Early New England.* New York, Toronto, and London: McGraw-Hill, 1963.

Stilgoe, John R. *Common Landscape in America, 1580 to 1845.* New Haven and London: Yale University Press, 1982.

Townsend, Gretchen Carol. "Protestant Material Culture and Community in Connecticut, 1785-1840." Ph.D. diss., Yale University, 1995.

Turner, Harold W. *From Temple to Meeting House: The Phenomenology and Theology of Places of Worship.* The Hague, Paris, New York: Mouton, 1979.

Walsh, James P. "Holy Time and Sacred Space in Puritan New England." *American Quarterly* 32, no. 1 (spring 1980): 79-95.

White, James F. *Protestant Worship and Church Architecture: Theological and Historical Considerations.* New York: Oxford University Press, 1964.

Williams, Peter W. "Architecture and Landscape." In *Encyclopedia of the American Religious Experience,* edited by C. H. Lippy and P. W. Williams, vol. 3, pp. 1325-40. New York: Charles Scribner's Sons, 1988.

Discussion Following Peter Williams's Essay

Daniel W. Hardy: Would it be fair to say you have traced the evolution of confusion about space? It seems to me that is one of the patterns that emerges in the history you have given us. We begin in the time frame where people are fairly clear about the organization of space and the emplacement of a meetinghouse within the landscape, and probably fairly clear about the interior disposition and arrangement of space within a building for worship. We seem to have an evolution wherein, increasingly, space itself makes no sense; the only sense one can find, as for example on the question of the emplacement of a church building, is to identify the intersection of two interstate roadways — this seems to be the closest one can get to making sense of space these days. And I wonder if there is a parallel contemporary sense of confusion regarding the interior disposition of space? My question is about spatiotemporality and the confusions that seem to typify much of contemporary culture. I wonder how, if at all, the Calvinist tradition contributes to this contemporary blurring of boundaries which you have just described.

Peter Williams: You have suggested that the Calvinist tradition began with clarity on the issue of space and then gradually unraveled. But I wonder: Is there not ambiguity at the very beginning? This is a tradition that appropriates and reconfigures already-existing spaces. Calvin seems to have promulgated an impossibly austere ideal that is at the root of his teaching. Perhaps I am indulging in history-of-religions speculations, but there seem to be certain impulses in *homo religiosus* that are very hard to expunge. Calvin tried, but they keep popping up, as in the example of consecrating a meetinghouse or sacralizing its space. Part of what is at issue here is the question already raised; namely, are we still dealing with Calvinism, or are we dealing with some other phenomenon? How many authentic Calvinists are there today? Mostly what we encounter today is not Calvinism but groups that still in some ways are linear descendants of the Calvinist or Reformed tradition, but that are not really Calvinist, so that the original purity of the message has been so dissolved in the solvents of modernity that this confusion you are talking about is very evident.

NEW WORLD COMMENTARY

Comments on the
New World Presentations

JOHN F. WILSON

How should one comment on papers that diverge dramatically both in the forms of their construction and their modes of argument? It seems best to take each one in turn, attempt briefly to engage with it, and then offer some more general observations that compass all of them. Such a "bifocal" approach — attending to each in order but broadening the conversation to bring them into relationship — should appreciatively underscore the richness of the materials presented to the readers of this volume. It should also point toward an effectively argued position which they share implicitly and which they contributed to the conference on which this volume was based.

Gretchen Buggeln develops her essay around a discussion of the new building constructed by the First Congregational Society of Hartford in 1807. It was, in her characterization, a "provincial manifestation of the Wren-baroque style common in English church building." The strength of this study is that it finds in this local development an exemplary event, one that illuminates a far more extensive cultural shift. In effect, it holds forth in microcosm the numerous and similar replacements of older church buildings by new-styled ones, a process that took place in New England and across much of the continent beginning in the late eighteenth century and continuing well into the nineteenth. Repeating the author's argument is unnecessary — it is available to read, and a summary presentation would fail to do justice to its nuances. But the question raised is, what is to be said to explain "this significant change, a transformation experienced by literally hundreds of New England Calvinist congregations following the Revolution"? There are several conventional views Gretchen Buggeln eschews in order to advance the explanation she proposes.

If we assume that the First Church's eighteenth-century meetinghouse had manifested architecturally the essential Calvinism of the Reformed tradition in New England (and eventually America), this dramatic shift to a metropolitan-inspired type of church building seems susceptible of two explanations. One is that the original "presence and force" of Calvinism "declined," and presumably the change in style of church building manifested a broader and deeper change in the culture. So the "plain style" of colonial buildings is taken to be an intentional expression of a theological impulse. Such a position simply assumes that an original, undiluted, essential Calvinist impulse determined cultural forms, including architectural ones. This kind of interpretation both derives from and reinforces the well-known (but routinely challenged and now largely discredited) "declension thesis."

Of course, a view that Calvinist theology had not changed is also wrong. For, in fact, whatever the labels — whether self-designated or the outcome of polemical interchanges among Consistent Calvinists, New Divinity, or even evangelicals — the emerging party structure of the New England religious world was a marked development within the broader Reformed tradition. Theology did change by way of engagement with changing times, and no one was more an agent of it than the most exemplary Calvinist America produced, namely, Jonathan Edwards. Such change was not a simple falling away from canonical positions, however, but a recasting, a reformulation, and a reassertion of the tradition in the process of being newly appropriated.

Another conventional explanation is that Calvinism ceased having a connection to religious architecture. On closer inspection, however, this turns out to be a variant of the declension thesis, indeed its specification. For, decoded, it is simply asserting (to make use of the sociologists' terms) that differentiation of the social order was occurring. The earlier edifice of the 1730s had originally served a number of community functions — place of town meetings, court of law, social gathering place — as well as meetinghouse of the religious society. The new metropolitan-inspired building was dedicated to religious purposes alone, and primarily for the members of the First Society or for those susceptible of recruitment to their numbers. Other religious groups were developing their own places of worship in a Connecticut now experiencing the reality (albeit in a severely limited version) of the religious pluralism that challenged the Congregational hegemony of an earlier era. So both of these conventional explanations — either declension in theology or its disconnection from architecture — in fact reduce to one, and that is simply in error.

Therefore the essay develops a "different way of looking at these buildings." As an approach it is a much more plausible and helpful reading of the construction of the new Hartford church. In explicating this position, Gretchen Buggeln reaches for the kinds of cultural and theological shifts taking place in the eighteenth century among Americans who made the Reformed tradition their own in that age. She invites us to recognize the idioms of the time, and to presume that their decisions about the architectural style for the new edifice were self-conscious. The early nineteenth-century members of the First Society of Hartford were, in fact, religious actors "appropriating architectural style[s] for their own purposes, an element of which was always spiritual." In this deceptively simple framing of the issue, we are gently reminded that Calvinists, whatever else they were, were not only re-sponders or re-actors; in addition, and this is basic, they were also not simply acting out Calvinist doctrine(s). These were complex human agents for whom spiritual concerns interacted with other purposes. Utilization of the Reverend Nathan Strong's sermon at the consecration of the new church literally takes us within the consciousness, albeit an elite one, of the time. His emphasis upon the necessity for the people of the First Society to worship God truly and glorify him is the point of connection to the Calvinist impulse, we should judge, rather than the specific forms utilized in the construction of the building or the specific theological formulations used in explicating that action.

This seems the natural point at which to introduce a fundamental observation about the subject at hand, Calvinism and the arts, no less than about the subject of Calvinism itself. And this point is simply that Calvin's thought is inherently dialectical, even though some adherents of Calvinism have failed to grasp it! Not only must any relationship between Calvinism and the arts be viewed as dialectical, but Calvinism itself must be interpreted as a dialectical intellectual program. Of course, the ultimate source for this dialectic lies in Calvin's understanding of God's creation and redemption of the world. This dialectical relationship is mediated to humanity, and available for comprehension, through nature as well as through Scripture. Thus Calvin's stance continuously eludes reification, or reduction to simple formulas, including any about Calvinism and the arts! This is an enduring aspect of the subject, with special relevance to the additional papers about New World subjects.

In turning to the papers by James White and Peter Williams, we find marked contrasts. The first is between their papers and Gretchen Buggeln's essay — which was organized in terms of framing and interpreting a particular event, namely, the erection of a particular church edifice. By way of contrast, both of these papers take the long view, moving with considerable imagination and skill across several centuries of time, and from an old world island or continental domain to an opening new world, as well as across religious or cultural traditions at first seemingly remote from Calvinism. Indeed, we can imagine the delight James White takes in proposing that post–Vatican II Roman Catholic liturgical practices manifest the Reformed "plain style" more fully than modern Protestant formulations! But there is also a marked contrast between the papers in the way they take the long view. We might dwell on that for a moment.

511

Peter Williams's long view is comparative in at least two ways. First, he opts to give us several case studies rather than the one that Gretchen offered. One is a broad view of the architectural trajectory from early colonial meetinghouse to securely national church. A second is close attention to Welsh Calvinistic Methodists as immigrants to the "western reserve" of the new nation, namely, Ohio. A third draws us to our own time and the religious structures of the Southern Baptist tradition. So in one respect his comparative inquiry engages us with a broad tapestry that begins with early New England meetinghouses and leads us to the "interstate tabernacles" of our contemporary landscape.

But his work is comparative in another dimension also, and it is imperative to draw out explicitly what he is practicing at or below the surface of his paper. This other approach to comparative work depends upon making use of typologies, framed to distinguish different kinds of religious structures in terms of the divergent logics — theologics, we might say — that they embody. In particular, Peter Williams adopts Harold Turner's distinction between the temple as a house of God and the meetinghouse as a congregation's worship space. But he also proposes that there is a third, perhaps intermediate, type, grounded in the tabernacle, that in the modern world "houses" charisma. In passing I cannot resist the temptation to observe that there are parallels between H. Richard Niebuhr electing to supplement Troeltsch's church-sect typology with the ideal of the denomination to make New World experience explicable, and Peter Williams's adding to Turner's temple-meetinghouse typology the ideal of tabernacle. But that is for another discussion! The basic point is that Peter is engaged in several dimensions of comparison: comparison among concrete cases and comparison as informed by theoretical constructs. Such an agenda sets high challenges for author and reader alike.

If there is an element of the synchronic in Peter Williams's paper, chiefly through his use of typology, James White's approach to comparison is a much more sustained diachronic endeavor. Indeed, White begins with the *Institutes* itself, invoking Calvin's moderate, and almost modern, sensitivity to context as well as text. While framed with respect to discussion of worship, he offers an interpretation in terms of the principle he proposes using to explicate a Calvinist approach to church architecture in the most encompassing sense: where true worship is truly accommodated. And that is the taproot of the iconoclasm we find manifested in and around the Reformed tradition. The real core of the paper, however, takes shape around his characterization of a "totally new vision of what the liturgy consisted of, a focus on the service of the Word reinforced occasionally by the service of the table and baptism." He adds, "The purpose . . . is not plainness for the sake of plainness; instead the goal is to enable all to participate in the liturgy instead of being distant onlookers to an unheard mass."

From this point of view, White interprets the "plain style," which concerned the rhetoric and style of preaching more than the setting of worship, as the core of the Reformed tradition. He argues that it was sustained in and through the simple and unadorned early "meetinghouses" in the new world of the seventeenth century. With the eighteenth, he finds reorientation of internal spaces (and the service of the Word within them) as well as a series of variations and adaptations. These explorations lead him to search for a term other than "plainness": "what is at stake in the first two centuries of American meetinghouses is a focus on the essentials of Reformed worship. The worship spaces and the architectural ornament declare the hierarchy of Reformed priorities culminating in the preaching of the Word of God. These buildings are splendid reflections of the worship purposes for which they were built."

The significant changes in the liturgical architecture of the Reformed tradition in America took place, in James White's view, beginning with the 1830s. And the driving forces were those elements of voluntary religion that were perfected in the new republic; namely, revivalism as a religious system, the elements of associationalism especially in and through the powerful and influential Sunday school movement, and the broad romantic reaction that transformed the past while incorporating so much of it. These elements turned Reformed Christianity away from its genius of concentrating on the essentials of accommodating true worship. I need not repeat his catalogue of the consequences that flowed from these changes, for his real point is to reach an ironic conclusion; namely, that modern Catholicism over the last century and a half has, perhaps unwittingly, come to embrace an ideal for its liturgy very like Calvin's original impulse.

There are twin temptations for one commenting on this paper; namely, either to endorse James White's suggestive claim or to roundly critique it. For many will undoubtedly be stimulated and challenged by this argument, indeed, will wish to argue these points for themselves to determine whether finally to agree or to disagree with him. For my part, I offer the comment that his proposal is reminiscent of the grand vision that the great historian Philip Schaff came to hold; namely, that in the wisdom of God the branches of Christendom might find reunion in the New World on terms that drew the best from all while allowing the worst to disappear. This would be an "evangelical Catholicism" — or perhaps a "Catholic evangelicalism." Whether James White sees it this way, I cannot say, but at least he has in Schaff a distinguished and weighty ally — albeit from the last century!

Where does all this leave us? The three papers on Calvinism in the New World vary significantly in the subjects they have taken up and even more in the manner the topics have been analyzed and presented. Yet all three embody a basic skepticism that we can identify in any simple sense a Calvinist aesthetic — in art or architecture — in the manner, for example, we are comfortable in identifying a particular aesthetic with the Shaker tradition that derived from Calvinism. Indeed, we might point to that Shaker aesthetic as one which fixed "plainness" as the objective, and in so doing decisively excluded the commitment to dialectical thinking so central to the original Calvinist impulse. No one of our authors seems at all comfortable with the notion that Calvinism could be reified or rendered static and still remain true to its genius — in the manner that is represented by the Shaker movement. Here we return to the observation that at its heart Calvin's legacy was dialectical in the ways suggested above.

If Calvinism is to be explored as a cultural force (which is to say, as an ingredient in cultures of the New World as well as the Old), we must be prepared to search for dynamic and shifting impulses that have exercised influence well outside strictly theological circles and ecclesiological institutions. At least in the study of New World Calvinism, the name of Perry Miller is necessarily invoked to signal the modern beginning of appreciation for its intellectual range and cultural power. Citing Miller is not to suggest that he got it altogether right. But he did capture the force of the insights and ideals Calvin voiced as effectively as anyone has, at least as they challenged the early New World Puritans. These ideas were certainly not first discovered by Calvin, nor have they been at play exclusively in the Reformed tradition that looks to his work, among others, for inspiration. But the notion of a dialectical relationship between God and the world, and the consequences that flow from human attempts to comprehend that relationship, have been and continue to be a cultural force of enormous consequence whatever the particular means of expressing it.

Contributors

Sibylle Badstübner-Gröger, Professor of the History of Art, Forschung-zentrum Europäische Aufklärung, Berlin, Germany

Philip Benedict, Professor of History, Brown University, Providence, Rhode Island

Gretchen Townsend Buggeln, Assistant Professor of Art History, Henry Francis du Pont Winterthur Museum, Winterthur Program in Early American Culture, Winterthur, Delaware

Jane Dempsey Douglass, Immediate Past President, World Alliance of Reformed Churches; Hazel Thompson McCord Professor Emerita of Historical Theology, Princeton Seminary, Princeton, New Jersey

Reindert Falkenburg, Professor of Art History, Netherlands Institute for Art History, 's-Gravenhage, The Netherlands

Paul Corby Finney, Professor of History, University of Missouri, St. Louis, Missouri

Hélène Guicharnaud, Conservator, Palais du Louvre, Paris, France

Daniel W. Hardy, Professor of Theology, Cambridge University, Cambridge, England

Matthew Koch, Department of History, The Johns Hopkins University, Baltimore, Maryland

James Lomax, Keeper, Temple Newsam House, Leeds, England

Raymond A. Mentzer, Jr., Professor of History, Montana State University, Bozeman, Montana

Betsy Rosasco, Associate Curator of Later Western Art, The Art Museum, Princeton University, Princeton, New Jersey

George A. Starr, Professor of English, University of California, Berkeley, California

Christopher Stell, Consultant, Royal Commission on the Historical Monuments of England

James R. Tanis, Director of Libraries, Bryn Mawr College, Bryn Mawr, Pennsylvania

Ilja M. Veldman, Professor of the History of Art, Free University, Amsterdam, The Netherlands

James F. White, Professor of Liturgy, Notre Dame University, Notre Dame, Indiana

Peter W. Williams, Professor of Religion and American Studies, Miami University, Oxford, Ohio

John F. Wilson, Collord Professor of Religion, Princeton University, Princeton, New Jersey

Mary G. Winkler, Associate Professor, Institute for the Medical Humanities, University of Texas Medical Branch, Galveston, Texas

516

Photo Credits

Figures

1. Courtesy C. F. Stell. From Bloxham, M. H., *Companion to the Principles of Gothic Ecclesiastical Architecture* (1882), 175.
2. Courtesy C. F. Stell. Photo: RCHME.
3. Courtesy C. F. Stell. Photo: RCHME.
4. Courtesy C. F. Stell. Photo: RCHME.
5. Photo: C. F. Stell.
6. Photo: C. F. Stell.
7. Courtesy C. F. Stell. Photo: RCHME.
8. Courtesy C. F. Stell. Photo: RCHME.
9. Photo: C. F. Stell.
10. Photo: C. F. Stell.
11. Photo: C. F. Stell.
12. Courtesy C. F. Stell. Photo: RCHME.
13. Photo: C. F. Stell.
14. Photo: C. F. Stell.
15. Photo: C. F. Stell.
16. Photo: C. F. Stell.
17. Photo: C. F. Stell.
18. Photo: C. F. Stell.
19. Courtesy C. F. Stell. Photo: RCHME.
20. Photo: C. F. Stell.
21. Photo: C. F. Stell.
22. Photo: C. F. Stell.
23. Courtesy C. F. Stell. Photo: RCHME.
24. From Bernard Picart, *The Ceremonies and Religious Customs of the Various Nations . . .* Vol. V (1733). Courtesy of the John Rylands Library, Manchester.
25. Courtesy of Castle Museum, Norwich.
26. From E. A. Jones, *The Old Silver Sacramental Vessels of the Foreign Protestant Churches in England* (London, 1908).

27. From E. A. Jones, *The Old Silver Sacramental Vessels of the Foreign Protestant Churches in England* (London, 1908).
28. Courtesy of The Museum of London.
29. Courtesy of The Museum of London.
30. Courtesy of The Museum of London.
31. Courtesy of Christ Church, Oxford.
32. The Victoria and Albert Museum, London; reproduced by courtesy of Saint Dominic's Priory, Haverstock Hill, London.
33. Courtesy of The Victoria and Albert Museum, London.
34. Courtesy of The Ashmolean Museum, Oxford.
35. Courtesy of Leeds Museums and Galleries, Leeds (Temple Newsam House).
36. Courtesy of The Manchester City Art Gallery, Manchester.
37. Courtesy of The Manchester City Art Gallery, Manchester.
38. Private collection on loan to the Bowes Museum, Barnard Castle, County Durham. Courtesy of Bowes Museum.
39. Courtesy of The Manchester City Art Gallery, Manchester.
40. Courtesy of The Victoria and Albert Museum, London.
41. Courtesy of The British Museum, London.
42. Courtesy of the Bibliothèque nationale, Paris.
43. Courtesy of the Bibliothèque nationale, Paris.
44. Courtesy of the Archives nationales, Paris.
45. Courtesy of the Bibliothèque nationale, Paris.
46. Courtesy of the Bibliothèque nationale, Paris. The author thanks Professor Philip Benedict for his gracious assistance in providing this illustration.
47. Courtesy of the Bibliothèque nationale, Paris.
48. Courtesy of the Bibliothèque nationale, Paris.
49. Courtesy of Centre historiane des Archives nationales, Paris.
50. Courtesy Direction Régionale des Affaires Culturelles Provence-Alpes-Côte d'Azur, Aix-en-Provence. Photo: Roncaute-Heller (Inventaire Général).
51. Courtesy Direction Régionale des Affaires Culturelles du Languedoc-Roussillon, Montpellier. Photo: J. M. Périn, © 93 (Inventaire Général-SPADEM).
52. From *BSHPF* 37 (1888): 372. Photo: John Blazejewski.
53. From *BSHPF* 37 (1888): 323. Photo: John Blazejewski.
54. From *BSHPF* 37 (1888): 486. Photo: John Blazejewski.
55. From *BSHPF* 37 (1888): 377. Photo: John Blazejewski.
56. From *BSHPF* 37 (1888): 376. Photo: John Blazejewski.
57. From *BSHPF* 37 (1888): 485. Photo: John Blazejewski.
58. From *BSHPF* 37 (1888): 380. Photo: John Blazejewski.
59. From *BSHPF* 37 (1888): 371. Photo: John Blazejewski.
60. Courtesy of the Collection of Frederick H. Schultz. Photo: Bruce M. White.
61. Courtesy of the Collection of Frederick H. Schultz. Photo: Bruce M. White.

62. Courtesy of the Collection of Frederick H. Schultz. Photo: Bruce M. White.

63. Courtesy of the New York Public Library, Astor, Tilden and Lenox Foundations.

64. Courtesy of William O. Harris, Speer Library, Princeton, NJ. Photo: John Blazejewski.

65. Courtesy of William O. Harris, Speer Library, Princeton, NJ. Photo: John Blazejewski.

66. Courtesy of William O. Harris, Speer Library, Princeton, NJ. Photo: John Blazejewski.

67. Courtesy of William O. Harris, Speer Library, Princeton, NJ. Photo: John Blazejewski.

68. Courtesy of William O. Harris, Speer Library, Princeton, NJ. Photo: John Blazejewski.

69. Courtesy of William O. Harris, Speer Library, Princeton, NJ. Photo: John Blazejewski.

70. Courtesy of Volkmar Billeb, Berlin.

71. Courtesy of Volkmar Billeb, Berlin.

72. From E. Muret, *Geschichte der Französischen Kolonie in Brandenburg-Preußen* (Berlin, 1885), p. 271. Photo: Ilka Schuster.

73. From E. Muret, *Geschichte der Französischen Kolonie in Brandenburg-Preußen* (Berlin, 1885), p. 271. Photo: Ilka Schuster.

74. Courtesy of S. Badstübner-Gröger, Berlin.

75. Courtesy of Martin Detloff, Berlin.

76. From *750 Jahre Architektur und Stadtebau in Berlin,* catalogue of the Internationale Bauausstellung 1987, ill. 121. Photo: Ilka Schuster.

77. From H. Börsch-Supan, *Die Kunst in Brandenburg-Preußen* (Berlin, 1980), pl. 26. Photo: Ilka Schuster.

78. From *Hugenotten in Berlin,* ed. G. Bregulla (Berlin, 1988), p. 249. Photo: Ilka Schuster.

79. Courtesy of Martin Detloff, Berlin.

80. Courtesy of Ilka Schuster, Berlin.

81. Courtesy of Volkmar Billeb, Berlin.

82. From Attila Komjáthy, *Felső-Tisza-Vidéki Templomok I* (Churches of the Upper Tisza Region I) (Budapest, 1983), pl. 8.

83. From Ilona Tombor, *Magyarországi Festett Famennyezetek és Rokonemlékek a XV-XIX. Századból* (Hungarian painted wooden ceilings and related monuments from the fifteenth to the nineteenth century) (Budapest, 1968), table 38.

84. From Tamás Hofer and Edit Fél, *Magyar Népművészet* (Hungarian folk art) (Budapest, 1975), fig. 26.

85. From Hélène Balogh, *Les Édifices de Bois dans l'Architecture Religieuse Hongroise* (1941), fig. 20.

86. From József L. Novák, "A temetők népi művészete" (The folk art of cemeteries), in *A Magyar Nemzeti Múzeum Néprajzi Osztályának Értesítője* (Announcements of the Ethnographic Section of the Hungarian National Museum), vol. 11 (1910), p. 7.

87. From Judit Szabadi, *A Magyar Szecesszió Művészete: Festészet, Grafika,*

Szobrászat (Art of the Hungarian secession: Painting, graphics, sculpture) (Budapest, 1979), pl. 248.

88. From Szabadi, pl. 249.
89. From Szabadi, pl. 247.
90. From László Debreczeni, *Erdélyi Református Templomok és Tornyok* (Transylvanian Reformed churches and towers) (Kolozsvár, 1929), pl. 42.
91. From *Heves Megye Műemlékei* (Historical monuments of Heves County), ed. Pál Voit (vols. 7-9 of *Magyarország Műemlékei Topográfiája* [Topography of Hungary's historical monuments], ed. Dezső Dercsényi), 3 vols. (1969-78), 3:529, fig. 696.
92. From J. István Kováts, *Magyar Református Templomok* (Hungarian Reformed Churches), vol. 1, p. 300, fig. 23.
93. From *Szabolcs-Szatmár Megye Műemlékei* (Historical monuments of Szabolcs-Szatmar County), ed. Géza Entz (vols. 10-11 of *Magyarország Műemlékei Topográfiája* [Topography of Hungary's historical monuments], ed. Dezső Dercsényi), 2 vols. (Budapest, 1986-87), 2:128.
94. From Rózsa Tóth Feuer, *Reneszánsz Építészet Magyarországon* (Renaissance architecture in Hungary) (Budapest, 1977), fig. 177.
95. From Marta Nemes, "Még egyser a debreceni református Nagytemplomról" (About the Reformed Great Church of Debrecen once more), *Műemlékvédelem* (Historical monument protection), vol. 30, no. 1 (1986), pl. 2, p. 41.
96. From Anna Zádor and Jenő Rados, *A Klasszicizmus Építészete Magyarországon* (The architecture of classicism in Hungary) (Budapest, 1948), pl. 3.
97. From Zádor and Rados, pl. 2.
98. From Zádor and Rados, p. 309, fig. 1.
99. From Gyöngyi Eri and Zsuzsa Jobbágyi, *A Golden Age: Art and Society in Hungary, 1896-1914* (Budapest, 1989), p. 192.
100. From *A Ház* 1, no. 1 (1908).
101. From *A Ház* 2, no. 1 (1909).
102. From Balázs Dercsényi, *Árkay Aladár* (Budapest, 1967), pl. 11.
103. From Eri and Jobbágyi, p. 89.
104. From Eri and Jobbágyi, p. 75.
105. From Sándor Bíró, Endre Tóth, Mihály Bucsay, and Zoltán Varga, *A Magyar Református Egyház Története* (History of the Hungarian Reformed church) (Budapest, 1949), p. 59.
106. From Bíró et al., p. 136.
107. © A. C. L., Brussels.
108. © A. C. L., Brussels.
109. Photo: Archive Doucet.
110. Courtesy Rijksmuseumstichting, Amsterdam.
111. Courtesy Rijksmuseumstichting, Amsterdam.
112. Courtesy Rijksmuseumstichting, Amsterdam.
113. Courtesy Kleinhempel, Hamburg.
114. Courtesy Rijksmuseumstichting, Amsterdam.
115. Courtesy Rijksmuseumstichting, Amsterdam.
116. Courtesy Rijksmuseumstichting, Amsterdam.

117. Courtesy Rijksmuseumstichting, Amsterdam.
118. Courtesy Rijksmuseumstichting, Amsterdam.
119. Courtesy Statens Museum for Kunst, Kopenhagen.
120. Courtesy Kunsthalle, Bremen.
121. © A. C. L., Brussels.
122. Courtesy The Minneapolis Institute of Art, Minneapolis.
123. Private collection of J. Böhler, München. Photo: Dr. W. Bernt, München.
124. Courtesy Stichting Atlas Van Stolk, Historisch Museum, Rotterdam.
125. Courtesy Rijksprentenkabinet, Rijksmuseum, Amsterdam.
126. From James Tanis and Daniel Horst, *Images of Discord: A Graphic Interpretation of the Opening Decades of the Eighty Years' War* (Bryn Mawr, Pa., and Grand Rapids: William B. Eerdmans Publishing Co., 1993), p. 36.
127. Courtesy Stichting Atlas Van Stolk, Historisch Museum, Rotterdam.
128. Courtesy Hessisches Landesmuseum, Darmstadt.
129. Courtesy Stichting Atlas Van Stolk, Historisch Museum, Rotterdam.
130. Courtesy Rijksprentenkabinet, Rijksmuseum, Amsterdam.
131. The Elisha Whittelsey Collection, The Elisha Whittelsey Fund, 1951. Courtesy Metropolitan Museum of Art, New York.
132. Courtesy Konigelige Kobberstiksamling, Statens Museum for Kunst, Copenhagen.
133. Courtesy Stichting Atlas Van Stolk, Historisch Museum, Rotterdam.
134. Courtesy Stichting Atlas Van Stolk, Historisch Museum, Rotterdam.
135. Courtesy Stichting Atlas Van Stolk, Historisch Museum, Rotterdam.
136. Courtesy Rijksprentenkabinet, Rijksmuseum, Amsterdam.
137. Courtesy Rijksprentenkabinet, Rijksmuseum, Amsterdam.
138. Courtesy Rijksprentenkabinet, Rijksmuseum, Amsterdam.
139. Courtesy Rijksprentenkabinet, Rijksmuseum, Amsterdam.
140. Courtesy Rijksprentenkabinet, Rijksmuseum, Amsterdam.
141. Courtesy Rijksprentenkabinet, Rijksmuseum, Amsterdam.
142. Courtesy Rijksprentenkabinet, Rijksmuseum, Amsterdam.
143. Courtesy Rijksprentenkabinet, Rijksmuseum, Amsterdam.
144. Courtesy Rijksprentenkabinet, Rijksmuseum, Amsterdam.
145. Courtesy Royal Library, The Hague.
146. Courtesy Institut Néerlandais, Paris.
147. Courtesy Kupferstichkabinett, Berlin.
148. Courtesy Kupferstichkabinett, Berlin.
149. Courtesy Rijksprentenkabinet, Rijksmuseum, Amsterdam.
150. Courtesy Institut Néerlandais, Paris.
151. Courtesy of Hervormde Kerk, Schoonhoven.
152. Courtesy Rijksprentenkabinet, Rijksmuseum, Amsterdam.
153. Courtesy Rijksprentenkabinet, Rijksmuseum, Amsterdam.
154. Courtesy Rijksprentenkabinet, Rijksmuseum, Amsterdam.
155. Courtesy of the Connecticut Historical Society. Hartford, CT.
156. Courtesy of New Haven Colony Society.
157. Photo: G. T. Buggeln.
158. Photo courtesy of Columbia University Press. From J. F. Kelly, *Early Connecticut Meetinghouses* (New York: Columbia University Press, 1948).
159. Courtesy G. T. Buggeln. Photo: John Giammatteo.

521

160. Photo courtesy P. C. Finney. Photo: © Steve Rosenthal.
161. Photo: Peter W. Williams.
162. Photo courtesy P. C. Finney. Photo: © Steve Rosenthal.
163. Photo courtesy P. C. Finney. Photo: © Steve Rosenthal.
164. Photo: Peter Vanderwarker.
165. Courtesy Library of Congress, Historic American Buildings Survey.
166. Photo: P. W. Williams.
167. Photo: P. W. Williams.
168. Photo: P. W. Williams.
169. Photo: P. W. Williams.
170. Photo: P. W. Williams.
171. Photo: P. W. Williams.
172. Photo: P. W. Williams.
173. Photo: P. W. Williams.
174. Photo: P. W. Williams.

Plates

1. Photo: C. F. Stell.
2. Photo: C. F. Stell.
3. Photo: C. F. Stell.
4. Photo: C. F. Stell.
5. Photo: C. F. Stell.
6. Photo: C. F. Stell.
7. Photo: C. F. Stell.
8. Photo: C. F. Stell.
9. Courtesy of The British Museum, London.
10. Courtesy of Leeds Museums and Galleries, Leeds (Temple Newsam House).
11. The Victoria and Albert Museum, London. Reproduced by courtesy of the Guild Church of St. Mary Aldermanbury, London.
12. Courtesy of The Dean and Chapter of Durham Cathedral.
13. Courtesy of The National Trust (Dunham Massey, Cheshire).
14. Courtesy of Leeds Museums and Galleries, Leeds (Temple Newsam House).
15. Courtesy of Trustees of the Chatsworth Settlement, Chatsworth.
16. Courtesy of The Victoria and Albert Museum, London.
17. Courtesy of Leeds Museums and Galleries, Leeds (Temple Newsam House).
18. Courtesy of Leeds Museums and Galleries, Leeds (Temple Newsam House).
19. Courtesy of Leeds Museums and Galleries, Leeds (Temple Newsam House).
20. Courtesy of Leeds Museums and Galleries, Leeds (Temple Newsam House).
21. Courtesy of the Bibliothèque publique et universitaire, Genève. The au-

thor thanks Michel Piller for his gracious assistance in providing this illustration.

22. Photo: Conservation Régionale des Monuments Historiques, Aix-en-Provence.
23. Courtesy Comité Départemental du Tourisme de Tarn-et-Garonne, Montauban.
24. Courtesy Comité Départemental du Tourisme de Tarn-et-Garonne, Montauban.
25. Courtesy Comité Départemental du Tourisme de Tarn-et-Garonne, Montauban.
26. Courtesy Comité Départemental du Tourisme de Tarn-et-Garonne, Montauban.
27. Courtesy Musée des Augustins, Toulouse.
28. Courtesy Musée des Augustins, Toulouse.
29. From György Domanovszky, *A Magyar Nép Díszítőművészete* (Decorative art of the Hungarian people), 2 vols. (Budapest, 1981), 2:348-49.
30. From Ilona Tombor, *Old Hungarian Painted Woodwork, Fifteenth-Nineteenth Centuries* (Budapest, 1967), pl. 1.
31. From Gyöngyi Eri and Zsuzsa Jobbágyi, *A Golden Age: Art and Society in Hungary, 1896-1914* (Budapest, 1989), p. 139.
32. From J. István Kováts, *Magyar Református Templomok* (Hungarian Reformed churches), 2 vols. (Budapest, 1942), vol. 1, pl. 10.
33. From Balázs Dercsényi, Gábor Hegyi, Ernő Marosi, and Béla Takács, *Calvinist Churches in Hungary* (Budapest, 1992), p. 118, fig. 332.
34. Courtesy Stichting De Nieuwe Kerk, Amsterdam.
35. Courtesy of I. M. Veldman.
36. Photo: © Polyvisie Hilversum.
37. Courtesy Frans Halsmuseum, Haarlem.
38. Courtesy of G. T. Buggeln. Photo: John Giammatteo.
39. Courtesy Connecticut Historical Society, Hartford, CT.
40. Courtesy of G. T. Buggeln. Photo: John Giammatteo.
41. Photo: G. T. Buggeln.
42. Courtesy of the Society for the Preservation of New England Antiquities and P. C. Finney. Photo: © Steve Rosenthal.
43. Courtesy of the Society for the Preservation of New England Antiquities and P. C. Finney. Photo: © Steve Rosenthal.
44. Courtesy of the Society for the Preservation of New England Antiquities and P. C. Finney. Photo: © Steve Rosenthal.
45. Courtesy of the Society for the Preservation of New England Antiquities and P. C. Finney. Photo: © Steve Rosenthal.
46. Courtesy of the Society for the Preservation of New England Antiquities and P. C. Finney. Photo: © Steve Rosenthal.

General Index

Architecture Index

Artist Index

(architects, burnishers, chasers, designers, draftsmen, engravers, gilders, goldsmiths, painters, sculptors)

Iconography Index